1877

Also by Michael A. Bellesiles

Arming America: The Origins of a National Gun Culture

Documenting American Violence: A Sourcebook
(co-edited with Christopher Waldrep)

Ethan Allen and His Kin: Correspondence, 1772–1819
(co-edited with John Duffy)

Lethal Imagination: Violence and Brutality in American History (editor)

*Revolutionary Outlaws: Ethan Allen and the
Struggle for Independence on the Early American Frontier*

A Survival Guide for Teaching

Weighed in an Even Balance

1877

America's Year of Living Violently

MICHAEL A. BELLESILES

THE NEW PRESS

NEW YORK
LONDON

For Nina
"What is essential is invisible to the eye."

Requests for permission to reproduce selections from this book should be mailed to:
Permissions Department, The New Press, 38 Greene Street, New York, NY 10013.

Published in the United States by The New Press, New York, 2010
Distributed by Perseus Distribution

LIBRARY OF CONGRESS CATALOGING-IN-PUBLICATION DATA
Bellesiles, Michael A.
1877 : America's year of living violently / Michael A. Bellesiles.
p. cm.
Includes bibliographical references and index.
ISBN 978-1-59558-441-0 (hc. : alk. paper)   1. United States—Civilization—1865–1918.
2. Social conflict—United States—History—19th century.   3. Violence—United States—
History—19th century.   4. Racism—United States—History—19th century.   5. United States—
Race relations—History—19th century.   6. United States—Economic conditions—1865–1918.
7. Railroad Strike, U.S., 1877.   I. Title.
E671.B47 2010
973.8'3—dc22

2009052949

The New Press was established in 1990 as a not-for-profit alternative to the large, commercial publishing
houses currently dominating the book publishing industry. The New Press operates in the public interest
rather than for private gain, and is committed to publishing, in innovative ways, works of educational,
cultural, and community value that are often deemed insufficiently profitable.

www.thenewpress.com

Composition by NK Graphics
This book was set in Adobe Garamond

Printed in the United States of America

2   4   6   8   10   9   7   5   3   1

Contents

Acknowledgments

In times of great grief, we learn anew the value and extent of friendship. There are those who cannot bear to witness pain and understandably step quietly away, while others display such kindness and personal loyalty as to lighten the burden of loss. I have been fortunate to have far too many of the latter to thank each in turn, but I would be sorely remiss if I did not express my profound debt of gratitude to a few people who have rendered aid in a time of need. I can never thank Kathy Hermes enough for getting me back into the classroom where I belong. But more than that, her courage in standing up to bullies has been an inspiration and a valuable reminder of why teaching and writing are so important. Stephen Wasserstein, my boss at Cengage Learning, has become a valued friend who keeps me grounded in both the needs of readers and the merit of clear prose. From death row, Eric Wrinkles remained a rock of friendship, patient and understanding until the moment he was put to death. Forever upbeat and positive, Carol Berkin evokes awe; her brilliance and boldness are matched only by her loyalty as a friend. I owe Carol a special debt for introducing me to her agent, and now mine, Dan Green—it is hard to imagine a finer agent. I have learned to rely on his wise counsel and blunt honesty; it has been a rare pleasure working with such an insightful critic. His connecting me with The New Press and my editor Marc Favreau was particularly fortuitous; their integrity and forthright nature have made writing this book a pleasure. My thanks as well to Sarah Fan and Cathy Dexter, whose editorial work improved this work considerably. I hope that all my other friends realize how much their time, patience, and continuing support have meant to me. I look forward to thanking you each in person.

Immersing oneself in a single year as I have done with 1877 can lead to a feeling of fellowship; at times it seems as though I know many of these people personally. The appalling villains are matched by the many admirable and courageous people who fought for their beliefs in a troubled time. In letters, journals, memoirs, and the decaying newspapers from the past, I also came to know a number of people who insisted on living joyous lives despite the darkness around them. As an historian, it is my task to do these people justice, to treat them with respect and let them speak for themselves. I hope that I have succeeded in attaining these goals. Similarly, one of the pleasures of research is rereading favorite books—such as those by Henry May, Kevin Kenny, and Elliot Gorn—and discovering new authors like Rebecca Edwards, Susan Jacoby, and Edward Blum, who bring history to life. I trust that my debt to other historians is abundantly clear in the pages of this book; their scholarship and intelligence have served as my guide.

Ultimately, the contents of a book are the responsibility solely of the author, and I embrace that burden. However, I could not have taken on this task without the support of my family. My father, Jacques, my siblings, Matt, Mark, Kathleen, and Lisa, and my patron saint Raymond have kept the faith and seen me through. My daughter, Lilith, becomes ever more brilliant while remaining gracious and loving. My wife, Nina K. Martin, to whom this book is dedicated, has had to live with my obsession with 1877, and has done so with good humor. Her love, loyalty, and honesty sustain me; her intelligence inspires me; and her appreciation for my cooking reminds me what matters most in life, the joyful company of loved ones.

Preface

The year 1877 may rank as one of the blackest in the nation's annals.[1]
—Allan Nevins

As Carl Sandburg observed, the Civil War had been fought over a verb: does one say "the United States is" or "the United States are"? In 1865 the matter seemed settled in favor of the former. At the expense of more than six hundred thousand lives, the idea of national unity based on the principle of freedom had apparently triumphed. But just a dozen years later that certainty was fading fast as angry and committed Americans pulled the country in divergent directions. In the South, white racists rose again in an attempt to seize power through violence and intimidation, seeking to negate the newly won rights of one-third of the region's inhabitants. Out on the Great Plains, the U. S. Army suffered repeated defeat at the hands of migratory Indians, while in Texas public officials from the governor on down issued panicked calls for federal troops in the face of a Mexican invasion that threatened a new war. In the far West, white demagogues linked the rights of labor with racism, calling for both labor unions and war against Hispanics and Asians. Meanwhile the entire country was in the grip of the century's worst depression while the specter of communism and aggressive labor agitation threatened to topple the very foundations of the capitalist order. Around the country Americans killed one another in record numbers previously seen only in time of war. And to top it all off, it looked as though the country would not have a president by inauguration day, March 4, 1877. As the historian Henry May wrote, "The year 1877 remained a symbol of shock, of the possible crumbling of society."[2]

This book examines one of the most tumultuous years in American history, arguably the most violent year in which the United States was not in the midst of war. Some years in a specific country take on an identity of their own, such as 1848 in much of Europe or 1968 in the United States, with every aspect of society and culture facing challenges and teetering on the verge of transformation. The year itself has no character of its own, of course, but contemporaries attach value to the calendar and frame events through the personality they impart to their time. The centennial year of 1876 was supposed to have been significant for the United States, yet most observers felt like the country had just been holding its breath. Despite the many parties and celebrations, the country was in the midst of a terrible depression, with business failures and unemployment reaching new heights. But 1877 was different. With the party over, the guests seemed intent on trashing the house.

For contemporaries, 1877 was a year unlike any other, and it continued to haunt their memories. From the day the year started, with news of the Ashtabula rail disaster, through its end and threats of a communist rebellion, it seemed that everything that could go wrong did.[3] Those who lived through 1877 thought it a fearful year. More than just the ongoing depression and the rising murder rate disturbed the public; in 1877 the United States almost came apart, twice—first politically and then over deep class tensions. The nation's political and economic leaders were determined to impose order, with force if necessary—or even where it would just be quicker or more effective. To all sides it appeared obvious that the country would never be the same. Looking at the turbulent events of 1877, the English scholar Goldwin Smith wrote, "The youth of the American Republic is over."[4]

It did indeed seem as though the whole country had suddenly changed direction. Since at least the Missouri Compromise of 1820, the nation had pivoted around race and slavery. Now, twelve years after the end of the destructive but liberating Civil War, racial relations gave way to class conflict as the primary political and social issue facing the United States. That is not to say that race was no longer important, but rather that the majority just did not want to talk about it anymore. Clearly many white Americans were frightened by the world they had created and hoped to turn back the clock to a less threatening time, as the democratic expansion of Reconstruction unleashed dangerous impulses. In 1877 a white woman in Alabama named Julia Green was jailed for two years for marrying a black man.[5] Throwing someone in jail for a private marital decision speaks volumes about the type of culture being created in 1877 and the limitations Americans accepted on their freedom. White America allowed this wholesale violation of the most basic freedoms because they no longer cared about racial equality or the fate of the freedmen. It is little wonder that Mississippi's last Republican congressman until the later twentieth century felt that "the war was fought in vain."[6] For the next fifty years, the consequences of industrialism would dominate the national discourse, while the rights of African Americans would be largely forgotten.

Just as the former slaveholders battled to regain their authority in the Southern states, so did the powerful industrialists of the North and the great landowners of the West assert their version of order in 1877. The "captains of industry," as they were starting to be called, found themselves contending with the "Great

Upheaval," the railroad strike that spread over much of the country—the closest thing the United States ever had to a general strike, and the only labor action in American history that came close to toppling the nation's economic structure.[7] While this dramatic and violent strike deserves a great deal of attention, there is much more that happened in this year that helped to determine the future course of the United States. A regular complaint lodged against books on American history is their bias toward incidents that occur on the East Coast, but the events of 1877 require a more national point of view. In this year, at least, occurrences in California and on the Great Plains, in Texas and West Virginia, had as great an impact on the country and its future as anything occurring in New York or Boston. Because the year 1877 sits right in the midst of the crisis of the accelerating industrialization of America, it is impossible to confine one's perspective to a single region.

Henry May observed that contemporaries found the proceedings of 1877 "impossible to ignore and difficult to explain away." Even ministers, who should have had some sympathy with the lives of the poor, were stunned by the many upheavals of 1877; "the sudden outbreak of large-scale labor warfare was at first completely unexplainable, except in terms of human depravity."[8] Many people responded by turning to imagined versions of their country. It was a year that witnessed the birth of numerous national mythologies: of the Wild West and glorious Indian wars, of corrupt Reconstruction governments and the South's heroic redeemers, of violent workers and an economy molded by rugged individualists— and for some reason they are always rugged. The richest people in the country became heroes, no matter how they made their money, while the poorest and most powerless became the source of violence and disorder, and a dangerous drag on the nation. Those who held to this vision constructed the most significant of all mythologies, social Darwinism, an ideology that not only accepted but celebrated violence.

Near the end of 1877, the YMCA offered a prize for the best essay on the year's key episodes. The winner, Joseph Nash, highlighted the significant changes the country had experienced in 1877, arguing that they marked "a new phase in our social order." What he saw was a completely different country from the one that had existed in 1876. While an exaggeration to be sure, Nash's essay points to the popular sense that everything had changed in these twelve months, and not necessarily for the better.[9] Liberal critics would spend the next century battling the "Solid South," the all-white Democratic polity of Southern states created in 1877 that forcibly pushed the entire country to the right and effectively blocked or watered down progressive legislation for decades. Conservatives found the country delicately balanced above class warfare, requiring the full force of the state to keep dangerous and un-American political and social forces in check. People across the political spectrum worried about the violent forces unleashed in 1877 and sought some route to a more harmonious future. Writing a decade later about worsening conditions in the United States, an advocate for the new Social Gospel movement—which had its origins in 1877 and sought to reconcile capital and labor—warned, "Another 1877 may be the prelude to another 1793," referring to the Reign of Terror in revolutionary France.[10]

While this book focuses on the violent disruption of the United States and on the country's desperate search for order, a lot else was happening that often influenced the main events described here. It is worth remembering what a phenomenal year 1877 was overall for the United States. Some of these acts may appear trivial now, but they often tell us a great deal about the contemporary culture. For instance, a major cause célèbre galvanized around the arrest and prosecution of contraception crusader Ezra Hervey Heywood by Anthony Comstock, America's self-proclaimed moral guardian. In the landmark *Munn v. Illinois* decision, the Supreme Court upheld government regulation as necessary for public safety. Ignoring such details, John D. Rockefeller began his illegal secret rebate and drawback system while signing an exclusivity contract with the Pennsylvania Railroad that gave him a virtual monopoly over the oil industry and made him the richest man in America; he also broke the coopers' union with extensive pay cuts and the nightstick-wielding Cleveland police. In this single year, the Bessemer steelmaking process was applied to barbed wire and sales jumped from 840,000 pounds to 12.86 million pounds, leading to the transformation of the West. Alexander Graham Bell started the Bell Telephone Association, which leased its first telephones, leading to the first telephone switchboard in Boston and Bell's first competitor, New England Telephone and Telegraph. Thomas A. Edison shouted "Hello," creating the first recorded message; later that year his assistant John Kruesi built the first phonograph, onto which Edison would recite "Mary Had a Little Lamb." Mary Jacobi, the first woman to receive a pharmaceutical degree (no American medical school accepted women at the time), published her groundbreaking *Question of Rest for Women during Menstruation*, challenging the popular notion that women were incapable of any activity during their menstrual periods. Sarah Orne Jewett wrote the elegiac *Deephaven*, evoking a vanishing, preindustrial America. Lewis Henry Morgan published what is often considered the first work on cultural evolution, *Ancient Society*, a study of Native American kinship systems. And for the first time in its history, the Senate approved the appointment of a black man to public office when Frederick Douglass was named United States Marshal for the District of Columbia.

In this same year John Wanamaker opened the first modern department store in Philadelphia, the first cantilever bridge opened for traffic across the Kentucky River, Albert Augustus Pope started the first bicycle factory, Johns Hopkins University began the first academic press with *The American Journal of Mathematics*, the American Museum of Natural History opened, the black poet Albery Allson Whitman published *Not a Man and Yet a Man*, the *Washington Post* began publication, the cakewalk was introduced into minstrel shows by Harrigan and Hart, the Westminster Kennel Club hosted its first dog show, the swan boats first floated onto the Boston Public Garden pond, Asaph Hall discovered Mars's two satellites, Gustavus Franklin Swift sent his first shipment of beef from Chicago to Boston, the Oneida Community began selling tableware, margarine appeared on the market, the New York legislature outlawed selling margarine as "butter," James A. Folger started making really bad coffee in San Francisco, John Jossi invented brick cheese in Wisconsin, the Quaker Mill Company began making oatmeal, and James Harvey Kellogg invented granola. Meanwhile, workers had taken over the nation's rail system and were threatening revolution.

Americans fashioned a unique voice in various creative fields in 1877. Henry James won recognition as a major literary talent with *The American*, though he was appropriately outraged when his German translator gave the book a happy ending.[11] At the same time, his brother William worked on an article that would set forth a new philosophy he called "pragmatism." William Dean Howells and his good friend Samuel Clemens, known to everyone as Mark Twain, were busily transforming American literature, while Anna Katherine Green finished *The Leavenworth Case*, the bestseller considered the first American detective novel. New York was taking over from Boston as the center of culture, and for artists it was an exciting time, as Thomas Eaton and Winslow Homer grabbed the American art world by its stuffed shirt and gave it a firm shaking. Their bold realism suggested a new direction to American art finally free of Europe's guiding hand and disapproving voice. To many literary critics, such as William Dean Howells and Richard Dana, it seemed that the country was finally fulfilling the goals Emerson set out in his 1837 essay, "The American Scholar," by creating an autonomous and authentic American culture. While there is not sufficient room to give these developments their due in this book, they speak to the vibrant and disorienting qualities of this dramatic year of change.

It is hard to mistake the importance of what happened in 1877. Americans struggled to come to terms with their new industrial society and the violence it generated. Class superseded race as the primary area of conflict; abolitionists became social Darwinists; onetime liberals came to see the wisdom of social control; those who had fought for freedom now demanded prohibition; elites battled to maintain their power in every part of the country. That is not to say, however, that more democratic forms of politics and culture came to a screeching halt. Nothing in history is predetermined, and no society can truly be shoved back into long-standing ruts after a decade of dramatic change. Blacks and Hispanics, workers and farmers, women and immigrants—all learned valuable lessons from the events of 1877. We may debate whether they learned the correct lessons, but there is no denying that a diversity of reform movements responded to the up-heavals of 1877 and sought to effect change without inviting the violent reprisals so common in that lethal year.

Writing more than thirty years later, the evangelist T. DeWitt Talmage, one of the more eccentric ministers of his age, remembered the upheavals of 1877 as some troubling nightmare: "For hundreds of miles along the track leading from the great West I saw stretched out and coiled up the great reptile which, after crushing the free locomotive of passengers and trade, would have twisted itself around our republican institutions, and left them in strangulation and blood along the pathway of nations."[12] For Talmage and so many others, 1877 was a bloody nightmare from which they struggled to awake. For others, it was the cat-alyst that drove them to claim their rightful place in a fully democratic nation.

1

On the Edge of a Volcano

I can not say that I am in the slightest degree impressed by your bigness, or your material resources. As such, size is not grandeur, and territory does not make a nation. The great issue . . . is what are you going to do with all these things? What is to be the end to which these are to be the means?
—Thomas Huxley, inaugural address, Johns Hopkins University, 1876[1]

Hard Times

A Scottish immigrant to America, Andrew Carnegie, recorded the September 1873 advent of the nineteenth century's worst depression as the interruption of a lovely summer holiday: "All was going well when one morning in our summer cottage . . . a telegram came announcing the failure of Jay Cooke & Co." Carnegie sat at the telegraph office as each hour "brought news of some fresh disaster," as banks and investment firms went under. Over the next several days, the only question seemed to be "which would go next?" Rushing back to work, Carnegie found near chaos in every aspect of the economy, as some of the most revered financial institutions collapsed in a matter of days. "Every failure depleted the resources of other concerns," he wrote. "Loss after loss ensued, until a total paralysis of business set in."[2] The Panic had begun.

Economic historians speak of "the Panic of 1873," an oddly limited name for an economic crisis second in duration and severity only to the Great Depression of the 1930s.[3] The depression that started in 1873 lasted until 1879 and had a massive impact on the United States. While contemporaries often referred to the "financial depression," they mostly preferred to call upon Charles Dickens's popular novel *Hard Times* to describe what they were going through.[4] As one Georgia paper put it, they were experiencing "Hard Times and No Money." Local businesses made few sales, one formerly successful merchant stating that "it was hardly worth while to open his doors as the sales did not pay the salaries of his clerks." Merchants were reduced to barter, taking cotton in payment, with cash seldom seen "except as a curiosity." New York's superintendent of the poor reported on October 25, 1873, that there were twenty thousand people in his city "who are utterly destitute," and he expected the number to quickly rise to fifty thousand.[5] By the time visitors arrived for America's great centennial, the country was in its third year of economic depression. How had the fabulously wealthy land of promise come to this dire crisis? For most foreign visitors the answer was obvious: that same avarice that imparted such ceaseless energy to the American people had driven them straight over a cliff.

The years from 1865 to 1873 had witnessed extensive prosperity and economic growth. It was also a time of notable expansion in railroad and building construction, and in immigration, as tens of thousands of people came to the United States to take advantage of the high demand for labor. Northern banks largely had capitalized the Civil War, giving them significant control over the money supply at a time when the federal government understood neither economics nor the concept of conflict of interest. Bankers like Jay Cooke, judged the most creative investment banker of his era, shifted to railroads at the war's end. So lucrative did railroads appear, and so much capital did they require, that Cooke and others did not hesitate to borrow heavily. The economy appeared fevered in its growth, increasing from 431,000 businesses in 1870 to 609,904 in 1871; there were 364 railroads at the beginning of 1873—260 of which paid no dividends—representing a total investment of $3.7 billion, tripling the industry's capitalization in just six years. Banks were loaning five times their money supply; major fires in Portland, Boston, and Chicago led each of these cities to increase their borrowing in 1872, funding their rebuilding projects by increasing their debt to historically high levels. All of that collapsed in September 1873, with no sign of recovery until 1879.[6]

Cooke's commitment to the Northern Pacific Railroad led him to bribe politicians, buy newspapers, and lie shamelessly about the qualities of the northern plains, all of which earned him numerous government subsidies. Cooke banked heavily on his reputation as the man who financed the Civil War to pour other people's money into the Northern Pacific, which faced enormous obstacles on its way to being the second transcontinental railway. An additional challenge arose when a young competitor, J.P. Morgan, sought to torpedo Cooke's schemes by circulating stories intended to scare away investors. The railroad operated over just 500 miles, with a thousand-mile gap between its two sections, despite expending $15 million. Embarrassed in early 1873 by the Credit Mobilier scandal, in which the Union Pacific Railroad bribed numerous elected and appointed officials from both political parties in order to cheat the United States out of vast sums of money, Congress temporarily stopped taking bribes from the railroads and cut off federal subsidies. Further revelations of corruption and the misuse of government funds followed, as the public learned that Cornelius Vanderbilt had received federal subsidies for not developing rail routes.[7]

Foreign visitors were awed by the sweep of American political corruption in 1876, from the spectacles of the Whiskey Ring and Secretary of the Interior William Belknap taking money for patronage, to several lesser scandals that touched every corner of the Grant administration. In Albany, the lobbyists for the horse railways defeated the Husted transit bill by buying votes in the legislature for as little as $250. Leaders of both parties, Sir George Campbell wrote, "carried into politics what I may call joint-stock morals," or the view that a political office exists to make its holder a profit. During 1876 the "gas ring" stole $8 million from Philadelphia, a legislative committee found New York City police not simply accepting bribes from criminals but also taking a portion of the stolen goods, while Connecticut's Democrats sold a Senate seat to William H. Barnum for a $20,000 contribution to the party.[8] As Denis Tilden Lynch wrote, "The nation was off on a moral holiday" in the years Mark Twain and Charles Dudley Warner called the Gilded Age.[9]

The economy started to wobble in the summer of 1873 as the money market tightened. Congress had decided that paper money—greenbacks—posed a danger to society and began withdrawing them from circulation, moving the United States onto the gold standard. It was in this context that Jay Cooke, no longer able to get loans, began using his clients' money without bothering to tell them. By September 1873, he had used up most of the bank's resources.[10]

The papers carried bad news nearly every day that September, beginning with the collapse of the New York Warehouse and Securities Company on September 8. Rumors flew and the stock market slipped, though the warnings were quickly dismissed by such stalwarts of the status quo as the *New York Herald* and the *New York Times*, both of which continued to report that the stock market was doing just fine. Unknown to these papers, Cooke and other financiers had attempted to persuade the Treasury Department to release an additional $40 million in greenbacks but were soundly ignored. Predictions of a coming crisis picked up, while the *Times* insisted on September 17 that "Money and Stock affairs in Wall Street are again reported free of exciting rumors."[11] That same day, President Ulysses S. Grant spent the evening in Jay Cooke's 75,000-square-foot Philadelphia mansion, Ogontz. Grant and several members of his family had borrowed heavily from Cooke, and the president expressed public confidence in his host's integrity. But the very next morning, Thursday, September 18, Harris Fahnestock, Cooke's partner and manager of the New York branch of Jay Cooke & Co., began diverting his personal holdings to his wife to avoid seizure. He then ordered the doors to the bank closed and suspended operations, admitting to a reporter that the bank had been using depositors' money to keep the Northern Pacific afloat for some time. "Where else could we get the money?" he demanded to know. Within a few hours Cooke ordered his Philadelphia house closed, followed by his Washington office and the First National Bank, the city's largest bank, presided over by Jay Cooke's brother Henry.[12]

The collapse of Jay Cooke & Co. was "a financial thunderbolt"[13] and "as un-expected as an earthquake,"[14] reported newspapers in New York and Philadel-phia. The bank and the man had appeared impervious, the bank's "name was everywhere the synonym for strength and solidity."[15] When the president of the New York Stock Exchange announced Cooke's suspension of business, there was "an uproar such as has scarcely filled the Exchange since it was built. Messengers fled every way with the story of ruin, and down came the stocks all along the line."[16] Crowds of thousands gathered in Philadelphia and New York. Members of the Philadelphia Stock Exchange rushed out into the street to check for them-selves that Cooke's business had actually shut its doors. Judges adjourned trials to hurry to their banks. A police officer in Philadelphia arrested a newsboy for spreading the rumor that Jay Cooke had gone out of business.[17] General Alvred Nettleton, an executive with the Northern Pacific and longtime confidant of Cooke's, read in the following morning's newspaper of the suspension of Cooke's bank. "If I had been struck on the head with a hammer," he wrote his wife, "I could not have been more stunned." He rubbed his eyes in disbelief and then set about firing people.[18]

Once those in the economic community figured out that their debts far ex-ceeded the nation's total money supply, panic spread. A run on the banks ensued as depositors frantically attempted to get their deposits out before the doors closed, driving more banks under. During the run on the Mellon Bank of Pitts-burgh, Thomas Mellon did not close his doors, but he did refuse to give his de-positors their money, sending them off with promises that they would get it at some point in the future while he hastily sent his agents to demand immediate repayment of every debt owed his bank. The failures racked up over the next few days: a run on Fiske & Hatch in New York led to its closure; the Lake Shore Rail-road went bankrupt, as did the Union and the National Trust companies; twenty more New York and twelve Philadelphia firms followed within a week. One of these institutions, the Fourth National, held millions in deposits from other banks, so that these smaller banks could no longer access their funds, leading to further collapses in the weeks ahead. The remaining banks worked together to try to stem the flow, attaining some control by early October.[19]

The swell from these failing banks capsized other businesses, while even those that stayed afloat were in serious trouble. The stock market slid into free fall, a "mad terror" taking hold of Wall Street, *The Nation* reported, as "great crowds of men rushed to and fro trying to get rid of their property." Like many other lead-ing stocks, Western Union lost one-third of its value in a few days, and fully one-half before the markets stabilized at the end of October; most railroads lost one-fifth to one-third of their value during the same period. A total of forty fi-nancial institutions failed in September 1873, and on September 20 the stock market suspended all trading for the first time in its history, remaining closed for ten days. Henry Clews & Co., one of the most prestigious Wall Street firms, collapsed September 23. As Theodore Roosevelt Sr. observed the next morning, Clews's life work "is swept away in a day."[20]

As stocks sank, banks unloaded investments and called in loans, propelling more investors to sell off their holdings. Railroads, which required credit to expand and operate, faced an immediate crisis and could not, in their turn, pay for purchases they had made for goods, such as those from Andrew Carnegie's new steelworks. In order to pay his employees, Carnegie had to sell his stocks at a loss, cease construction of his new mill, and take out loans at high interest rates.[21] A further drain on Carnegie's resources was his friend Tom Scott, who ran the Texas & Pacific Railroad. As that railway began to crumble, Scott turned to Carnegie and Edgar Thomson's Pennsylvania Railroad for help with his $7 million debt. The Pennsylvania came through with a $4 million loan, but Carnegie refused to endorse a loan, leaving the Texas & Pacific to stumble along and exert a curious influence on the election of 1876. The stress of the panic proved so great on Carnegie that he became seriously ill in late October and took to his bed. When he made it to the end of the year with his company intact, Carnegie, like most of the rich, was confident that "the foolish panic" was behind them and that "the spring will see things prosperous again."[22] He was completely wrong.

Though the actual "panic" was brief, its consequences were extensive. With their total capital reserves reduced by 23 percent within a month, banks became more skeptical about lending money and tended to hoard their funds over the next several years, further tightening the credit markets. Real estate markets collapsed as thousands of mortgages were foreclosed. The surviving banks took advantage of the crisis to seize properties at historically low prices, with Thomas Mellon even grabbing the property of James Kelly, the revered elderly patriarch of Wilkinsburg. Like Kelly, tens of thousands of Americans saw a lifetime of investment vanish in a few minutes at a sheriff's sale. Bankers like Mellon felt no sympathy, as clearly the losers were to blame for the "bad habits and extravagant living" that left them unable to pay their mortgages. Mellon made no connection between these failed mortgage payments and the fact that businesses nationwide found it difficult to meet their payrolls and to acquire loans, leading to layoffs and wage cuts, both of which reduced demand, leading to production cuts, leading to further layoffs. Those who failed had only themselves to blame.[23]

The waves of crisis ran westward, with five national banks suspending business in Chicago and many western banks going under. The president of the Bank of California, William A. Ralston, lost his entire fortune and committed suicide. By the end of the year, five thousand businesses had gone bankrupt, taking $228,500,000 in liabilities with them, while bank deposits fell $100 million, and eighty-nine railways defaulted on bonds worth $400 million. As each fell, it took another with it; by June of 1876, 40 percent of all railroad bonds, valued at $789,367,000, had defaulted. The economic crisis just would not let up as some of the oldest institutions in the country, such as New York's City Savings Bank, went down in flames. In 1874, 5,830 businesses went under; in 1875, that number was 7,740, rising to 9,000 a year in 1876 and 1877. Overall, business declined by one-third during these hard times. A spate of frauds and embezzlements further undermined public confidence, as when the deputy treasurer of New York fled with $300,000 of public monies and a teller at the Union Trust succeeded in absconding with a quarter of a million dollars. Meanwhile a very few speculators with large cash reserves, led by Russell Sage and Jay Gould, prospered as they picked up control of the Union Pacific, Western Union, and numerous other large firms, while J.P. Morgan triumphantly stepped into Jay Cooke's shoes as the nation's leading investment banker.[24]

Hard times spread through the industrializing world, from Argentina to Japan to Germany, forming, in the words of Allan Nevins, "a black dividing line" across postwar America. "On the one side lies the sunshine of buoyant commercial prosperity; on the other the gloom of depression, economy and poverty" lasting six years.[25] In the immediate aftermath of the Panic, people blamed federal and private extravagance; some believed, as Sir George Campbell reported, "that recent hard times will have a very good effect on the habits of the American people."[26] Cornelius Vanderbilt charged that the railroads had overexpanded, exceeding the demands of the economy: "Building railroads from nowhere to nowhere at public expense is not a legitimate undertaking." For others, alcohol was clearly to blame, following Dickens's Thomas Gradgrind in seeing any expenditure on nonessentials as violating reason and ensuring failure.[27] The leading business journal, the *Commercial and Financial Chronicle*, pinned the blame on the new Granger movement and its talk of government regulation, but admitted that some railroads had expanded their operations "in sections of the country where they were not yet needed" and had no hope of success. Many blamed the banks for funding far too many risky enterprises; the *New York Times* held that "banks have been departing from their legitimate line of business," fed by the irrational "railroad mania."[28]

The general air of corruption fed the crisis, with numerous "gross swindles" destroying confidence in the stock market. It was definitely the case that the new, mysterious area of finance was increasing in size and importance. No one quite understood what these brokers did, playing around with obscure trading mechanisms and manipulating the stock market. The commissioner of revenue, David A. Wells, declared that such speculative finance was undermining the ability of the United States to produce goods.[29] The depression, Andrew Carnegie wrote, revealed every "weak spot" in the economy as even sound businesses "were borne down largely because our country lacked a proper banking system."

Without a central bank capable of protecting businesses and the stock market from the mass recall of loans, banks had no security against sudden runs on their resources. As a consequence, the whole financial structure experienced a domino effect, as first one business and then another toppled, knocking over those linked to each collapsing enterprise. President Grant and Congress stood by helplessly and watched.[30]

Corporate leaders attempted to deal with their lost revenue through collaboration, meeting to set levels at which they would all agree to cut production and wages. For instance, in December 1874 the American Iron and Steel Association met in Philadelphia and resolved that all furnaces would reduce production by half, following that up with wage cuts. Though publicly opposed to such actions, Carnegie saw no alternative, as his company teetered on the brink. "It was impossible to borrow money," he said, as he was forced to enter these agreements and sell off all his other holdings. He resolved to acquire more capital and hold it in reserve to avoid such a crisis in the future, becoming one of those lucky survivors who benefited from the hard times. "When the cyclone of 1873 struck us we at once began to reef sail in every quarter," Carnegie wrote, putting a halt to all construction projects and buying up the shares of his partners as they went under. "In that way control of the company came into my hands." The depression thus aided Carnegie in consolidating control of his company and of steel production in the United States.[31]

In the years ahead the rich once more gained access to loans, but not so the middle class, and the poor paid the heaviest price for the depression, losing not just purchasing power but employment. Rail construction fell one-third to 1,940 miles in 1874, costing a half million railroad workers their jobs. Within six months 266 of the 666 industrial furnaces in the United States closed, each closure leading to hundreds of unemployed workers. In the absence of reliable statistics, it is impossible to know the unemployment rates, with estimates running from 15 to 30 percent of the workforce, while those lucky enough to hold jobs rarely enjoyed a full year's employment.[32] Overall, prices fell 20 percent during the depression; pig iron, an essential item in industrial construction, fell from $53 a ton to $16.50, and steel from $120 per ton to $42, between 1873 and 1877. Manufacturing and mining output both fell steeply during the depression, the only significant decline in the otherwise massive acceleration in production from the end of the Civil War until 1900. As agricultural output doubled between 1866 and 1878, prices fell 45 percent, driving thousands of farmers off their land. The contraction of currency following the demonetization of silver by the Coinage Act of 1873 worsened the situation considerably—and led to that legislation being called "The Crime of '73."[33] At the end of the Civil War, $31.18 in currency circulated per capita; by 1878 that number fell to $16.95. A significant proportion of the population literally did not have money. Wages collapsed, falling at least 15 percent during the depression, though such statistics are notoriously unreliable. The increase in the number of homeless was unmistakable, and there were numerous reports that many young women found no alternative but prostitution. The pressure on charitable organizations and public assistance increased dramatically, though what most worried the elite was the spread of radical ideas among the poor.[34]

In one of the surest signs that times were indeed hard, immigration dropped precipitously, and by 1874 tens of thousands of recent immigrants had returned to their homelands. The influx fell to its lowest point in 1877, with just 130,000 immigrants coming to the United States, compared with 450,000 in 1872. Sir George Campbell, a Scottish Liberal member of Parliament, advised his constituents that America "is a country only for those who are willing to work with their hands, and work very hard indeed." With the economic crisis there was no-room for anyone seeking "to earn his bread by his brains only" or expecting a traditional European workday. American employers would simply fire anyone who quelled at working twelve-hour days for minimal wages, as there was such a surplus of workers. The only demand for workers he witnessed was for female servants, who had become popular among the prosperous classes. Those who thought they might turn to farming suffered from a serious "delusion," as the best farmland was already taken, and here too the standards of long days and extremely hard work prevailed. Only the communal settlements of Scandinavians and religious groups like the Mennonites prospered in the context of falling produce prices and rising land values. Campbell predicted a future of industrial farming, in which large corporations owned the land, employing migratory workers as needed. The depression slashed the incentives for immigration.[35]

Americans who lived through these hard times bore witness to the suffering around them. "There have been few periods in the history of the world," the editor of one western newspaper wrote, "when hard times have been so prevalent everywhere as during the past three years." Following "the failure of Jay Cooke in the autumn of 1873," all the experts had predicted "that the flurry was merely temporary and that we would soon recover from this shock." But that had not happened. Since the Civil War the American people had believed theirs was a prosperous nation with a sound structure, but they now knew that "We had for some years been standing over a volcano and the bankruptcy of one house broke the crust which had alone been supporting us, and we have ever since been going down, and apparently have not yet reached bottom." Papers warned of famine stalking the streets of America's cities, and as one headline at the beginning of 1877 read, "The Times Growing Worse and Worse." The signs of want were everywhere, with half the workers in the industrial areas of the country either out of work or only haphazardly employed, reduced to begging for food and waiting patiently for things to turn around. But just how long would they wait?

Would there come a point when America's poor had enough and would demand change?[36]

Anyone who looked closely at American cities would see disease, defeat, and death. Visitors to Baltimore may have noticed that the streets reeked of sewage, but they did not know that the drinking water was contaminated and contagious diseases found a breeding ground in the cramped apartments of the poor, killing up to 139 infants in a single week. There was little help for these suffering poor, especially when many charitable organizations were subject to embezzlement. For instance, the Chicago Relief and Aid Society, set up after the great fire of 1871, became a major scandal a few years later when it was discovered that the society's board members, including industrialists George Pullman and Marshall Field, invested these charitable funds in their own companies. The reality of the depression could be overwhelming; for instance in 1876 New York City's police stations sheltered 72,285 women and 114,591 men, for a total of 186,876 homeless people—the equivalent of just under one out of every five New Yorkers.[37]

The Centennial Exhibition

As the United States reached the milestone of its first century, serious stress fractures appeared in its foundation. Many of the foreign visitors, who came to observe this hundred-year-old republic, saw America being dragged under by "the cult of the Greenback," as Jules Leclercq called it. Those who fell beneath the wheels of the industrial machine could expect no help, as the United States had no fallback for the poor, no workhouses or social services, no major public works projects, and only a small army to absorb the unemployed. Every aspect of American society, from the inadequate public schools to the numerous churches, bore witness to stark class divisions, with ministers insisting that those who fell into poverty deserved their fate.[38] Even those who had jobs could not expect to earn a living wage. Goldwin Smith, an advocate of free-market economics, found American corporations "impersonal and morally irresponsible."[39] The Polish writer and future Nobel Prize–winning author of *Quo Vadis?*, Henry Sienkiewicz, was appalled by the poverty he saw in a land that claimed to be the home of opportunity. The majority of Americans "live without steady wages, working irregularly, looking with envy and certainly with hatred at the millionaires who have more money than they can count." Public officials even told him that the poor often committed petty crimes "for the sole purpose of getting into prison where at least food and shelter are assured."[40] Sienkiewicz, at least, saw little for the Americans to celebrate in 1876. Yet, despite the deepening financial distress and widespread suffering, the country went ahead with its planned birthday party at the Centennial Exhibition in Philadelphia.

Officially the centennial event was intended to celebrate one hundred years of the American republic. However, there was little actual commemoration of the past other than George Washington's false teeth, and not much honest consideration of the future. But then, as William Randel wrote, "The truth is that in 1876 the nation's schools and even the colleges paid scant attention, if any at all, to American history."[41] Instead, the Centennial Exhibition was a triumphal self-congratulation for where the United States was in 1876, a celebration of a commercial and industrial society with the majority of its exhibits showcasing all the wonderful things that one could buy and the machinery that made those goods; it was also a concerted effort to reject the reality of the depression.

The exhibition was enormous; with 60,000 exhibitors covering 285 acres, it was the most extensive exposition until the Chicago World's Fair of 1893. The main building was the largest structure in the world at the time, covering twenty acres and measuring 1,880 by 464 feet, with displays numbering in the thousands.[42] At a time when there were few paved streets in the United States, the exhibition's asphalt walks struck many as extravagant, while others strolled delightedly along their smooth surface. The Japanese Building, with its beautiful examples of Japanese products and art, started a fascination with all things Japanese. The *Atlantic Monthly* described the Japanese working their exhibit as "the sweetest-voiced, gentlest-mannered folk," who made everything else at the Centennial Exhibition seem slightly vulgar. The exhibition tried to spread the joy by giving prizes to nearly everyone involved. *Harper's Weekly* noted three separate advertisements in New York's newspapers on one day, each claiming the title of the best piano in the world based on a medal won at the Centennial Exhibition.

The highlight of the exhibition was without doubt the giant twin Corliss engines—the world's largest steam engines—that moved seventy-five miles of belts and shafts to drive long rows of machinery, from presses printing daily editions of the *New York Times* to a candy machine; from a popcorn maker to a Pyramid Pin Company machine operated by a small girl that stuck 180,000 pins into paper every day; from a machine that made 40,000 bricks a day to a chewing tobacco machine run by four blacks who sang hymns while working.[43] Every day thousands of people stared in awe at the new machines as though trying to reassure themselves, wondering what would come next as they entered the first year of their second century.

The Corliss engines were started up on opening day, May 10, 1876, by President Ulysses S. Grant and Brazil's emperor Pedro II. The emperor, one of the first people to enter the exhibition when the grounds opened at 10 A.M., won over the crowd with his plain style and friendly interest in all he saw. At the urging of the exhibition's music director, Theodore Thomas, the exhibition commissioned Richard Wagner to write a "Centennial March" for the opening ceremony, paying the famous composer $5,000 for a stunningly mediocre piece that made evident Wagner's disinterest. (Thomas, who had done so much to promote Wagner's music, indicated that he hoped this piece might never be played again.)[44] Dom Pedro was one of the few people to hear Grant's short speech, as the president never raised his head from the page before him. Grant promised that the exhibition would showcase the nation's progress in "law, medicine, and theology; in science, literature, philosophy, and the fine arts," little of which was actually on display. Grant's closing sentence may have impressed Pedro with its modesty, however: "Whilst proud of what we have done, we regret that we have not done more."[45] The emperor watched as on several occasions the impatient crowd almost got out of hand and had to be forced back by troops armed with bayonets. He also saw the hand and torch of Frederic Bartholdi's unfinished tribute to the United States, the Statue of Liberty.

Dom Pedro, who had translated several of Henry Wadsworth Longfellow's poems into Portuguese, wanted to know why the poet was not present. None of the officials cared to admit that Longfellow was not interested in attending and had refused to write anything for the occasion. Pedro also wanted to translate the "Star-Spangled Banner," and pressed several prominent Americans, including Secretary of State Hamilton Fish, for the lyrics, but he met no one who knew them right through. He kept his humor, however, and after being told the number of revolutions per minute of the Corliss engines, Dom Pedro drawled, "That beats our South American republics." At some level one suspects that Pedro was having a grand time pulling everyone's leg with his seemingly innocent but often disturbing questions, though it is hard to be certain. Privately, he thought the exhibition "huge, as everything is here. Good taste is what is almost always lacking."[46]

It seems likely that Pedro did not see Thomas Eakins's *Gross Clinic*, arguably the single most important American painting of the period. Its stark realism disturbed the judges so deeply that they not only refused to award it any kind of prize, they actually transferred it from the Memorial Hall to the much overlooked Army Post Hospital. Pedro did see several works by Winslow Homer, including *Snap the Whip* and *The American Type*, though he failed to record if those raised or lowered his opinion of America's artistic ability.[47]

Culturally the Centennial Exhibition was a stodgy affair. The literary figures invited to represent the country were all safe and from the East Coast; the one Southerner, Sidney Lanier, was from Georgia. The West was ignored as too outrageous; Joaquin Miller, Bret Harte, and Mark Twain were all considered and rejected. Even the Midwest was too edgy for the organizing committee, which passed over William Dean Howells. And it almost goes without saying that no women, such as Helen Hunt Jackson, were considered. But then, most of those invited, like Longfellow, refused to attend. Despite writing a hymn for the opening day ceremony, which he sent "with many misgivings," John Greenleaf Whittier also chose to stay away from the exposition. "The very thought of that Ezekiel's vision of machinery and the nightmare confusion of the world's curiosity shop appalls me." Though not invited, Howells felt a bit more pride in the exhibition. It is "in these things of iron and steel that the national genius most freely speaks," he wrote in the *Atlantic Monthly*. With time the nation would turn to art, but "for the present America is voluble in the strong metals and their infinite uses." Reflecting on the giant Corliss engines, Howells was convinced that "no one can see the fair without a thrill of patriotic pride." On the other hand, he thought the Centennial Exhibition lacked cohesion or an underlying principle, and the absence of national unity was amply expressed by the fact that most of the Southern states refused to participate.[48]

The celebration of the one hundredth anniversary of the United States would have been the logical time for disgruntled Confederates to put aside their grudges and join in the national festivities. But they did not feel like it. On January 6, 1876, Congress had stated the ideal, adopting a resolution praising national harmony as "a most auspicious inception of the centennial year" and urging the people's representatives to "do no act which would unnecessarily disturb the patriotic concord now existing and increasing, nor wantonly revive bitter memories of the past." Though it passed the House unanimously, this resolution proved an empty gesture; there was no national harmony and the members of Congress did their part to increase the divide, as was amply illustrated when Democratic representative Samuel S. Cox called Republican James G. Blaine "the honorable hyena from Maine" during one debate. The same persistent sectional animosity largely lay behind Southern Democrats blocking congressional funding for the Centennial Exhibition. A bill to loan the exhibition $1.5 million passed only after an amendment was added requiring full repayment to the government before funds could be distributed to stockholders. The bill passed 37 to 20 in the Senate and 146 to 130 in the House, which was far from a harbinger of national unity.

Indeed, the celebratory tone of the centennial did not go unchallenged. In Charleston, only blacks celebrated Independence Day; in Lawrenceburg, Kentucky, a Confederate flag was hung from the county courthouse; in Oronogo, Missouri, a riot greeted the raising of a Confederate flag; while Vicksburg, Mississippi, refused to celebrate the Fourth of July until 1963.[49]

It is impossible to state how many people attended the exhibition, a fact that hasn't stopped people from trying to do so. Dee Brown confidently asserted "one of every five Americans came to celebrate the glories of his Republic" in the six months the Centennial Exhibition was open, basing this calculation on the 9,910,966 people who passed through the self-registering turnstiles, assuming that no one ever passed through twice. A ticket holder could leave the park and return later the same day, and many did so after taking a look at the menus of the exhibition's rather bland but stunningly expensive restaurants.[50] Nonetheless, many people did go to see the exhibition and were dazzled by its wonders. Longfellow finally overcame his objections and was thoroughly bored by the industrial displays. Ralph Waldo Emerson was "dazzled and astounded" by the Centennial Exhibition, while Fukui Makoto, the Japanese commissioner to the exhibition, found the whole affair a bit undignified. The crowds, he wrote, "come like sheep, run here, run there, run everywhere. One man start, one thousand follow. Nobody can see anything, nobody can do anything. All rush, push, tear, shout, make plenty noise, say damn great many times, get very tired, and go home."[51]

What most fascinated these pushing, rushing crowds was America's technological inventiveness. Some visitors gravitated toward unusual items such as Plummer's Patent Fruit Dryer, "an Oregon invention for extracting all the moisture from fruit without impairing the flavour," which caught John Leng's attention, as did a new process so mysterious he put it in quotes: "canning." Leng praised the Americans for their skill with agricultural implements, finding it hard not to "admire the 'knackiness,' compactness, and neatness of their innumerable inventions." However, he thought that the Americans should concentrate on what they did well, which was farming, and leave the manufacturing to the British, who knew what they were doing.[52] It was difficult to reconcile that limited view with the many wonders on display, and no other visitor who wrote on the exhibition suggested that the United States just pack it in and get back to the farm. Instead they marveled at the numerous recent inventions, such as an automatic baby feeder and a gas-heated iron operated by foot bellows. Also on display were such new developments as dry yeast and ready-made shoes, as well as two food items popularized by the exhibition: the banana and hot popcorn. Much attention was paid to the typewriter; for fifty cents a letter could be written for the visitor on this amazing machine. (However, typewriter sales were slow, even after Mark Twain bought one and his *Tom Sawyer*, the bestselling book of 1877, became the first novel published from a typed manuscript.) Popular with visitors from around the world was the newspaper pavilion with its ten thousand pigeon holes, each holding a different newspaper and all available for free reading. And thousands of children watched in awe as Old Abe, the eagle mascot of a Wisconsin Civil War regiment that witnessed thirty battles, was fed his daily live chicken.[53]

The single most important display at the exhibition aroused little attention at first, until the ever enthusiastic Dom Pedro stepped in to give it a nudge. On June 25, as the exhibit judges, accompanied by the Brazilian emperor, were completing a day of awarding medals, Pedro saw a teacher from the Boston School for the Deaf with whom he had earlier conversed. As the judges headed for the door, Pedro went in the opposite direction. "How do you do, Mr. Bell? And how are the deaf-mutes of Boston?" When Alexander Graham Bell hastily told Dom Pedro that he had to return to Boston that evening, the Brazilian persuaded the senior judge, Sir William Thompson (later Lord Kelvin), to examine the young man's telephone at once. They were duly impressed and gave Bell a medal. Dom Pedro became a sponsor of the inventor, being one of the first to purchase a telephone and helping to see that Rio de Janeiro installed a phone system in the early 1880s.[54] The Brazilian emperor deserves a great deal of credit or blame for what followed in the communication revolution.

In contrast to the exhibition's triumphant materialism, Sabbatarians kept the grounds closed on Sundays, while health authorities forbade smoking and prohibitionists attained a ban on the sale of alcohol. No aspect of American life evoked such relentless foreign criticism as Sabbatarianism. Few visitors claimed to understand it, and all resented it as the cities became tedious places on Sundays. On a side trip from Philadelphia to Baltimore, George Augustus Sala found nothing to do on Sunday but go to church, and that he would not do, preferring to stay in his room and curse all the church bells. Baltimore on Sunday might be theologically admirable, but "it was undeniably most deplorably and desperately dull." He could not understand how people spent the day: "Beyond church-going there was nothing to do; and one could scarcely go to church morning, afternoon, and evening." Americans had reached a smug perfection with "not a cigar shop, not a fruit or candy or cake store, or ice-cream saloon" open. What made it all the worse was that he could not get a cocktail in Maryland on Sunday.[55] A few communities made an exception for "the eternal American game of base-ball," but entire states found that sport far too frivolous for a proper Sabbath.[56] Even New York, bustling six days a week, grew eerily quiet on Sunday as the shops closed up and people stayed home. Leclercq soon learned that Americans got around their own laws through silly subterfuges, like buying liquor from the side door of bars—an example of the "American pharisee."[57] Visitors to the exhibition complained bitterly that Philadelphia closed on Sunday and that the city itself "is very rectangular."[58] "How gay it was!" Offenbach stated with heavy irony. "The few people you met were coming from church with funeral faces and their Bibles in their hands." And should you be "unfortunate enough to laugh, they would have you arrested."[59]

To foreign observers, the exhibition's Sunday closing was just another example of the middle-class bias against workers. The only way a laborer, who had just Sunday off, could visit the exhibition was by taking a day off without pay—though some companies organized group outings. A French workers delegation reported that American workmen are "the slaves and drudges of Capital." The demoralization of American workers baffled the French, given that the ideology of the country held that "every workman is in a sense his own master." But workers in the United States could not escape a life of ceaseless toil. "The probability is that if he starts business for himself, however hard he worked for another, he will work still harder on his own account," wrote the sympathetic Leng. "Hard work is the rule in America."[60]

The exhibition sought to avoid all possible controversies by giving in to the forces of religious purity and focusing relentlessly on technology. The only explicitly political exhibit was the Women's Pavilion, which represented the one social division in America that openly troubled the placid façade of the exhibition. Everything in the Women's Pavilion was built and operated by women—which made it a cause of some wonder and hostile humor—and it faced the government building, where a pair of cannon aimed directly at the women across the way. The women's committee invited Empress Teresa of Brazil to open the pavilion, though she arrived a bit late as Julia Grant had made off with her carriage. The empress pulled a tasseled gold cord to start the steam engine that ran the looms, spinning frames, and printing press. This central engine was overseen by Emma Allison, who became a popular attraction as thousands of visitors stared in amazement at this talented and charming engineer who politely answered even the most foolish and misogynist questions.

The pavilion's prize exhibit was a collection of etchings made by Queen Victoria, but far more popular and significant was the weekly magazine *New Century for Women*, every issue of which was printed at the pavilion and which condemned the iniquities of the male-dominated economy, proclaiming that equality for women would come through financial independence. The journal pulled no punches and did not defer to polite gender conventions. In a society in which women were legally segregated in advance of blacks, the accomplishments of the Women's Pavilion had a substantial impact and served its purpose, getting visitors to think and talk about the role of women in modern America.[61] Li Gui, sent by the Chinese government to report on the Centennial Exhibition, was impressed by the mechanical wonders, but it was the women's building that captured his imagination. He found it "novel and ingenious," as it displayed items made entirely by women and "even the people in charge of this exhibition hall were women." These women were friendly and well informed, but had "the spirit of men; I greatly respect and like them." Most surprising to Li Gui were the conversations he had with those who wanted political rights for women. While acknowledging that "their arguments are very novel" and their opinions occasionally extreme, he insisted that "after hearing them they seem reasonable." His conclusion was a strong recommendation to his government that China start educating women. "If we do not teach and encourage them, their talents will be buried; does this not go against Heaven's intention in creating people?"[62]

The German scholar Friedrich Ratzel shared much of Li Gui's enthusiasm for American women, whom he found more cultured than the men. "[A]lmost without exception, women here stand far above men in everything that one usually calls education or culture." However, he saw a danger in the greater "intellectual tastes and noble sentiments" of women in that they made females "dissatisfied in marriage and leads to an exaggerated opinion of one's self and causes them to misjudge their true position in life." Too much education would lead women to realize the degree to which they were not equal. Exaggerating wildly, Ratzel traced the recent increase in women converting to Catholicism "to the dissatisfaction of women with their fate." As a consequence, "one convent after the other is being filled up." Major M. Philips Price was also charmed by the American women he encountered, who had excellent manners "and talk quite freely and easily." Unlike Ratzel, he did not see them rushing into nunneries, but rather becoming interested in marrying Europeans. For those European men who want "beauty, money and talent," the United States was the place to look, "and I shall certainly advise my friends to patronize the American matrimonial market, and so infuse a little fresh blood into our sluggish old country." Paul Toutain understood female dissatisfaction, as American men paid almost no attention to women, especially not to their wives, which helped to make attentive Frenchmen like Toutain all the more attractive.[63]

On the same day that the Women's Pavilion opened, the National Woman's Suffrage Association met in New York City. From the Quaker minister Lucretia Mott to the popular romance novelist E.D.E.N. Southworth, most of the country's prominent women spoke in favor of granting women the vote. The guests of honor were Julia and Abbey Smith, two scholars in their eighties from Glastonbury, Connecticut, who refused to pay any taxes until they gained the right to vote. Even as their cows and property were seized by local officials, the two women remained true to the principle of no taxation without representation. As one speaker said, "To women this government is not a Republic, but a hateful oligarchy." The meeting approved a series of resolutions that began, "That the women of this nation in 1876 have greater cause for discontent, rebellion, and revolution than our fathers of 1776." The battle for women's rights was potentially the most radical movement of the age, as Susan B. Anthony called on America's women "to meet in their respective towns and districts on the 4th of July 1876, and to declare themselves free and independent, no longer bound to obey the laws in whose making they have had no voice."[64]

Former allies saw no reason to aid women. Sarah Spencer, the first lobbyist for women's rights in American history, attended the 1876 Republican convention in Cincinnati. On the opening day, June 14, she approached two of the speakers, Senator John Logan and Frederick Douglass, both supposedly supporters of a woman's right to vote, and demanded to know why neither had mentioned that issue in their speeches. Each gave an incredibly lame response, Logan insisting he had "entirely forgot," while Douglass said, "I would have spoken for you if I had thought of it." Spencer forcefully pushed herself onto the platform and spoke to the convention, which ignored her. The lawyer Phoebe Couzins received the same response from the Democratic convention in St. Louis two weeks later.[65] American independence had its limitations, even in the centennial year.

At the exhibition, the July 4 parade was reviewed by General William T. Sherman, Prince Oscar of Sweden, and General Saigo of Japan; the president of the United States was nowhere to be seen. Word quickly spread that Grant did not show up because of the heat. Once-sympathetic journals such as the *Atlantic* condemned the president: "It was the most condensed yet crudest statement of his estimation of the dignity of the country, the occasion, and his office. The credit of the day and nation could only gain by his absence."[66] Again, the guests of honor, Emperor Pedro and Empress Teresa, sat through one boring speech after another with their usual polite dignity. In the midst of the ceremonies, the monarchs were surprised to see a woman march boldly up to the stage where Senator Thomas Ferry was about to read the Declaration of Independence and hand him a sheet of paper. The woman was Susan B. Anthony, and she presented Ferry with a copy of the Women's Declaration of Independence. When Ferry took the paper without saying a word, Anthony and four companions walked through the crowd, handing out more copies of the document, and as Ferry began to read Jefferson's words, Anthony got on the musician's platform at the other end of the hall and read hers.[67]

While the Civil War had convinced many people that the young republic was not viable, within a few years of the end of the war it appeared that the United States was on the verge of becoming the world's first multiracial democracy as freed slaves gained the right to vote. The country continued to grow and extend its power and wealth, population, economy, railroads, and international reach. And yet, even as the centennial celebration drew to a close in November 1876, it seemed that the whole edifice was collapsing. Depression, government corruption, racial violence, stolen elections, the defeat of the United States Army, class conflict, and myriad forms of potential violence appeared to be tearing society apart. Numerous visitors held to the conviction that trouble lay ahead.[68] Who knew what the new year of 1877 might bring?

The Coming Storm

Americans seemed caught in a search for meaning in their rapidly industrializing nation. Now that the country was reunified after the horrendous Civil War of 1861–1865, they struggled to decipher the signs that might indicate the direction in which they were headed. Who were they as a people? What made them truly American? What meaning could the American people take from the celebration of one hundred years as a republic? Who better to answer these questions than the president of the United States?

On December 5, 1876, Ulysses S. Grant delivered his final State of the Union address to Congress. Grant offered what amounted to an apology for having held the office of president. He began by noting, "It was my fortune, or misfortune, to be called to the office of Chief Executive without any previous political training." As a consequence, "Mistakes have been made, as all can see and I admit." Those mistakes, however, were made not by him but by those he appointed, and there was nothing unusual there since "history shows that no Administration from the time of Washington to the present has been free from these mistakes." Grant would leave it to history to determine the worth of his presidency, confident that historians would find that "failures have been errors of judgment, not of intent."

Grant reminded Congress that when he assumed the presidency, the Civil War had ended just four years earlier. The leading issue of those years was whether "Government should be thrown immediately into the hands of those who had so recently and persistently tried to destroy it, or whether the victors should continue to have an equal voice with them in this control." Reconstruction meant only this, "except that the late slave was enfranchised, giving an increase, as was supposed, to the Union-loving and Union-supporting votes." That reconstruction—to guarantee the life of the union and the freedom of everyone living in the South—began in earnest once he became president. Those who remained supportive of the national government faced grave danger, with even federal officials subject to threats of violence. Postmasters serving in the Southern states were so often intimidated that they "have specially requested that their reports of apprehended danger should not be made public lest it should result in the loss of their lives." In such a situation, Grant indicated, the very maintenance of peace and the protection of the Southern electorate was an enormous accomplishment.

Now the country was stable and peaceful, Grant asserted, and the centennial had gone off very well; the Philadelphia exhibition accounted "a great success" that should engender "pride of country." But in that context he finally referred to what must have most dominated the thoughts of his audience: the need to reform their method of choosing a president. "Under the present system there seems to be no provided remedy for contesting the election in any one State." His recommendation, though, was strangely off-topic: "the disfranchisement of all who can not read and write the English language, after a fixed probation." Leaving Congress to ponder that curiously irrelevant recommendation, Grant ended his speech with palpable relief: "With the present term of Congress my official life terminates."[69]

Looking entirely backward, Grant gave no thought to the future. But then few of those enmeshed in the events of 1876 did so. They had had a fine party in Philadelphia, but with surprisingly few thoughts to the future beyond the technological. Several observers used the metaphor of a volcano to describe the problems America faced politically, in the South, and with race and class relations.[70] Southern white racists appeared intent on terminating democracy and establishing a phalanx of one-party states united by their loathing for their former slaves and for those who would support the blacks' rights as citizens. Management seemed bent only on its own aggrandizement, while the frustration of workers built like lava held in check too long. And though the country held an election in November, challenges to and investigations of the results meant the United States would have no idea who would be the next president until the spring of 1877. After one hundred years, could they really claim to be united states?

Thus, as the year 1876 ended, the nation, or so it seemed in America's newspapers, was gripped by despair and crisis. As the *Philadelphia Inquirer* noted in its last issue of the year, 1876 had begun with "great enthusiasm" generated by the centennial celebration but had not gone as so many had hoped, with "prosperity and happiness" widely spread. Some individuals had profited from the exhibition, but far more were caught in "adversity, grief and privation, much of which, caused by man's inhumanity to man, could have been prevented." Now came the "racket made by guns and pistols with which the old year will be fired out." The *Baltimore Sun* similarly observed that the year that began with such celebration ended with the current "crisis of affairs involving the free institutions of the republic."[71] John Swinton, the editor of the *New York Sun*, looked at the United States and saw poverty for most and excess power in the hands of too few. "The power of money has become supreme over everything," he wrote. Spreading its influence through the corridors of state legislatures and Congress, the elite acquired "all the special privileges and special legislation which it needs to secure it complete and absolute domination." This moneyed elite "must be broken or it will utterly crush the people."[72]

Workers had been particularly hard hit, as unemployment rose and wages declined. Even the exhibition had been a threat to workers. As a reporter for the *Philadelphia Inquirer* wrote of a workers' day at the exhibition, the men looked "with amazed interest" at the assembled technology in Machinery Hall, fully understanding that "unless he elevates himself above the low level of a thoughtless laborer for the bread of the passing day, he and his offspring must continually sink lower in the social scale, and perhaps perish in the end of starvation." Samuel Gompers remembered 1876 ending with "the seemingly impossible," more layoffs and wage reductions, with workers reduced to "a starvation level." The centennial year ended not with celebrations but with privation, and the sort of "misery and want that made the Christmas season of 1876 one that long haunted our memories."[73]

The whole country was on "the ragged edges," as the *Wheeling Register* put it, wrapped up in the current electoral crisis. In its last issue of the year, the *Macon*

Weekly Telegraph's headline screamed "President Preparing for War," while the *Duluth Weekly Tribune* reported on its front page that the Democrats were declaring "Tilden or War." The *Salt Lake Weekly Tribune* reported "Rumors of War," as "dark clouds" gathered that "threatened violence" ahead. In Chicago, the journalist Mark "Brick" Pomeroy, a man not known for temperate behavior, published a laundry list of disasters facing the nation: the political parties were "manipulating" election returns, the nation "is filling up with tramps," "bankruptcies are the order of the day," the people were afraid to defend their rights, the prisons were packed, "famine and despair are entering thousands of homes" while "rich men are growing richer and the poor men are growing poorer." Unemployment, foreclosures, alcoholism, "rape, robbery, murder," all were on the increase. With "women going into prostitution for bread" and "men going to vagabondage for lack of opportunity to labor," there seemed little hope for the nation with the government in the hands of "the Money Power that rules to misrule." Tilden was the Rothschilds' attorney, Hayes was "the bank owner's dummy," while Grant was likely to "whip out his sword and try to be Emperor."[74] The *Harrisburg Patriot* warned of "revolutionary plots," while the *Philadelphia Chronicle* maintained that "to talk of compromise is to condone crime."[75]

Many newspapers found a fitting symbol for the state of the country in the last days of 1876. Other than the deadlocked election, just about the only other news that found its way into these last newspapers of 1876 was the terrible train wreck in Ashtabula, Ohio, on December 29. The Lake Shore's Pacific Express had plunged seventy feet into a ravine when a recently completed bridge collapsed as a result of avoidable structural errors, killing at least eighty people in the process. For editorial writers nationwide, the collapse of the Ashtabula bridge was not simply an indication of the malfeasance of the railroads and the misplaced confidence of the public, but of the potentially unsound structure of the whole country. They were all watching a giant train wreck and could not avert their eyes. Across the country many observers would have agreed with the way one newspaper ended its list of disasters: "The storm is coming!"[76]

2

Seeking White Unity

The year 1877 dawned on a world of unrest and gloom.

—Samuel Gompers[1]

Henry Adams kept a list. It was a long list, and one that kept growing. Every time whites committed a violent act against blacks in his northern Louisiana parish of Clairborne, Adams would add a new entry. There was number 323, Manuel Gregory, who was hanged for "talking to a white girl," and number 333, Abe Young, who boasted that he was going to vote Republican, for which crime he was "shot by white men." Number 453, Jack Shanbress, was whipped and then shot "because he was president of a Republican club." Ben Gardner, number 454, was "badly beaten by white men" for refusing to work another year on "Mr. Gamble's plantation." Eliza Smith, number 486, was "badly whipped by Frank Hall" for "not being able to work while sick," while a black man known only as Jack, number 599, was "hung dead, by white men," for having "sauced a white man"—talking back after having received instructions. By the time Henry Adams presented his list to a committee of the United States Senate in 1878, there were 683 violent incidents.[2]

When the committee asked Adams what they could do to help, he responded that only federal troops proved effective in curbing violence. The white terrorists, called "bulldozers" in Louisiana, had no reason to fear local law enforcement, which they dominated. When federal troops came into his parish during the 1876 election, the bulldozers "stopped killing our people as much as they had been; the White Leagues stopped raging about with their guns so much."[3] But only the governor could request federal assistance, and that office had fallen into the hands of the terrorists themselves.

Henry Adams had been a slave for twenty-two years and knew well the anger of Louisiana's whites. But when he joined the United States Army, he met whites worthy of his respect, and in 1869 at Fort Jackson he began attending a school for black soldiers run by a white woman named Mrs. Bentine. Adams learned to read and write, and felt a new world opening before him, one that promised greater equality and opportunity. The following year he voted for the first time and perceived the potential of democracy, becoming a leader in his community and a successful businessman. As an organizer for the Republican Party, he found a number of whites with whom he could work and whom he esteemed for their honesty and courage, but the majority of whites belonged to the Democratic Party and sought to silence those with whom they disagreed. Reconstruction gave the former slaves hope for the future, but it aroused the rage of the defeated Confederates who despised the new order.[4]

Adams attempted to defend that order, the one that, under the Constitution's Fourteenth Amendment, promised freedom to all citizens. At every step he and his fellow blacks confronted a wall of hatred. The Democrats were not just political opponents, they were bitter enemies in a deadly struggle for the future of their country. They had no interest in compromise or in the traditional workings of a democratic government premised on accepting the peaceful exchange of power between political parties; they wanted it all, every office and complete political, social, and cultural control, with no room for any dissenting voices. Those who did not share a conviction in the inherent right of white men to rule totally were to be silenced and the South would speak with a single voice. These whites, so often the same people who had supported slavery and secession in the past, did not hesitate to use violence to attain their ends—thus Adams's list.[5]

Joe Johnson was another name on that list, but also Adams's friend. He had been elected constable in East Feliciana Parish on the Republican ticket in November 1876. When Adams went to visit his friend in the first days of 1877, he found a grieving widow standing by the smoldering ruin of Johnson's house. She told him how more than fifty white men had come to their house and killed her husband "because he refused to resign his office as constable." They set fire to the house with Johnson inside, leaving him for dead. But Johnson crawled from the house into a pool of water, even though "all the skin was burnt off of him." The terrorists saw Johnson and shot him several times, though he lingered on for several days before dying. Adams had to admit to Johnson's widow that there was little chance for justice, "as I knew that white men had been killing our race so long, and they had not been stopped yet." Standing with her children, Mrs. Johnson wept, "O, Lord God of Hosts, help us to get out of this country and get somewhere where we can live."[6] It would be a cry heard in different forms repeatedly through the South in 1877, and would start a movement with enormous long-term consequences for the entire country.

One of the unpleasant constants of American history is the willingness of whites to promote unity at the expense of black Americans. As Edmund Morgan pointed out for the colonial period, C. Vann Woodward for the late nineteenth century, and Dan Carter for the mid-twentieth century, class tensions can be sidestepped by appeals to racism.[7] The United States in its centennial year was deeply divided not just along racial and class lines, but also politically and geographically. The nation may have officially been reunified by the Civil War, but at the time of the 1876 presidential election there was every indication that the divide between the white South and the North remained as wide as ever, with the Democratic Party firmly identified as the party of Southern white racists.[8] Theoretically, such a division should not have mattered, as democracy handed power to the majority. In 1876 the majority in several Southern states consisted of Republicans, black and white. But from the point of view of white Democrats, such a vision of democracy was inaccurate and traitorous to the race, for the South belonged to white men, and among that group Democrats predominated. White racists therefore felt completely justified in using any means necessary, from legal barriers to violent intimidation, to keep blacks from the polls. For several years, the only thing preventing the Democrats from forcefully seizing control of all the Southern states was the United States Army. In the election of 1876 and its immediate aftermath, Southern Democrats succeeded in one of the most significant political maneuvers in American history: creating a one-party region that would consistently block social progress for the next century. This chapter documents the crushing of the democratic hopes raised by the Civil War, and the heroic efforts of African Americans determined to hold on to their hard-won status as citizens of the United States.

Democracy Defeated

In the aftermath of the Civil War, many Americans came together in an effort to remake the United States as a true democracy. The Republican Party—the party that had swept Abraham Lincoln into power on the eve of the Civil War—benefited from this effort, as many whites joined the South's blacks in opposition to racists in both the North and South. For a dozen years there was a substantial effort to integrate the South's four million freed slaves into the civic life of the nation. Southern white supremacists came to hate these Northern whites (often referred to as "carpetbaggers") and their Southern allies—whom they called "scalawags"—as much as they despised blacks, for these "race traitors" threatened the mythology of white unity and black inferiority.[9] The educational efforts of the "New England school marms" especially drew their ire for directly undermining a half century of proslavery propaganda based on the intellectual inferiority of blacks. Those opposed to Reconstruction united in a reenergized Democratic Party, while those favoring progressive programs enthusiastically supported the Republican Party.[10]

For a decade the two parties fought for the future of the South. The Democrats claimed that only they spoke for the South since they included the majority of whites. Backed by the forces of the federal government, the Republicans operated on a democratic principle based on the humanity of the freed slaves. So long as the federal government protected the rights of the South's black citizens, they and their white allies tended to win open elections in the Deep South. Frustrated by this adherence to democratic ideals, the Democrats responded with violence and intimidation, sending the Ku Klux Klan into the field on a terror campaign aimed at keeping Republicans, black and white, from voting. This struggle came to a head in 1871, with President Ulysses S. Grant requesting and fighting for legislation to end the Klan's reign of terror. Congress acted to protect the nascent Southern democracy with the Ku Klux Klan Act, which made it a federal crime to prevent citizens from voting, holding office, or attaining the equal protection of the laws. Thanks to Grant's vigorous enforcement and the dramatic federal trials in South Carolina, Klan violence diminished dramatically over the next four years.[11]

Temporarily defeated, the Democrats regrouped in 1874 and 1875 with "the Mississippi Plan," a carefully orchestrated effort to seize political control of the Deep South states through fraud, fear, and violence.[12] They found an additional useful weapon in exaggerating charges of corruption against the Southern Republican governments, helping to undermine Northern support for Reconstruction. While there were notable examples of malfeasance among these governments, the real issue for most Southern whites was that for the first time in their history state governments were spending money on infrastructure, most annoyingly on education for the freedmen and poor whites. This governmental activism required higher taxes, much as in the northern and western states, and threatened to undermine the absolute authority of the traditional Southern elite, who transformed these expenses for the improvement of their states into examples of fraud and outrageous waste. Through control of the press, Democrats crafted a mythology of criminal carpetbag governments bankrupting the Southern states for their own benefit that lasted for the next century.[13]

By 1876 the Democrats had reclaimed control of all the Southern states except for Louisiana, Florida, and South Carolina, though their hold on the South remained tentative in the face of persistent Republican opposition. In 1876 the Democrats aimed, as many foreign visitors observed, at nothing less than a "solid South," control of the entire region, with the intent of reestablishing white supremacy. In 1877 they expanded that goal to include the total suppression of dissent and the creation of fourteen one-party states.

The first step was to convince the North that the Confederacy was truly dead and gone. Though they had opposed funding the Centennial Exhibition, Southern Democrats used it to their advantage, manipulating sentimentality and Northern hopes of reconciliation as a cover for racism and the restoration of white supremacy. "Moderates" traveled through the North promising national harmony and evoking the centennial at every turn while blaming the Republicans for disrupting the atmosphere of reconciliation with their wild charges of

violence against blacks, displaying their hurt feelings for all to see and commis-
erate.[14] As Attorney General Amos Akerman of Georgia wrote, "When speaking
for effect at the North," Southern Democrats "say much about accepting the results of the war in good faith, and respecting the rights of everybody." But back
home they contradicted their own words with "drastic policy and unguarded ut-
terances."[15] Many observers realized that the promised centennial "reconciliation," or what the Concord, New Hampshire, *Independent Statesman* called the
"centennial gush fever," was a sham. A Missouri Republican observed that no
one could hope to attain public office who had not served in the Confederate army. He was "sick and tired" of all this talk of reconciliation, as it ended
with Republicans being disenfranchised. "What some optimistically viewed as
mutual reconciliation," William Gillette wrote, "might have actually been a
peace settlement on southern terms."[16] Stated bluntly, those who violated the
law won.

In contrast to the sympathy Southern Democrats received, Southern Republicans found little support in the North for their plight, where even their fellow
Republicans were losing interest in the rights of the freedmen and democracy in
1876 and 1877. Northern whites wanted sectional peace, so long as the cost was
borne by nonwhites. Northern newspapers stopped reporting acts of white violence, following the lead of the *New York Times* in insisting that aging abolitionists like Wendell Phillips and William Lloyd Garrison "represent ideas in regard
to the South which the majority of the Republican party have out-grown." Even
in Massachusetts, public opinion shifted away from supporting the aspirations
and even the lives of the freedmen. At a public meeting in Faneuil Hall called to
protest General Philip Sheridan's use of troops to evict five Democrats from
disputed seats in the Louisiana legislature, Wendell Phillips confronted the gathering: "My anxiety is for the hunted, tortured, robbed, murdered" blacks of
Louisiana. A heckler shouted, "That's played out, sit down." The crowd favored
the heckler.[17]

Congress retreated from Reconstruction in 1875 by defeating the Force Bill
intended to protect blacks from intimidation, especially in the exercise of their
right to vote. The Supreme Court abandoned Reconstruction the following year
with *U.S. v. Reese*, in which the court effectively terminated the enforcement of
the Fifteenth Amendment, Chief Justice Morrison Waite ruling that the federal
government could act only to prevent intentional racial discrimination and
lacked any authority over suffrage.[18] Incredibly, Justice Waite wrote that "the Fifteenth Amendment does not confer the right of suffrage upon any one," but
only protected an individual from having his vote taken away because of race,
leaving Congress with no avenue for ensuring a right to vote. In the midst of a
national election, the Supreme Court made clear that it valued order over
democracy and justice, giving the Southern Democrats a green light to proceed

with the process of disenfranchisement. In such a context, the only way the Republican Party could hope to remain alive in the South, and that black men could continue to exercise their rights, was through the authority of the executive branch to protect constitutional rights. President Grant had done a fairly good job in defending the freedmen from violent whites—thus the vital importance for the Southern Republicans to win the 1876 presidential election and maintain a friendly executive in Washington.[19]

Unfortunately for those hoping for continued Republican dominance of the executive branch, the party of Lincoln had two strikes against it in 1876: corruption and the depression. Deeply divided over the former, the party had little understanding of the latter as Congress voted to return to the gold standard, which further deflated the money supply. The country appeared gripped by malaise, a sense that the technological accomplishments celebrated at the Centennial Exhibition did not match the country's political immaturity. Corruption and inefficiency were not limited to the Grant administration; every social institution seemed marked by greed and dishonesty. There was a widespread sense—well expressed in such popular literature as Mark Twain and Charles Dudley Warner's *The Gilded Age*, and John De Forest's *Honest John Vane* and *Playing the Mischief*—that the country's top-heavy prosperity and moral decay went hand in hand.[20] Former Republican senator Carl Schurz found it "painfully obvious" that the government "is fairly honeycombed with corruption." Schurz admitted that the Republican Party appeared to embody this ethical decay and had lost anything approximating moral authority, but he and many other Republicans hoped for a revival of the moral basis of both their party and their country. At a meeting of reformers Schurz laid out the work of the centennial generation: "Our generation has to open the second century of our National Life, as the Fathers opened the first. Theirs was the work of independence, ours is the work of reformation." Reform did seem to be the leading issue of the time, at least among the intelligentsia; Mark Twain gave one of the few political speeches of his life late in the campaign, speaking in favor of reform.[21]

Though the Republican reformers initially gravitated to former treasury secretary Benjamin Bristow, they found much to recommend Rutherford B. Hayes, who had just been elected to a third term as Ohio's governor. He was honest, well liked, from a pivotal state, and the least divisive of the candidates. Hayes astutely understood that the corruption and ineptness of the Grant administration made both parties "more disposed to look for candidates outside of that atmosphere." He also benefited from a solid record as a "radical Republican" who had fought bravely in the Civil War and supported Reconstruction yet favored government reform and sound money policies. Party leaders immediately saw him as a logical compromise candidate without the baggage of the other leading candidates. Judge William M. Dickson wrote that Hayes's primary qualification for the nomination "is his intuitive perception of what at the moment is practicably attainable"; Hayes agreed with that pragmatic evaluation. When General Philip Sheridan, who had commanded Hayes during the Civil War, wrote that he hoped for a "Hayes and [congressman William] Wheeler" ticket, Hayes expressed no surprise except to admit to his wife, "I am ashamed to say, who is *Wheeler?*"[22] A few months later, in June 1876 at the Republican National Convention in Cincinnati, New York congressman William A. Wheeler would indeed be selected as Hayes's running mate.

Hayes, Wheeler, and the Republican Party talked constantly of reconciliation in 1876, forgiving the Southern Democrats for all their previous sins, from slavery to secession to suppression of black votes. Frederick Douglass bravely responded to this forlorn hope in a speech to the Republican convention on June 14, in which he asked: "What does it amount to, if the black man, after having been made free by the letter of your law, is unable to exercise that freedom; and after having been freed from the slaveholder's lash he is to be subject to the slaveholder's shotgun?"[23] He wanted to know if the whites would "make good on the promises in your Constitution," and made a telling comparison between Russia's serfs, recently freed by the czar and given "a few acres of land on which they could live and earn their bread," and America's slaves, who received nothing. "You turned us loose to the sky, to the storm, to the whirlwind, and, worst of all, you turned us loose to the wrath of our infuriated masters." It was a powerful speech. The *Cincinnati Commercial* answered Douglass by insisting that the "colored people are free—they have the ballot—and they must learn to protect themselves."[24] Such views represented the majority Northern perspective and an astounding willingness to not look at what the Democrats had done the previous year in Mississippi, blatantly stealing the election through violence and fraud.

The Democratic Party also nominated a strong reform candidate, New York's governor Samuel Tilden. Tilden played a major role in bringing down the notorious Boss William Tweed of Tammany Hall as well as in breaking the state's corrupt "Canal Ring." While Tilden supported "hard money," which is to say the gold standard, his running mate, Thomas A. Hendricks of Indiana, stood with the western branch of the party in favoring "soft money," or an inflationary paper currency based on silver. Given Republican weaknesses, Tilden seemed assured of victory as he could draw on his own considerable wealth, well-known organizational skill, and the ruthlessness of the Southern Democrats.[25]

Both centennial candidates were conservative and conciliatory, politically and personally. Neither spoke nor wrote with any great eloquence, distrusting emotion almost as much as they did one another. Both candidates ran excruciatingly dull and cautious campaigns that covered over the substantial passion at play throughout the country. Though a brilliant organizer who personally oversaw every stage of his national campaign, Tilden demonstrated a debilitating lack of energy at key moments—for instance, mysteriously waiting a month before delivering his official acceptance of the nomination in a well-documented and largely unreadable letter that was three times the length of the party platform. Bogged down in administrative details and specific ways to reduce government expenditure, Tilden's letter was far from a call to righteous battle. When the editor of the *New York Star* suggested to Tilden that his letter was a bit dense for most people to read, Tilden snapped, "It was not intended for *people* to read."[26] Repeatedly, Tilden would procrastinate in responding to even the most outrageously falsehoods levied against him. As a corporate lawyer, he preferred to present his case in a carefully formulated fashion, thick with detail and supportive evidence, weak on rhetorical flourish. This caution may reflect a becoming dignity, but it is also possible that Tilden suffered a stroke or from Parkinson's disease.

Hayes's letter accepting the nomination was not as ponderous, but equally dreary, declaring that he, too, would work for civil service reform and keep the nation's currency on a sound footing—reassuring reform-minded Republicans who had left the party to vote for Horace Greeley in 1872. Unlike Tilden, Hayes pledged to protect the civil rights of all citizens, but the only surprise in Hayes's letter was his promise to not seek a second term, which he argued ensured against his using patronage for purely political advantage.[27]

Since presidential candidates were not supposed to demean themselves by actual campaigning, these letters pretty much marked the end of their public engagement until after the votes were cast. That did not stop each from carrying on active behind-the-scenes efforts to influence voters. Hayes recruited the young novelist and editor William Dean Howells to write his official campaign biography. But when Howells appeared a bit too enthusiastic, Hayes threw cold water on the author by warning him to avoid controversial topics. In a sentence that must have baffled Howells, Hayes told his biographer, "Silence is the only safety." Similarly, he advised his friend and campaign surrogate Representative James Garfield to speak only of "general principles," as "I think explanations and defenses are bad things." In other words, it was best to keep the voters in the dark and appeal solely to party loyalty.[28]

Within party circles, though, Hayes actively promoted a strategy of focusing on the one issue he believed would unify and activate the North: "The danger of giving the Rebels the Government." Hayes wrote key Republicans that "waving the bloody shirt," as reminders of the Civil War were called, guaranteed success. He wrote James G. Blaine, "Our strong ground is the dread of a solid South, rebel rule," which serves to lead "people away from 'Hard Times,' which is our deadliest foe." Hayes felt justified in keeping the Civil War alive eleven years after its end since the Democrats fielded former Confederate officers and officials in every Southern state; in South Carolina every Democratic candidate was a

Confederate veteran. Hayes found his party divided on this strategy, with many angrily arguing that "waving the bloody shirt" diverted attention from reform, while others adhered to the advice of Charles Nordhoff of the *New York Herald* that they should appeal to conservative white Southerners, "the old Whigs," and build a new national coalition. As Nordhoff wrote Hayes, "The darkies you'll have any how; the white Whigs are what you want to capture." Frederick Douglass completely disagreed, writing the party's chair, Zachariah Chandler, "It is the same old conflict: Liberty, union and civilization on the one hand and Slavery disunion and barbarism on the other." The result was an unorganized and largely incoherent Republican campaign, though among rank-and-file Republicans the decisive issue was not the corruption of the Grant administration but, as Hayes predicted, a fear of the consequences of a "Solid South."[29]

The Democrats, in contrast, had a geographically focused message: reform in the North and white rule in the South. Their northern campaign was based on Tilden's voluminous position papers generated by the "Literary Bureau" he operated out of his home, while in the South they relied on intimidation and violence.[30] When Attorney General Alphonso Taft investigated events in the South, he reported to Hayes that the Democrats were using murder to win the election. Taft was doing his best to protect black citizens but the Democratic majority in the House of Representatives crippled this effort by refusing to appropriate funds for the army. In September Taft told Hayes that it had now become "simply a question whether the Fifteenth Amendment shall be given up." Hayes felt even more certain that the Republicans should be trumpeting this violence as their premier issue, but said nothing in public.[31]

With the election just two weeks away, Hayes had little doubt that he would be beaten by criminal conduct, including "violence and intimidation" in the South. Except where the candidates were concerned, the election of 1876 was passionate, vicious, violent, and chaotic. The campaign proved most corrupt and brutal in the Southern states, where the Democrats launched what one historian called "the most violent, disgraceful election in American history."[32]

There was little secret that Southern Democrats sought to create a one-party region by any means necessary. Shortly before the election the *New York Tribune* began an editorial on the subject: "A solid South—what does it mean? Why does it alarm all thoughtful men?" Benjamin Bristow wrote in answer to this question that it "portends mischief for the country." Democrats saw no reason to alter Chief Justice Roger Taney's *Dred Scott* reasoning that blacks had "no rights that the white man was bound to respect." In the South they aimed less to elect Tilden than to seize control of state governments, and never give them up again. As one observer stated: "If by trading him [Tilden] off to certain defeat they could get control of South Carolina they would cheerfully do it. All they want is to get it once, knowing very well that they can hold it forever."[33] Southern

Democrats were comfortable with their opposition to democracy. The *Augusta Constitutionalist* stated that "a minority of white men, when united in a common purpose, never fails to drive from power a semi-barbarous majority." The Pine Bluff Democratic Club boasted the tautology, "This is a white man's country and as such has to be ruled by the white men."[34]

The Democrats used an impressive variety of illegal methods to undermine democracy in the South, developing techniques that they would employ for the next hundred years. Since the bulk of Republican support came from the freedmen, the Democrats did all they could to limit the black vote, starting with organizing gun clubs to, as one Louisiana paper put it, place "control of the state government in the hands of the white people." South Carolina alone had nearly three hundred such clubs, which reported to General James Conner.[35] Military in organization, the gun clubs were well armed, generally included numerous Confederate veterans, and served as "the armed wing of the Democratic party."[36] Several Republicans favored the creation of their own gun clubs, but the party's leadership feared that such an effort would provoke further bloodshed.

Unopposed, Democratic gun clubs undertook night attacks on black communities in every Southern state, firing random shots into houses and targeting influential opponents. Democrats also used boycotts and proscription, signing resolutions swearing not to buy from any business operated by a Republican and refusing to sell to, rent to, or hire any Republicans. Any white who refused to sign on to these efforts was deemed an enemy and ostracized as well. Nor were they above purchasing votes; Democratic clubs boasted of the number of votes or promises to not vote that they had purchased. Democratic election officials "forgot" to open polls in black areas, or failed to provide enough polling places or ballots.[37]

Democrats did all they could to undermine the ability of the freedmen to defend themselves. Democrats worked in the Southern state legislatures to cut off funding for the militia or to defeat militia laws outright. Wherever Republicans dominated the militia, former advocates of the states' right to field military forces suddenly took the position that they no longer needed such an outdated military organization. In Tennessee, Democrats disbanded the state militia outright; in North Carolina and Mississippi Democratic judges issued injunctions forbidding state officials from paying the militia for their service. With white mobs seizing militia arms, Southern Republican governors found it necessary to sneak guns into their states in boxes marked with false identifiers such as "books," in much the same way abolitionists had once smuggled their "Beecher's Bibles" past Democratic inspectors.[38]

A surprising degree of creativity went into demoralizing Southern Republicans. In parts of South Carolina, blacks were forced to buy red shirts, the uniform of the racist gun clubs in that state; those not wearing the red shirt were considered fair targets for violence. In Louisiana blacks found in public without "protection cards" promising to vote Democrat were beaten. Throughout the South Democrats attended Republican meetings, taking down names for future retribution, and circulated rumors of "Dead Books," in which they recorded the names of blacks targeted for eventual execution. Gun clubs paraded through towns with coffins bearing the names of prominent Republicans, acquired cannon and fired them off in public as a warning to freedmen, and routinely surrounded Republican meetings, seeking to intimidate the participants into fleeing, often firing shots to hasten their departure. Far too often the threats accelerated from intimidation to economic discrimination to violence. T.M. Shoffner, a prominent Republican in the North Carolina legislature, was first ostracized by his fellow whites and then became the target of an assassination plot. Doubting the ability or willingness of local officials to protect him, Shoffner moved to Indiana.

As in the days of slavery, the First Amendment ceased to exist in the South; only opinions supportive of white supremacy were allowed and Republicans feared expressing their views in any public setting. "The Colored Citizens of Laurens" petitioned for protection from local Democrats, as no one "dares to speak nor act with respect of his franchise privileges without being in extreme danger."

That silencing of dissent extended to poor whites, a significant percentage of whom welcomed the increased state spending brought in by the Republicans, as well as the pleasure of watching the traditional elite slapped down. Thus, once they gained the majority in a legislature, Democrats usually began by passing a poll tax, effectively denying the right to vote to the state's poorest residents, black and white. Two-thirds of Kentucky's adult black males were immediately disenfranchised by the poll tax. Those who could pay found themselves in the unusual position of having their tax refused.[39]

George Tillman led his gun club in disrupting a rally in support of South Carolina's incumbent governor Daniel Chamberlain. Pointing at Chamberlain, Tillman called on his followers to hang him immediately. Such methods proved effective, as Chamberlain stopped appearing in public. Democrats delighted in the circular reasoning that their silencing the governor proved that he could not govern and that the state therefore had to have a Democratic government. In Louisiana a Democrat took a more direct approach and shot Republican governor Stephen B. Packard. Similarly, Democrats assassinated Joseph Crews, the leader of the militia in Laurens, South Carolina, and North Carolina's militia commander Colonel Sheppard, a Union army veteran.[40] Republican governments appeared helpless to respond to these acts of violence.

Terrorism swept the South in the weeks leading up to the election. It is difficult to know how many Southern Republicans were killed outright during the 1876 election campaign. In South Carolina an estimated 150 blacks were murdered in the weeks before the election, with no evidence of Republicans using violence or disrupting any Democratic meetings in that state. Some acts of violence threatened to become national scandals and revive Northern support for federal action, such as the Hamburg Massacre. Hamburg, a South Carolina town on the Savannah River settled by many black Union veterans, was celebrating Independence Day when two local whites demanded that the black militia company move aside for their carriage to pass. After an exchange of a few choice words, the militia parted for the whites, who went to Augusta, where they complained vigorously about the militia's uppity conduct. The following day, several hundred angry whites led by former Confederate general Matthew C. Butler attacked the town, leaving twelve blacks and one white dead, including the town's marshal.[41] When asked by a congressional committee to explain his conduct, Butler said that blacks had "little regard for human life." He failed to mention that Marshal James Cook's tongue had been ripped out and placed in his hands by members of the white mob.[42]

Several Democratic members of Congress as well as the party's chair, Abram Hewitt, begged their Southern brethren not to kill anyone else until after the election, lest the Republicans make it an issue. There were those in the North who perceived that the Democrats "had initiated a program to shoot the Republican Party into a minority in South Carolina," yet few demands for action issued from the press or the political leadership.[43] President Grant, like most Northern whites, condemned the crimes but failed to respond with force, writing Governor Chamberlain that "the scene at Hamburg, as cruel, blood-thirsty, wanton, unprovoked, and uncalled for, as it was, is only a repetition of the course which has been pursued in other Southern States." Yet Grant rejected Chamberlain's appeal for more federal troops. Instead, the governor was told to rely on "the better judgment and co-operation of [the] citizens" of his state to bring the criminals to trial "without aid from the Federal Government." Seven men were indicted, but none were ever brought to trial. On October 17, 1876, Grant issued a proclamation ordering the gun clubs to disband within three days—a meaningless gesture lacking any enforcement mechanism.[44] The gun clubs mocked these proclamations, disbanding only to re-form themselves as the "Allendale Mounted Baseball Club" or the "Columbia Musical Club with Four Twelve Pounder Flutes."

Southern Republicans such as South Carolina's Cass Carpenter felt betrayed by their party and government. "We who have borne the brunt of their persecution are no longer willing to be targets for assassins unless the republican party of the North will stand by us, and in such a way as will be of some avail to us." Such pleas fell on deaf ears, as Northern Republicans saw no hope for the survival of their party in the South. In many Southern states the Republicans just gave up, often not even fielding local candidates. The absence of substantive response emboldened Southern Democrats, who saw that violence worked and accelerated their use of force over the next several months—long after the election was over.[45]

The most graphic indicator of this renewed enthusiasm for violence came on September 19 in Ellenton, South Carolina. Hundreds of armed whites descended on this town where the local blacks had organized a militia unit. Following a running battle along the area's roads, three hundred whites cornered one hundred blacks in the nearby woods. Just as the whites were about to launch their assault, Captain Thomas Lloyd arrived with a detachment of U.S. infantry and dispersed the gun club. When Lloyd surveyed the town he found dead bodies scattered about; somewhere between thirty and fifty blacks had been killed over two days by members of the gun clubs, while the black militia killed three whites. Among the dead was state representative Simon Coker, who had been shot in the head while on his knees praying.[46]

In Texas the election provided the opportunity for settling a number of long-simmering feuds. One of the first targets of Democratic anger proved to be the German settlers of east Texas, who had remained loyal to the Union during the Civil War and supported the Republican Reconstruction government. Vigilantes launched an ethnic war against the Germans of Mason County, killing an unknown number of Republicans and driving the sheriff from his job and the county.[47] The governor sent in the Texas Rangers to restore peace, but, as the adjutant general reported, the newly installed Democratic grand jury refused to bring indictments, even in cases with numerous witnesses, and the rangers had to release all their prisoners.[48]

Though it upset their Northern brethren, Southern Democrats made little effort to disguise their willingness to kill. The editor of the *Charleston News and Courier*, himself a member of a gun club, wrote that electoral victory would come "in only one way, BY ARMED FORCE."[49] In Mississippi Democrats expressed their determination "to carry the election at all hazard, and in the event of any blood being shed in the campaign, *to kill every white Radical in the county.*"[50] Unlike the Ku Klux Klan earlier in Reconstruction, the new Democratic movement of 1876 and 1877, often called the White League or the White Man's Party, was not secretive, holding its meetings in the full glare of day without hoods. Clearly the Democrats felt they had nothing to fear from local, state, or federal officials no matter how outrageous or deadly their actions. There was no secret to their violent or partisan nature. The South Carolina Democratic election plan publicly stated the role of the gun clubs in the upcoming election: Martin W. Gary's "No. 1 Plan of the Campaign" called on every Democrat to be armed and held responsible to keep one black from voting Republican "by intimidation, purchase, [or] keeping him away" from the polling place. At all

times blacks were to be shown "that their natural position is that of subordina-
tion to the white man." Gary advised against threatening a Republican: "If he
deserves to be threatened, the necessities of the times require that he should die."
He reminded his readers that "A dead Radical is very harmless." This "Shotgun
Plan," as it was known, was a public invitation to violence from one of the nation's two political parties.[51]

Southern Democrats united in their effort to steal the election of 1876 and
"teach the negroes a lesson," ignoring state borders to establish white hegemony.
As a telegram from a gun club in Louisiana to the board of supervisors in Trin-
ity, Texas, promised: "Can raise good crowd within twenty four hours to kill
your negroes."[52] It is not surprising that violence marred the election from Virginia to Texas as Democrats insisted that those who would stand in their way
"must be exterminated." As Congressman A.S. Wallace said, "Intimidation is the
order of the day and terrorism reigns supreme."[53]

Many Republicans wondered what had happened to the hard-won victories
of the Civil War, and could not understand why there was no national outcry
against this illegal insurrection by the war's losers. The Democrats, according to
Republican John Meeks, had transformed American politics into a system based
not on "the number of votes but the number of guns."[54] Grant tried to intervene, but with the U.S. Army already spread thin, the best he could do was send
one thousand more soldiers south and instruct General Sherman "to hold all the
available force under your command, not now engaged in subduing the savages
on the Western frontier, in readiness" to protect voters "without distinction of
race, color or political opinion." Unfortunately, that "available force" was a small
number of troops; General Thomas H. Ruger had just 1,144 soldiers under his
command in South Carolina.[55] Power in the South was shifting away from the
national government, as revealed by Wade Hampton's march through South
Carolina. The former Confederate general undertook what Richard Zuczek called
a "perverse reversal of Sherman's" march, "with the same message: you are powerless against us, and we will do as we please." Hampton rode at the head of long
columns of red shirts, entering towns under banners reading "Carolina, Home
of the White Man," and ending with a massive show of strength in Charleston.
The purpose of the march, according to General Conner, commander of the gun
clubs and candidate for attorney general, was to "scare the darkies."[56]

Probably the single most remarkable feature of this terror campaign is the extent to which it did not stop the democratic spirit of the courageous freedmen and
their white allies. Despite the massacres at Hamburg and Ellenton, and the many
other acts of intimidation and brutality by the Democrats, Republicans bravely
trooped to the polls throughout the South. Democrats found it necessary to steal
the election by other means and make absolutely certain that the majority of blacks
would never have the chance to vote again. Those with delicate consciences even

persuaded themselves—and tried to persuade their Northern brethren—that trampling on the civil rights of the blacks was for their own good.[57]

As Election Day approached, astute observers such as Horace Redfield, who was covering the election in the South for the *Cincinnati Commercial*, thought it made little difference to the blacks who won. Tilden would withdraw troops immediately and leave the blacks to white tyranny, while Hayes would do exactly the same. But black voters put their faith in the party of Lincoln. Wherever troops were present, the black vote went overwhelmingly Republican; where there were no troops, even the blacks seemed to be voting Democratic, at least according to the tabulation by white officials. In Augusta, Georgia, blacks were required to vote at separate ballot boxes and produce proof that they had paid their taxes, while whites did not need to offer such evidence; officials turned away half the blacks but not a single white man. Not surprisingly, Tilden carried the district by a three to one margin. As Redfield reported, Democratic fraud was widespread and thorough, taking every means possible to secure victory for Tilden and the state tickets. Redfield dismissed the election as "a farce," and just hoped that the electoral results were obvious. On Election Day, November 7, Redfield wrote: "God grant that the American people have chosen a President to-day by so large an electoral vote that there can be no contest. I am fearful."[58]

Stealing an Election from Thieves

With 81.8 percent of eligible voters casting their ballots, the election of 1876 produced the highest voter turnout in a presidential election in American history. More than eight million voters cast ballots, two million more than in 1872— and that despite the enormous effort of Southern Democrats to prevent Republicans from voting.

Nationally, the Republicans did well, despite the theft of the election in Southern states, picking up thirty-three seats in the House, leaving the Democrats with a slim lead. Hayes won eighteen of the twenty-two non-Southern states with 52 percent of the vote and a majority of 255,640. It is highly probable that a fair election in the South would have produced a substantial victory for Hayes and a narrow Republican majority in the House of Representatives. For instance, if the black majority had not already been disenfranchised in Mississippi, Hayes would surely have carried that state and its twenty-three electoral votes. Horace Redfield did not doubt that a "fair election" in the South would have left Tilden "without a majority of the popular vote." Officially, Tilden ended with a national majority of 251,746 for 51.5 percent of the vote.[59]

On Election Day, Hayes wrote in his diary, "I still think Democratic chances [are] the best." Nonetheless, he feared that the result would be so tainted by Democratic corruption that the election would produce a "contested result," and might even lead to bloodshed. He added that he and his wife Lucy "felt more anxiety about the South—about the colored people especially," and was certain that a Democratic triumph would mean that "the amendments will be nullified, disorder will continue, prosperity to both whites and colored people, will be pushed off for years." There was little doubt in his mind that the only ones to benefit from a Tilden victory would be the old elite who bore responsibility for the Civil War. As news arrived that Tilden had carried New York, New Jersey, Indiana, and Connecticut, as well as the entire South, it appeared that the Democrat had won with 203 electoral votes. Hayes and his wife calmly headed for bed, comfortable with the knowledge that they would not have to move anytime soon.[60]

While Hayes, certain of defeat, slept through the Ohio night, General Daniel Sickles precipitated a national crisis. Sickles, one of the most notorious men in the country for having murdered his mistress's lover and gotten away with it, wandered from a late-night party to the now quiet headquarters of the Republican National Committee in New York City. Looking over the returns, Sickle observed that, with all the Pacific states going for Hayes, the Republicans could still pull off a one-vote victory in the Electoral College if they held on to South Carolina, Florida, and Louisiana. Entirely on his own authority, he sent off telegrams to Republican officials in these states and Oregon all saying the same thing: "With your state sure for Hayes, he is elected. Hold your state." At 6 A.M. on the morning after the election, he received responses from South Carolina and Oregon promising to stall the announcement of official election results in their states that might favor Tilden. Sickles sent several additional telegrams and headed home for bed, having successfully launched electoral challenges in all four states.[61]

Just at Sickles was leaving Republican headquarters, William E. Chandler, a member of the Republican National Committee, and John C. Reid, the editor of the *New York Times*, came rushing in. The paper had received sufficient information to question Democratic victories in the three key Southern states and the *Times* had proclaimed the election results "doubtful." Going over the telegrams on the desk of Zach Chandler, the party's national chairman who had passed out from too much whiskey, the two men concluded that Hayes could actually win. Finally waking up Zach Chandler, Reid and William Chandler explained the situation and persuaded the chairman to send off a barrage of telegrams intended to assert victory in the questionable Southern states. In New York that morning the *Tribune*, *Sun*, and *Evening Post* all declared Tilden the winner, but the *Times* and the *Herald* each insisted that there was no clear winner, the latter paper's headline reading, "The Result—What is it?"[62] The Republicans had launched a process that would keep the nation in suspense over the fate of the presidency for the next four months.

"If the decision to contest the election had been left to Hayes," his biographer

Ari Hoogenboom wrote, "Tilden would have been president." Hayes had no doubt that the Democrats had carried the South through "fraud and violence," but perceived no alternative to acquiescing in his defeat as he could not conceive how the Republicans would persuade the nation to accept his election by a single questionable vote in the Electoral College. Hayes wanted nothing to do with a contested election and insisted that there "should be no taint of dishonesty" on the part of the Republicans. The party leadership, however, proved less scrupulous, and fought diligently and ably to steal the election right back from the Democrats. In contrast, Tilden was certain he had won, but his party's leadership had no idea how to proceed.[63]

Over the next few weeks, all attention focused on the Southern election boards. Republican boards in the three contested Southern states used Democratic fraud as sufficient reason to throw out the results in several counties, while Democratic boards threw away those from black precincts.[64] There can be little doubt that the Southern election boards, whether dominated by Republicans or Democrats, were corrupt, but the Louisiana board made corruption into performance art. Throughout the South the election boards included members who were themselves running for office or were the recipients of government patronage that they hoped to see persist. But in Louisiana they simply offered themselves to the highest bidder, receiving competing offers from Tilden's nephew Colonel William T. Pelton and a Republican delegation led by Senator John Sherman and Representative James Garfield and backed by the well-stocked wallet of Chicago businessman Charles B. Farwell. Over the ensuing weeks, the two parties used every method, fair and foul, to capture the votes of Louisiana, Florida, and South Carolina. Republicans, who had deeper pockets, triumphed in all three states. Democrats rejected the official tallies and called together their own election boards, which validated a slate of Tilden electors, also setting up rival governments in opposition to the victorious Republicans.[65]

Historians continue to debate who actually won the elections in these three Southern states, with the deciding factor generally being the degree of legitimacy granted to African American voters. Like Mississippi, South Carolina and Louisiana had black majorities and significant numbers of white Republicans, indicating that Democratic claims of victory resulted from an unfair and corrupt electoral process.[66] Democrats definitely stole the gubernatorial election in South Carolina, proclaiming Wade Hampton the winner over incumbent Republican William Chamberlain by the slim margin of 92,261 to 91,127. But most counties required voters to sign in by race, showing that more whites voted in twenty-six of South Carolina's thirty-one counties than were eligible to vote, a disparity that did not result for blacks in any county in the state. The most recent and sophisticated effort to accurately access the vote in South Carolina gives the victory to Chamberlain by at least five thousand votes.[67] Horace Redfield made a fine distinction in the case of Louisiana: if the election had been fairly conducted, Hayes would certainly have won, but a fair count of the votes returned would have given the victory to Tilden.[68] The results in Florida are more difficult to determine at this remove, especially as both sides in the contest were remarkably corrupt. What is definite is that all three states started 1877 with competing state legislatures, governors, representatives to Congress, and presidential electors.[69]

As the new year of 1877 dawned, the nation appeared hopelessly deadlocked. Officially Tilden had 184 electoral votes and Hayes 165, leaving 20 votes up for grab. Hayes needed them all; Tilden required only a single vote to be president. The framers of the Constitution had not considered such a situation, simply stating that the electoral votes should be "directed to the President of the Senate," typically the vice president of the United States, who "shall, in the presence of the Senate and House of Representatives, open all the Certificates and the votes shall then be counted." But who decided which votes to open and read if there were two—or, as with Florida, three—sets?[70] Since Vice President Henry Wilson had died in 1875, Michigan Republican senator Thomas W. Ferry became president of the Senate. Hayes and many Republicans thought that the Constitution left it up to Ferry alone to decide which votes to accept; most members of Congress, Republican and Democratic, objected to putting such power into the hands of one man. Suggestions for resolving the mess multiplied, from a congressional investigation of the actual ballots to holding a new election. President Grant felt that the evidence indicated that Hayes had carried Florida and South Carolina, but that the corruption on all sides in Louisiana was so extensive it was impossible to accept its electoral votes, giving Tilden a lead of 184 to 177 and throwing the election, as the Constitution requires, into the House of Representatives—a proposal with which Samuel Tilden agreed. Given the Democratic majority in the House, Grant's fellow Republicans were horrified by this suggestion and quickly hushed up that proposal.[71]

Further complicating matters, the parties were far from unified, many members of Congress putting out feelers to the other side to see what they could get in return for their support. Just as New York's Republican senator Roscoe Conkling conferred with Democrats about the level of patronage he might enjoy under President Tilden, so did many Southern Democratic congressmen inquire about what they stood to gain from a Hayes administration. This latter group had a simple but deeply disturbing price: Republican acquiescence in "home rule," Democratic control of the Southern states. Such a deal did not translate into a typical political trade-off as it meant that the Republican Party would have to abandon both democratic principles and millions of blacks to the harsh mercies of white supremacists. It also seemed clear to many Northern Republicans that, in return for the presidency, their party would lose several states to the opposition. Putting aside these concerns, prominent Republicans close to Hayes began quiet negotiations with representatives of the Southern white elite. Hayes personally believed that, with economic incentives, he could lure Southern whites to join a bipartisan effort remaking the South. He had some grounds for this optimism, as many Southern Democrats hoped to further regional development through the improvement of their rail networks. Tom Scott's Texas & Pacific Railroad, which promised to connect the southeast with California, particularly interested many prominent Southern Democrats. Scott, one of the most powerful railroad men in the country, did his best to grease the wheels of compromise in Hayes's favor.[72] Historians still debate the particulars and significance of these negotiations, though it is at least fair to say that a number of Southern Democratic leaders reached an informal understanding with key Republicans. A great deal of ink has been spilt attempting to disentangle the agreement that resolved the electoral crisis of early 1877, but the results validate the suspicion that some sort of deal was reached.[73]

Meanwhile, Congress struggled to find a solution, remaining in continuous session into March. In January, each house appointed a committee to investigate the election. The House committee, dominated by Democrats, discovered that corruption in the three questionable states meant that all three should go to Tilden; the Senate committee, dominated by Republicans, concluded that fraud and voter suppression in the three states meant that all should go to Hayes. This was not helpful. The House Judiciary Committee then suggested the appointment of a joint special commission, which, after some very careful negotiation, led to a commission of five House members, five senators, and five Supreme Court justices. Originally the five justices were to be drawn from a hat, but Tilden killed that plan with the bon mot, "I may lose the Presidency, but I will not raffle for it."[74] While Tilden and many other political leaders doubted the constitutionality of the commission, a consensus emerged that there were so many recipes for disaster that some resolution was required as quickly as possible, no matter how tenuous the legality of the process.[75] Hayes and Tilden reluctantly accepted the commission in order to avoid a civil war. When one of Tilden's advisers suggested publicly opposing the commission, Tilden shot back, "What is left but war?"[76]

Tilden's fears found validation in the increasing calls for violence circulating through the country. It was a time of rumors, disturbing and bizarre—and occasionally true—as well as loud demands for violence. Reportedly, President Grant was planning a coup, while Confederate general Joseph Shelby supposedly announced in St. Louis that he would lead an army on Washington to put Tilden in the White House. Hearing this latter story, Confederate hero Colonel John S. Mosby, the "Gray Ghost," went to the White House and offered Grant his services to help ensure Hayes's inauguration. Indiana's Republican senator Oliver

Morton would soon bring charges of treason against Tilden and Hendricks for having been members of the pro-Confederacy Knights of the Golden Circle, while the state's newly elected Democratic governor James D. Williams predicted that civil war would be the "inevitable consequence" of Republican actions. In Cincinnati, Union veterans, suspecting a conspiracy by former Confederates, invaded a Democratic meeting, sparking a brawl.[77] Democratic representative Fernando Wood called for the impeachment of President Grant, while Donn Piatt, editor of Washington's *Sunday Capital*, was arrested for sedition after he called on the people to "take up arms" and demanded "Tilden or Blood!"[78] "The political situation was never so critical as now," Georgia Democratic representative Benjamin Hill, a former Confederate senator, wrote in an open letter to his constituents. "Our constitutional system is on a magazine of powder, and 10,000 fools, and some that are not fools, are striking matches all around it." He warned that unless they all behaved calmly and patriotically, "the most horrible civil war that ever disgraced and destroyed liberty and humanity" would ensue.[79] Looking back over nearly fifty years in Washington, the prominent journalist David Barry declared the election crisis of early 1877 the "preeminent" event of his lifetime—the only one capable of destroying the United States. The congressional sense of urgency grew from the conviction that they were on the verge of "a civil war more desperate than the one that had closed but twelve years before." This "would not have been a war of sections," as every state divided into partisan camps, resulting, "most public men think, in the destruction of our political institutions." In his whole life, Barry wrote, "I may truthfully say that no scenes made a deeper impression upon me than those" surrounding the Electoral Commission.[80]

Troubled by the professed willingness of his fellow Americans to take up arms so soon after their devastating Civil War, President Grant prepared to defend the capital. Grant could call on only 25,000 unpaid troops, most of them in the West, and had to tread lightly. He could not afford to alienate the Democrats, but they gave every indication of deliberately weakening the ability of the federal government to protect its democratic institutions. Grant adroitly maneuvered his available units to send a message of resolve while not appearing aggressive, ordering artillery companies placed on all the entrances to Washington, D.C., the streets of which, as the *New York Herald* reported, "presented a martial appearance." Grant ordered the man-of-war *Wyoming* to anchor in the Potomac River by the Navy Yard, where its guns could cover both the Anacostia Bridge from Maryland and the Long Bridge from Virginia. Meanwhile, a company of Marines took up position on the Chain Bridge. General Sherman told the press, "We must protect the public property, . . . particularly the arsenals." There was no way Sherman was going to let white Southerners get their hands on federal arms without a fight, and his clever placement of a few units helped to forestall possible coups in Columbia and New Orleans.[81] Grant avoided recognizing either of the two candidates as the winner, while making certain that everyone understood his willingness to use force to protect the government. He publicized his orders to Sherman and the movement of troops, effectively keeping the crisis within the halls of Congress while forestalling any hasty rush to settle the matter with force.[82]

Members of Congress began bringing pistols to the Capitol, and in Columbus, Ohio, a bullet was shot through a window of the Hayes home while the family was at dinner. General Sherman transferred more troops to the capital and paraded them daily on the city's main roads. When Abram Hewitt asked Sherman if he would continue to take orders from Grant if no one became president on March 4, Sherman responded in his usual blunt style: "The term of President Grant ends at twelve o'clock on the 4th of March. He will then be in no position to give orders to me, and I shall receive no orders from him." Of course, that left open the question of what would happen if no one was inaugurated president.[83]

The deliberations and political maneuverings of the Electoral Commission have been closely and extensively studied. The key fact is that the Democratic Party made a catastrophic error in judgment in deciding to back the only independent vote on the commission, Justice David Davis, who belonged to the Greenback Party, for the Senate seat from Illinois. Tilden's nephew Colonel Pelton reasoned that if the Democrats supported Davis in his bid for the Senate, the justice would side with Tilden on the commission, never imagining that the justice might act with integrity. Acknowledging his debt to the Democrats, the newly elected Senator Davis declared it a conflict of interest to serve on the commission, and his fellow justices then selected Republican Joseph Bradley to take Davis's place. The commission suddenly found itself with an eight-to-seven split in favor of the Republicans, which would end up being the tally on every vote by the commission and led to the election of Rutherford B. Hayes as president.[84]

The commission finished its deliberations at 7 P.M. on Tuesday, February 27, voting eight to seven to give South Carolina's electoral votes to Hayes and Wheeler. The March 1 congressional session considering these final votes was long and raucous. "It was," in the words of one journalist, "a stormy night both inside and out of the great marble building." Crowds gathered, many growing angrier by the minute. "Thousands of excited citizens fought with the police for admission to the building already over-crowded, and the galleries were fairly bursting with the throngs that besieged the doors."[85] In the Senate, Kentucky's Joe Blackburn called on the people to "rise in their majesty and might, not only to rebuke and spurn, but to punish, aye, if need be in blood, the perpetration of all the villainy and scoundrelism of this proceeding." One observer reported that Blackburn's speech "aroused the Democrats, those on the floor as well as those in the gallery, almost to a frenzy."[86] In the House of Representatives, several Democrats attempted to force a recess and tried numerous devices to stall acceptance of Hayes as president, but Speaker Samuel Randall refused to recognize any of these motions. Louisiana's Democrats called on Grant to withdraw the troops in their state immediately. Grant responded by showing one of their number a telegram to Republican governor Packard telling him that troops would no longer be used in support of his government, promising to send it as soon as the electoral count was finished. Thus bribed, Representative William Levy announced on the floor of the House that "The people of Louisiana have solemn, earnest, and, I believe, truthful assurances from prominent members of the Republican party, high in the confidence of Mr. Hayes, . . . that he will not use the federal authority or the Army to force upon those States governments not of their choice." No one spoke up for the black citizens about to be denied their rights. Levy called for the completion of the electoral count. At 4:10 A.M. on March 2, 1877, Senate president Ferry announced that Hayes and Wheeler had 185 electoral votes to Tilden's and Hendricks's 184 votes. The great electoral crisis was over. As David Barry wrote, "It was a test of our republican form of government more severe than any to which it has been or has since been subjected."[87] Now the question was: who would pay the price?

Selling Out Southern Blacks

Rutherford Hayes waited until he was certain of the outcome before leaving for Washington. He and his family left Columbus on the afternoon of March 1 in two special rail cars provided by Tom Scott, arriving in Washington at 9:30 the following morning. So sudden were the events concluding the election of 1876 that there was no time to plan an inaugural ball, and the inauguration was postponed a day to Monday, March 5. In his inaugural address, Hayes celebrated his selection as president following such a disputed election as an indication of a spirit of compromise, which he thought indicated a future of peace and prosperity in "a union depending not upon the constraint of force, but upon the loving devotion of a free people." Still, Hayes promised to use his full Constitutional power to protect the rights of all citizens, calling on the races to behave themselves, as Southern unrest could only be "remedied by the united and harmonious efforts of both races." Hayes failed to mention that he had to rely on the kindness of racists since there was no way he could enforce Constitutional rights in the South because Congress had adjourned on March 3 without appropriating funds for the army.[88] Reversing his own election strategy, he did not dwell overmuch on the establishment of a solid South, but rather talked at length about civil service reform. It was in the context of reform that he delivered the only memorable line of his speech—"he serves his party best who serves his country best"—and the one real surprise: a proposed Constitutional amendment limiting the president to one six-year term. Hayes's inaugural address acknowledged that while the Republicans may have won the election, they had lost the South.[89] After delivering his speech, Hayes, in a moment of unbridled passion, turned to his wife and shook her hand.[90]

Not everyone accepted Hayes's inauguration gracefully. Justices Stephen Field and Nathan Clifford boycotted the ceremony. Charles A. Dana, editor of the Democratic *New York Sun*, printed a picture of Hayes with the word "fraud" written across his forehead, and appears to have begun the habit of referring to him as "Rutherfraud B. Hayes," a usage adopted by Republican senator Roscoe Conkling.[91] The *Cincinnati Enquirer* charged, "By the grace of Joe Bradley, R. B. Hayes is 'Commissioned' as President, and the monster fraud of the century is consummated." Though Democratic Speaker of the House Samuel Randall would always put Hayes's title in quotation marks, his party quietly accepted "President" Hayes.[92]

The Democrats had every reason to be satisfied with the deal, for the presidency was the only election challenged by the Republicans. Hayes made good on his promises not to intervene as, over the next two months, the Democrats moved to seize those local governments still in Republican hands and to perpetuate their dominance of the South for a century to come. The only part of the deal Hayes could not fulfill was the building of the Texas & Pacific Railroad, but that was largely because Dana, through the *Sun*, made public the negotiations between Southern Democrats and Republicans. The ensuing outrage ensured that Congress would never agree to subsidize Scott's proposed line.[93]

By the middle of March, Southern Republicans realized that they were definitely being sacrificed on the altar of national reconciliation. "There is little effective opposition to the policy of surrender," Governor Chamberlain wrote, as the "North is tired of the Southern Question, and wants a settlement, no matter what." Amos Akerman angrily observed that the Southern Democrats took everything Hayes offered them "and laugh at him for being so easily taken in." Hayes gave it all away and got nothing in return.[94]

Many Northern Republicans also felt betrayed by their own party, especially when Hayes announced his cabinet. Secretary of State William M. Evarts had been Andrew Johnson's supportive attorney general; Secretary of the Interior Carl Schurz had supported Greeley over Grant in 1872 and long called for an end to Reconstruction. But worst was the former Confederate officer and Democratic senator David M. Key, selected for the lush patronage position of postmaster general. Robert Ingersoll asked in amazement, "What party do I belong to now?!" Many Republicans wondered why they had worked and voted for Hayes, one stating that the "whole cabinet is a gathering of icebergs or men with blood no hotter than that of a toad."[95] Except for Secretary of the Treasury John Sherman, the cabinet consisted completely of outsiders, suggesting Hayes's commitment to building a nonpartisan conservative coalition. Shortly after Hayes's inauguration, Representative Benjamin Butler declared Hayes's policy not a "happy compromise but a square and profitless sell-out."[96]

Hayes's patronage policy buried the Republican Party in the South. Ignoring competent and honest Southern Republicans, Hayes appointed mostly Southern Democrats to federal positions. In an area of the country where Republicans were not only ostracized but generally denied jobs, federal positions had provided the only security for most party activists in the South. Eliminating that support kicked the party's supporters while they were down. Hayes tried to make good on the deal he thought he had made by going on a speaking tour before the 1877 elections, traveling through the South in September and October. He promised that his policy was permanent, which his white listeners knew was the case, and assured the assembled blacks in Atlanta that in "no six months since the war have there been so few outrages and invasions of your rights." The president ignored the fact that the color guard did not bear the American flag.[97] Hayes even downplayed the Civil War as a misunderstanding, one in which both sides could feel pride. It was "no discredit to you [Southerners] and no special credit to us [in the North] that the war turned out as it did." It was an amazing act of groveling for a former officer who had seen so much combat, and it gained him nothing.[98] Hayes felt certain that his approach would help the Republicans win North Carolina, and possibly the border states as well. After a brief trip to Richmond, he wrote confidently that the South had "thousands of intelligent people who are not Democrats and who would like to unite with the conservative Republicans of the North." He also expected that the Southerners would keep their part of the bargain and elect Garfield Speaker of the House. He was completely wrong on all counts.[99]

Furious Southern Republicans insisted that Hayes had a moral duty to support them or he would aid in crushing "the very men who elected him to office." If South Carolina's Daniel Chamberlain, Louisiana's Stephen Packard, and Florida's Marcellus Stearns had not been elected governors of their states, then Hayes had certainly not been elected president—especially as Packard received more votes than Hayes. To do otherwise than support these three governments would be to hand victory to the failed rebels of 1861. As Chamberlain said in his inaugural address, the sympathy of many Northern Republicans had been chilled to the point "that they stand coldly by," finding that the "peace of political servitude is better than the abuse and disquiet which newly-acquired freedom has brought."[100] President Hayes explained his Southern policy in a widely published interview with the *Cincinnati Times*. Not only was he aware of the violence committed by Southern Democrats as "white Republicans as well as black were shot down during their political contests," but that was the very reason he chose to withdraw the protection of federal troops. He was convinced that those committing these acts of violence "are Christians, not thieves nor cut-throats," so by withdrawing the troops he assured them that they were no longer at war and "peace and ultimately harmony" would follow. When the reporter expressed doubt that these Southern Democrats would abandon the use of violence, Hayes responded, "How do you know?" Hayes remained confident that "most of the people of the South . . . are more disposed to encourage fraternal, harmonious social and business relations."[101]

Not everyone was impressed with Hayes's explanation. As one Western newspaper headlined the interview, "Hayes tells how he came to weaken so terribly," while an Ohio paper led with Hayes offering a "Compact with the Master Class of the South."[102] Southern Democratic papers treated his comments with contempt. The New England Conference of the Methodist Episcopal Church passed a resolution against Hayes's policy and his negotiation with the likes of Matthew Butler, "the chief . . . KuKlux instigator of the Hamburg massacre," and Wade Hampton, "who long since ought to have been hanged for treason." Former senator Benjamin Wade felt "a bitterness of soul that I never felt before"—that he had worked so hard for Hayes's nomination and angrily accused Hayes of betraying the very people who had risked their lives by voting to put him in the White House. Like many Republicans who had fought hard for civil rights, he thought, "I have been deceived, betrayed, and even humiliated" by Hayes's capitulation to the Democrats.[103]

In the showdown with the Southern Democrats, Hayes consistently gave in. He made it clear that he could not hope to uphold the law in the South and publicly pressured the three Southern Republican governors to resign their offices and hand them over to the Democrats. On March 10, less than a week after his inauguration, Hayes met with a delegation of blacks that included Congressmen Joseph Rainey, Richard Cain, and Robert Smalls, and, in words that were reprinted throughout the South, announced that "the use of the military force in civil affairs was repugnant to the genius of American institutions, and should be dispensed with if possible."[104] Curiously, Hayes would change his mind on the use of military force within three months, though in a different context.

The standoff in South Carolina paralyzed that state. Wade Hampton called on whites to pay no taxes as long as the Republicans remained in power, but to turn over a portion of those taxes to him to support his competing government. It was a brilliant move, one that starved the state government of funds and could fail only if the state enforced the law; however, the state did not have the power or will to do so. The *Spartanburg Herald* joined Hampton's crusade, warning that anyone who paid their taxes would give "aid and comfort to the enemy," which they defined as the government of their state.[105] With whites controlling most of the capital, there was little doubt in the mind of the paper's editor that the Republican government "is bound to fall to pieces."[106]

Hayes invited competing governors Chamberlain and Hampton to the White House for consultation, lending legitimacy to the Democrat's claims. Hampton played Hayes, promising the president whatever he wanted in return for federal acquiescence in his seizure of power. Hampton assured Hayes that his government would of course protect the lives and property of all its citizens including blacks and would support their civil rights in court, and that he personally would help make Garfield Speaker of the House. But as he offered the carrot, he also held up a big stick. When Hayes asked Hampton what would happen if the president recognized Chamberlain's government, Hampton supposedly replied, "The first thing would be that every [Republican] tax-collector in the State would be hanged in twenty-four hours."[107]

Heroic on the battlefield in the Civil War, President Hayes now favored surrender, confiding to his diary that he wanted to "withdraw troops and leave events to take care of themselves." Hayes announced the withdrawal of federal troops from the South—which he called his "pacification" policy—when the Senate was not in session, so as to limit the outrage from fellow Republicans.[108] On April 2, Hayes met with his cabinet and they agreed that he had little choice but to remove the remaining troops in South Carolina. The next day Hayes wrote Secretary of War George W. McCrary that "there does not now exist in that State such domestic violence as is contemplated by the Constitution as the ground upon which the military power of the national government may be invoked for the defense of the State." Therefore, he said, all troops were to be removed to their duty stations at noon on April 10. Hampton launched his coup the following day, replacing the elected government with one led primarily by former rebels. As Hampton moved into the capitol, the Democrats quickly took over both houses of the legislature, impeaching enough Republicans to give them an overwhelming majority.[109] As he was forced from his office, Governor Chamberlain issued a poignant and prescient farewell. The federal government, he declared, had abandoned the majority of South Carolina's citizens, forsaking "the lawful Government of the State to a struggle with insurrectionary forces too powerful to be resisted." The lesson was obvious: "If a majority of the people of a State are unable by physical force to maintain their rights, they must be left to political servitude." The following day the state's seal was delivered to Wade Hampton and democracy came to an end in South Carolina. In the biting evaluation of former attorney general Amos T. Akerman of Georgia, Hayes's policy followed the logic of curing "lawlessness by letting the lawless have their own way."[110]

Events in Louisiana followed a similar, though less dramatic, trajectory. A petition signed by hundreds of citizens including bishops and leading businessmen persuaded Hayes to withdraw his support from Louisiana's duly elected Republican government. "If local self-government is given us," these prominent citizens assured the president, "we pledge ourselves for the loyalty of Louisiana to the

Union, for the protection of life and property and civil rights of all her citizens, and for the equal benefits of her laws, without distinction of race, color, or previous condition." John Marshall Harlan, in Louisiana as one of Hayes's personal representatives, was appalled by the conduct of the state's Democrats, yet he urged Hayes to accept the promises expressed in the petition as sincere in order to finally remove "this Southern question from politics." From his headquarters in the Odd Fellows Hall, Francis T. Nicholls, the Democratic claimant to the governorship, swore that he "earnestly sought to obliterate the color line in politics, and consolidate the people on the basis of equal rights and common interest."[111] That was good enough for Hayes, who ordered the withdrawal of federal troops on April 20. On April 24, the troops left the capital; the next day the Democrats seized control of the state and its legislature and did not give it up for one hundred years, moving immediately to renege on all their promises. Governor Packard surrendered "only to superior force," admitting, "I am wholly discouraged by the fact that one by one the Republican State governments of the South have been forced to succumb to force, fraud or policy."[112] Reconstruction had been effectively killed by the Democratic counterrevolution.

In April 1877, the North capitulated to the South. In many ways, the Civil War had not ended in April 1865; it had continued as a battle for control of the region's future through 1877. Supporters of the Confederacy acknowledged that they could not have their own country after Appomattox, so they shifted their sights to reestablishing an all-pervasive white hegemony. As Richard Zuczek astutely observed, "The revolution that had begun in December of 1860 . . . finally came to an end in the city where it had begun: in Columbia in April of 1877." They might not have slavery any more, but they had a social system built on the nearly absolute subjugation of the black population. "Let us admit," editorialized the St. Louis Globe-Democrat, that "the untiring hate of the Southerners has worn out our endurance, and that though we staked everything for freedom under the spur of the rebellion, we have not enough of principle about us to uphold the freedom, so dearly bought, against the persistent and effective opposition of the unrepentant and unchanged rebels."[113]

Responding to Terror

A Darwinian vision was sweeping America in 1877. The *Washington National Republican*, which had often favored federal intervention in the South, now called for peace with the white South, holding that future disputes would be "decided according to the Darwinian theory, 'survival of the fittest.'" Within this racialist vision, African Americans did not qualify to enjoy the benefits of democracy. The problem with blacks was that they were poor, and that was clearly their own fault. Northern liberals could have easily drawn attention to the heroism of the freedmen and -women in rising from slavery, working together to create self-sustaining communities, and fighting for their rights, but instead they simply emphasized black poverty, blaming blacks for not being more prosperous.[114]

Throughout the country, former supporters of civil rights turned their backs on African Americans. One of the most prominent historians of this period, James F. Rhodes, criticized the Republicans for giving the vote to "an ignorant mass of an alien race." For support, Rhodes turned to the leading American scientist of the age, Louis Agassiz, who wrote: "We should beware how we give to the blacks rights, by virtue of which they may endanger the progress of the whites. . . . Social equality I deem at all times impracticable, —a natural impossibility, from the very character of the negro race." Agassiz, who found his evidence for black inferiority in the absence of organized states in Africa, warned that giving blacks rights would rebound "to their own and our detriment." In this "age of science," Rhodes found it ridiculous that the Republicans thought they could "make negroes intelligent by legislative acts." The liberal faith in education was absurd and could not overcome "the great fact of race." Though they found Darwinism repugnant in every other way, Southern Democrats embraced its bastard child, social Darwinism. As Wade Hampton told enthusiastic crowds throughout South Carolina, it was time that government passed to those "strong enough to sustain it."[115]

Not surprisingly, black Republicans generally felt betrayed; they could not understand how Hayes would refuse to stand by them after they had stood up for him. As a petition from a group of Louisiana blacks complained, the whites had enacted laws and then broke them without consequence, while blacks respected the law and suffered as a result. At every turn, the Republican Party compromised with the Democrats, but "what good are the compromises doing?" All they could see is that "conciliation" gave the Democrats "more power to steal from us and to whip us and to kill us." Their bitterness was tangible and easily understandable. One Ohio Republican compared Hayes's policy to throwing children to the wolves. There would be peace in the South, but at what cost— and what kind of peace? There would be no dissent, because none would be allowed; there would be no political battles anymore because there would be but one party. Seeing that the deal that brought Hayes the presidency had led directly to the denial of civil rights to blacks, George T. Downing righteously complained, "We realized that we were offered up."[116] The best Hayes could give these men was the appointment of Frederick Douglass as the first African American U.S. marshal. Douglass, the first black man ever voted on for approval to a federal office by the Senate, became marshal of Washington, D.C., by a vote of thirty to twelve despite the opposition of a powerful group of Washington lawyers. Douglass used the extensive patronage power of his office to bring ever more blacks into the government as civil servants, fostering the creation of a black middle class in the capital city. On the other hand, when Hayes appointed Douglass shortly after the inauguration, he eliminated one of the marshal's traditional duties, which was to stand next to the president introducing each guest at all formal White House receptions. Clearly Hayes was not completely comfortable with the idea of a black man standing next to him that often.[117]

Douglass's term in office almost proved a brief one. On May 8, 1877, he gave a speech in Baltimore on life in Washington, D.C., that nearly cost him his job and demonstrated the rapidly changing attitude toward racism in the United States. Though a long speech, just a few passages aroused the ire of many whites, North and South, by observing the obvious: that the nation's capital was home to both institutionalized and individual racism. Whites were outraged that Douglass questioned the wisdom of the founders in placing the capital "between two of the oldest slave states, each of which was a nursery and a hot-bed of slavery; surrounded by a people accustomed to look upon the youthful members of a colored man's family as a part of the annual crop for the market." As a consequence, it remained "southern in all its sympathies, and national only in name." Washington "has been, and still is, a most disgraceful and scandalous contradiction of the march of civilization." He pointed out that prior to the Civil War there was neither free speech nor a free press in the capital, as "Slavery was its idol, and . . . its people howled with rage, when this ugly idol was called in question." Little had changed among the whites in the capital, who resented the emancipation of the slaves "and would fight today if, by that means, they could bring back the old slave system." The heritage of slavery tainted everything, and Douglass found evidence that "its footprints are yet visible and deep."[118]

The Washington press, especially, exploded in fury, demanding Douglass's immediate firing. Even the party's standard-bearer, the *National Republican*, accused Douglass of "traveling through the North, spitting out spite and slander," and started a petition drive for his removal that garnered hundreds of signatures.[119] Douglass responded to the attacks as "malicious and silly." While every Southern Democratic paper joined in the chorus of denunciation, many Northern newspapers came to his defense, including the *New York Times* and *Tribune*, and the *Philadelphia Press*. The *New York Times* thought the whites of Washington were angry because "Mr. Douglass reminded them that they were rebels and slave dealers in the prehistoric ages."[120] The *Times* accurately observed that the controversy arose because Douglass "said some things about Washington which everybody knew to be true." The paper sarcastically added that "the conduct of this dark-skinned official was simply monstrous" as he "actually said just what he thought." Fortunately for Douglass, President Hayes stood by his appointment and the controversy died quickly in the crisis of June 1877.[121]

But Douglass keeping his office was the only significant political victory for America's blacks in 1877. Anyone paying attention knew that there was no turning back, that the Democrats, once in control, had no intention of ever letting go of power. The nineteenth-century Democratic Party loathed democracy for anyone but white men. As Chicago's *Inter Ocean* commented, "For the first time in the history of this country the doctrine is promulgated that not he who has the most votes, but he who has the strongest battalions, shall be recognized as the legal authority."[122] Writing in the *Philadelphia Weekly Times*, George Alfred Townsend noted that throughout the South it was "status quo ante bellum, or things as they were before Lincoln, slavery excepted: such is the tendency every-where." It was the death of democracy, at least in one part of the country.[123]

The end of Reconstruction empowered white Southerners. As one freedman told a congressional committee, "The white people in Louisiana are better armed and equipped now than during the war, and they have a better standing army now in the State of Louisiana than was ever known." They made no effort to dis-guise either their militancy or their connection to the rebellion. "You see them parade the streets of New Orleans with their gray uniforms on, and with their improved Winchester rifles and their Gatling guns, and they have now got everything except the rebel flag." Southern Democrats did not even pretend to favor democracy; now that their gun clubs were the official, all-white state militia, they could be called out to prevent Republican meetings with loaded weapons and claim they were acting within the color of the law to prevent a riot.[124]

Despite the terror, blacks remained determined to vote. In the extended state and national elections of 1876 and 1877, Southern whites had fully realized the utility of violence in attaining political ends, and employed it to effect in the state elections of 1877 and 1878. Without hesitation, they "bulldozed" any Repub-licans who went anywhere near the polls. Since state elections were staggered throughout the year, Democrats in one state could call on whites in neighboring states for support in keeping blacks from voting, resulting in lynchings across the South. In one of the worst of these events, death squads from the Shreveport area, including whites from nearby Arkansas and Texas, converged on the town of Caledonia for a "negro hunt" that killed twenty blacks. Even to report these acts of violence was to risk one's life. Two blacks called to testify before a federal grand jury were murdered on the way to New Orleans; no one was ever arrested for these crimes. A Senate committee investigating the extensive use of violence by Southern whites during the 1878 election concluded, "The right to vote is a priv-ilege more highly prized by the colored voter than by voters of any other class; and he will make sacrifices to exercise this privilege that few white men will."[125]

It is important to emphasize that whites were beaten into line as well by Dem-ocrats. Black influence had transformed the Republicans into the de facto work-ingman's party in the South, but the white elite did not want anyone voting who had a class interest contrary to theirs. Abandoning their Jacksonian heritage, Southern Democrats began pushing in late 1877 for poll taxes that would keep both blacks and whites from voting. The Brenham, Texas, *Weekly Banner* openly stated the advantages of a poll tax, which "would work like a charm in the counties where there is a large negro population," while keeping poor whites from the polls, "without any serious detriment to the public good."[126] Many working-class whites perceived that they, too, faced disenfranchisement and entered into a short-lived but often successful Greenback-Republican alliance. Fearing that class-based politics might supersede their race-based structure, Democrats successfully extended their terror campaign to include whites in the Greenback Party. When Louisiana state senator A.R. Blount, a black Baptist minister, was driven from office in the Democratic takeover of 1877, he promoted a fusion ticket with the Greenbacks. In 1878 this economically based alliance won over a large number of white votes. The White League complained that Blount was "not only controlling the negroes, but duping the white men." Horrified at the prospect of poor whites and blacks uniting, local elites hired "bulldozers" to attack the leadership of this alliance, forcing Blount and many others to flee the area before the elections.[127]

Since by the end of 1877 the Democrats controlled the Southern press and legal system, no one was prosecuted for these acts of violence, making it difficult to grasp the level of bloodshed. In one Louisiana county alone at least thirteen blacks were murdered during the 1878 election. When the *New Orleans Times* called for efforts to protect blacks from politically motivated assaults, critics attacked the newspaper for even acknowledging that there had been acts of violence. Democrats argued that the way to avoid such violence in the future was to disenfranchise all blacks, leaving the whites with no reason to kill them. That proved not to be the case, as lynching actually accelerated with the disenfranchisement of blacks.[128]

As did the 1877 elections, those of 1878 demonstrated that whites had inculcated the uses of violence, as they broke up Republican meetings, threatened and intimidated those identified as planning to vote, and practiced every sort of corruption to ensure victory. On many occasions, Democrats threatened violence if Republicans even fielded a candidate, especially if he was white. President Hayes received a flood of letters complaining of this violence, one white Republican stating, "You know how the Democrats have carried other parishes, and I know that if I run on the Republican ticket here I will be killed and I don't propose to put myself up as a target to be shot at."[129] Throughout the South, armed whites drove away black voters who dared to appear at the polls. The Democratic leadership insisted that they did not want to have to kill anyone, but they would if any effort was made to prevent their electoral victory; if blacks wanted to avoid violence, they simply should stay home. The chairman of the Louisiana Democratic Committee allegedly said in 1878, "I make no declaration of war; we don't mean to hurt anybody unless there is opposition made to the election of this ticket and if there is we will quietly wipe it out or move it aside." Such an attitude, while distant from standard democratic practices, proved highly successful. Southern Democrats stole the election of 1878 by the same means as they had those in 1876 and 1877.[130]

As if political disenfranchisement and uncontrolled violence were not sufficiently damaging, Southern whites also moved to return blacks as closely as possible to the form of coerced labor they had experienced under slavery. First introduced immediately after the Civil War, sharecropping became the favored system of black farming wherever the Democrats seized power, becoming standard throughout the South starting in 1877. Sharecroppers labored on someone else's land, paying their rent and accumulated debt from the resulting crop yield. It was rare for sharecroppers ever to accumulate sufficient surplus to save money toward buying their own land, with landlords doing their best to ensure the permanence of dependence.

Like slavery, sharecropping reached beyond the job to the worker's "home, his recreation, and his daily relations with others." Democrats in Congress acted to aid this economic oppression in the South by repealing the Homestead Act of 1866, which had aimed in part to help freedmen acquire their own land. The Southern state governments determined that blacks were no longer entitled to those lands that they had legally settled and improved, and began a process of forced eviction in 1877. Nearly half of the 2,012 blacks who owned homesteads in Florida at the beginning of 1877 were driven from their property, most of them ending up as sharecroppers.[131]

Those who attempted to get around the new economic system found themselves confronting the full fury of white supremacy. The new sharecropping system effectively took away freedom of movement for blacks, as those in debt were not allowed to leave the county. In certain Louisiana parishes blacks even had to carry passes in order to be on public roads, as during slave times.[132] When John Solomon Lewis of Louisiana found himself deeply in debt, he set out in search of better employment, just "like white workingmen." But he made the mistake of telling the landowner of his intentions. "He got very mad and said to me: 'If you try that job, you will get your head shot away.'" Seeing no alternative, Lewis and his family snuck into the woods that night as a first step out of the South.[133]

The white elite colluded in and paid for terrorist acts aimed at keeping blacks in line. Appearing before a Senate investigating committee, William Murrell of Delta, Louisiana, reported that landowners employed "nightriders" to terrorize blacks. "The class of men that do the bulldozing" were terrorists for hire, traveling through the South making "money by murdering and bulldozing generally." These costs were met by the local "rich men." Murrell noted, however, that these terrorists could prove just as dangerous to other whites. When one local businessman fell behind in his payments, the bulldozers warned him, "If you don't settle up we will do to you as we done to the niggers!" He paid up.[134]

With state support withdrawn from black militia companies, these units obeyed the law—unlike their white counterparts in the gun clubs—and disbanded. Efforts to maintain some form of self-defense force were met with the harshest repression, now backed by the full force of the state governments. Except for a very few counties, black political movements came to an abrupt end in 1877. Black leaders who attempted to keep the cause of equal rights alive were intimidated, prosecuted on trumped-up charges, driven into exile, or killed. U.S. marshal J.R.G. Pitkin reported to his superiors in 1877 that Southern blacks were "in a state of siege." The terror campaigns of 1876 and 1877 altered black politics, driving those politically involved into the shadows, reversing a general modernizing of American politics. As Nell Painter points out, in the South after 1877, with few exceptions, "each generation of modern political activists . . . was forcibly exiled or assassinated."[135]

Within a few months of Hayes's accession to the presidency, a number of Southern blacks had concluded that their only hope was to leave the South. Some blacks thought the United States was hopeless, and that they had no choice but to leave the country entirely. Thinking of Liberia, some contacted the old white-operated American Colonization Society. In May 1877, Harrison N. Bouey of Edgefield, South Carolina, wrote the Reverend Henry M. Turner of the Colonization Society of his interest in Liberia, as it had become clear "that the colored man has no home in America" since whites "believe that my race have no more right to any of the profits of their labor than one [of] their mules." That same month Bouey joined with George Curtis of Beaufort and the Reverend B.F. Porter of Charleston in organizing the Liberian Exodus Joint-Stock Steamship Company, quickly raising $6,000 of the $10,000 they estimated they needed to launch their migration. Meanwhile, a group of Alabama blacks petitioned President Hayes for funds for transportation to Liberia so that they might once more live as free men, while others sought foreign aid to help their emigration. By the summer of 1877, U.S. Representative Richard H. Cain of South Carolina reported there was "a deep and growing interest taken by the Colored people . . . in the subject of Emigration."[136]

Many whites supported this idea of emigration. In his final State of the Union message to Congress, President Grant insisted that one of the positive aspects of acquiring Santo Domingo, which he had long sought to annex to the United States, would be giving America's blacks a state of their own. Bidding farewell to the freed slaves appeared the path of least resistance for Northern whites. The *Chicago Times* hoped that the "removal of a large proportion of the blacks would have a tendency to remove the negro question from politics." Ultimately, however, few blacks left the United States for foreign climes; a great many decided to migrate only out of the South. Individuals and families reached this choice on their own in the months after the end of Reconstruction, serving as pioneers of the great migration to the northern cities that would transform urban America in the early twentieth century. Many others entered into a collective endeavor that would lead to the formation of communities where blacks could raise their families in peace, free from the constant terror of white racism. Like so many other groups, religious and cultural, in American history, thousands of Southern blacks looked west and dreamed of creating their own towns on the broad frontier far from the unending cruelty of the South. Forming black towns from scratch, however, required resources, planning, initiative, and enormous courage.

A few remarkable individuals stepped forward to lead their people west in a movement that became known as the Exodusters, with heavy emphasis on the parallel of Moses leading his people out of the Egyptian bondage. In Louisiana, Henry Adams proved the pivotal figure. After the 1876 election, Adams tried to organize Republican clubs for self-protection in Clairborne Parish, arguing that they should stay and fight. But his black neighbors found "it useless to try any longer; for the white men of Clairborne Parish [have] killed every good black man in our parish that tried to lead us right." Adams had to agree that the violence of the 1876 election and its aftermath left them little alternative to leaving the South. In May 1877, a Louisiana Colonization Council held its first public meetings in response to what Nell Painter called "a ground swell of despair."[137] As Henry Adams told the Senate, "We found ourselves in such condition that we looked around and we seed that there was no way on earth, it seemed, that we could better our condition" in Louisiana. There were no alternatives in the South, for every state had fallen into the hands of "the very men that held us slaves." Their choice was both obvious and rational: "Then we said there was no hope for us and we had better go."[138]

There was no clearer confirmation of the wisdom of leaving than the simple fact that they had to hold their meetings in remote locations, in swamps and deep woods scattered through the South, and dared not even ask for outside help for fear they would be discovered and become the targets of white terror. That terror drove many freedmen who had initially opposed migration to change their minds. As William Murrell told the Senate, it was when the bulldozers came to his house and "committed such outrages, then I gave up all hope" of staying in his home state.[139]

As Democrats became more confident in their power, realizing that the North would not act to protect Southern blacks, they accelerated their terror campaign. In Louisiana, the area of the greatest violence other than New Orleans was Caddo County, which included the town of Shreveport. In September 1877, after repeated acts of violence, the county's blacks petitioned President Hayes for protection. Their petition began poignantly by calling attention to their service to the Union during the Civil War and how the product of their labor had made America rich while they were in chains. They regretted that it was necessary to remind Hayes of their rights guaranteed under the Constitution, and of the federal government's duty to protect those rights. Now those rights had been lost. "If that protection cannot be given and our lost rights restored, we would respectfully ask that some Territory be assigned to us in which we can colonize our race; and if that cannot be done, to appropriate means so that we can colonize in Liberia or some other country," for "we cannot live in the South." To make certain that Hayes understood the cost to the Republicans of his failure to act, the assembled blacks promised to stop voting "unless we have full protection and our own officers to guard our interests and rights." The people of Caddo never received an answer from the president. They had ceased to exist in the eyes of the nation and had no choice but to act on their own behalf.[140]

Initially there was no coordination between the various groups seeking to leave the South in 1877. Blacks came together throughout the region, trying to determine how to pool their meager resources. Repeatedly, these gatherings reached the same conclusion: that they should move west—now. The closest western state, and the one that carried a positive image in their minds because of John Brown and the pre–Civil War battles to keep the territory free, was Kansas. In May 1877, Benjamin Singleton and Columbus Johnson of Tennessee toured Kansas looking for an area where blacks might settle. Returning to Tennessee, they called a meeting on migration for May 30. Singleton told his audience, "It is now high time to be looking after the interest of our downtrodden race." So great was the response that they held their next mass meeting in Nashville over two days, July 31 and August 1, emphasizing racial unity and the need for collective action to build "our future welfare" outside the South. Enthusiasm for the move was intense, propelling this group to begin the migration from Tennessee to Morris County, Kansas.[141]

At the same time that Singleton and Johnson were looking for a place to bring Nashville's blacks, W.J. Niles and W.R. Hill were also traveling through Kansas looking for a new home for blacks from Lexington, Kentucky. That summer five groups from the Lexington area who had been acting independently of one another united their efforts and founded the town of Nicodemus, which would become the most prosperous and well known of Kansas's black communities. The first group, which could not get away from the South fast enough, arrived in July 1877.

Disgusted with the violence and corruption of Louisiana politics, Alfred Fairfax, a former slave and Republican activist, led several families to Chatauqua County, Kansas, where he became the first black man to serve in that state's legislature. Word was spreading fast through the South that, as one migrant from Texas wrote Governor John St. John, Kansas was "a free state in which a colored man can enjoy his freedom." That turned out to be a fairly accurate assessment.[142] In a year in which the United States turned its back on both democracy and its black citizens, Kansas stood as a shining beacon of hope. While the rest of the country threw aside the promises of the Constitution when it came to black people, Kansas welcomed them, and those fleeing the South came to enjoy their freedom and some degree of prosperity in the state. It is difficult to ascertain the number of Exodusters, especially as many more headed further west. Estimates of the total number who joined the Exoduster migration of 1877 to 1881 hover around fifty thousand, though that figure may be low. One study found that six thousand African Americans left Louisiana, Mississippi, and Texas for Kansas in the three months of March, April, and May 1879; another found 13,500 blacks entering Kansas in 1877.[143] Whatever the exact number, it is evident that many thousands of black Americans saw no future for themselves in the South. "Fleeing from oppression and bondage," as former Louisiana state senator Andrew Pollard put it, they found on the prairie a better life, one free from terror and violence.[144]

In the face of unrelenting violence and oppression, resistance took different forms. The determined drive of black Southerners to educate their children and to create autonomous educational institutions must be seen in this light. Since whites now monopolized nearly every avenue of prestige in the South, teaching remained one of the few professional positions to which black men and women could both aspire, as well as one of the few ways in which dedicated radicals, white and black, could continue to aid Southern blacks. In addition to ending internal improvement projects, disarming black state militia companies, and removing blacks from juries, Democratic "redeemer" governments cut funding to all public schools, wanting to educate neither poor whites nor blacks, though black schools were hardest hit, with some state governments cutting off nearly all funding for black schools in 1877. The American Missionary Association and black churches stepped into this gap—the former sending volunteer teachers, the latter opening schools throughout the South. Numerous Northerners continued to make the trip south to work in the schools for the freedmen and their children; additionally, many blacks educated during Reconstruction turned their attention to helping other blacks learn the same skills. Robert C. Martin of Mississippi described his classes in May 1877: During the week he taught "forty-nine scholars" who worked hard to master reading and writing with the assistance of two other teachers. On Sunday he drew eighty-three "Sunday Scholars," as he called them, who ranged in age up to fifty-one years old, "and only a few of them are ever absent." That same year Winslow Homer paid tribute to this dedication to learning in his powerful painting *A Sunday Morning in Virginia*.[145]

No matter what their position on the question of migration, black leaders continued to emphasize the importance of education. Their success is evident in the shift in school enrollment in the 1870s. In 1870, 56 percent of white males and 52.7 percent of white females aged five to nineteen were enrolled in school, compared with one-tenth of the nonwhite children. While the white enrolled population increased by seven percentage points during the 1870s, the nonwhite figure increased to 34 percent by 1880, rising to 40 percent in the decade after 1877. In 1865, less than 10 percent of Southern blacks could read; by 1870 that figure had risen to just 18.6 percent, but by 1890, 55 percent of the South's African Americans were literate. This accomplishment is particularly impressive when compared to the situation in other contemporary societies, or even to the level of white literacy in the South, which was only marginally higher. For instance, in Spain the overall literacy rate hovered around 25 percent, while Italy could boast 31 percent.

Over two million Southern blacks were taught to read in the last quarter of the nineteenth century, which stands as a notable testament to the resilience and dedication of a population hammered by racism at every turn. By 1892 there were 25,000 black schools in the South and more than 20,000 black teachers—13,000 of whom had themselves been educated in these schools. Those educational advances occurred within a context of racism that reached incredible levels of hypersensitivity on the part of whites. In 1879 the faculty of Atlanta University voted that they would stop referring to their students as gentlemen and ladies and would in the future call them "young men" and "young women" so as to avoid upsetting local whites who were known to turn violent when blacks were given respect.[146]

W.E.B. Du Bois called these educational efforts a "crusade" and the female missionaries who often ran these schools "women who dared," celebrating the "thread of brave and splendid friendship from those few and rare men and women of white skins, North and South, who have dared to know and help and love black folk." Booker T. Washington, who generally shied away from anything that might be considered radical or challenging to white rule, wrote: "The part that the Yankee teachers played in the education of the Negroes immediately after the war will make one of the most thrilling parts of the history of this country."[147] Some small comfort could be found in the 1892 report of the secretary of the American Medical Association: "In 1865 there were two negro attorneys; there are now 250. Twenty-seven years ago there were three colored physicians; now there are 749." Despite white efforts to close down black schools—from undermining their funding to threatening the teachers—autonomous black education persisted, the only light in a long, dark night.[148]

Turning Their Backs on Progress

In 1877, Southern whites accepted union and Northern whites accepted racism. Hayes, who had waved the bloody shirt of rebellion in the election of 1876, referred to Southern whites as "my Confederate friends" in 1877. *The Nation* rejoiced that the "Compromise of 1877" meant that blacks "will disappear from the field of national politics. Henceforth, the nation, as a nation, will have nothing to do with him." That liberal magazine was convinced that now the South would fade as a separate section, as control reverted to white men, where it belonged.[149] Racial violence spread north, inspiring Democratic election officials in Cincinnati to beat blacks who attempted to vote—right at the polls.[150] By the end of 1877 it appeared fairly clear that the majority of whites in the North and West no longer wanted to hear another word out of the South that was not part of a romantic novel. Protestant Christianity, which had played such a large role in promoting the abolition of slavery, proved as indifferent to the rights of freedmen as most secular institutions. Some Northern leaders had been preaching complete forgiveness and acceptance of Southern white violence for several years, none more prominently than the former abolitionist Henry Ward Beecher. The Southern whites had erred, but they were still his people, and Beecher mourned "for those outcast States," which he defined solely in terms of their whiteness. Beecher went on: "The bitterness of their destruction, the wrath that has come upon them; their desolation"—these inspired his sympathy more than the travails of the freedmen. Beecher oozed compassion for the defeated whites as he insisted that their violence must be ignored as you would ignore a young child misbehaving. "You must not be disappointed or startled because you see in the newspapers accounts of shocking barbarities committed upon these people," he advised Northern whites. Racist violence was understandable as Southern whites adjusted to their new environment. Until that adjustment was complete, the people of the North must have "patience with Southern men as they are, and patience with Southern opinions as they have been, until the great normal, industrial, and moral laws shall work such gradual changes as shall enable them to pass from the old to the new."[151]

Turning their backs on a moral understanding of freedom and basic rights, many prominent Northern religious leaders followed Beecher's lead in preaching white solidarity as the premier social value. "A growing number of white Protestants," writes Edward J. Blum, "came to rationalize second-class citizenship for blacks as divinely sanctioned." Whiteness replaced loyalty to the Union and the promotion of freedom as determinant. Put another way, white Christian Northerners sold out, and for a very low price. Withdrawing financial support for missionary and educational efforts in the South saved money or allowed for its diversion to what Dwight Moody and others saw as the more important task of saving white souls.[152]

Harriet Beecher Stowe—author of the phenomenally popular abolitionist novel *Uncle Tom's Cabin*—initially opposed her brother's blanket forgiveness for all Southern transgressions. By the late 1870s, however, she came around to his position after she established a winter home in Florida. As her private letters reveal, she not only knew of the racial violence but asked her friends not to mention it in public, as she did not. Where once she had felt sympathy for the enslaved, she now felt passionate concern for her wealthy white neighbors. She encouraged her peers to purchase vacation homes of their own in Florida and not worry about the blacks any more. Throughout the latter half of the 1870s, Stowe wrote fondly of the ideal of the old South, complete with plantations and servile blacks, even positively comparing her own property to a slave plantation.[153] Stowe now offered her Northern white audience "a South much more to their liking, a place that needed no more reconstructing." In 1877 Stowe invited her fellow whites to join her in retiring from the field of political activism and enjoying a mint julep on the veranda, describing Southern whites as a "remarkably, quiet, peaceable, and honest set of people, who believe in the apostolic injunction, 'Study to be quiet and mind your own business.'" She had come a long way from *Uncle Tom's Cabin*.[154]

While Northern Protestant leaders were willing to forgive, Southern whites were not—forgiveness had to be on their terms. In the years before the Civil War, the Methodist, Presbyterian, and Baptist churches had separated into Northern and Southern branches; in 1877 many Northern clergymen called for denominational reunification. The editor of the *Atlanta Constitution*, insisting that Southern churches must not lose their sectional identity, doubted the sincerity of Northern churchmen, whom he called "imposters who brought the country to grief, and who were most appropriately named the 'hell-hounds of Zion.'" Presbyterian minister Robert Lewis Dabney of the Union Theological Seminary in Virginia, like so many Southern whites, framed the issue in terms of sex, warning that for the Southern Presbyterians to unite with the Northern branch of the church would be "a step which would seal the moral and doctrinal corruption of our church in the South, and be a direct step towards that final perdition of Southern society, domestic amalgamation"—by which he meant interracial sex—producing "a mulatto South." The Baptists and Methodists also refused to merge with their Northern brethren, insisting on their sectional identity in the face of Northern desires for reconciliation.[155]

In Augusta, Georgia, the evangelist Dwight Moody, in the midst of launching what historians call the Third Great Awakening, was forced to choose between justice and a successful revival; he chose the latter.[156] At the start of Moody's Augusta revival, blacks and whites mingled without incident, infuriating a number of prominent whites who demanded that Moody build a literal fence between the races. Moody gave in immediately, and his revivals—and all others in the South until Billy Graham's in the 1950s—remained segregated. The *Atlanta Constitution* perceived the significance of this event, putting it on the front page, praising Moody for arousing piety among the roughest people but warning him that any effort to interfere with their racial relations "would bring down upon him the contempt and abhorrence of our entire people." In contrast, a Western newspaper accused Moody of abject cowardice for placing "southern prejudice" above his Christian beliefs.[157]

Once Moody made the correct adjustments, Southern racists enthusiastically welcomed his revivals; the founder of the *Southern Review*, the Reverend Albert Taylor Bledsoe, called Moody "the astonishment of the world," and "the most wonderful phenomenon of the nineteenth century." But then, there was no reason why they should not be pleased; not only did Moody refuse to condemn slavery, he also made it clear that blacks would never rise from their poverty or deserve equal rights. Moody's message of quiescence freed all whites from feeling guilty over the condition of the nation's blacks; equality would be found in heaven, not on earth. In the name of white reconciliation, Moody slaughtered the notion of integrated Christianity at its inception.[158]

African American ministers saw what Moody's choices meant for them. After Moody's Charleston revival, where he refused to invite the black churches to participate, one minister complained to the annual A.M.E. conference that Moody's "conduct toward the Negroes during his Southern tour has been shameless, and I would not have him preach in a barroom, let alone a church," as Moody "placed caste above Christianity." Frederick Douglass observed that while the agnostic Colonel Robert Ingersoll insisted on integrated audiences, the Reverend Moody "turned his back upon his colored brothers" North and South. Noting that blacks could still enter theaters or a lecture by Ingersoll without being segregated, Douglass labeled Moody a rank hypocrite: "Of all the forms of Negro hate in this world, save me from that one which clothes itself in the name of the loving Jesus." Moody's segregated revivals legitimated Jim Crow years before the Southern states institutionalized the practice in law.[159]

Like Beecher and Stowe, Moody ignored any information that countered his vision of a peaceful South, actively avoiding reports of the terror campaigns in the South and speaking without reference to the battle for the future of the nation being fought around him. His calls for white unity drowned out any suggestion of justice for blacks. "This was a reversal of great importance," Blum has written, "for northern and southern whites were coming to believe that God desired peace among whites far more than justice for all citizens." Blum makes a compelling case that within a few years the idea of a national democracy had been completely destroyed, replaced by a unified white republic.[160] It is certainly the case that Moody encouraged Northern whites to forget their commitment to social justice and to join in a Christian embrace of racial unity. Culturally at least, the Confederacy won the Civil War in 1877, as white supremacy became the accepted national standard.

The Civil War launched a struggle for national identity. One vision framed the country as a multicultural democracy, and the South benefited from that experiment through Reconstruction, as activist governments improved the region's schools and sought to build an infrastructure more supportive of economic development. However, the traditional white elite and many corporations perceived advantages in preserving sectionalism. The Southern white oligarchy regained political power by crushing the aspirations of the freedmen and seizing control of the state governments through violent means. At the same time, the expanding Northern corporations fought the centralizing power of the federal government, which had a tendency to limit their reach through regulation. They found great advantage in manipulating weak state governments and playing one state off against another to win special concessions; it was also far easier and cheaper to buy a few state legislators as compared to Congress. That Southern congressmen served as a brake on progressive legislation for the next hundred years is no coincidence.

In many ways the "restoration" of white racial hegemony is the culmination of the Civil War. The Democratic theft of the election of 1876 amounted to a counterrevolutionary war against federal policy and Constitutional protections. The Civil War brought freedom to the South, but the majority of Southern whites rejected democracy in favor of oligarchy. Northern whites abandoned the fight for a united and democratic nation in 1877; Southern whites kept right on fighting for their vision of a divided, racist nation for another hundred years. W.E.B. Du Bois ended his history of Reconstruction by observing that both justice and democracy were defeated in 1877. That year marked the "triumph of men who in their effort to replace equality with caste and to build inordinate wealth on a foundation of abject poverty have succeeded in killing democracy, art and religion." In summarizing the Democratic counterrevolution in the South, Du Bois simply said, "God wept."[161]

3

Bringing Order to the West

Judge Lynch is the judge wanted by the workingmen of California. I advise all to own a musket and a hundred rounds of ammunition.

—Denis Kearney, 1877[1]

Out on the frontier, in a town that had just been founded six years earlier, the single most contentious political issue was prohibition, with the opponents of alcohol winning the elections.[2] Colorado Springs was one of the many fast-growing new frontier towns in post–Civil War America. Founded in 1871, the town by 1877 already had a population of several thousand, with two newspapers, several churches, and no saloons. Though part of the mining boom sweeping the West at the height of the famous "Wild West" period, Colorado Springs was a dry town and wanted to stay that way. No subject agitated the Republican *Colorado Springs Gazette* more than alcohol consumption; no issue of the paper passed without reference to the benefits of temperance and the horrors of demon rum.[3] Chief among the disordering crimes of alcohol was violence. Repeatedly the paper pointed out the direct connection between drinking and violence, holding drunkenness responsible for 90 percent of the homicides—a figure not far off the mark, as recent historical research finds that 80 percent of those in prison for violent crimes in the West committed their offenses while under the influence of alcohol. In her travels across the country, Miriam Leslie found Colorado Springs one of the most civilized towns she visited, its "morals . . . guarded by the sternest of liquor laws," and home to "two of our most cherished American female authors," Helen Hunt and Grace Greenwood.[4]

Though a Republican town, Colorado Springs included many Democrats who preferred government regulation of the liquor trade to prohibition. The opponents of temperance consistently pointed out that alcohol could be acquired anyway by those who wanted it, so how much better to have just a few licensed saloons in town where the community's citizens could purchase safe alcohol. While it printed these opinions throughout 1877, the *Colorado Springs Gazette* rejected the reasoning as avoiding the problem. It was true that many people did buy alcohol illegally, but that did not make it less of a crime; and a town did not drop laws against robbery just because some people insisted on stealing from their neighbors.[5]

Colorado Springs did not match the classic image of a Wild West town. The majority favored temperance, the economic development of the community, law and order, and women's suffrage—which the paper supported as "simple justice." In the popular construction, the Western town is rarely run by prohibitionists, as was the case in Colorado Springs. But these Western Republicans aimed above all else for order, which they saw as necessary for business to thrive, and which alcohol and the violence it produced so clearly disrupted. Located in the middle of the West, the people of Colorado Springs could look in every direction and see violence threatening their society, as the newspaper regularly reminded them. The obvious increase in violence troubled the *Gazette*, which noted with alarm that there had been three murders in the area in the previous year.[6] In addition to the disruption threatened by the unresolved election of 1876 and the horrors committed on the South's black population, the paper reported on violent labor actions back East and the tramp scare nationwide. To the town's north the army continued its war against the Sioux, who had slaughtered Custer's command at the Battle of the Little Bighorn, while in the northwest the military pursued the Nez Perce, with whom the paper sided, seeing these Indians as the victims of white criminality.[7] Farther west an anti-Chinese "communistic rising" undermined the economy and international relations, while news arrived from the south that Mexico had invaded Texas![8] The *Gazette* agreed with the *Greeley Tribune* that "our social and political affairs have become so demoralized that we are breeding robbers and scoundrels at an astonishing rate." All this violence led to an increase in lynching from California to Florida, illegal actions the paper struggled to understand but could not bring itself to condemn entirely.[9]

The West seemed to be out of control in 1877, but not in the way generally pictured in films and novels. There are indeed few myths harder to dispel than that of the Wild West. Despite nearly a half century of scholarship demonstrating that gunfighters in showdowns and Indians racing around and around circled wagon trains are bunkum, the public remains wedded to this imagined past. Most Western towns were established quickly, with government and law enforcement firmly in place from the start. For instance, the town of Tombstone was founded in 1877 and enjoyed its first year without any bloodshed as it saw its population boom to four thousand people. Homicide rates were much higher in the rural South and urban East than in the West. It was not one-on-one assaults that accounted for Western bloodshed, but state-sanctioned and crowd violence, generally committed against nonwhites.

The West was not a lawless society, though it was not yet a stable society; individual gunmen did disrupt communities on occasion, but solitary acts of homicide were not the primary concern of the majority of those living in the West. The army did fight a brutal war with several Indian nations, but the public was not unified in support of these conflicts. Rather, the year 1877 witnessed a struggle for the future development of the West and the form of its social order. The ethnic structure of democracy and the control of land and resources dominated this conflict. Those who sought to impose white supremacy often acted outside the law, yet they found the local government sympathetic to their cause, as did those who sought to incorporate the West, to concentrate its land and resources under the control of a wealthy elite. The courts consistently stood on the side of those working to bring the West's resources into a few hands, as exemplified by the Court of Private Land Claims returning only 5 percent of the 35 million disputed acres in the Southwest to their original Hispanic owners. In 1877, Republican-dominated governments—territorial, state, and national—rushed to bring a WASP order to the West, and did not quell at using violence to attain their ends.[10]

The federal government also intended to bring order to the West, if only because its huge expanse represented a possible source of dissolution and could easily defy central control. The federal organizational impulse was expressed in many ways, some of them benign. For instance, in 1877, Congress established the U.S. Entomological Commission in an effort to eradicate the grasshoppers devastating Western farms and rangelands, while John Wesley Powell led the first geological surveys of the West in an effort to figure out just what exactly the government owned.[11] And then there were the Indians, who—in the eyes of those on the East Coast—appeared far too restless, moving about the Great Plains without apparent pattern or reason.

Those working for the incorporation of the West into the national economic and political order knew that they needed the support of at least a majority of Western settlers. The quickest way to buy them off was to increase the supply of inexpensive land available to them. The traditional route to that end in North America was to take the land from the native peoples. As in the past, that goal led to warfare, in this instance the last two sustained battles for Western dominance, each of which began very poorly for the United States.

War on the Plains

When 1877 started, the United States government was in the midst of one of its least successful and most embarrassing Indian wars. The majority of the country's military personnel were engaged in chasing various Indian peoples around the West, suffering several defeats at the hands of their poorly armed opponents. The Western Indians wanted to be left alone to enjoy their traditional lands in peace. Unfortunately for them, the United States government intended to move them all onto government "agencies," as the areas set aside for the Indians were then called. The Supreme Court facilitated these efforts by ruling that Congress no longer had to negotiate treaties with Indians, but could enact legislation without their consent. This convenient policy allowed the government to negate all previous treaties in the name of "peace." President Grant instituted his "Peace Policy" in order to corral the Indians into the agencies and bring stability to the West by destroying Indian culture. Indians were to settle on government land, where federal agents administered aid, taught them to farm like whites, and educated their children to be "Christian citizens." To assist the government in these endeavors, which everyone knew would be resisted, Congress appropriated funds for just 25,000 soldiers—a level that would remain the authorized size of the army until 1898. Then, in order to apply pressure on Presidents Grant and Hayes to withdraw all remaining troops from the South, Congress refused to pay the soldiers.[12]

White relations with the Indian peoples were further complicated by the federal government's highly inconsistent policy. Sometimes agents worked to protect the Indians from an aggressive military commander keen for glory and from avaricious whites anxious to seize their property; sometimes these agents were in league with speculators and thieves, leaving the army to step in and protect the Indians. For instance, in northern California in early 1877, J.L. Broaddus, agent for the Hupa Indians, conspired with local interests to seize the Hupa lands. When the Hupa refused to cooperate, he decided, without authorization from Washington, to simply close the agency and move the Indians to some distant lands. When the Hupa refused to budge, Broaddus stripped the agency of every movable object, selling their tools, livestock, even their harvested crops, and pocketed the proceeds. Then in May 1877 he declared the agency closed and left. Lieutenant James Halloran, commander of the garrison at nearby Fort Gaston, stepped in and promised to protect the Hupa from the whites. With help from the U.S. Army, the Hupa rebuilt their homes and within a few years were again self-supporting. But the Hupa people never received any compensation for all the property stolen from them by the federal agent responsible for their well-being.[13]

Such corruption was not a secret. Anyone paying the least bit of attention knew that the Department of Indian Affairs specialized in sleaze. Contrary to a negative perception fostered by some scholars that the white West was unified in its racism, many newspapers routinely reported on and condemned the mistreatment of the Indians. The regular exposure of scandals in the Department of Indian Affairs troubled some members of Congress, as did Othniel Marsh's powerful 1875 exposé, *A Statement of Affairs at the Red Cloud Agency*, which correctly predicted that the government's abusive policies would soon drive the Sioux to rebel. Other critics of the policy felt that the agencies, as E.L. Godkin of *The*

Nation wrote, "degrade the tame Indians into lazy and filthy paupers, preparatory to their extinction through disease, drunkenness, and the loss of that vital power which results from total lack of occupation." Given this slow death, which also demoralized whites, Godkin favored a policy of immediate extermination, which would be better for all involved. "In fact," he wrote, "our philanthropy and our hostility tend to about the same end, and that is the destruction of the Indian race." Having defeated Custer, the Indians deserved a "rapid slaughter" and should be "hunted down persistently" to facilitate that end.[14]

The overburdened and underpaid U.S. Army was charged with the task of forcing the Indians onto agencies. According to the U.S. Census of 1870, there were 383,712 Indians in American territories, 234,740 of whom remained free in the West. These "nomads," as the government labeled them, were concentrated in a few territories: Alaska, 70,000; Oklahoma, 34,400; Arizona, 27,700; Dakota, 26,320; Montana, 19,330; Nevada, 16,220. The Plains Indians who relied on buffalo for their survival faced the imminent end of their way of life as the extermination of bison formed an essential part of the politics of conquest, one supported by General William Tecumseh Sherman, who looked forward to the day when "all the buffaloes are extinct" and the Indians would have no choice but to move onto government agencies in order to survive. By 1877 the southern herd was near extinction and the northern was on its way to obliteration.

The United States did not speak with one voice on this issue. On the one hand, Congress attempted to protect the bison by passing a law in 1874 prohibiting the shooting of female bison by non-Indians; on the other hand, the Grant administration refused to enforce the law. Fully encouraged by the government, hunters went on a killing spree unlike any seen in human history with the possible exception of the extermination of the passenger pigeon. For instance, in two months in 1876 Orlando Brown killed 5,700 bison, firing his rifle so often that he went deaf in one ear. The public fully understood these policies and their goals, the "wanton slaughter" evoking the approval of the *Colorado Springs Gazette* in February 1877, though with the caveat that the whites lost as well since now "a herd of buffaloes is a most unusual sight in places where within the memory of those who are still young, myriads of them have passed and repassed."[15]

The army further accelerated the dispossession of the Plains Indians in 1874 when General Philip Sheridan violated the treaty with the Sioux and sent Colonel George A. Custer with a column of Seventh Cavalry into the Black Hills to determine if the rumors of gold were true. Custer confirmed the presence of gold and started spreading the good news to anyone who would listen, drawing thousands of prospectors, speculators, and settlers onto Sioux lands. The population of the Dakota Territory increased from 14,000 whites in 1870 to 135,000 in 1880. As required by their treaty, the U.S. Army, which had created the problem, began removing white intruders with as little enthusiasm as possible. Meanwhile, the Grant administration began pressuring the Sioux to sell the Black Hills for $6 million and move onto land set aside for them by the government. The Sioux rejected this offer, leading the government to abrogate its treaties and enter into a chthonic pact with those seeking to exploit the region for their own advantage, instructing the army to stop defending Sioux lands. The whites moved in, set up mining towns—including Deadwood and Custer City—and began behaving badly toward their Indian neighbors. Hoping to avoid conflict, the Sioux moved farther north, but they clashed with a group of prospectors, resulting in the deaths of three or four whites. The government now had the excuse it needed to act not just against the Sioux but against all Western Indians. At the urging of the military high command, the government ordered that all Indians should report to agencies by January 31, 1876; those that did not would be considered "hostiles." Hundreds of Indians refused to follow these orders.[16]

Here, as with so many other issues at this time, the level of violence hung on the action or inaction of the United States Army. There were those who urged a more restrained policy on the army, one based on negotiation rather than coercion. But the army was commanded by two notably bloody-minded generals, Sherman and Philip Sheridan, neither of whom had much use for either diplomacy or Indians. The lawyer Perry Belmont had dinner with Secretary of War Don Cameron and General Sherman at the beginning of the year and was appalled to hear the general repeat "the only too familiar phrase, 'The only good Indian is a dead Indian.'" Belmont expressed concern that a man with that attitude held the official mandate to impose the government's "Peace Policy."[17] As the historian Paul Wellman wrote, "If ever any people was goaded into war, it was the Sioux in 1876." Wellman was certain that had there been a World Court available, "the United States would have been ruled an 'aggressor nation.'" Sherman's response to any concern with the rights of the Sioux was blunt: "We must act with vindictive earnestness against the Sioux, even to their extermination, men, women, and children."[18]

The Sioux had risen in rebellion against a blatant effort to steal their land. Led by the clever Unkpapa chief Sitting Bull[19] and the charismatic Oglala warrior Crazy Horse, the Sioux won a pair of notable victories, first at the Battle of the Rosebud on June 17, 1876, where George Crook's forces were saved only by the heroism of his Shoshone and Crow scouts, and then most dramatically at the Battle of the Little Bighorn on June 25, 1876, which saw the slaughter of Custer's command.[20] After these battles, many hoped the whites might offer a new treaty that would respect Sioux lands, but no such diplomacy ensued. In the face of white intransigence, Yellow Grass, an Indian holy man who claimed to channel the spirit of Custer and who had been a proponent of a negotiated peace, called for continuing war. He acknowledged that he had always been "a great friend of the whites. . . . But now I see they are determined to destroy all our peace and happiness, and my advice will be to my people, as long as I live, never submit to the whites."[21]

The country as a whole was equally divided over how to proceed with the war against the Sioux. The army, seeking to capitalize on Custer's fame, reburied their reckless colonel at West Point in 1877, and a stream of books and poems flowed out to feed the mythology. Edward Clarence Stedman began his epically dreadful poem in Custer's honor: "Young lion of the plain, / Thou of the tawny mane!" Captain Jack Crawford, Buffalo Bill Cody's sideshow assistant, wrote a more economical "Death of Custer": "Did I hear news from CUSTER? / Well, I reckon I did, old pard; / It came like a streak of lightnin', / And, you bet, it hit me hard." With such eulogies, it is a wonder that anyone would read more, yet within a year of Custer's death he had been elevated to heroic stature for having led his command blindly into the largest concentration of Indian warriors ever known to have gathered in the American West. A more lasting aspect of the glorification of Custer was Cassily Adams's famous painting *Custer's Last Stand*, which Budweiser Beer distributed to nearly every bar in the country.[22]

There were voices of dissent in this Custer celebration. One anonymous officer claiming to speak for his fellows told the *New York Herald*, "We all think, much as we lament Custer, . . . that he sacrificed the Seventh Cavalry to ambition and wounded vanity."[23] The commander of the Seventh Cavalry, Colonel Samuel Sturgis, whose son died with Custer, shared this view, dismissing his subordinate as "a very selfish man" who "was insanely ambitious for glory." Sturgis's commander General Alfred Terry would have court-martialed Custer had he survived. Lewis Henry Morgan, the lawyer whose 1877 book *Ancient Society* founded the field of social evolution, wanted to know how anyone could blame the Sioux for defending themselves. Corruption and a lack of intelligence on the part of the federal government created the crisis in the West.[24]

Similarly, the country was divided between those sympathetic to the Sioux and those who thought they should be exterminated. For instance, Emily FitzGerald, the wife of an army surgeon based in Idaho, called for genocide. "Don't let anybody talk of peace until the Indians are taught a lesson and, if not exterminated, so weakened they will never molest or butcher again," she wrote a friend. "I wish they would kill them all."[25] John Finerty of the *Chicago Times* thought Montana capable of supporting "millions of people . . . if the whole tribe of Indians, friendly and otherwise, were exterminated." Finerty did not disguise his racism, admitting that "I detest the race."[26] Others thought the campaign against the Sioux was, in the words of Charles Diehl, also of the *Chicago Times*, "a miserable fiasco," and the region hardly worth all the trouble. James O'Kelly dismissed it as "patent humbug campaigning." In fact, after being on the trail with Crook's army for a few months, Finerty himself declared eastern

Montana unworthy of all the trouble, a terrain so "hard, repulsive, sterile" that it made "one's heart sick to look at the place."[27]

General Crook deeply resented the sympathy for the Sioux that he read in many newspapers. In orders issued to his troops, he complained at length about the ingratitude of a public that failed to realize that "Indian warfare is, of all warfare, the most dangerous, the most trying, and the most thankless," largely because Congress refused to recognize it as war, bypassing the need to issue a formal declaration against their enemies. Meanwhile, he continued, "Your savage foes are not only the wards of the nation, supported in idleness, but objects of sympathy with large numbers of people." But he assured his troops that they were "on the side of the weak against the strong," though he did not explain that unusual role reversal.[28]

After the Sioux and their Cheyenne allies destroyed half of the Seventh Cavalry at the Little Bighorn, U.S. forces, staggered by such a horrendous defeat just eleven years after the end of their Civil War, were immobilized for months. Morale plummeted throughout the army—the "humiliation of defeat," as the *Chicago Times* called it—undermining the troops, who understood that the public recognized the "utter failure" of the campaign against the Sioux as their fault.[29] James O'Keely, who had traveled widely with the Brazilian emperor Dom Pedro, joined the army out on the plains and was shocked to discover that "if one listens to the soldiers as they discuss among themselves the campaign, the conviction is forced that they no longer look upon victory as certain." According to Reuben Davenport of the *New York Herald*, "A dull apprehension of disaster reigned" in the army.[30] While General Sheridan, commander of the Military Division of the Missouri, moved as many of his forces north as possible, the overall commander, General Sherman, transferred reinforcements from the Pacific coast and the South. Settlers on the plains verged on panic and welcomed the reinforcements with demonstrations of support and appreciation, though they also criticized the army for not acting with greater energy. Phocian Howard, writing for the *Chicago Tribune*, found Custer's defeat and the power of the Sioux the primary topics of conversation everywhere he went in the West, with everyone elevating the size of the Sioux force, generally by three to five times their actual number of some thousand warriors, creating a consensus that the army was outnumbered.[31]

By the fall of 1876 the army had the largest force it had ever put into the field against the Plains Indians. General Terry commanded 1,600 men, while General Crook led 2,100 soldiers and 225 Shoshone in pursuit of the Sioux, and Colonel Nelson Miles fielded 500 infantry. Davenport declared "All other Indian wars sink into insignificance compared with this [one]."[32] But for the rest of the year these armies basically blundered around the plains looking for the Sioux and

Cheyenne. In every action they undertook over the next year, the army would be haunted by the memory of the Little Bighorn.[33]

Meanwhile, only the organizational skills of Sitting Bull and the inspiring military leadership of Crazy Horse held the Sioux coalition together. But for the supplies they had stripped from Custer's dead troops, the Sioux would have been reduced to fighting with traditional weapons. Pursued by three armies, they saw little hope for success. Still, Sitting Bull kept them on the move while Crazy Horse filled many with the conviction that victory was possible. Opponents realized that Crazy Horse was one of the great warriors of his age, while even Sioux opposed to his militaristic policy looked on him with awe, both for his courage and for his famous generosity. As Captain John Bourke said, "I never heard an Indian mention his name save in terms of respect."[34]

As 1877 dawned, Crook and Miles worked to revitalize American forces and isolate the Sioux and Cheyenne. They benefited from the individualistic nature of the Plains Indians, who even in wartime lacked a clear chain of command and respected dozens of equal leaders. These weaknesses were evident at the Battle of Wolf Mountain in January 1877. Crazy Horse, who had fewer than one-third of his original warriors, set up an elaborate ambush of Miles's two regiments but could not control his forces, while Miles, who had built a strong defensive position, used his artillery to good effect. Both sides fought well, but as Miles's troops retreated in the midst of a blizzard, Crazy Horse could not persuade his warriors to press the attack, and the Indians also withdrew, badly battered.

There was a clear dialectic to the Sioux way of war; their individualized style produced astounding feats of courage yet also undermined anything like tactical or strategic vision. Few commanders could hold their units together for more than one day, generally for little longer than a few hours on the field of battle. Having won honor in individual combat, the warrior rarely felt the need to stick around to aid others. In the aftermath of the Battle of Wolf Mountain, which both sides appeared to have lost, Sheridan and Crook happily predicted that this war "will be a short and decisive one," as the Indians "are discouraged and feel that their case is hopeless." Rumors circulated that Crazy Horse was on the verge of surrender. As the *Colorado Springs Gazette* stated, "If this be true, the power of the Sioux will soon be a thing of the past."[35]

With ammunition running out for his 250 remaining warriors, and with more than six hundred noncombatants to feed, Crazy Horse knew that he could not hold out much longer in the harsh winter weather—though he did. Over the next few months the Sioux alliance fragmented, the steady departure of forces—most seeking food and shelter by moving onto the agencies—crippling Crazy Horse's military plans. Ultimately it was the lack of food and ammunition that defeated him, not the army.[36] Dr. Thomas Williamson, who lived with the Sioux for many years, wrote on March 15, 1877, "Since the fall of Custer, Sitting Bull and his associates never had enough ammunition for a regular battle, and have avoided fighting whenever it is possible." Crazy Horse made several efforts to capture supply trains in order to arm and feed his troops, but Crook kept them well guarded. Miles attempted to end the war by meeting personally with Sitting Bull, but the two men had too much pride to speak coherently to one another. Miles just could not understand the continued resistance of the Sioux, while Sitting Bull could not comprehend the ruthlessness of the army against a people who were not the aggressors. Sitting Bull explained that peace was easily attained, all that was required was for the whites to leave Sioux land. Miles countered that only the unconditional surrender of the Sioux would end the war. The negotiations broke down at this point and the two men returned to their war.[37]

In February 1877, Sitting Bull and his Sioux followers headed north to Canada. He tried to persuade Crazy Horse to join him, but the latter felt he could make it through the winter best by staying put and continuing the war in the spring. Crook, a clever negotiator, promised the Sioux that he would persuade the new president to establish a separate agency for the Northern Nation of the Sioux people. By March it was clear that the Indians had little choice but to surrender. Iron Horse spoke for the emerging consensus: "You see all the people here are in rags, they all need clothing, we might as well go in." In April the Cheyenne gave up, won over by Crook's promises, which were never fulfilled.[38]

At the beginning of the year, Crazy Horse had rallied his forces by proclaiming, "This country is ours"; by mid-April an exhausted and dispirited Crazy Horse acknowledged, "All is lost anyway . . . the country is lost."[39] Crook sent Sioux messengers, including Spotted Tail and Red Cloud, to Crazy Horse with offers of his own agency along the Powder River if he gave up the fight. On May 6, Crazy Horse surrendered, leading his remaining followers into Red Cloud's agency and agreeing to go to Washington to meet with the president about establishing his own agency. As Crazy Horse passed Fort Robinson, thousands of agency Indians poured out to cheer their hero. One army officer, watching this procession, angrily complained, "By God, this is a triumphal march, not a surrender." The soldiers counted 889 Sioux with a total of 46 breechloaders, 35 muzzle-loaders, and 33 revolvers among them. The following day, Miles defeated the last group of resisting Sioux, Lame Deer's village, near the Powder River, and Sitting Bull led his adherents across the so-called Medicine Line into Canada. Perry Belmont found it highly significant that when United States officials met with the Plains Indians, they required a body of armed guards, while Canadian officials met Sitting Bull's Sioux at the border accompanied by two Mounties.[40]

President Hayes's administration refused to uphold Crook's promises and put Crazy Horse on the Red Cloud agency rather than on his own. At the end of August Crook showed up with what struck many Sioux as an outrageous request:

that they aid him in fighting other Indians. "We are tired of war," Crazy Horse said, "we came in for peace." Nonetheless, he offered to fight for "the Great Father" until none of their enemies remained. The translator rendered this statement of support as "We will go north and fight until not a white man is left." Many Sioux felt that the translator's error was an intentional one, aimed at removing Crazy Horse from a leadership position. The error was corrected, but Crook remained suspicious, especially when an exasperated Crazy Horse threatened to lead his people north to Canada if promises were not met. Crook was not pleased and instructed that a close watch be placed on Crazy Horse, making arrangements to have the Sioux warrior imprisoned in Dry Tortugas, Florida.[41]

On the morning of September 4, 1877, Crazy Horse left the agency, either to take his sick wife to a doctor or to avoid arrest. The agency's white officials panicked and ordered his arrest, sending four hundred Indians and eight companies of the Third Cavalry to bring him back. Crazy Horse made it to the agency of his uncle Spotted Tail, where the pursuing force caught up with him and brought him back to the Red Cloud Agency. When Crazy Horse saw that he was about to be placed in a three-by-six-foot windowless cell before being shipped off to Dry Tortugas, he turned to fight his way out, knife in hand. "Kill him!" some shouted. "Stab the son-of-a-bitch!"[42] While three Indians held his arms, a soldier ran Crazy Horse through with his bayonet. Crazy Horse staggered forward, and another soldier bayoneted him in the back. Crazy Horse fell to the ground. Little Big Man and some others tried to help him up. "Let me go, my friends," Crazy Horse gasped. "You have got me hurt enough." It grew silent, as hundreds of Sioux gathered outside, watching in shock. Seven-foot-tall Touch-the-Clouds, who had worked for peace so often in the past, held the others back. "He was a great chief, and he cannot be put in a prison." He then bent down and picked up the fallen warrior, carrying him to the adjutant's office, where Crazy Horse's friend Dr. V.T. McGillicuddy gave him morphine. It took several minutes for Crazy Horse to die, during which time it is recorded that he said, "All we wanted was peace and to be left alone."[43]

With Crazy Horse dead and the Sioux insurrection ended, the government officially terminated the Fort Laramie Treaty of 1868, took the Black Hills from the Sioux, and transferred the survivors to a number of "reservations"—a new word coined in 1877 to replace "agency." Securing control of the northern plains, the army constructed two forts in the Yellowstone area, Fort Keogh and Bighorn Post, which were deliberately built in the center of what had been the lands of the Sioux and Cheyenne with the clear purpose of ending their power for good.[44] Defeating the Sioux had enormous long-term consequences for the development of the plains, facilitating government control and opening the entire region to further settlement and exploitation. With the Sioux safely contained on reservations, there seemed nothing to hinder American expansion and the government's desire to impose order on the West.

During the summer of 1877, a group of civil engineers and workers traveled up the Missouri River to Cow Island with instructions to remove a number of obstructions to river traffic. They were accompanied by a company of twelve troopers from the Seventh Infantry out of Fort Benton. Steamboats had ferried fifty tons of government equipment and supplies to Cow Island, where they sat under tarpaulins until they could be sent overland to various government posts. The engineers set about clearing the river for the flood of migrants expected to pour into the Indian-free Black Hills. But then, suddenly, on September 23, Indians appeared on the south bank of the river.[45]

The commander of the troopers, Sergeant William Molchert, watched anxiously as hundreds of Indians forded the river above and below his base and set up camp nearby. He quickly discovered that these were not Sioux but a completely different people who had traveled all the way from eastern Oregon and Idaho. Several approached the camp and Molchert went out unarmed to meet with them. He was stunned that they "spoke English as well as any one could" and expressed their friendship, politely asking if they might have some food. Molchert got a sack of hardtack, added a side of bacon, shook hands with their chief, who was named Joseph, and hoped they would all go away. Desperate with hunger, some of these Indians snuck into the engineers' camp, stealing food and other supplies. One of the chiefs expressed his regret that they had to steal, but he saw no choice as they were starving. He was upset, though, that some "bad boys" set fire to a stack of five hundred sacks of bacon, which created a huge blaze that could be seen and smelled over a great distance. The fire lit up the area sufficiently to allow the defenders to see the Indians and drive them off. There were no casualties and little loss other than the bacon, but it was evident that the government's "Indian problem" was not over. Within a month of Crazy Horse's surrender, the limited resources of the U.S. Army would once more be stretched in pursuit of an errant tribe—in this case the peaceful, respected, largely Christian, and even more elusive Nez Perce.[46]

The Nez Perce Take On the United States

The whole nation followed the flight of the Nez Perce. Just twelve years after massive armies had battled across the landscape of the East, the technologically advanced United States Army suffered repeated defeats at the hands of a poorly armed band of a few hundred Indians. The war became a national drama, with the public hungry for every possible detail of their military chasing these ghosts within the very borders of the United States, newspapers rushing reports of their movement into print on a daily basis. It quickly became general knowledge that these Indians had been defrauded by the government and neighboring settlers, leading many whites to perceive nobility in the Nez Perce search for safety, and transforming one of their chiefs, Joseph, into a heroic symbol of the native peoples. While a few papers called for the sanguine defeat and punishment of the Nez Perce, the majority, even in the West, cheered them on and urged the government "to let them go in peace," even as the Indians inflicted humiliating defeats on American forces.[47] When the *Denver News* called for the immediate "extinction" of the Nez Perce, the *Colorado Springs Gazette* pointed out that these Indians acted in the most humane fashion. The *Gazette* expressed the common sentiment that the Nez Perce "have been systematically imposed upon" by avaricious whites, and reminded its readers that the Nez Perce had always been "friendly to the whites" since they first fed the starving Lewis and Clark expedition seventy-two years earlier; that they always protected whites from "the attacks of less friendly tribes; that they were of great service to United States troops during the Modoc War; that they are the most manly, candid, brave, and least treacherous of North American Indians." The government tried to raise panic among the people of the West over this supposed terror, but the value of "our civilization and the feeling of security that our power gives us, should makes us prudent and merciful rather than mean and revengeful."[48]

The United States government repeatedly recognized the Nez Perce as friends and allies, signing two treaties that guaranteed them possession of their lands in Idaho and Oregon in perpetuity. Yet, like the civilized tribes of the Southeast who had been forced onto the Trail of Tears in the 1830s, the Nez Perce became the target of white envy. In violation of treaties and a presidential proclamation from Ulysses S. Grant, white settlers encroached on Nez Perce territory in the 1870s, often resorting to violence to drive away the native owners. In 1875, when the state of Oregon demanded title to all Nez Perce lands within its borders, President Grant caved in, revoking his executive order. More white settlers rushed in, killing several Nez Perce in the process of expropriating their lands. When one of these murderers confessed and turned himself in, no charges were brought against him, demonstrating to the Nez Perce that they could not expect justice in white courts.[49]

Joseph, one of the primary chiefs of the Nez Perce, called for restraint, finding an ally in 1876 in General Oliver O. Howard, commander of the Military Department of the Columbia. Howard sent a commission of army officers to confer with Joseph and investigate the situation, approving their recommendation that the Nez Perce receive recompense for their losses and surety in their lands. Howard turned to the Bureau of Indian Affairs to "effect a just and amicable settlement," but the bureau demanded that the Nez Perce give up their Oregon lands and move to the Lapwai reservation in Idaho. "We are not to be trampled upon and [our] rights taken from us," Joseph proclaimed in opposition to this land grab. "The right of the land was ours before the whites came among us."[50] The United States government refused to negotiate and in January 1877 ordered the removal of the Nez Perce from their land. General Irwin McDowell, commander of the Military Division of the Pacific, ordered General Howard to personally oversee the operation "to occupy Wallowa Valley *in the interest of peace.*"[51]

In May, when the Nez Perce still had not left their land, Howard came to meet with their leaders. Toohoolhoolzote, a Nez Perce spiritual leader whom Howard's aide Lieutenant Melville Wilkinson described as "six feet and over of badness," got into an argument with the general over the origins of land ownership. For Howard, the question was simply one of power—the United States had it and the Nez Perce must adjust to that reality. Howard arrested Toohoolhoolzote on the spot, telling the Nez Perce that the only question was "will the Indians come peaceably on the reservation, or do they want me to put them there by force?" It was not the most diplomatic language or action, but then Howard was a soldier, not a diplomat.[52]

Howard was an unusual man. He had seen extensive action during the Civil War, from the first Bull Run through Sherman's march to the sea, losing his right arm at the Battle of Fair Oaks. Deeply religious, Howard encouraged his soldiers to attend prayer meetings and practice temperance, earning the nickname "the Christian soldier." After the war, he headed the Freedman's Bureau and helped found Howard University, taking pride in aiding the former slaves in the transition to freedom. General Crook was "very much amused" by Howard's self-image, Howard having told him "he thought the Creator had placed him on earth to be the Moses to the Negro. Having accomplished that mission, he felt satisfied his next mission was with the Indians." For the Nez Perce, he was not Moses but one of the pharaoh's commanders.[53]

Trying a more gentle approach, Howard rode with Joseph and his fellow chiefs Looking Glass and White Bird up to the Lapwai reservation for an inspection. It was a lovely area of small farms, but, as Joseph reported, "We rode all day upon the reservation, and found no good land unoccupied." Nonetheless, Joseph and his co-chief and brother Ollokot continued to favor a peaceful move to the reservation, and all those involved expected Nez Perce capitulation. "Quiet peace reigns," Sergeant Michael McCarthy wrote on June 12. "Joseph has put his pride in his pocket," and began collecting his livestock for the move to the reservation.[54]

The very next day, an old warrior named Red Grizzly Bear mocked some of the young men for not avenging the deaths of relatives killed by whites. Three of these young men immediately set out for the white settlements along the Salmon River seeking revenge, killing four white men and raping two women.

These crimes destroyed any hopes for peace and divided the Nez Perce. Some wanted to turn the criminals over to the army, but most followed the lead of Joseph and Ollokot in heading east, aiming to reach the plains, where they would join their old friends the Crow in living off the buffalo they thought were still plentiful.[55]

The violence committed by these three young Nez Perce sparked what the government saw as an "uprising," but there were deeper causes. As the scholar Jerome Greene has written, the events of June 1877 "represented the culmination of a cultural crisis" among the Nez Perce that had simmered for years, as many of them had learned English, become Christians, and settled on individual plots of land to farm, verging on full assimilation into white society. Yet they suffered heavily at the hands of the whites, from property theft to repeated acts of rape, and found no justice in the white legal system. Their culture was undermined by the ill effects of alcohol, decades of "repeated land swindles," and the "usual litany of broken promises." For many of these people, it was long past time to get away from this abusive relationship with the whites; what they failed to appreciate was how difficult it would be to elude white power.[56]

On June 15, Captain David Perry, commander at Fort Lapwai, received frantic messages from white settlers reporting the murders and rapes and begging protection. "We want arms and ammunition and help at once," the settlers cried. "Don't delay a moment." The army, caught completely by surprise, was ill-prepared for this sudden outbreak of hostilities. Most of its units were still scattered across the plains, exhausted from the yearlong war against the Sioux. General Howard moved quickly to organize his forces, reassuring General McDowell that his soldiers "will make short work" of it, which proved to be one of his lesser prophesies.[57]

Howard's forces were well supplied with all the latest in munitions and led by a coterie of experienced veterans—not just the commanders but the field officers as well. Captain Perry had served with distinction in the First Cavalry since the Civil War, Captain Joel Trimble had been at Gettysburg and Cold Harbor, and Lieutenant William Parnell, a native of Ireland, had first seen action in the notorious charge of the Light Brigade at Balaclava before joining the U.S. Army during the Civil War. Their first confrontation with the inexperienced Nez Perce began by accident at White Bird Creek on June 17, where Joseph's people had set up their village at the base of a canyon near the Salmon River. As Perry's force, which consisted of a hundred troopers and eleven citizen volunteers, descended the canyon toward the village, six Nez Perce came forward under a flag of truce. One of the civilians began firing, and the Nez Perce scattered for cover. Sixty-five Nez Perce—armed with weapons ranging from bows and muskets to Winchester repeating rifles—returned fire. Perry had no time to place his forces, which were spread out along the ridge, so he simply ordered them to dismount and take protective cover. But the civilians panicked and fled, exposing Perry's flank. The Nez Perce accentuated the confusion by sending some of their horses rushing along the ridge, stampeding many of the troopers' horses. Perry struggled to restore order, but, he later wrote, many of the men, "seeing the citizens in full retreat . . . were seized with a panic that was uncontrollable, and then the whole right of the line, seeing the mad rush of the horses on the left, also gave way and the panic became general." Remarkably well led, the Nez Perce sustained their attack, picking off individual soldiers, and cutting off and killing an eight-man contingent. Finally Lieutenant Parnell succeeded in organizing a skirmish line, which halted the Nez Perce pursuit and saved Perry's command as the Nez Perce pulled back and the troopers fled to Mount Idaho.[58]

The army had acted with an excess of confidence, leading to what General Howard called a "rout . . . , a kind of Bull Run, on a small scale." Sergeant Michael McCarthy gave a more precise explanation of the disaster: the troopers were just not ready for the campaign. The soldiers had gone without sleep for two nights, and "We were marched into a deep cañon and to a country strange to us, and familiar to the enemy," without any plan of operations. They had just stumbled into the Nez Perce, resulting in thirty-four dead and two wounded. In contrast, the Nez Perce suffered two or three wounded and no fatalities. The low number of wounded spoke to the incredible marksmanship of the Nez Perce, a skill that would plague the U.S. forces for the rest of the campaign. The Nez Perce proved calm in battle; having no reserves of ammunition, they chose their shots carefully, did not make the mistake of firing from horseback, as did the soldiers, and consistently used the terrain to their advantage.[59]

The national press excitedly reported on the Battle of White Bird Creek, which came so soon after the army had announced an end to all Indian hostilities in the West. Parnell's action drew praise for having prevented another Little Bighorn, the *New York Herald* stating, "There is no doubt but the Indians would have pursued and massacred every one of the command were it not for the bravery and determined pluck of Lieutenant Parnell."[60] The press was hungry for heroes in this otherwise disastrous start to yet another seemingly pointless war. Sergeant McCarthy, who had attempted to organize a rear guard, had been left behind, eluding the Nez Perce for two days before walking back to rejoin his company. A grateful nation awarded Parnell and McCarthy Congressional Medals of Honor. But there was no escaping the fact that the U.S. Army had once more been beaten by "savages." And yet these savages acted oddly. In a widely reported incident, Isabella Benedict became caught up in the chaotic battle at White Bird Creek as she rode to Mount Idaho with her two children. A Nez Perce named Sounded Head swept her up and kept Benedict and her children safe until the battle was over, then escorted them to safety. Such contradictory narratives of murder and rescue confused the sympathies of many, winning the Nez Perce a reluctant respect. Even hardened foes of the Indians like *The Nation* moved within a month from blaming the war on the "pure cussedness" of the "savages" who acted with "hostile intent" against innocent settlers to castigating the government for conducting a criminal war against the mistreated and blameless Nez Perce.[61]

Realizing that he now faced a major Indian uprising, Howard got immediate approval for the transfer of troops that had been stationed in the South, leaving his freedmen to fend for themselves. On June 23 he took personal command of the pursuit of the Nez Perce, leading four hundred soldiers and a unit of civilian volunteers. From the start, the Nez Perce completely outmaneuvered Howard, often toying with him in much the same way General Nathanael Greene had with Lord Cornwallis during the Revolution. At one point Joseph turned back, crossed the Salmon River, and came behind Howard, forcing the general to reverse direction in a "Horrible retrograde march." The troopers were immensely frustrated by the whole exercise, and baffled by the ease with which the Nez Perce moved through this daunting terrain. "How the whole tribe of Indians with horses, women, papooses, etc., got across [the Salmon] was a puzzle," Sergeant McCarthy wrote after the war. "It is yet a puzzle." Even with all their "engineering skill," the army could not cross the river where the Nez Perce had. The press took a little too much delight in Howard's troubles, the *Colorado Springs Gazette* observing, "The rotundity of the earth has been proven beyond a doubt by the campaign of General Howard against the Nez Perces." With the Nez Perce constantly appearing behind Howard's forces, "it is difficult to discover at this distance whether Howard is after Joseph or Joseph after Howard."[62]

Howard worsened the situation by launching a preemptive strike on Looking Glass, who had no intention of joining Joseph in his flight east. Looking Glass, who had earned a reputation as a talented warrior when he helped the Crow defeat the Sioux in 1874, wanted nothing further to do with war and felt confident the whites would respect his peaceful inclinations. After all, he and his people— 20 adult men and 120 women, children, and old men—ran a prosperous dairy business at their village of Kamnaka. What possible threat could they pose? But Howard suspected that Looking Glass would soon join Joseph and sent Captain Stephen Whipple with sixty-six troopers and twenty civilian volunteers to forcibly remove these Indians to the reservation. On the morning of July 1, 1877, the U.S. Army attacked Looking Glass's dairy farm. Whipple rode up and demanded that Looking Glass surrender immediately. Bird Alighting spoke for Looking Glass, telling Whipple, "He does not want war! He came here to escape war." At that moment a civilian volunteer shot a villager and bullets started flying wildly, sending Whipple and his officers diving for cover. The Nez Perce fled into the nearby woods to escape the violence. The troopers killed three Nez Perce, suffering no casualties themselves, and stole most of their livestock, which they took to Mount Idaho in triumph.[63] Looking Glass and his people saw no choice but to join Joseph in his war against the United States.[64]

Innovative tacticians, the Nez Perce used small units to tie down much larger commands. At the Battle of Clearwater on July 11 and 12, Toohoolhoolzote and twenty followers brought Howard's army to a screeching halt for two days. "The Indian battle formations were excellent," Sergeant McCarthy wrote. "Commands were mostly given by signals," as they operated in groups of three or four men, each squad working as "an independent unit." McCarthy was most impressed with the way the Nez Perce "rolled off the pony to the ground, took deliberate aim and crawled on again, the pony remaining quiet and patient during the firing." They also built stone emplacements with amazing speed, "horseshoe shaped, high enough for a man to stand up in, and on the top willows were so placed as to cover a gun barrel and shade the eye." The Nez Perce kept at a safe distance from the Gatling guns, taunting their opponents to waste their ammunition in fruitless firing, while covering the migration of the noncombatants. Their rapid mobility often led to the troopers firing on one another in the confusion of battle. The Nez Perce fought unlike any other Indians the army had yet encountered; many of their methods anticipated insurrectionary tactics of a later era.[65]

The United States Army had three decisive advantages: ammunition, artillery, and reinforcements. As with their war against the Sioux, the army could send its troops into combat with hundreds of rounds of ammunition, while the Nez Perce generally had only a few rounds, with no access to more except from dead U.S. soldiers or captured supply wagons. The army expended ammunition as though it would never run out. Yellow Wolf recalled one battle in which the troopers fired ceaselessly: "We could not count the soldiers. There must have been hundreds. Bullets came thicker and thicker." The army could build on that advantage by charging with artillery support, as at Clearwater. But above all else, the Nez Perce had no source of reinforcements, while the army had several thousand additional troops to draw upon in their war against the Indians.[66]

However, the army bore one significant handicap: Custer's defeat. Little Bighorn taught officers to be exceedingly cautious, generally avoiding both an arrogant certainty of victory and a willingness to take chances on the battlefield. Such caution led to the occasional victory, such as they claimed at Clearwater, but permitted the Nez Perce repeatedly to escape. Bird Alighting described the end of the Battle of Clearwater: "Everybody was running, some leading, some falling behind! All skipping for their lives, for the camp! . . . They followed the families, the moving camp, guarding them from the pursuing soldiers. The cannons boomed and the Gatling guns rattled, sending out shot after shot after the fleeing families." Having cleared the Indians from the field, an understandable caution held Howard back from following up on his victory; he instead waited for reinforcements. Army casualties were twelve dead and twenty-seven wounded at Clearwater, half of those part of the command structure, as the Nez Perce targeted officers. "Their fire was deadly," Lieutenant Charles Wood wrote, "the proportion of wounded to killed being but two to one." The Nez Perce incurred four dead and six wounded.[67]

After these initial battles, the Nez Perce were divided on how best to proceed. Joseph and Ollokot favored heading east and then turning back to their homelands; White Bird proposed heading for Canada; Looking Glass wanted to head out onto the plains. After much debate, the Nez Perce chose the latter course, believing that once they passed out of General Howard's territory they would successfully escape. This strategy indicated a cultural failure to understand the nature of the United States, as they saw each army as essentially a different tribe. Looking Glass later said he "did not want to fight either soldiers or citizens east of the Lolo [Trail] because they were not the ones who had fought them in Idaho." They had no grievance with the people living hundreds of miles across the Salmon River.[68]

Crossing into Montana, the Nez Perce faced a second army commanded by Colonel John Gibbon operating out of Fort Shaw, one of the new bases intended to complete the pacification of the West.[69] Gibbon entered into an alliance with the Flatheads, traditional friends of the Nez Perce, and sent Captain Charles Rawn with two hundred largely unenthusiastic men to intercept Joseph. "It was the belief of most of us," one volunteer reported, "that in case of a fight, especially before reinforcements arrived, it would have been another Custer massacre." When the Nez Perce made clear their intention to pass in peace, most of the civilians cheerfully went home, leaving Rawn with just thirty regulars, an equal number of volunteers, and twenty-one Flathead scouts. These men watched from inside what everyone would soon call "Fort Fizzle" as the Nez Perce rode calmly by. One soldier reported that "I saw squaws and children with camp stuff going up" the ridge past the fort, looking unconcerned—some even waved. Rawn tried goading his men to attack, but "the truth was, some of our citizens were pretty badly scared"; the Nez Perce already had a fearsome reputation.[70]

The failure at Fort Fizzle amused those papers sympathetic to the Nez Perce and infuriated those hostile to the Indians. "The Nez Perces, fresh from the victorious slaughters of Idaho," reported one paper, "were permitted to pass an entrenched camp . . . under command of a Regular army officer without a shot being fired." The *Helena Herald* found the troopers "as useless as boys with popguns." Thomas Sunderland, embedded with Howard's forces, thought, "There is no earthly excuse" for the escape of the Nez Perce. What the press did not know was that Rawn's inaction persuaded Joseph and the other chiefs that they had been right to believe all would be well once they reached the plains, a perspective reinforced by the willingness of many whites to sell them goods, including ammunition. Yellow Bull assumed from the "friendly talks we had had with the soldiers" they met that there would be no "more fighting, especially if we did not disturb the settlers." By July 30 the Nez Perce had increased their lead in advance of Howard's army to one hundred miles. But at this point, convinced that their troubles were literally behind them, they slowed down, not realizing that Gibbon was racing to cut them off with a large force of troopers and volunteers. Seeking to avoid the humiliation of Fort Fizzle, Gibbon ordered that there were to be "no negotiations whatever with the Indians, and the men should have no hesitancy in shooting down any armed Indian they meet."[71]

Gibbon intercepted the Nez Perce at Big Hole, boldly sneaking up on the Nez Perce camp in the predawn hours. His troops raced among the tipis, firing indiscriminately. "Fortunately for us," one soldier reported, the Nez Perce were "a little dazed and nervous from the shock of surprise." The Indians were more surprised than the troopers knew, for they did not realize that they were still at war and had failed to set out pickets. Yellow Wolf, sleeping soundly when he heard shots, thought he had to be dreaming.[72] But the Nez Perce recovered quickly and the fighting turned fierce. "Men, white and red, women and boys, all take part in the fight, which is actually hand to hand, a regular melee, rifles and revolvers in full play, men are powder burned, so close are they to death dealing guns," wrote one officer. Soon the ground was "covered with the dead and dying, the morning air laden with smoke and riven by cheers, savage yells, shrieks, curses, groans." Boys frantically attempted to protect their families with knives; the more humane soldiers knocked them aside, while others fired without hesitation.[73] The soldiers poured a heavy fire onto the fleeing Nez Perce with no regard for age or gender in what Gibbon called "the greatest slaughter." Tipis were pulled over so that soldiers could shoot at cowering occupants, in one instance killing five children. Captain William Logan rushed forth to put a stop to the shooting of noncombatants and was shot in the head by a woman whose husband had just been killed; she was also killed instantly.[74] After just twenty minutes, the fighting ceased and the troopers set about destroying the village. Young White Bird saw a little girl standing in the river, confused and cold, holding her arm in the air. As he approached he saw "a big bullet hole" in her arm, and knew there was nothing he could do to help her.[75]

Clearly defeated in a horrific battle in which everyone was a target, the Nez Perce did not give up. They fled into the brush, re-formed, and counterattacked. Gibbon reported on the deadliness of their fire: "At almost every crack of a rifle from the distant hills some member of the command was sure to fall," including Gibbon himself, who was wounded. Suddenly surrounded by the Nez Perce warriors, the troopers huddled within hastily erected defenses, listening as the Nez Perce packed up the remains of their village and headed south, but not before disabling Gibbon's howitzer and taking two thousand rounds of ammunition.[76]

General Sheridan called the Battle of the Big Hole "one of the most desperate engagements on record." Gibbon lost thirty-one men with forty wounded and the Nez Perce lost somewhere between forty-five and ninety people, mostly women and children. The military moved quickly to frame the Battle of the Big Hole as a heroic victory, awarding numerous citations, including six Medals of Honor. Nonetheless, Idaho and Montana were in an uproar; panic spread with wild rumors of volunteers "cut to pieces" by the Nez Perce. The Lemhi Shoshones moved into a fortified canyon to protect themselves from the Nez Perce and the whites, the latter tending to treat all Indians alike.[77] White settlers sought safety inside forts with nicknames like Fort Skedaddle and Fort Run. They begged territorial governments and the army for guns, but openly questioned the justice of the war. Even a group of volunteers with Gibbon's force in the Bitterroot Valley got into a debate over whether it was appropriate to pursue peaceful Indians. There were many who felt that the United States should just leave the Nez Perce alone.[78]

Through July and August the Nez Perce won skirmishes against the pursuing armies and then melted into the surrounding country. In early September they entered Yellowstone National Park, just recently opened to the public, coincidentally interrupting Sherman's tour of the park.[79] After fighting a ferocious battle with Colonel Samuel Sturgis's Seventh Cavalry at Canyon Creek on September 13, the Nez Perce finally decided to turn toward Canada. However, Looking Glass, concerned that his people were on the verge of collapse, convinced his fellow chiefs to slow their pace, confident that they had long since outstripped General Howard's pursuit. On September 29, the Nez Perce settled in heavy fog on the northeast side of Bear's Paw Mountain near Snake Creek, just forty miles from the Canadian border.[80]

While the Nez Perce rested, Colonel Nelson Miles rushed his force of more than five hundred soldiers north to intercept them before they crossed the border. Cheyenne and Lakota scouts, many of whom had been among those just defeated by the army, took the lead among Miles's troops. Miles planned to use the traditional cavalry charge straight into the Indian village at dawn, shooting everything that moved. Custer had developed this technique of shock and awe at the Washita in 1868 when he notoriously slaughtered a village of peaceful Cheyenne living under the protection of the U.S. government, though such an approach had proven less successful at the Little Bighorn.[81]

On the morning of September 30 the 700 Nez Perce prepared for their final move to Canada. They did not feel in a hurry, and several of the 250 warriors went off to hunt. Joseph and his twelve-year-old daughter went to catch some horses while others packed up the camp. Suddenly scouts came rushing in, reporting the swift approach of troopers. Women and children fled the camp while warriors rushed to secure the horses and take up defensive positions. Yellow Wolf remembered, "Soon from the south came a noise—a rumble like stampeding buffaloes," as Miles's cavalry came charging toward the village. Rushing to high ground, Yellow Wolf saw "hundreds of soldiers charging in two wide, circling wings," surrounding the camp. Joseph put his daughter on a horse and told her to ride north while he raced back to the village, bullets ripping his clothes and shooting his horse from under him. "As I reached the door of my lodge," Joseph recalled, "my wife handed me my rifle, saying: 'Here's your gun. Fight!'"[82]

Though Miles caught the Nez Perce completely by surprise, the Battle of Bear's Paw Mountain was no repeat of the Washita, except in replicating Custer's lack of reconnaissance. The cavalry charged in without bothering to check the terrain or enemy positions, and met Nez Perce warriors firing from concealed positions. "Those Indians stopped our charge cold," said trooper John McAlpine. "We met those soldiers bullet for bullet," Yellow Wolf said with pride. "We held those soldiers from advancing. We drove them back." Though the Nez Perce recovered quickly, they remained baffled as to who was attacking them, and why. A warrior shouted to Lieutenant Lovell Jerome, "Who, in the name of God are you? We don't want to fight."[83]

Ignoring this call for peace, Miles renewed the attack that afternoon, only to be once more forced back by stiff resistance. Expecting Sitting Bull to appear at any moment and join the Nez Perce, Miles shifted to a siege, though he need not have worried, as Major James Walsh, superintendent of the North-West Mounted Police, persuaded Sitting Bull that he would lose his welcome in Canada if he took part in the war south of the border. Miles ordered Lieutenant Edward McClernand's cavalry to chase down the fleeing women and children, but they were hurled back by a small group of Nez Perce. A Cheyenne riding with the troopers described how the "Nez Perces were very brave and crowded on the soldiers," moving in so close that the cavalry dared not fire for fear of hitting one another. Because of this action, many Nez Perce made it safely to Canada.[84]

The battle dragged on as the Nez Perce's accurate fire kept the soldiers pinned down. Scout Louis Shambo thought these warriors "the best shots I ever saw." Any soldier who exposed himself for even an instant was likely to be wounded, his medical care consisting of "a stiff drink of brandy and opium." The wounded caught between the lines were certain that the Nez Perce would mutilate them during the night, and their opponents did sneak through no-man's-land in the dark, but to grab weapons and ammunition, not to kill. One wounded sergeant was reassured by a Nez Perce speaking to him in English that he would not hurt him, while another soldier begged the Nez Perce stripping him of his ammunition belt for water and was left with a full canteen. These were hardly the savages about whom they had been warned.[85]

Both sides shivered through the cold night as snow fell in the darkness. Yellow Wolf recalled "Children crying with cold" as they could not build a fire. On the other side a trooper found it "frightful to see so many dead soldiers, Indians, horses & ponies lying about." The siege lasted from the evening of September 30 until October 5.[86] Miles shelled the camp with exploding shells that missed the warriors in their entrenchments, killing several noncombatants; Yellow Wolf watched in horror as a shell killed a girl and her grandmother. Still, the Nez Perce held on. "They fight with more desperation than any Indians I have ever met," Miles wrote. The Nez Perce debated making a break for it, which would mean leaving the wounded and elderly behind. "We were unwilling to do this," Joseph stated. "We had never heard of a wounded Indian recovering while in the hands of white men."[87]

On the evening of October 4, General Howard arrived at Bear's Paw and urged negotiation. The next day Joseph delivered his famous speech of surrender, which began with the generous statement that he knew General Howard's heart and trusted him.

> I am tired of fighting. Our chiefs are killed. . . . The old men are all dead. . . . It is cold and we have no blankets. The little children are freezing to death. My people . . . have run away to the hills, and have no blankets, no food; no one knows where they are—perhaps freezing to death. I want to have time to look for my children. . . . Maybe I shall find them among the dead. Hear me, my chiefs. I am tired; my heart is sick and sad. From where the sun now stands I will fight no more forever.[88]

Joseph was right: his people were exhausted, starving, and worried about their families; surrender was their only option. Miles and Howard agreed to do all they could to help the Nez Perce, promising Joseph that his people would be kept through the winter at the Tongue River Cantonment and then returned to Idaho. Joseph presented his Winchester to General Howard, who stepped back and pointed toward Miles, who accepted the gun from Joseph. Sixty-seven other warriors and many noncombatants followed behind Joseph, surrendering their weapons to the troopers. Howard described this "forlorn procession, . . . covered with dirt, their clothing was torn, and their ponies, such as they were, were thin and lame."[89] Joseph, according to Major Henry Tilton, was "in great distress" over the fate of his daughter. Miles was jubilant, boasting in a dispatch to General Terry, "We have had our usual success."[90]

Nearly 250 Nez Perce, including Joseph's daughter, escaped Miles's encirclement and later pursuit to the Canadian border, joining Sitting Bull. One Nez Perce woman described how they hid through that first night, "cold and chilly, we stood or sat holding our horses. We cried with misery and loneliness, as we still heard the guns of the battle." White Bird told the Mountie Major Walsh that the Nez Perce had not wanted war but were forced to it because "the white man wanted the wealth our people possessed; he got it by the destruction of our people." Walsh, who thought White Bird an intelligent and sympathetic man, was moved as the Nez Perce concluded, "We have no country, no people, no home."[91]

The battle cost the U.S. Army two officers and nineteen troopers; four officers, forty-six troopers, and two Indian scouts were wounded. The Nez Perce lost twenty-five, and between forty and sixty were wounded. The war lasted from June through October, the U.S Army officially losing 6 officers, 101 enlisted men, and 6 civilian employees; the wounded totaled 13 officers and 125 enlisted men. The war cost $1,873,410.43, an enormous amount for the period; there is no estimate of the property destroyed or lost. Howard's forces marched 1,700 miles in pursuit of the Nez Perce, while the Nez Perce themselves, including their journey after their capture, ultimately marched 7,000 miles. The number of Nez Perce who died in the nineteen battles over three and a half months is unknown but probably numbers between 96 and 145 people, at least 36 of whom were women and children, though many estimates run much higher. Included in that total killed were all three of the original murderers who had launched the war, as well as Looking Glass, Toohoolhoolzote, and Joseph's brother Ollokot. The Nez Perce had faced not just the U.S. Army in battle, but also the Crow, Sioux, Bannock, Gros Ventres, and Assiniboines. Only the Plains Cree are known to have aided the Nez Perce by taking some in as refugees and helping them into Canada.[92]

The betrayal of the Nez Perce did not end with the war. Miles wrote General Terry recommending friendship with the Nez Perce, whom he described as "decidedly [the] most dangerous Indian enemies" the country had faced, combining "the cunning of wild Indians, and many of the arts of civilized warfare," with an unnerving ability to speak English. He reminded his commander that "as this trouble was commenced with fraud and injustice I am satisfied these Indians can be made loyal friends of the government in six months" if only they are treated "with anything like honesty and justice."[93] Terry agreed, but General Sherman nullified the surrender agreement and ordered the Nez Perce to Fort Lincoln in Dakota Territory. Miles protested that it was "inhuman to compel them to travel farther" in such weather, but he was overruled; Sherman wanted to make an example of the Nez Perce by never allowing them to return home.[94]

As Miles predicted, the journey to Fort Lincoln was cruel, and many Nez Perce died along the way. Lieutenant Frank Baldwin described the winter march as "most inhumane," to the extent that Miles "can't sleep or take any comfort thinking as he does of their suffering." But Miles felt much better when they reached Bismarck, where hundreds of people turned out to welcome the Nez Perce, providing a generous feast for the prisoners and their military escort. Joseph stood next to Miles as the band played the national anthem. As a further testament to the celebrity status of the Nez Perce, the town threw a banquet for Joseph and the other chiefs, serving salmon as a reminder of their home country. Spurred on by this demonstration of public support for his prisoners of war, Miles requested that he be allowed to accompany Joseph to Washington, D.C., to present the case for the Nez Perce to be returned home. But Sherman, annoyed at all the attention awarded these defeated Indians, would have none of it, ordering the Nez Perce to Fort Leavenworth. When Joseph learned of this new destination for his people, he gave way to a rare show of frustration, asking, "When will these white chiefs tell the truth?"[95]

During their forced march to Fort Leavenworth and then to the Indian territory of Oklahoma, more than a hundred Nez Perce died, a great many of them children. Sherman was practicing a slow genocide against the Nez Perce in this miniature Trail of Tears. Joseph devoted himself to trying to get his people home, visiting Washington, D.C., writing an article in the *North American Review*, and finding an unlikely ally in the newly promoted General Miles, who lobbied President Hayes and Secretary of the Interior Carl Schurz on behalf of the people he had defeated in battle. Miles finally got through to General Sherman, who declared the Nez Perce war of 1877 "one of the most extraordinary Indian wars of which there is any record." He had to admit that he admired the Nez Perce for displaying "a courage and skill that elicited universal praise." Now that they were properly chastised, Sherman thought they deserved special consideration as "they abstained from scalping; let captive women go free; did not commit indiscriminate murder of peaceful families, which is usual; and fought with almost scientific skill, using advance and rear guards, skirmish lines, and field fortifications." Finally, in May 1885, after nearly eight years of battling for their rights, the remaining 268 Nez Perce boarded a train for the journey home.[96]

Secretary of War George W. McCrary declared that Joseph's surrender "ended Indian hostilities for the present, and, let us hope, for the future as well."[97] But the very next year the army turned its anger on the Bannock and Ute people in separate, though less dramatic, campaigns. Confident of their power, the U.S. Army sowed the seeds of future conflict. For instance, in 1877 General James Carleton forcibly moved the Apache from their Chiricahua reservation in Arizona Territory to San Carlos in the middle of the desert, inspiring a young man named Geronimo to lead a decade-long struggle against what he saw as an effort to destroy his people. However, with the defeat of the Sioux and Nez Perce in 1877, the government had confronted and destroyed its last significant challengers for control of the West.

And what of Sitting Bull, that scourge of the white man and terror from the north? The Unkpapa chief finally descended from his refuge in Canada, but he did not return to the United States to continue the war; rather, he came to settle peacefully at the Standing Rock Agency and later to become the main attraction in Buffalo Bill Cody's Wild West Show, which helped craft the image of Western violence. In 1890, authorities became concerned that Sitting Bull would join the new Ghost Dance religion and disrupt their acculturation plans, preemptively ordering his arrest. When other Sioux rushed to Sitting Bull's defense, a chaotic fight ensued and Indian police shot and killed the old warrior. It was an ignoble and entirely avoidable death for such a heroic figure. Chief Joseph lived on to fight with his words for the rights of his people, standing as a constant reminder of their dignity and courage. He died at his home at the Colville reservation in eastern Washington in 1904.[98]

The Trouble with Mexicans

The Indians were just the most visible and dramatic challengers to white hegemony in the West in 1877; for many whites, the sizable Hispanic population of Texas and the Southwest threatened to introduce multicultural confusion into the North American republic. It was even conceivable that they could use democracy to their advantage and elect one of their own to Congress, or even, in the most frightening scenario, unite with other dissatisfied elements of the population and gain control of an entire state.

The most likely location for Hispanic domination was New Mexico. During the negotiations resulting in the Treaty of Guadalupe Hidalgo ending the Mexican War in 1848, Secretary of State James Buchanan promised that New Mexico would be admitted into the Union as a state "the moment it can be done with safety." The treaty itself promised full civil rights to all Hispanics and pledged that New Mexico would be brought into the Union with equal status as a state "according to the principles of the Constitution." It certainly had the requisite population; the 1880 census found 110,565 people living in the territory, which gave it more inhabitants than two established states. The *Hispaños* were included in the white population, but estimates place their number at 70 to 80 percent of that total. Therefore it was perfectly logical to imagine that New Mexico would have a largely Hispanic legislature and perhaps even Hispanic senators. Many powerful figures trembled at that vision.[99]

The Republican Party officially favored statehood for New Mexico, seeing its Hispanics as natural allies in the struggle against the white supremacist Democrats. But every effort to bring the state into the Union had been blocked by Democrats and a few East Coast Republicans. Several efforts to gain statehood for New Mexico in the 1870s failed because Democrats repeatedly charged that too many of its citizens were Mexican first and American second. New Mexico came closest to statehood in 1875, when the Republicans attempted to gain admission for both Colorado and New Mexico. The *New York Times* was appalled at the idea of letting in such an "ill-regulated" territory, where "a large part of the people is ignorant and utterly destitute of enterprise and public spirit." The *Cincinnati Commercial* was more pointed, and nasty, in its criticism of the territory, with its preponderance of people of "Mexican descent" who were "almost wholly ignorant" of English and where "popular ignorance prevails like a pall throughout the whole territory." Particularly disturbing was the fact that a majority of New Mexico's newspapers were published in Spanish, indicating that the New Mexicans "are aliens to us in blood and language." Nor could the *Commercial* help but point out that 152 of the territory's 158 churches were Catholic. Repulsed by the idea of making a state "out of a handful of half-breeds, miners and squatters in these remote Territories," the *Commercial* hoped to hear no more of such a ridiculous proposal. The Senate approved both states, but the House passed only on Colorado, rejecting New Mexico by seven votes.[100]

New Mexico's next effort to gain statehood was seriously undermined when it grabbed the national spotlight in 1877 with the justly famous, though much mythologized, Lincoln County War. This battle for economic and political control of the southern half of New Mexico had it all—gunslingers, murder, mayhem, cows, water rights—the whole story of the Wild West in its popular formulation. What the popular story usually leaves out, however, is the reason for the war and its consequence. Most accounts end with then-sheriff Pat Garrett shooting "Dirty Little Billy" (William Bonney, also known as Billy the Kid), but the war continued for another year and ended with the largest landowners in New Mexico territory gaining a political dominance that would last until the mid-twentieth century. Order in New Mexico, as in Texas, Arizona, and every other Western territory, was imposed from outside with the assistance of federal authorities. That dynamic is amply demonstrated in the events of 1877.[101]

Lawrence Murphy dominated the economy and politics of Lincoln County, which covered much of the southeastern quarter of New Mexico. In addition to owning the only store in the county, he controlled nearly every other business as well. This near-monopoly on trade did not sit well with John "Jinglebob" Chisum of Roswell, widely known as "The Cattle King of New Mexico" for his herd of more than 75,000 head. The competition for land and water in Lincoln County created a complicated array of shifting alliances and sporadic violence.[102] In December 1873, the murder of Lincoln's constable Juan Martinez by a group of white ranchers exploded into the Horrell War, which bordered on a race war. Murphy and his ally Sheriff William Brady, perceiving a threat to their dominance from Chisum, sided with the *Mexicanos* against Chisum and most of the white ranchers. The ensuing violence had a powerful ethnic and economic cast: Hispanics tended to herd sheep while the whites went with cattle, the two groups competing for scarce grazing lands.[103] The white ranchers who gravitated to Chisum's leadership instituted a terror campaign similar to that employed by the Klan in the South; houses were surrounded by masked gangs late at night, mysterious fires destroyed crops and structures, arrested Hispanics had a way of ending up killed "while trying to escape." A group of whites killed a local sheriff "for no other reason than that he had a Mexican wife." Supported by Sheriff Brady, Lincoln's *Mexicanos* formed a vigilante committee in order to defend themselves. Within a single month thirteen people had been murdered.[104]

In 1876, Chisum entered into an alliance with the town's new and only lawyer, Alexander McSween. With Chisum's backing, McSween opened a store and the county's first bank, and represented a number of locals in lawsuits against Murphy. Another new arrival in the region, a young Englishman named John Henry Tunstall, joined the alliance in challenging Murphy for control of the county. Suddenly the factions shifted, with the Hispanics and many small ranchers tired of Murphy's monopoly siding with Chisum and McSween; the latter chaired a meeting of the two groups that recognized "with inexpressible pleasure the good and united feeling that binds all our people Mexicans and Americans together."[105] Other small ranchers, who had resisted Chisum's efforts to drive them off their land in early 1877 or would not unite with Hispanics, went over to Murphy's side. Aided by his close friend and protégé James Dolan, and Sheriff Brady, Murphy also found a powerful ally in Chisum's main competitor in land acquisition, Thomas Catron. Known as the "most unscrupulous man in the Southwest," Catron also happened to be the U.S. attorney for the Territory of New Mexico and headed up what was known as the Santa Fe Ring, a group of powerful lawyers and landowners who ran the territory in their own interest. Catron proved a valuable ally to Murphy, backing him in the capital and giving his actions the cover of legality.[106]

Investments and lawsuits quickly became tangled, dividing the area into two hostile factions. Writing in 1882, Pat Garrett intelligently noticed that both sides claimed to speak for "the public" in 1877, when the conflict began. The Chisum alliance could accurately insist that they were standing up to a small wealthy clique that ran the territory without regard to the public good, while the Murphy faction just as correctly spoke for the "smaller cattle owners in Pecos Valley [who] charged Chisum with monopolizing, as a right, all this vast range of grazing country." At the beginning of 1877 Murphy sought to hit Chisum where it hurt by encouraging his workers to steal Chisum's cattle. So successful was this enterprise that people started referring to Murphy's "miracle herd": no matter how many cows he sold, the herd never got smaller. When Chisum's foreman, James Highsaw, found evidence of rustling in the public corral at Loving's Bend on March 28, he lost his temper and shot the suspected thief in the back of the head.[107] This was the second murder that year in the area, and the conflict accelerated, though Highsaw was never arrested.[108]

Both sides brought in hired guns, and, Pat Garrett wrote, "in the winter and spring of 1877 the war commenced in earnest." In April there were two gun battles between the factions that somehow left no casualties but lots of ill will. With Sheriff Brady serving Murphy, Chisum tried to get the military at Fort Stanton to intervene, but their commander absolutely refused, arguing that such conflicts lay outside his jurisdiction. Two more murders followed in May, with both admitted murderers escaping prosecution. The contest between these powerful and wealthy factions created chaos as violent acts multiplied, each crime evoking another in revenge for its predecessor. Garrett observed that "the unsettled state of the country caused by these disturbances called the lawless element, horse and cattle-thieves, footpads, murderers, escaped convicts, and outlaws from all the frontier states and territories" to Lincoln County. Some came, tried their luck, and left. Sam Bass, the most famous outlaw in the United States after Jesse James, robbed a stage in Lincoln County, and was captured soon thereafter. But in January 1877 he escaped from the jail in Santa Fe by unlocking his leg irons and jumping down the stairs when the guard's back was turned. An angry U.S. Mail agent and a Nebraska sheriff who showed up the following day to arrest Bass on charges of robbery and murder respectively were, as the local paper reported, "rather disgusted when they heard of his escape." Bass fled to Texas, where he would continue his brief nefarious career.[109]

Another outlaw who came in search of opportunity in August 1877 was William Bonney, or Billy the Kid. "The reckless daring, unerring marksmanship, and unrivalled horsemanship of the Kid," an admiring Garrett wrote, "rendered his services a priceless acquisition" to whichever side won his services. The Kid was on the run for having killed a man who called him "a pimp" and took a job with the Murphy group. But then Bonney befriended John Tunstall—it was actually more like a romantic crush—and switched allegiances. Tunstall liked the Kid and put him in charge of a herd of cattle.[110] Several more gunfights resulting in at least another six deaths made 1877 a bloody year for Lincoln County; that there were not more deaths was not for lack of trying. Tunstall described Lincoln in September 1877 as "a den of thieves, cut throats & desperadoes & corrupt officials"; its main street became known as "the most dangerous street in America."[111]

But Murphy still controlled the local political apparatus, and he could deputize whomever he liked to operate under the cover of law. In February 1878, the new deputy sheriff, William "Buck" Morton, led a posse to arrest Tunstall. Morton and his posse came upon Tunstall out on the range while he was herding some cattle. Morton later claimed that Tunstall, who was alone and on horseback, fired on the posse, leading them to shoot back. His horse shot from under him, Tunstall fell to the ground wounded. A member of the posse named Tom Hill, a petty thief, went up to where "Tunstall was lying on his face, gasping, placed his rifle to the back of [Tunstall's] head, fired, and scattered his brains over the ground."[112]

Pat Garrett was convinced that Tunstall's murder turned Billy the Kid into a killing machine, the news of his friend's death sending him into a rage. "Breathing vengeance," Garrett wrote, Billy "quitted his herd, mounted his horse, and from that day to the hour of his death his track was blazed with rapine and blood." Such purple prose probably exaggerates the case, as Billy the Kid first sought vengeance in the legal system, attempting to have Morton and Hill arrested for murder. Bonney and McSween went to Sheriff Brady, demanding he arrest Tunstall's murderers, but Brady refused, as Morton had been on official business. Frustrated that they could not find justice, the McSween-Chisum faction organized a vigilance committee and appointed Constable Dick Brewer to head up these "regulators"; each side now had officers of the law upon whom they could draw for legitimacy. This alternative posse caught Morton and another member of his posse, Frank Baker—Hill got away only to be killed a few weeks later while attempting to steal some sheep.[113]

Brewer had given his word that he would bring the men in to stand trial and actually bullied Billy the Kid into not killing the two prisoners. Brewer brought his prisoners to the Chisum ranch, where they heard that the Murphy faction had organized its own posse to liberate the two men. Brewer pressed on immediately for Lincoln, but Morton and Baker were both shot while "trying to escape," possibly by Bonney. Few people believed that story, and the revenge cycle continued; Brewer was killed three weeks later. Bonney sought further vengeance by joining the gang that killed Sheriff William Brady and his deputy on the main street of Lincoln. Murphy brought in even more hired guns, including a new sheriff, Pat Garrett, and in a battle often called "the Big Killing" that involved forty men and lasted over four days in July 1878 trapped McSween and several of his followers in his house. Murphy ruthlessly set fire to the house, killing McSween and three others as they fled the flames. Bonney made his escape along the Bonita River, living to kill many more men over the next three years.[114]

Like much of the nation, President Hayes was outraged by these events, especially when he learned that Governor Samuel Beach Axtell had intervened on several occasions in support of Lawrence Murphy. Hayes fired Axtell and replaced him with General Lew Wallace, who arrived in September 1878 and set about cleaning up the mess, starting by removing Thomas Catron from office as U.S. attorney. Wallace followed up by declaring martial law in Lincoln County and issuing a general amnesty to all those who renounced the use of violence. Backed by the governor, Sheriff Garrett pursued Bonney relentlessly, finally catching him in 1881. Tried and convicted of killing Brady, Bonney escaped after killing two deputies. Garrett surprised Billy the Kid on the night of July 14, 1881, shooting him dead. The Lincoln County War ended shortly thereafter when the Murphy faction agreed to Governor Wallace's compromises and saw that even greater profit resulted from working with Chisum and the other large ranchers. This alliance between merchants and the great landowners would dominate New Mexico for the next century, while the ethnic violence persisted for many years to come. The Lincoln County War fed the public's image of New Mexico as an "ill-regulated" territory, as the *New York Times* expressed it.[115] The public was fascinated by gunslingers like Billy the Kid, but showed less awareness of the racial undertones to Bloody Lincoln. When Gregorio Valenzuela called Ham Mills a "damned gringo," Mills shot him dead; when John Riley shot Juan Batista Patron in the back, the judge dismissed the case as "self defense."[116]

Texas and the Salt War

Conflict had regularly disrupted the border between Mexico and the United States ever since Texan independence from Mexico in 1836. Even following Texas's statehood in 1845, Hispanic citizens of the United States maintained a list of long-standing grievances, starting with the perceived theft of their land under the color of law or through violence and intimidation, to a tendency for U.S. courts to treat the murder of Hispanics with indifference. Decades-long land battles in the previous Mexican territories of New Mexico and Colorado often erupted into violence.[117] On one notable occasion in 1877, the Hispanics fought back, vigorously. Though largely forgotten today, Texas's "Salt War" terrified the white leadership of the state, unifying a majority of whites under the Democratic banner in fear of the consequences if the Hispanic majority of a region actually succeeded in exercising their rights. The Salt War also reminded the Texans of their continued reliance on federal troops for border security, and they deeply resented it.

Texas is, in many ways, a special case. Not only is Texas part of the West, but it is also a Southern state with a history of slavery and the use of violence to maintain white supremacy. Once the Democratic Party seized control of the state in 1874, the legislature cut funding for law enforcement, eliminating the state police, gutting the militia, and even threatening the survival of the legendary Texas Rangers, who found themselves often serving without pay. Republican governor E.J. Davis's state police had outraged the Democrats, who saw far too many black officers for their liking. They were similarly disturbed that the U.S. Army had posted the soldiers of the all-black Tenth Cavalry, the renowned "Buffalo Soldiers," in Texas. As Texas Ranger James Gillett complained, these soldiers "thought themselves the equals of white men," and thus should not have been stationed in Texas. In eliminating the state police, the Democratic Texas legislature, in the words of one historian, "cleansed itself of carpetbaggers, scalawags, and negroes."[118]

But getting rid of the all-white Texas Rangers was another matter. In 1876 Texas adopted a new constitution "which limited the state government so severely that it could hardly function." In April 1877 prominent legislators suggested disbanding the Rangers entirely to save money. Large landowners were horrified and applied pressure to squash this effort at frugality. The West Texas Stock Association took a more direct route, meeting in Goliad and pledging more than seven thousand dollars to see the Rangers through the next few months, while Richard King, owner of the largest cattle herd in Texas, bought new Winchester repeaters for the Rangers. The Democrats agreed to save the Rangers, though they voted insufficient funds to last the year and forced through legislation calling on the citizens to organize themselves into "minute companies" to defend the state against Indians, Mexicans, and "other marauding or thieving parties."[119] These companies were to provide their own weapons, supplies, and leadership, which was a recipe for, as it turned out, both ineffective law enforcement and vigilantism. In effect, the Texas government, unlike the rest of the West in 1877, moved to undermine public order.

The bigotry of the Rangers could be extreme, to the point that an educated Ranger like James Gillett firmly believed that "it is a strange fact, but one beyond question, that no wild animal or bird of prey will touch the body of a Mexican." The Rangers felt little hesitation in using violence against those they identified as inferior. In early 1877 Lieutenant N.O. Reynolds confronted a group of black men in a saloon over a stolen pistol. When one of the blacks fired his gun, the Rangers opened up, killing four men "and a little girl."[120]

The Rangers had no more respect for the border with Mexico than they did for human life. In May 1877, Lieutenant Lee Hall led his men into Mexico, arresting their suspect in the main plaza of Piedras Negras. A few months later Hall demanded that Colonel Manuel Gomez of the Mexican army help him capture some escaped prisoners. Gomez wrote General Antonio Canales that Hall had even threatened to invade Mexico if he did not receive assistance. Outraged Mexicans rallied to the flag, hundreds of border residents pledging to "sacrifice themselves for the independence and dignity of their country." Hall in turn complained to the state's adjutant general, William Steele, that the Mexicans sheltered cattle thieves and other criminals who raided Texas.[121]

These provocative actions by the Rangers aggravated already tense relations with Mexico. In 1876, General Porfirio Díaz overthrew the elected government of Mexico with funding from United States railroad companies frustrated that President Sebastian Lerdo de Tejada refused to serve their interests. But Díaz moved slowly in showing his appreciation to his U.S. backers, and the Grant administration refused to recognize Díaz as president. Instead, in May 1876, the U.S. Navy insulted the honor of Mexico by landing a force of sailors and Marines at Matamoros, Mexico, to protect American citizens and property. In his final State of the Union address, President Grant warned that these "commotions" along the border could lead to much worse if not addressed. These increasing "acts of violence by citizens of one Republic on those of the other" were complicated by the changing course of the Rio Grande. "These changes have placed on either side of that river portions of land which by existing conventions belong to the jurisdiction of the Government on the opposite side of the river."[122] Grant hoped for a diplomatic solution, but his successor went in the opposite direction. On June 1, 1877, President Hayes poured fuel on the fire by authorizing U.S. troops pursuing Indians or other "lawless bands" to cross into Mexico. Díaz objected and sent troops to the border. Colonel Joseph H. Potter took his president's permission to heart and ordered Captain James Randlett not to let the border hinder his operations: "If you catch the thieves, hit them hard"; if they cross the Rio Grande, "follow them into Mexico." Randlett did as instructed.[123]

The border became more volatile as vigilantes crossed both ways in pursuit of thieves and sought revenge for previous acts of violence. Posses quickly turned into murderous criminals, killing Mexicans indiscriminately. For instance, an attack on Corpus Christi by a group of Mexican thieves that left five dead resulted in one of the new "minute companies" lynching several local Hispanics suspected of aiding the Mexicans. Efforts to charge members of this minute company with murder and robbery resulted in no convictions. In August 1877, a group of fifteen Mexicans rode into Rio Grande City, shooting the judge and a jailer and escaping with "two notorious outlaws." The U.S. Army gave chase, crossing into Mexico, but failed to catch the outlaws. The *Galveston News* thought this "flagrant outrage" sufficient cause for war, and newspapers around the country took up the cry. Adjutant General Steele reported to the governor that a state of war existed between Texas and the "Mexican banditti."[124]

Several newspapers in Texas and elsewhere in the West argued that the only way to bring peace to the border was to move it further south. Such calls for the annexation of the northern part of Mexico paid little attention to the consequences of another war with Mexico, but spoke to an aggressive nationalism on the rise in the West. Those favoring immediate military action were frustrated with the caution of General Edward Ord, commander of U.S. troops in Texas. The *Colorado Springs Gazette*, for instance, criticized the liberality of the general for thinking it "'impolitic' to chase Mexican cattle thieves across the border with colored troops"—an insult to the Mexicans. The *Gazette* sarcastically congratulated the general on respecting the sensibilities of the "Greaser."[125]

As calls for military action spread to the Eastern press, many critics feared that President Hayes secretly hoped and planned for a war with Mexico to distract attention from pressing economic issues or to seize the northern Mexican states for incorporation into the United States. General William S. Rosecrans, reviving the language of manifest destiny, encouraged the latter idea but said that the United States should try to buy the land before taking it militarily. A group of exiled Mexican soldiers took all this talk of annexation as a chance to launch a counter-attack on Díaz and began mustering on the Texas side of the border. In July General Ord arrested the exiled General Mariano Escobedo and his followers, who were recruiting troops in Texas for an imminent invasion of Mexico, while the Texas Rangers broke up another group of would-be liberators. It was in such a climate that the Salt War around El Paso briefly threatened to plunge the two nations into a broader conflict.[126]

In 1877 El Paso—which the Anglos insisted on calling Franklin—was the westernmost town in Texas, home to some six hundred people. Across the Rio Grande lived an estimated seven thousand Mexicans in several villages, with the Texas town of San Elizario, twenty-one miles to the south, the largest settlement in the area, with some two thousand people. The entire county claimed only eighty Anglos. These isolated communities stood on the far fringe of Texas, 580 miles from Austin—a distance that required two weeks of hard travel.[127] Several salt lakes sat on public land at the foot of the Guadalupe Mountains, a hundred miles east of El Paso. For the previous century, residents on both sides of the Rio Grande had collected salt from these lakes as a communal right. The salt was one of the few sources of surplus cash available in this hardscrabble area, and in 1862 residents of the valley got together and built a road seventy miles long to facilitate the movement of this precious commodity.[128]

The few non-Hispanics in the area were bitterly divided between the Republican supporters of Reconstruction led by the Italian immigrant Louis Cardis, the town's representative in the state legislature, and the Democratic opponents of equal rights, dominated by Judge Charles Howard, who arrived in El Paso in 1872. Howard had nothing but contempt for most of the Spanish-speaking majority: "It is like talking to a lot of jacks, all braying at once."[129] Most historians, even recent ones, treat the area as divided between "Americans," which consisted of just those eighty Anglos, and "Mexicans" (everyone else). As Walter Prescott Webb put it, "It is not difficult to see that in a race war the handful of 'Americans' would have rough sledding with the Mexican horde."[130] And yet, oddly enough, it was the Anglos who began the war.[131]

With the Democrats firmly in control of Texas in 1877, Charles Howard became El Paso's judge and saw a major moneymaking opportunity in those salt flats at the foot of the Guadalupe Mountains. Inspired by visions of controlling the region's salt trade, Howard had his father-in-law make the necessary claims in Austin. With land titles in hand, Judge Howard threatened to prosecute anyone who hauled salt from *his* lakes without payment. In September 1877 Howard even brought charges against two Hispanics for stating that they were going to get salt from the lakes. Though this action was a violation of the First

Amendment, Howard had the law on his side when it came to the ownership of the lakes, which had been up for grabs—though no one knew it. In defending the traditional salt rights of residents, Louis Cardis put forth a different perception of the law, one that valued the common good over claims of individual landownership. He also offered a traditional approach to politics, calling on the general public to act in support of these rights. On October 1, a crowd in Ysleta first arrested the county judge and justice of the peace in the name of the people, forcing them to resign their offices, and then went in search of Judge Howard. They found him and his agent, John McBride, holding armed positions on the roof of Sheriff Charles Kerber's house. With the situation growing potentially violent, the three men surrendered.[132]

In a letter published in the *Mesilla Independent*, the only newspaper in the region, Howard described how he was "surrounded by forty armed men, hooting and jeering at me," and forced to accompany them to San Elizario. A mob of between two hundred and four hundred angry Hispanics quickly formed to demand action, "and a more sullen, ferocious looking body of men, I never saw." Placed under guard for three days, Howard could hear the crowd "raving and raging like hungry coyotes."[133] The priest at San Elizario, Pierre Bourgade (later archbishop of Santa Fe), and Cardis rushed to the scene and persuaded the crowd not to hurt Howard but to reach a deal with him. Howard claimed he was warned that the life of every "American" in the region was endangered unless he signed a document agreeing to leave the area and to not interfere with the free use of the salt lakes until the state courts had decided on the issue. Leaders of the crowd insisted that they were justified in these actions "because they were the people and the people were the law."[134] Under duress, he signed the paper and promised not to bring charges against any member of the mob. With an angry crowd still occupying the streets of San Elizario, Father Bourgade thought it best to walk with Howard, one arm protectively over his shoulder, and escort him out of town. Howard made it safely to Mesilla, New Mexico, where he telegraphed the governor of Texas that Mexico was invading the United States—a story picked up and amplified by newspapers around the country. Philadelphia's *North American* headlined "Mexican Invasion of Texas," while the *Arkansas Gazette* charged the "battle cry of the Mexicans who have invaded Texas" is "Death to Gringos!" Transferring fantasy to fact, the paper asserted that "the lives of all white men are threatened . . . and a horrible massacre is imminent." The next day the paper reported that Mexico had "claimed and occupied" El Paso.[135]

The commander of U.S. forces in the region, Colonel Edward Hatch, ordered Lieutenant Louis Rucker to investigate the situation. Rucker reported that a mob of both United States and Mexican citizens had overthrown legal authority in the region, putting Anglo lives at risk. Sheriff Kerber, released unharmed by the mob, sent inflammatory messages to the governor and warned that Cardis was telling the Mexicans that they had a right to bear arms. "None of the American citizens are safe so long as we have no troops here to enforce law and order," the sheriff concluded, excluding the Hispanics from the rights of citizenship. District Judge Allan Blacker wired Governor Richard B. Hubbard, "Civil authorities powerless in El Paso County" in confronting a mob that is "quiet, but organized and unyielding. Life and property still in danger and will be until military protection is awarded."[136] Cardis also sent a telegraph to the governor, assuring him that "the late disturbance in this Co. is over and everything seems to be quiet." To ensure that peace, Cardis organized local committees to work out any remaining differences.[137]

In addition to feeding the stories of a Mexican invasion of the United States and congratulating themselves for helping to elevate sentiments for war to a "fever heat," the *Galveston Daily News* purported that "Mexico will never be well governed, nor properly developed, until it is conquered and annexed to the United States." The *New York Times* mocked this new version of manifest destiny, which argued "that a friendly State must be invaded and subjugated for the purpose of illustrating the value of republican institutions."[138] Some Northern papers realized that the Associated Press stories they ran described not a Mexican invasion but a political protest by American citizens, and suspected that there were those in Texas attempting to use the war scare to further their own interests. General Philip Sheridan attempted to dampen some of this enthusiasm for war by declaring the trouble in El Paso as little more than a "brawl" over salt rights, and ordered Colonel Hatch to act only against "encroachments upon American soil of armed bodies of Mexicans." Sheridan and his second in command, General John Pope, told Hatch to have nothing to do with "local disturbances of the peace."[139] Sheridan appeared to be right when Rucker and a platoon of the Tenth Cavalry rode into San Elizario on October 8 and determined that order had been restored. However, Rucker reported that the Hispanics had been misled by unnamed interested "parties," rather than acting on the basis of any real grievances. He confidently assured his commander that there would be no further trouble if the people were just left alone.[140]

The whole matter would have probably ended there had Howard not felt so aggrieved. Howard's servant Wesley Owens later testified that the judge had been planning to kill Cardis for several months. Humiliated by his treatment at the hands of a mob, Howard told the *Mesilla Independent* "that infamous monster [Cardis] had designed and arranged long before" this uprising by the "poor, ignorant, deluded and credulous people" of El Paso County to take total control of the region. "I can think of nothing in Earth or Hell bad enough for him."[141] In contrast, the monster Cardis recorded in his diary that his efforts to resolve the conflict appeared to be working with recent discussions "showing good disposition on the part of people to meet us and harmonize." He then wrote the last sentence in his diary, "Captain Courtney advised me to be on my lookout, for Howard is making 'desperate threats at my life.'"[142]

Judge Howard returned to El Paso with a military escort and settled back in his home. The very next day, October 10, 1877, he got up from his lunch and said to his servant, "Wesley, I feel very restless and must have my revenge." Grabbing his double-barreled shotgun, Howard walked into the Schultz Brothers store and fired both barrels into Cardis, killing the Republican leader before numerous witnesses.[143]

Solomon Schutz immediately sent a telegram to Colonel Hatch, reporting that "Don Louis Cardis was killed this moment by Chas. Howard, and we are expecting a terrible catastrophe." He feared that every non-Hispanic would be slaughtered if troops were not sent at once to El Paso.[144] Sheriff Kerber not only did not arrest Howard as he rode out of town, he praised him, stating that a monument should be erected to the judge "for delivering us from a tyrannical, unscrupulous scoundrel."[145] If, as seemed likely, the Anglo population of El Paso wanted a violent confrontation with the Hispanic majority, they were about to get their wish.

Defining chutzpah for his generation, Howard fled back to Mesilla and called on Texas governor Hubbard to send Rangers to restore the order he had disrupted in El Paso. The governor agreed and ordered Major John B. Jones to send a company of Rangers to El Paso. Even at this point, affairs in El Paso County need not have turned violent; there were many Hispanics who considered themselves proud citizens of the United States. In San Elizario, Gregorio Garcia, a former captain of the state police during Reconstruction, organized a company of men to support the Rangers. Had Texas issued a warrant for the arrest of Judge Howard for the murder of Louis Cardis, the region would in all probability have returned to its quiet ways. But the state of Texas never enforced the law against the murderer of a member of its legislature. Instead, Major Jones rejected the advice of many local Anglos and refused to appoint Garcia, a Republican and an Hispanic, to command the Rangers in the region.[146] Jones may have been acting on the advice of Sheriff Kerber, who warned him, "Be on the lookout, Major, these greasers are very treacherous," as he selected the inexperienced John B. Tays to lead the Rangers in restoring order at San Elizario.[147] Then Howard, rather than being arrested for murder, joined the Rangers at their encampment and rode into El Paso. There could not have been a more direct provocation, but Howard added to the fire by filing charges against those who had taken salt in his absence: "If they take salt, I will prosecute them."[148]

San Elizario's Father Bourgade warned Major Jones that angry Hispanics had gathered in town, determined to drive Howard away for good. "Three fourths of these fellows are already starving in consequence of their bad crops and are determined to get something from the salt or fight to the death." More troubling, most of Bourgade's congregants believed that the Rangers were actually the employees of Howard rather than state officials, since he had rode into town at their head. Bourgade went with Jones to meet with some of the Hispanic leaders. When the major asked them to disarm, one of them produced a copy of the Constitution and pointed out the Second Amendment, which gave them the right to bear arms. Jones was deeply disturbed that someone had given these people a copy of the Constitution, a clearly incendiary document. He failed to appreciate what it meant when these frustrated Mexican Americans said that they would rather have U.S. cavalry than the Rangers patrolling their streets, rejecting out of hand the notion that Hispanics had reason for not trusting the Texas Rangers.[149]

The leaders of San Elizario did not give up in their effort to preserve peace, trying their luck with John Tays. They offered to raise a company of men from both sides of the ethnic divide, and Garcia once more proffered his assistance to the Rangers. Tays not only rebuffed any assistance from Hispanics, but also sent ten of his Rangers to aid Howard in arresting a group of men who had gone to get salt from the lakes. Clearly a simple economic endeavor had taken on the cast of obsession for Howard. When Father Bourgade passed on the information that a group of armed men were camped right outside of town, Tays finally listened and called for help from Captain Thomas Blair, who was stationed at El Paso with twenty U.S. cavalrymen. On the night of December 12, Blair rode toward San Elizario but found the road blocked by some fifty civilians. Assured that this was an entirely civil matter involving solely U.S. citizens, Blair returned to El Paso.[150] Troubled that the cavalry had so willingly turned back, Sheriff Kerber called on Governor Hubbard to send help. Though he was a committed Democrat opposed to federal intervention in state affairs, Hubbard barraged President Hayes with appeals for the full force of the U.S. Army to descend on the Mexican border to "repel this invasion of our territory." Hubbard was careful to frame the message so as to imply that Mexico had launched a military operation, informing the president that they were desperate for aid, the "Mexican force being too strong to be repelled by the Texas troops, and it being impossible to raise a civil posse from the citizens, who are nearly all of Mexican blood and sympathy." Hubbard also sent Sheriff Kerber to New Mexico to raise forces for the defense of Texas.[151]

Fearing an actual war, the Mexican government tried to defuse the situation by ordering that no Mexicans were to cross the border into Texas. This gesture was as futile as Howard's efforts to stop the exploitation of the salt lakes. The political protest in San Elizario expanded, drawing many Mexicans across the border to join the several hundred Hispanics surrounding the Ranger outpost, demanding the surrender of Howard. Garcia and his followers established themselves in Charles Ellis's store, still hoping to somehow restore order. When Ellis went out to negotiate with the crowd, he was met with the shout, *"Ahora es tiempo!"* (The time is now!) A man on horseback threw a lasso around Ellis and dragged him down the street before dismounting and slitting his throat.[152] The protests had turned into a siege.

The following morning, December 13, the Rangers saw that the crowd had arrayed itself into platoons and set themselves up in defensive positions. For two days the crowd exchanged fire with both the Rangers in their adobe stronghold and Garcia in Ellis's store; at least one Ranger and three to six members of the crowd died. On the night of December 14, after three times repelling direct attacks and having his son die in his arms, Garcia surrendered.[153]

Hearing that there was trouble of some kind in San Elizario, Captain Blair again rode into town. Leaders of the crowd politely informed him that all the Mexicans had gone home and that no one had been killed in the battle. Their assurances were good enough for Blair, who rode back to El Paso without making contact with the Rangers. Tays held out for two more days; on the morning of December 17, he met with Chico Barela and a few other leaders of the crowd, who assured him that if Howard surrendered and promised to abandon his claims to the salt lakes, he would be allowed to leave and no one would be hurt. Tays relayed this message to Howard, who understood the situation. "I will go," he told Tays, "as it is the only chance to save your lives, but they will kill me." Tays then surrendered his command—the first and only time that a unit of the Texas Rangers surrendered.[154]

Violating all their promises, the crowd seized Howard, his agent McBride, and an unpopular local merchant named John Atkinson and stood them each in turn in front of a firing squad. When the crowd called for more murders, Barela stepped in front of the Rangers and shouted, "No, no other man shall be killed." With some resentful grumbling, the mob turned its attention to looting buildings belonging to Anglos and those Hispanics who had stood by them.[155] The Rangers were then assembled to watch as the Hispanics paraded and delivered speeches denouncing the Anglos. Disarmed but allowed to keep their horses, the Rangers were ordered out of town. They rode to El Paso where, in Tays's bitter words, he found Captain Blair "making preparations to start to my assistance with his command of 18 men some time next Spring."[156]

While President Hayes did not order federal troops to the area, General Sherman decided that Governor Hubbard's request for aid was sufficient to justify military action, ordering units in west Texas and New Mexico to rush to El Paso by forced marches. Thus began "the invasion of San Elizario."[157] On December 22, Colonel Hatch started down the Rio Grande toward San Elizario with sixty cavalry and artillery. That same day a vigilante group from New Mexico led by John Ford swept through the area killing numerous Hispanics and committing other outrages including looting and rape. They were followed by Sheriff Kerber's band of forty volunteers who furthered the state's policy of retribution by killing a number of Hispanics and confiscating all firearms in Hispanic possession. Kerber's band, which included Lieutenant Tays, shot their first two prisoners while they were "trying to escape." When Colonel Hatch, riding nearby in his buggy, heard the gunfire, he confronted Kerber, who insisted that all the shooting had been in self-defense. Hatch looked at two nearby bodies, both shot in the back: "I then denounced this inhumanity in no measured terms." Hatch assumed command of all forces in the area, issuing orders that "outrages in the name and under the color of the law, and by those who ought to be its representatives and guardians, will not be tolerated." The army spent the next week slowly restoring order to the region and driving the vigilantes back into New Mexico. Most of the Hispanics in the area fled to Mexico, and then the Anglo militias turned on one another, battling over stolen goods and settling old scores. There were many injuries and at least one murder when the Rangers' Sergeant J.C. Ford killed a Sergeant Frazer.[158]

On December 19, 1877, Governor Hubbard requested a full inquiry into the participation of Mexican citizens in the "El Paso Troubles," as they were being called. President Hayes turned to the army, which sent colonels John H. King and William H. Lewis to investigate. Hubbard sent Major Jones to join them and begin the official cover-up. When Jones discovered that the officers were looking into the conduct of the Rangers and other state officials, he wrote an official protest; when the two colonels ignored him, he prepared his own narrative of events. The colonels thought the lesson of the Salt War was clear, that federal troops should be permanently stationed in the region. They were confident that the area's Hispanics would never have fired on the blue coats, while the Rangers were seen as a tool of local elites. Warrants were issued for the arrest of nearly one hundred members of the mob that killed Howard, but they had all fled to Mexico. They returned quietly over the next two years without consequence or prosecution. The new owners of the salt lakes appointed an accommodating agent, the same Sergeant J.C. Ford who had gotten away with killing a fellow Ranger. Ford worked with the local Hispanics to reach an equitable pay schedule for collecting salt and there was no further conflict over the issue.[159]

The Salt War briefly threatened to plunge the United States and Mexico into a larger war; instead, it served as a prime impetus in the improvement of relations between the two countries. Over the next year, Mexico's president Díaz exerted greater control over the border, ameliorating much of the tension between the United States and Mexico for the next forty years. Equally helpful from the point of view of the U.S. government, Díaz gave the U.S. railroad companies exactly what they wanted, which amounted to 80 percent of Mexico's railroad stocks and bonds and tens of thousands of acres. By the turn of the century, non-

Mexicans would own a third of Mexico, with three-quarters of that total being in the hands of U.S. citizens. In appreciation of Díaz's efforts, President Hayes revoked his orders to the army to ignore the border in early 1880.[160] Meanwhile, the state of Texas instituted a number of repressive measures that kept the Hispanics second-class citizens for more than a century. The Democratic government of the state ensured that, so long as they held power, the voice of the majority would be silenced along the Mexican border.[161]

Rejecting Diversity

While newspaper accounts—and subsequent histories—of the West have focused on Indians and Mexicans as the sources of disorder, white people created far more difficulty for the government than did any other group. Nowhere was this disruptive nature of white settlement more apparent than in California, considered the most settled and civilized of the Western states, with a complex and diverse population of whites, blacks, Hispanics, Asians, and Indians. In this setting, white Californians took it upon themselves to turn the state into a cauldron of violence in 1877, rising up to crush those they saw as outsiders and determining the pattern of ethnic relations that would last for many decades.

For California's Hispanics, 1877 was "the year of lynching." Lynchings had occurred before in California—two a year was the average in the state prior to 1877—but never to such a degree. At least nine Latinos were lynched by mobs in California in 1877.[162] These extralegal acts of violence were emblematic of a pattern throughout the Southwest of using violence to keep Hispanics in line. Even the idyllic seaside resort of Santa Cruz witnessed a dual lynching. Francisco Arias, thirty-eight, and Jose Chamales, twenty-two, had just been released from San Quentin prison after serving three years for manslaughter and robbery, respectively. On May 2 they shot and killed Henry De Forest, a man neither of them knew, in order to get money to go to the circus. Taking about $20 from De Forest's corpse, Chamales and Arias went to the circus and had a good time. Chamales then went home and told his mother all about the murder. Chamales's mother reported the crime to the police, who arrested the two young men and put them in jail, where they both confessed. The police judged these two men to be mentally disturbed. A crowd gathered outside the jail and worked itself into a fury, demanding instant justice. At 2 A.M. on May 3 the crowd rushed the jail, overpowered the jailer and sheriff, and seized Arias and Chamales. Dragged to the Water Street bridge, Arias and Chamales again admitted their guilt, whereupon they were hanged from a crossbeam; they were left dangling until the following day when there was sufficient light for a photograph to be taken. Someone in the crowd put hats on the two men, and a number of children can be seen in the front of the crowd staring up at the bodies. This photograph became the first postcard of a lynching from the West Coast, and by the following day the U.S. mail had widely distributed these photographs of two men hanging by their necks. It was a society that tolerated the graphic representation of extreme levels of cruelty.[163]

No effort was made to discover who had participated in the lynch mob and no charges were ever brought. Local papers justified the hangings and insisted that the lynch mob included many respectable citizens, implying that the members of the mob were well known. While acknowledging that "Judge Lynch is a very dangerous magistrate," one editorial argued that "he is the terror of outlaws and desperadoes, and a most able defender of public safety."[164] In nearby San Juan Bautista on July 12, Justin Arayo confronted Manuel Butron over a long-standing debt. When Butron refused to pay up, Arayo shot and killed him. Despite a detachment of guards, the jail holding Arayo was overwhelmed by a mob around 1 A.M. and Arayo was hanged from a nearby tree. Once more the local press voiced its support for this action, one paper even treating it humorously as an enjoyable day's entertainment. Later in the year some citizens of Bakersfield went on a rampage, lynching five Hispanics they accused of horse theft, again with no charges brought against members of the mob. The targeting of Hispanics continued into 1878, when there were five more lynchings.[165]

The bigotry against Hispanics was widespread. The noted philosopher Josiah Royce admitted that Anglos accused of crimes, "civilized men," generally received fair trials, but that Hispanics were not so fortunate. It was "considered safe by an average lynching jury in those days to convict a 'greaser' on very moderate evidence if none better could be had." In an extreme form of racial profiling, Royce stated, "One could see his guilt so plainly written, we know, in his ugly swarthy face, before the trial began."[166]

If white Californians despised Hispanics, they reserved their most extreme hatred for the Chinese. Initially the U.S. government encouraged Chinese immigration, welcoming the cheap labor on behalf of the Western railroad and mine owners, and negotiated the Burlingame Treaty of 1868, which allowed unrestricted Chinese immigration. The Chinese came to the United States for roughly the same reason as did Europeans—economic advancement. But the Anglos—which in this instance includes Irish workers—saw Chinese immigration as substantively different from that of any other group. As many foreign visitors observed, the Chinese embodied the American ideal of hard work, a quality vocally appreciated by employers. But being neither white nor Christian, they aroused an animosity among West Coast Anglos with deep racist and economic roots. The Chinese were too hardworking, accepting jobs for wages well below what even black and Hispanic workers in the West would accept.[167]

Though the Chinese made up 7.5 percent of California's population, nearly 30 percent of those Chinese lived in San Francisco; and since the vast majority of Chinese immigrants were adult men, they accounted for nearly one-fifth of California's labor force. Their numbers were increasing, with a record 22,781 Chinese arriving in 1876, just 4,142 of whom were women; still, even this peak number accounted for just 4 percent of the total immigration to the United States that year. But this relatively small community wielded significant local power. Chinese immigration was dominated by the "Six Companies," private organizations that maintained a tight control over the process. The Six Companies acted outside of American law, enforcing their own regulations and arbitrating disputes among their members, and also backing up their decisions by keeping a special unit of the San Francisco police on their payroll.[168] In return for this dominance of the immigrant community, the Six Companies sought to protect the Chinese from the hostility of the whites, hiring detectives and lawyers to defend those denied access to usual legal channels, winning significant court cases, including several that overturned restrictive legislation. Such demonstrations of power reassured the Chinese and further inflamed many whites.

In the 1876 elections, the national platforms of both parties had racist anti-Chinese planks. Early in 1877, a joint congressional committee recommended a renegotiation of the Burlingame Treaty to put an end to further Chinese immigration. The decision was not too surprising, given that two of the committee's five members were honorary vice presidents of San Francisco's Anti-Coolie Union, while a third had made numerous public statements against Chinese immigration. San Francisco sent California's former attorney general Frank M. Pixley as their representative. Pixley declared the Chinese "the inferiors to any race God ever made" and had no objection to lynching them all and burning the ships bringing them from China. The committee heard no Chinese witnesses, and instructed other witnesses to not talk about what California gained by the presence of Chinese workers, directing them instead to focus on moral and social questions. The committee then concluded that the very presence of the Chinese discouraged the migration of white Americans and immigrants to the state—a point made by Henry George, who added that the blacks and Chinese could never hope to attain the level of civilization enjoyed by whites.[169] James P. Dameron, a lawyer who claimed to be an ethnologist, informed the congressmen that the Chinese hordes would soon reverse Darwinian principles as the inferior but more numerous "vegetable-eating" Chinese overwhelmed the perishing though superior "flesh-eating" Caucasians.[170] The committee's 1,200-page report was heavily influenced by Pixley and Dameron, referring to the Chinese as an "indigestible mass in the community."[171]

California's labor unions, just starting to organize, found particular danger in these Chinese workers, blaming them for their appallingly low wages. Led by the Irish immigrant Denis Kearney, the unions created their own Workingmen's

Party in October 1877 under the slogan, "The Chinese Must Go!" The young California journalist Henry George gave voice to many of these working-class fears, writing that there was no way non-Chinese workers could hope to compete with the Asian immigrants, who by pooling their earnings and living in inhuman conditions got by on less than subsistence wages.[172] George warned that Chinese immigration was a national problem that would soon spread east, forcing all workers to accept lower wages and "crush our working classes into the dust." But these economic arguments were not sufficient for George; he felt the need to link them with a harsh racism, as he charged that the Chinese are "utter heathens, treacherous, sensual, cowardly and cruel" and practice every manner of "unnamable vices."[173]

Anti-Chinese organizing was backed up with violence. In March 1877, a particularly disturbing incident took place in Chico, California, which had just elected an anti-Chinese town council. A group called the Order of Caucasians warned the farmers and businessmen of Butte County to fire all their Chinese workers and replace them with whites, backing up their threats with a series of arson attacks on the homes of Chinese workers. When Christian Lemm, a German immigrant, could not find any whites to clear wood, he hired six Chinese. On the night of March 14, six white workers burst into a shack housing the six Chinese woodcutters and opened fire, and then set the building on fire. Two of the Chinese escaped the flames with serious wounds, and the other four were killed. Shortly after these murders, messages appeared on the doors of those employing Chinese workers warning them that their buildings would be burned to the ground if they didn't purify their labor force. When the attackers were identified, hundreds of Chinese came to watch their trial, and the Six Companies hired a private detective to gather evidence against them. The judge, admitting his sympathy for the men, refused to order their execution and sentenced them to twenty to twenty-five years in San Quentin; they were pardoned by Governor George Perkins, who was also from Butte County, in 1881.[174]

The Lemm Ranch Murders grabbed national attention, only to be surpassed a few months later by an even more dramatic series of events. In San Francisco on the night of July 23, 1877, white workers attacked the city's Chinatown. Over three nights crowds ransacked dozens of buildings, setting many on fire. A great many Chinese were severely beaten and several killed. The city's business leaders feared that the fires could easily spread to other buildings and sent in the fire brigades. When the mob attacked the firefighters, William Coleman, a leading businessman, revived the organization he had led in 1856: the Vigilance Committee. Over the following week an estimated four thousand volunteers patrolled the city, imposing order but also coming to an arrangement with the workers. The city's elite joined the crusade against the Chinese, giving it respectability and authority, in return for the workers curtailing acts of racial vio-lence within San Francisco.[175]

The Specter of Class War

In some ways, the anti-Chinese agitation sparked competing bigotries. Those supportive of the rights of the Chinese often attacked Kearney's followers as ma-lingering Irish, unwilling to work hard and aiming to stop the Chinese from raising the expectations of employers. As the *Colorado Springs Gazette* editorial-ized that November, "Nothing angers the average Irishman so much as seeing a Chinaman working for his living." On other occasions, criticisms of the anti-Chinese movement barely concealed contempt for all workers; attacking the Chinese constituted "a safety-valve for the pent-up passions of angry hoodlums." Regardless of the alleged motivation for a strike, generally seen as a "communis-tic rising" by the mainstream press, Western workers could not resist using the occasion as an excuse to attack the Chinese: "Whenever a riot takes place there the crowd goes off to the Chinese quarters and murders a few of the pig-tailed Orientals." There was cause to fear these working-class crowds, which could just as easily turn their attention to the rich and powerful. After witnessing a group of poor men shout at Leland Stanford, the most powerful man in California, the journalist James Ayers worried that he could be witnessing the first moments of a new French Revolution.[176]

Ayers picked up on an essential quality of the California workers' anti-Chinese movement: its connection with anticorporate sentiment. Kearney did not direct his ire just at the Chinese; he also targeted the state's political corruption, which he linked to the expansive power of its largest corporations, particularly the Cen-tral Pacific Railroad. Henry George saw that Kearney's sudden rise to power in the summer of 1877 was "the natural result of social and political conditions toward which the country as a whole steadily tends"—the concentration of wealth. George warned his readers that events in California presaged the future: "We have great and increasing accumulations of wealth," as capital became bet-ter organized to the point that a single "railroad company dwarfs the State." This concentration of wealth and power into a few hands produced social instability and would lead to greater violence unless stopped; until such time, demagogues like Kearney could agitate the poor with righteous indignation. Rejecting the political establishment, Kearney called on workers to launch a movement to re-claim the state for the common people. Demanding violence in the name of class and racial solidarity, Kearney mixed socialism and racism, lashing out at the Chinese and those who employed them. "The rich have ruled us until they have ruined us," he told his followers, saying they think nothing of employing "a standing army to shoot down the people." But that was about to change, as "the republic must and shall be preserved, and only workingmen will do it."[177]

Kearney used a shared hostility to the railroads to build an alliance with the state's farmers. The near monopoly of the Central Pacific, which controlled 80 percent of all California rail traffic, had allowed it to use the depression to lower wages while raising freight rates; the first antagonized the workers, the second the state's farmers. Kearney charged that the corporate elite promoted Chinese immigration to undercut both wages and unions, using its increased profits to purchase legislators who did their bidding. At a rally on San Francisco's Nob Hill, provocatively sited in front of the mansions of several of the state's richest men, Kearney labeled the rich "thieves" who "will soon feel the power of the Working-men" as they marched through the city and reclaimed what was rightfully theirs. Kearney warned that if their demands were not met he would lead the city's workers to "City Hall, clean out the police force, hang the Prosecuting Attorney, burn every book that has a particle of law in it, and then enact new laws for the workingmen." His language growing more violent, he proclaimed, "The dignity of labor must be sustained, even if we have to kill every wretch that oppresses it." Kearney also promised that his Workingmen's Party would rein in the economic and political power of the railroads. Driven by this goal, California's farmers and workers united in calling for a new state constitution.[178]

In the election held on September 5, 1877, 62 percent voted for a constitutional convention. Both the Republicans and Democrats were terrified of Kearney, uniting in a Fusion or "Non-Partisan" ticket to defeat the "communists," as they called the Workingmen's Party. The *San Francisco Evening Bulletin* warned that the city was threatened by "a reign of hoodlums, incendiaries and murderers." Kearney undermined San Francisco's peace and prosperity in his "attempt to organize the vicious elements of the city into an open warfare against property and personal safety," which justified the authorities in putting an immediate end to his public assemblies.[179] The police did break up his next meeting and arrested Kearney, who received numerous visitors, including many journalists, at the city jail. He was charged with sedition, and his trial was a sensation; even Emperor Norton, the famous eccentric who believed himself ruler of North America, attended in full regalia. The trial did not last long as the judge declared the recently passed sedition act invalid and dismissed the case. The workers held another rally in celebration. The city's government responded by calling out the militia, banning public meetings—an ordinance roundly ignored—and arresting Kearney once more, something they would do several times in an effort to silence him. The state legislature joined in, passing an act making it illegal to encourage riotous behavior and another funding the expansion of the San Francisco police.[180]

As California's economic elite quickly realized, they had erred in making Kearney a martyr, as he drew ever larger crowds.[181] They did their best with the

Fusion ticket to confuse the voters, their "nonpartisan" candidates winning 77 of the 152 seats, compared to 51 Workingmen, 11 Republicans, 10 Democrats, and 3 independents. But many of these nonpartisan delegates despised the railroads, which would prove a decisive issue. As Leland Stanford told Collis Huntington, the convention "is a dangerous body, and it will not intentionally do railroads any good."[182] The Workingmen's Party found a large number of allies among representatives from farming districts with backgrounds in the collectivist Granger movement. These delegates shared the Workingmen's perspective that the railroads had already inflicted serious damage on republican values, particularly by weakening the traditional independence of farmers and skilled workers. Conservative delegates found just cause to fear the violent direction of many debates; for example, one delegate was of the opinion that if an official should "sell out and betray us, let the people rise and crack their worthless necks on the first tree they can find." Another sought to put into the constitution the words that any railroad official who ignored state regulations should be "hanged by the neck until he be dead."[183] These members of the Workingmen's Party had learned that violence, or at least the threat of violence, was a very effective political tool. As the historian William Deverell wrote, "The specter of violence stalked the halls of the constitutional convention."[184]

The resulting constitution, approved by 54 percent of the voters, was the longest in the United States to that date and included numerous limitations on corporations, including granting the state legislature eminent domain powers over corporate property, outlawing stock watering, placing restraints on land speculation, forbidding corporations from violating individual rights or "the general well-being of the state," authorizing regulation of railroads by popularly elected railroad commissioners, and ordering that a corporation could only conduct business for which it was expressly authorized by its charter. Most of these particulars were negated by the courts, which sided with the corporations in finding them vague and unconstitutional, and the truly important labor issues, such as an eight-hour day, were all defeated at the convention. As Henry George wrote just two years later, "The new Constitution has proved a bitter disappointment to those who expected so much from it." But one part of the new constitution remained in place and influenced federal law: the section denying the Chinese the right to vote or work for any government agency.[185]

Both political parties realized that there was much to be gained from appealing to racism and actively joined in the effort to terminate Chinese immigration. The Democratic Party shook off its historic links to coerced labor, focused their appeal to the Western unions, and became the voice of white racism in the West just as it was in the South. In February 1878, the U.S. House of Representatives, after just one hour's debate, passed a law limiting the number of Chinese passengers allowed on any ship to fifteen. Hayes vetoed the act on legal grounds for violating the Burlingame Treaty.[186]

Though Kearney himself fell from power, his bigotry gave the established parties an effective tool with which to misdirect the energies of the workers. With both parties striving to gain favor among California workers by attacking the Chinese, an alteration in the status of these immigrants was inevitable. Though some Chinese were naturalized as allowed by the Burlingame Treaty, the courts interpreted the naturalization law of 1790 as limiting citizenship to whites. In September 1879 California held a referendum in which 96 percent voted for excluding the Chinese from the state; a similar vote in Nevada resulted in 99 percent favoring restrictions on Chinese immigration. As an early historian of the labor movement wrote, these results "indicate a remarkable uniformity of public opinion." Using the referendum as sufficient validation, the California legislature passed legislation in February 1880 prohibiting the employment of Chinese workers.[187]

In 1880 the United States entered into a new treaty with the government of China, which slammed the door shut, followed in 1882 by the Chinese Exclusion Act banning all Chinese workers, skilled and unskilled, from the United States. It was the first explicit restriction on immigration in American history. The treatment of those Chinese still living in the United States became equally restrictive; for instance, in 1885 the Chinese of Humboldt County were rounded up and forcibly exiled from the county. They did not return until the 1970s.[188]

Throughout the West, fearful whites beat back the threat of multicultural democracy. While there were divisions over how best to deal with disorder in the West and continuing debate over the sources of violence, there was a shared sense that democracy could not be allowed to get out of hand through a universal extension of rights. The very size of the West posed numerous challenges to the maintenance of the law and federal authority; the U.S. Army supplied the weak bond holding the region within the national union. In 1877, the West faced dozens of alternative paths forward, many of which would have led to a more democratic society. In every instance, local elites put aside suspicions of one another and of the federal government to unite in keeping a lid on social change, working to build a mild West friendly to economic development. However, neither they nor others hesitated to employ violence to attain their ends. In their willingness to use force for political, social, or economic ends, elite whites were little different from Billy the Kid.

4

The Terror of Poverty

Only the man who stands utterly alone, friendless, moneyless, ill clad, shelterless and hungry, looking at the sun sinking red in a mid-winter snow, can know what it is to be a real tramp. That experience was mine, through no fault of mine.

—Terence Powderly[1]

Lafcadio Hearn, one of the great journalists of the late nineteenth century, was a young reporter for the *Cincinnati Commercial* in 1877 when he became interested in the lives of the poor. On the first day of the year, Cincinnati's overseer of the poor guided Hearn through the city's most destitute quarter. Every one of the decrepit rooms Hearn entered looked roughly identical, with the same few pieces of decaying furniture shared by far too many people. Hearn was both appalled and delighted with the impoverished people he encountered—stunned by their suffering but impressed by their creativity in getting by and fascinated with the authenticity of character he found in the poorest neighborhoods. He heard memories of plantations from former slaves; one old woman even had memories of Africa, where she had been kidnapped as a child and taken into slavery. Despair shadowed the poverty Hearn witnessed: "These wanderings in the haunts of the poor, among shadowy tenement houses and dilapidated cottages, and blind, foul alleys with quaint names suggesting deformity and darkness, somehow compelled a phantasmal retrospect of the experience, which cling[s] to the mind with nightmare tenacity." The people who lived here were subject to every disease, with hints of "the mercy of death" in every room. He could hear children being ruthlessly beaten, and no one acting to stop it. As one Irish woman said, "Shure there's no ind to it at all, at all."[2]

Hearn had found his calling: to report on the effects of poverty in the land of plenty. When his paper sent him to New Orleans to cover the political battle for Louisiana's electoral votes, Hearn devoted himself instead to studying the city's different ethnic groups.[3] Writing a friend from New Orleans in 1877, Hearn was astounded by the totality of poverty, but found some comfort in it: "as everybody is poor in the South, my poverty is no drawback." He quickly perceived, however, that there was an enormous difference between his poverty and that of the Italian immigrants and the freed blacks: he had a way out, they did not. His articles drawing attention to poverty and ethnic differences proved deeply disturbing to his middle-class readers and he lost his job as a consequence. Before the year was out, Hearn would find other venues for his work, showing his readers a part of America they rarely, if ever, saw, anticipating later committed journalists such as the *New York Tribune*'s Helen Campbell and Jacob Riis.[4]

Often credited with bringing ethnography to America, Hearn provided graphic portraits of the decrepit heart of the nation's industrial cities and helped to make a generation feel a little guilty, while inspiring many, for instance Jane Addams, to want to work to alleviate poverty. Hearn's task was not an easy one, and it cost him heavily. Years later, after he had settled permanently in Japan, Hearn looked back on his defense of the downtrodden and saw that "I had been opposing a great national and social principle without knowing it." As a consequence, even people he counted as friends "stopped speaking to me."[5] Hearn discovered that middle-class Americans feared the poor, most especially the transient poor, and sought to punish those they could not control. That fear built through 1877, the year of the first great hysteria over the homeless, known at the time as the "Tramp Scare."

The persistent depression destabilized America, increasing unemployment and underemployment to levels never previously known. The middle class felt threatened, in danger of sinking down into the undistinguished mass of the poor. Separated from the workers because they received salaries rather than wages, working five days a week rather than six, owning homes rather than crowding into tenements, the middle class held a precarious position manning the decks of the great industrial ship or managing the retail emporiums of the nation. Doctors, lawyers, and ministers were part of the middle class, but the majority worked for large corporations or the new service industries. There is no precision to the class categories used in the late nineteenth century, no social scientists or census bureau ready to give class divisions an exact financial definition. Historians attempt to calculate their numbers but always stumble over the measurements and delineations—are farmers or self-employed artisans middle class? Contemporaries felt they knew what it meant to be middle class: not rich and not working class. They "comprise the mass" of American society, were conservative and hardworking, and formed what Senator Oliver P. Morton called "the balance-wheel in our political machine" and economy. The middle class was consistently described as "industrious," possessing all the more positive social qualities and forming "the bulwark and defense of a free government." They valued conformity in conduct and uniformity in their possessions, as demonstrated by one of the few successes of 1877, John Wanamaker's first modern department store in Philadelphia, which quickly became a mecca for middle-class consumers. Middle-class values were held to be American values, and they were even taking over American literature, much to the annoyance of many critics who resented the growing number of stories of middle-class life.[6]

But their grip was uncertain, and lately the middle class had become caught up in the speculative fever, trying to secure their place with unwise investments. The depression clarified the distinction between an upper and a lower middle class, the former belonging to the professions and the upper reaches of management while the latter stood just a few missed paychecks away from the working class. Publicly everyone spoke in favor of the middle class; political opponents agreed on its importance to the nation and its current precarious position. Republican governor Alexander Rice of Massachusetts warned that the United States was in danger of losing "that great middle class of population, who are neither so rich as to be sordid, nor so poor as to become objects of charity," and whose characteristics of sobriety, loyalty, and religion sustained society. According to Rice, only the development of new industries and economic opportunities would save the middle class and the republic. Lewis H. Bond, candidate of the Workingmen's Party for governor of Ohio, also warned that the middle class "is speedily disappearing from American society," though he blamed the manipulations of the "moneyed oligarchy" for its decline. Henry Carey Baird of the Greenback Party warned that the middle class was approaching "extinction," a view shared by many Democrats.[7]

While far from extinction, the middle class certainly felt uneasy. Many saw their salaries cut or even lost their jobs just like any worker, and the whole class was in danger of being "beggared." A reporter who visited secondhand furniture dealers around New York City found that middle-class families were selling off their possessions, "and, while there is a constant stream of persons desiring to sell, the list of those who wish to buy is very small." Visits to dealers in jewelry and other luxury goods revealed the same pattern, as the middle class, fearful of falling into poverty, bought fewer consumer goods. They had even stopped buying homes, which were seen as essential to middle-class identity. The real estate crisis and absence of readily available loans made it difficult to purchase a home, leading to proposals for legislation that would help the middle class buy houses, proposals that were consistently defeated as inappropriate government interference in the marketplace. There were those who hoped that the middle class could take advantage of the hard times to buy property for low prices, but the reality was that the real estate market remained "apathetic," as few people could afford to buy anything beyond necessities.[8] The middle class failed to fight for this legislation, though, because, in Wendell Phillips's analysis, its members had lost their political commitment in their desperate scramble to stay afloat financially and had fallen for the "bubble and chaff" of free-market ideology.[9]

The one thing those in the middle class could agree on was that they did not want to be poor. Perhaps as a consequence they had little sympathy for the unemployed. When Chicago's *Inter Ocean* reported that thirty thousand workers had lost their jobs and were anxious for employment, one city alderman rejected the number and the characterization as "humbug" since "no industrious man need be without work." Unemployment was the product of laziness and nothing more; workers just needed to adhere to middle-class values of "living pretty close up to their income."[10] In 1877 the middle class was in the process of constructing an ideology that blamed the poor for their poverty as a moral failing. Such a worldview made the concept of falling economically all the more terrifying. With no end to the depression in sight, a frightened middle class lashed out at the easiest target, the homeless.

They were everywhere, these wandering poor, and theft and violence followed in their path. To the press, the tramps "are bold, numerous and troublesome," "an unpleasant and dangerous scab upon the body-politic," "the terror of the New England, as well as the New York housewife."[11] "The 'tramp nuisance' has swollen to the dimensions of a great and threatening social peril," as these "marauders" instituted "a reign of terror" wherever they went, with the streets of every city "infested by vagrants." It was impossible to avoid "the tramp question," which "forces itself on the newspapers as well as on the people and public authorities."[12] Anyone reading the newspapers in 1877 would agree that the tramp threat was real, and growing.[13] By that summer the New York Board of State Charities declared "that there never were so many of this class on the road," and their number was steadily increasing. Some solution had to be found "or the people will be overrun with these hordes of vagabonds" who are "a cause for alarm and anxiety to the woman of the house."[14] As Southern white men justified racial violence by claiming that they had no choice but to protect their womenfolk from a mythologized "black beast," so middle-class men throughout the country insisted that their war on the homeless grew from the danger posed to the nation's housewives. Rather than admitting that they were scared, these heroes acted out of concern for the danger posed by this media-generated terror to their wives and daughters. At the same time, the fear of tramps served to keep women at home, establishing a geography of fear that quickly engulfed all public spaces, most especially the roads and railways.

That the tramps appeared so suddenly on the American scene is easily explained. The depression that started in 1873 devastated the American working class. Those lucky enough not to lose their jobs saw their wages cut. Those who lost their jobs enjoyed no social safety net beyond the generosity of some churches and the willingness of the local jail to put them up on a cold night. Not surprisingly, many jobless workers took to the road and the rails in search of work; tramping was thus a rational response to unemployment. As Eric Monkkonen wrote, "Tramps were, in other words, the ordinary working people of the United States on the move between jobs and residences."[15] There had been migratory workers in the past, but never in such extensive numbers nor traveling over such great distances; the depression accounted for the first, the recent completion of the transcontinental railroad for the latter.

Finding jobs in industrial America required more than pounding the pavements; it required hitting the road. When Jay Cooke's business empire collapsed, all work halted at the terminus of his Great Northern Railroad in Duluth. Within a month the population of that town dropped from 5,000 to 1,300, the remaining 3,700 people leaving with their families in search of work elsewhere. Entire mining towns were shut down and everyone thrown out of work—and out of their houses, which belonged to the mine. Such communities almost always lacked any form of charity or public relief. For example, when the mines in Bethel, Pennsylvania, closed in late 1876, most of the workers went to Clay County, Indiana, where they had heard there was work. They found unemployment just as high there, and were now far from home without any hope of a job. Lacking an alternative, these men had to walk home, becoming along the way "the much dreaded and despised tramps."[16] They might have thought of themselves as miners, but to the people they passed they were tramps.

The Tramp Scare was thus a direct consequence of the depression. The word "tramp" had long been a mundane verb or a romantic noun; one tramped across fields into town, while Thoreau went on a tramp in the Maine woods. But by the end of 1873 "tramp" had become a pejorative noun.[17] By the end of 1874, the religious magazine *The Congregationalist* was making the first reference to "the vast army of tramps" moving across the country, which the *Lowell Citizen and News* picked up on in August 1875 in first referencing the "tramp nuisance" as a threat to the country. While "tramp nuisance" appeared often in the press during the centennial year, the imagery of a tramp army with all its connotations of warfare did not become common usage until 1877, when "tramp evil" made its appearance.[18]

The Tramp Scare

According to Philadelphia police records, the peak year for tramps in that city was 1877. The number of vagrants counted by the police increased more than four times from 1873 to 1877, and fell by 50 percent by 1880; these statistics reinforce the connection between the depression, which ended in 1879, and the Tramp Scare. In 1880, the first year for which there is anything like accurate national data, 631,637 people stayed in police stations as guests rather than prisoners—and that at a time of decreased homelessness.[19]

At first, municipal authorities encouraged the police to put up the tramps both as a cost-saving expedient—police stations being a relatively fixed cost while homeless shelters would have to be built and staffed—and because local industries and farmers welcomed access to this unorganized and highly mobile labor force. In the years prior to the Civil War, Pennsylvania's jails had a reputation as congenial refuges for the homeless. But starting in 1874, Philadelphia's authorities decided to put an end to this image, which they thought was attracting far too many homeless to their city, by sending arrested vagrants to a new house of corrections where they were put to rough labor such as quarrying stone, and were subject to brutal punishments. Similarly, the railroads initially shared a positive attitude, allowing tramps to ride in their boxcars unhindered, making use of them for seasonal work and for union busting. However, when the supply far outstripped the railroads' demand, as happened in 1877, management ordered its police forces to crack down on the tramps. This added hostility from the railroads intensified the antitramp sentiment in 1877.[20]

The fear of an army of unemployed emerged in a specific political context. In the aftermath of the Franco-Prussian War in 1871, the people of Paris had declared their city a commune. Briefly, until the government of France turned on the commune with military aid from the victorious Prussians, it looked as though communism would enjoy its first great triumph. The Paris Commune lasted just two months but loomed as large in middle-class imaginations as the embodiment of all that is violent and disruptive as the French Revolution once had. The Paris Commune was the most covered foreign story in the American press during the 1870s, becoming a byword for the dangers of the left and feeding a hysteria among the upper and middle classes. As the depression of 1873 deepened, references to the Paris Commune increased, with every call for reform being seen as akin to the attacks on property rights by the Paris communists. The tramp fit into these visions of a working-class conspiracy as the harbinger of similar lower-class excesses in the United States. In this context, the tramp was not a vague social evil; he was a tangible threat to society itself. "As long as he remains, he is a perpetual menace; for he is the incarnation of social revolt," the *Arkansas Gazette* editorialized in January, 1877. "It was the tramps who led the awful dance of death which whirled the monarchy and aristocracy of France to the arms of the guillotine," and then brought down the rule of law in Paris in 1871. If swift action was not taken, the same would happen in the United States before the year was through.[21]

The acts attributed to the tramps covered the criminal spectrum, though specific examples always seemed to be occurring in some other part of the country. Usually newspapers spoke of the generic tramp "in our midst every day," and of "the evils" he inflicts "increasing with an alarming rapidity." Newspapers regularly reported that their area was "overrun with tramps," with "stores and dwellings being plundered and robbed," though rarely with the sort of exact details that invite verification. Rather, the same story describing the tramp armies sweeping through the neighborhood would go on to warn that the problem was national in scope: "From all parts of the land comes accounts of the depredations committed by these roving bands of thieves."[22] Tales of these "depredations" generally lacked a location. Both the *St. Louis Globe-Democrat* and the *San Francisco Evening Bulletin* reported that tramps pursued a farmer in order to rob him, only to express their disgust once they caught the farmer and discovered that he had no money. Neither paper stated where this event occurred, though both implied that it was nearby. Papers routinely reported on "hordes" of tramps descending on a specific area, generally at least a thousand miles away. For instance, papers in San Francisco and Buffalo reported that "The tramps are going to the Black Hills in hordes, without a bit of fear of the Indians."[23] Meanwhile, the *Arkansas Gazette* was reporting that the hills of Pennsylvania were "overrun with the tramping squads of ruffians and robbers since the advent of the summer." It seemed that "No part of Pennsylvania has escaped the invasions of these violators of the law," though the Pennsylvania papers remained surprisingly ignorant of these outrages, which they often found occurring out West. Western papers reported that these crimes were concentrated in the East, while East Coast papers found them mostly in the "thickly populated districts of the West."[24] Southern newspapers consistently reported on the many tramp transgressions in the North, while Northern newspapers had articles on depredations in the South. In a single article, *Frank Leslie's Illustrated Newspaper* established that the tramps favored the Northeast and the West, while "Ohio is the paradise of tramps," thanks to its excellent roads and "comfortable farmhouses."[25]

The Tramp Scare is an irony-rich vein in American history. The country thrived on mobility, but tramps were too mobile, taking American ideals to a frightening and unpredictable extreme. Americans moved a lot, but usually to settle someplace new. Tramps just moved, without apparent purpose, though usually to travel to agricultural jobs determined by season, or just in search of any type of work. Most tramps were not, as the public perception had it, lazy and shiftless, avoiding work and stealing what they wanted; rather, they were either underemployed seasonal workers trying to find jobs that would keep them going for another few months or unemployed workers desperate for employment.

The press refused to acknowledge these economic realities. It was widely agreed that the tramp chose to be a tramp. He was not the victim of deprivation or misfortune; he was just lazy. There was no shortage of work in America, despite the depression, or so the employed middle class thought. A Milwaukee paper wanted the police to "keep a close eye upon these fellows, as there is no excuse, this time of year, for a man to be out of employment, if he is disposed to work, as every farmer wants from one to three hands."[26] Those who thought the tramps chose their way of life made no connection between the deepening depression and the increase in tramps. To a worker, the depression of 1873 meant enormous cuts in pay or the loss of a job. Entire industries cut workers' wages by a quarter or fired the majority of their employees. To members of the upper-middle class, the depression was an inconvenience, with some positive aspects—such as the increased availability of servants. In January, the novelist Henry James, who rarely took notice of the matters that troubled most people, wrote his brother William from London after reading about the hard times in the United States. "From here it all looks shocking bad." And he hoped that the depression did not prove "a serious discomfort" for William.[27] He then moved on to a description of his gentlemen's club.

The tramp took on the quality of an all-purpose supercriminal, seemingly capable of every transgression. "The versatile tramp," the *Albany Argus* held, "changing his demeanor and adapting his occupation to suit the changing seasons, no longer appeals" for table scraps, but waits for an opportunity to steal from the home owner. Tramps, it was widely reported, typically take a job as a cover for theft. Thus an unnamed farmer hired a tramp to do some whitewashing, but the scoundrel stole $150 in cash and fled. Since the only reason a tramp would ever agree to work was as subterfuge for some greater crime, it was obvious that one should not give a job to the homeless. The line between criminals and tramps vanishes within such logic. To the general public they were one and the same, but there are cases where it would appear that a criminal gang earned the label of "tramps" without actually being of the fraternity of the homeless. In one instance, a group of vigilantes from Quakertown, Pennsylvania, raided the house of one Thomas Widfrife, finding several thousand dollars' worth of stolen goods and arresting a number of "tramps" belonging to his gang. But were these men tramps if their leader owned a house and they focused their criminal attentions on the neighboring area? By treating all criminals as tramps, newspapers promoted the equation that all tramps are criminals.[28]

Much of this tramp terror had a quality of convenience, since every crime could be blamed on a tramp. Thus Chicago's *Inter Ocean* reported "an outrage . . . committed . . . on the person of a young lady" outside Bradford, Ohio. Though the criminal had not been apprehended and no one knew who he was, the paper had no doubt that it was a tramp who attacked this poor woman. Local authorities knew *what* rather than *who* they were seeking, and thus conducted their search "for the tramp." When a home in Foxborough, Massachusetts, was burglarized, the police searched "for all suspicious characters" and arrested nineteen tramps; a judge sentenced them to sixty days in jail, and the newspaper proclaimed them "the thieves." And yet, "None of the stolen articles were recovered." The evidence for crimes by tramps could be bizarrely circumstantial, as when the *St. Louis Globe-Democrat* charged that tramps were arsonists as "we don't remember to have ever heard of one of these numerous travelers getting killed by jumping from the fifth story window of a hotel to escape the flames."[29]

Tramps were expert at every form of theft, from stealing food placed on Chinese graves to riding trains without paying. Tramps rode freight trains not to get around but to break into cars in order to throw their contents out to cronies along the way. On the other hand, tramps felt justified in riding the rails for free, appropriating entire trains. There were several reports of gangs of 50 to 150 tramps boarding a train at once and refusing to pay. In one instance in an unstated location, the conductor refused to go on until the tramps paid their fare, and the engineer let the fire go down. "The tramps drew revolvers and ordered the engineer to fire up or they would fire him up." The engineer started the train back up and the tramps got off at the next town.[30] In another instance, 150 tramps took over the town of Mason City—either Iowa or Illinois—and "informed the citizens they would be civil and quiet" if furnished with food and lodging. The citizens complied and two days later the tramps appropriated a train headed north. In Delaware one hundred "ragamuffins"—probably the least intimidating name for tramps—threatened to tear up track if not taken aboard a freight train. So common had this danger of tramps riding trains without paying become that many trains began running through stations at high speed. What is shocking in each of these stories is that there is no indication that any police force, not even the railroads' notoriously brutal private police, gave chase. Americans appeared to be at the mercy of an invading barbarian army. The level of concern over the tramp threat was evident when a leading urban newspaper like the Chicago *Inter Ocean* thought it newsworthy to cover the story of a tramp arrested for breaking into a home in Sioux City, Iowa, and stealing a loaded rifle.[31]

The theft of a loaded rifle spoke to what the public most feared from the tramps: violence. Papers often reported on assaults that had no seeming motive, not even theft; tramps appeared dangerous, unhinged, and unchallenged by the forces of law and order. The *Boston Advertiser* reported that an unknown tramp shot and killed a teenaged boy in Brandon, Vermont, with a revolver, and then committed suicide, all for no known reason. A few months later another tramp shot and killed "an Inoffensive Young Man" in the countryside outside New Haven, Indiana, again for no discernible reason, and without being seen or caught. A "Villainous Tramp" entered the home of a Mr. Gilpin, a farmer near Dubuque, Iowa, surprising the farmer's young daughter, and "attempted to outrage her person." Fortunately, Gilpin and his son returned home just in time "and gave the villain an unmerciful flogging and pitched him outdoors, where he lay some time before he was able to crawl away."[32] The public had cause to fear some tramps, but no systematic effort was made to discover the extent of tramp violence nor the accuracy of the stories circulating in the papers.

The tramp armies that "swarm thick along the lines of the railroads" aroused public terror. As the ever hysterical *Arkansas Gazette* reported, tramp armies mobbing relentlessly through Pennsylvania were committing "Fearful outrages," including "robbery, arson, rape, and murder by wholesale." Recent—unspecified—crimes by these organized bands of tramps "outstrip in enormity any previous crimes" by "this class of nomadic outlaws." In a series of highly unlikely events reported by a Texas paper, one hundred tramps supposedly attacked a single isolated farm somewhere in Lancaster County, Pennsylvania. The farmer opened fire on the tramps, who returned fire. Suddenly "Policemen and citizens from Lancaster" came to the farmer's aid and a fierce gun battle ensued, ending when the police "charged on them, the tramps retreated, leaving five wounded." In difficult-to-swallow imagery, a Georgia newspaper warned that "swarms of well dressed tramps are reported in the passes of the Blue Ridge, wending westward."[33]

There were some verifiable crimes committed by gangs of tramps, though they were rarely as dramatic or as violent as the most repeated stories. For instance, in late September a group originally reported to consist of twenty tramps robbed a building at Warrenton Junction, Virginia, and then attempted to board a passing train. Railroad employees seized what turned out to be six tramps and turned them over to authorities. Not much of a gang, these six starving tramps came from six different cities and had just recently met. A few days later five tramps attempting to board a train near Manassas were chased off by the conductor—not much of a story had the miscreants not been tramps who appeared to be operating with criminal intent.[34] Similarly, there may be another way of looking at a story the *Inter Ocean* published in its crime column on the "Ingratitude of a Tramp" named Barth Hayes who was given a job by R.B. Watkins of Dixon, Illinois. Hayes repaid this kindness when "Mrs. Watkins eloped with him."[35]

By the summer of 1877 this certainty that tramping represented a giant criminal conspiracy had reached the point that papers began reporting evidence of an extensive "brotherhood of tramps" that ominously exchanges "confidences and items of information," dividing the country into criminal fiefdoms.[36] This brotherhood made its headquarters in New York City, from which an estimated fifteen thousand professional tramps fanned out every summer to commit crimes. Though this was a significant understatement of the number of tramps in the country, these outlaws constituted "a formidable force to let loose upon the country." By splitting up, this tramp army could cover an extensive territory, ensuring that no one grasped the true size of their criminal conspiracy.[37] Another common story reported that the state of Massachusetts or the mayor of Lowell sent undercover detectives pretending to be tramps to infiltrate this dangerous "swarm." The detectives learned from other tramps—who, one assumes, recognized cops when they saw them—that the vagrants maintained "a perfectly organized brotherhood" that controlled all illegal activity in the Northeast. "They are under orders of a chief and each tramp has a special duty assigned to him" in a precise criminal division of labor. Members of the brotherhood of tramps "are even instructed what to steal and whom to steal it from," and have secret signs and words.[38]

Because of the expansion of the nation's rail system, tramps were showing up in rural areas unused to homelessness. In the first few years of the tramp phenomenon, 1874 and 1875, farmers and their families welcomed these visitors, if not with a few days' work, then at least with a meal and a place to spend the night. The hospitality of rural people who had few visitors from outside their home counties was well known and may have been abused by some tramps, and stories of ungrateful and even hostile tramps spread quickly. By 1877 newspapers were warning their readers that tramps "move in concert and avoid places where the police regulations are strict," preferring to attack "isolated farm houses." Tramps did steal, but probably not to the extent imagined, and petty thefts had been common in cities for decades but were relatively unknown in rural areas. The tramp brought this urban practice of the homeless to country towns, elevating the theft of some clothes left out to dry into a disturbing national trend.[39]

More than one paper asked, "What are we to do with the tramp? How are we to get rid of him, or better, if possible, convert him into a useful citizen?" Or, as another paper put it, they should find ways of "Utilising the Tramps."[40] "It is evident," the Hartford Times editorialized, "that something must be done to protect the industrious and well-to-do from these professional mendicants." The search for solutions to the "chronic tramp nuisance" took many forms. Cincinnati enacted "an ordinance that enables tramps to divide themselves into two classes—those who are willing to earn a living and those who are not." The city ordered the arrest of all vagrants; those willing to work were to be put to public tasks like clearing the roads of ice in return for room and board, while those unwilling to work "are treated as vagabonds and punished accordingly."[41] In contrast, Chicago's superintendent of police M.C. Hickey maintained that the solution to the tramp evil was to find them all guilty of a crime. He supported a new vagrancy law, one that would allow him "to give these fellows a warm reception whenever they show themselves in the city, and transfer their labors to the House of Correction." To Hickey, tramps were all thieves who could easily pay the current $20 fine for vagrancy; for that reason he favored a $200 fine for vagrancy with a jail term of up to one year if the fine was not paid. That would get them off the streets fast, Hickey assured the public. The state government responded to Hickey's call to arms by passing a new vagrancy act giving the police

the power to arrest tramps on sight and ordering that tramps found guilty of vagrancy be put to hard labor. Eighteen states passed explicit antitramp laws, all of
which, in the words of the late-nineteenth-century scholar John J. McCook, had
"a panicky look," suggesting "a pressing evil, real or imaginary."[42]

Such endeavors to "abate the tramp nuisance" came up against the perception that the vagrancy laws were far too lenient for the poor.[43] With the jails
bursting with tramps, and the new workhouses unable to take even a fourth of
their number, many tramps arrested for violating vagrancy laws were immediately released by the overburdened courts. As a consequence, there were widespread calls to build more workhouses and put the tramps to labor on public
projects. The South was in danger of being "overrun" by tramps as the weather
turned colder in the North "unless special laws are at once enacted to check the
evil." Yet calls for greater enforcement of vagrancy laws confronted the enormous scale of the homeless problem; in the single year of 1877, New York City
police made one million vagrancy arrests (there were no doubt many repeat offenders). In Philadelphia, arrests for vagrancy rose from under 2 percent of all arrests in 1872 to 12 percent in 1877, from less than one thousand to more than
five thousand vagrants arrested. In most cases the police could do no more than
bring the vagrant in for the night and then release him or her, for to try all these
vagrants would have overwhelmed the legal system. Given the great number of
vagrants, the *New York Tribune* favored setting up "colonies of tramps" in under-
populated areas. The *North American* took a far tougher approach, calling for the
restoration of the "whipping-post" to punish tramps.[44]

Starting with New Jersey, several states passed new vagrancy laws in 1877
aimed directly at the tramps, exploiting their inability to pay fines in order to get
cheap labor for public projects.[45] These new vagrancy laws were among the
harshest in American history and aimed at exercising more control over the poor.
The new Southern Democratic state legislatures passed convict labor in 1877,
establishing the notorious chain gangs as tools of repression targeting both
blacks and tramps. Convict labor quickly became a major source of income for
Southern states, often equaling tax revenues. States and towns were also ruthless
in their treatment of those arrested for vagrancy and other crimes; between 1877
and 1880, 285 convicts worked on the Greenwood and Augusta Railroad in
South Carolina, 128—or 45 percent—of whom died. In contrast, the contemporary death rate in Northern prisons was just over 1 percent. The South established a system that pretty much allowed them to keep prisoners as long as they
wanted. For instance, the Texas vagrancy law allowed the state to hold the arrested tramp until his fines and costs had been satisfied by working at a set rate
of $1 per day. Just as the company store in mining districts always managed to
keep workers in debt, so the "costs" of a vagrant arrested in Texas always seemed
to exceed the dollar earned.[46]

Antitramp laws were not limited to the South, or to states. Connecticut's new law created an innovative legal category (the "tramp"), encouraged arrests by paying a $5 bounty for every tramp detained, and raised the maximum punishment to three years in the state prison if a tramp was found in possession of a "dangerous weapon." The town council of Manassas, Virginia, found tramps "so troublesome" that they saw no alternative to enacting an ordinance forbidding any vagrants from coming within the limits of the town.[47] Several states lumped tramps together with "persons *non compos mentis* or dissolute of habits," who "may be prohibited from carrying weapons." Ohio's law was even tougher, mandating three years in prison for kindling a fire on the highway or entering anyone's property uninvited.[48]

These laws ended many basic rights for the unemployed. A Civil War veteran who had become a tramp from necessity held that "the right to live honestly is more sacred than the right to hold 'property.'"[49] Another asked what happened to the right of workers to travel and seek a job. J.E. Emerson wrote the *National Labor Tribune* that the new antitramp laws make it "a crime to be out of employment and money at the same time," and compared this legislation to the notorious Tudor vagabond laws. But in 1900, Ohio's Supreme Court upheld that state's vagrancy act by declaring that "the genus tramp . . . is a public enemy."[50] Antitramp legislation, in the words of Michael Davis, "was criminalizing the indigent unemployed without distinction."[51]

Cities and towns across America criminalized poverty in 1877. The emerging ideology justified cutting aid to the poor while increasing the cost of law enforcement. As they closed places where the homeless could spend the night, municipalities ordered the arrest of those same people—now called vagrants—for having no place to sleep. But even such efforts appeared insufficient; self-proclaimed tramp experts insisted on a national effort to eradicate this menace.

The Antitramp Crusade

The antitramp movement took form in July 1877 with a meeting at Bryn Mawr of "95 gentlemen" from several eastern Pennsylvania counties. This gathering of leading citizens from Philadelphia and its environs drew national attention as it expressed well middle-class anxieties over the "the Tramp Nuisance."[52] Many explanations were given for this convention; one common story held that it was the result of a tramp murdering a family in Gore, Ohio, in June. Another story circulating stated that the convention convened after three tramps raped and killed a young woman in Unity, Pennsylvania. An angry crowd supposedly caught these tramps in a train yard, debated lynching them, but instead took them before a local judge, who released them after they denied committing the crime. Each of these stories carried the subtext that the law proved incapable of dealing with tramps, requiring the public to act in its own defense.[53]

Speaker after speaker at the Bryn Mawr convention vented his anger not only against the tramps but also against those they saw as enabling the tramps to continue their parasitical way of life: generous liberals. "A strong point is made in denouncing the indiscriminate supply of food and money to the vagabonds prowling through the rural districts as being calculated to encourage them in vagrancy and render them insolent and vindictive toward those who do not accede to their demands." Gestures of fellow-feeling and charity were seen as grotesquely misplaced with the tramps, who exploited such sentimental weakness and would eventually bite the hand that fed them—or worse. Insisting that they were part of a larger national "movement against the tramps and rogues infesting the country," attendees at the Bryn Mawr meeting issued a resolution calling for the energetic enforcement of Pennsylvania's recently passed Vagrant Act, demanding, in the language of the act, the arrest of "all persons wandering abroad and begging who have no fixed place of residence in the township"; all should be put to work on public projects. In addition to calling for the arrest of tramps, these gentlemen demanded that the railroads work with local authorities to "prevent the going of disreputable persons about upon freight trains from station to station." They further recommended that officers be placed at stations "to arrest all vagrants found getting on or off the trains or lounging around the depots or along the line." The *North American* felt that these resolutions "showed that the participants in the movement mean business and that the tramp nuisance has become intolerable."[54]

This "War on the Pestiferous Tramp" gained steam and encouragement from around the nation over the next few weeks. The executive committee selected at the Bryn Mawr meeting organized their campaign against the tramp, which included a call for more constables as well as "a special force of mounted policemen," to arrest the "gangs of tramps." Their enthusiasm for the chase led these gentlemen to delve into the minutiae of their effort, even to the types of signals used by their special police. They demanded that local magistrates see to "the rigid enforcement of the law," which drew the ire of many who felt that the committee was not vigorous enough in relying on the law to solve the tramp question. The *North American* criticized these gentlemen for "contenting themselves with passing resolutions" rather than acting as vigilantes. Anyone who read the many stories of tramp crimes knew full well that the law had proven inadequate to the task and it was up to the people to take justice into their own hands.[55]

But according to papers in other states, that was precisely what the people of Pennsylvania were doing. As legal authorities did nothing to punish the tramps, respectable citizens "have formed themselves into vigilance committees to protect their lives and property from the regularly-organized companies of traveling brigands that have spread terrorism" in the area around Huntington, Pennsylvania—or so papers outside Pennsylvania reported. A group of miners in some unnamed Pennsylvania valley battled a gang of tramps, killing one of the miscreants, while farmers in Pleasant Valley lynched a tramp for an unspecified crime. In reporting on the "March of the Tramps" that September, a San Francisco paper declared the Pennsylvania vigilantes so successful that the "the army of brigandish tramps" had been driven out of that state into neighboring Delaware and Maryland, where they committed "flagrant deeds of outlawry" in these unprotected states.[56]

These stories of imagined vigilante action in Pennsylvania spoke to the violent fantasies of many Americans, who wanted this new criminal element dealt with pitilessly and immediately and were no longer content to let the law deal with such matters according to traditional procedures. Citizens had to turn to vigilantism in self-defense, as the tramps had "no fear of the regularly constituted authorities." Enthusiasm for extralegal action filled America's newspapers in 1877 with calls for the "formation of vigilance committees in places where the police regulations are inadequate to secure the summary arrest and severe punishment of these lazy outcasts."[57] Declaring tramps "a deadlier peril than Chief Joseph or Sitting Bull," a Macon, Georgia, newspaper cited the "several battles royal" that had taken place in Pennsylvania in calling on home owners to "take down their guns and go out to fight the tramps." Even racial boundaries bent a little in the shared "War on the Tramps." An ordinarily racist Southern newspaper reported with approval on the action of the blacks of Hanover, Virginia, who "have invented a remedy of their own for the tramp nuisance," beating "one of their color" who was begging with a "stout stave." The fear generated by the Tramp Scare was so intense that thousands of otherwise law-abiding Americans thought that the rule of law was no longer sufficient. "The householder is powerless to defend his home, and the tramps are strong enough to give battle to the Sheriff and his posse," one paper warned. In their frustration, many people called for "A War on the Nomads."[58] Vigilante action against tramps did occur, as it did against ethnic minorities in the South and West in 1877, but the flood of such stories far exceeded the actual supply of antitramp vigilantism.

The reality was fear. The more honest newspaper accounts noted that people were afraid, even while feeding that dread with apocryphal stories. In November, the *Boston Advertiser* observed that selectmen and city authorities throughout New England had to "meet the problem of how to dispose of tramps when cold weather comes," Maine particularly being "overrun with vagabonds." While the paper found no verifiable acts of violence attributable to these tramps, they did lack proper respect for property. Using the passive voice, the paper reported that "Barns are commonly entered, poultry is stolen, clothes-lines are robbed, and there is an uneasiness and insecurity which should not be endured in a peaceful

State." While there was disagreement over the best course of action, there was little doubt that something had to be done about the tramp, "and done at once." The sense of urgency was profound; the very security of the country appeared at risk, and the sacrifice of the rights of these few tramps appeared a small price to pay "if we are to have any comfort by day or safety by night." That the danger from the tramps "is present and urgent there is no doubt, nor that society needs better means of dealing with it than the law now provides."[59]

One rarely considered response to the tramp problem was aid. In fact, many commentators expressed outrage over the willingness of far too many otherwise respectable citizens to extend assistance to these undeserving poor, with several ministers delivering sermons condemning charity as a dangerous impulse. Very quickly the antitramp movement morphed into an anticharity campaign. The taxpaying citizen should not be "supporting the worthless life of the tramp."[60] A Boston newspaper complained that "Country people," out of fear or false charity, made the situation worse by feeding the tramps: "All help should be withheld by private citizens, and every one asking it referred to the authorities."[61] In the opinion of the *New York World*, "If we are to get any good out of the tramps who will not work if they can avoid it," people must stop feeding them.[62] In reporting on debates in the Boston newspapers over "the question of giving food to tramps and beggars," the *Lowell Citizen* declared that those who worked with the poor in benevolent organizations opposed the policy. In a story repeated in many forms, this paper reported that one local charitable organization had recently put up twenty-five tramps for the night and offered them breakfast in return for a few minutes' work clearing snow. Twenty of these tramps refused, indicating "that they could just as well get a breakfast without work at the back door of some citizen." With righteous anger, the paper declared, "Giving a breakfast to such men is simply putting a premium on vagrancy."[63] The *St. Louis Globe-Democrat* agreed that giving aid to tramps was a dreadful mistake, an "encouragement and perpetuation of this lowest type of degraded humanity." The police protest that while half of the householders "are complaining of the tramps, the other half are feeding them." Charity "is merely an encouragement to vagrancy and crime, and the real duty of the citizen is to hand him over to the police." Ironically, even as the St. Louis press spoke out against giving aid to tramps, eastern papers condemned St. Louis for its generosity in establishing a "Tramp's Paradise," and "the best loafing-place they could find."[64]

The fact was that St. Louis had "no poor relief system under the control of the Government." When a local minister suggested that there should be some form of public assistance given the current economic "emergency," Mayor Henry Overstolz rejected the idea out of hand. Government-operated soup kitchens and workhouses were both impractical and unnecessary, the mayor insisted, though he did offer to ask the police to provide shelter "in cases of absolute destitution."

Nonetheless, the eastern press preferred to believe their own stories and continued to castigate St. Louis for feeding the homeless. There are those, the *Boston
Advertiser* admitted, who feel "that society owes every man food, clothing and
shelter." To them, the *Advertiser* responded, "Society owes no man a living, not
a crumb, nor a shred." The policy of some cities to feed tramps for fear that they
might starve, which the paper called "the St. Louis principle," is not just wrong,
it "is downright communism." Some charities responded to this new sentiment
by refusing services to unknown transient poor. One New York charity took advantage of the stated objection that handouts would be spent on alcohol by selling tickets that could be exchanged only for food and lodging.[65]

A surprising number of Christian ministers, such as Henry Ward Beecher,
showed a less than charitable attitude toward the tramps. The Reverend W.H.H.
Murray of Boston even objected to the presence of tramps at Dwight Moody's
revivals, as they sought only to enlist the sympathy of the benevolent. Murray
demanded that doorkeepers prevent those so obviously in need of charity from
entering Moody's Tabernacle. Another minister warned of a tramp conspiracy
that planned to "sack and burn whole communities." In the midst of the hot,
violent summer of 1877, New York's Reverend Robert B. Hall delivered a sermon on the "tramp question" that drew his congregation's attention to these
"men who have the taint of sin about them, the stamp of crime upon their fore-
heads. Poor outcast tramps and vagabonds!" Having established their dangerous
character, Hall called on his auditors to "look upon them tenderly," as they
"loathe themselves, they hate the world, and are ready at times to curse God and
die."[66] Nowhere in his sermon did Hall ask for more than pity for the tramps,
and devoted much more time to justifying their shared fear of the homeless.

A few astute observers suggested that "the tramp" as a stereotype served a specific social purpose. "Society must always have a scapegoat for its sins," the *St.
Louis Republican* argued; "just now it is tramps." Based on newspaper accounts
and political speeches, the tramp concentrates in himself all the evils known to
man, plus a few extra. Amidst the many remedies suggested for the tramp threat,
"none are based on the assumption that possibly he may be as much sinned
against as sinning." The *Republican* felt it necessary to point out the obvious,
that just "because a man is wandering about the country homeless, hungry,
ragged and importunate, it does not follow that he is a thief or bloody-minded
villain." No doubt there are a number of bad men among the tramps, the paper
admitted, but most are tramps because they are unemployed. Where there is
prosperity, there are very few tramps; the paper reminded its readers that no one
had heard of tramps until a few years ago. "The tramp is the legitimate outcome
of what is commonly called 'hard times.'"[67]

As the depression worsened, social services diminished. New York City, for instance, ceased its "outdoor relief" programs in 1875 as one reaction to the Boss

Tweed scandals. In the summer of 1877, New York's Association for Improving the Condition of the Poor dropped two thousand poor people from its rolls, even though the number requesting aid was increasing. In Indianapolis, the Committee on Benevolence refused to open a soup kitchen because they thought it "impossible to discriminate between the worthy and unworthy poor" and felt that they needed to do so. In Chicago, 60 percent of those applying for aid were rejected as "not deserving relief." There were too few private "soup kitchens" to fill the gap, and those that existed were quickly overwhelmed by demand. As more cities dropped their policy of letting the homeless stay in police stations overnight, more tramps turned in desperation to the commission of some crime, generally stealing an item from a store and then waiting patiently for the police, in order to spend time in jail. Such arrest-oriented crimes tended to occur in the winter, but on occasion starvation drove tramps to provocative acts. In August two immigrants—one a thirty-three-year-old Dane and the other a forty-year-old Englishman—set fire to a barn in Milford, Pennsylvania, and then waited to be arrested. In court, the two men said they had been "tramping for several months, had been unable to secure work, and, being almost starved, concluded to fire the barn and get into prison, where they would get something to eat." The state had no choice but to oblige.[68]

Social Darwinism

The new angry and dismissive attitudes toward charity went hand-in-hand with and found their greatest justification in the development of social Darwinism. Impressed with what they took to be the hard, scientific fact of natural selection, many prominent American intellectuals, politicians, and businessmen followed Herbert Spencer in wanting to extend Charles Darwin's insights on nature to society. To those who enjoyed the benefits of American prosperity, unrestrained capitalism appeared a law of nature, and one that should be obeyed by all and not altered, as to do so would undermine social progress. Daniel S. Gregory's popular *Christian Ethics* argued that "The Moral Governor has placed the power of acquisitiveness in man for a good and noble purpose," so that interfering with greed was actually a sin. Not surprisingly, the rich and their acolytes crafted an ideology from this perception that equated wealth with morality and poverty with a defective character. No one gave voice to this belief system better than the Reverend Henry Ward Beecher, the most famous—and highly paid—minister in America: "The general truth will stand, that no man in this land suffers from poverty unless it be more than his fault—unless it be his *sin*."[69]

Though it had its origins in England with Spencer's writings, social Darwinism became an obsession among educated Americans in the late 1870s. While scholars place the first use of the phrase "social Darwinism" in Europe in 1879, it is telling that the phrase actually first appears in the public press in the United States in 1877—and then in the context of the tramp menace.[70] *The Nation* converted to social Darwinism in 1877, its editor, E.L. Godkin, declaring that nothing of value "is not the result of successful strife." Those who are successful in life deserve their wealth, while trying to lift up the weak undermines this natural struggle and thus social progress.[71]

In discussing his own youthful delight in social Darwinism, Henry Adams had no trouble explaining its attraction. "Such a working system for the universe suited a young man who had just helped waste five or ten thousand million dollars and a million lives, more or less, to enforce unity and uniformity on people who objected to it," he wrote in reference to the Civil War. "The idea was only too seductive in its perfection; it had the charm of art."[72]

So popular had evolutionary theory become in 1877 that *The Congregationalist* complained that too many "preachers seem to think it their duty to give their congregations dilutions of Tyndall and Huxley and Herbert Spencer," the leading promoters of Darwin's work. They noted with concern that Harvard students are now expected to read Spencer. Later in the year, Harvard's professor John McCrary, who held the chair in geology, resigned in opposition to this cult of Herbert Spencer.[73] But his was a lonely voice, as readings of Spencer became common at high school exercises throughout the country, even in Milwaukee.[74] Despite their rejection of evolution, most Protestant ministers and intellectuals were entranced by social Darwinism. The Reverend William A. Halliday used Darwin to point out that progress is certain, but that not everyone advances together; "the survival of the fittest is nothing the unfit can cheer about."[75] Newspapers nationwide excitedly covered the news that the first volume of Spencer's *Principles of Sociology* was about to be published by Appleton's. A mine owner in Colorado named one of his sites the Herbert Spencer Lode. Out in California a man walking with a longtime friend of the family was discussing Herbert Spencer, "illustrating the survival of the fittest by examples within their own knowledge," when suddenly he proposed marriage to his companion and she accepted.[76] The newspaper does not so state, but it is likely that the couple observed Darwinian advantages in participating in the process of natural selection.

As Susan Jacoby has pointed out, one reason social Darwinism became so popular in late-nineteenth-century America was its ability to appeal to both sides of the emerging cultural divide. On the one hand it based its claims on scientific validity; on the other, Herbert Spencer had insisted that science cannot comprehend the "Unknowable," which everyone took to mean God. The dual characteristic of social Darwinism is evident in two of Spencer's biggest fans in the United States. William Graham Sumner found in Spencer scientific justification for his extreme version of laissez-faire. Sumner could thus claim it was a fact, "fixed in the order of the universe," that government intervention threatened to disrupt the workings of natural selection—from the eight-hour day to public education, protective tariffs to the post office, they all thwarted progress. Appearing before the House of Representatives, Sumner was asked, "Professor, don't you believe in any government aid to industries?" To which he emphatically replied, "No! It's root, hog, or die." That answer evoked the intelligent follow-up: "Yes, but hasn't the hog got a right to root?" But Sumner denied even that right of survival: "There are no rights. The world owes nobody a living." He then dismissed any view of economics other than his own as "fallacies." Meanwhile, Henry Ward Beecher turned to Spencer to argue that economic success is evidence of the working of both God's will and natural selection. Given that double authority, no one should attempt to ameliorate economic inequality. Science proved God's will in making certain that "the poor will be with you always."[77]

Henry James at least was baffled by this fascination with Herbert Spencer. Both his father and brother William kept telling him that Spencer was a genius. When James arrived in London in 1877, he became a member of the Athenaeum Club, to which Spencer also belonged. In one letter to his father he reported, "On the other side of the room sits Herbert Spencer, asleep in a chair (he always is, whenever I come here)." Two weeks later he wrote William, "I often take an afternoon nap beside Herbert Spencer at the Athenaeum, and feel as if I were robbing *you* of the privilege." He tried reading Spencer, but found him too tedious to bother. Among prominent American intellectuals, James was unusual in his disregard for the great man.[78]

It was an age enamored with the aura of science, and also with a great deal of tolerance for pseudoscience. In 1877 Yale professor William Graham Sumner discovered the work of Herbert Spencer, and through him the concept of social Darwinism. Sumner, emerging as the founder of American sociology, felt certain that science and statistics could prove that what is, is good. Some people might look at a statistic like only 100,000 Americans attending high school, with just 12,000 young people—2,000 of them women—graduating from college, and see massive inequality, a glass 95 percent empty. Not William Graham Sumner. To this advocate of extreme laissez-faire, these numbers indicated the winnowing out of the qualified from the masses in the struggle for survival. Like most people, Sumner saw in the 76,808 miles of unregulated railway the marker of the most extensive rail system in the world and America's future glory. Similarly, Sumner took as a sign of the nation's strength the fact that, despite the United States being in the midst of its worst depression, the country still managed to attract 169,986 immigrants (his statistic counted only those who came through federal facilities, some 75 percent of the total), more than 60 percent of whom came from northern and western Europe—though he and many others were troubled by the ethnic background of that other 40 percent. Life expectancy in the United States was just forty years, but then the average was dragged down by

industrial accidents, which were a sign of economic progress. It was more difficult to frame the bright side of the high infant mortality rate; in northeastern
Pennsylvania's coal fields, one-third of all newborns died during their first year.
Sumner mulled over these numbers and worked to fit them into his theoretical
understanding of the world, insisting that the government had no role to play in
the battle among these millions of people fighting for survival as part of a natural process in which the fittest triumphed and society benefited.[79]

Not everyone was enamored of social Darwinism. Darwin, for instance, was
far from pleased with those applying natural selection to everyday social interac-
tions.[80] Others were taken aback by Spencer's ruthlessness. "If they are not sufficiently complete to live," he wrote of the poor, "they die, and it is best they should
die." It appeared that the marketplace could justify nearly every inhuman act
imaginable as a scientific necessity. Henry Demarest Lloyd sarcastically framed
this revolutionary new theory as "the doctrine that you can do anything with
your fellow-man provided you do it in the market."[81] Plenty of Americans with
little grasp of science discovered deeply disturbing flaws in the popular simplifi-
cations of Darwin. When Sumner delivered a talk in Bloomington in January
1877 attacking government intervention, only an embarrassing thirty people sat
in cavernous Washington Hall. The Chicago *Inter Ocean* dismissed Sumner for
having "a very small appreciation of great things and a very great appreciation of
small things," and felt "we can hardly afford to trust his opinion" given his disturbing indifference to human suffering. Sumner did not lose heart, publishing
several articles in 1877 mocking the notion that government action could do
anything but retard social and economic progress. By year's end Sumner was
speaking before large, enthusiastic audiences, receiving petitions for this "colos-
sus from Yale College" to come speak in Chicago.[82]

The Tramp Scare fed the social Darwinian movement, offering powerful evidence that nature removed the weak from society, for clearly those who wandered
aimlessly through a land of such plenty had to be weak. The consensus held that
the tramp crisis had its root either in the sinful character of the deliberately unemployed or in the Civil War. Many contemporaries thought the majority of
tramps were veterans "fired with unquenchable and irresponsible wanderlust" by
the war, made dangerous by their military experience, and yet weak of character.
The Civil War left the country, *Scribner's Monthly* argued, with "a great number
of men utterly demoralized." The depression "cut them loose from remunerative
work, and they have become rovers, nominally looking for employment, but
really looking for life without it." The experience of war followed by unemployment destroyed their character, as they lost their self-respect and "their sense of
manhood and of shame, and have imbibed the incurable disease of mendicancy."
Acknowledging that many of these tramps were women, *Scribner's* saw no hope for
the tramps, who "can never be restored to sound manhood and womanhood."

This "evil" would not "be cured by returning national prosperity" as it "is a hopelessly demoralizing mental disease." The only option was for the state to force these diseased men and women to work.[83]

This vision of the dangerous veteran, crazed by his experience of war and an inability to fit back into civilian life, filled middle-class America with dread. The war had taught bad habits to veterans, introducing "a new element" into the national character. Before the war, "it was thought that every able-bodied man could support himself by his industry, and it was a rare sight to see a native-born citizen driven to the extremity of asking for alms." But soldiers were used to just hanging around the camp, to receiving their food and lodging without having to work except for the occasional firing of guns. They sought to maintain that life of ease and abandoned prewar values of self-reliance in the process. "To beg was regarded as almost as discreditable as to steal" prior to the war, "but now stout and healthy men . . . demand their rations of house-keepers, . . . with an air of authority that can hardly be tolerated." The answer to this problem was clearly the application of the same standards of discipline that had kept these men in line during the war; they would have to be forced to work by the superior authority of the government. Given the military service of these veterans, though often on the opposing side of the author of any given critique, it is rather shocking how little sympathy even these tramps inspired. So deep was the contempt "for men who are so demoralized as to beg from choice," and so frightened was the public of the assumed proclivity of veterans for violence, that the veteran tramp was seen as having "but to take a single step to land in ruffianism." The country was not to blame for the war affecting many thousands of veterans adversely, as only those of weak character could so easily shake off the coverings of civilization for this life of theft and violence. "Already they intimidate, and rob and murder, to get the means to support their useless lives."[84]

While their numbers are surely exaggerated, a great number of America's homeless were indeed veterans of the Civil War. The presence of large numbers of veterans among the tramps was evident in the "military" organization of the tramp camps, which tended to be a lot neater than observers expected. Their use of military titles, clever maneuvers to avoid detection and arrest, and indications of leadership in tramp bands persuaded many who came in contact with the tramps that they were a criminal conspiracy, whereas the reality was a reversion to military standards. From the left, the labor press attempted to arouse some sense of national responsibility for these homeless veterans who had served their country, comparing the tramping armies of unemployed with the Union forces. Those who are now tramps, the *National Labor Tribune* wrote, "once tramped at Gettysburg . . . where their present defamers would not dare to tramp." Veterans wrote in to the labor press to express their bitterness. "Was it for this [poverty] we traveled the seas for a land of Liberty? Was it for this we fought?"[85]

But who were the tramps and where did they come from? Were they in fact largely Civil War veterans, or criminals, or lazy ne'er-do-wells, or the victims of hard times? Surprisingly little contemporary effort was made to discover the reality of these people perceived as such a social threat. A few police officers did attempt to discover the truth of the threat facing America. In St. Louis, a Captain Lee of the First Police District conducted a survey in January 1877. In that month, his jail put up an astounding 1,652 different tramps for the night. Of these, 567 were native-born Americans, 624 German immigrants, 278 Irish immigrants, and the rest from elsewhere in Europe and Canada. Despite their poverty and the high percentage of immigrants, fully 80 percent of these tramps could read and write English. What they shared was a desire to find a job or, in the absence of paid labor, food and a warm place to spend the night. In Philadelphia, native-born tramps tended to be literate single males without dependents, 80 percent of them under the age of forty; 71 percent were tested as literate. A similar study in Columbus, Ohio, found roughly a quarter of the tramps in their twenties, with just under half foreign-born, mostly Irish and German. But nearly a third of the tramps were locals desperate for aid, most of them skilled workers.[86]

Few people took as much care as Captain Lee to discover the tramps' precise origins. In September 1877, the Conference of Charities organized a special session at the American Social Science Association meeting in Saratoga Springs on the "tramp question." The scholars involved made no effort to explore the social reality of homelessness, comfortably demonizing the poor as "lazy, shiftless, sauntering or swaggering, ill-conditioned, irreclaimable, incorrigible, cowardly, utterly depraved savage[s]." These words came from the star of the conference, Professor Francis Wayland, dean of Yale Law School and author of *The Elements of Moral Science*. Wayland dismissed sympathy for the poor, since, as everyone knew, "It is very rare that employment of some kind cannot be obtained by any one really anxious to secure work" in the United States. Public fear was completely justified as the tramp considered "himself at war with society and all social institutions," and would not hesitate to commit any crime to support his idleness. Society needed to act firmly to protect itself from the tramps' "daily spectacle of lawless violence."[87] Wayland immediately became *the* authority on the tramp menace, cited, quoted, and called upon to buttress every argument for the harsh treatment of this dangerous element. Within two weeks of the conference, antitramp laws based on Wayland's harsh recommendations began appearing before state legislatures, backed by emphatic calls to end all charity for the poor.[88]

In 1877 the terror of the tramps became a national obsession among the middle class. Understanding the depths of this fear requires an appreciation for the broader perceived "threat" posed by workers in 1877 within the context of the deepening economic crisis. The tramp terrified the middle class by living outside the accepted rules and control mechanisms imposed by employment. Only wages and workplace discipline prevented the mass of workers from becoming as dangerous as the tramps. Like the freed blacks in the South, workers appeared a frightening class of rough, barely controlled, primal beings who could easily slough off the thin constraints of Christian culture and rise up to create the horrors of the Paris Commune in America. By 1877, those who did hard physical labor were coming to be identified as a dire threat to a well-ordered society. In January of that year, this dread of the working people found its clearest embodiment in that most horrifying of all groups, the Molly Maguires.

The Molly Maguires

Just as with the tramps, it is difficult to separate the reality of the Molly Maguires from the elaborately constructed mythology. As every crime from the pettiest theft to murder led to shouts of "tramps!" throughout the United States, so in the mining districts of Pennsylvania everything from industrial accidents to bar brawls produced charges of Molly Maguire involvement. The consensus among historians is that the press and management greatly exaggerated every aspect of the Molly Maguires, from their numbers to the extent of their criminal activities. Newspapers routinely identified the Ancient Order of Hibernians as "the official name" of the Molly Maguires, with secret headquarters in New York and London. "The society," the *San Francisco Daily Evening Bulletin* explained, "which is, of course, Irish in origin—exists, under the form of a benevolent organization, simply for the purpose of outrage and murder," and maintains "powerful political influence," controlling votes, swaying elections, and filling "important offices with its own members," even to state governors.[89]

Such astounding projections of power onto the powerless ignored the reality that, as unskilled immigrant workers, the Irish found few allies and felt isolated and abused by the larger society, as was in fact the case. Far from an international organization, the Molly Maguires were a loose alliance of Irish Catholic workers in Pennsylvania's coal region, most of whom also belonged to the Ancient Order of Hibernians. The Molly Maguires fought to maintain the wages and job security of miners at a time when management was doing its best to cut both drastically. They definitely committed acts of violence, but nothing like the number of which they were accused. And most important, the only reason they ever gained prominence is because management succeeded in destroying the miners' union.

In the years from 1868 through 1874, the Workingman's Benevolent Association rose to prominence among coal miners. It is telling that in those same years there was little violence in the coal mining areas, as workers overcame ethnic divisions and for the first time found a peaceful avenue for expressing their grievances, a fact widely recognized at the time. The Pennsylvania Bureau of Industrial

Statistics praised the union for its pacifying work, crediting it with having "forced into reformation or removal . . . reckless and turbulent" workers. It was the union that ended the "carnival of crime" in the region in the 1860s. For the first time the workers had a powerful voice speaking on their behalf, and they took full advantage of it as union leaders presented themselves as an alternative to the violence of the Molly Maguires—and of the mines. Violence was a daily aspect of the miner's job, made worse by the complete absence of safety standards and a hospital. John W. Geary, Republican governor of Pennsylvania until his sudden death in 1873, blamed the negligence of the owners for much of the violence done to workers, and the union placed safety on the top of its list of demands, for which it was routinely accused of interfering in the free market. The union opposed the use of violence and sought to reach common ground with the employers; the employers did not hesitate to use violence to crush the union, as they did in the strike of 1875, which saw an end to the union and its mediating influence.[90]

Destruction of the union opened the door to violence, by both the corporations and the workers. With the union destroyed, the historian Kevin Kenny wrote, "a minority of Irish workers turned to violence as the sole remaining strategy for winning some sort of rudimentary justice in the mines." From their perspective, the Molly Maguires fought for justice; from that of the general public, their violence was entirely criminal. Two books published at the beginning of 1877 set the tone of fear, elevating the sixty to seventy Irish workers who belonged to the Molly Maguires into an international conspiracy intent on destroying the American way of life. Though there was little substance to their charges, the two books proved very effective in heightening public terror of the poor. The journalist Francis P. Dewees's study of the Molly Maguires drew largely on newspaper accounts and court records, completely misrepresenting the group as little more than foolish Irish workers who had brought their traditional anti-English conflict with them and committed acts of violence "without cause, or pretence of a cause." Much more interesting, if only because it was written by a key participant in the war on labor, was Allan Pinkerton's *The Molly Maguires and the Detectives*, which portrayed the Molly Maguires as ruthless gangsters closely connected with the union movement.[91]

Allan Pinkerton, the founder of the detective agency bearing his name, was an immigrant from Scotland who had originally been a barrel maker and supporter of the Chartist labor movement. In the United States he became an abolitionist and served during the Civil War as the head of President Lincoln's intelligence service. After the war Pinkerton discovered that there was a great deal of money to be made working for the nation's largest corporations infiltrating and crushing unions. His abandonment of former sympathies was so complete that he even worked for the Spanish government in 1872 helping to put down a revolution in Cuba that sought to end slavery. Pinkerton's greatest success, though, would come with the destruction of the Molly Maguires. To maximize the publicity value of this coup, and to exaggerate his services to the nation by expanding the danger posed by the mine workers, Pinkerton wrote the deeply distorted and biased *The Molly Maguires and the Detectives*, which quickly became the cited authority on the Irish group.

Pinkerton constructed the narrative followed by the majority of newspapers and most early historical accounts, characterizing the Molly Maguires as a terrorist organization intent on controlling the mines. The Molly Maguires, in Pinkerton's telling, dominated Pennsylvania through their front organization, the Workingman's Benevolent Association, and by manipulating the inherent flaws in a democracy that allows the poor to vote. Any who opposed the Molly Maguires met a violent end, as they performed "deeds that might make angels weep"; they were also "communists."[92] Pinkerton fails to mention that the first agent he sent to investigate the union, P.M. Cummings, reported that not only did the union oppose violence and the Molly Maguires, but it had also established order among the workers throughout the region. But then, Pinkerton was not interested in telling his story from the perspective of the workers.[93]

As the Pennsylvania Bureau of Industrial Statistics observed, the peace of the state's coal mining region was transformed in the mid-1870s when Franklin B. Gowen of the Philadelphia & Reading Railroad decided to take complete control of coal production in Pennsylvania, crushing both small operators and the labor union in the process. Gowen's strategy for dealing with the Workingman's Benevolent Association was to equate the union with the Molly Maguires. Even while the Reading Railroad was establishing its monopoly in the coal regions, Gowen was attacking the union as terrorists seeking to destroy small businesses.[94] The Reading Railroad's monopoly changed the nature of work, increasing industrial accidents, lowering wages, and destroying the workers' standard of living. A reporter for the *New York Labor Standard* visited St. Clair, Pennsylvania, in 1877 and described one of Gowen's mines. He entered town through "a great cloud of black dust [that] is ever streaming, settling on everything." The division of labor had been firmly established, with each worker performing the same, closely regulated task, "just as a steam engine or a clock." When the workday was over, the "black silent men" went home "in the regular groove, just as the steam goes out of the boiler when its work is done, and then dropped off into sleep, his only pleasure." The reporter was appalled by what he saw: "I have seen far more cheerful bodies of men in prisons." Of all the places he had been, this was the one to which he would least like to return; depression hung over the town like a heavy, suffocating blanket. "It may be their black and dreary surroundings; it may be their knowledge of constant and terrible danger; it may be the strain of great physical labor—I know not what it is, but something there is about these mines that wears the life and soul out of the men, leaving only the weary, blackened shell."[95]

In the absence of a union, the Molly Maguires, who did have a tendency to resolve conflicts violently, found greater acceptance as the only organization willing to act on behalf of the workers, particularly the Irish laborers. Several historians have noticed the ethnic nature of violence among miners, with the lower-paid Irish battling with the higher-paid English and Welsh workers; British and American workers could take advantage of the apprenticeship program at the mines, but the Irish need not apply, even in the late 1870s. Kevin Kenny traced the tradition of collective violence back to Ireland, where the targets were those who held power—the landlords—or those who acted on their behalf, including constables and magistrates. There is no evidence that the Molly Maguires as an organization was imported from Ireland; rather, Irish workers drew upon that heritage in response to conditions in the Pennsylvania coal fields and the group never expanded from that area. In this context, the violence of the Molly Maguires makes sense as a reaction to the disparity of power, which lay entirely in the hands of Gowen and the other large industrialists. Others have pointed to the violence between 1875 and 1877 as class warfare, with the workers battling management and their agents, the police. James McParlan, the Pinkerton spy who infiltrated the Molly Maguires, was badly beaten by a policeman acting on behalf of management during one labor action, and had to sneak out of town to get proper medical care for his wounds.[96]

The Molly Maguires intimidated, beat, and on several occasions probably killed representatives of management. The owners responded with private police, strike breakers, and vigilantism. Pinkerton notes the murder of two workers, Charles O'Donnell and a pregnant Ellen McAllister, by agents of management, but dismisses it as "fighting fire with fire," and effective, as the Mollie Maguires now "experienced a new feeling of dread." He had to admit that "vigilante" violence "was a breach of the law," but he insisted that murdering an innocent worker and a pregnant woman "was in the interests of humanity and the law, and . . . had a wonderfully tranquillizing effect upon the society, which, during the preceding months, had disported itself riotously in human blood."[97] Pinkerton failed to mention that his agency was supplying the vigilantes with the names and addresses of those to be targeted. Nor did he mention the response of James McParlan to the murder of Ellen McAllister. Since McParlan had supplied the information that led to the murder of McAllister, he accounted himself equally guilty and resigned his position, as "I am not going to be accessory to the murder of women and children." Pinkerton ignored McParlan's resignation and mentions it nowhere in his book; nor was anyone ever convicted for any of these vigilante crimes committed in the name of social order, though McParlan was willing to testify. Those with less of a conscience than McParlan, such as Allan Pinkerton, blamed the victims for their fate.[98]

The reality of the Molly Maguire "reign of terror" did not match the hyperbole rushing into print in the early part of 1877. Prosecutors reached back fifteen years to charge the seventy Molly Maguires arrested with having committed sixteen murders between 1862 and 1875, six of those in the last of these years. The state charged that each of these crimes formed part of a long-established and extensive labor conspiracy aimed at taking control of the mines; yet the victims were a diverse group, several with no obvious connection to the conflict between workers and management. A few of the victims belonged to management, while another was a despised police officer, one was a justice of the peace, another anonymous, and several were Welsh workers struck down, according to McParlan, in revenge for violent acts against Irish workers. The only connection between the defendants, other than McParlan's charge that they were all members of the shadowy Molly Maguires, was membership in the Ancient Order of Hibernians.[99]

In the view of many jurists and historians, the Molly Maguires trials bordered "on a travesty of justice," though it is hard to see how they did not cross over that demarcation.[100] As one scholar wrote, "The Molly Maguire investigation marked one of the most astounding surrenders of sovereignty in American history."[101] A criminal investigation instituted by a private corporation operating through a private detective agency, using a private police force to maintain order, had only the vaguest hint of legal standards. That the crushing of the Molly Maguires was largely a private enterprise is evidenced by the fact that the seventy arrests were made by Captain Robert Linden of the Pinkerton Agency, and the lead prosecutor in four of the trials was none other than Franklin Gowen, who delivered impassioned speeches on the massive and dangerous Molly Maguires conspiracy.[102] The remaining four prosecutors all worked for railroad or mining companies; one of them, Charles Albright, equated labor unions with treason. As Harold Aurand wrote, "The state provided only the courtroom and the hangman."[103]

In addition to this astonishing privatization of American law, news coverage hostile to the Molly Maguires and workers in general marked every step of the trial. The *New York Times* framed the case in a manner that left little doubt of the desired outcome: "The revelations of the doings of the Mollie Maguires . . . are appalling" and "uncover a state of brutish ignorance and superstition which one might think could not exist in this Republic. The Pennsylvania authorities owe it to civilization to extirpate this noxious growth, now that its roots have been discovered." The judges who oversaw the trials saw nothing wrong with excluding Irish Catholics from the juries, since they were bound to be biased, yet perceived no problem including many German Protestants, some with little command of English.[104]

The exact details of the crimes were often hazy, and the precise connection of the accused to the victims tended to be circumstantial. The state's entire case against the Molly Maguires was based on evidence from James McParlan and informants turning state's evidence to avoid prosecution. Throughout the trials, the defense argued that McParlan's evidence should not be accepted, as he had instigated and helped plan several of the murders, a position rejected by judges and juries. The most notorious of the informants were Daniel Kelly and Jimmy Kerrigan, both of whom had backgrounds that should have called their credibility into question. "Kelly the Bum," as he was known around the mining community, had been convicted of a number of previous crimes, including robbery and grand larceny, and admitted to taking part in the murder of Alexander Rea in 1874. Pennsylvania governor George Hartranft pardoned Kelly on the larceny charge on January 6, 1877, and Kelly first appeared as a witness for the prosecution in February.

Everyone hated Jimmy Kerrigan, including his wife, who on the witness stand called him "a dirty little rat." Despite repeated witnesses, including Mrs. Kerrigan, disputing his credibility, Kerrigan's evidence was used to convict several Molly Maguires.[105] At one trial, Captain Linden of the Pinkerton Agency admitted that he gave informants the option of testifying and receiving their freedom or being tried for murder with the probability of execution. He also stated that he gave money to the informants' families. Patrick Butler, the primary witness against Dennis Donnelly, testified that he had received immunity in return for his evidence, and was currently employed by the Pinkerton Agency as a detective in Philadelphia. The defense not only produced an alibi for their client, but also evidence that Butler had ordered the murder. Nonetheless, Donnelly was found guilty and hanged. It is little wonder that most scholars of the Molly Maguires hold that at least some of those executed were innocent, though it remains impossible to know for certain.[106]

The trial of John Kehoe, identified as the leader of the Molly Maguires, was the main event in 1877, with Franklin Gowen serving as prosecutor. Kehoe was charged with murdering a mine foreman named Frank Langdon in 1862.[107] There was no evidence linking Kehoe to the crime other than the fact that he had been working at the same mine and may have been docked pay by Langdon.[108] Kehoe offered a firm alibi establishing that he had not been present at the beating that led to Langdon's death; his attorney presented further evidence that Langdon, who had walked home after the fight, died as a consequence of his doctor administering an excess of stimulants, which produced a heart attack. The prosecution attacked the very idea of an alibi, making the word sound like a criminal dodge. Gowen called it a tool "which comes most readily at the beck and call of every criminal who knows himself to be guilty; for, when every other defense fails, the ever-ready *alibi* is always on hand to be proved by a crowd of relatives and retainers." Reversing the standard understanding of an alibi as proof of innocence, Gowen insisted that "it is always the defense that is resorted to by the guilty." Capping this triumph of illogic, the judge told the jury that it did not matter whether Kehoe was present at the beating, as the prosecution claimed that he had helped to plan it and that was good enough for him—and for the jury, which found Kehoe guilty of first-degree murder on January 16, 1877. "The King of the Molly Maguires . . . never flinched," though his wife, "whose loyal devotion to her husband has gained her much admiration, wept bitterly." The judge sentenced Kehoe to be hanged.[109]

Kehoe delayed his execution for more than a year by appealing his conviction all the way to the United States Supreme Court, which decided against him in October 1877. Kehoe's attorneys presented the Pennsylvania Pardon Board with statements from two of the men who admitted taking part in the beating of Langdon, swearing that Kehoe had nothing to do with the affair. The Pardon Board rejected the appeal, as did Governor Hartranft. Kehoe insisted on his innocence from the scaffold just before the state killed him in December 1878.[110]

The newspapers gave the impression that the country was in the grip of a war between order and anarchy in 1877, with the poor on the side of chaos. In such a conflict, almost any means were justified to preserve social stability. In the case of the Molly Maguires trials, prosecutor Francis W. Hughes, an employee of the Reading Railroad, insisted that if the Molly Maguires were not destroyed, "organized society must itself perish." Organized gangs of workers were a "moral cancer as deadly as any physical one," and must be cut out of the body politic. In such a situation it was of course "better that five, ten, or five hundred Molly Maguires should be suspended by ropes from the end of the gallows, than that civilized society should disappear." All legal standards were irrelevant in such a Darwinian struggle for survival. The prosecutors blithely explained away all irregularities as necessities in this war against terrorists. This rejection of the rule of law found validation in the *American Law Review*, which even upheld guilt by association as a legitimate means of securing a conviction.[111]

In this battle for civilization, the railroads found a powerful ally in the Catholic Church, which joined in condemning not just the Molly Maguires but even the Ancient Order of Hibernians, accepting as fact Gowen's assertion that they were one and the same. Archbishop James Frederic Wood of Philadelphia stayed in regular contact with Gowen and supported his efforts to crush the union along with the Molly Maguires. In February 1877, Scranton's Bishop William O'Hara excommunicated all members of the Ancient Order of Hibernians in his diocese.[112] In an atmosphere of heightened paranoia and terror, the church turned its back on its poor Irish communicants.

The state, intent on demonstrating its power as a warning to workers everywhere, planned the first ten executions of Molly Maguires to be held on a single day, June 21, 1877. Known as "Black Thursday," the hangings were a public spectacle and the subject of extensive media coverage. The press crawled over every aspect of the process—the rejected appeals, the preparations for the executions, and the executions themselves. A great deal of space was given over to the special scaffold erected at Mauch Chunk so that all four men could be hanged at once (the six at Pottsville were hanged in three pairs).[113] Journalists, doctors, and other interested professionals petitioned for the right to attend the executions. A few hundred people watched within the prison, while several thousand gathered outside the prison walls to witness the first executions in the history of Carbon and Columbia counties. Wild rumors, apparently promoted by Allan Pinkerton, circulated that the Molly Maguires would attack the prison. The state responded by calling out extra police, public and private, and the Easton Grays, a volunteer militia company patrolled the area. After the executions, a bulwark of the railroad's Coal & Iron Police surrounded the burials to prevent any political displays.[114]

The priest who attended the executed men at Pottsville, Father Daniel McDermott, had originally accepted the guilt of all the convicted men, and condemned the Ancient Order of Hibernians as a tool of the Molly Maguires. But as the executions approached, he came to believe that at least two of the men were innocent. There was no doubt in his mind that James Carroll and Thomas Duffy had not committed the crimes of which they were accused; Carroll had not even been charged with being present at the murder of the policeman Benjamin Yost in 1875. Both men had been convicted solely on statements by the informer Jimmy Kerrigan, who had in all probability planned the murder. Immediately after the executions, a shattered Father McDermott told the press that the hanging of these two men had been a terrible miscarriage of justice. The following week, McDermott and Father Mark Sheridan wrote an article for the *New York Herald* that was republished in several other newspapers, arguing that the Molly Maguires had arisen from the "antagonism of Capital and Labor," and that the oppression of the latter by the former had led to the violence in the coal districts of Pennsylvania. Theirs was the minority view.[115]

With headlines like "The Molly Maguires Will Swing" and "Artistic Neckties," newspapers nationwide proclaimed popular satisfaction with the mass executions. In celebrating these hangings, the *New York Sun* even pointed to another miscarriage of justice, the 1822 mass executions of African Americans in the alleged Denmark Vesey "conspiracy," seeing both as positive acts in which appropriate "tribute [had] been paid to the gallows" by the state.[116] The *Philadelphia Public Ledger* celebrated June 21 as "a day of deliverance from as awful a despotism of banded murderers as the world has ever seen." The *Philadelphia Inquirer* exulted in the destruction of "the most relentless combination of assassins that had been known in American history." These papers had no qualms over the use of the death penalty, the purpose of which in their minds could not be clearer:

vengeance and prevention. "The fate of these wretched men should be a warning to their associates, for there are many men in the mining districts who are just as ready to imbrue their hands in human blood as were they, and it is necessary that a terrible example should be set them, both for the protection of the community, of property and for the vindication of justice."[117]

The Working-Class Terror

The Molly Maguires trials jostled successfully for front-page coverage in 1877. Even out in Newark, Ohio, "the recent prominence given to the discussion of the Molly Maguire crimes" had thrown the community "into a fever heat." This rural town in the middle of the state, a safe distance from the nearest mines, lived in terror of this "oath-bound organization" with its "hellish-secrecy" that sought not workers' rights but to become rich by "pillage and plunder." It was particularly disturbing that the Molly Maguires had moved about in public without anyone reporting their dastardly deeds to the proper authorities. Even in Newark, "the public pulse throbs feverishly for vengeance." Insisting that it did not want to bias its readers against the accused, the *Newark Advocate* described one of the murders in gruesome detail, stating that the accused were possessed by "demons" when they attacked their innocent victim. A San Francisco paper labeled the Molly Maguires "the best organized gang of criminals in existence."[118]

As with the tramps, the Molly Maguires were often blamed for acts of violence for which there was no evidence of their involvement, even after they had been crushed as an organization. When a group of "desperate characters" attacked a Maryland saloon keeper, the press assumed the villains must be Molly Maguires since a mine was nearby. Similarly, when workers in Erie, Colorado, attempted to prevent strikebreakers from entering the mines, the Denver press labeled it an example of Molly Maguireism, declaring "Ruffianism Rampant at Erie."[119] As far as any historian has ever determined, the Molly Maguires never organized in Colorado.

There were more Molly Maguires trials in Pottsville starting in November 1877, resulting in another ten executions that aroused a brief flurry of media attention. But by 1878 the press had lost interest in the Molly Maguires conspiracy. When Dennis Donnelly was hanged in 1878, the *Miner's Journal* reported the fact under the headline "Hanging No Longer Attractive," pointing out that not a single reporter from outside the region attended this latest execution of a Molly Maguire.[120] As if to balance some imagined scale of justice, two of those hanged by the state had been informants—the state reneging on its promise of leniency.[121]

The general public perceived an obvious link between tramps and the Molly Maguires. Both consisted of dangerous men who would rather commit acts of violence than work; they were, in the *New York Times*'s succinct headline, "The

Vilest of the Vile." From there it was a short leap to including labor unions among these threats to civilization—a jump that most American newspapers were happy to make. By doing so, the press was serving the interests of the railroads, as Gowen fostered the myth of a Molly Maguires–type conspiracy in order to prevent a resurgence of labor unions in the mining districts and to help destroy the unions affiliated with his railroad. The *Irish World* saw this effort clearly, charging that the Molly Maguires hysteria was the product of Gowen's "greed and rapacity," and that the owners of the railroads were the true conspirators, acting contrary to the public good. The *Boston Pilot* took a slightly different line, one more in keeping with the view of many prounion journals: that Gowen's monopoly power had driven the miners to "Molly Maguireism and murder, and then virtuously hounded them to scaffold." Two days later the paper added that Molly Maguireism was "the direct outcome of the contest between labor and capital." Many newspapers had a conflicted view of the trials, in that they reported on poverty and corporate corruption, yet condemned the Molly Maguires. At a time when few groups publicly defended the Molly Maguires, New York's Cigarmakers' Union held a public meeting in January 1877 that adopted a resolution of support. Their leader, Samuel Gompers, insisted that everyone present knew why the Molly Maguires had arisen: "The mining corporations and the railroads had crushed every vestige of organization among miners," so they had no choice but to organize a secret society. When management destroys unions, Gompers warned, violence follows.[122]

The tramp scare and the Molly Maguire trials presaged the collapse of the ideal of American exceptionalism. No longer could the United States boast to be free from the danger of class warfare. "The tramp nuisance," wrote the *Galveston News*, is "a symptom of a social disease." Lawlessness and violence follow in their wake and they serve as "the herald of a mighty wave," an aroused working class. "A dissatisfied, menacing proletariat has long been the nightmare" of Europe, and now here they were on America's shores. The United States had long boasted "that our free institutions furnished a complete safeguard against the growth of a pauper class and a revolutionary proletariat." Now there could be little doubt that this "complacent fancy has been pretty thoroughly exploded." The tramps were not patient, they did not wait upon charity, private or public; they seized all the "good things in reach of a strong and lawless hand." This paper had no idea how to respond to the tramp menace except forcefully, and they found their fears amply reinforced by the advice the radical Socialist Lucy Parsons gave the tramps: "Learn the Use of Explosives!"[123]

Molly Maguires and tramps both violated middle-class conceptions of the world. The presence of thousands of homeless people wandering the country and the willingness of workers to turn to violence indicated some flaw in their economic system or in the poor. Despite the persistent depression that started in

1873, the majority of white Americans could not blame the system, for the free-market economy operated as a law of nature, a great scientific fact that could not be questioned; on this point all the prominent thinkers and leading public officials agreed. It was therefore not the system that was flawed, but the people. Individuals either could not or would not find work because of some defect in their character, and acted to game the system by begging or violence. Individual tramps and Irish workers challenged middle-class sensibilities and evoked contempt and fear; but when thousands of workers organized in resistance to the free market, the middle class perceived revolution.

5

The Great Insurrection

Pittsburgh & the riots neither surprised nor greatly disturbed me; for
where the government is a sham, one must expect such things.

—Mark Twain[1]

"Communistic ideas are now widely entertained in America," the *Washington
National Republican* warned in 1877. A "great communist wave" was sweeping
over the country. Several newspapers went further, warning that the nation's
workers were on the verge of establishing "communism in America."[2] W.W.
Grosvenor accused the Granger farmers' cooperative movement of being secret
communists and blamed them for the depression, fearing for the future of the
country as the "communistic spirit in Congress" grew.[3] The "spirit of communism" had spread even into Kentucky, though "the cool audacity and impudent
effrontery of the Communists have nowhere shown so conspicuously as in St.
Louis."[4] In any given city, some local commentator perceived his hometown as
the locus of the international communist conspiracy; "the workingman in Pittsburgh is really a communist, and there is no doubt that communistic ideas have
widely spread." Around the country, the press and politicians, businessmen and
ministers saw a "secret Communist cabal" disrupting social peace in 1877, inspiring otherwise content and law-abiding workers to rise up against management to make outrageous demands for a reversal of wage cuts. Clearly only
communists could contend that workers had the right to strike in order to intimidate employers into paying higher wages. Such an approach would not only
lead to workers taking over the running of corporations; it was little more than
extortion. As Secretary of the Navy Richard W. Thompson wrote the president
of the Pennsylvania Railroad, strikes are "nothing more or less than French communism . . . so entirely at war with the spirit of our institutions that it must be
overcome."[5]

The year 1877 witnessed the first widespread enthusiasm for Marxist socialism in the United States, largely in response to the depression and the evident
hostility of state and federal governments to the needs and concerns of workers.
For the first time, a "red scare" swept through the country as political leaders and

journalists perceived a nationwide threat to capitalism, religion, and social order when workers pushed back against the unfair distribution of the depression's burden, most of which seemed to fall on their shoulders. The middle class imagined the poor seizing New York and Philadelphia as they had Paris in 1871. Though America's economic and political elite only briefly believed that the workers would triumph, it was obvious to them that they needed to fight vigorously against the spread of subversive communist ideas such as the eight-hour day, workers' safety, and the right to organize unions.[6]

But the efforts of corporate leaders to smother unionism in its cradle only fed the fury and heightened a sense of injustice among their workers. As if to make abundantly clear who was boss, management from the smallest enterprises along America's docks to the largest industries announced further wage cuts, taking more out of pay packets already lightened by four years of depression. Fueled by a combination of worsening economic conditions and the harsh labor practices of management, the animosity between workers and management built through early 1877, exploding in violence in July in city after city, sweeping America into what everyone from the president on down called an "insurrection," and what historians tend to call "the Great Strike."

The Great Strike of 1877 was unique in American history. Within a few days the pent-up frustration of the previous years poured forth in a spontaneous shout of "Enough!" Within a week, some five hundred thousand workers walked off their jobs from New Jersey to San Francisco in the first nationwide strike in American history. Precision suggests that its usual name of "the Great Strike" is inaccurate; in fact, dozens of different strikes overlapped and then collided in July 1877. But on the other hand, it is worth treating it as a single event since the action of strikers in one part of the country inspired others to finally take a chance on demanding what they saw as their rights.[7]

Management responded to these events not with negotiation but with force. When local and private police forces proved insufficient to compel the workers to return to work, management turned first to the state militia, and then to the United States Army (corporate leaders expected their voices to be heard and heeded at all levels of government, and they were rarely disappointed). The Great Strike of 1877 marked the first use of federal troops to crush a strike on a national scale. The only previous uses of the army against strikers had come first in 1834, when President Andrew Jackson sent troops to end a strike on the Chesapeake & Ohio Canal, and then on five occasions during the Civil War when local commanders had made troops available to management to put down strikes.[8]

The Great Strike began along America's extensive railroad system, the largest employer in the country. From the start, railroad officials would argue that a strike against them was an assault on the nation's circulatory system; any retreat on the part of the railroad would have a devastating impact on the entire economy. President Rutherford B. Hayes, who owed so much to Tom Scott and other prominent railroad officials for his recent inauguration, understood the precedent he was setting and felt real sympathy for the plight of the nation's workers. Yet he had to act quickly, and reflection on the justice of his decision would come only later, and would haunt him for the rest of his life.

Workers with Few Options

The key to America's industrialization, the railroads were the nation's largest enterprise—with the most workers and highest capitalization—and the primary form of transportation. The *Chicago Tribune* called the railroads "the very heart and life of the modern system of commercial existence." Some fifty corporations ran over 79,000 miles of track in 1877, representing some $5 billion in capital, $2.26 billion of which was bonded debt (the national debt that year was $2.1 billion). Topping this powerful ziggurat was the Pennsylvania Railroad, the single largest corporation in the United States, controlling 6,600 miles of track and employing nearly 200,000 workers.[9] The depression had hit the railroads hard; collectively they defaulted on $800 million in bonds and their stock value dropped to half of what it had been at the beginning of 1873. Despite these considerable losses, the railroads continued to pay dividends of 6 to 10 percent, while wages for workers fell between 20 and 50 percent. The Baltimore & Ohio Railroad never missed or decreased a dividend through the depression, while it cut wages 50 percent. The year 1877 looked to be a very good one for the railroads, with the end of the depression in sight—at least as far as management was concerned.[10]

Any upturn in the economy would benefit management and the stockholders, not the workers, whom the railroads treated with contempt. Though the Pennsylvania Railroad contract with the Brotherhood of Engineers stipulated that wages could not be altered without consultation between the company and the union, Tom Scott cut wages repeatedly without bothering to even inform the Brotherhood. When a committee from the union came to see the railroad's superintendent, J.M. McCullough, to protest this violation of their contract, McCullough fired the lot of them. When the Brotherhood threatened to strike, McCullough told them, "Strike and be damned." As the superintendent of the Harlem Line of the New York Central told reporters, "If the engineers should strike, their places could be easily supplied, and the public not feel the change."[11]

As the summer of 1877 heated up, railroad workers found their pay shrinking while corporate profits increased. Grotesquely underpaid, the workers also had to contend with the epic cupidity of management. Because railroad workers had to meet their own expenses, not even receiving discounts on return trips, their actual salaries often ended up being less than those of unskilled factory workers. Firemen on the Baltimore & Ohio saw their wages fall from $55 a month in 1873 to $30 in 1877, while the wages of brakemen fell in those years from $70 to $30 and conductors from $90 to $50—reducing wages to where they stood in 1842. Even in the depths of the depression, factory workers could expect to take home $40 a month. One of these Baltimore & Ohio workers wrote, "We eat our hard bread and tainted meat two days old on the sooty cars up the road, and when we come home, find our children gnawing bones and our wives complaining that they cannot even buy hominy."[12]

The workers on the Pennsylvania line appealed to Tom Scott for help, pointing out that their wages had been repeatedly cut so that many of them were now earning 75 cents a day: "We have sympathized fully with your directors in all their past efforts to further the interests of your company, and accepted the situation so long as it guaranteed to us a bare living, but in the last move too many of us was guaranteed a pauper's home." When a grievance committee of workers met with Scott, he told them that the railroad was being run "simply that the men might be employed," and that there was not "one iota of profit to the owners." Thus reassured, the workers accepted the wage cuts. When some engineers struck anyway, the firemen took their places, demonstrating the sort of divisiveness that so often benefited management.[13]

To address this debilitating lack of unity, a group of workers met secretly at Dietrich's Hall in Allegheny City, Pennsylvania, on June 2 and, under the leadership of a young worker named Robert Adams Ammon, formed the Trainmen's Union, open to all railroad workers regardless of skill level. The assembled workers resolved that if the wage cuts and doubleheader policy (doubling the size of a train without additional workers) were not reversed, they would "leave the trains standing just where they were, and go home." Credit for this move toward worker unity is owed to the energizing presence of Ammon, an unusual leader for the working class. The twenty-five-year-old son of a prominent Pittsburgh insurance executive, Ammon had been expelled from college at the age of sixteen, served with the U.S. cavalry, traveled through Asia and South America, and just the previous year had become a brakeman for a subsidiary of the Pennsylvania. A brilliant and charismatic organizer, Ammon spent June traveling the various railroad lines in Pennsylvania and the Midwest recruiting members to this new secret union, inducting several thousand workers before the end of the month.[14]

Management quickly learned of the union, paid some workers to be their spies, and began firing any of its members they could discover, including Ammon. On June 25 five representatives of the union met with management to present their grievances and were immediately fired. The union membership met the next day and debated whether to strike. Management's hired plants resisted this call for a strike and disrupted the meeting, effectively ending the short-lived union.

However, on one of his recruitment trips, Ammon had met with Baltimore & Ohio workers in Martinsburg, West Virginia. These workers had taken a 10 percent wage cut the previous November, bringing their wages down to half of what they had been in 1873, and vowed that if their wages were cut any further they would strike. Ammon had already become used to such bold talk leading nowhere. "They talked most loud at Martinsburg, but I thought it was all wind," Ammon recalled. "I didn't think they would strike at all." On Monday, July 15, John W. Garrett, president of the Baltimore & Ohio, happily told the railroad's board of directors that the previous twelve months had been very good for business and signed off on a 10 percent dividend for the company's shareholders. Later that day Garrett announced another 10 percent wage cut, telling the papers he felt confident that his workers would "cheerfully recognize" the necessity of reducing wages. It proved one cut too many.[15]

The Great Strike of 1877 began at Camden Junction, a switching point two miles from Baltimore. Lacking a union, the workers had no plans. The events that followed on Garrett's announcement of another pay cut emerged spontaneously from workers reading newspapers on the morning of July 16 and coming together to complain bitterly. A fireman on Engine 32 got off his train at Camden Junction and refused to go any further. Firemen on other trains in the switching area quickly joined him and began persuading their fellow workers to also strike. Management immediately requested police assistance from Baltimore mayor Ferdinand Latrobe, a stockholder in the Baltimore & Ohio. Latrobe complied, ordering his police to arrest the strike leaders. When a judge questioned the legality of Baltimore police operating outside their jurisdiction, Garrett simply empowered the officers as "special" railway police and sent them to crack a few heads and make some arrests.[16]

Meanwhile, Garrett's son-in-law John King, vice president of the railroad, gathered together the requisite number of strikebreakers. Backed by forty Baltimore police officers, he fired all the strikers and replaced them with the strikebreakers. It was all treated as standard procedure and the trains were quickly rolling again. But workers had begun gathering at the B&O dispatch office in Martinsburg, a key rail junction, listening to reports of the quick crushing of the nascent strike in Camden Junction by Baltimore police. As evening approached, the workers in the Martinsburg rail yard declared themselves on strike and began uncoupling the engines from the trains. Moving the engines into the roundhouse, the workers declared that no trains would leave Martinsburg until management rescinded the wage cuts. Responding to B&O demands, Martinsburg's mayor, A.P. Schutt, followed the example of Baltimore's mayor and ordered the arrest of the strike leaders.[17]

But Martinsburg was a workers' town, one sympathetic to the strikers. The following morning, Tuesday, July 17, the *Martinsburg Statesman* accused Garrett of "putting wages down to starvation point" and urged the workers to resist. While the *Chicago Tribune* opposed any untoward behavior on the part of the workers, it added that all the railroads had behaved with "insanity" in "falling upon their employees and razed their already two-or-three-times-reduced wages down to the starvation line." A large crowd of locals gathered that morning at the rail yard to show their support for the strikers. Backed by their community, the B&O's brakemen joined the strike and the crowd aided the workers in halting all freight traffic; passenger trains were allowed to go through so as not to inconvenience the public. Though there had not been an act of violence nor had any property been destroyed, B&O's vice president King sent a telegram to West Virginia governor Henry Mathews stating that there was a "riot" in Martinsburg and requested militia to restore order. Mathews took King's word for it and called out the Beverly Light Guards, a local militia company consisting mostly of railroad workers.[18]

The militia was initially uncertain of what was expected of them but quickly had little choice. One striker, William Vandergriff, attempted to halt a train, firing upon the militia. The militia opened fire and wounded Vandergriff so seriously that he died nine days later from his wounds. The *Martinsburg Statesman* blamed Mathews for the shooting and proclaimed Vandergriff "a martyr" killed for his beliefs, "shot down in sight of the lowly home whose inmates he was trying to shield from starvation." The engineer of the approaching train, a strikebreaker, witnessed the shooting and immediately got down from the engine, joining the strikers. The militia, as Colonel C.J. Faulkner complained bitterly to Governor Mathews, felt guilty over firing on a fellow worker, especially as they sympathized with the strikers, and refused to follow his orders. Finding the strikers "too formidable for me to cope with," Faulkner sent his men home.[19]

With the militia having deserted the field, B&O president Garrett demanded that Governor Mathews call for federal troops. Mathews was hoping to avoid an escalation of violence, so instead he ordered up the Moorefield militia, none of whom were railroad workers. Sending arms and ammunition to the hastily assembled troops, Mathews hoped that they would prove sufficient to stop the strike. Instead, by the time the new militia unit reached Martinsburg, the strike had spread all along the B&O line and from there was running "like a wave of fire along our principal lines of railroad."[20] In Keyser, white and black workers joined together and "soberly considered" their options, deciding that "at the present state of wages which the company has imposed on us, we cannot live and provide our wives and children with the necessities of life," and went out on strike. The governor's military deputy, Colonel Robert Delaplain, wired Mathews that the entire town of Martinsburg favored the strikers and that no one could be found willing to run the stalled trains, even when promised military protection. "The odds," he advised the governor, are "largely against our small force," and he joined Colonel Faulkner in recommending that two hundred U.S. Marines be sent to supplement the militia.[21] Mathews immediately took their advice and sent a telegram to President Hayes on July 18 requesting federal troops, as "it is impossible, with any force at my command, to execute the laws of the State." Garrett congratulated Mathews and sent a supportive telegram to Hayes encouraging the president to send troops immediately.[22]

But Hayes's willingness to use troops in a labor dispute could not be assumed. After all, in his inaugural address just four months earlier, the president had promised not to interfere in "the domestic affairs of the states." He had exercised this commitment to inaction in failing to respond to the disenfranchisement of blacks in the South, and many assumed he would take the same attitude toward the West Virginia strike, especially as there had been very little violence yet. But on the other hand, Tom Scott and other railroad leaders had played a significant role in winning the presidency for Hayes, and his cabinet was filled with men linked to the railroads: Secretary of State William M. Evarts and Secretary of the Navy Richard W. Thompson had both been railroad lawyers, while Attorney General Charles Devens and Secretary of War George W. McCrary had significant business connections to the railroads. Backed by his pro-railroad cabinet, Hayes acted swiftly, issuing a proclamation on the afternoon of July 18 giving strikers until noon the following day to desist and ordering General William H. French to lead the Second Artillery to Martinsburg. Hayes's proclamation declared the strike "unlawful and insurrectionary proceedings." The label "insurrection" quickly caught on and was used by many newspapers to describe events over the next two weeks.[23]

On the afternoon of July 19, the B&O prepared a train to leave Martinsburg for Baltimore under militia guard. Just as the engineer, N.B. Bedford, reached to open the train's throttle, his wife and daughter "climbed to the foot board, and pleaded, tears in their eyes, that he would not go." These women were declared "heroines" by the workers and were "applauded by other wives and children who had gathered around the engine." Bedford got down from the train and informed the railroad officials that he would not take the train anywhere. Vice President King fired everyone on strike, announcing that they would now be considered as trespassing on railroad property. He then rushed more strikebreakers to Martinsburg, informed the press that "the backbone of the strike has been broken," and succeeded in moving every train out of the company yards by the following day.[24]

Despite this defeat, workers met and resolved that they would rather "die by the bullet as starve to death by inches" and voted to continue their strike. A "manifesto" issued at Westernport, Maryland, on July 20 warned the B&O management that if they didn't restore the workers' wages, "we shall run their trains and locomotives into the river; we shall blow up their bridges; we shall tear up their railroads; and we shall consume their shops with fire." As if these threats of violence were not sufficient to get management's attention, the strikers also called on "the God of the poor and the oppressed" to stand with them against a company that had repeatedly and "unmercifully cut our wages and finally has reduced us to starvation."[25] The anguish of these workers resonated with other workers, regardless of industry, and that same day, Friday, July 20, the strike took an unusual direction, getting away from the control of the B&O's management and becoming the first national strike in American history.

In Cumberland, Maryland, striking rail workers, all of whom had been fired by a corporation that seemed to have power and the law on its side, faced the surprising vision of hundreds of canal workers and miners marching to join them. Declaring themselves on strike as well, these workers aided the railroad employees in uncoupling freight cars. These displays of working-class unity and frustration spread quickly along the line. At Keyser a train was run onto a siding and the crew taken off by angry strikers, their numbers greatly augmented by workers from other fields. The residents of Keyser thought "the whole thing grows out of too much pay and speculation among the head men—big salaries, wine suppers, free passes and presents to Congressmen for their votes," and all the while workers received starvation wages.[26] Events quickly proved the accuracy of strikers who claimed that "the working people everywhere are with us," as workers in factories and canneries throughout Maryland went out on strike. One local paper described the strikers as "a respectable body of men," who "receive every encouragement" in the state's towns. Those on the scene agreed that most people sided with the strikers: "There is no disguising the fact that nine-tenths of the people of this place sympathize with the strikers."[27] B&O president Garrett met with Governor John Carroll of Maryland and demanded that the militia be called out. The governor immediately followed Garrett's orders and called on General James R. Herbert to lead the Baltimore militia to Cumberland.[28]

That night, the emergency militia bell at Baltimore city hall was rung for the first time in the city's history. General Herbert had made a terrible mistake, as the bell was rung at 6 P.M., just as most workers were heading home. By 6:30 several thousand people had assembled at Camden Station, and they were not reporting for militia duty. Another crowd gathered in front of the Sixth Regiment Armory on Fayette and Front Streets, where recent road construction had left piles of rocks handy for the angry men and women to hurl at the gathering militia, who retreated inside. Everyone knew why the militia was being called out, and most of Baltimore did not think it right that their city's militia should be used against fellow workers, especially not those striking against the hated B&O.

That lack of enthusiasm had spread to the troops; Herbert found that just 120 men had reported for duty. Issuing twenty rounds to each soldier, he ordered his force to march to the train station. Even with the added protection of a company of police, the militia was twice driven back into the armory by the furious crowd. Ordered forth once more, the militia came out firing. "The streets were quickly deserted and the detachment passed by the *Sun*'s office, still firing random shots over their shoulders with apparent recklessness," shattering windows along the march route and killing eleven civilians and wounding at least forty more. Most of those shot were bystanders, including a fourteen-year-old newsboy for the *Baltimore News*, which declared that he was the sole support of his invalid mother. Half of the militia deserted on the way to the station, leaving Herbert with just fifty-nine men. As the soldiers boarded the train at Camden Station, a crowd estimated as several thousand angry citizens destroyed the telegraph office adjacent to the station and began hurling rocks and other projectiles at the train. The train crew hastily fled the scene, leaving the militia surrounded and taking cover in a nearby shed while the crowd turned its fury on the B&O, setting fire to numerous coaches and stoning the firemen and police who came to battle the flames.[29]

Prodded by Garrett, Governor Carroll sent a telegram to President Hayes requesting immediate federal assistance to restore order to Baltimore. Just before midnight, Hayes ordered General William Barry, commander of historic Fort McHenry, to gather all available soldiers and move immediately to relieve the encircled militia at Camden Station. Hayes then ordered three companies of regulars from their posts in New York and instructed General Winfield Scott Hancock to take personal command of the situation. But by midnight the crowd had dispersed and Carroll wired Hayes that the situation appeared to be under control. Hayes did not revoke his orders, fearing another outbreak of violence on the following day.[30]

By Sunday, July 22, some 1,200 federal troops patrolled Baltimore's streets, aided by the Maryland militia, which poured into the city. Camden yards enjoyed a guard of several hundred soldiers and a pair of Gatling guns. The police arrested scores of people, none of whom were strikers. B&O management made it clear that they would not compromise with the strikers, all of whom would be considered trespassers if they came onto company property. The strike continued, and the B&O continued to lose tens of thousands of dollars a day as their freight trains were unable to move through Baltimore despite the military presence.[31]

If the strike against the B&O had been the only significant labor action in July 1877, it would have been but an historical footnote, interesting primarily for the support it evoked from workers in other industries. But the actions against the B&O proved to be just the initial push that overcame a natural inertia-resisting action and set off an ever-accelerating sequence of labor actions unlike anything ever seen in the United States. As the St. Louis newspaperman Joseph A. Dacus later wrote in his book on the Great Strike, newspapers gave primacy to the coverage of these events from the first protests at Camden Junction on July 16 until the strike drowned out all other news, drawing "exclusive attention to social *emeute* [insurrection] on this side of the Atlantic, unparalleled in the annals of time." The front page of every paper in the country carried headlines—starting on July 19 in the *Rocky Mountain News*—on what was being called "the Great Strike." From coast to coast, Americans picked up their newspapers with headlines screaming, "King Mob, the Strike Degenerating into Lawlessness," "The Strike Spreading," "The Great Strike: It Is Still Spreading with Frightful Rapidity," "The New Rebellion," "Riotous Outbreaks Still Increasing," "The Contagion Still Spreading," "Bloodshed," "Fire and Blood, Pillage, Confusion, Anarchy," and "Chaos Reigns Supreme." In areas unaffected by the strike, newspapers fed a sense of panic. Even in remote Colorado Springs, the paper aroused its readers with tales of "murder and arson" while blaming the greedy railroads for driving their workers to desperation.[32]

Throughout the nation, workers read of the actions of the railroad strikers and identified with their long-standing grievances. As most contemporaries reported, that sympathy spread even into the middle class, not least because everyone seemed to hate the railroads, even other businessmen. A Pittsburgh doctor wrote that the city's business leaders "have been bitter enemies of the road [the Pennsylvania Railroad] on account of the discrimination in freights that existed." It was cheaper to ship from Chicago to Philadelphia than to Pittsburgh, even though the trains passed through the latter city on their way east. The same rate inequalities, which appeared capricious to most observers and perfectly logical to rail management, applied nationwide. Only those living in the major hubs of Boston, New York, Philadelphia, and Chicago benefited from the high-volume discounts offered by the railroads. The self-interest of local businessmen thus melded humanistic sentiments that the railroads had reduced workers' wages "to a starvation point" and treated them unjustly.[33]

At one level the emerging "Great Strike" was actually a series of local strikes, most started by the refusal of a few men to move their trains. But the absence of any organizing body should not indicate that this national upheaval was little more than a coincidence of unrelated events. Quite the contrary; in the many individual labor actions of 1877 we witness the American working class struggling to form some sort of common bond among workers based upon their shared sufferings over the previous four years. While there is no shortage of evidence of increased class consciousness—of workers coming to identify themselves by their economic position regardless of other variables, including skill level and race—American workers sought above all else practical ways to negotiate with their employers for safer and fairer workplaces, and for a living wage. The danger of working on America's railroads was greater than in any other industrial nation in the world, all of which had some measure of government oversight of work conditions. In contrast, the United States left safety entirely in the hands of the employers; it was up to each company to determine if they wanted to protect the lives of their workers. The attitude of most American employers—a perspective consistently upheld by the nation's courts—was well expressed by the Pennsylvania Railroad's official rules for employees: "6. The regular compensation of employees covers all risk or liability to accident. 7. If an employee is disabled by sickness or any other cause, the right to claim compensation is not recognized." Like other American railways, the Pennsylvania refused to equip its trains with readily available safety devices, resulting in hundreds of unnecessary deaths every year.[34]

In these hard times, labor was just another entry on a balance sheet to the leading industrialists, a cost that could be reduced through layoffs or wage cuts. This attitude is well revealed in a typical report to Andrew Carnegie from one of his managers in March 1877: "Had an unfortunate accident this morning," William Jones wrote. "Rope on cupola hoist broke and cage fell catching the Hoist Boy in the act of crossing under, crushing him to jelly." Rather than expressing anything approximating sympathy, Jones blamed "the boy's carelessness" for his death, which "Delayed Works slightly. Damage slight." Carnegie expressed his contempt for his workers in other ways, determining that he would have no unions in his plants. In November 1876 he closed his plants for maintenance, sending the workers off on a five-week furlough without pay, a common event at the time. When the workers returned in December, they found that they could get their jobs back only if they signed an agreement to not join a union and to quit if they already belonged to one. Those who refused to sign were blacklisted for life from working for Carnegie.[35]

While management embraced an unabashed laissez-faire attitude—that workers individually contracted with management and if they did not like their situation, they should just leave—workers hoped to avoid this harsh choice of accepting starvation or jumping off a cliff. Neither option appeared sensible to America's workers, and limiting the choice in that fashion could only politely be termed ludicrous. But in the absence of national unions, workers perceived few options but the traditional ones of taking to the streets, just as their predecessors had done in Boston and Philadelphia in the 1770s or in France in 1789. Confident that it held all the trump cards, management did not expect its workers to act in any serious sustained fashion. As the superintendent of the western division of Pennsylvania Railroad, Robert Pitcairn, stated on July 16, he expected no problem, as his workers "were always complaining about something" but never did anything. A few days later he left Pittsburgh just two hours before that heritage of urban protest exploded, briefly threatening to tear apart the nation's social fabric.[36]

Pittsburgh in Flames

On the morning of July 19 two brakemen and a flagman in the Pennsylvania Railroad's Pittsburgh yards refused to leave on a scheduled doubleheader. When the dispatcher sought replacements, the other workers displayed solidarity and refused to replace the three strikers, instead declaring that they were also on strike. Just as the workers on the Baltimore & Ohio had done in Martinsburg, the workers then surrounded the switches, uncoupling engines and refusing to allow any trains to leave. Within a few hours the railroad workers had been joined by striking miners and crowds of the unemployed. Together they blocked the tracks throughout Pittsburgh, bringing all freight traffic to a halt. As in Maryland and West Virginia, they allowed passenger and mail trains to continue their journeys. When an engineer attempted to start up one train, a crowd surged onto the tracks in front of it, and the engineer stepped down from the cab. "It is a question of bread or blood," one worker told a hesitating engineer; "if I go to the penitentiary I can get bread and water, and that is about all I can get now." When the senior Pennsylvania Railroad official on site, David Watt, called on Mayor William McCarthy to provide fifty police for protection, the mayor regretted to say that recent budget cuts had reduced the police force from 236 to 116 officers and that he could spare only 11 officers; just 6 showed up.[37]

Dissatisfied with this paltry police presence, Watt tried to talk with the mayor, only to learn that McCarthy had left the city. Watt then turned to Allegheny County sheriff Hugh M. Fife for help. Fife came to the scene and spoke to a crowd of about five hundred workers, ordering them to go home. The crowd roared back for Fife to go home, which he did. Watt frantically sought protection for the nine hundred loaded cars sitting in the rail yard, without success. A mass meeting of the suddenly revived Trainmen's Union, which the Pennsylvania Railroad had killed just a month earlier, welcomed every level of railroad employee, from yard worker to engineer, and unanimously adopted resolutions setting forth their goals of restoring wages and ending doubleheaders. They found their strike solidly supported by the local press. "The people of this city sympathize with the strikers," wrote the *Pittsburgh Critic*. "They are incensed beyond measure, with the cold, corrupt legislation which has fostered the colder and more corrupt organization known as the Pennsylvania Railroad Company." Sheriff Fife judged that "the whole laboring class" and most of "the responsible portion of the people of Pittsburgh" sided with the workers. Many people found management guilty of being "reckless to the verge of criminality," using corporate profits to gamble on the stock market, form "crushing combinations, and generally scheming to enrich themselves."[38] This perception of broad-based community support would be seconded after the strike by the legislative committee appointed to investigate these events, which discovered "a large portion of the people also believed that the railroad company was not dealing fairly by its men in making the last reduction in wages."[39]

Public support found practical expression when a group of leading Pittsburgh businessmen approached the railroad about putting forth some counteroffer in order to begin negotiations with the workers. But the Pennsylvania Railroad dismissed the suggestion as ridiculous; management would not talk with the workers. Instead, the railroad decided to look outside the city for support. The company's lawyer, John Scott, wrote a telegram requesting troops which he then persuaded Sheriff Fife to send to the state's adjutant general, James W. Latta. Left in charge by Pennsylvania's governor George Hartranft, off touring the West on Tom Scott's personal train, Latta complied, ordering General A.J. Pearson to muster the Sixth Division of the state militia, based in Pittsburgh. Only 250 of the division's 326 men reported for duty, and General Pearson wired Latta warning that most of the men were on the side of the strikers and suggested that troops be sent from Philadelphia to buttress his efforts. Latta agreed and ordered the First Division to leave for Pittsburgh immediately. At 2 A.M. on July 21, six hundred militia left Philadelphia, stopping at Harrisburg to pick up ammunition and two Gatling guns.[40]

The morning of Saturday, July 21, found strikers camped along the railroad line and companies of Pittsburgh militia nearby, mostly with their arms stacked. The imposition of outside troops infuriated the people of Pittsburgh, especially as word spread that the Philadelphia militia boasted of teaching Pittsburgh a lesson. Crowds of sympathetic citizens milled around, and a friendly atmosphere surrounded the strike as the local militia chatted comfortably with the workers about the inequities of the Pennsylvania Railroad. Again a group of prominent local businessmen attempted to persuade the railroad to operate with some degree of diplomacy, this time suggesting that they not try to move any trains until Monday to give tempers time to cool and to ensure that those with jobs would be at work rather than milling around the strikers. They also pointed out that no reliance could be put in the Pittsburgh militia, which included far too many workers. But the railroad's vice president, Alexander Cassatt (brother of painter Mary Cassatt), refused to hear of anything that might smack of giving in to workers and stated flatly that it was the government's responsibility to make sure that the railroads ran without hindrance. Meanwhile, a workers' meeting pledged to avoid the use of violence and not to interfere with passenger trains or mail cars, while insisting that the strike would last "until we are allowed sufficient wages for our labor to keep our families from actual want." They also thanked the "public at large" for "the sympathy so fully tendered us."[41]

The Philadelphia militia arrived at the Union Depot at 1 P.M. and quickly took positions along the line so that the Pennsylvania Railroad could start running its freight trains at once. Rumors flew as hundreds of people, including curious Pittsburgh militia, gathered at the Outer Depot, site of the loaded freight trains. At 5 P.M. columns of Philadelphia militia with bayonets fixed, led by Superintendent Robert Pitcairn of the Pennsylvania Railroad, moved on the Outer Depot. Sheriff Fife accompanied the troops, carrying a warrant issued at the request of the Pennsylvania Railroad for the arrest of unnamed individuals on the charge of rioting. The crowd began hissing and hurling insults at the Philadelphia militia. Suddenly, without prior warning, the lead militia units charged the crowd with leveled bayonets, stabbing people indiscriminately. As civilians fell to the ground, rocks began flying at the troops. An officer shouted "Fire!" Without hesitation, the militia fired directly into the crowd, which fled in every direction. Twenty people, including one member of the Pittsburgh militia, a woman, and three children, lay dead on the ground, with at least another twenty-nine wounded. A grand jury later found this initial militia fire "an unauthorized, willful and wanton killing," and declared that they could call it "by no other name than murder."[42] Local papers condemned "the Roughs of Philadelphia" who shot down citizens in cold blood, and labeled the massacre "The Lexington of the Labor Conflict."[43]

As the screams of the wounded replaced the sound of gunfire, the crowd dispersed, spreading the word of this outrageous atrocity. News of the militia's actions blazed through the city, and thousands of workers from the many factories and mines in the area rushed to the Outer Depot. Throughout Pittsburgh, furious workers broke into gun shops, appropriating arms and ammunition. Within the hour a massive crowd, enraged over this latest injustice, drove the Philadelphia militia into panicked retreat. The Philadelphia officers, seeing that scores of civilians were armed, searched for aid, but the police and the Pittsburgh militia had evaporated. The city was in the hands of the crowd. Rushing for the roundhouse in the nearby depot, the Philadelphia militia attempted to take defensive positions while the crowd surrounded the building and smashed every window. Avoiding a direct attack on the well-armed militia, the crowd began setting fire to all the railroad property in the area. While some set fire to the freight cars, others looted them, emptying everything they could before the cars were engulfed in flames. As the railcars burned, the fire department rushed to the scene, only to be stopped by the thousands of citizens blocking access to the rail yards. The crowd allowed the firefighters to save property across from the Union Depot, but not the property of the Pennsylvania Railroad.[44]

The fire burned out of control, spreading over three miles from the depot to the city limits, destroying 39 buildings belonging to the Pennsylvania Railroad, 104 engines, 46 passenger cars, and more than 1,200 freight cars. Every building from the Union Depot to 28th Street between Liberty and Penn suffered fire damage. The massive Union Depot itself fell to the flames, as did the enormous grain elevator adjacent to the depot, which rose 150 feet and took several hours to burn. Throughout the conflagration, the crowd kept up a steady barrage of small-arms fire and hurled rocks and other projectiles at the barricaded militia. An effort was made to send a blazing boxcar into the roundhouse, but it derailed before it broke through the closed doors. At first light the following morning, smoke from the fire began filling the roundhouse and the troops decided to take their chances on escaping the siege and making their way to the U.S. Arsenal at the end of Penn Avenue. The arsenal housed tens of thousands of firearms, cannon, and masses of gunpowder behind strong stone walls. As the militia marched down Penn Avenue, they drew fire from windows, rooftops, and alleys. The militia returned fire, their training demonstrating its value in their deadlier shots, which claimed another twenty civilian lives as three of their number fell dead (the number of wounded is unknown but probably reached two hundred). But the militia's ordeal did not end at the arsenal, for its commander, Major A.R. Buffington, refused to open his door to the militia, telling them that he did not want the crowd turning their fury on his building. He did agree to take in the wounded but forced the militia to continue their hazardous march over the river and out of the city, where they finally threw themselves down in exhaustion on the hills facing Pittsburgh. From this vantage point they could see the pall hanging above the smoldering ruins of the train yards.[45]

Nothing like the Pittsburgh riots had ever happened in the United States before, with the possible exception of the 1863 Draft Riots in New York City. Militia then had fought a ferocious battle through the streets of a major American city and been defeated. Though they had inflicted many more casualties than they themselves suffered, the Philadelphia militia had been chased out of town and goaded a crowd into destroying the property they were supposed to be protecting. Fearing another Pittsburgh, other cities took numerous precautions, such as canceling all police leaves and calling for militia support before their own workers set fire to the city.[46] The press outside of Pittsburgh went into hysteria mode over this vision of "Pittsburgh Delivered Up to the Mercies of the Mob," proclaiming the "reign of anarchy" a victory for "madness" and "Barbarism" and the imminent collapse of Western civilization. A few journals perceived a legitimate protest, but kept their support muted.[47]

In Pittsburgh, the workers felt they had won an important victory over the railroad, and their strike spread to other industries. Of particular significance was the participation of the large labor force from the National Tube Works, who marched from mill to mill pulling the workers out on strike. By Monday evening most of the workers in the city were out on strike. That same night the railroad workers met and placed blame for the destruction on Tom Scott for refusing to negotiate and once more called on the company to parlay. The editor of the *Pittsburgh Post*, James P. Barr, supported the workers' call for arbitration and personally contacted Scott to request some sort of compromise. Barr urged Scott not to place all his faith in the military. Scott dismissed Barr as a meddling liberal and remained certain that military force could rein in his workers.[48]

But the strike spread to Philadelphia, the Pennsylvania Railroad's home city. On July 22 rail workers in Philadelphia walked off the job and called on the company to halt its freight traffic. With much of the militia in Pittsburgh, and fearing that the same sort of destruction could strike his rail yards in Philadelphia, Scott reluctantly conceded to the workers' demand, and the Pennsylvania Railroad came to a halt. In Altoona, a crowd of strikers and their supporters attacked two trains carrying militia to reinforce Pittsburgh. The troops on one train surrendered, were fed by the victorious workers, and then agreed to return to Philadelphia. On their return journey, they were again captured by workers, this time in Harrisburg, given another meal, and sent home.[49]

Urged on by Tom Scott, Pennsylvania adjutant general James Latta first called for federal troops on July 22, but he received no reply from President Hayes. At 7 P.M. that night, Governor Hartranft wired the president from Wyoming, requesting regulars for duty in his state. Hayes, a stickler for Constitutional form, still refused to act because two key words were missing from both of the previous telegrams. So Hartranft, on his way back to Pennsylvania, sent another telegram from Nebraska: "I amend my requisition from the general government by adding the words domestic insurrection." To buttress the governor's plea for aid, Tom Scott suggested to the president that the strikers were waging war against the country and should be treated as enemies of the United States. Hayes made the U.S. Army available to the railroads.[50]

Workers in Reading were emboldened by the news from Pittsburgh and seized the property of the hated Philadelphia & Reading Railroad on July 22. Railroad president Franklin Gowen immediately called on the militia to beat off the workers, but the members of the Reading Rifles announced that "if ordered to fire, they will lay down their arms; that they are workingmen and do not desire to kill other workingmen." The city of Reading embraced their militia for what they perceived as an act of courage while the state acted on Gowen's behalf by sending General Frank Reeder with the Fourth and Sixteenth regiments to protect the railroad's property. The Reading newspaper reported on the ensuing events with a mix of anger and sorrow: "The EAGLE has never been called upon to chronicle a more horrible slaughter of its peaceful and law-abiding citizens as is its duty to-day." In what the paper called "one of the most terrible butcheries that has ever disgraced the pages of Reading's local history," the imported militia marched from the depot in the early evening of July 23 to where the strikers blocked the tracks and, without warning, fired several volleys into the crowd. The casualties included strikers and bystanders, women and children, and five police officers who had succeeded in keeping the streets clear and the crowd peaceful. The militia wheeled about and fired randomly up 7th and Penn Streets, killing ten and wounding forty. "It was the old story of military interference and military blunder," the newspaper lamented, as "the innocent are shot and the guilty escape." Reading's sheriff R. Yorgey shared the newspaper's outrage, as neither military nor civil authorities had informed him of the imminent arrival of the militia or of their plans, nor had his aid been requested to maintain order, and several of his officers were among the victims. The city was in an uproar over what the newspaper called "cold-blooded murder," and the coroner launched an investigation into General Reeder's actions. Since it appeared that the citizens of Reading were about to turn on the militia and do battle, General Winfield Hancock sent federal troops into the city to restore order.[51]

Meanwhile, out in Terre Haute, Indiana, members of the Brotherhood of Locomotive Firemen, which included a young worker named Eugene V. Debs, met on July 22 to discuss the recent strikes back East. Their employer, the Vandalia line, had cut their wages by a third during the depression. The Brotherhood voted to request a 15 percent pay increase for all employees, threatening that otherwise they would follow the example of their eastern colleagues and strike. When Vandalia's president, Riley McKeen, refused to respond, the workers went on strike, stopping all freight cars and vowing to drink no alcohol until they had won. McKeen surprised everyone by announcing that he would stop all traffic on his line, except mail cars, until the dispute was resolved. The striking workers professed their faith in McKeen's "honor and integrity," as well as in his willingness to resolve the strike amicably, and assured the people of Terre Haute that they would do nothing to interfere with the city's business, would protect all railway property, and would return to work as soon as their wages reached a level that could support their families. They asked for support from their fellow citizens in "our resistance to the encroachments of capital upon unprotected labor." However, they added, they did not welcome support from "irresponsible parties such as tramps and roughs." An odd mixture of the language of class warfare and class harmony, the strikers' manifesto placed all the blame for the current problems on the monopolistic practices of Tom Scott's Pennsylvania line, and aroused wide public support.[52] Mayor H. Fairbanks and Senator Daniel Voorhees both called for McKeen to meet the workers' demands and praised the strikers for their adherence to nonviolence. Workers proclaimed that they were battling against the eastern monopoly controlled by Tom Scott and did not blame their own bosses for being unable to resist this tyrant.[53]

Meanwhile the strike had spread to several other lines in the Midwest, including those in Indianapolis, known as the "City of Brotherly Freight Trains" for the many lines that came together there. Nervous military commanders, seeing themselves outnumbered by the thousands of rail workers in the area, moved all arms out of the Indianapolis Arsenal to prevent their seizure and stationed fifty regulars at the arsenal to be on hand in case of trouble. When a crowd stopped a train on the Indianapolis, Bloomington & Western line, a railroad in receivership, Judge Walter Q. Gresham of the Seventh Circuit used this action as sufficient excuse to swear in a pack of new U.S. marshals, including his friend and future president Benjamin Harrison, and arm them with guns from the federal government. The judge wired Hayes that the situation was "most critical and dangerous," with the public entirely on the side of the workers and distrustful of local officials, and the mob the "supreme authority" in Indianapolis. He called on the president to send more troops. Though Hayes knew from Signal Corps officers that there was "not the least sign of violence" in Indianapolis, as the workers were doing little more than protecting railroad property and abstaining from drinking, he sent two hundred troops anyway in support of Gresham's contention that a strike against a railroad in receivership was contempt of court and an affront to the national government.[54]

While Judge Gresham was panicking, General Benjamin Spooner was talking with the strikers at the Vandalia yards in Terre Haute, explaining to them the legal complications of interfering with companies in federal receivership. The workers understood and handed over control of the rail yard. The Third U.S. Infantry arrived on Friday, and Gresham ordered the arrest of strike leaders and the opening of all lines, even those not in receivership. The following day the strikers capitulated, putting an end to their hopes of attaining a commonalty of interests with their employer. Judge Gresham sentenced four strike leaders to six months in jail. The chief prosecution witness was Riley McKeen.[55]

In early July the Louisville & Nashville and the Louisville, Cincinnati & Lexington railroads both cut wages 10 percent. On July 23, workers of the latter railroad went to the judge overseeing the bankrupt line, H. W. Bruce, and requested that he reverse management's wage cut, which, amazingly, he did. The following day, workers of the Louisville & Nashville met with that line's president, Dr. E.D. Sandiford, to present similar demands and also received satisfaction. Excited by these developments, workers in several other Louisville industries struck for the reversal of pay cuts. Mayor Charles D. Jacob warned the workers that in other cities the tramps had incited trouble, leaving "poor workingmen" to pay the cost. The mayor and chief of police Isaac W. Edwards then began recruiting reliable citizens for a defense force and sent men to collect weapons from the Frankfort Arsenal. When Mayor Jacob tried to speak in front of the courthouse, he was shouted down by a mixed-race crowd of some six hundred workers, who began throwing stones from local excavations at streetlights and through windows. One of those shattered windows belonged to the family of a twenty-year-old Harvard Law School student home for the summer, Louis Brandeis. Outraged by this damage to their bay window, Louis and his brother

Alfred volunteered to serve in the mayor's hastily assembled militia and were provided with guns. (Given his complete lack of familiarity with firearms and appallingly bad eyesight, it was fortunate that young Louis was not called upon to level his weapon.) A thousand volunteers, including the Brandeis brothers, patrolled the streets while the mayor wired Governor James B. McCreary requesting arms, ammunition, and more militia. The governor sent four hundred state militia and an additional seven hundred rifles. Tensions ran high on Wednesday, July 25, as workers and militia marched through the city, though it was obvious who had the better weapons. When the workers marched on the depot, they were met by fifty police who opened fire on the crowd, which fled. Mayor Jacob called for federal troops, but they proved unnecessary as the strike lost steam before this display of force.[56]

Rail workers in western New York took a different stance, one aimed at avoiding both direct confrontation and abject capitulation. The Erie Railroad was in receivership, under the direct supervision of a federal judge. When workers struck against the Erie in late June, the head of the railroad, Hugh J. Jewett, warned them that they would be held in contempt of court if they persisted, and, on July 1, he fired the workers' representatives. Initially the workers buckled under and continued to go to work. But on July 19 the Erie's employees, emboldened by strikes elsewhere, met and demanded that their fired representatives be restored to their positions and recent wage cuts reversed. When the company once more refused even to talk with the workers, the latter voted to strike, took an oath to drink no alcohol, and informed the saloons in the railroad's home terminus of Hornellsville that they were not to serve alcohol to any railroad workers until the strike ended. Although there had not been a single act of violence, not even against property, New York's governor Lucius Robinson immediately responded to requests from Erie's management and sent militia units to Hornellsville to put down the strike. However, the strikers, many of whom knew members of the militia, greeted the state troops when they arrived in Hornellsville, and discipline collapsed. Jewett asked the workers to send a negotiator to meet with him and other railroad officials. As the workers' representative, Barney Donahue, left this meeting, he was arrested by a group of railroad detectives serving a warrant under Jewett's name charging Donahue with contempt of court.[57]

On July 22 the Erie attempted to run its trains out of Hornellsville, inspiring one of the most creative tactics of the Great Strike. Men and women from the town, workers and supporters, soaped the rails for a quarter of a mile up Tiptop Mountain, one of the steepest grades in New York. As the Erie's engines roared up the mountain out of town with their strikebreaker crews, the trains lost traction and began sliding downhill. Workers rushed aboard, pushing aside the confused militia, disabling the trains' brakes and forcing all the passengers and crew off. They then detached the passenger cars and sent them rushing back into the Erie yards, sending engines and mail cars on their way over soap-free tracks so the workers could not be accused of interfering with the federal mail. The passengers and militia were left to walk back to town. Erie officials tried two more times to send a train out of Hornellsville, but were defeated by soap both times and gave up.[58]

Disgusted with events in Hornellsville and the failure of the militia to fire upon the strikers, the *New York Times* called for the governor to send in militia prepared to use their guns, as had the militia in Pennsylvania. Governor Robinson agreed with the *Times*'s brutal analysis of the situation and ordered the Twenty-third Regiment from Brooklyn to Hornellsville. The train bringing the militia on July 23 came to a screaming halt several miles short of Hornellsville: the strikers had torn up the track. Rather than firing on ranks of workers, the soldiers found themselves pressed into repair duty. The militia finally reached Hornellsville that night and took up positions around the yard. When the strikers attempted to approach the soldiers, as they had done earlier, a single shot was fired over their heads and the workers retreated.[59]

But frightening the workers with armed troops ready to kill did not get any trains out of Hornellsville. Frustrated by the workers' inspired protests, the Erie's management finally agreed to meet with workers' representatives without firing them. The workers assured management that they would not use violence or damage any property, and were even willing to accept the wage cut, but that they would continue on strike until their previously fired representatives were restored to their jobs. Determined to leave no doubt as to who was boss, Jewett shouted that he would not allow anyone to tell him how to run his business and repeated management's party line: the workers should be pleased that the company allowed the strikers to return to work and if they did not like the conditions, they should quit. He also violated his pledge and had five labor leaders arrested for contempt of court. Not surprisingly, word of these arrests ended any willingness on the part of the workers to compromise with the Erie.[60]

As this battle dragged on, business owners in Hornellsville feared the sort of violence and destruction that had raged through Pittsburgh. Where Pittsburgh's business leaders had tried to talk reason to management, Hornellsville's businessmen projected the same sort of creative thinking as had the workers and attempted to resolve the strike by promising to support the strikers' representatives until they found new jobs. Making that offer public, they quietly applied pressure on the Erie's management to make some small concession. The railroad finally agreed that no workers would be dismissed as a consequence of the strike and reversed the wage cuts for many of them. With the backing of local businesses, the workers agreed on July 26 to end their strike. The Union Pacific, whose workers were also on the verge of striking, followed the example of the Erie Railroad and granted a similar list of minor concessions to avoid a strike. Most New

York newspapers thought the Erie had set a terrible precedent by even talking to the workers.[61]

The Strike Spreads

The hostility of most of the nation's press to workers grew from a very real fear of revolution. The *Brooklyn Eagle*, the paper once edited by Walt Whitman, thought, "It is not pleasant to think of men being mowed down by soldiers, but it will be a much worse spectacle for the country to have a mob triumphant in a state like West Virginia than to have the life blown out of men who refuse to recognize the right of every American to control his own labor and his own property." The nation's leading journals repeatedly called on the railroads to not give in to what they saw as extortion. *The Nation* declared that "it would be a national calamity" if business made any "concession as to wages or the retention of persons engaged in the strike." To restore wage cuts would be to surrender power to "a body of day laborers of the lowest grade." Nor should business negotiate with workers; violence was the correct response. The *Railroad Gazette* called for the strikers to be "shot on the spot like highway robbers."[62] Most East Coast and Midwest papers refused to acknowledge the slightest hint of legitimacy in the workers' claims, fully accepting the standard view that those unhappy with their jobs should just quit and look elsewhere. The *New York Times's* description of the strikers offers an impressive list of adjectives and pejoratives: disaffected elements, roughs, hoodlums, rioters, mob, suspicious-looking individuals, bad characters, thieves, blacklegs, looters, communists, rabble, labor-reform agitators, dangerous class of people, gangs, tramps, drunken section men, lawbreakers, and on through another twenty-four negative portrayals ending with "idiots."[63]

The prevailing free-market ideology allowed even a paper arguing that the workers' "scanty pay" was sufficient "proof of something widely wrong" with the economy to insist that "pity for the troubles which have disturbed the rioter, and for the blindness which leads him to violence, is not incompatible with the sternness which meets him with bullets." It is little wonder that labor leaders often charged the press with working for "the interests of the monopolies and tyrannical capitalists," while the Missouri legislator J.J. McBride condemned the press for taking the side of management against "American citizens, who endeavored to make an honorable living."[64]

Of course, not all of America's newspapers were terribly impressed by the arguments of railroad's management, especially their insistence that they were suffering too. "The officials can build palaces, the laborer can rent a hovel," charged the *Pittsburgh Critic*. "These railroad authorities can afford salaries that will secure the costliest luxuries and sustain an apish aristocracy, [but] cannot extend the salary to meet the commonest necessaries of life, to the beggared, starving, crushed laborer and his family."[65] The *Missouri Republican*, generally antagonistic to labor, felt that "if the laboring men of this country must choose between revolution and abject submission to the heartless demand of capital, they will certainly not be condemned by this journal if they prefer war to starvation." All four of Chicago's major papers initially supported the strikers, holding that the railroads gained their profits by cutting the wages of workingmen "to the starvation point."[66]

Chicago's officials did not share the confidence of the city's newspapers in the pacific intentions of the workers. In the aftermath of events in Pittsburgh, Mayor Monroe Heath met with law enforcement officials and, confidentially, with the commanders of the recently organized Illinois National Guard, ordering them to keep all armories under close guard and prepare for trouble. The mayor also persuaded Secretary of War McCrary to send the Twenty-second Infantry to Chicago even though there had not yet been any incidences of violence. These secret preparations became public on Monday, July 23, 1877, with the papers reporting on the mobilization of 450 policemen and 2,000 militia from the First Regiment, the so-called sons of capital, and the Second Regiment, known for its high concentration of workers. The Chicago Citizens' Association, a group of leading businessmen, gave the city a Gatling gun, four cannon, one hundred guns, and thousands of rounds of ammunition to be used in case of an uprising.[67] That same evening the socialist Workingmen's Party held a mass protest meeting drawing an estimated fifteen thousand people—making it probably the largest such public meeting yet held in the city. For three hours this "Grand Army of Starvation" marched around the industrial areas of Chicago carrying signs in German, French, and English with slogans such as, "We want work not charity" and "Why does overproduction cause starvation?"[68]

The *Chicago Tribune* reported that the workers were orderly and that the Workingmen's Party, "contrary to general expectation, counseled (at least openly) moderation, and deprecated any resort to violence." Nonetheless, the press found these socialists frightening, drawing attention to a speech by activist Albert Parsons that "bordered upon the inflammatory."[69] Parsons, a former Confederate officer married to a former slave and living in exile after fleeing Texas just ahead of a Klan lynch mob, praised the strikers in the East for standing up for their rights and refusing to become "vagrants and tramps." While he regretted the violence, Parsons understood that "our distressed and suffering brothers" were driven to these actions by desperation. He condemned the press for vilifying labor unions as communist and for being more interested in sex and crime than the hardship of their readers, and recommended that they "go to the factories and workshops to see how the toiling millions give away their lives to the rich bosses of the country." Proclaiming labor the source of all wealth, Parsons called on the workers to take control of the railroads and end their slavery: "It rests with us to say whether we shall allow the capitalist to go on [exploiting us], or whether we shall organize ourselves." The crowd enthusiastically endorsed a resolution condemning "our suicidal system of 'free competition.'"[70]

Later that night the Michigan Central switchmen went on strike and were joined the next morning, July 24, by workers in the Central's shops and freight yards. They marched together to the yards of the Baltimore & Ohio and the Illinois Central, pulling ever more workers into the strike and into a spontaneous meeting, where the crowd approved the statement, "We hope to gain our rights, bread for our families, and a decent living for ourselves." They then continued their march through the city, drawing out ever more workers and chanting, "Down with the Thieving Monopolies" and "Down with the Wages of Slavery." Workers from factories, packinghouses, and lumberyards joined the strike, and the crowd stopped all freight traffic through the city, persuading officials of several railroad companies to go along with the strike and make no effort to run their trains. Whenever they encountered squads of police, the crowds dispersed and went elsewhere, avoiding any provocation that might lead to violence.[71]

The strike briefly eradicated Chicago's bitter ethnic divisions, as class consciousness united many former enemies. More than a thousand Irish packinghouse workers, many hefting butcher knives, marched under a large banner reading "Workingmen's Rights" down Archer Avenue toward Halsted Street, where a battle raged between strikers and police at the viaduct. As they marched they entered and closed many lumberyards and other businesses, intimidating employers into promising pay raises for their workers. At Halsted they encountered both the police and a crowd of Czech workers, who broke into loud cheers for the Irish, a traditional ethnic adversary. Some of the Chicago newspapers were becoming nervous, fearful that the strikes they had supported might get out of hand and quickly produce a Chicago Commune, and expressed concern over this unity of workers who usually formed their gangs along ethnic lines. The *Chicago Tribune* called it "one of the most terrible, audacious, and unreasonable" events of the period, yet the reporter demonstrated his respect by writing, "They were men in every sense of the word, . . . brave and daring, and scattered terror in their way."[72]

On July 25 Mayor Heath closed all saloons and ordered the fire bells rung to summon the militia. The Grand Army of the Republic, veterans of the Civil War, sent volunteers, and Heath, as did so many mayors, organized companies of the "better class of citizens" to combat the workers. Gun stores were selling out of their wares as the middle-class prepared for class war. Police swinging clubs broke up a Workingmen's Party meeting of an estimated five thousand workers; "the neighborhood was given over to riot and skull-smashing." Neither the police nor the city government had any patience for First Amendment rights at such a time, and another workers' rally at the corner of Market and Madison

Streets was scattered by the police when they fired a warning volley. The day ended with three workers dead and eight seriously wounded.[73]

The city's Common Council held an emergency session, declaring "a rebellion against lawful authority." The council called upon loyal citizens to join the special police to battle the insurrection and gave Mayor Heath authority to spend any funds he thought necessary to restore order. Matching this stick with a carrot, the Common Council admitted that "thousands of workingmen are idle in the city of Chicago at the present time, whose families are suffering for the necessaries of life," and authorized the city to borrow $500,000 for construction projects. The mayor addressed a meeting at the Moody and Sankey Tabernacle, calling for five thousand volunteers, especially those "who have served during the War." Reverend Robert Collyer blessed this enterprise "in defense of order and of our homes" from a mob that had stopped "the great wheel of commerce." Two hundred veterans immediately formed a volunteer force, the police supplying them with Springfield rifles and forty rounds each, while one hundred German volunteers formed themselves into a cavalry unit. The Twenty-second U.S. Artillery arrived, followed by four hundred men from the First Regiment of the Illinois National Guard.[74]

At every level, public officials were terrified that Chicago would go the way of Pittsburgh. Mayor Heath appealed to Illinois governor Shelby Cullom to request further federal help, and the governor telegrammed President Hayes, who immediately ordered the Ninth Infantry under General R.C. Drum to the scene. By July 26 an estimated twenty thousand men were ready to battle the strike in Chicago: the National Guard, private militia companies, volunteers, the police, and the U.S. Army. The *Inter Ocean*, which had been sympathetic to the strikers just four days earlier, was now demanding that the city "squelch them out, stamp them out, sweep them out of existence with grape shot."[75]

What ensued was the Chicago Police Riot of July 26. Strikers near the Halsted Street viaduct began stopping streetcars, which drew a large detachment of police who forced the crowd away. More strikers and their supporters appeared and pushed back against the police, who were reinforced in their turn. Clubbing furiously, the police drove the crowd over the viaduct and down to 16th Street, but a crowd of some five thousand workers arrived and the police fled to the high ground of the viaduct and began firing on the crowd, shooting at least six men. Running out of ammunition, the police turned and fled, running into militia and more police coming to their aid. The militia charged the crowd, the police following, clubbing every civilian they could reach. People scattered before this onslaught, with the police and militia in pursuit. In the midst of this violent chaos, U.S. Army units and the Second Regiment of the Illinois National Guard arrived, complete with a pair of cannon. The fleeing civilians reached 12th Street where another crowd had gathered to attend a meeting of German cabinetmakers at

Turner Hall. Police and volunteers rushed into this crowd and then ran into the building, beating bystanders at random. The Chicago police attacking Turner Hall were commanded by a pair of sergeants named Householder and Brennan, the former leading the charge inside while the latter directed forces out in the street. When the hall's owner protested to Householder, that officer brought his club down hard on the man's head and ordered his forces to carry on with the attack on the German cabinetmakers. Several officers opened fire with their revolvers as the cabinetmakers frantically leapt out of windows. Meanwhile, according to numerous witnesses, Sergeant Brennan calmly shot at anyone he saw escaping from the hall.[76]

The Second Regiment tried to restore order by clearing the street with their bayonets, but the battle simply parted around them and raged on. Chicago's workers, who appear to have lacked firearms, fought as best they could; when the police and soldiers dispersed a crowd, "guerrilla warfare" ensued. Small groups of workers attacked the police and their allies in quick strikes and then melted into nearby buildings. The police finally took the unusual step of ordering all windows and doors closed and rooftops cleared. Peace was secured with the arrival of the Ninth U.S. Infantry and the rest of the Twenty-second U.S. Artillery. Mayor Heath swore in an additional two thousand volunteers and ordered the arrest of more than four hundred workers. The strike dragged on for a few more days, but the battles had ended with the death of at least eighteen workers. The cabinetmakers brought charges against Sergeants Householder and Brennan for their attacks; a judge found them guilty of inciting a "criminal riot," but fined them each just six cents.[77] The riots of July 26 convinced the Chicago press that the strikers were all communists who deserved to be on the receiving end of official violence. The *Tribune* held that "the Fight with the Communists is at an End" thanks to the courage of the city's police. Only the *News* among the major papers remained loyal to the workers, proclaiming the bloodshed the result of "a uniformed mob."[78]

Briefly it had looked as though the strike would succeed, not just in Chicago but nationwide. On July 25 John Hay wrote his father-in-law that it appeared probable that the railroads would have to give in to workers' demands as a "disgraceful" necessity. Two days later he reported the country in "the gravest danger." Several corporations avoided strikes by responding positively to the demands of their workers. For instance, J.H. Devereux, president of the CCC&I Railroad, revoked his recent 10 percent wage cut, as did the Union Pacific, some smaller railroads, and several mine owners in Pennsylvania, while other industrialists, including Andrew Carnegie, changed their minds about further wage cuts.[79]

The decisive moment came on the evening of July 26, when President Hayes met with his cabinet, gaining their approval to use all necessary military force to end the strike. The following day, July 27, Pennsylvania's governor Hartranft loaded trains furnished by Tom Scott with three thousand federal troops and six thousand state militia and made his way to Pittsburgh. He brushed aside the strikers' effort to speak with him and ordered the restoration of order by military force. From Pittsburgh, he traveled from town to town, making certain that the strikers were dispersed and the trains back in operation with strikebreakers. These troops occupied much of Pennsylvania through the next several months, until the last coal miners gave up in late October.[80] President Hayes's commitment of much of the U.S. Army to the task of restoring order proved the critical factor in putting down the labor insurrection. With law enforcement entirely behind the corporations, many nascent strikes never got off the ground. In Kansas City a massive meeting of railroad workers demanded that wages be restored to their former levels or they would strike, but they abandoned those plans the following day when the company announced that it would deploy federal troops.[81]

However, in a few places, the strike began anew despite the threat posed by the U.S. Army. Employees of the Delaware, Lackawanna & Western Railroad had seen their wages fall 35 percent from September 1876 to July 1877. When fifteen hundred workers of the Lackawanna Iron & Coal Company in Scranton went on strike, the rail workers followed suit—a reversal of the usual pattern. By Sunday, July 29, all of Scranton had joined the strike—an estimated 35,000 workers. One worker told a reporter that low wages had reduced them all to the verge of starvation, but that "death is too expensive, a funeral too costly a heritage for the living, and so they struggle on to keep body and soul together as a matter of economy."[82] The general manager of the Lackawanna Iron & Coal Company, W.W. Scranton, wrote a friend: "I trust when the troops come,—if they ever get here,—that we may have a conflict, in which the mob shall be completely worsted. In no other way will the thing end with any security for property here in the future."[83] Impatient to get started, Scranton's businessmen organized a volunteer group that shot and killed six miners. General Robert Brinton arrived on August 2 with the First Division and suppressed public protests by workers. Though Scranton's miners did not give up until early October, they found themselves unable or unwilling to combat armed troops and an enforced silence. In Scranton, as throughout most of the country, management consistently refused to negotiate in any way with their workers and relied entirely on military force to settle the contest. But also as in much of the country, the animosity of workers toward those who had served in the militia was intense; the people of the town of Scranton, according to one militia captain, referred to his company thereafter as "the firing squad."[84]

The Brief Life of the St. Louis Commune

Nowhere did the concept of a general strike come closest to fulfillment than in St. Louis, where a united working class shut down the city. Enthusiasm for joining the spreading national strike boiled over first across the river in East St. Louis. On the night of July 22 a meeting of railroad workers from several lines voted to join the Brotherhood of Firemen in striking for the restoration of their wages. The workers left Traubel Hall and marched to the Relay Depot, where they joined a crowd of St. Louis workers excited by events in East St. Louis. The crowd selected a machinist to be their president, and he delivered a rousing speech calling attention to the example of strikers in the East and issuing a battle cry for class warfare: "The capitalist was trying to starve the workingmen, and was educating his children to look down on them, despise and grind them under foot at every chance."[85] The strikers seized the depot, using it as their headquarters for the rest of the strike. The workers also took over the town itself, closing most of the saloons and preventing the movement of trains through this vital transit point. The strike quickly spread to other industries, encountering only enthusiasm from the local population, excited that the workers were finally taking on the hated railroads. Mayor John Bowman, who had only twelve police officers and had been elected as a friend of the workers, cleverly suggested that he appoint strikers as special constables to protect railroad property. The workers greeted this proposal as a sensible course of action and, as a consequence, no property was damaged or stolen during the duration of the strike in East St. Louis.[86]

On Monday, July 23, the Missouri Pacific line gave in to the workers and restored their wages. James H. Wilson, the receiver of the St. Louis & Southeastern Railroad, was outraged by this betrayal of capitalist solidarity and vowed to never surrender to his workers' grievances, for if the railroads did so, "there would be no end to their demands, and the railroads would have to submit to the being controlled by their employes." The East St. Louis strikers' executive committee also rejected the agreement with the Missouri Pacific, issuing "Order No. 2," stating that no one could negotiate with a railroad except the executive committee, which would only accept a general agreement with all the lines passing through East St. Louis. This insistence on unity undercut a number of negotiations.[87]

Across the Mississippi in St. Louis, the Workingmen's Party, led by the Danish immigrant Peter A. Lofgreen, denounced the federal government, which had "allied itself on the side of capital and against labor."[88] The St. Louis papers were astounded by the size of the meetings organized by the Workingmen's Party. At one such rally Albert Kordell told the crowd, "I believe that our railroad monopolies today have no other object in view than to take the government in their possession and rule it for the next fifty years to come, to the injury of our free institutions." If violence was required to stop them, then workers had a patriotic duty to take up arms. An English Marxist named John E. Cope shared this view that violence might be required, especially as there was a flaw in the American system that honored those who murdered workers, just so long as they worked for the rich. "A man who stole a single rail is called a thief, while he who stole a railway is a gentleman." Speaking in German, Albert Currlin worried over the quiescence of American workers in the face of outrageous injustice, failing to act while the railroads were "robbing the laborer of his products and filling the land with paupers, vagrants and tramps." Several speakers attacked St. Louis mayor Henry Overstolz for not supporting public works projects. Briefly sympathetic to the plight of the working class, the *Missouri Republican* held "it was the sight of the wives and children, hungry and unprovided for, which was driving them to assert what they believed to be their rights."[89]

The crowd the following day was even larger, estimated as at least ten thousand. Reverend John Snyder of the St. Louis Church of the Messiah criticized his fellow clergy for being "pious conservators of social selfishness in high places." Speakers saw the St. Louis strike as part of a great national uprising by the producers of wealth. When someone in the crowd wanted to know if these calls for worker rights meant "Negroes too?" the crowd screamed "Yes!" and called to hear a black worker speak. The assembled thousands then voted, without apparent dissent, to establish a general strike in order to win legislation ending child labor and establishing an eight-hour day. They took a more radical stance than most other strikers in calling not just for the revocation of recent pay cuts, but for the restoration of wages to their 1873 level. The management of several companies immediately agreed to the demands of their workers, winning the reversal of wage cuts for several groups, from roustabouts to skilled craftsmen. But those first successes brought quick opposition from the guardians of middle-class mores. When strikers at a beef cannery demanded an increase in wages from seventy-five cents a day to $1.75, the *Missouri Republican* labeled them "Mad Strikers."[90]

Such demands for a seemingly insane $1.75 a day highlights the real motivation of the strike nationwide: privation. In the terrible slough of the depression of 1873, the poor, even those with steady work, verged on starvation. It took just the smallest push to topple them over the edge into dire want. The workers' consistent demand for "a living wage" was not an empty slogan but an absolute necessity. A German-language publication from the St. Louis strike asked, "Has our government done anything for us workingmen?" It answered: "Emphatically no! Therefore, fellow-workingmen, we MUST act ourselves, unless we want starvation" in the future. On July 25, a mixed-race crowd marched through the streets of St. Louis to Lucas Market. Along the way a worker ran into a bakery and emerged with a loaf of bread atop a staff. The crowd cheered the bread as "the symbol of the strike."[91] As in the classic bread riots of Europe in the eighteenth century, the American worker had established an economic morality in stark contrast to the ruling paradigm that consistently favored the wealthy.

The crowd following the loaf of bread into Lucas Market swelled to ten thousand people. With repeated supportive shouts, they listened as leaders of the

Workingmen's Party told them that they were not taking part in a strike but in "a social revolution." The crowd approved a statement calling on the federal government to nationalize the railroads "for the general welfare," and vowed once more that their goal was to aid all workers, including blacks. Setting a pattern that would persist in the Southern press well into the twentieth century whenever any group called for reform, the *Missouri Republican* declared the presence of these black workers sufficient negation of everything for which the workers contested. They charged that the strike was controlled by "notorious Negroes," and then turned around and blamed the Workingmen's Party for violating the community's core values by allowing race mixing.[92] After the strike, Albert Currlin, the leader of the German segment of the Workingmen's Party, blamed the blacks for undermining the strike and proclaimed his adherence to racist rejections of blacks and whites associating together. He also admitted that the executive committee on which he served "didn't mean to fight, and wouldn't fight," despite their rhetoric of social revolution. They had every intention of giving up at the first appearance of the police, Currlin maintained.[93] Had city authorities known the nonviolent predilections of these perfidious socialists, they would certainly have acted much sooner.

By July 26 nearly every manufacturer in St. Louis, some sixty factories, had closed. The executive committee of the Workingman's Party ran the city. The British consul reported that the strikers had seized the railroads and were "running the trains and collecting fares," and deplorably, "a large proportion of the public appears to regard such conduct as a legitimate mode of warfare." The workers appeared formidable in their unity, and the rhetoric of revolution terrified the city's leadership. When railroad management asked Mayor Overstolz to arrest the strike leaders, he bluntly stated that he did not have the strength to do so.[94]

Throughout the strike the executive committee of the Workingman's Party continued to insist on nonviolence. Even while demanding "justice . . . or death!" worker pamphlets warned against using violence and promised to "do all that lays in our power to assist the authorities in keeping order and in preventing acts of violence." Some strike leaders admitted that while "united in purpose," they were "undecided what course to pursue." At a July 25 mass meeting, a speaker called on the assembled workers to begin arming themselves in order to counter attacks by the police and military. The executive committee immediately silenced the speaker and attempted to have him arrested. The following day the executive committee called on the mayor to feed the poor in order to "avoid plunder, arson or violence by persons made desperate by destitution," promising to assist the mayor "in maintaining order and protecting property," and assuring the public that they would hold no demonstrations to avoid riling up the workers.[95] Since the strike had drawn its unity from such mass meetings, this decision to forgo further public assemblies guaranteed their failure.

While the executive committee dithered and issued tame proclamations calling for peaceful protest, the city's merchants armed themselves to destroy the workers. On the night of July 24, three hundred soldiers of the Twenty-third U.S. Infantry arrived in St. Louis with two Gatling guns. But their commander, Colonel Jefferson C. Davis, stated that he was there to protect government property and had no intention of quelling the strike or running the trains. To clarify his distance from the conflict, Davis moved his troops into the old federal arsenal two miles from the city center. St. Louis's business leaders were astonished by the colonel's attitude and Mayor Overstolz hastily called a (briefly) secret meeting of the city's "respectable elements." He told the assembled businessmen that the police and militia could not hope to deal with these "thirty thousand fully armed socialists," and the U.S. Army appeared reluctant to get involved. The mayor therefore created a "Committee of Public Safety," consisting of a judge and five former generals, to restore order. Overstolz found substantial backing from James H. Wilson, the receiver of the St. Louis & Southeastern Railroad, who sent hysterical telegrams to Secretary of the Interior Carl Schurz, who forwarded them to Secretary of War McCrary, who ordered Davis to act in case of violent disorder.[96]

The following day Sheriff John Finn began putting together a private militia that would soon number five thousand men. At the Committee of Public Safety's request, Missouri governor John S. Phelps sent fifteen hundred rifles and ammunition from the state arsenal. When the committee called for a further ten thousand rifles, two thousand revolvers, and cannon from the secretary of war, McCrary, while supportive, wired back that there were not enough arms left in government hands to meet this request. The nationwide strike had exhausted the government's military resources. To fill the gap, business leaders raised $20,000 to arm their militia, the St. Louis Gun Club contributed shotguns, and the federal arsenal at Rock Island supplied some small arms. Mayor Overstolz looked forward to sending his army into combat.[97]

On the afternoon of Friday, July 27, some two thousand strikers were milling around outside Schuler Hall, where the executive committee met. At 3 P.M. shouts that "the soldiers are coming!" ran through the crowd. A reporter from the *Missouri Republican* climbed onto the balcony and looked up Fifth Street, where he could see mounted police trotting toward him. Behind the horses came two columns of police carrying muskets with bayonets attached, a cannon in their midst. Mayor Overstolz rode at the rear of his forces. The police, "with their forest of bayonets, advanced with regular, measured tread, presenting a very pretty column." As the police rode into the crowd, swinging their clubs without restraint, their commander shouted, "Cut 'em down, if they don't go." The crowd quickly fled as the police arrested all those they found in the building. Not a shot was fired.[98]

To the regret of the now uniformly venomous press, the police did not recognize the members of the executive committee, who escaped while several reporters were arrested. Early on the morning of July 28, U.S. troops invaded East St. Louis and seized the Relay Depot without resistance, arresting some hundred workers. The St. Louis general strike collapsed. The British vice consul contemptuously dismissed the workers for giving up without a fight; "the illegal arrest of a few men met together to talk in a hall was sufficient to bring the whole affair to an end." The police rounded up the entire executive committee and they were speedily brought to trial, but the case was dropped for lack of evidence. In October the St. Louis grand jury investigated the strike and concluded that, while they would like to punish the strike leaders, they could not find any legal grounds for doing so.[99] It was an anticlimactic end to a movement that had struck icy fear into the hearts of corporate America.

After two weeks of living in terror of the workers, the St. Louis press now found them comical. "Communism in St. Louis received a very black eye," the *St. Louis Globe-Democrat* proclaimed, having been defeated by "only a small squad of police" who found no need to shoot anyone. If there had been effective leadership, by which they meant leaders willing to use violence, St. Louis would have become the first "American Commune." Still, as was widely acknowledged, the workers had staged a revolution, demonstrating to everyone what America's workers might accomplish. Now that it was safely over, the St. Louis papers took a sort of perverse pride in pointing to "the St. Louis Commune" as the "only *genuine* Commune" in 1877.[100] But Secretary of the Treasury John Sherman dampened any such enthusiasm by seeing the shadow of the French Revolution in the strike, warning that the continuing and "irrepressible conflict" between capital and labor could once more threaten the American way of life.[101]

Cold-Blooded Americans

At a meeting of workers at the Cooper Union in New York on July 26, J.P. McDonnell, editor of the *Labor Standard*, argued that from the beginning of the depression in 1873, America's working class had been conducting "a sort of guerrilla warfare for their rights" and survival. All their previous hard work had been overwhelmed by the combined forces of capital and the state, so that now they stood on "the verge of starvation." But these labors had served a valuable purpose, having "culminated in the present revolt against oppression." The strike's greatest accomplishment was to show the commonalty of interest among all workers, for it arose spontaneously "because the workmen of Pittsburgh felt the same oppression that was felt by the workmen of West Virginia," and Chicago, and St. Louis. The strike had already proven that class consciousness could eliminate "barriers of ignorance and prejudice" that previously had kept workers powerless. "It was a grand sight to see in West Virginia, white and colored men standing together, men of all nationalities in one supreme contest for the common rights of workingmen," McDonnell told a crowd of cheering workers. But victory would have to wait for another day, and required planning.[102]

Very few strikers called for violence at any time in 1877, and what bloodshed occurred either originated with the police or troops, or came in response to the violent actions of law enforcement. With the exception of the California followers of Denis Kearney, there are no significant instances of workers instigating bloodshed. Nonetheless, the Great Strike was the deadliest labor action in American history. The extent of casualties remains unknown, though the number is usually put at a minimum of 117 killed and many hundreds wounded.[103] The strike tied up two-thirds of the country's 79,000 miles of railroad track and transformed several major cities into military encampments. In eight days, nine governors labeled the strike an insurrection and called for federal troops; militia had been called out in eleven states, involving at least 45,000 state troops in strike suppression, the largest use to that date of militia in America's peacetime history. The army had forced open rail lines throughout the Midwest, the Chesapeake Bay area, Pennsylvania, and New York. Governors threatened strikers with criminal prosecution, while judges formed a new legal concept, declaring workers in contempt of court for striking against companies under court receivership.[104] Prior to 1877, federal troops had been used only to guard federal property at the request of governors; now they acted on the request of corporate leaders to protect private property. "The corporations have the law on their side," observed the *Reading Eagle*. "They own the Legislatures, they retain the ablest lawyers, they control most of the newspapers, and manufacture public opinion." And, most importantly, they did not hesitate to use violence. Those workers who dared "contend for the rights of human nature and American citizenship, . . . are branded as rioters, met by force of arms, provoked to violence, and then shot dead."[105]

The strike had brought the nation's transportation network to a screeching halt, affecting nearly every industry in the country. Starting with the major eastern railroads—the Baltimore & Ohio, the Pennsylvania, the Reading, the New York Central & Hudson, and the Erie—the strike had spread out to affect every line from the Wabash to the Union Pacific, the Texas & Pacific to the Northern Pacific, the Louisville & Nashville to the Canadian Southern. The nation's political and economic elite had seen a giant stir in 1877, and were terrified. Their fear was both tangible and realistic. John Hay, soon to be President Hayes's assistant secretary of state, wrote, "Any hour the mob chooses, it can destroy any city in the country—that is the simple truth."[106]

The series of strikes that swept through the country in 1877 revealed a great deal about the United States. The most obvious fact was the precariousness of life for the average worker, whose income was repeatedly slashed at the whim of corporate officials in distant offices. And yet workers consistently appealed to middle-class ideals, as when they began strikes by resolving to drink no alcohol and even ordered taverns closed for the duration. The workers also forswore violence, an attitude not shared by management, which never hesitated to use force rather than negotiation and assumed that police, militia, and even the United States Army existed to enforce their will. Nor, even in the worst confrontations, did striking workers ever attack U.S troops. It appears that their respect for the blue uniform, which many of them had worn during the Civil War, stayed their hand.

In most regards, the strike was a failure, with thousands of workers fired and blacklisted. The Pennsylvania Railroad succeeded in having one hundred former employees arrested and thrown in jail; other railroads were less spiteful but also arranged for the arrest of dozens of workers. Most commentators were stunned at the speed of the strike, which started in West Virginia on July 18 and had spread across the Midwest to St. Louis by July 24. It was generally estimated that eighty thousand railroad workers and half a million other workers had gone out on strike. It scared many people silly. The Christian *Independent* called for years of "hard labor in state prisons" for those identified as leaders of the strike in order to demonstrate "the punitive power of the law."[107]

But what did the Great Strike mean? Clearly there were lessons to be learned, but no one could agree on what instruction to take from these events. The *Martinsburg Statesman* thought that the railroads should learn something from the strike, especially in the way it spread rapidly from a local dispute on the Baltimore & Ohio: "Heartless and selfish railway corporations" needed to understand "that there is a point in oppression beyond which it is not safe to go." The young New York labor leader Samuel Gompers felt that workers learned the hard way that they were on their own and could rely on no one but one another. During their strike, the Cigarmakers Union ran soup kitchens for strikers until their food ran out; the city offered no assistance. The Pennsylvania Railroad's Tom Scott thought the strike showed the need for a larger army in the service of industry. He warned that this "insurrection" would likely lead to more violence as "now, for the first time in American history, has an organized mob learned its power to terrorize the law-abiding citizens of great communities," and called for routine federal aid to the railroads to meet this threat.[108] A great many newspapers, even in the South, felt that the strike exploded the fallacy of states' rights once and for all. "The inefficiency and weakness of State Governments in struggling against a concerted uprising of the mob classes," the *Chicago Tribune* editorialized, "have been abundantly demonstrated." Mark Twain thought the strike showed clearly what happened when the government lost touch with the people it was supposed to serve.[109] America's leading religious figure, the Reverend Henry Ward Beecher, thought the lesson was that American workers were spoiled.

Having rebounded from the most notorious sex scandal of the 1870s, Beecher had settled into a comfortable life as the highly paid minister to the rich at Brooklyn's Plymouth Congregational Church. Like his sister Harriet Beecher Stowe, he had moved a great distance from the radicalism of his youth, and now enjoyed the luxuries garnered from his well-recompensed speaking tours and his $25,000 annual salary. On Sunday, July 22, 1877, Beecher delivered a sermon, "Hard Times," that set forth a merciless Christianity, one that mocked and derided the poor. Standing before his well-heeled and well-fed congregation, Beecher lectured those workers disrupting the nation's peace with their irrational strike and their fancied grievances. "The great laws of political economy cannot be set at defiance," he assured America's workers, whose manhood he then questioned for not being content to live on bread and water. Surely, Beecher insisted, anyone could survive on a dollar a day, which should be sufficient for bread and water; and "a man who can't live on bread is not fit to live."[110]

Coming in the midst of the strike, Beecher's sermon became an instant polarizing sensation, covered by newspapers coast to coast.[111] Many well-to-do people and leading Christians applauded his sermon, crediting him with saying what needed to be said, that Christianity had no patience for the poor who failed to know and keep their place. Prominent religious journals such as the *Congregationalist, Independent, Presbyterian Quarterly*, and *Christian Union* published extracts or the entirety of Beecher's sermon and agreed that this was no time for charity and mercy toward the poor. Other ministers delivered their own denunciations of the downtrodden masses. The Reverend Joseph Cook, a popular Chautauqua speaker, condemned the strikers as violent communists, loafers, and "enemies of the human race." His careful examination indicated that the "American lower ranks contain three different sets of men—the unenterprising, the unfortunate, and the unprincipled." Echoing social Darwinist principles, Cook maintained that, since anyone can rise in America, those who do not succeed economically lack "either energy or principle," and their "shiftlessness . . . needs sometimes the spur of hunger."[112]

Beecher did find his critics, even among the wealthy. The *Commercial and Financial Chronicle* felt that Beecher did not "show either a wise head or feeling heart." Workers and their advocates were naturally outraged; the *Sun*'s prolabor editorial writer John Swinton addressed a workers' meeting in New York called specifically to protest Beecher's sermon, attacking the minister as a false Christian and unfeeling monster.[113] But Beecher garnered much harsher criticism from newspapers apparently delighted by the chance to turn tables on the righteous New York minister. The *Raleigh Register* thought that Beecher's wealth made it unlikely "that he could appreciate the gnawing pangs of hunger that afflict so many" of his less fortunate fellows. That was the only excuse they could find for this "Reverend brute" and "hoary headed old hypocrite" who was "totally unfit to expound the doctrines of holy writ to a Christian people." The *New York World* was caustic in its denunciation, finding Beecher's "folly . . . immeasurable" in taunting the poor at the very moment they are in the midst of revolution. It seemed as though he wanted to throw fuel on those flames. The *Indianapolis Sentinel* called Beecher "fiendish" and predicted he would suffer "the fires of hell" for his callousness. With mordant concision, the *Independent Statesman* called Beecher "about the craziest man in this country."[114]

Beecher accused those criticizing his contempt for the poor of being communists and then clumsily tried to get out of the controversy by delivering another sermon the following Sunday defending his position. With thirty undercover police in his congregation, Beecher felt safe to demonstrate even greater insensitivity in this sermon, "Communism Denounced." Portraying his critics as dangerous radicals intent on destroying the country, he repeated his faith in the status quo: "God has intended the great to be great, and the little to be little." Rejecting any government regulation of industry as "insane," while government aid to the poor is "communistic" and "un-American," Beecher found no class distinctions in America, calling on the poor to grumble less and work more. Insisting that his comments had been taken out of context, Beecher went ahead to insult the disadvantaged: "I don't say that $1 per day is enough to support a working man, but it is enough to support a man." Samuel Gompers wrote that Beecher's sermon "made the working people think the Church had no consideration or understanding of our welfare or problems."[115]

Many contemporaries lacked Beecher's certainty, and for them, the meaning of the Great Strike remained elusive. Scores of commentators agreed that the strikes showed that communists were everywhere—for to go on strike was to be a communist. But they disagreed about whether the strike demonstrated the power of those communists, or their weakness, since the strike had largely failed. Taking leave of its senses, the *New York Tribune* actually argued that "Communistic hatred of the rights of property has enlisted the votes of a majority of the people of the United States," and that the only reason they had not yet taken over the country was because they could not agree among themselves how best to do so. Positing a different apocryphal vision, members of the Harmonist commune south of Pittsburgh speculated that "this reign of terror marked the beginning of the harvest-time spoken of in Scripture," with the Day of Judgment ahead.[116] The *Labor Standard* hoped that the strike was but the first step in a revolution, predicting that "the occurrences during the last portion of July, 1877, will, in the future history of this country, be designated as the beginning of the second American Revolution, which inaugurated the independence of Labor from Capital." John Swinton thought the strike unique; there had been "nothing like it in any history whatsoever."[117]

The strike had certainly disrupted many certainties. Victorian sensibilities on the domestic roles of women found little validation in the Great Strike. Respectable middle-class observers were deeply disturbed by the active participation of women in these events. Sometimes the nurturing characteristics traditionally ascribed to women overlapped with more dramatic public actions, as when women in Pittsburgh served tea, coffee, and sweets to the men destroying the trains, and also helped in the looting of freight cars. There is little doubt that women did not hang back while men did the heavy lifting. The *Chicago Times* reported that roughly one-fifth of the crowds in that city were women. In a charge typical of mainstream reporting on crowds since the eighteenth century, the *Tribune* claimed that "the women had been exciting the men to action throughout the morning," often behaving more violently than the men, "cursing and howling like demons," and attacking the paper's reporters.[118] Women supporting the strikers in West Virginia "looked famished and wild, and declare for starvation rather than have their people work for the reduced wages."[119]

A report by the *Inter Ocean* on women in the Chicago crowds attracted national attention and was widely reprinted. Sexual images mixed freely with the newspaper's insistence that women lost their gender identity by their involvement in the strike. "Enraged female rioters," some carrying babies and many barefoot, flowed through the city's streets, "their disheveled locks streaming in the wind." Adding to this provocative portrayal of harridans and harlots on the march, the *Inter Ocean* described dresses "tucked up around the waist," revealing the women's underclothing and exposed breasts similar to the classic image of Madeleine at the barricades. But on the other hand, "Brawny, sunburnt arms brandished clubs," while "female yells, shrill as a curlew's cry, filled the air." Powerful and erotic, this "unsexed mob of female incendiaries rushed" to call the men out on strike. In a scene straight out of the Paris Commune, the fence surrounding the Goss & Phillips Manufacturing Company "was carried off by the petticoated plunderers in their unbridled rage." When the police came to meet this "Amazonian army," the women hissed and let lose a "shower of missiles" and profanities that temporarily staggered the police, who were shocked by such foul language. "Expressions were made use of that brought the blood mantling to the cheek of the worst-hardened men in the crowds," the paper gasped. "It was awful." The police finally drove the women away with their clubs.[120]

Those involved in the strike could not mistake its core lesson: as Mark Twain said, the government was not on their side. Workers did not mistake the message they received loud and clear from President Hayes's actions—that the federal government was making publicly apparent its bias toward industry. Hayes tried to reassure workers that the federal government was not their enemy by telling a press conference that he saw "no spirit of communism" in the strike, which did not attack "property in general, but merely . . . that of the railroads with which the strikers had difficulty." These sentiments were apparently sincere, as Hayes wrote in his diary, "The railroad strikers, as a rule, are good men, sober, intelligent, and industrious." But the president's words fell flat with most workers agreeing with the *Martinsburg Statesman*: "Presidents, judges, governors, mayors and legislators are but cats' paws nowadays in the interest of rings and corporations."[121]

It was also apparent that supposed Constitutional protections did not extend into the poorest neighborhoods. In most large cities, public officials moved quickly to silence anyone or any group they felt capable of inciting the workers. In Philadelphia Mayor William S. Stokley violated state law, as well as basic First Amendment rights, when he banned all public gatherings. Without any authorization, he more than doubled the police force to 1,400 men and armed the city's 400 firemen; together they patrolled Philadelphia's streets along with 700 regulars, 125 Marines, 2,000 special police, and the 500 volunteers of the Veteran Corps. Stokley ordered these forces to confiscate all copies of the *Labor Standard* and to attack meetings of the Workingmen's Party, at one of which a young worker named William McBridge was shot in the back of the head by a policeman. When a delegation from the Workingmen's Party met with the mayor to protest this violence and obvious violations of their rights, the mayor repeated that all meetings were banned and would be broken up by the police. With that, the dangerous Marxists of the Workingmen's Party surrendered and announced that they would hold no more meetings until the crisis passed.[122] Oddly, not even the prolabor newspapers pointed out that the city of Philadelphia was the single largest holder of Pennsylvania Railroad stock and that Mayor Stokley generally chaired the annual stockholders' meeting.[123]

After the strike collapsed, local officials and corporate leaders pressured President Hayes to keep U.S. troops on duty in the occupied cities. Though by July 31 it was fairly obvious that management had won their battle with labor, Tom Scott wired President Hayes, "Please do not be misled by any news of peaceable settlement of existing troubles." Scott warned that if federal troops were removed, workers would again rise in rebellion. Hayes chose to ignore this and other dire warnings and slowly withdrew federal troops by the end of October. However, by backing with the power of the U.S. Army an interpretation of the law that allowed federal courts to forbid strikes against railroads in receivership, Hayes had given the corporations one of their most powerful weapons against workers in the years ahead: the strike injunction.[124]

The bloody-mindedness of the middle class stands in stark contrast to the nonviolent conduct of most workers. The nation's leading newspapers and magazines called for the use of extreme force to put down the strike. Even Lucy Stone, a prominent suffragist, insisted, "The insurrection must be suppressed, if it costs a hundred thousand lives and the destruction of every railroad in the country." The nominally Christian *Independent* turned gory when it came to workers: "If the club of the policeman, knocking out the brains of a rioter, will answer, then well and good; but if it does not promptly meet the exigency, then bullets and bayonets, canister and grape—with no sham or pretense, in order to frighten men, but with fearful and destructive reality—constitute the one remedy and the one duty of the hour." A newfound respect for Napoleon repeated itself in numerous religious and secular journals: the *Independent* praised the French tyrant for clearly having it right in stating that "the way to deal with a mob was to exterminate it." The *Independent* concluded with an affronted sniff, "Rioters are worse than mad dogs."[125]

Hayes and many other political leaders thought that the best way to avoid future national strikes was to expand the nation's ability to react militarily. The terror generated by the strike did not die down, but calls for enlarged police and military arose in every part of the country. By early August 1877 both the Chicago police and Illinois National Guard had been enlarged. Many states quickly acceded to the National Guard movement and transformed their traditional state militia into this more professional, better-armed military force that was not so directly tied to the local community. There was general agreement that the militia, as currently constituted, "is very unfit for the task" of dealing with workers. Governor Hartranft reorganized the Pennsylvania militia into the National Guard, buying more Gatling guns for his forces and dismissing for "cowardice and mutinous conduct" companies and even some of his senior officers for showing sympathy to the strikers; many of these men were also fired by their employers. The War Department issued its first manual on "Riot Duty," while the *Army and Navy Journal* began running articles on "Street Fighting," and pamphlets such as *Suggestions upon the Strategy of Street Fighting* appeared.[126]

But many people questioned the loyalty of the police and the militia, both of which had too often sided with the workers and had clearly failed to maintain order. New York boasted the best prepared militia in the country, yet in New York City half those called up refused to report for duty. One officer noted that half of his regiment consisted of "Irish workingmen in perfect sympathy with their oppressed fellow workingmen." So few troops turned out when called by an upstate regiment that its commander called it "unfit to bear arms," and recommended its disbandment. The performance of the Pennsylvania militia ranged from "disgraceful" to "pitiable." Its Sixteenth Regiment gave ammunition to strikers in Reading and proclaimed their "intention, in case of further trouble, of siding with them," while a company of Philadelphia militia captured near Harrisburg stripped itself of its arms and paraded through the streets—"a humiliating spectacle," in the words of the adjutant general. The militia did not turn out at all in Indiana, and disobeyed orders in Ohio, Pennsylvania, Illinois, and West Virginia.[127]

The new heroes of the industrial middle class and corporate elite were the troops of the United States Army, who had clearly saved the day. Certain that there would be more labor insurrections in the future, public figures such as Carl Schurz, Tom Scott, and Horace White called for the expansion of the standing army to at least twice its current diminutive 25,000 soldiers, and recommended they be stationed permanently near all large cities and industries. Their position was supported by a fanciful pamphlet that came out in 1877 called *The Commune in 1880: Downfall of the Republic*, in which communist strikers rise again and overthrow the government by infiltrating the National Guard. The narrator muses that the country could have been saved if only they had enlarged the army, as "the real safety of a country lies in her regular army."[128] Many prominent figures felt the need not just for a stronger military but for a strong military leader, and began a movement to secure the 1880 Republican nomination for that failed president Ulysses S. Grant.[129] Others spoke openly of their contempt for democracy. George Vest, the author of Missouri's defeated secession ordinance who would be elected to the U.S. Senate in 1879, proclaimed: "Universal suffrage is a standing menace to all stable and good government. Its twin sister is the commune with its labor unions."[130]

Not surprisingly, the labor press opposed the expansion of the army. "What they demand is a well organized body of trained soldiers, who know and care nothing about the grievance of the people, and who stand ready to defend railroad and other corporations in their career of plunder and oppression." Lewis H. Bond of the Ohio Workingmen's Party felt that "Gatling guns and glistening bayonets are not efficacious agents in righting the wrongs of labor," and warned the advocates of a standing army "to overawe our people, and shoot down our fellow-citizens whose protest against starvation is their only crime," that those forces could easily turn on them someday to establish a tyranny in America. The probusiness *Commercial and Financial Chronicle* agreed with Bond that an army employed on behalf of specific economic interests could eventually be turned against anyone, including business; only "the law-abiding disposition of the people" will preserve social order. Many newspapers shared this skepticism for a variety of reasons. Those sympathetic to labor charged that "Mr. Hayes and his railway managers" sought to crush all forms of protest by enlarging the army, presenting the "sad spectacle . . . [of] a government with one hand driving laboring men to desperation, [and] the other bayoneting back their acts of despair."[131] Others found a large standing army "nothing less than a radical revolution of our whole republican system of government." The *Railroad Gazette* doubted the efficacy of an enlarged army, as ultimately the public order depended on the goodwill of the people. In a surprisingly evenhanded formulation, this voice of management perceived "a delusion prevalent among railroad officials and the community generally that a strike is an abnormal condition of things, somewhat like a pestilence or an invasion of potato bugs, and that if we could only employ sufficiently destructive means to kill the bugs . . . we would always be free from the evil." But strikes were unavoidable as "inseparably associated with our present economy and must be regarded as the natural outgrowth of the existing relations between employers and employed."[132]

Ultimately, all calls for military growth floundered not because of the compelling arguments of the press and labor leaders, but because of staunch Democratic resistance. Representative Joseph Blackburn of Kentucky opposed using the army for "the subjugation and slaughter" of "impoverished citizens"; Hendrick Wright of Pennsylvania had seen the army used against "the workmen of my district," and had no desire to see that oppression repeated; Auburn Pridemore of Virginia did not want the military to "control the labor of the country"; and T.T. Crittenden of Missouri opposed using force to subject the "laboring men of this country" to the control of management. Of course, the Southern Democrats also had no desire to see a strong army being used to restore the rights of African Americans, a point not lost on many Republicans who linked the Democratic Party with both the Ku Klux Klan and communist workers.[133] But the Democrats' winning arguments proved to be the cost of a larger army and their majority in the House of Representatives. As a consequence, nothing came of the repeated calls for military growth until another major nationwide strike raised elite fears in the 1890s.

Through the rest of the year, the press continued to ask what the strikes meant and how to prevent their recurring. Few considered for a moment paying workers a living wage as a possible solution. Rather, the press looked elsewhere, blaming the character of the working class—as irrational and/or inebriated—for their poverty, recommending tighter controls or temperance, and sought outside agitators, unions and communists, to explain the strikes. In speaking of "the formidable insurrection of different classes of laborers" in July 1877, the *Galveston Daily News* blamed the unions, though few of the workers who struck belonged to unions. But then, the unions had been infiltrated by communists who rejected "the natural forces" of the free market. Other papers saw international conspiracies, and the New York City police were apparently convinced that "the secret inspiration" of the strikes could be found in the "famous International Society which played such havoc in Paris." A few days after the Great Strike ended, the *Chicago Tribune* looked around and saw that the United States was no different from other industrial societies: "We, too, have our crowded tenement houses, and our entire streets and neighborhoods occupied by paupers and thieves," as a consequence of industrialization and hard times, which have left so many poor people desperate, rough, brutal, and "enamored of violence." Tramps were everywhere, and were ever "ready for theft, or rape, or incendiarism, and sometimes for murder." All dreams of an egalitarian society to the contrary, "the extremes of wealth and poverty are now to be seen here as abroad; the rich growing richer and the poor poorer,—a fact to tempt disorder." The United States was definitively home to class conflict; the *Tribune* warned, "We now have the Communists on our own soil." The government had missed a major opportunity in not acting with greater force to crush the workers' uprising; they must not make that mistake again, as only "repressive measures" will keep the poor in line. The *Tribune* thought the hanging of the Molly Maguires marked "a good beginning," but insisted it was not enough. They needed gunpowder "to teach the dangerous classes a needful lesson." Bullets "and the love of God" will maintain order in this violent new world.[134]

The First Red Scare

"By the light of flames at Pittsburgh, we may see approaching a terrible trial for free institutions in this country," wrote the economist William M. Grosvenor. "The Communist is here." The United States was in the grip of its first Red Scare in 1877. Any talk of meeting the workers halfway or taking their grievances seriously led to accusations of giving in to the "communists." By easy extension, anyone who showed the slightest hint of humanity toward workers became a communist as well.[135] Naturally, all Republican reformers, like Judge West of Ohio and Secretary of the Interior Carl Schurz, were communists, but so were the Democrats, especially their Chicago leader F.A. Hoffman, who mouthed "communistic gibberish" about workplace safety. Anyone who questioned any aspect of American society, such as Lucy Stone, was a communist, despite her call for killing the workers; in fact, all suffragists were communists.[136] Efforts to eliminate the chain gangs were communist. The press and political leadership entered onto an orgy of finding communists in the most unlikely places. The communists were of course intent on destroying religion, but a surprising number of ministers were communists.[137] Some Republicans were communists, the entire Greenback Party was communist, as of course was the Workingmen's Party, and most Democrats. Denis Kearney was a communist, Senator Hendrick B. Wright of Pennsylvania was "that gray-bearded communist," and the Indian was "the Communist of the Plains."[138] These accusations reached bizarre extremes, such as the oft-repeated charge that "Citizen Schwab, the New York German communist, . . . thinks men who won't buy beer ought to be shot."[139] That made sense to most prohibitionists, who linked communism with alcohol consumption, a dangerous two-way street that justified eliminating both.[140]

Obviously, one man's communist is another's "man of the people," a point made by a few of the more worker-friendly newspapers and political leaders. Self-interested parties were attempting to frighten the public into believing that the United States was on the verge of a communist revolution. "The Commune

Nonsense," as the *Pittsburgh Post* put it, had been used to alarm "timid people, by insinuating that the American working classes are influenced by the teachings of the Paris Commune." In Pittsburgh, at least, there was no evidence that any communist had played a significant role in planning or carrying out the strike, which "originated in well ascertained grievances." The *Galaxy* also found no evidence of communist conspiracy in the strike: to construe the uprising as "indicative of the presence of a communistic element . . . is something that the facts in the case do not warrant." Lewis H. Bond, the Workingmen's Party candidate for governor of Ohio, charged that the defenders of the status quo were using the charge of "communism" to try to discredit those standing up for reform. "Capital has started that refrain to drown the appealing voice of labor." The Red Scare was just a distraction from the real issues facing the country. "When millions of people are unemployed . . . we are told that the law of supply and demand regulates everything, and that as there is no demand for labor, it must—what? Starve?" Better to starve to death than to become a communist appeared to be the message workers received, Bond charged. The government subsidizes business in ways worth millions of dollars and can supply business with convict labor, but when starving people demand jobs they are labeled communists.[141]

But the perception of those like Bond who thought the threat of communism overblown and a distraction rarely made the newspapers. Most of the country was repeatedly reminded of the grave danger posed by the communist menace and learned that the only way to deal with these people was violently. "Every communist is a traitor to this government, and should be dealt with accordingly," declared the *Inter Ocean*, which favored hanging all communists. The press did its best to make every labor leader a communist and then to dehumanize them all. "The so-called communist is a sore upon the face of society, a cancer in the blood of honest thrift," the *Inter Ocean* maintained, with language that invited further violence. There was a general sense that the country had just dodged a bullet and would not be so lucky next time. One newspaper blamed the rising tide of violence in 1877 on modern technology, as workers had taken advantage of the telegraph and railroad to spread their strike. A well-organized uprising exploiting modern communication and transportation could seize control of the country. Something had to be done to prevent such an occurrence; the most efficient step would be to make sure that any future unions be killed at birth.[142]

Despite the angry rhetoric of the Red Scare and calls for the execution of strike leaders, the courts proved lenient, juries forgiving, and grand juries sincere in their understanding of the law. Outside the corridors of power and offices of opinion makers, there seemed to be a general sense that the strikers had been justified in their actions, but that it was a good thing they had lost and now should go back to work. Cautious local officials who had to deal with their communities on a daily basis feared a revival of the conflict if they created any martyrs, so they quietly let almost everyone arrested off with a warning. Even Judges Walter Q. Gresham of Indianapolis and Thomas Drummand of Chicago relaxed with time. Immediately after the strike they held a joint session to try fifteen strikers on contempt-of-court charges. The judges asked the defendants if they could prove their innocence (which they could not), heard evidence from railroad officials, and sentenced thirteen of them to six months in jail. In succeeding trials, these judges, as well as a Judge Jennings of New York, lectured those they convicted of interfering with the U.S. mail, criminal conspiracy, and contempt of court, and then ordered the release of all these men by the end of August. Juries were even more lenient. Sixty strikers arrested in Harrisburg were ordered to pay small fines and released. In St. Louis most charges were dismissed and a few workers sent to the workhouse for short terms.[143] Hundreds of people had been arrested in Pittsburgh; most were released and the remaining handful sentenced to brief terms in the workhouse. Of sixty-three workers indicted in Reading, only three were convicted. There was extensive evidence that the jurors sympathized with the strikers, which may explain why so many prosecutors eventually dropped all charges against striking workers.[144]

The majority of railroad executives failed to share this forgiving nature, expressing outrage at the leniency of the law and adding hundreds of names to their blacklists. Railroads also instituted "the ironclad oath," by which workers swore they would never join a union or go on strike. The labor movement had seemingly been dealt a crippling blow. By the end of the year, the *Labor Standard* could identify only nine national unions, most of which met in secret. "The recent troubles have given a great impetus to the growth of secret labor organizations and workingmen by the hundreds are paying their necessary dues and taking strange oaths—but all in secrecy."[145] While most of the older craft unions declined or disappeared as a consequence of the strike, one general union, the Knights of Labor, grew rapidly. At its general assembly in January 1878, the Knights of Labor became a national organization dedicated to organizing workers regardless of gender, race, ethnic background, or skill level. As a consequence, it became the most important labor organization of the 1880s.[146] Though their numbers had been reduced, labor unions were on the verge of a major rebirth. For the first time, workers heard criticisms of capitalism and understood exactly what the critics meant. Their experience of the Great Strike gave credence to some of the most telling critiques of the system, and in the years ahead they would gravitate toward a number of political movements, including the Grangers, socialism, and the Populists. But perhaps the most important political lesson they learned was that winning local elections was not sufficient; they needed also to create organizations that stood for their interests on a daily basis.

Furious at their treatment during the Great Strike, workers in cities around the United States mobilized to punish public officials who had called the troops down on them. At its September 1877 convention, the surviving remnant of the Brotherhood of Locomotive Firemen—most of whose members had been fired and blacklisted—condemned the attacks on the strikers in July as the work of "banditti." It was not the workers who turned to "Springfield rifles and Gatling guns as a means of preserving their rights: They have a more powerful and effective weapon—the ballot box." Many observers assumed that the great number of workers, if organized into a single political party, could seize power politically. Karl Marx wrote Friedrich Engels on July 24, 1877, that the Great Strike was "the first uprising against the oligarchy of capital which had developed since the Civil War," and predicted that it could lead to the creation of a great labor party in the United States.[147]

To many workers it seemed obvious that they would never win any rights unless they took a more effective political role. Their most famous success came in Scranton, Pennsylvania, where the young labor leader Terence V. Powderly won a stunning victory, becoming the first Irish American city mayor in U.S. history.[148] But the most impressive triumph of worker organization came in Louisville, Kentucky. With state elections slated for early August, workers in the city held a mass meeting on August 1, declared themselves the Workingmen's Party, agreed to a platform that began by condemning both political parties for having turned their backs on "the working class," and nominated a slate of candidates consisting entirely of workers. These candidates pledged themselves to an eight-hour day, arbitration of labor disputes, an end to child labor and chain gangs, and "the liberal application of funds for educational purposes." They promised "a better financial policy than the one which has impoverished the masses, brought utter stagnation upon commerce, and thrown out of employment millions of people."

The local press was terrified of this development and called on voters to reject this new political party. While acknowledging that the workers had cause for complaint and that it was better that they use the ballot instead of violence, the *Louisville Courier-Journal* warned that workers needed to act through the existing parties or face certain defeat.[149] As the election approached, the *Courier-Journal* lost all semblance of objectivity, warning that a victory for the Workingmen's Party would lead to a "Kentucky Commune" and "will be a signal for all the secret societies of Communists in this country and abroad to head for our fair state and begin their work of wreckage." The duty of all citizens was thus to "vote for men who are upholders of civilization." To the paper's horror, the Workingmen's Party, or the "mob movement" as they called it, won a sweeping victory, winning five of the seven offices and earning 8,850 votes compared to a combined total for all other candidates of just 4,728 votes. Clearly the "Kentucky Commune" was forthcoming. The paper attributed the victory to "the bitterness of the defeated strikers."[150]

Inspired by the Louisville victory, other labor parties formed and won local elections through the fall of 1877 and into 1878, often electing men who had been leaders of the strike.[151] Many of these labor parties formed coalitions not just with the Greenback Party and middle-class reformers but also with black workers. In Cincinnati, the Workingmen's Party nominees included a native-born worker, a Czech, a German cigar maker, an Irish stonecutter, and Peter H. Clark, the African American principal of the city's segregated Colored High School. As the Socialist paper the *Emancipator* wrote in endorsing Clark, America's blacks had experienced most directly the "robbery and murder" that disgraced capitalism and the United States.[152]

Clark traveled widely in the Midwest, campaigning for labor and Socialist party candidates, gaining the respect of many observers, and the label "strictly a communist" from others. His stump speech argued that the Great Strike proved that the government at every level was the tool of the capitalists, regardless of which party held power, and that the workers therefore needed to reject the logic of acquiescence and elect their fellow workers to office to ensure that the army would not be used against them in the future. In one particularly fiery speech, Clark maintained that the violence during the strike all originated with the government and corporations. The *Cincinnati Commercial*, which praised Clark's speech and reprinted it in full, dismissed his failure to "understand why it is that the military are always against the strikers." The paper offered the standard explanation that the dissatisfied worker could quit, but if he attempted to strike, he damaged the property of his employer and thus broke the law.[153] Clark responded to the paper with the words of Ecclesiastes: "I beheld the tears of such as were oppressed and they had no comforter." America's workers had suffered repeated pay cuts under the logic that the railroads were losing money, Clark wrote, "But when they see high railroad officials receiving the salaries of princes, when they hear of dividends on stock and interest on bonds, they cannot understand why there is no money for the man whose labors earn these vast sums." And then if they dare to complain, "they are told that they are at liberty to quit and take their services elsewhere. This is equivalent to telling them that they are at liberty to go and starve." America would be a weaker country if its workers accepted "wage slavery."[154]

Clark received more votes than anyone else on his ticket, but he could not break the statewide lock of the two major parties. Workers' parties won office only at the local level, as they did in Louisville, Chicago, Milwaukee, Scranton, San Francisco, and a few other cities. In Toledo, the labor candidates swept the city, even sending two representatives to the state legislature. The biggest surprise came in St. Louis, where the Workingmen's Party carried five of the city's wards, despite the Democrats' racist campaign. But in statewide races, the labor parties made a poor showing, polling 52,854 votes in Pennsylvania, 20,000 in New York, and just 17,000 votes in Ohio.[155]

The value of the ballot box was further undermined by the consistent negation of reform legislation by the federal courts. Nearly every effort of workers to pass legislation protecting their rights or ensuring workplace safety in the late nineteenth century fell before the courts' fiat. Jane Addams, who founded Chicago's Hull House a decade later, understood perfectly the cynicism she saw among the poor when it came to democracy. They sensibly distrusted the integrity of the court system, being well aware "the judges have so often been trained as corporation attorneys," with sympathies and interests aligning with their former employers.[156] The great legal scholar Roscoe Pound also realized that labor violence after 1877 resulted from the inability of labor to find justice in the court system. But America's workers did not need intellectuals to tell them what was obvious: that politics and the courts were both rigged against them at every level.[157]

Electoral politics appeared limited without some organization to apply steady pressure on behalf of America's workers. Terence Powderly, who guided the Knights of Labor through most of the 1880s, and Samuel Gompers each looked back over their long careers and saw 1877 as the landmark year for labor; both men saw hope growing from the smoldering ruins of the Great Strike. Though the year presented "a picture of cumulative misery," Gompers wrote, the "revolt brought a whisper of hope."[158] Gompers, who fought a long, bitter, and losing strike for cigar makers in New York City in late 1877, felt that the Great Strike was the true beginning of the rise of American unions. The government called it an insurrection; Gompers called it "rebellion."[159] Ultimately the cigar makers' strike collapsed as the New York police used tactics they had learned in July, arresting workers without charges, beating them on their way to jail, and holding them well past the period allowed by habeas corpus standards. When the strike finally collapsed, the Manufacturers Association issued public thanks to the police commissioner for acting on its behalf. Samuel Gompers countered that the railroad workers' "rebellion . . . was the tocsin that sounded a ringing message of hope to us all." They bravely rose up "against conditions that nullified the rights of American citizens," clearly demonstrating the strength of the workers. The Great Strike saved Gompers' Cigarmakers' Union, which had fallen to just five hundred members at the beginning of 1877, but rebounded fourfold that fall.

The lesson of the Great Strike could not have been clearer for Gompers: the need for workers to organize. Gompers saw how the small scattered unions did their best to support one another through the many strikes of 1877, and he was certain that if they could combine their courage, resources, and ambitions, they could win more victories in the future. From this perception eventually emerged the American Federation of Labor, with Samuel Gompers as its founding president.[160]

"The late strike was not the work of a mob nor the working of a riot, but a revolution that is making itself felt throughout the land," said the *Washington Capital*, which thought "that America will never be the same again." Something had changed in the country when so many thousands of workers were so desperately dissatisfied that they would risk all they had in order to reverse what appeared such a minor pay cut. Using language repeated in numerous newspapers and journals, the *Capital* concluded, "For decades, yes centuries to come, our nation will feel the effects of the tidal wave that swept over it for two weeks in July."[161] The Great Strike had changed everything, though it was not yet clear just how. Management nationwide was delighted with how matters had turned out, as in 1877 "labor is under control for the first time since the war."[162] The British ambassador thought that vision incredibly short-sighted. He felt that the key fact was the suppression of the strike; the use of military forces acting at the behest of the largest corporations to address a labor dispute indicated a significant shift in power, but one that carried its own negation. "The power wielded by the great corporations in this country is almost incredible, and in their treatment of their subordinates they ignore entirely the principle that property has its duties as well as its privileges." The ambassador predicted that such an attitude could lead to the future growth of the unions, which ultimately had the power of both numbers and justice.[163] His prediction would prove correct, but it would take several decades for the workers to overcome the seismic shift in economic and political power represented by the successful crushing of the Great Strike. The alliance between big business and the federal government would hold firm for the next twenty-five years, before it was shaken up, though not terminated, by the progressive movement.

Writing in his diary on August 5, 1877, President Hayes observed, "The strikers have been put down by *force*."[164] While he had ordered the use of federal troops against the strikers, Hayes was deeply disturbed that it had taken the military to address what he saw as the violent actions of thousands of workers. Like so many others, the president wondered if the Great Strike was yet more evidence of an apparently increasing willingness of Americans to kill one another.

6

Homicidal Nation

We doubt not a man's fortune may be read . . . in the lines of his face, by physiognomy.

—Ralph Waldo Emerson, 1877[1]

Cassius M. Clay, the former United States minister to Russia who had arranged the purchase of Alaska, was a tough old bastard. He was also a notoriously violent man; but then he had needed to be aggressive in order to survive the many attacks upon him over the years. The Kentucky editor had been an early and pugnacious voice of abolitionism in a slave state, an advocate of the Republican Party and Abraham Lincoln, and had beaten off several physical attacks over the years and even faced down a mob. For several decades he stood at the radical end of the political spectrum, publicly pressuring Lincoln to emancipate the slaves, favoring the nationalization of the railroads, supporting José Martí's independence movement in Cuba, and attacking wealthy financiers for corrupting the American economy. Disgusted with the corruption of Grant's presidency, he switched to the Democratic Party and became a serious contender for vice president as Tilden's running mate. In 1877 he added murderer to his résumé.[2]

One of the most spectacular homicides of 1877, Clay's shooting of Perry White was full of ironies and uncertainties. Few facts of the case remain unquestioned other than that White was a black man whose parents, Sarah and David White, had been fired by Clay just the day before the shooting. Even Clay's version of events shifted with time. Initially he charged White and his mother with stealing from him and then seeking revenge after they had been caught, though he could offer no proof of the thefts. Later Clay insisted that White's parents had attempted to poison his son, Launey, apparently at the behest of the Republican Party. While he never explained how murdering his son served the interests of the Republicans, Clay stuck with this story when he wrote his memoirs years later in an account dripping with paranoia as "every one was a traitor and an enemy," and he came to the conclusion that a long list of family members must have been poisoned.[3] Another version of events published in several newspapers held that

Clay, a notorious womanizer, and White were competing for the affections of the same young woman, and that Clay shot his adversary to get him out of the way. Clay gave some credence to this latter motivation in his muddled memoir by claiming he came upon the plot against him and his son when he intercepted a letter from Perry White threatening to kill Clay in the belief that the woman in question "would marry him if she was removed from my employ."[4]

Similarly, Clay's accounts of the actual shooting varied widely. Clay insisted that he saw White standing next to a horse by the side of the road and suspected an imminent attack. He therefore dismounted from his own horse, drew his gun, and, when White came running toward him with a raised pistol, Clay fired in self-defense (though he admitted he shot before White had had a chance to do so).[5] Friendly papers published this version of events, insisting that "Mr. Clay has public sympathy in his favor, the negro whom he killed having been notorious as a thief and desperado." Nevertheless, papers that accepted Clay's account took advantage of the shooting to publish stories on Clay's colorful and violent past.[6] Unsympathetic papers argued that Clay shot White without proper provocation, reporting that other witnesses had seen an unarmed White retreating from Clay before the latter fired. "Kentucky justice," asserted the *Boston Globe*, "does not regard the killing of a negro by a man of Mr. Clay's standing as a very serious matter." The *Inter Ocean* reversed Clay's conspiracy theory and charged that Clay killed a black man in order to gain credibility with his new friends in the Democratic Party. As his trial approached, stories appeared that Clay had grown "gloomy," believing "that the colored people are rapidly decreasing in number and must finally become extinct." Clay's lawyers put up a vigorous defense despite the many different and often contradictory versions of events circulating, and he was found not guilty by reason of self-defense.[7]

Cassius Clay may have garnered numerous headlines and found himself with a number of new Democratic friends sympathetic to his need to kill a black man, but his fame and popularity as a murderer was nothing compared with that of the most notorious psychopath of the period, John Wesley Hardin. Though he looked nothing like the typical image of the coldhearted killer—he was thin, handsome, well educated, and possessed of an easy smile—Hardin probably holds the record for most individual murders in the last half of the nineteenth century, with totals ranging from twenty to fifty (the lower end of that scale being more probable) by the time he was twenty-six years old. Hardin, "the champion desperado and one of the most noted personages in Texas," according to the *Galveston Daily News*, and "A Bad 'Un" in the eyes of the *St. Louis Globe-Democrat*, demonstrated his talents during the last years of Reconstruction in his native Texas by shooting down a number of black police officers, his homicidal racism earning the respect of many whites.[8] One of these fans invited Hardin to take part in the long-running Sutton-Taylor feud, which Hardin joined with zeal. In 1877 he murdered deputy sheriff Charles Webb, which finally attracted the attention of the state's authorities, forcing Hardin to flee Texas for Alabama.[9]

Lee Hall of the Texas Rangers recruited Dallas policeman John R. Duncan to find Hardin. Going undercover, Duncan befriended Hardin's father-in-law and managed to find a letter addressed to "John Adams" in Alabama, which he assumed was Hardin's pseudonym. Learning that John Adams was returning to Alabama from Florida, Duncan and Lieutenant John B. Armstrong staked out a train station outside Pensacola, Florida, with eight deputies on August 23, 1877. They observed Hardin sitting in the smoking car on the train with three friends and entered the car from opposite ends. When Armstrong pulled his Colt revolver, Hardin shouted and reached for his own pistol, which became caught in his suspenders. One of Hardin's friends tried to escape through the window and was shot dead by a deputy. As Duncan and two other deputies grabbed Hardin from behind, Armstrong bashed him over the head with his revolver and then manacled the murderer.[10]

People curious to see the notorious John Wesley Hardin thronged the train stations on the journey back to Texas. Hardin, who was friendly with the Rangers and happy to talk with reporters, found "his patience sorely tried by the gaping crowds who gathered" wherever they stopped "to stare him in the face, with a curiosity that knew no sense of delicacy." The crowd outside the Travis County jail proved so thick that the Rangers had to lift Hardin and carry him above their heads to his cell. No previous Texas trial had attracted a greater number of spectators or a heavier Ranger presence. Hardin and his companion James Taylor fielded a team of four defense lawyers, including Waco judge S.H. Renick, but could not overcome the eyewitness testimony of respectable citizens who had seen Hardin and Taylor goad and then gun down Sheriff Webb. The jury convicted Hardin within an hour and the judge sentenced him to twenty-five years in prison for murder.[11] A few critics, including Bill Longley, found this sentence too lenient. Longley was sitting in the Galveston jail awaiting his execution for murder when he wrote to dispute Hardin's "superiority . . . as a high toned murderer" and his light sentence.[12]

In an interview with the *Galveston Daily News*, Hardin stated that he had received a fair trial "considering the fact that they were not simply trying a man charged with crime, but John Wesley Hardin." The reporter added that Hardin wept often during the interview. Curiously, Hardin became a model prisoner, studied law, and following his pardon in 1894 by the governor of Texas became a lawyer. But he had little chance to show how well he could translate his talents to his legal practice, as within the year he was shot in the back by Constable John Selman, a former outlaw seeking fame.[13]

Acts of murder, violence, and aggression filled the newspapers in 1877; it was almost as if they served as a kind of safety valve for pent-up anger over the class antagonism that defined the era. A sensational demonstration of this dynamic involved Wall Street's leading financier, Jay Gould. It is difficult to find anyone who had a kind word to say for Gould. About the best that could be said of him was that he got his start on Wall Street by marrying the daughter of the president of a railroad. More typically, he was called "infamous," and the "prince of the railroad schemers," who had done "more to hatch communism, breed riot and destroy Republican government than all other causes combined." He was described as looking like "a satisfied ogre," though a tiny one—"that pint of peanuts," as one broker called him—with a smile that "is not pleasant to see."[14] With a nationwide reputation as a manipulator of the economy, Gould's comment that he would give a million dollars to see Grant back in the presidential chair did not arouse enthusiasm for his view of democracy for hire.[15]

At the end of July 1877, Major A.A. Selover, a Christ Church vestryman who worked at the Shirley and Dunham brokerage firm, did what so many Americans longed to do by thrashing Jay Gould. Selover and James Keene, a renowned Wall Street speculator, considered themselves Gould's good friends and trusted him in a number of business transactions, which initially earned respectable profits. They therefore did not hesitate to follow Gould's advice to short-sell Western Union stocks, little suspecting that Gould was using them to drive up the price in order to increase his own profits. One day, in an apparently unplanned encounter with Gould near the corner of Broad Street and Exchange Place in New York, Selover began, in a friendly manner, inquiring about the transaction. But witnesses reported the conversation quickly turned testy, with Selover grabbing Gould by his lapels and shouting, "I'll teach you what it is to tell lies!" He slapped Gould in the face and struck him in the chest, sending Gould's gold pencil and bejeweled scarf pin flying. Selover hit Gould several more times, calling him "a damn liar!" He then lifted the diminutive Gould off his feet and threw him into a nearby construction pit. Some witnesses stated that a crowd that had gathered cheered at the sight of Gould lying still at the bottom of the pit. A policeman who had rushed to the scene let Selover go upon learning the victim's name. Gould, bruised but not seriously injured, returned to his office and immediately hired a pair of armed body guards who went with him everywhere.[16]

Selover also returned to his office, where he spoke calmly with reporters about beating Gould, insisting he had no intention of killing the man he had until recently considered his friend. He did not hesitate to admit that he had been caught in Gould's speculative web, but felt that Gould had taken advantage of their friendship: "It would exhaust the capacity of the English language to fittingly characterize the meanness, the duplicity, and the treachery with which this scoundrel has treated me." He and James Keene had consistently shown kindness to Gould, standing by him through the many attacks on his character and trusting him with their life savings. However, their friendship clearly had a sharp edge to it, as Selover had "helped Gould at one time out of the tightest place he ever was in, and I told him if ever I found him deceiving me I would thrash him, and I have done it." Selover felt completely justified in his actions: "I kept my word, even if he could not keep his."[17]

The public reaction to the attack was largely favorable, with many writers expressing the wish that they had been in Selover's position. "A jubilant feeling seemed to prevail" on Wall Street as news of the attack spread.[18] Most brokers confirmed that Selover and Keene had displayed "good faith but Gould, as usual, betrayed his companions." The prestigious former congressman and broker Russell Sage described his company's previous business relations with Gould in less than laudatory words: "Gould gave us his contract; that was no good. He gave us his word, and that was no good." As one gossipy account reported, "Even the ladies to-night were talking of the matter, and expressed much sympathy for Keene, who is said to have lost much through Gould's duplicity." In a widely repeated summary, Keene proclaimed Gould "the worst man set on earth since the beginning of the Christian era. He is treacherous, cowardly, false, and a despicable worm incapable of a generous motive." With no one rushing to Gould's defense, and the millionaire refusing to speak on his own behalf, no newspaper disputed Keene's judgment, writing instead that Gould had a long history of betraying trust and was known to have driven at least one old friend to suicide.[19] Gould had built his vast wealth through fraud, as demonstrated by his destruction of the Erie Railroad. As one New Hampshire paper maintained, Gould's profits "are made out of the losses of others. When he rejoices, some one must mourn." Though a few papers reported that Gould had earned some undeserved sympathy for having been attacked by a much bigger man, the general sentiment was that Selover had behaved appropriately, and had forestalled Keene's plans to shoot Gould.[20]

Gould did not die as a consequence of the attack, though many people wished he had. It is difficult to know which is the more striking aspect of this event: the complete lack of sympathy for the victim or the unhesitating justification of illegal violence. In contrast, no one attempted to justify John Wesley Hardin's homicidal actions, though the public was clearly fascinated by this celebrity criminal. And public figures were divided largely along political lines over Cassius Clay's shooting of a young black man, with Democrats defending his use of deadly force to resolve his dispute with Perry White and Republicans condemning as racist both Clay and the jury that exonerated him. Yet no one spoke publicly on Gould's behalf, few condemned the use of violence by a private individual seeking to punish the financier, and even those critical of Selover faulted him because Gould might receive sympathy as a consequence—a result they need not have feared. Some newspapers even recommended the extension of Selover's approach; as one cynical newspaper observed, "No one need pity these Wall Street thieves when caned by each other."[21] Unlike Clay and Hardin, Selover was never brought to trial for assault on one of the richest men in America.

Such endorsements of interpersonal aggression are all the more remarkable as a consensus built through 1877 that the nation was in the grip of a dangerous epidemic of violence. There were numerous sources of violence: the Molly Maguires, strikers, tramps, Southern Democrats, private security forces, public police forces, the militia, Indians, lynch mobs, and vigilantes. On top of these many threats to public order came the traditional acts of homicide that seemed to be rising beyond anyone's ability to get them under control. The perception of increased violence in 1877 led many newspapers to begin running columns like the *Inter Ocean*'s "Casualty Calendar" and "Criminal Calendar" or the *St. Louis Globe-Democrat*'s variations on "Rogues and Roughs," listing recent acts of violence.[22] While the violence of the Great Strike and the Indian wars received the most attention, the daily papers routinely carried accounts of what H.V. Redfield called "ordinary killings."[23]

A public perception grew that the United States was becoming a homicidal nation. Contemporary observers and later scholars noted the sudden rise in murder in the years surrounding the centennial of the country.[24] The *Cleveland Leader* reported that no murder had been committed in the area between 1815 and 1867, when the number of homicides began increasing every year: "How can we account for this almost sudden eruption of murders during the last eight years?"[25] The explanations ran the gauntlet from declining church attendance to the increased availability of firearms, with the recommended solutions equally diverse. It occurred to few people that there was something within the United States itself that could explain American violence; after all, there was nothing particularly exceptional about America any more, as the Great Strike had proven. For most people, the fault lay not with Americans but with humanity.

The Dangerous Class

There were murders galore. In St. Louis, Patrick Develin, a soldier brought in to restore order during the Great Strike, was robbed of fifty cents by a prostitute, Sylvia Hammon. Develin went back to camp, took a gun, returned to the "bawdy-house," and shot and killed Hammon and another prostitute who came to her aid. In Edenville, Michigan, a local physician, Dr. Rockwell, got into an argument over a horse with a local farmer and kicked him to death. In Bryan, Texas, a newspaper editor murdered his business partner in an argument. In the bayous of Louisiana someone was going around "indulging a very peculiar and diabolical propensity for cutting off people's heads," claiming six victims. People were murdered for love, gain, and revenge, and mostly during the killer's drunken rage.[26]

Newspapers reported with shock in April that there were eight homicide cases before the Philadelphia courts, including the murder of a police officer and an infanticide. When a Philadelphia man was killed in a barroom brawl, one paper lamented, "The newsboys will have a fresh cry of 'all about the murder' this morning."[27] Other localities expressed the same concern over the rising level of violence: four homicides in the San Francisco area in three months, two murders a year in Colorado. A headline in a Raleigh, Virginia, paper said it all: "Another Homicide."[28]

For far too many people, violence seemed the best solution to any problem. Most disturbing, young people were picking up the example of their elders and starting to carry guns. In reporting on a recent school shooting, the *Galveston Daily News* expressed outrage that nothing was done after a recent inspection at a Houston school "revealed that quite a startling percentage of the pupils were carefully provided with weapons" by their parents. In one widely covered case in April, four-year-old Dudley Kimball in Boston shot a neighboring two-year-old named Cox through the head. The police insisted that the shooting was definitely not an accident; rather, the "act was premeditated by young Kimball." The two boys were quarrelling when Dudley went and got his father's gun and "deliberately and coolly pointed the muzzle of the revolver at his [Cox's] head and fired."[29] The *Milwaukee Sentinel* worried that the phrase, "'That small boy with a pistol' will become a colloquial monstrosity equal in hideousness to the mother-in-law, the tramp, and the insurance agent."

Sometimes these gun-related deaths were accidental; others, like the Boston case, appeared to be intentional. There had been two shootings in Ohio alone on Christmas day involving boys who had received pistols as gifts. The *Sentinel* lamented that "men are foolish enough with weapons, boys can hardly be expected to be wiser," leading the paper to conclude that firearms should be kept out of the hands of the latter. "There are laws against carrying secret firearms," the paper noted, encouraging an additional "prohibition on youngsters carrying or playing with firearms." While such laws could not prevent all such shootings, they could certainly reduce the number, the paper maintained.[30]

This spreading stain of violence fed a growing dissatisfaction with the efficacy of the law. Particularly annoying to a vast swath of the public was what they took to be a liberal court system that too often demonstrated leniency to criminals, letting them off because of "technicalities" such as the absence of evidence. Though most lynchings occurred in the South for reasons of racial control—such as when a black man was lynched before two thousand people for an alleged rape in Columbus, Tennessee—the popular imagination focused on vigilante action in the West.[31] Even in law-abiding Republican towns such as Colorado Springs, the public often took the law into its own hands. In July, the police arrested Marcus Gonzales for "one of the most brutal" murders "in the annals of crime," according to the *Colorado Springs Gazette*. Gonzales had purportedly killed an elderly couple named Brown and left their daughter, Mrs. Rice, for dead. She recovered and identified Gonzales, who had killed her parents to cover the theft of $4. At the jail, a group of seventy-five men "over-powered" the guard—which was generally a face-saving performance rather than an actual attack on the police—took Gonzales from his cell, and hanged him from a telegraph pole in the town square. The newspaper approved of the conduct of the "vigilance committee," as they remained "quiet and orderly but determined" throughout the lynching. In December the newspaper reported on a man accused of murder taken from the jail in nearby Georgetown and hanged. The *Gazette* noted that many people denounce such lynchings without reference to the cause, "and that cause is the great number of acquittals of criminals of the most desperate character by some irregular legal technicality, or by the winning eloquence of the prisoner's lawyer, addressed to a soft-hearted jury." The paper insisted that such leniency did nothing to address the increasing homicide rate; there had been a dozen murders in the last six years in Colorado. "Whenever the people of any town or county feel assured that justice will be meted out to every violator of the law, untrammeled by false sympathy," the *Gazette* stated with certainty, "there will be but little danger of that community being shocked and disgraced by the performance of Judge Lynch."[32]

Those who defend lynching often argue that lynch mobs function in the absence of the law, but the opposite is almost uniformly the case. Lynch mobs operate in defiance of the law, most particularly when they feel that the courts may let an accused man off with too light a sentence, or may even free the accused as innocent. As Michael Pfeifer has written, lynch mobs "did not respond to an *absence* of law but rather to a *style* of criminal justice that was careful and deliberative, ostensibly impersonal and neutral, in which the rights of the defendant, the reform of the criminal, and humanitarian considerations were factored in beyond the punitive demands of communal opinion." Lynching sought to preserve order in a certain way, "to uphold the hierarchical prerogatives of the dominant residents of the locality."[33] While not all lynchings were racially motivated, there was a high correlation between lynching and racism, which was by no means limited to the South, nor did it solely target African Americans. Southern elites had always preferred a weak judicial system as a justification for their acts of vigilantism; as long as the courts had little real authority, white supremacists could establish a perfect rationalization for their extralegal violence. And, as noted in chapter 3, Hispanics and Chinese were disproportionately targeted by Western lynch mobs. Bigotry was widespread and warped every standard of American law and conduct.[34]

But the public was divided on the legitimacy of lynching. For instance, the double lynching in Santa Cruz in May 1877 (also discussed in chapter 3) led to an angry exchange between newspapers in that city and in San Francisco. The Santa Cruz paper defended the lynchings as a necessary action undertaken by respectable people: "property owners and tax payers, representatives of almost every trade, profession and business interest" had acted to uphold justice before the courts could muddy the waters. The *Daily Alta California* in San Francisco condemned these actions as an unjustified taking of the law into private hands, which could easily lead to injustice. While it was true that these men "may have, under our laws, deserved death," the "mob which hung them had no authority nor right to violate the law and good name of the state by inflicting punishment which takes the character of personal vengeance." The advocates of vigilantism rejected what they saw as the middle-class sentimentality and an excess sensitivity to due-process rights, putting forth instead the conviction that lynch mobs operated as an effective deterrent against illegal violence. Opponents of lynching pointed out that the mobs themselves were committing illegal violence, as they well knew; otherwise why would they, as the *Alta California* observed, carry out their deeds under the cover of darkness, and then sneak home "afraid to take responsibility for their act"? Putting forth an insistence on the formal operation of the law as the best guarantor of justice, opponents "bitterly attacked lynchings as atavistic, prone to miscarriages of justice, and destructive to the cause of law and order."[35]

The role of the police proved decisive in lynchings. There is little doubt that the police in Santa Cruz and Colorado Springs stepped aside and let the mobs take their prisoners to be hanged. Other officers of the law were not so accommodating. When William M. Davis shot and killed Louis Ash in a drunken rage in Virginia City, friends of Ash organized a lynch mob; but the sheriff placed a guard at the jail and the mob went home after exhausting themselves by shouting their intention to kill Davis. In San Antonio the sheriff frustrated a lynch mob by hiding its prey. In several states, law enforcement came to the conclusion that vigilantes were themselves often gangs of criminals bent on intimidating witnesses into not testifying and judges and juries into acquitting gang members. Texas Ranger Lee Hall stated that he could not leave his prisoners in the hands of a sheriff whom he felt led the local vigilantes as a front for criminal activities, and there are several instances of vigilante mobs, which often included sheriffs, freeing those arrested by the Rangers. On another occasion Hall reported that, though he had recovered twelve hundred stolen hides, he would not waste his time arresting anyone since the sheriff and county prosecutor were almost certainly part of the gang. Meanwhile the great cattle barons used vigilantes for their own purposes; for instance, in Nueces County cattlemen organized vigilantes to launch a terror campaign against Mexican shepherds and workers.[36] The *Galveston Daily News* held that "nine-tenths of the anarchy and lawlessness which has existed in Western Texas for the past twenty-five years, has grown out of the action of mobs and vigilant committees." Generally, though, the Rangers shared the public's contempt for the laxity of the courts, and became notorious for shooting suspects in the back while they were "attempting to escape."[37]

The perception that liberal judges stymied the best efforts of law enforcement was not limited to the West. While the cities of the Northeast experienced vigilante action only in response to strikes, their middle class and elite shared the sentiment that far too many criminals received light sentences or were freed outright. Anthony Comstock, in his third year as director of the Society for the Suppression of Vice, complained that most of his efforts were in vain because of the leniency of the courts, which released most of the people he arrested while even the "worst criminals" found it easy to obtain pardons. Attempting to respond to this perceived leniency, the New York legislature passed an indeterminate sentencing law in 1877 mandating that a felon would be held until prison officials decided that he had been reformed, effectively transferring the sentencing power from judges to prison bureaucrats.[38]

Yet the jails and prisons themselves often seemed part of the problem. On the whole, American jails were not very formidable, with escapes common in the 1870s and 1880s. When judges or juries did not release criminals, gangs of their friends occasionally did so. For instance, in Nevada's Carson Prison, convicts working in the shoe shop grabbed the deputy warden, shouted "Liberty or death; you shall die, but we will be free," seized two guards as hostages, and attempted to break out of the prison. Their effort failed when the other guards opened fire, killing one prisoner and wounding two of the hostages. More successful was the "Connecticut Borgia," Lydia Sherman, who simply walked out the front gate of the Connecticut State Prison where she was serving a life sentence for murdering "three consecutive husbands and seven children."[39] Two months later another prisoner escaped from the same prison, this time by going out a window. In May twelve men broke into Texas's Brownwood jail, released six prisoners, and fled the scene, all of them eluding capture by the frustrated Rangers. In August a self-proclaimed vigilante group held a "jail opening" in Rio Grande City, freeing all the prisoners, who fled to Mexico. In 1877 there were additional successful jail breaks in Texas, Colorado, California, Kansas, Kentucky, Mississippi, Missouri, Wisconsin, Ohio, Pennsylvania, Massachusetts, New Hampshire, and Iowa, where a sheriff helped a convicted murderer escape.[40] When not porous, jails appeared to be schools of crime. The Reverend Tilton called jail "the very worst kind of school of vice," where those who committed a petty crime "come in contact with the very worst of criminals." Jails "produce more criminals than they prevent."[41]

Scholars have attempted to bring precision to the perceptions of contemporaries witnessing a rise in homicide. It is difficult to craft confident generalizations about violence in nineteenth-century America, an age before the systematic calculation of criminal conduct. But many historians have approached the subject with localized studies. Thus Roger Lane found that the homicide rate in post–Civil War Philadelphia peaked in the years of the depression, with 205 murders from 1874 to 1880. But, as Lane points out, there is significant under-counting of homicides in the later nineteenth century. Lane thinks that most murders were committed by poor transients, though it is difficult to determine. Of those tried for murder between 1860 and 1880 in Philadelphia, only thirty-three can be found in the city directories, and just a quarter of those remained in the directories for four years or more. Lane hypothesizes that those most prone to violence were those least attuned to the "rhythms of the new economic order," living outside the discipline and rigid time constraints of industrialism. At its most basic level, only those who do not have to be at work early, six days a week, can afford to get drunk and rowdy on any night of the week, and alcohol was the most common precipitator of homicide in these years. These findings give credence to the period's tramp fears.[42]

Contemporaries had little doubt that violence was spreading in the United States in 1877, but many experts hoped that science could provide answers to criminal detection and prevention. The vast majority of nineteenth-century writers and officials who attempted to understand the roots of violence blamed the criminals. Flaws in their character or heritage explained their behavior, not larger social arrangements or the environment. The dominant paradigm of the period, adhered to even by Karl Marx, was that most crime originated in the low-est orders of society—what Marx called the "lumpenproletariat" and the general public referred to as the "dangerous class" or "criminal class." These tramps, pro-fessional criminals, and vagrants were dangerous not simply because they had no respect for property or life, but also because they were so demoralized that they became parasites in any society. Marx saw them as "social scum," a "passively rot-ting mass" that collected in the most filthy areas of large cities. "This rabble," he warned, "is absolutely venal and absolutely brazen," and had no compunction against using violence to gain immediate gratification. His words were replicated in every middle-class newspaper in the United States.[43]

The police claimed primacy as the experts on violence and perceived the pres-ence of a "criminal class" that bore responsibility for the vast majority of crimes against both person and property. Newspapers picked up on this notion and gave it wide credence, though it proved difficult to pin down exactly who con-stituted this class and what explained their actions.[44] In short, the concept of a criminal class sidestepped the larger issue of causality. The police's experience with criminals led many officers to feel that they could recognize them on sight. This confidence took physical form in New York with Inspector Thomas Byrnes's famous "Rogues' Gallery" of photographs, which allowed the public to identify malefactors in their midst. Anyone could stop by police headquarters and step into the gallery to see what the criminal class looked like—and in 1886

Byrnes published his collection in book form, bringing these faces to a wider public.[45] Byrnes ordered his detectives to gather as much information about those they arrested as possible to aid in their later apprehension—for Byrnes was confident that few of those he arrested would ever be turned away from breaking the law. This vast accumulation of data persuaded Byrnes that criminals operated according to no pattern other than greed, and he rejected two popular theories of the sources of crime: physiognomy and ethnicity.

The first theory, developed by the Italian Cesare Lombroso, held that physical appearance indicated character, and that depravity and criminality were both easily evident to the trained eye. Byrnes thought that notion nonsense. "Look through the pictures in the Rogues' Gallery and see how many rascals you find there who resemble the best people in the country."[46] Similarly, the people captured on film by Byrnes's detectives are all white, predominately WASP, with a number of Irish and Jews, and just a few Italians. But then, Byrnes was fascinated by the "professional" criminal, by the miscreant who carried on his or her trade with skill and talent, whether robbing banks or pulling confidence scams; he had much less respect for those so lacking in professional standards as to resort to violence.

The newspapers spoke with much more confidence than the police about the nature of the criminal class. Generally they were perceived as dangerous "nonproducers," and "members of a standing army continually at war with the community which supports it." There was an obvious tautological quality to the concept of a criminal class, as every study defined it as those who commit crimes, and attempted to determine its nature by looking at those who were in prison. Thus, alternate causes for incarceration such as racism are lost in the explanation that those in prison are there because they are criminals and therefore indicate the nature of criminality. For example, the report of the California Prison Directors in August 1877 found that most criminals were between twenty-five and thirty, with half native-born Americans. One-sixth of the prison's population was Chinese, followed by Irish and Germans.[47] The *San Francisco Evening Bulletin* ignored most of the material gathered in this report and focused on a single reference to literacy in order to reject the logic that education lessens crime since the majority of criminals can read and write. Moving beyond the statistics, the paper held that the prevailing characteristics of the criminal class were a "deficiency of conscience" and self-control, an innate viciousness, and laziness. The criminal acted "in strict accordance with his instincts," and was thus beyond reform: "He has neither the natural regard for others which lies at the base of conscience, nor has the sufficient self-control to enable him to consider his own selfish interests in the long run."[48]

While the criminal class could be found in every city in the country, it took on slightly different qualities in each locale. Oddly, some cities felt a certain pride in claiming that its criminal class was the vilest (Denver), or the most daring (San Francisco), or the largest as a percentage of the population (Boston).[49] Each state had its own variation on those identified as belonging to the "criminal class"—immigrants in the Northeast and on the West Coast, and blacks throughout the South. Generally, however, the membership of the criminal class depended on which group was the target of contempt at a particular moment; thus the *San Francisco Evening Bulletin* proclaimed in the immediate aftermath of the strike that the local hoodlums are known by their "willingness to murder Chinese on short notice, or to fire buildings for the mere love of the thing," and a month later stated that there was a high concentration of Chinese among the city's criminal class.[50] Confident of the identity of the criminal class, some papers called for laws to constrain them, though specifics remained vague, while others just called for sterner child discipline. Several politicians in 1877 attacked the notion of allowing members of the criminal class to vote, since voting gave them control over the passage and enforcement of laws that they would no doubt break at some point. The *Lowell Citizen* noted with approval that the new constitution of Georgia permanently took away the franchise from those convicted of any criminal offense—failing to notice the intention of diminishing the number of black voters.[51]

No public figure made a connection between crime and the growing economic disparity and poverty of America's cities. The 1870s saw the building of shoddy tenements to house the poor in most cities, the construction proceeding in tandem with the rise of numerous juvenile gangs. New York's Lower East Side around Chatham Square and the Poverty Lane area near Ninth Avenue had particularly bad reputations in this regard, being home to notoriously vicious gangs of boys who quickly grew into the city's leading thugs. The Dutch Mob worked the area east of the Bowery in New York until Captain Anthony J. Allaire took command of the Eighteenth Precinct in 1877 and brought the gang down through the unhindered use of his officers' billy clubs.[52]

New York City appeared to be the center of, and perhaps even the spur to, the crime wave sweeping the country. The daily accounts of beatings, murder, and mayhem captured the attention of visitors to New York, a surprising number of whom sought out statistics to back up their impressions. The British traveler George Sala spent time pursuing the matter, eventually learning that the police courts of New York City arraigned 56,004 men and 22,529 women on criminal charges in the year ending October 31, 1878, but he could not get a precise count on the different types of crimes committed. Though lacking comprehensive statistics, the city remained a particularly good place to study crime, as it was in the public perception "a thieves' paradise," or, as Herbert Asbury put it, the Gilded Age was "when New York was really wicked."[53] The city's high concentration of immigrants persuaded many observers that the foreign-born constituted the major component of the criminal class, with each nationality possessing its own characteristics. For instance, English thieves carried a reputation for successful criminality, gathering in taverns like the House of Lords on Houston Street. There the likes of Chelsea George, London Izzy Lazarus, and Charles "Cockney" Ward connected with fences and made temporary partnerships. One of the latter ended badly for Lazarus, who was killed by Barney Friery in a fight over the division of the spoils from a jewelry store heist. Inspector Byrnes praised Cockney Ward, whose real name was Charles Vallum, as holding "the distinction of being the only man in his line who can play the confidence game successfully on women." Ward's career came to a temporary end in April 1877 when he was caught raising money for the Presbyterian Hospital—without its knowledge or approval—and was sentenced to five years in prison.[54]

In 1877 the Charlton Street gang of river pirates terrorized those traveling by water around New York. They were known for their violent methods, and the police suspected that many of the unidentified bodies that washed ashore had fallen victim to this gang. Led by Mike Shannon, who enjoyed political influence in the city's Eighth Ward, the gang was broken up by the unusual expedient of a joint operation by the New York City and Hoboken police. However, Shannon walked because of a hung jury—even after two of his accomplices testified against him. Frustrated police felt certain that bribes had determined the outcome of the trial.[55]

Modern Policing in 1877

Police work in 1877 was a world away from *CSI*. There was little recognizable as solid policing or detective work, and little success in catching criminals unless they were apprehended on the spot. The police generally relied on brute force alone to get the job done; advanced methods followed the line suggested by Denver marshal David J. Cook as his first rule of good policing: "Never hit a prisoner over the head with your pistol, because you may afterwards want to use your weapon and find it disabled."[56]

It was a time of tough police, men who did not hesitate to shoot to kill drunks who got out of hand, with coroners ruling such actions "justifiable homicide." In St. Louis, Officer Jerry McCarty shot and killed a twenty-year-old vandal, John Shelley, as he fled. Father M.J. M'Cabe, a Catholic priest, testified to the shooting but justified the actions of Officer McCarty as "it was a matter of surprise to him that the officers had not killed one-half of the 'Castle Garden' neighborhood, as they mostly consisted of the vilest and lowest class of people, who are fighting and quarreling continually." The jury agreed with the priest and acquitted McCarty. In Houston, an Officer Morris shot and killed a suspected horse thief, Andrew Washington, who was running away. Despite the overwhelming evidence that Washington was unarmed and running when Morris shot him in the back, the jury, which expected their police to use their guns, returned a verdict of not guilty.[57] Sometimes, as George Sala observed, the press would abuse the police "for the addictedness of 'clubbing' people—that is to say, to brain them on slight provocation with their truncheons," but generally there was little objection to more excessive violence. Sala personally witnessed a fight between police and a crowd of workers in New York in which the police drew their revolvers to hold off the crowd. Sala insisted it was clearly a friendly brawl, as the police "did not use those weapons; while on the part of the mob not a single shot was fired."[58]

Curiously, developments in police procedure in New York were matched in Texas. In an effort to stem the rising tide of violence in Texas, Major John B. Jones, commander of the Rangers, and Adjutant General Steele compiled a written version of Byrnes's Rogues' Gallery. Their "Black Book," or "Crime Book," a copy of which was given to every Ranger, listed all the men wanted by the Rangers with as much description and other information as they could compile. The book attempted to bring some control to the wave of violence sweeping through Texas after the new Democratic legislature cut the Rangers' budget by half. Responding to this crisis, Jones ordered his men in March 1877 to discontinue all operations against the Indians and shift their attention to crime. They found few allies as the Democratic-controlled courts tended to let white defendants walk free, no matter what their offense. The Rangers arrested hundreds of men but found it difficult to attain convictions against any of them, if only because witnesses refused to testify for fear of retribution. The Rangers did enjoy one legal tool that they employed freely: the law against bearing arms. While the state constitution protected the right of citizens to own firearms, it granted the legislature "the power by law to regulate the wearing of arms with a view to prevent crime." Throughout the 1870s the Rangers used these gun laws to arrest many men against whom they could prove no other crime.[59]

Major Jones hoped to avoid bloodshed as much as possible, fearing that it would just feed further violence; thus the Rangers' basic method for capturing criminals was to sneak up on them while they were sleeping. For instance, John King Fisher, a leader of a particularly successful gang of cattle thieves, was captured when Captain Leander McNelly and several of his men woke up Fisher and eight of his crew by nudging them with their drawn pistols. But so compliant was the local court that Fisher was released that same day. Lieutenant Lee Hall proved a bit more clever, charging Fisher with a bewildering array of crimes, keeping the cattle thief busy rushing back to various courts for four years from 1877 to 1881.[60]

The primary challenge the Rangers faced was a pair of feuds that spanned several years and produced numerous deaths. In DeWitt County, the Sutton-

Taylor feud was entering the third year of what Captain McNelly called "a per-fect reign of terror." After a "posse" killed a doctor and his son for treating a member of the opposite side, the governor sent Lee Hall and a company of Rangers to restore order. Hall quickly discovered that while everyone knew who the murderers were, no one would testify, out of loyalty or fear; with two of the suspected killers serving as deputy sheriffs, public reticence was understandable. Hall acted boldly, bursting in on a wedding to seize the accused and crowding the courtroom with his armed Rangers, strong-arming the judge into rejecting bail and sending the defendants to be tried in a separate county. But this success was short-lived as most of the accused were freed when the court records and ev-idence mysteriously vanished. Only one man was convicted, and he was imme-diately pardoned by the governor because of his service in the Confederate army. Nonetheless, pressure by the Rangers suppressed the Sutton-Taylor feud and, in combination with the high-profile capture of John Wesley Hardin, earned the Rangers grudging respect and economic support from the legislature, which fi-nally awarded them a permanent spot in the budget.[61] Public support for the Rangers proved less forthcoming.

The Horrell-Higgins feud in Lampasas County, northwest of Austin, was more extreme. Back in 1873 two of the five Horrell brothers and some friends had gunned down four state policemen. A crowd broke them out of jail, and the Horrells took off for New Mexico before returning to stand trial for the murders, of which they were acquitted. In January 1877, the overconfident Horrells made the mistake of stealing cows from Pink Higgins, one of the meanest men in Texas. On January 22, Higgins walked into the Gem Saloon in Lampasas, lev-eled his Winchester at an unarmed Merritt Horrell, and calmly shot him four times. When the remaining brothers swore revenge, Higgins and some of his pals ambushed Mart and Tom Horrell, shooting them in the back. Though wounded, the Horrell brothers got away and planned retribution.[62]

In May a gunfight raged through the town of Lampasas, leaving two dead and one wounded. With so many bullets flying about, some local businessmen called on the Rangers, who tried to arrest the leaders of both sides but found that no one would testify. Deciding to ignore "the strict dictates of the law," Major Jones launched another of his predawn raids. When the Horrell brothers awoke on July 28, 1877, they found themselves facing Winchester rifles. The following day Jones arrested Higgins and his chief henchmen. The commander of the Texas Rangers then did something astonishing and creative. He wrote out a pair of letters, each apologizing and promising an end to violence, and addressed to members of the other side in the feud.[63] Jones then forced the men in his cus-tody to sign and exchange letters, and published the whole affair in the local pa-per. Incredibly, this gambit worked, and the Horrell-Higgins feud ended with a pair of polite letters.[64]

Public fascination with these "Western desperadoes" grew through 1877. Reporters covered the violent and often bizarre Texas feuds, interviewed the Younger Brothers, and exaggerated the exploits of the James Gang while elevating sheriffs such as Wyatt Earp to heroic stature. In late summer, a minor outlaw named Sam Bass gained sudden national notoriety. The depression turned many people to a life of crime, including Bass. Unable to find a job in his native Indiana, Bass found sporadic work in Denton County, Texas, until he and some friends thought to take advantage of the disorder the Great Strike generated by robbing a train. Riding north to Nebraska, twenty-six-year-old Bass and five others undertook what Texas Ranger James B. Gillett called "one of the boldest train robberies that had ever occurred in the United States." On September 18 the gang stopped a Union Pacific passenger train at Big Springs, stealing $60,000 in newly minted twenty-dollar gold coins. They then walked through the train, taking another $5,000 in property off the passengers. Bass drew national attention for convincing an accomplice not to hurt the guard in the baggage car.[65]

The response to the robbery was quick and brutal. At the behest of the Union Pacific, the United States Army joined in the chase, undertaking the task of law enforcement. The army quickly found, shot, and killed two of the gang, recovering a third of the gold. A third robber, shot and captured the following month in Missouri, snitched on the rest of the gang. Bass made it back to Texas, where he led the Texas Rangers and the army on an extravagant chase, robbing two stagecoaches and four trains by April 1878, all within twenty miles of Dallas. While none of these robberies gained anything like the wealth of the first strike against the Union Pacific, they served to solidify Bass's national reputation as a successful criminal and drew down the full fury of Texas's corporate elite.[66]

With large rewards drawing scores of bounty hunters, the state mobilizing law enforcement, and the corporations bringing in the Pinkertons, the U.S. Army, and U.S. Marshal Stillwell Russell and nineteen special deputies, Bass found himself pursued by hundreds of armed men. Major Jones coordinated a ruthless policy to remove anyone who might give aid to Bass, arresting not just every known accomplice but also several lawyers charged with "harboring train robbers." If a judge released one of these men, Jones simply ordered him arrested again. Captain June Peak, whom Jones described as "a terror to evil doers," scoured the countryside for Bass, arresting all suspicious persons and killing one member of the gang, Arkansas Johnson, in a dramatic shoot-out. But Bass eluded capture and rumors of his presence swept through the state and beyond.[67]

It was an informer who brought down Sam Bass. Promised a full pardon and a piece of the reward, gang member James Murphy sent a letter to Major Jones with Bass's plans to rob a bank in Round Rock. Jones, determined that his Rangers would capture the elusive bandit, failed to inform anyone else of his information.

On July 19, 1878, the Rangers scattered through Round Rock failed to recognize Bass and two members of his gang who entered town on a reconnaissance mission before hitting the bank. When a local deputy responsible for seeing that everyone checked their guns with the sheriff noticed a suspicious bulge under a stranger's coat, he asked Sam Bass if he had a pistol. Bass answered, "Yes," and the three outlaws opened fire, killing the deputy and wounding a second. Rangers came rushing from all directions, firing scores of bullets at the fleeing outlaws. One was killed, one escaped unscathed, and Bass was seriously wounded. The next day a company of Rangers found Sam Bass sitting at the base of an oak tree, dying. They took him into custody, where he was pleased to talk about anything but his companions. He died the afternoon of July 21, his twenty-seventh birthday. It was hardly the Rangers' most brilliant manhunt, but the published versions of the battle finally won them the respect Jones sought.[68]

Whether in New York or Texas, California or Michigan, law enforcement in the years after the Civil War was, as the historian David R. Johnson wrote, "thoroughly decentralized, thoroughly democratic, and thoroughly chaotic." The police were encouraged to make arrests no matter what the offense, as statistics measured success. Chicago police commissioner Mark Sheridan boasted, "The police are efficient; they made 28,000 arrests last year." Rates of prosecution or effective crime prevention mattered less than the body count. It is not surprising, therefore, that the most common arrest was for drunkenness, which accounted for about half those picked up by urban police. Depending on the city, only 10 percent to 15 percent of total arrests were for felonies. That low arrest figure did not translate into a paucity of property crimes. Quite the contrary—many studies of reported crime indicate a steady increase through the depression years, while a few scholars argue that the crime rate held steady.[69] But there is also general agreement that crime did not pay during these years. Eric Monkkonen found that "almost exactly as many criminals were reduced to poverty by their crime as paupers were driven to crime by their poverty." Despite a tendency at this time to glorify criminals, especially Western desperados, most of the country worried about these rising crime rates and sought solutions, though it was rare for anyone to publicly suggest that the source of increased levels of violence might be found, as the Colorado Springs Gazette worded it, in "the great number of men who have been thrown out of employment." Cities and towns throughout the country passed laws aimed at tightening enforcement and hired more police. For example, in 1877, Dodge City hired Wyatt Earp to put a lid on the violence; Earp brought in his friends Doc Holliday and Bat Masterson to help out.[70]

What was not clear to some observers was why, if the police knew who constituted the criminal class, they just did not arrest the lot of them. There was a widespread suspicion that the police were often a little too chummy with the dangerous class, arresting petty criminals while working with and sometimes for the criminal elite—charges made against all three of the Dodge City sheriffs in 1877. Rumors—many of which would later turn out to be true—swirled about Inspector Byrnes and other leading police officers in the nation's largest cities, suggesting an array of profitable arrangements with criminals. Just as the police were supposed to prevent crime rather than create it, so did the public feel that they should respond to violence rather than being responsible for it. Yet it was impossible to escape the fact that the police were themselves a significant source of violent behavior. When not denying that they ever responded with excess brutality, police officers tended to justify their use of force by insisting that they had to be tough because of the vicious nature of criminals and out of a sense of frustration with liberal judges. Many accepted this logic, while others compared America's police to organized criminal gangs, with heavy press emphasis on their corruption, and held them to an unfavorable contrast with the professional police forces of London and Paris.[71]

New York's Captain Alexander "Clubber" Williams was the embodiment of the brutal, corrupt, and enormously successful cop. His nickname came from the enthusiasm with which he clubbed suspects first and made inquiries later, his fame rising when he ended the power of the Gas House Gang by the adroit application of his legal theory, "There is more law in the end of a policeman's nightstick than in a decision of the Supreme Court." In 1876 he succeeded in becoming captain of the Twenty-ninth Precinct, and gave the west side area between 14th and 42nd Streets its name when he rejoiced, "I have had chuck for a long time and now I am going to eat tenderloin." His new Tenderloin District was home to the city's leading theaters, clubs, restaurants, hotels, and brothels, all of which were major sources of graft for a clever officer like Williams. As the *New York Sun* sarcastically observed, Williams was "very thrifty," saving more than $100,000 on a salary of $2,000 a year. When pressed by an official inquiry to account for his affluence, Williams explained that he had made some fortunate investments in Japanese real estate.[72] The *Police Gazette* had no room for humor in condemning Williams as a "brutal British bully" who terrorized the city's working class. Though hundreds of formal complaints and repeated lawsuits for assault were filed against Williams, he consistently received the protection of the Police Commission's Republican members, who viewed him with great favor. Despite setting records for the number of brutality and corruption charges, Williams was actually promoted to inspector.[73]

Most victims of police violence in New York City were "white males from non-Anglo backgrounds." Surprisingly, just 4 percent of those subject to police brutality were African Americans.[74] Put another way, the police tended to vent their anger primarily at immigrants and members of the working class, the latter accounting for 70 percent of those filing complaints.[75] The working class perceived this bias and saw the police as tools of the wealthy who had consistently proven themselves hostile to workers. Workers did not forget the Tompkins Square Riot, nor the Orange Day Parade of July 1871, when the militia protecting Irish Protestant marchers opened fire on a crowd of protesters, inflicting one hundred casualties. These events led to widespread distrust of the police and militia in New York, and loud calls for the democratic reform of both. In contrast, middle-class reformers saw the police as working-class thugs, the tool of Tammany Hall and corrupt immigrants, and wanted less democracy, favoring the establishment of oversight boards with no connection to politics. The very use of this new phrase "police brutality" indicates the judgment of the middle class, which saw the police brutally employing force against the innocent. Accounts of police brutality often emphasized the animal-like and massive physical appearance of the police.[76] Even poor victims of the police earned the sympathy of the urban press, so long as they were not striking at the time. For instance, in the spring of 1877 the secretary of New York's German benevolent society, Edward Dierks, was discovered by police unconscious and bleeding. Rather than considering that he might have been the victim of an attack by robbers, the police assumed he was drunk and arrested him. Receiving no medical care, Dierks died the next day. The city's papers attacked the police for doing more harm than good, the *World* charging them with "such stupidity, brutality, and neglect of duty" as befits "a monstrous satire upon our civilization." However, middle-class reformers had no objection in 1877 to the police using that brutal force against disruptive workers.[77]

This hostility between police and public was heightened by the layers of corruption in most American cities. In 1877 New York's police commissioner Joel B. Erhardt, a Republican, publicly objected to Tammany Hall levying a tax on every member of the Police Department for the Democratic Party's campaign fund. His complaints were dismissed by the Democratic *Star* as "sheer political hypocrisy," since the Republicans would do the same thing if they ever got into power. After all, the *Star* pointed out with what its editor surely assumed was killer logic, "somebody has to contribute" to the political campaign, so why not the well-paid police.[78] Though many Democratic police officers also resented paying for Tammany Hall's campaigns, public contempt for the police grew.

Neither brutality nor corruption was limited to big-city police forces. In Texas, the poorly paid Rangers supplemented their income in a number of ways, most profitably through rewards. On December 7, 1877, Rangers John B. Armstrong and Thomas Deggs, lured by the large reward involved, went to arrest John Mayfield, a murder suspect. Coming upon Mayfield in the corral at his ranch, the Rangers shot him "when he resisted arrest." Mayfield's neighbors were so outraged by this violent arrest that they chased the Rangers off and buried Mayfield in a secret location so the Rangers could not claim the bounty.[79] The Rangers also had a reputation as the most brutal police force in the country, not hesitating to use torture to acquire information. One favored method was putting a noose around a prisoner's neck with the other end of the rope over a tree branch, repeatedly pulling the defendant off the ground until he confessed or supplied information. Ranger William Callicott confidently reported that "this treatment always brought out the truth," sanguinely adding that after getting what they wanted the Rangers generally hanged their suspect until he was dead. General Edward Ord, commander of U.S. troops in Texas, carefully acknowledged that the Rangers gathered information "by means which I could not legally resort to, but which were the only means of getting at the actual facts." He added that, after seizing a suspected Mexican criminal, Captain Leander McNelly "hung him up until he was made to confess where the rest of the raiders were [located]."[80]

The police in most cities were inadequate, poorly trained, and distrusted. The population of New York City had tripled between the 1840s and 1877; yet while the old city watch had put 548 men on the streets every night, the 1877 police force mustered just 769 officers. Nor did the police yet employ any "matrons" to aid women victims or deal with female suspects. Grotesquely overworked, most police spent nine-hour shifts on the street and seven hours on reserve in a station house, six days a week. They were generally rather grumpy as a consequence, having little patience for anyone who complicated their task. Such men were likely to resort to their clubs at the slightest provocation.[81]

Inventing the Science of Criminology

In the face of corrupt and violent police, a rising crime rate, and perceived liberal courts insistent on upholding technical points of law, many Americans found the task before the country daunting, requiring not only sterner methods but more scientific ones as well. The nineteenth century was an age of scientific racism and misogyny, of taking the appearance of people and biological differences as determinative. Many scientists established racial hierarchies based upon deviation from the perceived white norm, while others worked hard to establish the inferiority of women. Among those seeking to determine the roots of criminal behavior, two names loomed large in the United States starting in 1877: Cesare Lombroso and Richard L. Dugdale.[82]

For Cesare Lombroso of Turin, whose *Criminal Man* was first published in Italy in 1876, crime was biologically determined. Lombroso rejected Enlightenment notions that the punishment should fit the crime; instead he insisted that the punishment should fit the criminal. Crime is not a product of free will, he said, but the result of biological factors, and, most important, we can perceive this biological inheritance simply by examining the face of the subject. Lombroso spoke to a vision of crime as a disease, a perspective finding voice in 1876 and 1877 in France, Germany, England, and the United States. Lombroso's contribution was to layer a patina of science over this popular bias. Building on the emerging ideas of social Darwinism, Lombroso argued that criminals were atavistic errors in evolutionary development, the embodiment of man's savage heritage, and as such could be identified by their physical appearance. In a sense, the "born criminal" cannot help himself, as his animal nature forces him to act savagely. But because his atavistic nature takes both mental and physical form, the criminal carries the features of an ape or other inferior animal, allowing the police to identify and isolate criminals early in their careers in order to protect civilized society. Making such an argument required Lombroso to demonstrate that animals are themselves guilty of criminal conduct, a task to which he devoted the first part of *Criminal Man*. As Stephen Jay Gould wrote, in what "must be the most ludicrous excursion into anthropomorphism ever published," Lombroso found adultery, rage, theft, rape, and criminal conspiracy among a wide variety of animals.[83]

Though Lombroso's *Criminal Man* did not appear in English for many years, its concepts spread quickly across the English-speaking world through the promotion of his admirers and had enormous popular influence in the last quarter of the nineteenth century. The first hints of this influence can be found in discussions of criminals and tramps in 1877, with references to their having "a distinctive type of character, physiognomy and aspect which unites them in one class, although they are gathered from all races and conditions." Even Ralph Waldo Emerson wrote that year that "a man's fortune may be read . . . in the lines of his face, by physiognomy."[84] Within fifteen years, Lombroso would be credited with founding the field of criminal anthropology, which accepted as scientific fact the idea that physical characteristics are accurate indicators of criminality. Still more intriguing, different kinds of criminals shared distinctive features. Thus Lombroso's investigations found that murderers almost always had large noses, thick hair, thin lips, and well-developed canines. Once a scholar mastered Lombroso's photographs, he could enter a prison and "distinguish almost at a glance those condemned for theft and those condemned for murder."[85]

The woodcuts and photographs that accompany Lombroso's work exaggerate the features of numerous European criminals to illustrate their savage appearance. Lombroso could never have imagined a Ted Bundy or a John Wesley Hardin, for the concept of the "handsome criminal" was an oxymoron.[86] His theory of criminal physiognomy influenced most American police departments, which began compiling "Lombroso Books"—compilations of descriptions and photographs of criminal types—and calling on physiognomy experts to appear in court cases as early as 1878, while the public embraced the notion that criminals looked the part, a bias reinforced by most contemporary literature as novelists enjoyed the right to portray their villains in the broadest brushstrokes. However, with time, the physical evidence of photographs began to overwhelm Lombroso's theory, particularly in the most famous of these collections, Thomas

Byrnes's *Professional Criminals of America*. Yet even though Byrnes rejected Lombroso's argument that you could tell a criminal just by looking at him, supporters of Lombroso found validation for the master's theories in Byrnes's book.[87] When the Chicago police followed Byrnes's lead and opened their own Rogues' Gallery in 1877, a local reporter thought it "a fine place to study the human physiognomy in its vilest phase." The criminals all looked "as though their crimes were stamped on their countenances," even though many looked inconspicuous and some had "intelligent faces."[88] Early criminologists, at least, found it easy to ignore the evidence of their own eyes in favor of their ideology.

In 1877 a young, adventurous social scientist named Richard Dugdale presented a paper on the "Hereditary Transmission of Vice and Pauperism" at the same Saratoga conference that promoted the criminalization of tramps. Dugdale's paper summarized the research in his new book *The Jukes*, which had appeared at the beginning of the year and was already in its third edition. Few books have had such a deleterious effect on our understanding of crime and justice as Dugdale's *The Jukes*. While conducting research for the Prison Association of New York, Dugdale visited an Ulster County jail and came upon a family he called the Jukes that had produced seven generations of criminals, prostitutes, and paupers; "all, or very nearly all, became devoted to a life of crime." Beginning with five sisters in the mid-eighteenth century, the Juke family produced 709 descendants that Dugdale could discover—though he estimated that they produced 1,200 progeny—128 of whom had been prostitutes and 76 convicted criminals, while some 200 had received poor relief and between 72 and 175 had syphilis.[89] In the current generation, 58 percent of the adult males were criminals. Dugdale concluded that any given member of the family was thirty times more likely to be a criminal than the average citizen. Within a few years *The Jukes* was widely accepted as the single most influential work on criminology in the United States, referenced by all experts on the subject. Writing in 1891, Robert Fletcher credited Dugdale with making it "impossible to doubt that criminal propensities can be and are transmitted by descent," a conclusion unchallenged by any prominent contemporary scholar.[90]

In a series of pull-out family trees, Dugdale described each member of the family. He also established a pauper line and a criminal line, the former constituting a class of nineteenth-century welfare cheats long before the term was coined. In the criminal line of the family, the "men prefer the risks and excitements of criminality and the occasional confinement of a prison where they meet congenial company, to the security against want and the stagnant life of the alms-house." The criminal line followed from Ada Juke, 60 percent of whose descendants were criminals and 35 percent on relief, while 61 percent of the pauper line of Effie Juke got relief and 53 percent were criminals. But the crimes of the Ada Juke line were much more violent, while Effie's descendants engaged only in "petty misdemeanors."[91] Similarly, not all of the Jukes were mentally defective; there were "crime capitalists" among their number who violated the idea that crime doesn't pay by making a steady income from their illegal activities. Dugdale sought to measure the "social damage" of the Jukes, constructing elaborate charts to quantify the impact of their misbehavior. He calculated that by 1877 their crimes had cost the state of New York $1,308,000, not counting the effect on future generations damaged by these crimes.[92]

Neither the particulars nor the accuracy of what Dugdale discovered about the Jukes matters as much as the uses to which he put this family portrait. The history of the Jukes proved to Dugdale's satisfaction the power of inherited traits: "capacity, physical and mental, is limited and determined mainly by heredity." Dugdale did allow, however, that genetics is a matter of probabilities rather than certainty, since environmental forces can ameliorate hereditary ones, though the environment can alter people only to the extent that hereditary allows it.[93] The scientist's task therefore is to examine this relationship: "The objective point is to determine how much of each results from heredity, how much from environment."[94]

Dugdale was fleshing out social Darwinism as he focused on the negative impact of heredity in constructing a detrimental home environment, leading to the obvious logic of his recommended solution: remove the children from the care of hereditary criminals and paupers. Society had a duty to remove children from the homes of immoral parents just as it would take a child from a plague house, because both criminality and pauperism were diseases passed from the parent to the child. Criminals are diseased and lazy, he said, and given to "sexual excess," which diverts energy from honest labor. This laziness and sexuality creates "a vicious circle, making idleness and fornication reciprocal causes of each other as hereditary characteristics which can only be eliminated from society by the advent of uncompromising death—the wages of sin."[95] But pauperism is even worse than criminality, he believed, as the latter as least indicates some degree of vigor. The ambitious children of paupers turn to crime, while the lazy children remain paupers, influenced by the licentious habits they learn at home: "Pauperism is an indication of weakness," and there is no hope of reforming someone caught in its debilitating snare.[96]

Quite simply, to Dugdale, the gravest danger paupers and criminals posed to society was reproduction, which was about the only thing they undertook with any energy. "In the training of certain idiots, one of the great impediments to ameliorating their condition is found in the sexual orgasms to which they are addicted, the practice of which perpetuates their idiocy." With adults, the only solution was to divert all that energy into forced labor. But the best way for society to address the problem was not to wait for adulthood, but to remove the children of these defectives: "Any child of habitually criminal parents should be withdrawn from the influence of such a home, and the younger the child, after it is weaned, the better the chances of success." These children should be put into industrial training, by which Dugdale meant more than "formal instruction in a trade." Those taken from the homes of criminal parents should receive a thorough education imparting the morality of hard work to create "a moral infant."[97] In this regard Dugdale did give a nod toward the broader environment in his call for public health and education programs, but within the context of overcoming hereditary influence. The expansion of public education, starting with kindergarten, would combat deleterious parental instruction, while public health programs would make up for the failure of parents to care adequately for their children. Healthy, educated, hardworking people could not commit crimes—they just did not have the leisure time to do so—and once habituated to labor they were unlikely to fall back into poverty. Giving the poor a taste for steady work was "the best possible safeguard against the unbridled indulgence of the passion, and with this, an effectual check to the formation of criminal practices which are, in a majority of instances, the direct result of indulgence in exhausting vices."[98]

Insistent that his readers not see the Jukes as an isolated historical anomaly, Dugdale crafted larger generalizations about criminality. He turned first to official statistics and found them wholly unreliable, criticizing "the inefficiency of the police" as well as "the falsification and defectiveness of the records." He guessed that the state recorded details of only one-fourth of the total number of cases heard in the courts, which were themselves but a fraction of the crimes reported. Most troubling was the failure of the states to record and track habitual criminals. Despairing over the lack of scientific rigor, Dugdale called for a new effort to understand crime and its consequences, and offered a first step and model for that project.[99]

Undertaking what was probably the first personal survey of criminals in American history, Dugdale interviewed 251 convicts at New York's Sing Sing and Auburn prisons. Confident of his own abilities to tell when the prisoners lied, he dismissed 18 men from his sample as hopeless prevaricators and based his statistics on 233 of those he interviewed, collecting the data onto a series of tables that imparted an aura of precision to all his statements. His categories and definitions were occasionally very different from modern understanding, as when he found a "close relationship between nervous disorders and crime." For Dugdale, nervous disorders ran from excessive drinking to epilepsy to debilitating insanity. "Habitual drunkards" were defined as "all such persons as get drunk at least once in three weeks," a definition that included 40 percent of Dugdale's criminals. But his most important finding, one that linked this study back to the Jukes, was that 79.4 percent of these prisoners were habitual criminals, though just 26 percent were listed as such in the official records.[100] This figure, in combination with 89 percent having been "neglected children"—abandoned, orphaned, or, in 51 percent of the cases, children of alcoholic parents—confirmed the hereditary nature of crime and the need to do something about the "criminal stock."[101]

What then was to be done? Dugdale rejected the existing penal system, which began badly and just kept getting worse. Given that four-fifths of all prisoners were repeat offenders, it was obvious to Dugdale that prisons just did not work, a view widely held in 1877.[102] New York's prisons were marked by "corruption, ignorance and perhaps still more dangerous indifference, until it has neither philosophy, ascertained experience, justice, public advantage, or common sense to recommend it." America's prison system, undermined by "vast perfunctory incompetence, [massed] an army of moral cripples, cursed with contaminating characteristics," and brought them together in "an environment of criminal example." In other words, the prisons trained criminals. Dugdale believed the prisoners should be treated like any diseased person, with treatment attuned to individual need, preferably in solitary confinement. "What is wanted," Dugdale insisted, was "treatment in accordance with the ascertained deficiencies of each person, . . . adopting any passion or emotion which is yet sound or serviceable for the purpose as a point of departure in the new education." But if this effort failed, they should be eliminated: "In dealing with the typical habitual criminals who are contrivers of crime, criminal capitalists and panders, where we cannot accomplish individual cure we must organize extinction of their race." Those criminals not open to reform "must sternly be cut off from perpetuating a noisome progeny either by the propagation or perversion of the coming generation." That did not necessarily mean mass executions, which had been tried in the past and proved inefficient, but "perpetual imprisonment."[103] Dugdale essentially suggested an early version of the three-strike laws, but for a different purpose. Once a person was identified as a habitual criminal, he should be locked up for life to ensure that he did not propagate—the childless criminal thus being denied a long-lasting detrimental influence on society.

Thus a complete alteration in social norms was required if the United States wanted to deal effectively with criminality and poverty. The public must be involved in sweeping efforts to reform criminals, turning their backs on traditional standards of criminal justice and sentiment, and making the hard decisions to confiscate children from destructive families such as the Jukes. Dugdale offered both description and prescription, but the public proved interested only in the former as a way of demonizing an entire class of people.

The Jukes had enormous influence. As William M.F. Round, secretary of the Prison Association of New York, wrote in 1884, the year after Dugdale's death, The Jukes was valued wherever civilization "has advanced far enough to be alarmed at the increase of crime, and to be concerned in reducing the criminal classes." Round also made clear that Dugdale himself came from a "noble lineage" dating back to William the Conqueror.[104] Within a decade Dugdale had established the dominant ideology of American criminology, which saw heredity as the primary determinant of illegal conduct. As Robert Fletcher, the outgoing president of the American Anthropological Association, wrote in 1891 in praising "the New School of Criminal Anthropology," Dugdale established that the criminal "breeds criminals; the taint is in the blood," and nothing could change that fact. Dugdale left no doubt that the liberal justice system, which attempted to make the punishment meet the crime, was both contemptible and unscientific, as the criminal will always be a criminal. Thus recidivism could not be explained by any flaw in society, but by the "congenital physical and moral degeneracy" of the criminal.[105] The conclusion was therefore logical, Fletcher argued; society needed to protect itself and promote evolutionary progress through the expanded use of capital punishment. In part as a consequence of Dugdale's research, the death penalty enjoyed a revival in the late nineteenth century.[106]

The Jukes is not a long book—just 120 pages—and yet it appears that no one noticed that Dugdale had uncovered a significant statistic in his interviews: that 79.4 percent of his "hereditary criminals" were unskilled workers. Rather than linking that finding with the ill effects of poverty or the limited opportunities available in industrial America, Dugdale saw it as more evidence of "the inaptitude of criminals." In fact, he reversed the logic, perceiving this lack of skill as a free choice made by the average criminal who, as with most of the Jukes family, "adopts some kind of intermittent industry which requires no special training," if he worked at all, in order to allow for the unhindered pursuit of crime. Similarly, another statistic not mentioned in any contemporary review seemingly undermined Dugdale's recommendation that children should be taken from their families, as he found that 30 percent of the habitual criminals in his study had been "refuge boys," children sent to reformatories or industrial schools, which he labeled centers for "criminal training."[107] He insisted that children be taken from the families of criminals and paupers, but did not say where they should be sent. Each of these statistics suggest an alternate reading of The Jukes, one that finds four-fifths of prisoners from working-class backgrounds and one-third having been institutionalized as children as sufficient cause for further examination of the nature of the criminal justice system and the social roots of criminality. Dugdale did not make that connection. But in 1877 another writer began the research that would lead to the publication of one of the most significant books in the development of an autonomous school of American criminology, a book that would gain little attention at the time but that would, once the obsession with hereditary explanations burned out in the disreputable fires of eugenics and fascism in the 1930s, be rediscovered and suggest an alternative structure for understanding crime and poverty in the United States.

Discovering the Social Roots of Homicide

Horace V. Redfield had no intention of becoming a pioneer sociologist. In 1876, Murat Halstead, the influential editor of the *Cincinnati Commercial* who sent Lafcadio Hearn to New Orleans, appointed thirty-one-year-old Redfield the paper's Washington bureau chief. Covering the 1876 presidential election and its aftermath in the South, Redfield observed the power and effectiveness of violence, reporting on the ways in which the white Democrats had used intimidation and brutality to keep African Americans from the polls. Asking if violence defined the United States in some way, Redfield began searching for statistics. Like Richard Dugdale before him, Redfield found empirical research on crime rare, and what little there was proved highly unreliable. Even the director of the Census Bureau, General Francis A. Walker, had written, "Neither the statements of Crime nor those of Pauperism for the year are regarded as possessing any high degree of statistical authority."[108] Like so many observers of America at this time, Redfield could not escape the feeling that the number of murders kept increasing, though it was difficult to be certain as no one yet had begun to count. Redfield decided to count.

What Redfield found deeply disturbed those who read his seminal book *Homicide, North and South* when it came out in 1880. Whereas England and Wales, with more than 25 million people, had between 235 and 375 murders, depending how they were counted, Texas alone, with some 1.25 million people, had 475 homicides—and that number did not include lynchings, which Redfield did not list as homicides. Not only were there a lot more murders in the United States than in any other industrial country, they were concentrated in the South. According to Redfield's research, there were 40,000 homicides in the South between 1865 and 1880. In contrast, there were 750 murders in the six New England states combined during those years. Redfield studied only what he called "ordinary killings," deliberately leaving out the political murders that had first attracted his attention.[109] He sought to get at the norm of American behavior, to discover the national standard of violence.

Where foreign visitors in 1876 came to see the Centennial Exhibition and the glories of the young republic, Redfield took his readers on a guided tour of homicidal America. Dipping into specific accounts of murders and examining particular communities, Redfield painted a stark portrait of a violent country. But individual homicides and even statistical tables did not make clear the nature of the country's relationship with violence until they were compared, one region to another. In 1877 in Galveston, which had a population of 13,000, there were 5 arrests for murder and 54 for assault with intent to commit murder, while in Rochester, New York, with a population of 85,000 and one of the centers of the Great Strike, there were only 2 manslaughter and 6 assault arrests. While 14 percent larger than Louisiana in population, Maine had just 9 murders in 1877 compared with 152 in Louisiana—giving Louisiana a murder rate 1,500 percent that of Maine. There were 219 homicides in Kentucky in 1878, compared with 50 in the six New England states. South Carolina was, in Redfield's view, simply insane: in the four years from 1875 through 1878, there were 87 murders in Massachusetts, while South Carolina, with half the population of Massachusetts, reported 113 homicides in 1877 alone, with a further 68 severely wounded. The murder rate among the white people of South Carolina was 1,500 percent higher than that among the native-born citizens of New England.[110]

But Texas claimed the championship, with 450 to 475 murders a year during the period of Redfield's study. In Harrison County, Texas, there were 13 arrests for murder in 1877, in a county with a population of just over 13,000 people.[111] Redfield felt the numbers were so much higher in Texas for two significant reasons: "the habit of carrying concealed weapons," and, more important in Redfield's view, "the great laxity in the administration of the law." In a confrontation between two Texans, Redfield reported, an unarmed man suggested they fight without guns. The other "replied that they did not fight that way in Texas" and thereupon shot his opponent. Despite the reputation of the Texas Rangers for doggedness in pursuit of criminals, law enforcement was grossly underfunded in the state, and the courts were consistently forgiving acts of violence. Those arrested on homicide charges "are treated with extraordinary leniency," and almost any excuse was accepted by the courts to justify murder. The consequence, according to one Texas newspaper, was that at least eight hundred murderers, "many of whom have killed more than one man," were loose in the state.[112] "Among other curiosities of crime in Texas," Redfield wrote, "we find that to be a peace-officer in that State is about as dangerous as to be a soldier in active service," as sixteen officers were killed in the line of duty in 1877. New York had just under one hundred homicides; "with some five times the population of Texas," Redfield writes with a hint of sarcasm, "they get along with one-fourth the homicides."[113]

The violence extended beyond homicide, of course. In Louisville in 1877 the police arrested 107 people for "cutting with intent to kill." Based on such numbers, there was no doubt in Redfield's mind that the South had a culture of violence, one that extended to all aspects of Southern life. Redfield also found domestic violence common, and a "brutal feature of these Southern murders is the frequency of relatives killing relatives." In explaining why southern Indiana was so much more violent than the northern part of that state, Redfield observed that they commited murders of "the Southern type,—that is, two men, often intoxicated, have a 'difficulty,' and one shoots or stabs the other."[114] There was just no escaping the impact of his statistical study: Southerners accepted a far higher level of violence than did any other region of the country, including the Western states. Redfield concluded that "there is nothing that so distinguishes the Southern civilization from the Northern as this one matter of homicide."[115]

What, then, accounted for this differential level of violence? According to Dugdale, the explanation would have been found in a different pattern of inheritance, the presence of more habitual criminals in the South passing on their behavior to their children. Where Dugdale looked at the "home environment" as determinative, Redfield looked beyond the home to the larger social environment. The standard explanation for violence, Redfield wrote, was immigration, yet he found no solid evidence to support that view. Similarly, there was no evidence to support the notion that the frontier somehow accounted for American violence, since New York City had more homicides than any of the Western territories except Texas. Redfield felt certain that the difference between the South and the rest of the country was that the Southern legal system literally allowed people to get away with murder.[116] Incarceration figures throughout the South had initially baffled Redfield, with very few people serving time for homicide despite all the murders. The 1870 census reported that there were 323 homicides that year in Texas, yet only 70 people were in prison "for all offenses!"[117] But the more he studied, the more Redfield became convinced that this failure to jail violent criminals was part of a larger culture that had no respect for the law and a great deal for violence. Redfield's basic point was that a lack of order and enforcement in the South encouraged violence, as the certainty of punishment was vital for diminishing violence. In the South, most accused murderers got off, usually by pleading self-defense; in the North, they were generally sent to prison or executed, which Redfield found "wholesome."[118]

Part of that laxity of law enforcement that multiplied the murder rate considerably was allowing the carrying of concealed weapons, which was in fact illegal in almost every state. "Let the Legislature make the carrying of concealed weapons a penitentiary offence," the *Louisville Courier-Journal* wrote. "This is the only remedy" to the rising murder rate. Similarly, the *Galveston News* complained, "As long as men see fit to carry concealed weapons the practice will be kept up, for the law, whatever it may be in theory, is not effective in practice."[119] In South Carolina an argument over "positions on the floor" at a dance led to five men drawing concealed pistols and opening fire, resulting in one death. "Five men go to a dance loaded with pistols," Redfield wrote, "in case one of the pistols would be useful for 'self-defense'!" Redfield clearly felt that the country was making a mistake in not enforcing the concealed-carry laws with greater rigor. On a single street in Vicksburg, eight people were killed and eight more seriously wounded over the space of a single year. With one exception, "the shooters and their victims" were all armed "with concealed deadly weapons, so that it does not appear that these hidden instruments of death carry with them any protection against murder." Allowing the carrying of concealed weapons, which persuaded each man of his own power and right to stand above the law, promoted lawlessness, according the Redfield. The events on this Vicksburg street highlighted "the uselessness of carrying concealed weapons," as the "carrying of arms does not prevent murder, but causes it." For Redfield, it seemed too obvious that the reason Vermont had so few murders was its enforcement of its concealed weapons law.[120] Redfield believed in the efficacy of the law, when enforced, to effect change; he also believed that the failure to enforce the law would pass on a disregard for its strictures to the next generation. In this regard, at least, Redfield appeared to agree with Dugdale in perceiving the power of the home environment, since children learn attitudes toward violence from their parents. Redfield quoted a Texas paper on a school shooting in which a mere child shot another in the breast with a small pistol" that he had brought concealed to school. "An investigation led to the discovery that two boys, who had a quarrel, came to school armed, just as if they were grown up and the school were a mere legislative assembly."[121]

This lack of respect for public safety raised a larger question of the root of such self-destructive disregard for the rule of law. Redfield suspected that it could be found in the Southern heritage of slavery and violence, a view that has been bolstered by subsequent historical studies. He perceived the racial component to murders, but admitted it was difficult to disentangle, as few white-on-black murders found their way into either the newspapers or the courts. As Redfield traveled through the South he noticed local newspapers attributing violent crime to blacks. Yet, based on their own reporting, the exact opposite was the case, with whites murdering one another and blacks in far greater numbers. "Measured by relative population, homicide is very much more frequently committed by whites than by blacks," he stated.[122] In Texas in 1878 there were six black-on-white murders, and fifty-three white-on-black murders, "so far as we are able to learn." As Redfield observed, "When a negro kills a white man the law is enforced with rigor, if the mobs, usually at hand upon such occasions, allow the law jurisdiction in the case at all." Redfield identified the race of the victims and murderers in 109 South Carolina cases in 1877: in a state with slightly more blacks than whites, whites murdered 45 whites and 24 blacks, while blacks murdered 35 blacks and 5 whites.[123]

The death penalty served as an effective deterrent when carried out quickly and uniformly, demonstrating the power and certainty of the law, yet the Southern states used it only rarely against whites. Raising the example of the Molly Maguires, Redfield pointed out that Pennsylvania executed more accused than there were murder victims. The state showed admirable ruthlessness, hanging three men for one murder and sending eleven to prison for the attempted murder of another man who "escaped with slight wounds." Pennsylvania prevented further outbreaks of violence through the "wholesome wholesale hanging and imprisonment of the guilty."[124] Until the Southern states reacted as sternly with its white killers, there would be no letup of violence in the region.

To understand the roots of this extraordinary attitude toward law and violence, Redfield looked back to slavery. Though he could just as easily have quoted Thomas Jefferson on the way slavery made every slave owner a tyrant and taught the utility of violence, Redfield turned instead to Charles Dickens. Traveling through the South in 1842, Dickens had been horrified by the routine violence of Southern life, and linked it directly to slavery. As the slave owner "is a coward in his domestic life, stalking among his shrinking men and women slaves armed with his heavy whip, so he will be a coward out-of-doors, and, carrying cowards' weapons hidden in his breast, will shoot men down, and stab them when he quarrels."[125] Slave owners saw themselves as a law unto themselves, justified in committing acts of violence in order to maintain racial order and personal honor. Slavery may have disappeared but racism remained, still imparting the same lessons that the law could be ignored at will.

But Redfield insisted that such racial explanations were secondary to the simple fact that Southern courts always operated on a presumption of self-defense in any killing, as was the case with the Cassius Clay murder case. Between the unhindered carrying of firearms and the revolving door of the courts—and the former was certainly understandable in light of the latter—the law offered little protection to anyone, regardless of race, and had a "demoralizing effect" on society. A violent cycle was created, in which Southerners felt justified in using violence since the state would not act on their behalf, and the state accepted that violence as a necessary act of self-defense. The Texas Baptist minister James B. Cranfill well expressed this notion that each man was responsible for his own defense: "I put my revolver in my pocket every morning when I put on my trousers. Indeed, I would have felt much more comfortable going up the street without trousers than I would without the gun."[126] It had reached a point, Redfield argued, where juries on murder trials often included men who had themselves been acquitted on homicide charges.[127] The result was an increasing flood of violence in the South.

Taken together, these Southern murders amounted to a policy of terrorism that operated in complete defiance of the law. "Some of the assassinations appeared to be for no other reason than that the victim was a witness in a murder case, or had been efficient in having murderers arrested," Redfield wrote. "In this way quiet, law-abiding citizens are often kept in terror, and dare not take active steps in the suppression of lawlessness." The entire South paid for this contempt for the law. The only solutions, Redfield insisted, were gun control statutes and the energetic use of the death penalty.[128] The convicted murderer, Redfield wrote, "should never be taken out of prison unless it is to be hung."[129]

Many contemporaries shared Redfield's perception of the social supports for homicide. Justice Samuel Miller of the United States Supreme Court insisted that federal troops had to stay in the South became of the "fiendish hatred" of whites for blacks. The nation could not "trust the South with the power of governing the Negro and the Union White Man without such guarantees in the federal constitution as secure their protection." He bluntly asked his Texas brother-in-law to "show me a single white man that has been punished for murdering a Negro." Justice Miller was quite correct in holding that murders by whites went unpunished even in such notoriously outrageous examples as the Chisholm or Kemper County Massacre in 1877. The U.S. attorney in Alabama wrote Attorney General George Williams that most people in the state believed that "any man may murder a Republican, for political reasons without the slightest reason to fear that he will be punished, but with every reason to believe that he will be applauded for the act."[130] In the South, Democrats perceived Republicans as fair targets, and anyone who read Southern newspapers, as did Redfield, noted a relaxed attitude toward shootings. For instance, one Texas newspaper stated of the victim of a shooting: "Moore is not dead, but is dangerously wounded. The weather is delightful now." Similarly, in a strange case of product placement, an article on another murder suddenly recommended Dr. Bull's Cough Syrup as "the best medicine in use."[131]

The murder of blacks by whites, lynchings excepted, rarely found their way into the papers unless the purpose was to terrify other blacks. When the opposite occurred, the act tended to get attention and leave little doubt as to the guilty party. Redfield took the standard justification for lynching, that the law was too lenient, and flipped it over, arguing that the leniency was an intentional construct of the white community intended to allow them to commit acts of violence without fear of legal retribution.[132]

The law proved endlessly forgiving of white violence throughout the South, even when the courts themselves had been targeted. In April 1877 a group of outlaws sought to prevent the Kimble County Court from sitting by intimidating the judge and jurors. The Texas Rangers moved quietly into the county and over three days arrested forty-one men without firing a shot. Encouraged by this show of strength, "decent citizens" promised their support and witnesses stepped forward to testify at the trials of numerous local criminals. The Rangers' commanding officer, Major John B. Jones, confidently predicted that a single term of court would "make Kimble a civil and law-abiding county, safe for good people." The grand jury quickly issued twenty-five indictments, including ones against the sheriff and county judge, both of whom were forced to resign, but only nine citizens appeared to serve on the jury, and none of those forty-one men arrested at great cost to the state were tried. Jones, like Redfield, felt that such failure to act undermined the rule of law.[133]

Thanks to the research of H.V. Redfield, we know more about homicide in the years 1877 and 1878 than in any other years in the nineteenth century. Of course there are all sorts of problems with the statistics, as Redfield acknowledged. Redfield used census data, criminal, court, and prison records, and newspapers, attempting to determine the particulars of every homicide and render an accurate count. The Southern states were particularly difficult, their official records erratic and the news accounts colored by numerous biases. Despite these difficulties, Redfield's findings have held up well over time.[134] However, perhaps because of his sudden death shortly after the publication of *Homicide, North and South*, Redfield had little impact on the study of American violence until he was rediscovered after World War II. Since then, *Homicide, North and South* has exerted a great deal of influence, though not all of Redfield's insights have been fully appreciated.[135]

In a particularly astute observation, Redfield argued that the country misperceived the nature of violence due to a bias in the coverage of crime. In the South "homicides are so frequent that it is only now and then a case attracts much attention outside of the very narrow circle where it happens." For that reason, Northern murders, being rarer, attracted far more media attention and gave the impression that the Northeast was home to many "shocking crimes."[136] Thus the "notoriety of New England in respect to horrible crimes is to be attributed more to their immense publicity than to their frequency." Redfield compared Charles Freeman's murder of his daughter on the supposed command of God in Massachusetts in 1879, a case that received national attention, with that of a woman in South Carolina who murdered her five children "so that they might all go to heaven"—a case that generated no press.[137] It is possible that the press highlighted exceptional Northern murders in order to avoid the larger questions raised by Southern violence and the rising homicide rate; or Redfield could have been right that editors just sighed, "Yet another murder in Louisiana," and moved on to some other story. Either way, "ordinary killings" found their way into the press every day.

In 1877 something snapped; violence overwhelmed the press and every issue contained tales of outrage and horror, from famous criminals such as John Wesley Hardin shooting down witnesses, to obscure and angry husbands murdering their wives; from organized acts of racist violence, to uncoordinated crowds of striking workers; from the very real actions of lynch mobs, to the imagined terror of tramps. As one newspaper declared, it seemed as though "the pastime of murder" had become a common activity. Another thought the country had "become so demoralized that we are breeding robbers and scoundrels at an astonishing rate."[138] When a particular violent act caught the public's interest, the press luxuriated in every detail of the crime and trial.

The quotation that opens this chapter is taken from one of Ralph Waldo Emerson's final essays, "Demonology." Emerson questioned whether humanity was yet ready for all its many technological advances, wondered if we had proceeded morally to a point where we could use wisely what we had created. Clearly he thought not, holding that "men are not fit to be trusted with these talismans." Disturbed by the events around him, Emerson expanded on the Tramp Scare by imagining "tramps flying through the air" in battery-powered balloons in order to descend on isolated farms and commit horrible crimes; we can make new weapons with ever more clever ways to kill one another, but "there are many things of which a wise man might wish to be ignorant, and these are such." Emerson pleads with his readers, "Shun them as you would the secrets of the undertaker and the butcher." People approach these improvements in our way of life and think that they will make no demands on us—all we see is the convenience. And yet it is evident, he continues, that we create more ways to damage ourselves and our world. Physical advances require a spiritual or moral price, but we refuse to acknowledge that debt and learn little from the ill effects of what we have wrought. "The history of man is a series of conspiracies to win from Nature some advantage without paying for it," Emerson observes, as humanity is "mad to grasp" power, but rejects the need to change its moral ideas. Everything we craft is subject to misuse; "the good genius may be there or not, our evil genius is sure to stay."[139]

One of the great minds of the nineteenth century, Emerson quietly spent his last days with his family and his books, yet had time to read the newspapers. Day after day, a trail of bloodshed led across the pages, from assaults to murders to arson to acts of rage and desperation. The human mind could invent new ways to do everything, including kill, but appeared incapable of reflecting on its own actions. Modern technology was "so fatal as to put an end to war by the threat of universal murder," but would we realize that danger in time? Emerson had little hope in that regard and found scant evidence in the events of 1877 to convince him otherwise: "Before we acquire great powers we must acquire wisdom to use it well."[140]

7

Breaking the Spell

I return to Young America, telegraphing, telephoning, and phonograph-
ing, and electric-lighting the world out of its mind.

—George Sala[1]

They were certainly happy 1877 was ending. At their most objective and dispas-
sionate, the majority of commentators agreed with Chicago's *Inter Ocean* that
the year drawing to a close marked an "era of unusual importance, . . . which
largely affected all classes of society." But it was hard to disguise the sense of relief that 1877 was over. Looking back over the year, America's newspapers largely
accepted that 1878 could only be better. When newspapers attempted to capture
1877 in just a few words, they saw it as a year of "chaos" or an "unnatural" year.
In nearly every respect it had been "a year of deep and sombre shadows." On January 1, 1878, the whole country was happy "to have seen the last" of 1877. "The
old year went out with her train somewhat draggled," wrote the *Boston Advertiser*, "leaving behind a feeling of relief that she was well out of the way." One of
the more genteel descriptions came from the *San Francisco Evening Bulletin*,
which thought 1877 "has been an eventful year." It had not been "among the
more prosperous, . . . there are more men out of employment than at any time
during the last ten years." Even given that the depression had been going on
since 1873, the year ending had been even worse, leaving people convinced that
the "best that could be done was to hold on for better times." Now, on the last
day of 1877, "We look hopefully upon the dawning of the New Year, trusting
that it will be more auspicious . . . than the last."[2]

It had been a year marked by depression and bankruptcies.[3] In an article titled
"Who's Next," the *Inter Ocean* reviewed the nation's persistent economic problems and wondered which bank would be the next to fail. "The end of our bank
troubles has apparently not yet come," as several more large banks went under
in 1877. The *North American* tried to put the best light possible on the number of bankruptcies, arguing that with so many businesses failing, the remaining
enterprises would benefit from the reduction in competition and cheaper labor.
As one of the few voices of optimism, the paper hoped that the era of "losses,

insolvency and decay" would make way to "a new era of activity" in 1878 and saw evidence that "Capitalists" responded to the collapse of competitors through concentration, building "up huge firms calculated to command general confidence." True, some "have been disposed to complain of these as monopolies," yet there was reason to believe that "a new and far more prosperous mercantile regime" would follow upon the creation of larger corporations. The paper added that the year also had its upside in the destruction of the Indian threat and the resolution of the "problem" with the freed blacks, "and even the Chinese are returning home." After so much "tumult," a little peace and prosperity would only be fair; at the very least, the situation could only improve.[4]

There was little debate that the depression continued to disrupt the nation as "the commercial world is out of joint." Politely stated, 1877 had been a year of "small profit," marked by "depression of trade, financial embarrassment and comparative commercial stagnation."[5] The economic disarray persisted—despite such positive signs as the largest crop yields yet recorded—as reports came from every part of the country of "one unvarying tenor," that there was a crisis of "over-production," growing unemployment, cutthroat "competition which made trade unremunerative," and the failure of old, well-established businesses. The contemporary economist Horace White wrote that by the end of 1877 the country's finances were frozen. Except for farming, "All else is a weary and aching mass of unemployed or half employed capital, misdirected talent, and underpaid labor, to which commerce gives the generic name of glut." As steel prices hit an all-time low, there were few indicators that the end was in sight.[6] Many papers could not understand why American goods did not sell better abroad given the falling labor costs, deflation, and declining value of the dollar. They saw any signs of economic recovery negated by "the savage and imprudent assaults made upon the national credit," and 1877 ended with the economy in worse shape than it had been at its beginning.[7]

There were those who found the root problem in the lack of regulation, the depression having been brought on by "crazy speculation." The financial markets had collapsed because of an "era of speculation, of fraud, or fortunes made and lost in a day." In 1877 "confidence fled, values shrank, capital became timid and repressive, want and penury came, labor could find no employment, crime lifted its hideous face everywhere"; in short, it was a year "of grievous financial distress." While some papers blamed the rich, most settled for a general collective castigation of "our own folly." The optimists said they had just been lucky that the year had not been worse, while the pessimists longed for the prosperity of 1865 to 1872 and feared that 1878 would be even more of a disaster.[8]

Even the hopeful mood of the *North American* soured when it turned its attention from economics to the related topic that had dominated its news coverage in 1877: violence. On this topic, Dr. Pangloss gave way to Eeyore on a bad day. "If the immediate past furnished the augury for the immediate future," the paper editorialized on New Year's Day, 1878, "it would needs be a cold welcome that should install the new year." The year ended had been colored red, marked by violence at every turn, twice disrupted by "fear of renewed civil war at home," first over the contested presidential election and then by the Great Strike. The entire year "witnessed unusual anxiety" as the country's full military force was required to suppress "labor troubles," and political crises gave way to "sweeping business difficulties." The very "foundations of business have been so violently interfered with and the confidence in political institutions has been so rudely shaken that other evils seem more natural," leading to a dangerous acceptance of violent means to resolve problems.[9]

Any summary of the year could not escape the incredible range of dramatic and violent events disrupting the nation's peace. "If the worst forebodings have not been realized, the record of the year is, nevertheless, a page full of suffering and misery, of disaster and death, of human hate and angry contention," summarized the *Boston Advertiser*. The paper confidently predicted that people would look back upon the year ending "as one of disaster and gloom," which had brought little happiness to anyone. Repeatedly, papers referred to the narrowly averted and "startling possibility of civil war." Though the presidential contest had not produced all-out war, many American citizens had died in the South attempting to exercise their right to vote, and the resolution of that political crisis worked to "keep alive old passions and to awaken new ones."[10]

Exhausted by the violent confrontations of 1877, the American people searched for explanations and solutions to the dramatic changes overtaking their country. Looking closely, the ever more activist press discerned a culture of violence with deep and troubling roots that extended to all aspects of society, from the treatment of animals and minorities to domestic and labor relations. Noting the intimate connection between alcohol and violence, many people thought the solution obvious: outlaw alcohol. Even while the country set off on its path of denying civil rights to a large segment of its population based on racial categorization, a major effort driven by eloquent new voices sought to extend rights to women. A conviction that women could bring a new moral clarity to American politics that would positively transform the country battled traditional perceptions of feminine subservience and masculine domination. While white society aimed both to marginalize blacks, Indians, and Hispanics and to romanticize their tragic past, these other Americans struggled to maintain their cultures and communities. Workers fought for more, for a place at the table and acceptance as Americans. But following the events of 1877, business found itself backed by the coercive power of the state, requiring labor to adopt new strategies. Henry George began work on *Progress and Poverty*, seeking fundamental economic reforms that would end the hopeless lives of bare subsistence that marked the existence of most American workers, while William Graham Sumner elevated the ideology of unregulated free markets to the status of immutable natural law. The elite were deeply disappointed with democracy, while the workers turned to it as their only option. Prominent conservatives, including James Garfield, John Hay, Emory Upton, Jacob Schiff, and Judge Walter Gresham, called for limitations on the franchise, an enterprise the Southern elite signed on to with enthusiasm, while in cities as diverse as San Francisco, Altoona, and Louisville, proworker candidates won election and labor unions started their slow revival. Samuel Gompers felt that the strike of 1877 was the true beginning of the rise of American unions as they both abandoned utopian dreams of a workers' state and embraced the virtues of national organization, while Andrew Carnegie credited the year's events with solidifying his mastery of the steel industry.

In the dozen years after the Civil War, democracy had spread across America, inspiring and invigorating numerous social movements and granting political roles to those who had once been exploited and abused. Those long used to exercising unchallenged authority did not appreciate these developments, which threatened both their power and the structures that maintained their dominance. In 1877, by manipulating fears and hatreds, America's elites created a country where railroads did not use the air brakes invented by George Westinghouse in 1869, a safety device mandated in every other industrialized nation, leading to the unnecessary deaths of several thousand workers over the next quarter century. Theirs was a country that excluded certain people from the full rights of citizenship because of their race and gender, a nation that used military force to end strikes and accepted—and often glorified—personal violence to a degree unknown elsewhere in the civilized world. The country that had celebrated its centennial with the highest voter turnout in its history rejected democracy in 1877 and handed power over to white supremacists and the corporate elite, granting them the right to use the state apparatus—from the legislatures to the courts to the United States Army—to maintain control. But the democratic activism that would eventually overthrow these systems of intolerance also took root in 1877. With that mysterious power of history to prove, as Theodore Parker so aptly put it, that the arc of the moral universe is long but it "bends towards justice," from the ashes of 1877 would grow the democratic revival of a dozen social reform movements.[11] The individual stories that follow indicate the ways in which the United States underwent significant changes as a consequence of events in 1877.

A Sober Suffragist

In June 1873, Northwestern University appointed a remarkable young scholar to be the first dean of their new Woman's College. Just thirty-three years old,

Frances Willard displayed a sparkling intelligence, formidable organizational skills, and a driving concern for the well-being of her students, and she quickly became one of the most prominent female educators in the country. But her tenure as dean proved short-lived, as harassment by male students and her fellow professors made teaching difficult and leadership impossible. The university's president—whose marriage proposal she had rebuffed—treated Willard with disdain and failed to act against male students disrupting her classes. It meant nothing, she publicly charged, to claim educational equality for women yet leave the college in the hands of men and "arrange its surroundings solely for men, give the instruction entirely by men," and then expect those few women students to do well.[12]

Looking around the country, Willard found few true opportunities for women. Before the Civil War, the University of Iowa had been the only public university to accept women; by 1875 the universities of Wisconsin, Indiana, Minnesota, Missouri, Michigan, and California had accepted the logic that women citizens should have an equal access to education. However, in many colleges women were not allowed to speak in classes, a prohibition extending to rhetoric courses. Even at Oberlin, the first coeducational college, women could not address audiences including men until 1877—and then it was considered a shocking innovation. There were signs that the male public disapproved of these advances, which they tended to dismiss as "novelties." For instance, Vassar College's women's baseball team, the Resolutes, succumbed to public pressure in 1877 and ceased playing.[13] Of greater consequence, the Supreme Court had just ruled in *Bradwell v. Illinois* that states could bar women from the professions, with Justice Joseph Bradley proclaiming that, under the ancient standard of *couverture*, "a woman had no legal existence separate from her husband," and could therefore not enter into contracts or conduct any business without her husband's approval. But more than that, the court declared the "paramount destiny and mission of woman are to fulfill the noble and benign offices of wife and mother. This is the law of the Creator." Given the "peculiar characteristics, destiny, and mission of woman," Justice Bradley wrote, the state had full power to determine "what offices, positions, and callings" were available to each gender. Women had no choices beyond motherhood; the woman who could not or chose not to have children was, in the language of common law, a relict.[14]

Depressed by an overwhelming "sense of injustice," isolated and undefended when local newspapers launched a scurrilous campaign against her, Willard resigned after just one year as dean. At a loss as to how to proceed, she sought a role free of male oversight and their patronizing sense of natural superiority. Willard carefully explored her options, which, as the Supreme Court reminded her, were notably limited because of her gender. However, events in Ohio created an opportunity never before available to women, and Willard would, in her words, walk through that "open door."[15]

For millions of Americans, the primary cause of American violence and disorder appeared obvious: alcohol. There was indeed a sound basis to this conviction. Contemporary and historical studies find a direct correlation between alcohol consumption and violent behavior. It was perfectly reasonable in this context for P.T. Barnum, who came out for temperance in September, 1877, to state that three-quarters of the crime in the United States "was attributable to drink." A Western newspaper declared drunkenness responsible for 90 percent of the homicides in their state, while the Maine State Temperance Convention needed only to refer to what everyone knew to be true—that inebriation promotes aggression—to justify a resolution stating that alcohol was at war with society.[16] Alcohol makes a man "incapable of controlling his powers of reasoning," the convention stated, and thus leads to insanity and murder. "When once the power of volition is lost the mind runs riots," declared the annual report of Boston's Washingtonian Home, "and may develop a thousand forms of crime and folly."[17] During the Great Strike, middle-class commentators assumed a direct connection between alcohol and violence; the rioters had to be drunk, and taverns therefore bore responsibility for the resulting violence. "To try to put down the rioters on Halsted Street and still keep the saloons open is foolish," the *Inter Ocean* proclaimed. "Close the saloons!" By this logic, liquor merchants were liable for crimes, "for he who furnished the demon which men put in their mouths to steal away their brains and burn up their manhood, is an accomplice in whatever villainies may flow from indulgence in intoxicating drinks." As this correlation between alcohol and violence spread, many confessed murderers defended themselves by insisting, in the words of one, that "drinking alcohol . . . made me crazy."[18]

With few questioning the destructive power of alcohol, it seemed obvious to many Americans that something needed to and could be done. "Since drunkenness is producing more crime, more insanity and a greater number of deaths than any one cause in our land," the *St. Louis Globe Democrat* asked, "should we not do what we can to lessen its destructive march?" The temperance movement had been active in the United States since the 1830s, but its focus had generally been on moderating drinking, had been largely a male preserve, and in the years immediately after the Civil War had suffered a number of serious setbacks as returning soldiers had found liquor a necessary anesthetic and solace. But in the last half of the 1870s temperance changed dramatically, shifting to prohibiting rather than tempering; it promoted public activism rather than moderate legislative efforts, and moved from a masculine exercise in self-control to a women's crusade.[19]

At the end of 1873, coincident with the start of the depression, the Women's Temperance Crusade burst forth in Ohio, drawing on the energy of women to combat the rising consumption of alcohol. To a large extent this increase in alcohol use resulted from the new pasteurized beer made by breweries with national distribution networks. Workers preferred this lighter, less expensive beer over the hard liquor of the past, but drank a lot more of it. By the mid-1870s, newspapers reported there was a saloon for every 280 people, or roughly 1 per 60 adult males. That increased consumption became a women's issue, as men drank up paychecks, became more violent when drunk, and abandoned families. Alcoholism became coded for domestic abuse, and the thousands of women who joined in the Women's Crusade as it spread from Ohio across the Midwest believed that reducing or eliminating alcohol's influence would lead to a more peaceful and civilized America.[20] In 1877 Elizabeth Boynton Harbert described the Women's Crusade as a response to the vice and violence men had learned during the Civil War: "Within our own homes a fearful conflagration was raging." In seeking to bring peace into the home—which was supposed to be "a haven in a heartless world"—the temperance movement took on the aura of a sacred mission as they fought and sacrificed for Christian ideals, generally defined in Protestant terms.[21] Though launched by the sermons of the Reverend Dioclesian Lewis, the Crusade differed from all previous reform movements in the United States in that it was led by women, and differed from prior women's events in its activist style. Yet these women maintained they were not challenging social norms; rather, they simply extended their traditional role of protecting the family, acting publicly to preserve the domestic sphere. It was a subtle argument, but one essential to the acceptance of their endeavors by the respectable middle class.[22]

The Women's Crusade eschewed traditional, deferential forms of female behavior in favor of direct public action. These women knelt in the street before tavern doors or marched boldly inside to place their Bibles on the bar and pray for the owners to stop selling liquor. As evidence of the power of prayer or of these women, many Ohio saloon keepers closed their doors permanently, several even pouring their entire stock of liquor out into the street. Some men responded with violence, hurling objects from rotten eggs to bricks at women, dragging their wives away from demonstrations or beating them for participating, and physically intimidating the Crusaders as they prayed. However, these martyrs emboldened many more women, demonstrating, as Annie Wittenmyer put it, that women "can face the cannon and the mob."[23] The largest public action by women in the nineteenth century, the Women's Crusade involved an estimated 50,000 to 150,000 women in nearly a thousand separate events. But most of these efforts were short-lived; towns generally remained dry for just six months to a year before someone took advantage of the continuing demand for alcohol by opening a new saloon. The Internal Revenue Bureau reported that 750 breweries went out of business between 1873 and 1875, which could just as well have been the result of the depression as of the Crusade, and alcohol consumption did dip for a few years, only to rise again during the centennial.[24] By the end of 1874 the Women's Crusade had faded from the scene, but not before playing a key role in founding the Woman's Christian Temperance Union (WCTU) in Cleveland in November 1874.[25]

Shortly before that Cleveland meeting, Frances Willard sat in a Portland, Maine, hotel, agonizing over her future. After several months of reflection, she remained uncertain of direction. She had observed but taken no part in the Women's Crusade, "this whirlwind of the Lord," as she called it. Out of work, she needed to make a living, yet she felt a strong pull toward the temperance cause. She had seen how easily her brother had abandoned his abstinence pledge; it seemed obvious that temperance had to be enforced by law.[26] She wanted to attend the conference in Cleveland and participate in the Crusade, but doubted that any income would match her commitment. Though a rational person who had weighed the pros and cons carefully, Willard had been raised in a religious home and turned, as many devout Americans would, to the Bible for an answer. Alone in her hotel room, she opened the Bible at random and read from Psalms, "Trust in the Lord to do good; so shalt though dwell in the land, and verily thou shalt be fed." That was all she needed to know; God would see that she survived.[27] The revelation that her path lay with temperance may have had divine origins, but as Willard's secretary and companion the talented musician Anna Gordon later wrote, Willard realized that the WCTU presented a major personal and social opportunity, capable of battling every "evil which threatens the home and strikes at our civilization." It would also prove "a great educational agency for women."[28]

Willard came to temperance from the perspective of "the woman question"— the debate over the role of women in the aftermath of the Civil War. She was definitely one of those who felt that women should enjoy an equality of rights, but was not yet certain how to reach that goal. She initially thought that the WCTU offered the means toward that end, with temperance benefiting women by granting greater safety and security at home. Willard saw herself engaged in a great struggle for the future of America: "Instead of peace I was to participate in war."[29] She began this campaign in the inner city of Chicago, working with the poor immigrants who poured into the city in the 1870s and would, by 1890, constitute one-third of the population. Though she witnessed this poverty close up, she still held to the traditional explanations that only moral rather than social reform could produce prosperity. She did, however, suggest to the head of Chicago's Relief Committee that some form of public works project might prove helpful, only to be dismissed as ill informed.[30]

Willard did not last long in the inner city, finding her true calling in giving temperance lectures. Even as dean of the Northwestern University Woman's College, she had thought it inappropriate for women to speak before a mixed audience, allowing men to read her addresses in her place. All that changed once she joined the WCTU. At the Cleveland convention, Annie Wittenmyer, a seasoned veteran of the temperance movement and editor of *Christian Woman*, was elected president. Surprisingly, Willard, who had been committed to the cause for only a month, was elected secretary of the new organization. Her skills must have been readily apparent to all who met her, and she quickly became the voice of the younger members tired of accepting that women could only be auxiliaries to male-led reform efforts. As Willard wrote Wittenmyer, "Our object is not by any means *only* to pull drowning men out of the stream, but . . . to make our influence felt at the fountains of power."[31]

Shortly after joining the WCTU, Willard met Anna Dickinson, the talented child orator for the Union cause during the Civil War who had spoken before Congress and President Lincoln, and was just about to embark on a career as an actress. Dickinson became Willard's guide to the most effective methods of public speaking, as well as her counselor toward a more political engagement. Dickinson persuaded Willard that she could make a living as a lecturer, a career that paid rather well in the late nineteenth century. Willard took voice lessons and concentrated on becoming a better speaker. Far more radical than most prominent women of the period, Dickinson was a secularist uninterested in temperance. Through 1876 Willard repeatedly tried to convert Dickinson to the cause and persuade her to abandon her plans to become an actress, but without success. Dickinson thought Willard "too serious," yet remained her close friend, while Willard was obviously attracted to Dickinson's larger-than-life, often outrageous personality.[32]

At the Centennial Exhibition in 1876, Willard gave a well-received lecture on temperance, which earned her a rare invitation to speak at Chautauqua, the morally toned speaking circuit headquartered in the New York town of the same name, despite the hesitance of its founder, John Heyl Vincent, to allow women to speak in his tents. Put off by Vincent's attitude, Willard rebuffed his effort to get her to come back in 1877. He acknowledged in his letter that he might "slight the lady-lecturers," but thought he was complimenting her by insisting that she was the great exception to the rule that women did not make good public speakers.[33] In November Henry Ward Beecher invited her to speak from his Plymouth Church pulpit, a sign of Willard's rising stature as an orator. Willard's big break came in January 1877 when Dwight Moody heard her speak. Moody and his Ed McMahon, the singer Ira Sankey, had just completed their triumphal centennial-year revival through America that culminated with the opening of the eight-thousand-seat Chicago Tabernacle in 1877.[34] Moody asked Willard to lead a prayer service before a packed house of women and then to introduce the famous temperance speaker John B. Gough, after which he brought her on as a full-time member of his revival.

Through the first part of 1877, Willard rapidly rose to become the preeminent woman evangelical speaker in the country, though Moody preferred that she speak to women-only audiences.[35] While they shared a commitment to temperance, Willard and Moody responded differently to the violence and disorder of their time. Moody placed no faith in legislation, believing that only a conversion to evangelical Christianity could effect change, and that solely at the individual level. But then the temperance movement was hardly uniform; the Reverend Dioclesian Lewis, who had sparked the Women's Crusade, thought the idea of prohibition a ludicrous violation of personal liberty and unenforceable, and Willard herself drank for "medicinal" purposes, often on a daily basis, and remained flexible on the best approach to temperance. While she was willing to defer to Moody on the issue of prohibition, Willard would not play down the effect of alcohol abuse on women. The more she framed temperance as a woman's issue, the more uncomfortable Moody became.[36]

Once more Willard balked at male control, even from the paternal Moody, who insisted that she speak only for his revivals and take no outside engagements. Moody grew testier on this point after Willard invited her friend Mary Livermore, a Unitarian temperance speaker, to join her on the platform. Moody, who had been raised a Unitarian, no longer considered them Christians, rejected the notion that women could be ministers, and demanded that the WCTU change its name to the Woman's Evangelical Temperance Union so as to exclude Unitarians. Willard, who tended to communicate with Moody through his wife, Emma, wrote, "The more I study the subject, the more I fail to see that it is for us to decide who shall work in this cause side by side with us, and who shall not." Willard also questioned Moody's attitude toward women, pointing out that at his meetings he called for the "brethren" to come forth to receive salvation, while his women's meetings "are a relic of an outworn regime." Moody probably resented Willard's words and tone, for he had his wife write Willard that she was fired.[37] In September Willard described the exchange to Vincent, writing that she could not devote herself to Moody and his "old, separatist, oriental idea of her place in the church by conducting his women's meetings!"[38]

Once more without a job, Willard decided to devote herself full-time to the WCTU. Camouflaged by respectability, the WCTU was in some ways one of the most radical organizations of its time, completely rejecting nineteenth-century gender arrangements. Only women could vote, hold office, and invest in WCTU enterprises. With offices in every city and most of the larger towns in the country, the WCTU offered hundreds of women jobs and leadership positions completely unavailable elsewhere in the United States. Their printing house and newspaper employed only women, which proved a major breakthrough, as women worked in jobs they could not get otherwise, from typesetter to the upper levels of management. The WCTU also set up some of the first child-care centers in the country and in Ohio organized a nondenominational "Woman's Church" that had a "shepherdess" rather than a minister.[39]

These deeply religious women challenged religious orthodoxy in numerous ways. Opponents routinely hurled at them the words of Paul that women must remain silent in church, cannot teach, and must rely for all instruction on their husbands.[40] In 1877 the Presbyterian Church convicted Reverend Isaac M. See of Newark, New Jersey, of allowing women to preach from his pulpit in violation of Paul's injunction.[41] The Reverend C.T. Berry criticized such out-of-control literalism, wondering "what shall become of women who have no husbands" or whose husbands "are spiritual numbskulls?" And were all those female "Sunday school teachers supposed to go home?" The WCTU responded to its ministerial critics with Paul's assurance that "There is neither Jew nor Greek, there is neither bond nor free, there is neither male nor female: for ye are all one in Christ Jesus."[42] Many WCTU women perceived the mainstream denominations as striving to keep women in their (silent) place, though some, such as the Congregational Church, officially endorsed the presence of women in the pulpit. Once they began exploring the historical relationship between women and religion, many prominent members of the WCTU reached dramatically militant positions. "Church and State unite in one thing if in no other," wrote Mary Lathrap, "in defining a position for women, and so far as possible keeping them in it."[43]

The debate over the right of women to speak in church was just part of a larger cultural denigration of women. Prized as mothers and wives who maintained the home, women found little room for themselves beyond that idealized domestic sphere. Those who stepped into the public world of politics, business, and intellect generally met contempt. The evaluations of women tended toward the contradictory. It was "well known" that women could not be trusted with money, bankruptcies often resulting from "silly women" addicted to "extravagant living," while they also tended to deny their husbands small pleasures through petty economies. Women who failed to adhere to their proper domestic role endangered society, while a woman who pampered her husband was "a foolish and selfish woman who . . . flatters his vanity." Women were not smart enough to understand politics, while women like Susan B. Anthony who spoke for the political rights of women were "busy-bodies" who offered the public "filth and nastiness."[44] Followers of the Reverend Moody were "silly sentimental women," while the Reverend Moody called those too concerned with the affairs of this world "silly women laden with sins, led away with divers lusts." Women, being better liars than men, were "most dangerous," though being so gullible and ignorant they more often fell prey to schemers. But above all else, men accused women of being excessively emotional and irrational, lacking the finer qualities of intellect displayed by men and incapable of excelling at math. As Dr. Oliver Wendell Holmes pithily put it, women tended toward hysteria, and "a hysterical woman is a vampire, who sucks the blood of the healthy people about her."[45]

Given such a context, one of the primary goals of the WCTU was improving the image of women, demonstrating that they had worth beyond giving birth and raising families. WCTU meetings celebrated historic women and one another, struggling to create a women's history, and promoting the building of monuments to heroic women. From Elizabeth I to Elizabeth Barrett Browning, from Joan of Arc to Harriet Beecher Stowe, the WCTU broadcast the talents and heroism of women, claiming a history for themselves that had been too often obscured by men. Frances Willard went further, insisting that the women of her generation were making their own history: "History! What attraction has its ancient record for you who are steadily making America a history more inspiring than any that her archives have yet furnished." Mary Lathrap flipped the stereotypes, raising women to heroic heights for their courage in working with the poor while "dainty" men ignored the precepts of Christianity and feared the poorest among them.[46]

Perhaps even more remarkable was the brilliance with which these activists began constructing a women's discourse, one that praised one another even in the midst of significant disagreements. Frances Willard led the way in constructing this ideal of supportive dissent. In 1877, even while battling Wittenmyer for the presidency, she made certain to repeatedly praise her as a great leader. Willard consistently called on even the shyest "sister," as she insisted they call one another, to give their opinions, and, like the finest teachers, found something to compliment in every statement. The WCTU rarely brought in outside speakers, calling instead for the sisters to "step to the front themselves." Willard addressed her audiences as "Women, Sisters, Mothers," drawing them into a shared bond rarely experienced or properly valued elsewhere, educating "women out of the silence which has stifled their beautiful gifts so long."[47] The language of sisterhood, as Carol Mattingly has written, "made positive use of cultural restrictions to create a sense of community, repeatedly using terms applicable only to women and inclusive of all women." Like the proverbial fish without a bicycle, these women got along just fine without men. As Willard said, they were "in nowise guided, moulded or controlled by men."[48] It is easy to understand why so many thousands of women joined the WCTU.

Though it was never its stated intent, the WCTU played a pivotal role in helping many women break free of the confines of the domestic sphere. Willard saw that "custom's pinched lips" declared, "Thus far and no farther," leading her generation of women to rebel. Eventually Willard would be forthright about her goal, which was nothing less than "reconstructing the ideal of womanhood."[49]

Through this reformulation of womanhood, the WCTU never lost sight of its primary goal: getting men to drink less for the safety and security of women. Members insisted on the right and ability of women to fight back against the "liquor lobby." The Illinois WCTU, of which Willard was president, resolved that "since woman is the greatest sufferer from the rum curse, she ought to have power to close the dram-shop door."[50] Their initial demands were modest—calls for Sunday closing and the licensing of taverns—but expectations shifted as temperance reached messianic heights in the late 1870s. Abstaining from alcohol would reduce the amount of violence while building a more rational and loving

society. As W.E. Clifford, president of the Evanston Temperance Union, proclaimed in 1877, America's women, armed only with their moral influence, will
soon "banish crime, pauperism, and misery from the nation." When it came to
temperance, "Women are the makers of public opinion." One consequence of
the temperance vision was the absolute conviction, widely shared, that women
were more ethical than men.[51] Temperance thus served as a socially acceptable
activism and demonstration of female moral superiority best represented by
Lucy Hayes, the first presidential wife to have a college degree, and who was well
known as "Lemonade Lucy" for banning alcohol from the White House. As
William Evarts said, the water flowed like champagne at state dinners.[52]

But the temperance crusade hit a wall. Resistance from the "liquor interests,"
"Rum Power," and "saloonists" generally defeated even their tamest efforts at the
state level.[53] The WCTU evoked a lot of anger not just from the liquor lobby,
but also from politicians, such as the Missouri Democrat who said that women
may be able to "teach an infant class, but not to speak or lead in prayer." Several
states, even the ever-sober Connecticut, repealed existing prohibitory laws, and
temperance advocates saw the liquor interests increasing their power in American politics.[54] "The whole temperance movement was characterized by vacilla-
tion and defeat," wrote an early historian of the antialcohol crusade, while "the
liquor interests, confident because of their victories, went forward like a con-
quering army, each year attaining additional political power."[55] The United
States Brewers' Association, whose annual meeting tended to be called the Beer
Congress, acknowledged their debt to immigrants in their battle against "puritanical tyranny." The 1877 Beer Congress resolved that those "who seek the support of the so-called temperance party [will] be earnestly opposed irrespective of
their political creeds."[56] It is true that individual towns, such as Colorado
Springs, with a strong Republican base instituted some controls by limiting the
number of saloons, requiring licenses to sell alcohol and instituting closing
hours. But such communities were in the minority, and only rock-solid Republican Maine went all the way in outlawing the manufacture and sale of alcohol.[57]

The temperance crusade appeared to be fading in 1877 when Frances Willard
had an epiphany. In her later telling, Willard was on her knees praying when she
heard a voice in her head: "You are to speak for woman's ballot as a protection to
her home and tempted loved ones from the tyranny of drink." In addition, in
that instant, Willard said, "for the first and only time in my life, there flashed
through my brain a complete line of argument and illustration."[58] Yet behind
this profound moment of revelation lay months of preparation. Several other
women had urged Willard to fight for suffrage, most particularly the controversial Unitarian Mary Livermore, president of the Massachusetts branch of the
WCTU.[59] Additionally, Willard found herself increasingly disagreeing with Annie Wittenmyer and the older WCTU leaders who adamantly opposed women's

suffrage and all else that Willard identified as modern. When Willard suggested to a WCTU meeting that they should discuss suffrage, the chair, Lucy Butler, instantly put the young upstart in her place, insisting that "we do not propose to trail our skirts through the mire of politics."[60] Wittenmyer's supporters found politics a lessening of the moral authority of women as well as a diversion from their true goal of temperance. To wean men from alcohol was to wean them from violence and corruption, and that was a sufficient duty. As one of them said at the 1877 convention, "By educating the children to temperance there can be but little doubt of what the men of the next twenty years shall be."[61]

Willard slowly formulated her position on women's rights, trying out arguments in search of an effective message. Initially she insisted that women needed to vote as "the Sabbath and the Bible are now attacked by the infidel foreign population of our country."[62] This nativist stance offended many other suffragists and would have alienated a large proportion of the voting males, and Willard soon abandoned it. Instead, she discovered a sisterhood with Catholic women based upon the cult of domesticity and "home protection." After all, she reasoned, Catholic women also had to protect themselves and their homes from the violent effects of alcohol. Willard's genius was to craft the argument for women's suffrage on the scaffolding of the cult of domesticity. Where Susan B. Anthony and Elizabeth Cady Stanton saw voting as a right, Willard framed it as a moral duty, expressed in ways that few could protest: the nurturing role of women, their higher moral standards, their sensitivity and compassion, with the ballot as "a weapon of protection to her home."[63] With women voting, society itself would become moral, cleaned of corruption, and much better behaved. Such a perspective held real attraction in a Gilded Age that appeared on the verge of greater violence and immorality. Willard used the separate sphere ideology to drag women into the public sphere. But underneath all these moral arguments lay an essentially practical one: "We have carried ballots to men year after year, urging them to vote; but we have made up our minds that it is just as easy for us to vote ourselves."[64]

Despite their intellectual differences, Anthony was thrilled with Willard's decision to tie the temperance crusade to the cause of women's suffrage, congratulating her in 1877 on "breaking the spell" that had fallen over American women. Anthony did not share Willard's faith in the efficacy of legislation to alter drinking habits; instead she held up the ideal of a better class of engaged mothers permanently improving society. Aiming lower than Anthony, who wanted to vote in national elections, Willard was content if women could vote at the local level, where they would battle the liquor lobby for the soul of communities. But after their mutual friend Mary Livermore brought them together, the two crusaders became lifelong friends, working together to make women a force in American life.[65]

Willard planned her campaign well, moving slowly, preparing the way for the complete transformation of temperance from a crusade for inner salvation to one for political transformation. She was unerringly polite to opponents, women and men, assuring the latter that their chivalry in seeking to protect women from the filth of politics was admirable but not required. In her contest with Wittenmyer for control of the WCTU, Willard behaved with great respect toward her elder while slowly shoving her off the stage. At the 1876 convention, Willard declined nomination for the presidency, yet still received thirty-nine votes to sixty for Wittenmyer. At the 1877 WCTU convention in Chicago, Willard welcomed the delegates with a riveting speech comparing alcohol consumption to the raging fires that had consumed Chicago in 1871, and held up suffrage as necessary to combat the conflagration. Ignoring Wittenmyer's objections, Willard introduced discussion of women's suffrage in the WCTU magazine *Our Union* in 1877. In that year and 1878 Willard made serious though polite efforts for the presidency, winning the support of most of the Midwest delegations, and almost beating Wittenmyer, becoming the dominant personality at the annual conventions. The 1879 contest for the presidency was not even close, with Willard winning ninety-nine votes to forty for Wittenmyer, pushing the WCTU into national politics. Within two years the WCTU would officially endorse women's suffrage as a priority, and Willard would be the most famous woman in the United States, a celebrity who attracted enormous attention.[66]

Under Willard's leadership the WCTU registered impressive growth, expanding from a few thousand members in 1874 to 13,000 in 1876, to 150,000 in 1883, with offices throughout the country. Its huge publishing house probably printed more women authors than any other press in the world. In 1877 the WCTU claimed a role in persuading Senator Henry W. Blair of New Hampshire to introduce the first constitutional amendment prohibiting the manufacture and sale of alcohol, and in aiding the first significant political victory of the decade by temperance forces when General C. C. Van Zandt, nominee of the Republican and Prohibition parties, was elected governor of Rhode Island for the first of three terms. By the end of the century, WCTU political influence led to every state in the country requiring schools to teach the dangers of drinking.[67] But what they could not accomplish was winning the vote for women.

Many American women who had fought long and hard for an end to slavery and the triumph of Union troops in the Civil War assumed that victory would win them the right to vote that they had first demanded at the Seneca Falls convention in 1848. But the ideal of universal suffrage was squashed during Reconstruction. Even onetime allies such as Wendell Phillips took the view that the country could only handle one major change in the aftermath of the war. "One question at a time," he insisted. "This hour belongs to the negro." Elizabeth Cady Stanton asked Wendell Phillips if he believed "the African race was entirely composed of males."[68] Apparently Congress did, as the Fourteenth Amendment began with its promise of universal human rights in Section 1,[69] and then suddenly turned away from that goal and limited those rights to men by introducing the word "male" for the first time into the Constitution.[70] Stanton presciently warned that "if that word 'male' be inserted, . . . it will take us a century at least to get it out." In the view of the suffragists, women actually lost ground with the Fifteenth Amendment, as it based suffrage explicitly on gender.[71]

Suffragists hoped that the courts would draw upon that first part of the Fourteenth Amendment, with its promise of equal rights to "All persons born or naturalized in the United States" to grant women the right to vote. But a unanimous Supreme Court rejected that logic in *Minor v. Happersett*, holding that suffrage was not one of the rights of citizenship.[72] Betrayed by male abolitionists who failed to see the logic or importance of extending the same rights to women as to freed black men, Susan Anthony railed against the "aristocracy of sex" working to keep women from equality. Stanton made the best of the situation and realized that at least now women were liberated from their inconstant male allies. Long convinced that women could never attain true reform in groups run by men, Stanton moved to organize women to act on their own behalf on many different issues, from politics to religion, keeping the right to vote as the premier goal.[73]

Suffragists were divided over the best strategy for winning the vote. Stanton and Anthony founded the National Woman Suffrage Association (NWSA), aimed at amending the Constitution, while Lucy Stone and her husband, Henry Blackwell, formed the American Woman Suffrage Association (AWSA), which devoted itself to battling in the states. The two organizations aided one another, but neither proved successful and they united in 1890. In 1877 Susan B. Anthony presented Congress with petitions from twenty-six states calling for a sixteenth amendment to the Constitution, but Congress refused to consider the matter; suffragists had little choice but to fight it out at the local and state levels.[74] Women in Toledo, Ohio, protested that the Board of Education "discriminated" against women by paying them 20 percent less than men for the same job but, typically, were ignored.[75] Undaunted, women's suffrage groups sprang up throughout the country in the late 1870s, placing the issue on the ballot in many states, garnering the votes of hundreds of thousands of men nationwide, though rarely earning the majority of votes.[76]

The suffragists' first successes came in Wyoming in 1869 and Utah in 1870, followed by several defeats. In 1877 came the crucial struggle for the ballot in Colorado. On election day, suffrage proponents canvassed the state, getting out the vote and standing near polling places making last-minute appeals. In Denver, Reverend T.E. Bliss, "the Woman Hater," who had just labeled suffragists "old hens" and warned that if women voted they would never marry,[77] confronted Lucy Stone as he went to vote and a bitter debate ensued, with Bliss telling Stone that she was "no lady" and had no right to be in Colorado, and Stone responding that he had hurt generations of women. It descended from there.[78]

The abuse Stone received was replicated in the official returns, with the proposal failing 14,053 opposed to just 6,612 in favor. Most of the votes for women's suffrage came from Denver and Greeley, the rest of the state rejecting it by sweeping majorities. The defeat killed the suffrage movement in Colorado; the *Rocky Mountain News* remained confident of eventual victory in the near future, though it recommended that next time all electioneering should be left in the hands of men, and then discontinued its "Woman's Column."[79] The struggle to extend the right to vote to women crashed in 1877, as the country moved to restrain rather than extend democracy. Colorado was the battlefield—and the suffragists lost. They came closest to success at the California Constitutional Convention the following year, where a women's suffrage clause was hotly debated before being defeated by ten votes. The movement did not revive in Colorado until 1893, when the sudden success of the Populist Party led the legislature to once more call for a referendum on women's suffrage. Firmly backed by the Populists, including Governor David H. Waite, the proposal won 35,698 to 29,461, making Colorado the first state to adopt women's suffrage by popular vote.[80] Women did not cease getting married.

For a few months in the fall of 1877 the Colorado campaign focused national attention on the role of women in America. Briefly, many prominent intellectuals and some leading newspapers argued that the country could now move beyond the near civil war of winter and the riots of summer, and was on the verge of significant change—which was precisely what terrified a great many people. For this latter group, the Colorado election had been an "unhappy disturbance" that fueled too much talk by women about their "rights" and just made everybody "very uncomfortable." *The Congregationalist*, one of the primary opponents of universal suffrage, expressed annoyance at foolish women unable to distinguish "between a moral and a civil government," the latter having "to deal with swords and guns, and police clubs, and with riots, conflicts and battle-fields," as recent events proved. Clearly the "peculiarities and weaknesses of the 'gentler sex,'" disqualifed them from "all participation in public affairs." Granting women an ethical role, *The Congregationalist* rejected as "sophistry and folly" Willard's logic that women could therefore bring "great moral influence" to politics. As evidence they charged that biblical "teachings relative to the sphere and responsibilities of woman, were scoffed at, and the sacred Book openly ridiculed" by the suffragists. Because the suffragists would not accept their subservient role as defined by *The Congregationalist*'s reading of the Bible, they were thus considered blasphemers and no longer moral—which was all the more reason why they should not be allowed to vote. The suffragists did not behave like women, speaking in public, campaigning, bullying men, and then "cowardly" hiding "behind the weaknesses and immunities of their sex." The violence of the South is "as nothing compared with the malignant spirit of some of these advocates of the millen-

nium of 'Woman's Rights.'" They particularly condemned Lucy Stone for confronting the Reverend Bliss with "a torrent of insult and abuse." But the voters
rejected "this corrupting, this wild and reckless phantasy of woman's political
suffrage." The journal concluded that three-fourths of the women in Colorado opposed the proposal, but since they could not vote, there is no way of knowing.[81]

The defeat of universal suffrage led many women to question the nature of
American society. Out in Colorado Springs, Georgianne E. Watson, a former
Vassar English professor, wrote, "A State, nominally democratic, which limits its
franchise, is . . . either an aristocracy or an oligarchy." Watson suggested a link
between economic and political power, with the elite battling against women's
suffrage in order to maintain the status quo. Watson was surprisingly public with
her views; only one other prominent contemporary suffragist proclaimed a radical economic vision: Frances Willard. Linking the many events of 1877 into a
chain of social causality, Willard saw women as no different from men in being
the victims of capitalism, calling on her temperance crusaders to support government regulation of the economy. "The rich idlers amusing themselves in New-
port while poor workers bury themselves in coal mines" demanded a response.
In a significant and radical break with the temperance tradition, Willard reversed
the old saw that drinking caused poverty. She was convinced that most workers
drank to escape the hardships they faced every day; so if the workers were raised
out of poverty and given a living wage and an eight-hour day, most would cease
drinking.[82]

Despite these many setbacks, Emily Faithfull, an English advocate of women's
rights who made three trips to the United States between 1872 and 1884, found
cause for hope. In 1884 she wrote how when Harriet Martineau visited in 1840,
"she found only seven occupations open to women; today, in Massachusetts
alone, there are nearly three hundred different branches of industry by which
women can earn from one hundred to three thousand dollars a year." The typewriter, developed in 1873, had changed everything: "These marvelous inventions are giving hundreds of girls throughout the States remunerative work." In
Macon, Georgia, Faithfull met a "Woman Switchman" renowned for not having
made a single mistake in the several years she held her job. Faithfull asked the
railway worker how she liked her work, receiving the answer: "Far better than
the wash-tub. I am never sick, and I know when my work is done."[83]

At the National Woman Suffrage Association convention in 1877, Susan Anthony presented what she hoped would be the Sixteenth Amendment to the
Constitution.[84] The following year Senator Aaron A. Sargent of California presented Anthony's amendment, which stated that "the right of citizens of the
United States to vote shall not be denied or abridged by the United States or by
any state on account of sex." Forty-two years later, fourteen years after Anthony's
death, women would finally win the vote with the passage of the Nineteenth

Amendment to the Constitution. In the previous year, Frances Willard's friend Anna Gordon, now president of the Woman's Christian Temperance Union, watched as prohibition became part of the Constitution as the Eighteenth Amendment.[85] Willard, who died in 1898, had hoped that these two measures would transform America, making it a more moral and less violent nation. While the results of the experiment of prohibition would have probably disappointed Willard, she could only have been enormously satisfied with the attainment of her other major end, the greater political involvement of women. In 1877 a woman's right to vote had been firmly rejected by the political leadership of both parties and by the voters of several states. Though the road to political equality was a long and uneven one, it was, as Willard appreciated, a journey worth taking—not just because the goal was worth reaching, but also for the sense of self-worth that individual women would gain by fighting for justice.

A Dedicated Teacher

In the summer of 1877, a former slave in West Virginia played a significant role in moving the state capital from Wheeling to Charleston. The state legislature had decided to put the location of the capital up for a vote. The issue was not so much political as geographical; since those living near each of the proposed capitals would most likely vote for that choice, victory depended on voter turnout. The white backers of Charleston realized that they could clinch the election if, rather than preventing the area's blacks from voting, as was becoming the norm, they encouraged their participation in the election. To attain that goal, they turned to a young teacher in nearby Malden named Booker T. Washington.[86]

Just twenty-one years old and a recent graduate of Hampton Normal and Agricultural Institute, Washington proved to be an excellent speaker and organizer. He gave numerous speeches and worked hard to get out the vote, helping to win the election for Charleston. Two aspects of the campaign impressed Washington: the ease with which whites and blacks could work together on an issue of mutual importance, and the respect he received from white leaders as a consequence of his hard work. Washington reflected on these lessons in a letter to the *West Virginia Journal* he titled "Can We Not Improve?" By "we" he meant "the colored people, for I am a colored man myself, or rather a boy."[87] Washington saw much of which the freedmen could be proud in the past decade, but also a number of failures. The most important task of all, education, reflected these strengths and weaknesses. "The time is fast coming when bondage can no longer be a plea for ignorance," Washington wrote. "Our many friends who have stood by us in the past . . . want to see us accomplish something ourselves." If they only persevered, it would not be long until a large number of blacks "will be equal in education, equal in wealth, and equal in everything that tends toward human advancement." They could not give in to despair, he reasoned, but must find the "courage and resolve" to succeed against the odds.[88]

Washington's optimism and faith in hard work is astounding against the background of racist violence he had witnessed. The Ku Klux Klan had been active in the Malden area and Washington recognized them as descendants of the slave patrols, only "more cruel." The Klan's primary goal was "to crush out the political aspirations of the Negroes, but they did not confine themselves to this, because schoolhouses as well as churches were burned by them, and many innocent people lost their lives." The Klan's brutality made a great impression on the young teacher who initially thought that "there was no hope for our people in this country."[89] Yet Washington came to believe that he could find a road for his fellow blacks, some way for them to carry on their lives in peace in a country that permitted such homicidal extralegal violence. He would find this route, like one of the old slave footpaths that ran hidden in the bushes next to the main highway, in a focused technical education.[90]

The freedmen, Washington argued, had relied too much on the federal government for support and not enough on themselves. "During the whole of the Reconstruction period our people throughout the South looked to the Federal Government for everything, very much as a child looks to its mother." Such faith and dependence were natural, for it was the government that had won them their freedom. But even as a young man Washington felt "that it was cruelly wrong" of Congress to not "make some provision for the general education of our people . . . so that the people would be better prepared for the duties of citizenship." Instead the slaves had been handed their freedom, given a metaphoric pat on the back, and been sent on their way, unprepared and ultimately unprotected. But the black people had made a terrible mistake as well; by focusing on politics over economics they had handicapped themselves for the long-term struggle for acceptance. The "political agitation" of the Reconstruction period "drew the attention of our people away from the more fundamental matters of perfecting themselves in the industries at their doors and in securing property." Seeking a wider sphere of influence than teaching in West Virginia, Washington enrolled in the Wayland Baptist Seminary in Washington, D.C., in 1878.[91]

Washington quickly determined that the ministry was not for him. He expected to receive a call to preach, "but, for some reason, my call never came." Washington was bothered by the differences between Wayland and Hampton; at the former the students dressed well and studied abstract matters, while at the latter they did not concern themselves with appearance and concentrated on learning a practical skill. The result, Washington felt, was that at Hampton the student made "the effort through the industries to help himself, and that very effort was of immense value in character-building." In a sense, the Wayland students did not seem to appreciate the society in which they lived and how far blacks had to travel.

"They knew more about Latin and Greek when they left school, but they seemed to know less about life and its conditions as they would meet it at their homes."[92]

Living in Washington, D.C., was an education, with its large black population seemingly more interested in appearance than in the improvement of themselves and their race. Young men and women threw their wages away on frivolous purchases and entertainments, rather than saving to acquire property and prepare for the rough times ahead. Washington wished he could send the lot of them into the countryside, where they would learn the hard lessons they needed in order to survive and prosper. He came to the opinion "that what our people most needed was to get a foundation in education, industry, and property," and he felt that he could contribute toward that end as an educator. So in 1879 he left Wayland to teach at Hampton Institute, being put in charge of the first class of Native American students. And then in 1881 came the call he had been waiting for, to open Tuskegee Institute in Alabama.[93]

Over the next thirty years, until his death in 1915, Booker T. Washington built Tuskegee into a center for technical education, crafting a vision for the future of black people in America that saw them attaining a place at the table by accepting the growing segregation of the South and working to find a safe economic niche within a hostile culture. At times Washington's calling could sound stunted, as when he famously said that blacks must "learn to dignify and glorify common labor," as "it is at the bottom of life that we must begin and not at the top." But his aim did not swerve from the goal of economic self-sufficiency—the need for African Americans to place their feet solidly on the American land so that their claims to citizenship would resonate with a society that measured worth by hard work and money. "At the bottom of education, at the bottom of politics, even at the bottom of religion itself there must be for our race, as for all races, economic independence."[94]

During the few years from 1877 to 1882, while Washington learned the lessons that would lead him to the conclusion that blacks had no choice but to accept their second-class status in the United States, the South was becoming a single-party state with serflike conditions for its black underclass. Black Americans saw what was happening and fought against these developments, which were generally identified as a consequence of "the President's Policy." A protest meeting of "colored persons" at Boston's Revere Street Church charged that Hayes's Southern policy disenfranchised black citizens while "the negro was treated as a serf."[95] It was clear that Northern industry found advantage in these policies as creating a steady supply of incredibly cheap labor. Even former white allies proved "willing to sacrifice the black race for the sake of commerce." If these policies were not reversed, within five years "the condition of the black race would be worse than that of the serfs in Russia."[96]

The charges made at this meeting generally proved accurate. Many former friends, from Harriet Beecher Stowe to powerful editors of the Republican press, were tired of the whole issue of black rights. Mostly these onetime white supporters refused to believe that Southern whites would keep blacks from the polls in the South, and remained confident that with time the "negro vote" would have its effect and that a "New South" in which whites accepted the civil rights of blacks would soon emerge. But it was time to slow down, for the blacks' own good; if blacks acted too "turbulently," they would "be met by violence." The burden was on the blacks to educate themselves and advance economically. "If the blacks remain ignorant, they will become mere serfs," and apparently deserved that fate. If they failed to "rise in morals and intelligence, they will become prey to idleness" and disappoint "the whole nation in the results of emancipation." In a way these voices from 1877 anticipated Booker T. Washington's approach, counseling the freedmen to rise "gradually" through "intelligent toil," avoiding politics until they had earned the respect of Southern whites. "Any other solution of the difficulty than this will give a temporary advantage to one of the political parties, to be followed by effective repression by the other."[97]

But it was too late, for one of the political parties, the Democrats, had already launched an active policy of repression, one widely labeled a "reign of terror" by the Republican press.[98] To the Republicans, these outrages reflected an inherent cowardice in Southern whites, who always targeted the weakest members of their society. Reporting on the lynching of a black woman, the *Rocky Mountain News* observed, "It does not take more than six Virginians to hang a woman."[99] Yet while condemning lynching and other forms of violence, Republicans did not fight back, contenting themselves with contempt and righteousness.

The election of 1878 shocked Republicans nationwide as they lost all but four congressional seats in the South and their vote total fell to its lowest level since the war.[100] Where many scholars argue that Gilded Age America had "an essentially conservative electorate," it was in fact a severely limited electorate. In Louisiana the black population grew 33 percent between 1870 and 1880, while the number of Republican votes decreased 47 percent; in Mississippi the black population grew 46 percent while the Republican vote declined 59 percent.[101] The South Carolina election typified this "New South":[102] the Republicans did not even put up a candidate against Wade Hampton, who won reelection 119,550 to 213.[103] After he was elected governor, Hampton promised to protect black voters, a vow he broke every day he was in office. Before Southern audiences he succinctly referred to Northerners as "those suckers."[104]

Contemporaries and later scholars would do their best to see the end of Reconstruction as a course correction, a termination of corrupt Republican governments, and just a brief bump on America's heroic march of freedom. Even sympathetic scholars framed the denial of black rights as "the shunting of the American Negro onto a long and roundabout road to freedom." The history of the period is thus all about white men, as "the entire country was weary of Reconstruction."[105] Until recently, historians of this period spoke of "the people" and "Southerners" as white only, consistently placing blacks outside the bounds of citizenship, robbing them a second time of their historic rights. Thus one historian wrote, "The people of the states in secession, once the Confederacy was crushed, desired nothing so much as to regain control of their states" and wanted an end to "Federal control, or 'occupation,' or 'military government.'" There is sufficient evidence that the freedmen did not feel the same way, for it was that "occupation" which protected their very lives. But it was vital to the mythology of the end of Reconstruction that black people remained unseen and unheard. Thus the monument erected by whites to the Hamburg Massacre is dedicated "to the only resident of Hamburg to be killed in the Hamburg riot of 1876," completely ignoring the twenty or more blacks murdered in that town.[106]

Not content simply to hold power, Southern Democrats worked to construct a mythology that would legitimate their racist seizure of power and social structure.[107] Proponents of the one-party South used the religious term "redeemers" to describe the politicians who restored white supremacy to the South after the "justified" overthrow of the corrupt Reconstruction governments. "Redeemers" must surely be one of the most twisted names ever given to terrorists, but for generations American history textbooks have used this phrase, and still do, though usually with the courtesy of quotation marks. The editor of the Rutherford Hayes papers gave voice to this mythology when he insisted, "Everyone can see now that the experiment of permitting a newly enfranchised and ignorant servile race . . . to govern American States in defiance of the intelligence, the culture, and the property interests of the Anglo-Saxon inhabitants, was bound to fail." President Hayes demonstrated not just the "wisdom but the moral courage" to let "the forces of civilization" violently crush democracy as he "answered for all time the obstinate and distracting Southern question."[108] While we may not care to inquire into a definition of moral courage premised on abandoning the rights of a large segment of the American population to racial serfdom and terror, it is important to recognize the power of the Southern mythology of "redemption" that pulls in even the most fervent advocate of its political opponents.

The Reconstruction myth served the purpose of covering the crimes of the Democrats in a blanket of righteousness, as former Mississippi governor Adelbert Ames understood. Benjamin Andrews, who was writing a critical history of Reconstruction, had been told by Democrats that Mississippi was $20 million in debt when the party retook the state. Andrews wrote Ames to ask how he had wasted so much money. Ames suggested that Andrews not take the word of those determined to discredit forever a government that had included black officials, but to look in the state records for himself, which would reveal that the state debt had been half a million dollars, a rather substantial difference. "Slandering the reconstructionists," Ames wrote Andrews, served to obscure and justify the fact that Democrats had "committed crime upon crime to prevent the political equality of the negro."[109] John R. Lynch, the former Speaker of the House of Mississippi and one of the handful of African Americans to serve in Congress during Reconstruction, wrote an angry rebuttal to Andrews called *The Facts of Reconstruction*. Ames's government, Lynch pointed out, had built schools and kept the debt low, without any evidence of fraud—unlike the succeeding Democratic government, the state treasurer of which stole more than $300,000. Ames thanked Lynch for setting the record straight, adding "Unfortunately greed, the father of slaves, was too much for us. He who was a slave is now a serf."[110] Both men felt they were up against powerful forces that preferred lies to historic reality, and indeed over the next century few people questioned the myth, which was enshrined in two of the most popular movies in American history, *Birth of a Nation* and *Gone with the Wind*.

On Memorial Day 1878, Frederick Douglass delivered a speech in New York in which he reminded the audience that the Civil War lived on. "A lawless and revolutionary spirit is still abroad in the country," he warned, and "the Constitution and the laws are . . . dishonored and disregarded," while "duly elected State Governments" have been "overthrown by violence." Carefully avoiding any criticism of President Hayes for "stepping to the verge of his constitutional powers to conciliate and pacify the old master class at the South," Douglass did suggest that it was reasonable to demand that some sign "of conciliation should come from the other side" as well. Inequality was tangible to Douglass, for while Southern whites could go anywhere they pleased in the United States, here was he, a federal marshal, unable to do the same because he was a black American.[111] Over the next decade Douglass's bitterness with the betrayal of African Americans in 1877 grew; in 1888 he furiously denounced "the So-Called Emancipation as a Stupendous Fraud."[112] Violence against blacks rose every year, as the heroic Ida B. Wells would soon begin documenting in her journal *Free Speech*. White lynch mobs were burning blacks at the stake, which is an "awful indictment against American civilization." In a fury, Wells wrote, "No other nation, civilized or savage, burns its criminals; only under the stars and stripes is the human holocaust possible."[113]

White Southerners rejected democracy and chose oligarchy and poverty in 1877, living with the consequences for a hundred years. And yet, somehow, African Americans retained their faith in America and its dream of democracy. Booker T. Washington clung to his ideals of acceptance and hard work into the twentieth century, influencing African American leaders around the country as he set up supportive networks and persuaded white philanthropists to fund his educational efforts. His insistence that blacks needed to avoid confrontation with whites frustrated those, such as W.E.B. Du Bois, who combated segregation; but, as Du Bois admitted, thousands of African Americans benefited from

Washington's unswerving commitment. Confident that education and labor were the safest, surest paths to prosperity within a segregated nation, Washington grappled with the reality that, while black Americans continued to struggle with the effects of two centuries of slavery, white America had turned its collective back on the Civil War and all it represented.

In 1886 Anna J. Cooper, a former slave and recent graduate of Oberlin, set down her thoughts on her native land. She spoke for many blacks in writing, "Our satisfaction in American institutions rests not on the fruition we now enjoy, but springs rather from the possibilities and promises that are inherent in the system, though as yet, perhaps, far in the future." African Americans had an equal claim to the United States and would someday attain full citizenship, for "there can be no doubt" that this "is the arena in which the next triumph of civilization is to be won; and here too we find promise abundant and possibilities infinite."[114] Cooper stayed true to her belief that she could make America live up to its promise, laboring as a teacher for black children and working women, earning a PhD from the Sorbonne, and in 1930 rising to become president of Frelinghuysen University in Washington, D.C. And still she fought on for her ideals and for her people, battling against lynching, supporting the NAACP in its struggle to end segregation, seeing the legal justifications come crashing down with *Brown v. Board of Education* in 1954, dying at the age of one hundred and six in 1964, the year that Martin Luther King Jr. became the youngest person ever to win the Nobel Peace Prize. Hers had been a life filled with hope and conflict, with accomplishments and bitter disappointments. Through it all Anna Cooper remained true to the vision she laid out in her youth and which she articulated so perfectly in 1902, speaking before the Friends General Conference. The United States, she had insisted, would yet be "the land of destiny for the descendants of the enslaved race, that here in the house of their bondage are the seeds of promise for their ultimate enfranchisement and development."[115]

So, in the years after the end of Reconstruction, the black community turned inward and sustained itself as best it could through the long dark decades of Jim Crow. But from this sustained tradition of hard work and shared struggle would emerge the slow, painful, and ultimately triumphant battle for equality that would save the soul of American democracy.

A President Confronts Corporate Capitalism

Rutherford B. Hayes found his first year as president challenging. First there was the fact that roughly half the country felt he had stolen the election and therefore did not deserve to be president—but he rode that one out. Then came the need to somehow negotiate the end of Reconstruction in such a way that the black Southerners who had put him in the White House did not fall victim to the hatred of their former masters; but he had solved that problem, he was certain. There had been the distractions of the Western wars against the Sioux, Nez Perce, and almost with Mexico; but they had all ended as triumphs for American arms, in his estimation. Of course the horror of the Great Strike had come close to tearing the nation apart and sending it straight into another civil war; but he had firmly suppressed the insurgents and restored order. And over it all hung the continuing nightmare of the depression; that was a problem that just would not go away and to which all sorts of people were offering completely unacceptable solutions. The economic situation posed a problem for Hayes and would dominate the rest of his presidency. However, it would not be the larger questions of unemployment, labor relations, bankruptcies, or industrial policy to which Hayes and Congress devoted themselves, but rather to what appeared on the surface to be the simple issue of coinage.[116]

The coinage issue was more than simply an esoteric economic detail; rather, it reflected a fundamental understanding of the role of government and a vision for the nation. It is fairly clear that no one completely understood the workings of the economy in the Gilded Age, as is revealed by the many efforts to explain the depression. The general public perceived the depression was brought on by personal corruption and greed, the blame lying with such people as Jay Gould, John Fisk, Tom Scott, and other avaricious corporate leaders.[117] Though some manufacturers blamed the unions for hard times since they disrupted the free market and raised wages to unnaturally high levels, the most common view among elites was that these things happen and are but the routine shrugging off of inefficient businesses by the market.[118] Critics of this sangfroid pointed out that the United States went on the gold standard in 1873, coincident with the start of the depression.[119]

When it came to currency, the prevailing nineteenth-century economic wisdom held that money needed to be backed by precious metals, preferably gold, otherwise it lacked "soundness"—a favorite phrase of the period.[120] There was little appreciation for the utility of money as an agreed-upon medium of exchange that feeds further activity as it circulates through the economy. Instead, it was believed that those with money should hold on to it and invest it carefully, while the government must back up every dollar with a dollar's worth of gold and be able to exchange one for the other. Those who favored this view of currency took the word of a few prominent economists and business leaders, such as the social Darwinist William Graham Sumner and the railroad magnate Tom Scott, who pontificated on the need for a "sound currency," while those who favored a more expansive currency backed by both gold and silver turned to old Jacksonians such as Senators Allen Thurman and George Pendleton and representatives of the mining interests such as Representative Richard "Silver Dick" Bland. It did not occur to all but a few of the "experts" that the whole debate over the need for a metallic base to currency was irrelevant and that money could circulate without being backed by any mineral or precious metals.[121]

One gets a good sense of this struggle to understand the workings of the economy in the diary of Rutherford Hayes. The president knew which side he was on, that of a strict gold standard, though he was never completely sure why that was the better approach. Hayes tried out an array of intellectual justifications, jotting down talking points that might work in his effort to publicly explain his position, but he appears to have baffled himself on several occasions. He knew that silver was demonetized in 1873, which some saw as related to the depression, though it was unclear what consequences followed from that step. Surely any effort "to pay the public debt in depreciated silver coin is a violation of public credit," and would add to the national debt. The country was set to abandon paper currency, "greenbacks," entirely on January 1, 1879, which would seriously limit the money supply. Hayes saw Alexander Hamilton's point, raised by advocates of silver, that coinage should not be "scanty," yet Hayes insisted that coins must have "intrinsic value—to be money and not a mere promise," and that "money" had to equal gold, because gold was an agreed-upon standard of exchange with some inherent value.[122]

When it seemed likely that the Bland-Allison Act for the "remonetization" of silver would pass Congress, Hayes wrote that he would definitely veto the legislation, though "I am not so opposed to silver coinage that I would veto a bill which guarded the rights of creditors." But he could not approve "a measure which stains our credit. We must keep that untainted." Since the United States was "a debtor nation," it was vital to keep interest rates low, which he gathered was best served by gold coinage—though the connection remained obscure. Hayes added that "expediency and justice both demand honest coinage," though he had to admit that there was no necessary reason why silver coins could not be honest. A few days later he tried again to explain it to himself by writing that the silver bill "will contract the coin of the currency by expelling gold, which will not remain in the presence of the depreciated silver." It is still not clear if he knew what he meant by that sentence.[123]

When the Bland-Allison Act passed the Senate, Hayes again insisted to himself that he would not sign it, though he suspected Congress would override his veto. "I ought to give a brief summary of the objections to it," he wrote in his diary, but immediately admitted that doing so would require further reflection. On at least one point he was certain, that "the first and great objection" to silver coinage was that it would be "a violation of the national faith," apparently because the United States had already committed to the gold standard. After receiving the bill, which passed both houses by large margins, Hayes met with his cabinet. Navy secretary Richard Thompson favored the bill on practical and political grounds, insisting that "the people [are] almost unanimously for it," expecting that silver coinage will lift them out of the depression. But Hayes insisted his was a principled opposition based on his perception that "the obligation of contracts was impaired by the law." He rested this argument on the notion that contracts signed prior to the Bland-Allison Act expected payment in currency backed by gold, not backed by gold and silver—a proposition Thompson dismissed as ridiculous. Secretary of War George McCrary worried that a veto would hand the Democrats a winning issue and lead them back to power. Secretary of the Treasury John Sherman favored a veto, but quoted the powerful Democratic financier August Belmont, whom Hayes called "the agent of the Rothschilds," as fearing the long-term effects of a veto and recommended that Hayes sign the act. Secretary of the Interior Carl Schurz "thinks a veto, if successful, will save the country from an immoral and dangerous measure," but doubted that the effects of the bill would be that devastating. With even those opposing the act hedging their bets so effectively, Hayes was thrown back on his own original reasoning and vetoed the bill as "dishonest." Both houses of Congress overrode his veto, with numerous Republicans joining the majority of Democrats.[124]

This cabinet meeting drove home to Hayes that opposition to his presidency had grown within his own party. In addition to divisions over the silver issue, leading Republicans objected to his Southern policy and his plans to make the civil service nonpartisan. Republicans and Democrats united on an ideology that government should serve the interests of the economic elite; they just had different notions of how to do so. The Democrats presented themselves as "the people's party," though in the South—their persistent power base—they more honestly called themselves "The White Man's Party." While their rhetoric maintained that they fought for the common man, their adherence to free trade served the interests of many components of the elite, including the largest cotton growers in the South.[125] Governments, state and federal alike, routinely aided business while proclaiming their adherence to laissez-faire standards. For members of both parties, laissez-faire meant no government intervention that would hinder business, though legislatures often responded to the demand of their constituents for some level of regulation, especially of the railroads. Such forays into economic regulation hit a barrier in the Supreme Court, the majority of which offered significant support to the free-market ideology. In an 1877 decision, *Munn v. Illinois*, the court upheld the importance and validity of state police powers, seemingly justifying a wide range of actions by the state governments; in practice the Supreme Court repeatedly overturned regulatory legislation. Justice Samuel Miller found "my faith in human nature" shaken by "the united, vigorous, and selfish effort of the capitalists" to manipulate every aspect of government to their benefit.

The bias of most judges in favor of corporations over communities was not difficult to understand, Miller wrote, since most judges came to the bench after decades of working as advocates "of railroad companies, and all the forms of associated capital." One could not expect them to be impartial when "all their training, all their feelings are from the start in favor of those who need no such influence." For Miller the world had divided between prewar idealism and postwar cynicism.[126] Rutherford Hayes essentially agreed, noticing that where just a few years earlier slavery and racial relations had divided the country, "Now the great problem is to rid our country of the conflict between wealth and poverty without destroying either society or civilization, or liberty & free government."[127]

The development of industrial America was not predetermined. There were many possible paths that the United States could have followed after the crisis of the Civil War; the events of 1877 determined that route.[128] Government repression in 1877 set the standard for the next sixty years. When similar crises occurred in the 1880s and 1890s, corporations called on federal troops to violently suppress strikes. When not using the U.S. Army to maintain complete control of the workplace, American corporations could call on the militia, police, the Pinkerton Agency, or simply hire thugs as needed, free from any government regulation or inquiry. For example, when workers on the Kansas Central Railroad went on strike in the fall of 1877, management persuaded Sheriff Williams of Jackson County to arm a posse of forty railroad employees with Winchester rifles to protect a train running the strikers' blockade. The posse was not even led by Sheriff Williams or any other officer of the law, but by a former U.S. marshal named W.S. Tough employed by the railroad to deal with workers. Outside of Circleville, Kansas, about sixty-five strikers blocked the tracks. The "rioters," led by "hard case" Bill Hartman, confronted the posse, which immediately attacked the workers. The reporter for the *New York Times*, F.W. Willard, redefined journalistic standards by joining the battle on the side of the railroad and claimed to have shot and killed Hartman.[129] That a reporter would publicly boast of killing a labor leader testifies to the devastating dehumanization of the poor in America. Workers everywhere were painted with the broad brush of communism and subversion, as law enforcement continued to find Molly Maguires wherever attempted strikes occurred over the next several years.[130]

Responses to the events of 1877 varied widely and included a number of cooperative movements. The Grange enjoyed a few years of success in the Great Plains in the late 1870s, but its effort to bring farmers together to protect themselves from the power of the railroads and large corporations intent on dominating the distribution of American food production fell apart in the 1880s. The Southern Farmers Alliance in Texas, founded in 1877, hung in for more than a decade, evolving in the early 1890s into the Populist Party. Perhaps because of the role they played in hanging the Molly Maguires, many leading Catholics became sympathetic to the unions, most particularly Baltimore's Bishop James Gibbons.[131] But his was an unusual case, as workers found few allies outside of their own ranks in the years ahead.

Out in California, Henry George perceived that the problem of American society was the unequal distribution of wealth, which he blamed on the rich monopolizing land ownership and speculators keeping huge areas off the market in
hope of future profits. His "single tax" plan called for a heavy tax on such unpro-
ductive land, which would raise revenue for the government while forcing more
land onto the market. George expected that as speculators realized that paying
taxes negated any future profit, workers would step in to buy these cheap lands
and become farmers—a rather unrealistic adherence to the traditional American
agrarian ideal. This redistribution of the nation's wealth would end class conflict
in America and bring social peace, George believed. Perhaps more important
than the details of his plan, George's *Progress and Poverty*, which he published in
1879, was one of the first popular books to suggest that American exceptionalism was at an end, that the United States could not avoid the class conflict that
accompanied industrialism. A failure to address economic inequality would lead
to accelerating class conflict in ways that Karl Marx predicted, though with a different result: the collapse of civilization. What made George's book so important
was not so much its recommendation for the future as its description of the present. Completely rejecting the triumphal celebration of wealth inherent in classi-
cal economics and social Darwinism, George insisted that one's social position
was dependent on circumstance rather than on character or superior evolutionary coding. George's work helped radicalize old reformers like Rutherford Hayes
and young ones like Cleveland's Tom Johnson, who would create the progressive
movement.[132]

America's workers took some important lessons from 1877. Primarily, it was
now evident to them that they could not rely on the government to represent
their interests unless they took an active role in politics. Jacksonian America was
definitely dead and gone, though it is doubtful that Andrew Jackson and his followers had ever been as sympathetic to workers as the Democratic Party maintained. Similarly, the courts had proven themselves to be the bitter enemy of labor,
as Justice Miller observed; even elected judges had a clear bias against workers
and an unqualified adherence to a free market ideology that allowed corporations
but not workers to organize on their own behalf. It was also evident that public
opinion mattered. Workers had started the Great Strike with the majority of
Americans on their side, but they had lost that support as disorder spread. The
ultimate lesson to be derived from the strike was difficult to dispute—that the use
of violence by workers brought the repressive power of the state down upon them.

All these lessons came together on January 1, 1878, when delegates from
around the country met in the labor-friendly city of Reading, Pennsylvania, to
organize the Knights of Labor. The union's constitution promised to fight the
"alarming development and aggressiveness of the power of money and corporation." Toward that end, members dedicated themselves to political action, the

pursuit of public opinion, the need to act within the law given the hostility of the courts, and nonviolence. Their Statement of Principles condemned antitramp legislation and called for the "abrogation of all laws that do not bear equally upon capitalists and laborers."[133] And even though announcements of their meetings appeared in the press, the Knights of Labor constituted itself as a secret organization in order to protect its membership from being blackballed by management.[134] They put their faith in democracy, confident that appeals to peaceful reform would win popular acceptance for the idea of a labor union—but they watched their backs.

Opponents came down hard on the Knights of Labor, condemning them as Molly Maguires and communists.[135] Despite their adherence to nonviolence, the Knights were routinely accused of "Warlike Preparations"; despite their clearly stated purpose to use the ballot box to win changes, they were charged with plotting to overthrow the government. Their secrecy was condemned, even though there was no hiding that they would all be fired if discovered. The very fact that they organized was seen as an attack on American values, though the nation's largest corporations often worked together to attain their ends.[136] Even the Knights' defense of tramps was seen as suspicious or foolish, the *New York Times* offering its opinion from on high that in recognizing the tramp as "the victim of our present economical system," the Knights failed to see him "as other people do, [as] the victim merely of a violent dislike to labor and a violent thirst for rum."[137]

Despite such superficial criticisms of the Knights of Labor, a broad consensus agreed that the "labor question" was the key problem facing the American people in the aftermath of 1877. In an oft-repeated metaphor, the country sat atop a volcano of class warfare, which was "more serious and dangerous" to the United States than the Civil War. The "conflict between labor and capital" was the "great problem" of the age—on this point most commentators and political leaders agreed.[138] There was no doubt that the events of 1877 were just "the beginning of a series of social problems—largely labor problems—which our country may next be called upon to solve." But what was to be done? How could the country avoid class conflict leading to the overturn of their institutions? They had to do something, because American workers were becoming ever more radical, and it was evident that "Communism is going to cause us much trouble in this country for the next decade, and possibly longer."[139] There were a few political leaders, such as William E. Smith, the Republican candidate for governor of Wisconsin in 1877, who insisted that it was of "transcending importance" that they take the complaints of labor seriously and act to "ameliorate the condition of the working class." More commonly, the press and public officials sided with business in holding that the obvious answer was the expansion of the military.[140]

The debate over the size and purposes of the U.S. Army remained complicated by the traditional distrust of a standing army. But the states had their enforcers as well, and the militia tended to be used for a single reason in this period other than parades: suppressing unions. From 1877 to 1903, state militias were called out more than three hundred times to put down strikes. States considered legislation to prevent strikes from even getting started, such as the rather vague New York law forbidding "the use of language intended to incite riot or violence to person or property," while Congress debated mandating the use of federal troops against any striking workers who disrupted rail transportation. The federal government moved in to supply arms and training to what was now being called the National Guard. The most visible result of the government's response to the Great Strike of 1877 was the armory movement, which led to the building of massive stone and brick structures in the heart of most American cities—modern fortresses devoted to avoiding a repetition of the Battle for Pittsburgh during the Great Strike.[141]

It is not difficult to understand why state governments made these new armories a high priority. Regardless of political position, nearly everyone was predicting further problems and perhaps even civil war. Jay Gould thought the strike of 1877 but the start of "a great social revolution" that would surely lead to "the destruction of the republican form of government in this country."[142] Labor papers such as the *Pittsburgh Leader* also predicted that 1877 marked the beginning of "a great civil war in this country between capital and labor." Inspired by the Great Strike and fearing further uprisings, states built new armories in nearly every city in America, from Boston to San Francisco; Portsmouth, Virginia, to Detroit.[143]

The importance every level of government gave to these new armories is best revealed in the ceremonial opening of the largest of them all, that of New York's Seventh Regiment in 1879. A Victorian gothic pile covering the entire block between Fourth and Lexington Avenues and 66th and 67th Streets, the armory was intended to give the impression of a fortress with its enormous towers, imposing portcullis, narrow windows behind iron bars, and six-inch-thick oak door. New York's mayor Edward Cooper was accompanied to the grand opening of the armory's huge gates by President Hayes and Secretary of State Evarts. George W. Curtis, editor of *Harper's Weekly*, spoke to the assembled militia: "In the last dire extremity behind the policeman's club glistens your bayonet." The events of 1877 informed most of his speech, as Curtis praised the militia for responding heroically to "the unpardonable sin" of riots. In a democracy, where "every wrong can be lawfully redressed," there was no excuse for public disturbances. If any group questioned that truth, then the militia, "these reservoirs of the will of the State," would pour forth from this "temple of peace" with overwhelming power. They acted for the whole nation, for "when you aim, the people aim, and your deadly volley is the stern and startling declaration that the will of the people, lawfully expressed, shall prevail." Curtis's call for the use of force against rioters was voiced throughout the country. In Wisconsin, Colonel Charles King advised his troops, "Do not shoot until you have to, but when you shoot, shoot to kill."[144]

In the 1850s and 1860s the Republican Party worked for free labor, free men, and national expansion. By 1877 it worked for business, using the federal and state governments to provide capital and aid them in keeping labor costs low. Among Republicans, the desire for social order replaced social justice; a new ideology seized the nation, one of each against all. It was thus easy for the likes of *The Nation*'s E.L. Godkin to consider himself a liberal and yet turn on labor and Southern blacks.[145] No one represents this shift in attitude among Civil War–era reformers to conservatism in response to the events of 1877 better than the man who had been Abraham Lincoln's personal secretary and close friend John Hay. A well-known liberal independent, often considered a radical in the first half of the 1870s, Hay was horrified by what he saw as spreading disorder in 1877, for which he blamed the poor. By the end of the year Hay had emerged as a bitterly "rigid" antidemocrat, having no sympathy for workers and questioning the wisdom of allowing just anyone to vote. Hay went further, scorning the open society Lincoln had championed, rejecting the notion that the country benefited from social mobility.[146] To express his contempt for labor, Hay wrote a novel based on the Great Strike called *The Bread-winners: A Social Study*. Hay saw class warfare tearing the country apart, with America's only hope being the organization of the upper class to smash the unions before the United States slipped into socialism. The Great Strike inspired many other novels, but Hay's struck a powerful chord among the middle class and elite, and has been credited as "one of the earliest fictional defenses of unfettered capitalism."[147]

While most of the Republican Party moved right in response to the events of 1877, President Hayes eventually headed left. He had not meant to be a tool of the oligarchs, but by 1879 he understood that he had been used by America's corporations. After he left the presidency, Hayes reflected on the events of 1877 and discovered a stark alternative between the railroads governing the country or the people governing the railroads. Extreme wealth undermined democracy and threatened to lead the country into class warfare as the concentration of capital and democracy were inimical; one had to give way to the other. Still struggling with economics, Hayes became nearly obsessed with the unfair distribution of America's wealth. "The question for the country now is how to secure a more equal distribution of property," Hayes wrote. Once out of office, the former president became a social radical, favoring taxation to prevent incomes above $15,000 a year and estates worth more than $500,000.[148] He called for government regulation of the railroads, a minimum wage and old-age pensions, universal education, and a progressive income tax, and even doubted the morality of the death penalty.[149] Hayes admitted to his wife that sometimes he sounded a little "communistic," but justice demanded that he speak out.[150]

Hayes went beyond these anticipations of progressivism, if not the New Deal, by blaming corporate greed for the violence suffusing America. Management drove workers to strike and then responded brutally, using thugs, the police, the U.S. Army, whatever forces they could employ to tame the workers. As he told the Prison Congress of 1888, "the crimes of the wealthy," their greed and ostentatious lifestyle, deprived workers of a decent wage while presenting a bad example to everyone. After meeting Cornelius Vanderbilt, who had inherited $100 million from his father in 1877, Hayes was appalled that "such vast and irresponsible power" would be lodged in the hands of one man.[151] Everywhere he looked he saw the increased influence of money: "Excessive wealth in the hands of the few means extreme poverty, ignorance, vice, and wretchedness as the lot of the many." He was outraged by Standard Oil, which he labeled "a menace to the people" that "attempted to seize political power and usurp the functions of the State."[152] He was equally upset with his fellow Republicans such as Hay who spoke down to the working class: "No man is fit to make or administer laws in this country who holds in contempt labor or the laborer." Yet Hayes had to admit that he had played a key role in handing power over to the rich and that the United States now had "a government of corporations, by corporations, and for corporations."[153] Of course, since he was no longer president, he could do little to limit corporate control of the federal government. Unlike Frances Willard and Booker T. Washington, his epiphany had come too late to help his country deal with the crises of the Gilded Age.

In 1877 the battle lines in the United States shifted. From the writing of the Constitution to 1877, race had been the primary problem facing the country. In 1877 white America largely declared itself done with that issue. For the next sixty-five years the conflict between capital and labor sat at the center of American life.[154] The structure of American strikes was established in 1877 and persisted through World War II. Workers tended to resort to violence reactively, when attacked, and were often almost touching in their innocence, as they expected management to respect and understand their arguments. They struck on the basis of old ideals and methods, the notion of just wages obtained through peaceful protest, while management responded in a new way, with lethal violence. In 1877 the enemy of American expansion ceased to be the Indians and became the workers, who had to wait for another, greater depression, to attain their goals.

An Immigrant

In 1870, a twenty-one-year-old Danish immigrant named Jacob Riis arrived in America, drawn by promises of prosperity and dreams of adventure fueled by the novels of James Fenimore Cooper. "It was a beautiful spring morning," he wrote thirty years later, "and as I looked over the rail at the miles of straight streets, the green heights of Brooklyn, and the stir of ferryboats and pleasure craft on the river, my hopes rose high that somewhere in this teeming hive there would be a place for me." The United States had an open immigration policy, so it was just a few hours before Riis was walking the streets of Brooklyn, confident that he would do well as he had strong hands and "a strong belief that in a free country, free from the dominion of custom, of caste, as well as of men, things would somehow come right in the end." But this was America, so the first thing Riis did was "buy a navy revolver of the largest size, investing in the purchase exactly one-half of my capital." With visions of Cooper's heroic Chingachgook of the Six Nations and expectations of "buffaloes and red Indians charging up and down Broadway," Riis set off for Manhattan to find a job. However, one of the first people he encountered was a friendly police officer who tapped the butt of Riis's revolver and advised him to keep the weapon at home as it was little more than an invitation for robbery. A bit confused, as he thought the gun was supposed to prevent crime, "I took his advice and put the revolver away, secretly relieved to get rid of it," as it had proven "quite heavy to carry around."[155]

With the gun ritual out of the way, and the discovery that there were neither buffalo nor jobs ready at hand in New York, Riis decided to head west. He got as far as Pittsburgh, where the factories appeared to have an insatiable demand for labor, the United States being in the midst of a major economic expansion and the steel mills pouring out thousands of miles of rails expanding the nation's transportation system to an extent previously unknown. Riis got a job at Brady's Bend, building housing for the growing workforce. But in 1873 the mill where Riis worked went bankrupt, its buildings abandoned, scavenged, and decayed, so that when Riis returned to the area several years later, all he found were some chimneys and a few shacks.[156]

Unable to find another job and his money quickly exhausted, Riis had no choice but to pawn his revolver and boots, and, "homeless and penniless, I joined the great army of tramps." In his later, prosperous life, Riis would condemn tramps as mostly lazy and unwilling to work, yet his own experiences as a tramp indicate the complete opposite, as he traveled around the country, begging for food and shelter, taking whatever odd jobs he could find, suffering the contempt of those lucky enough to have employment.[157] He could not find anything like a steady job, as "I was now too shabby to get work, even if there had been any to get." Riis slept in fields and barns, in doorways and flophouses in New York's slums, and often not at all as he spent "nights of hopeless misery with the policeman's periodic 'Get up there! Move on!'" Riis learned from the more experienced travelers along "the great tramps' highway" which towns to avoid and which might be good for a day's work and a meal.[158]

The trough of this tramping existence came on a cold rainy night in New York, when, soaked through to the skin, Riis appealed at the Church Street police station to be put up for the night. The sergeant on duty agreed to let him in, but Riis's dog had to stay outside. Reluctantly, Riis left his dog outside in the torrential rain, his companion curling itself up shivering on the police station stoop to wait for morning. During the night another tramp stole the gold locket containing a lock of hair from Riis's beloved Elizabeth Gortz, whom he left behind in Denmark. When Riis complained to the officer at the desk of the theft, the policeman refused to believe that a tramp could own a gold locket, "seized me and threw me out of the door, coming after to kick me down the stoop." Riis's little dog leapt at the officer, grabbing hold of his leg with a fierce bite that made the policeman scream in pain. The officer "seized the poor little beast by the legs, and beat its brains out against the stone steps." In a blind rage, Riis attacked the sergeant and had to be dragged off by two other police officers. Riis believed that the other officers must have felt guilty for the conduct of their chief, for rather than beating him senseless, they put him on the ferry to Jersey City. Depressed and alone, Riis resolved "that I would never return, and, setting my face toward the west, marched straight out the first railroad track I came to."[159]

Though Riis resented being identified as a tramp, he had to admit to the status as he wandered homeless and unemployed. As the depression eased in 1879, the "tramp menace" lessened, though it did not end. Those who thought that the tramps were not unemployed workers seeking jobs may have been puzzled by their rapidly diminishing numbers, but oddly never addressed the issue. In New York, the Night Refuge Association, founded to deal with the overflow of tramps from the police stations, closed their operation in 1878. However, historians who argue that the tramp largely vanished from newspapers by 1880 are incorrect, as the tramp remained a potent symbol of the danger posed to bourgeois society by the poor.[160] The middle class continued to vent its fury at the tramps, whom it blamed for every conceivable problem facing the nation. The tramp continued to be dehumanized in the popular press as a snake and a cancer. The *New York Tribune* described the tramp as a "creature, midway between the vegetable and animal world," not unlike "reptiles in general," while popular novels like Horatio Alger's *Tony the Tramp* portrayed tramps as thieves and cutthroats. "Scum" and "able-bodied loafers, who think the world owes them a living," tramps preferred "to make the summer one long picnic, strolling through the country begging and stealing."[161] Since "nearly all cases of violence may at once be set down as the work of 'a tramp,'" society had no choice but to "crush out this social evil at any cost." Feeding a tramp was, according to many, like "furnishing support to an enemy in war, it is aiding and abetting rebellion against the great laws of social prosperity." With the depression over, the continued presence of the homeless, though fewer in number, proved to most that they were not on the road because of destitution but because of "the dominion of appetite" and atheism over them.[162]

The events of 1877 had made the tramp appear ever more ominous, a dangerous subversive linked to strikers and communists intent on destroying American
society. Allan Pinkerton especially promoted this conspiracy theory with his
book *Strikers, Communists, Tramps and Detectives.* The *New York Tribune* charged
that tramps were inspired by "communistic literature which flatters the indolent
with the assurance that the world owes them a living"—a phraseology that would
not die.[163] Two books appearing in 1878 reinforced Pinkerton's portrait of a
communist/tramp conspiracy: Lee O. Harris's *The Man Who Tramps* and Frank
Bellew's *The Tramp.* Harris promoted the image of the tramp as a recent radical
immigrant who refused to work and understood socialism as a license to steal,
putting forth a taxonomy of tramps: the indolent, criminal, and political—all of
whom were hazardous to society. The political tramps tended to be refugees
from the Paris Commune, "vicious agitators, who had tasted of the intoxication
of anarchy and bloodshed." Neither poor nor hungry, tramps were well fed and
well organized, intent on becoming "rulers in this land." Bellew agreed that the
tramps were "under a most perfect system of organization, and ready at any moment, when the opportunity arises, to hurl their power at the throat of organized
society." Their secret society, with its passwords, oaths, and secret handshakes,
answered to a "grand central lodge somewhere out West." At any moment they
could bring half a million tramps to bear on a single point in support of strikers—
though, oddly, they had not done so during the Great Strike.[164]

Faced with both the tramp hysteria and the Great Strike, police work shifted
to battling crime and controlling the poor more directly through enhanced vagrancy laws. "This new emphasis on crime control itself was doomed to failure,
for it was the one thing at which the police had never been especially successful."[165] Police stations around the country stopped providing shelter for the
transient, unless they were charged with vagrancy, which became more common. The number of tramps arrested increased while the number of lodgers in
police stations declined after 1877. Acts such as New York's Raines Law terminating free lunches in bars, a main form of sustenance for the homeless, increased hardship for those without jobs. The "scientific charity" movement, as it
was known, aimed to cut off aid for the homeless for their own good. In 1879
Brooklyn and Philadelphia ended all "outdoor relief," with opponents of charity
immediately claiming victory when the number of homeless began declining—
choosing to ignore the increasing availability of jobs as the depression ended.[166]

Most states followed the example of New Jersey in passing antitramp laws.
New Jersey's law defined tramps as those who "live idly and without employment, and refuse to work for the usual and common wages, . . . or shall be found
going about from door to door, or placing themselves in the streets, highways or
roads, to beg or gather alms, and can give no reasonable account of themselves
or their business in such places." However, efforts to enforce antitramp laws gen-

erally collapsed. In New Jersey the Camden jail became so crowded with vagrants that the sheriff told the judge there was no room left and he had to release most of the tramps. Though these laws typically called for the establishment of workhouses, few towns could afford them. Even Boston's overseers of the poor put the law aside as they had "no means to set so large a number at work." State officials added that it was nearly impossible to determine "the character of the applicant, whether he is a vagabond or an honest laborer." It was far simpler to just give them some soup and a place to spend the night. There were flashes of sympathy among the general condemnation of tramps; in 1883 a New York supreme court justice rebuked Westchester County for arresting tramps, as "poverty is their only crime" and they travel "in search of employment." But the general fear and loathing of tramps continued through the rest of the century.[167]

Fortunately for Jacob Riis, he ceased being a tramp before the traumatic events of 1877. Through a series of different jobs and aided by complete strangers, Riis stumbled into a position working for a newspaper in New York City. In explaining why he became a reporter, Riis would often insist that he did so because most journalists, "themselves comfortably lodged, have not red blood enough in their veins to feel for those to whom everything is denied." Riis had experienced poverty and privation firsthand. "Some one had to tell the facts," so he aimed to become a reporter, and intended to keep at it "until the last of that ilk has ceased to discourage men from trying to help their fellows."[168]

In the summer of 1877, Riis was in Elmira, New York, when the Great Strike broke out. Within two days city officials had deputized dozens of civilians to act as police and "soldiers with fixed bayonets guarded every train" as well as the rail yards. The "Citizens Committee" battling the strike took Riis to be an ally of the workers and, probably fearing that he would write of the city's "semi-martial law," ordered him out of town and put him on the first train that made it through the siege. This train got as far as Scranton, where Riis walked up the main street and joined a large crowd of striking coal miners. He moved his way to the front of the throng and saw "a line of men with guns, some in their shirt-sleeves, some in office coats" blocking the strikers from marching on to the coal company's offices: "The crowd hung sullenly back, leaving a narrow space" between themselves and the armed volunteers. In between the two groups Scranton's mayor "was haranguing the people, counseling them to go back to their homes quietly." Without warning, someone in the crowd threw a brick that hit the mayor in the head. "I heard a brief command . . . and a volley was fired into the crowd point blank," one shot hitting the man standing next to Riis. "There was an instant's dead silence, and then the rushing of a thousand feet and wild cries of terror as the mob broke and fled." Riis joined that flight: "In all my life I never ran so fast."[169]

When Riis fled the gunfire in Scranton, he kept on heading east by foot, pondering the whole way what lessons this encounter had to offer. Above all else, he had witnessed the futility of violence, which just made any situation worse, but he also saw clearly the need for reform. That fall he found his "life-work" when the *New York Tribune* hired him as a police reporter. He often sat "praying that he may write a good murder story," but he would do much more than that.[170] Over the next two years he launched his own crusade, one aimed at exposing the corruption and tragedy of the treatment of the poor. Riis, like most Gilded Age reformers, believed that the primary barrier to change was "that people did not know and had no means of finding out for themselves" just how bad conditions were among the poor. Convinced that if they knew the truth that the majority of Americans would act, Riis set out to tell them what they needed to know. "Accordingly I went poking about among the foul alleys and fouler tenements" of New York, "sounding the misery and the depravity of it to their depth." What he found disgusted and repelled him—and his readers. People lived in the filthiest imaginable conditions, crammed into unsafe and overcrowded structures lacking running water, light, and toilet facilities. The Lower East Side had the highest population density in the world, with more than three hundred thousand people in a square mile. Contagious diseases, crime, and violence thrived while people died young; life expectancy in the United States declined during the Gilded Age by a decade, largely as a result of unsafe and unhealthy workplace and living conditions. It was often a dangerous job gathering this information, as when one of the leaders of the Why-o gang stuck a knife into Riis's ribs. But in 1879 came the first stirrings of the Social Gospel movement, and Riis finally had effective allies.[171]

The poor perceived that Jesus Christ might be on their side well before most ministers did. They saw hypocrisy and cant in the condescending sermons of prominent ministers the likes of Henry Ward Beecher, only too quick to tell them how to live their lives while violating so many of the precepts he insisted others follow. Even without Henry Ward Beecher, American Protestantism made few connections with the majority of poor people in the 1870s. Protestants had little room for social responsibility beyond temperance, and largely abandoned the field to Catholics and secularists. In fact, the Catholic practice of working with the urban poor lowered that religion in the eyes of many Protestant ministers, who gave standard sermons on the undeserving poor and accepted the notion that poverty was a sign of weak moral character. Newspapers' practice of publishing extracts from these self-satisfied Protestant sermons in Monday's editions convinced most American workers that the mainstream denominations were not on their side and confirmed for Catholics their opinion that Protestant ministers worked for the industrialists.[172]

The occasional sex scandal involving ministers aided this downward trajectory in ministerial reputation. In April 1878, Elizabeth Tilton issued a public statement acknowledging her adultery with her minister, Henry Ward Beecher.

The California labor leader Denis Kearney came east to speak to an anti-Beecher rally in Brooklyn, reading out to them from the book of James, chapter 5, which begins by telling the wealthy that "your riches are corrupted," and advises them to "weep and howl for your miseries that shall come upon you." Referencing the fears of the middle class, Kearney drew the lesson: "In those days all the saints were tramps." He then made a biting reference to Beecher's adultery: "If Henry Bread-and-Water Beecher had been compelled to live upon bread and water there would be no scandal to relate." Kearney concluded that the Bible made clear "that God almighty is with the workingmen of the United States."[173] Much to his surprise, the labor leader would soon be joined by a great number of ministers and theologians in this opinion that Christ was on the side of the poor, as the events of 1877 exerted a powerful transformation on American religion.

The first stirrings of the Social Gospel movement that finally brought Protestantism into line with the social realities of workers emerged in the immediate aftermath of the Great Strike. As Henry May wrote, the labor conflicts of 1877 "provided the drastic sudden shocks that were necessary to shatter Protestant complacency."[174] There are a few hints of conscience among some of the Protestant journals, such as the *Watchman*, which gently recommended a "feeling of responsibility and a purified moral sensibility on the part of those who manage capital and employ labor," but they still insisted that strikes could not be allowed. One sympathetic Christian response came from Charles Loring Brace, the Congregationalist minister who played a prominent role in developing the Social Gospel theology. Giving his impressions of the 1877 strikes shortly after their suppression, he wrote, "I believe myself that, in general, the laboring classes do not receive their fair share. Strikes are one of their means of getting more." Then there was the Presbyterian minister DeWitt Talmage, "the fiery, untamed pulpit orator" of the Brooklyn Tabernacle, who outraged most Southern Presbyterians with his "scandalous" sense of humor and social activism (it was difficult to determine which was worse). Such critics thought Talmage was "desecrating the pulpit and disgracing the religion by which he makes his money."[175] Talmage, who labeled New York City "the modern Gomorrah," often joined his friend Henry Ward Beecher in visiting the "shrines of wickedness" with a police escort, gathering material for their sermons. The two ministers spoke with one voice on most matters, including the error of silver coinage. However, on one issue they disagreed; Talmage, finding the excesses of the rich unworthy of praise, questioned Beecher's motivation in taking their side in all social issues: "I declare, in the name of Almighty God, that no man has a right to be worth $100,000,000."[176]

But Talmage and Brace were among the few professional voices of the time that acknowledged the right to strike, since the majority of ministers, like nearly all economists, held firm to the conviction that workers had no grounds for complaint as the United States was a land of equal opportunity. Ministers warned against being persuaded by those passages of the Bible that might, to the casual reader, appear to promote charity and social justice. The *Christian Union* warned that, rather than literally applying Jesus's call for charity in New York, "it would be a great deal better to burn down the city." In trade unions, the *Christian Advocate* maintained, one could find the "worst doctrines of Communism." The best course of action would be to "Legislate Trades' Unions out of existence." Beecher, who often repeated his ungracious homily that a working family could live on a dollar a day, did not receive a Christian response until three years later, when the *Christian Advocate* offered compelling proof that there was no way any family could hope to survive on so little money.[177]

The first indication of an organized Protestant concern for the poor came in 1878, when the Salvation Army started in the United States. Over the next several years, a group of Protestant ministers in New York City, led ironically by a Jewish doctor, Felix Adler, organized the Tenement-House Commission and attempted to force health standards onto the places where the city's poorest lived. Jacob Riis worked with Adler and his ministerial colleagues, reporting on the enormous resistance they encountered from the owners of the tenements, who kept arguing property rights in response to every critique. Property, Riis wrote, appeared to trump not just the lives of the poor but their souls as well. Since "you couldn't very well count souls as chattels yielding so much income to the owner," the very existence of the poor paled before property rights. With time, Riis's coverage of the appalling conditions of New York's slums would have national impact, as the inhabitants of other cities realized they also had slums that cut short the lives of thousands of people and that no one was safe from the diseases incubated in those open cesspits. In addition, Riis's use of photography completely transformed American journalism, providing visual evidence that imparted immediacy to each story. At one of the meetings of Adler's Tenement-House Commission, Riis came up with the title for his book that would document in word and image the reality of slum life: *How the Other Half Lives*.[178]

In so many ways, Riis had attained the American dream. During the 1880s he became a prominent reporter—well known for his accounts of violence and poverty—and earned a respectable income. He returned to Denmark to marry his childhood sweetheart Elizabeth Gortz, and together they established a middle-class home in New York. Riis also became friends with the chief of the Six Nations, General Ely Parker, the man who wrote the terms of surrender at Appomattox and had been President Grant's commissioner of Indian affairs. But Riis had seen reporting as a means to an end, a very personal objective: to close down the flophouses inside police stations. In Boston he had seen how the homeless could be treated humanely, given "a clean shirt and a decent bed and a bath, . . . and something to eat in the morning, so they did not have to go out and beg." He thought New York City should do the same and did not think it was too much to ask that the city "establish a decent lodging-house." But Tammany Hall, which still dominated the city, found too many opportunities for corruption by keeping the police in the business of putting up the poor, and finding many other uses for the money the city appropriated for building a homeless shelter. Riis would not give up, spending years battling "the walls of ignorance and indifference." He remained confident that it was "just a question of endurance," that if he kept at it with faith in his cause and in democracy that eventually reforms would be made.[179] It took until 1895, when the energetic new president of the police board, Theodore Roosevelt, read Riis's work and insisted on meeting the man he would come to call "the best American I ever knew."[180] Riis took Roosevelt on a tour of the slums, including to the Church Street police station, where he told an outraged police commissioner of his own experiences in that very room. Roosevelt declared "my whole life was influenced by my long association with Jacob Riis," who set him on his path to reform the worst effects of an unregulated economy, starting with closing down the police lodging rooms. Finally, Riis wrote, "The murder of my dog was avenged."[181]

A College Student

The country was changing fast, and the young man selecting his college wanted to play a role in that transformation. Harvard was the logical choice for this child of privilege, who would definitely be among his own kind, having grown up surrounded by the most prestigious families in America, attending church with Livingstons and Wolcotts. Harvard in 1877 was, David McCullough wrote, "as homogeneous an assembly of young men—and as unrepresentative of turbulent, polygot, post–Civil War America—as one could imagine." As all-white, mostly Protestant males from the families of the eastern elite, the students "all *looked* alike." One must search hard for distinguishing characteristics when examining their photographs. Two-thirds of the class of 1880 came to Harvard from a distance of less than one hundred miles. Richard Middlecott Saltonstall, who would become the applicant's best friend in college, was the sixth generation of his family to attend Harvard, stretching back to Nathaniel Saltonstall, who graduated in 1695.[182]

But the applicant to this stodgy bastion of wealth and entitlement had a sound academic reason for his choice: Harvard boasted the preeminent faculty in natural history in the United States. Though an opponent of Darwin's theory of natural selection, the college's Louis Agassiz had set a high educational standard that encouraged laboratory and field work, both of which appealed to the would-be scientist. Alexander Agassiz, himself a noted ichthyologist, directed the museum his father founded, the Harvard Museum of Comparative Zoology.

Among the elder Agassiz's most eminent students were the geologist Nathaniel Southgate Shaler and the polymath William James, both of whom taught at their alma mater. Harvard had made clear its priorities in 1869 when the overseers made the surprising decision to appoint a thirty-five-year-old scientist, Charles Eliot, president. Eliot transformed American education through the introduction of the elective system, his insistence that science was the equal to the humanities, and the radical notion that students should be treated as adults. It is little wonder that the aspiring scientist from a wealthy family would select Harvard. "I should like to be a scientist," Theodore Roosevelt confided to his diary, and Harvard was the best place to pursue that goal.[183]

Five feet eight inches tall and weighing just 125 pounds, eighteen-year-old Teddy Roosevelt arrived at Harvard in the fall of 1876 and wanted to do everything. His fellow students thought he either possessed incredible willpower or was demented; even friends questioned his stability, finding him far too passionate, while others "thought he was crazy."[184] In a time and place that prized the sophisticated, reserved, well-dressed gentleman who spoke with care and precision, Teddy defied all conventions. He was a rampaging whirligig of energy, who ran when others strolled, enjoyed both wrestling and dancing, demonstrated enormous enthusiasm where other students feigned bored disinterest, and spoke at such a frantic clip that the words spilled over one another in a waterfall of language. At a time when students were advised to not speak in class, the eminent geologist Nathaniel Shaler had to remind his most excited and excitable student: "'Now look here, Roosevelt,' he said, 'let me talk. I'm running this course.'"[185] Roosevelt boxed as well, though not very well. In fact he was not a very good athlete, but he showed startling resolve and perseverance, and was intensely competitive. He also taught Sunday school classes for more than three years at Christ Church, until the minister learned that he was not an Episcopalian but a Presbyterian. Unbothered by such distinctions, Roosevelt called the minister "rather narrow-minded" and switched his Sunday energies to a church in the city's poorest neighborhood. His love of nature and killing animals have been brilliantly explored in David McCullough's *Mornings on Horseback*, which makes sense of young Teddy's avaricious interest in nearly everything. He joined the Glee Club and the Rifle Club, where in 1877 he may have witnessed President Eliot, worried about the possibility of insurrection, personally drilling the riflemen.[186] He rowed, hiked, took part in almost every sport, and began work on what would be his first book, and through it all he excelled academically, graduating magna cum laude. And yet to some friends he seemed to be coasting, making it all appear so easy.[187] He may have looked like the other students, but he certainly did not behave like them.

Roosevelt clearly enjoyed life in Cambridge, including his classes. In 1877 he joined the Nuttall Ornithological Club and spent the last days of the year working on a paper describing the disruptive qualities of the English sparrow on the local environment. He took William James's anatomy class, but spent most of his time at the Museum of Comparative Zoology. Shaler's geology course, which included long hikes to experience the subject firsthand, proved particularly inspiring. Shaler, according to President Eliot, shared many characteristics with Roosevelt, being energetic and full of curiosity and good cheer. But something odd happened while Roosevelt was taking all those science courses: he also became interested in history and government. Charles Dunbar's class on political economy was among his favorites, and much to his surprise he also liked George H. Palmer's course on metaphysics. He may have initially attempted to avoid the subject, given his family influences, but politics drew him to its beguiling flame. His uncle Robert Roosevelt, a former Democratic congressman, gained widespread recognition when he turned on Boss Tweed in a dramatic speech at the Cooper Union, suggesting that the man caught tampering with a ballot box should be shot on sight. Uncle Robert was also an early conservationist who connected well with his nephew, the hunter who loved nature.[188] During the crisis of the depression in 1877, Robert Roosevelt called for government action such as massive public works projects to prevent an uprising by the starving poor. His ideas were dismissed out of hand by the *New York Tribune*: "Absolutely the only protection which we can have against the dangerous tendency of laborers to crowd into large cities is the sure punishment which nature brings, in want of work, suffering or starvation." Anyone who did not appreciate that hands-off approach to poverty should, according to the paper, just leave the United States.[189] The ideological division in American society could not have been clearer than Robert Roosevelt's pragmatic attempt to solve social problems versus the standard view that individuals must deal with any and all crises on their own.

But it was Theodore Roosevelt's father who most influenced the young man. A beloved, charismatic figure, the senior Theodore Roosevelt towered over his son's early life. A financier and philanthropist whose family owned vast tracts of New York City, the elder Roosevelt came down on the side of the ideological divide that favored action in the midst of the terrible depression. He contributed to the building of humane workhouses for tramps, visited and promoted reforms to hospitals, prisons, and the city's slums, served as the first chairman of the Bureau of Charities, and was deeply moved by the plight of the many poor children living on the city's streets. As he wrote his son, "All that gives me most pleasure . . . is connected with others, an evidence that we are not placed here to live exclusively for ourselves." The senior Roosevelt hobnobbed with the rich and powerful, serving on the committee chaired by Secretary of State William Evarts that raised money for the Statue of Liberty's pedestal.[190] As one of the leading figures in the construction of the new American Museum of Natural History in New York City, Roosevelt led President Hayes on the premier tour of the museum on May 15, 1877.[191]

And the Roosevelts were rich, emphatically rich. While at Harvard, Teddy's yearly allowance of $8,000 was 60 percent more than President Charles Eliot's salary of $5,000 a year. People looking for financing to help build the new America came to the senior Roosevelt for funding, though Teddy's father was far from infallible in that regard. Alexander Graham Bell, desperately trying to raise money for his new invention, visited Roosevelt. Bell hooked up a pair of telephones so that Roosevelt could talk from one room to another. The financier thought the telephone might have a future as a toy but was of no real utility, and Bell went away emptyhanded. Shortly thereafter, Bell made his first sale, found his first celebrity customer in Mark Twain (who had a phone line running between his home and the *Hartford Courant* office), and opened the first telephone exchange in New Haven in January 1878. Twain embraced the new technology, and may have been the first writer to make a telephone central to a short story with his "A Telephonic Conversation."[192] The Roosevelts, however, would not be part of that adventure.

The two Theodore Roosevelts seem to have been largely uninterested in politics until 1876, when the elder, outraged by the corruption of the Grant administration, joined other liberal Republicans in seeking to change the party's direction. When Harvard professor Henry Adams called together some of the nation's best and brightest to meet at the Fifth Avenue Hotel on May 15, 1876, the assembled luminaries included E.L. Godkin, Frederick Law Olmsted, William Cullen Bryant, William Graham Sumner, and Theodore Roosevelt Sr. While they did little more than talk, these gentlemen agreed that the Republican Party must nominate a reform candidate for president and that they would forward that objective. Roosevelt attended the Republican convention in Cincinnati, where he worked for the nomination of Secretary of the Treasury Benjamin Bristow but accepted Rutherford Hayes as a good alternative. However, in the process he made a bitter enemy of New York's powerful senator Roscoe Conkling.[193]

For the Roosevelt family, much of 1877 centered on the senior Theodore's nomination by President Hayes to replace Chester A. Arthur, seen as the tool of the corrupt Senator Conkling, as collector of the New York Customhouse. The most lucrative government post available, the collector oversaw a gigantic operation that took in nearly two-thirds of the total tariff revenue of the United States and employed more than a thousand people. While some employees, such as the writer Herman Melville, went about their jobs diligently, many others held their positions in consequence of political favors or in return for kickbacks. The corruption reached epic proportions and evoked congressional investigations that went nowhere, as Senator Conkling consistently derailed any attempt to interfere with his favorite plaything. Roosevelt's nomination provoked a pivotal battle within the Republican Party between the president and the Senate, reformers and party hacks, Hayes and Conkling—and the latter won.[194]

Widely respected as a man of sterling honesty and character, Roosevelt offered to serve without pay. The press, Democratic and Republican, praised Roosevelt as an outstanding choice for the office and precisely the man to end the corruption of the New York Customhouse. But Conkling set out to destroy Roosevelt and his reform-minded allies, pummeling them with a stream of effeminate labels and references to their mincing ways, women's magazines, and skirts. After hearing one such performance at the state Republican convention in September 1877, George William Curtis, editor of *Harper's Weekly*, questioned the senator's sanity. He wrote Charles Eliot Norton that, seemingly possessed by "a fury of hate" for Roosevelt, Conkling's features were contorted by his violent nature. But Conkling had his way—and the put-down that would last a generation: "When Dr. Johnson defined patriotism as the last refuge of a scoundrel, he was unconscious of the then undeveloped capabilities and uses of the word, 'Reform!'" In a secret session, the Senate listened as Conkling strode the aisle punctuating every sentence assaulting Roosevelt's integrity "with violent gestures." Bowing to Conkling, and delivering Hayes a stunning blow, the Senate rejected Roosevelt, 31 to 25.[195]

Roosevelt wrote his son Teddy that "a great relief was taken off my shoulders" by the Senate's vote. "To purify our Customhouse was a terrible undertaking which I felt it was my duty" to accept, but which he did not relish. His defeat clearly demonstrated "the power of the partisan politicians who think of nothing but their own interests." While happy to be free of the whole dirty affair, "I fear for your future," he told his son. "We cannot stand so corrupt a government for any great length of time." Many friends, including the artist Albert Bierstadt, stopped by to offer their support to Roosevelt, and most of his family expressed relief.[196] As Teddy wrote his mother, "I am glad on his account, but sorry for New York."[197]

Teddy Roosevelt's relief was short-lived, as his father became suddenly ill in February 1878. As word spread that he was dying, Teddy rushed home from Harvard and a crowd gathered outside the family home. Incredibly, the crowd included a large number of the poor children aided by Theodore Roosevelt's philanthropy, who stood sentry until word came that their benefactor had died. His father's death devastated Teddy, who lost his anchor in life and came to doubt his own worth in the depths of his grief. "How little use I am, or ever shall be," he wrote in his diary. "I am as much inferior to Father morally and mentally as physically." He turned bitter and angry, on one occasion pulling out a revolver and shooting a neighbor's dog that annoyed him. He set off on twenty-mile hikes, battling down his fury and sorrow. It took about six months for his natural ebullience to return. Not once in that period did he mention Roscoe Conkling or link his father's death with the senator who falsely accused Roosevelt of seeking office for his own benefit, yet it is very likely that the connection remained alive in young Theodore Roosevelt's mind and may have clarified further his own political inclinations.[198] In his diary he scrawled, "How I wish I could ever do something to keep up his name." But what could young Teddy do? When he told his friend William Roscoe Thayer that he wanted to get involved in reforming New York's government, Thayer wondered "whether he is the real thing, or only the bundle of eccentricities which he appears." Another student who admired Roosevelt figured he would someday become a first-rate professor of history.[199]

Of one thing Theodore Roosevelt was fairly certain: America needed reform, not just to end the corruption rife in the country, but also to bring order to its expanding industrial economy and somehow to control the violence it seemed to generate. Charles Francis Adams Jr. blamed the Civil War for America's love affair with violence. The war had transformed American character by undermining respect for law, teaching the utility of violence, and training several million men in the value of organization, resulting in "some of the most remarkable examples of organized lawlessness" in history. Adams was not speaking here of common criminals, but of railroad magnates, who had "reduced courts, legislatures, and sovereign States to an unqualified obedience to their will." The entire political system, Adams warned, would collapse if serious systemic reforms were not undertaken.[200]

Henry Adams, that haughty critic of a time that did not properly appreciate his talents, would later write, "The American boy of 1854 stood nearer the year 1 than to the year 1900." His education had not prepared Adams for what he would encounter, as the pace of history accelerated in the years after 1865. Those alive at the time noticed the dramatic change in America; for contemporaries, 1877 had moved a century from 1860 in nearly every regard, but nowhere more so than in terms of technological and industrial change. Where John Greenleaf Whittier and many other leading intellectuals looked backward in 1877, the editor of *Atlantic Monthly*, William Dean Howells, looked forward. He realized that the Currier & Ives world was long gone, if it had ever existed. As Howells became more aware of the violent impact of industry, he came to see that the realism he had been promoting had not been that realistic after all, leading him to write a powerful prolabor novel and attack the "ruthlessness of unbridled capitalism" in another.[201] Some embraced the changes, others resented and even resisted them, but they bore down on everyone with the speed of a freight train.

Teddy Roosevelt sought to jump onboard that train, but he also longed to connect with the past. Another fan of James Fenimore Cooper, Roosevelt wanted to head out west from the time he was a boy, seeking to take part in the nation's saga of expansion. By the time he made his trip west in 1883 the prairies had been swept clean of its native population.[202] Confined to reservations, their culture targeted by the government, America's Plains Indians had lost their way of life. Now that the last significant resistance to the expansion of the United States had been eliminated, whites could accelerate the process of romanticizing the Indians. In 1883 William Cody began his "Buffalo Bill's Wild West" show, an extravagant glorification of the white conquest of the West that included Sitting Bull as one of its stars. The show, which usually concluded with a staged "Custer's Last Stand," set the popular image of the "Wild West" for the next century.[203] Having missed the real Wild West, Roosevelt wrote about it instead, producing a bestselling four-volume history *Winning of the West*. Despite having written forty-six books, Theodore Roosevelt is rarely treated as an intellectual. Generally he is perceived as a man of action with a sentimental streak, portrayed reacting to Jacob Riis's dog story or Upton Sinclair's *The Jungle*, charging up San Juan Hill or shrugging off an assassin's bullet. But Roosevelt changed the way Americans think about themselves.

Roosevelt had wanted to be a scientist, and it was certainly an exciting time for that ambition. Othniel Marsh's 1877 discoveries of the Stegosaurus, Diplodocus, Brachiosaurus, and Allosaurus at the Como Bluff site in Wyoming permanently altered our understanding of prehistoric life in North America, provided dramatic support for evolutionary theory, and made the United States, with its alkaline soils that preserved bones so well, the center of paleontological research. But Marsh entered into a bitter and often bizarre conflict with another prominent scholar, Edward D. Cope, hiring spies and attacking each other at every turn, making a mess of paleontology that took a generation to clean up. Marsh also erred in creating the Brontosaurus with the bones of two different animals. Nonetheless, his discoveries accelerated interest in Darwinism, which rapidly became the dominant scientific paradigm. Darwinism continued to have its powerful enemies, particularly in the Southern churches. In 1878, the president of Vanderbilt College in Nashville, Alexander Winchell, published a surreal mix of religion and science called *Adamites and Preadamites*. He argued that blacks were too inferior to be the descendants of Adam, who had to have been white. Given that "fact," Winchell reasoned that the human race had to be older than the biblical Adam and blacks must be the descendants of an earlier stage in human evolution. That Winchell acknowledged the validity of evolution, even in the service of racism, was too much for the Southern Methodists who ran Vanderbilt and they fired their president.[204] Coincidentally, the annual meeting of the American Association for the Advancement of Science had met the previous year, 1877, in Nashville, and listened as the organization's vice president, Othniel Marsh, confidently stated, "I am sure I need offer here no argument for evolution; since to doubt evolution to-day is to doubt science, and science is only another name for truth."[205]

Interest in science spread well beyond academic circles, as indicated by the success of the Museum of Natural History in New York, one of the most visited sites in America within five years. It may be difficult to imagine the president of the United States delivering the formal welcome, as Hayes did, at a science museum;

it may be even more difficult to imagine a leading scientist expressing confidence that a museum would help to fill the public's need and desire for scientific knowledge, as Marsh did at the museum's public opening in December 1877. Similarly, rationality as an intellectual ideal appeared triumphant, at least in academic circles. As 1877 ended, G. Stanley Hall of Harvard University was finishing the first PhD in psychology awarded in the United States. At the same time William James and Charles S. Peirce independently sent off the final drafts of the first articles in the development of pragmatism, both of which appeared in January 1878. James and Peirce formulated what would become the paradigmatic American philosophy, arguing that philosophy is not a path to certainty, only a way to cope with life, and that truth is found not through logic but results. In all walks of life, from the police to philosophy, prisons to philanthropy, sports to sanitation, the United States had launched itself on what one historian has called "the Search for Order" in the aftermath of the near chaos of 1877. Johns Hopkins, with its dedication to the research ideal, finished its first year in 1877, as did the country's first professional organization, the American Chemical Society, followed in 1878 by the American Bar Association.[206] But the most significant aspect of America's intellectual development in 1877 and immediately thereafter was the triumph of a qualified social Darwinism, which would place even a country as anarchic as the United States into a logical historical structure.

The continued vibrancy of social Darwinism in America flew in the face of developments in evolutionary science. In 1880 William James used Darwinism against social Darwinism, determining that it was not science but "a metaphysic creed, . . . an emotional attitude, rather than a system of thought." But his evaluation was roundly ignored in the United States, which remained enamored of an ideology that appeared to justify everything the country chose to do. Not even the ongoing depression put a dent in the enthusiasm for social Darwinism. In 1878 William Graham Sumner appeared before a House committee investigating the causes of the depression. After five years, it seemed as though laissez-faire economics had been given a fair chance and been found wanting. But Sumner insisted on staying the course until all the dross in the economy had been eliminated, whereupon it would return to healthy progress. He found it necessary to remind the people's representatives that nature demanded social inequality, that there was just no way around that fact and any effort to try and change this natural law would lead to further disasters. Sumner confronted Congress with a stark alternative: "If we do not believe in survival of the fittest, we have only one possible alternative, and that is survival of the unfittest." Nature rode humanity with an "iron spur," he said, and the poor had to bear their suffering for the betterment of the race. Any failure on their part was entirely their own fault, because they tended to give way to vice so easily. "Nature's remedies against vice are terrible," Sumner said, complacently summarizing the workings of the world. "She removes her victims without pity. A drunkard in the gutter is just where he ought to be, according to the fitness and tendency of things."[207]

Americans struggled with two fundamental and seemingly contradictory aspects of the social Darwinist vision: primitive violence and progress. Herbert Spencer had thrown around words like struggle and conflict as he spoke of survival of the fittest, but he seemed unconcerned with what violence actually meant and how it related to his promised progress. Evolution, as presented by Spencer but not Darwin, marched forward, propelling humanity on an ever-upward trajectory. Yet the battle for survival required brutal conduct, which seemed to contradict progress. How did the events of 1877 fit into such a format? Where were the signs of progress in the continuing depression, the strike, the mistreatment of the homeless, the rising homicide rates, the slaughter of the Indians, the abandonment of the blacks? For most observers, 1877 had been a serious step backward, not part of some progressive development. If accepting social Darwinism necessitated living with uncontrolled violence then the majority of Americans wanted nothing to do with it.

Theodore Roosevelt presented the American people with the resolution to the Darwinian paradox, essentially by imposing his character onto the intellectual construct. In his writings and speeches, Roosevelt promoted the idea that conflict and action built character, and the strong man welcomed the righteous struggle as an essential aspect of the "strenuous life." On the one hand that meant a life of movement and doing: striking out into the wilderness, camping, hunting, undertaking any adventure that challenged the individual, behaving like Theodore Roosevelt. On the other hand, Roosevelt made a virtue of externalized violence as part of the struggle for survival that produces progress. This life of action extended to the nation as a whole, which also competed for survival against the other nations of the world and required that Americans be willing to do battle, not against one another but in combat against competing peoples. The stakes were enormous, for both the country and the citizen. "If we stand idly by," Roosevelt wrote, "if we seek merely swollen, slothful ease and ignoble peace, if we shrink from the hard contests where men must win at hazard of their lives and at the risk of all they hold dear, then the bolder and stronger peoples will pass us by, and will win for themselves the domination of the world."[208]

Roosevelt promoted athletics as a key component of the strenuous and manly life, tapping into a popular new conception of masculinity. The blood sports lost popularity not just because of middle-class disgust and their association with the poor, but also as a new attitude toward sports emerged in the late 1870s and 1880s. Responding to fears of the feminization of America, the idea that the country was growing soft as women gained cultural influence and more men took the desk jobs associated with industrialization, a cult of exercise gained millions of adherents. Men, it was charged, were losing their masculinity, becoming "overcivilized" to the point that they were ineffective and inert, victims of that new industrial-age disease "neurasthenia," a mix of fatigue and depression.[209] Doctors thought this new disease was particularly common in the United States, William James calling it "acute Americanitis." Real men were muscular, strong, and capable of violence—but controlled, rational violence.[210] A few years after Roosevelt graduated from Harvard, Henry James gave voice to the fears of the "damnable feminization" of America in his book *The Bostonians*. His character Basil Ransom complains that his "whole generation is womanised." Looking at America, he sees the "masculine tone is passing out of the world; it's a feminine, a nervous, hysterical, chattering, canting age" that "will usher in the reign of mediocrity." Men were becoming whiners, full of excuses for inaction and failure. But the "new man" pushed back against this weakness. As a young Harvard professor in 1877, William James received the following advice from his mentor: "Stop your sniveling complaints, and your equally sniveling raptures! Leave off your general emotional tomfoolery, and get to WORK like men!"[211]

Doctors, recipients of a newfound respect as they professionalized, promoted exercise to overcome the indolence of modern life and prevent neurasthenia. Clergy who had once criticized all sports as primitive distractions from a Christian life now embraced the idea of "muscular Christianity," and encouraged nonviolent sports.[212] The Reverend DeWitt Talmage, whose book *Sports That Kill* had played a prominent role in the campaign against blood sports, encouraged less bloody forms of exercise.[213] Instead of watching animals and men tear at one another, the muscular Christian should arise from his couch and work out. It was not incidental that alcohol hindered athletic excellence, leading many advocates of exercise to conclude that a healthy workout of any kind would reduce drunkenness. Colleges particularly seized on this new fad, which Louis Agassiz called "Peripatetic Learning": rather than limiting the student to studying the classics, an essential aspect of the student experience is exercise. Modern colleges "have incorporated the athletic sports, and under the flag of 'muscular Christianity,' have base-ball companies and miniature navies." Ministers jumped on board with educators in advocating this "new style of muscular Christianity," which Roosevelt took part in at Harvard by joining a dozen different athletic clubs. The theological justification built upon the notion that the body was the temple of the spirit and should be well maintained. The Reverend W.X. Ninde of Detroit told the graduating class of Northwestern University, "One of the worst of heresies—not against a human creed, but against God's blessed intent—is that scandalous judgment which puts dishonor in the human body, which counts it the soul's implacable enemy, and starves and scourges it into submission." It should be treated with respect as "the soul's fitting habitation." It was time to "dread physical feebleness and admire and envy the healthy man." Anticipating Roosevelt, Ninde "blessed the men who are well and strong and enduring—who work hard and love it, who live long and still bring forth fruit in old age."[214] Intellectuals embraced muscular Christianity as a sign of progress, the sloughing off of outdated notions and myths, applauding the growth of the YMCA in the 1880s, the spread of professional baseball teams to most American cities, and the adoption of football by the majority of colleges. This new emphasis on masculinity, whether Christian or secular, fit the Darwinian paradigm. A vital outdoor life and commitment to athletics allowed the prosperous to have both the benefits of civilization and, as Roosevelt formulated it, a firm connection to America's past of rugged individualism and heroic masculinity. Virility would balance industrial culture to create a modern man of strength, wealth, and vision, capable of triumphing in the battle for survival.[215]

Roosevelt went to college just as this new ideal of masculinity was gaining currency and intellectual legitimacy and would become its voice and embodiment. Sports, Roosevelt wrote, "develop such qualities as courage, resolution and endurance." He rejected bare-knuckle prizefighting as "simply brutal and degrading," noting that its audiences "hover on the borderlines of criminality; and those who are not are speedily brutalized, and are never rendered more manly." Those who enjoyed watching two men pummel each other with their bare fists were no different than those who attended cockfights and rat fights, all of which appealed to primitive tastes and blood lust. But boxing was a different matter, a functional art appropriate for the modern age.[216] Roosevelt saw nothing wrong with men battering one another, just so long as they did so according to a formal set of rules that maintained good order, separating the civilized boxing match from a primitive brawl with two pairs of gloves. The boxers entered and exited the ring as gentlemen, their fight a demonstration of prowess and ability rather than of brute force.

Just as gloved boxing fell within a respectable structure that gave it meaning and value, so Roosevelt's muted form of social Darwinism justified murderous violence within the larger context of an international struggle for primacy. He was not rationalizing individual acts of violence, for civilized societies existed to maintain order and prevent such random disruptive acts. But as part of "the law of strife," the manly responsibilities of citizenship, violence was a high calling. At times Roosevelt's bloody-mindedness sounded like an editorial written in 1877. For instance, he became convinced that the Populists were "plotting a social revolution and the subversion of the American Republic" in the 1890s and called on the United States to treat that threat as the French government had the Paris Commune, "by taking ten or a dozen of their leaders out, standing them . . . against a wall and shooting them dead."[217] Generally Roosevelt spoke more abstractly about the glories of war, the creation of national greatness through constant struggle, and the utility of ceaseless energy, but he left no doubt that the nation had a right to exercise its monopoly on violence, and Americans had a duty to take part in its wars when called upon.

The humanitarianism that marked abolitionism, most of the antebellum reform movements, and much of Reconstruction vanished in the late 1870s. When Cecilia O'Neill, a Populist from Nebraska, traveled through the East giving lectures on the plight of farmers and unemployed workers, she met with "heartless indifference." When she warned that privation could lead to violence, her listeners assured her that "the Army and our Militia will keep order." O'Neill was convinced that the comfortable middle class could not imagine that workers shared the same humanity, as was evident when the New York Charity Organization Society warned that soup kitchens would damage the morals of the poor. This shift from compassion to a strenuous adherence to social Darwinism helps to explain the conduct of the United States Army in the later Sioux war that ended so badly at Wounded Knee in 1890, and in the Philippines in the early twentieth century when an estimated 100,000 civilians were slaughtered by American forces.[218] The country had learned too well that violence solved its problems.

Coda: Three Poets

Huang Zunxian came to San Francisco as Chinese consul general in 1882, convinced that the United States was the most advanced country in the world. But disillusionment overtook him as he encountered lawlessness and violence, especially against his fellow Chinese. In frustration, he wrote a series of angry poems, challenging the Americans on their hypocrisy and betrayal of the ideals of their revolution: "They have sealed all the gates tightly, / Door after door with guards beating alarms / . . . Anyone with a yellow-colored face / Is beaten even if guiltless. / . . . The American eagle strides the heavens soaring, / With half of the globe clutched in his claw. / Although the Chinese arrived later, / Couldn't you leave them a little space."[219]

The English visitor George Sala puzzled over the obsession of white Californians with the Chinese, which appeared inexplicable to him. Critics of the Chinese pointed to the paucity of women other than prostitutes among their number and to the failure of the Chinese to assimilate to a society that treated them worse than dogs. It was true that, according to the 1880 U.S. Census, there were 71,244 Chinese men and just 3,888 Chinese women in California, but Sala found this logic evasive. It appeared to him that the anti-Chinese movement was really a form of class conflict, with white workers holding the elite responsible for the influx of Chinese as part of a plot to reduce workers' wages. While a fan of California in all other regards, Sala perceived the state "tied to no traditions and hampered by no prejudices:—except against John Chinaman." Every issue becomes embroiled in "the Chinese question," and labor erred terribly in allowing racism to defeat its other goals, even to breaking their own strike efforts in order to hurt Chinese workers. Sala saw no difference in the conflict between capital and labor in Europe and America, except in California, where the bitterness of the white workers had reached a point where they were willing "to burn Capital's house over its head" in order "to massacre its Chinese cheaply-hired labour." In response, capital threatened to "shoot Labour down by the hands of the State or of Federal troops, and, if need be, to hang Labour's . . . agitators."[220] Pressure from Denis Kearney's Workingmen's Party led to the Chinese Exclusion Act of 1882, the first legislation to ban a specific group from immigrating to the United States, though class animosity did not lessen as a result. The Chinese thus became America's first illegal aliens.

This was not the Golden Mountain as Huang Zunxian and so many Chinese had heard, but the "Land without ghosts," a nation where people lacked respect for their ancestors, seemingly had no history, and offered no refuge for the Chinese. Americans betrayed strange and contradictory approaches to immigration. On the one hand they had no general naturalization policy and often proudly proclaimed that their nation had been built by immigrants, while on the other they tended to make invidious comparisons between themselves, the children of immigrants, and the new arrivals. In the years ahead, millions of immigrants poured into America, altering the nation in fundamental ways, while many political leaders and intellectuals would demand that, in Huang Zunxian's words, they seal all the gates. But they would not stanch the flow of immigrants until the early 1920s, and even those limitations would be poorly enforced and ineffective, and the barriers remain porous.[221]

Above all else, the United States remained the land of which millions dreamed, a place where people could prosper and fulfill their promise, a land of constant change. Despite the depression of 1873, more than a quarter of a million people came to the United States every year through 1877; in 1878 that number rose rapidly to 525,000 immigrants a year through the 1880s. Many of the old guard still running the country felt open immigration boded ill for the future of the United States. The Reverend Josiah Strong was just the most prominent voice warning of this "social dynamite" pouring through the open gates. Despite his stated opposition to all government regulation, William Graham Sumner warned in 1878 that too many of the wrong kind of people were coming to the United States, threatening freedom itself. The prominent historian Francis Parkman took time from his massive history of the struggle between Britain and France for control of North America to write an article arguing that it was already too late, that democracy had failed because of America's inability to control immigration: "Two enemies, unknown before, have risen like spirits of darkness on our social and political horizon—an ignorant proletariat and a half-taught plutocracy."[222] While Parkman at least apportioned the blame to both sides of the social scale, most critics followed Sumner in heaping venomous scorn onto the Catholics, with many Protestants charging an international conspiracy to transform America into a papal colony. Some critics of open immigration worried that it was even conceivable that the United States would one day have a Catholic president! These Catholic immigrants certainly were changing the country, as the number of Catholics doubled between 1870 and 1900 to 20 percent of the population.[223]

Within the country as well, Americans began moving with ever greater frequency in search of better lives. While the government's temporary abdication of regulatory authority had many negative consequences, it also created a diversity of opportunities for those with their eye on the main chance. The migration from the countryside to the city altered individual lives and changed the nation's culture and structure forever in significant ways. No one in 1877 could have guessed which way the United States was headed; many worried that the country was on a road to ever more violence, some perceived bright futures of equality and prosperity, and still others placed the recent upheavals in a larger journey toward democracy that had started a century earlier and would wind on into the distant future. There was plenty of cause for both hope and despair, and room left over to wonder just how we had arrived at this place.

During Reconstruction, America tried democracy, deploying federal troops to protect citizens' rights against violence. In 1877 Americans wanted little more to do with the Civil War and all it represented, particularly the fight for equality and national unity and reform. The Civil War as a series of battles remained sharp in public discourse, but the war's purpose faded. The year started with a deal being cut, the Northern oligarchy handing the South back to its white elite in return for their compliance with this new power arrangement culminating in the destruction of democracy in the South. Blacks were driven from the polls, followed soon thereafter by poor whites, as is evident in the decline in voting. In the 1876 election, an estimated 82 percent of adult males voted; in the 1880s, voter turnout in the South was 64 percent; in the 1890s the states that had passed the most restrictive legislation targeting poor whites and blacks had a voter turnout of just 42 percent; by the first decade of the twentieth century only 30 percent of all eligible Southern voters cast ballots. As under slavery, the white elite got representation for people who they would not allow to vote. Their example was followed in Western states, where non-Anglos were denied rights and New Mexico was not granted statehood because of all the resident "aliens."[224] In 1877 the American public acquiesced in the destruction of their nascent democracy, doing nothing to protect the rights of Southern black voters and allowing armed gangs to terrorize and kill black citizens through the rest of the century. Whenever the federal government refused to act, as in the South in 1877, violence triumphed, but if U.S. troops intervened, as in the Great Strike, then extralegal violence failed.

Huang Zunxian would have found a warmer welcome had he made it to Walt

Whitman's home in Camden, New Jersey, where Whitman, suffering from a long illness, had just brought out the first commercial edition of *Leaves of Grass*. It sold well at first, but the publisher suddenly withdrew the book when a district attorney threatened to bring obscenity charges against the book in response to its sexual language. Fortunately for Whitman, he found another publisher in 1882 and sold thousands of copies. However, despite his success, Whitman had soured on the United States. His earlier optimism had faded in the glare of the new industrial society: "The spectacle is appalling." The atmosphere of the country was pure hypocrisy while the "cities reek with respectable as much as non-respectable robbery and scoundrelism." Where the Civil War and its immediate aftermath "show that popular democracy, whatever its fault and dangers, practically justifies itself beyond the proudest claims and wildest hopes of its enthusiasts," now "democracy" is just a sham and "looks with suspicious, ill-satisfied eye upon the very poor, the ignorant, and on those out of business." The new American nation had no patience for those lacking "cash in the bank."[225]

Whitman had long held to the notion of American exceptionalism, the idea that its democracy freed the United States from the burdens of class warfare that tore at Europe's vitals, a conviction shattered by events in 1877. As the contemporary historian James Ford Rhodes wrote, the American people "hugged the delusion that such social uprisings belonged to Europe." But the violence of 1877 "came like a thunderbolt out of a clear sky, startling us rudely." The Great Strike especially, in the words of *The Nation*'s editor E.L. Godkin, had shattered the American conviction that theirs was the one country where "there was no proletariat and no dangerous class." Now it was evident that the United States was no different from any other country; the conviction that they had "solved the problem of enabling capital and labor to live together in political harmony" collapsed beneath the weight of its many contradictions. The death of exceptionalism was acknowledged by radicals such as Henry George and conservative businessmen such as Tom Scott of the Pennsylvania Railroad.[226] The events of 1877 broke the spell of exceptionalism and Whitman watched his dream of the great democracy free of class conflict go up in smoke.

Whitman wondered what had happened to America's compassion. There were so many angry voices calling for violence, unexpected voices: ministers, suffragists, intellectuals, journalists, all demanding retribution against those who disrupted the country's good order, seemingly not appreciating the degree to which that disorder was the result of forces beyond the control of the powerless. The angry ones drowned out the voices of compassion, which were still present, especially among the youthful. It could be found in the young family headed west with the Exodusters, looking back at the only home they had ever known, a land of hate and violence intent on perpetuating a system of racism that would scorch another five generations. The young parents turned their eyes toward

Kansas, hoping that they could finally be free and build a home for their children. It was there in the mind of seventeen-year-old Jane Addams, challenging her father who wanted her to behave like all good young women from prosperous families by getting married and staying at home with her children. Addams saw the poverty and suffering around her and wanted to help, though she was not yet sure how to do so. It was there in the eyes of Sarah Winnemucca, the Paiute princess, who courageously and peacefully defended her people against the remorseless advance of white civilization, winning the respect of onetime enemies and eventually being called "the most remarkable woman" of her generation.[227] It was there in the hands of Terence Powderly, insisting, despite all provocations, that workers must remain nonviolent as he organized and led the Knights of Labor in the generations-long battle to win recognition for the right to unionize. Compassion was out there, Whitman was certain, but it had been obscured by the raging fires of violence and hate.

But what, Whitman demanded, had happened to democracy? Now just a word, it "sleeps" and "resides altogether in the future." Whitman was not yet willing to give up: "Democracy, in silence, [is] biding its time." He imagined himself standing on California's shores, with the great republic at his back. "Long having wander'd since, round the earth having wander'd," he wrote. "Now I face home again, very pleas'd and joyous." But Whitman added a final line in parentheses: "(But where is what I started for so long ago? And why is it yet unfound?)"[228] It would be found, his soaring democracy, but not just yet.

The same year that Huang Zunxian wrote about America slamming doors in the faces of the Chinese, another poet, inspired by the Russian and eastern European Jews she met in New York, penned a completely different poem of the "Mother of Exiles" lifting her "lamp beside the golden door." Just five years after William Graham Sumner worried that too many of the wrong kind of people were coming to the United States, Emma Lazarus presented the United States with the words for its Statue of Liberty that spoke to all that is finest in its heritage and its promise for the future. In a sweeping vision of her country that forgave so many recent acts of violence against immigrants and workers, Native Americans and blacks, women and dissidents, Lazarus spoke to a future of endless possibilities, calling on the world to "Give me your tired, your poor, / Your huddled masses yearning to breathe free." And they would come, and keep on coming. Millions of American families begin with tales of hardship as desperate men and women crossed the Atlantic or Pacific oceans or walked across the southern border, seeking and finding a promised land of opportunity. They would come, the poor, persecuted, forlorn immigrants grieving for all they had lost, and join with the millions already living here who, behind Lady Liberty's back, also yearned to breathe the free air of America.

Notes

A note on newspapers: nineteenth-century newspapers are notoriously difficult to cite. They change their names constantly, do not routinely number their pages, insert articles and editorials seemingly at random, and often do not bother with headlines. The practice of large, recognizable headlines was just coming into vogue in 1877 and had not yet caught on entirely. As a consequence, some of the following citations for newspapers and articles have titles and some do not. Unless otherwise indicated, the articles cited start on page one of the newspaper. I have cited the page on which the article begins even if it continues on another page as it is generally very difficult to locate an article fragment in these newspapers. Contemporary accounts often differ in minor and significant ways. I have therefore attempted to give multiple sources for events and quotations so that interested readers can compare versions and reach independent judgments.

Preface

1. Allan Nevins, *The Emergence of Modern America, 1865–1878* (New York: Macmillan, 1927), 304.

2. Henry F. May, *Protestant Churches and Industrial America* (New York: Harper & Brothers, 1949), 95.

3. See, for example, "The Ashtabula Calamity," *New York Times*, January 1, 1877; "The Railway Horror," *Boston Daily Advertiser*, January 1, 1877; "The Communists Preparing," *Chicago Daily Tribune*, December 17, 1877; "The Communists," *Chicago Daily Tribune*, December 20, 1877, p. 8.

4. Goldwin Smith, "The Labour War in the United States," *Contemporary Review* 30 (1877): 541.

5. Rebecca Edwards, *New Spirits: Americans in the Gilded Age, 1865–1905* (New York: Oxford University Press, 2006), 140.

6. Edwards, *New Spirits*, 28.

7. The earliest use of "captains of industry" that I can locate was in a brief article in the *Boston Daily Advertiser*, September 23, 1876.

8. May, *Protestant Churches and Industrial America*, 91.

9. Joseph Nash, *The Relations between Capital and Labor in the United States* (Boston: Lee and Shepard, 1878), 8.

10. T. Edwin Brown, *Studies in Modern Socialism and Labor Problems* (New York: D. Appleton and Co., 1886), 67.

11. Henry James to William James, June 28, 1877, in *Henry James Letters*, ed. Leon Edel, 4 vols. (Cambridge, MA: Harvard University Press, 1974–84), 2:116–17, 121n1.

12. T. DeWitt Talmage, *T. DeWitt Talmage as I Knew Him* (Teddington, UK: Echo Library, 2006), 49.

Chapter 1: On the Edge of a Volcano

1. Thomas Huxley, *American Addresses* (London: Macmillan, 1877), 125–27; "Views of an Impartial Observer," *Galveston Daily News*, September 23, 1876.

2. Andrew Carnegie, *Autobiography of Andrew Carnegie* (Boston: Houghton Mifflin, 1920), 189.

3. Rendigs Fels, *American Business Cycles, 1865–1897* (Chapel Hill: University of North Carolina Press, 1969), 107; A. Ross Eckler, "A Measure of the Severity of Depressions, 1873–1932," *Review of Economic Statistics* 15 (1933): 79; Robert Sobel, *Panic on Wall Street: A History of America's Financial Disasters* (New York: Macmillan, 1968), 192. Denis Tilden Lynch, *The Wild Seventies* (New York: D. Appleton–Century Co., 1941), 264, holds that the depression started in 1872, as measured by the great number of homeless crowding New York shelters and police stations that year. William Godwin Moody, *Land and Labor in the United States* (New York: Charles Scribner's Sons, 1883), 222–24, argues that the economic crisis began in 1867, based on the number of business failures.

4. I have located 522 newspaper articles with "Hard Times" in the headline from October 1, 1873, through the end of 1879, compared with 342 uses of "depression." The first history of the depression was F.W. Smith, *The Hard Times* (Boston: J.R. Osgood & Co., 1877).

5. "Hard Times and No Money in Georgia," from the *Columbus Sun*, in the *Little Rock Daily Republican*, November 3, 1873; "Hard Times in New York," from *New York World*, October 26, 1873, in the *San Francisco Daily Evening Bulletin*, November 5, 1873.

6. *Commercial and Financial Chronicle* (New York), January 24, 1873; Sobel, *Panic on Wall Street*, 156–73; Davis Rich Dewey, *Financial History of the United States* (New York: Longmans, Green and Co., 1931), 370–71; Moody, *Land and Labor*, 215–22; Allan Nevins, *The Emergence of Modern America, 1865–1878* (New York: Macmillan, 1927), 291–94; *Historical Statistics of the United States: Colonial Times to 1957* (Washington, DC: U.S. Department of Commerce, Bureau of the Census, 1960), 427–78; Alexander Dana Noyes, *Forty Years of American Finance* (New York: G.P. Putnam's Sons, 1909), 1–19; Fels, *American Business Cycles*, 86, 98–102; Oliver M.W. Sprague, *History of Crises Under the National Banking System*, 61st Cong., 2nd sess., Senate Doc. no. 538 (Washington, DC, 1910), 1–89; Henrietta M. Larson, *Jay Cooke: Private Banker* (Cambridge, MA: Harvard University Press, 1936), 383–411.

7. Sobel, *Panic on Wall Street*, 167–71; M. John Lubetkin, *Jay Cooke's Gamble: The Northern Pacific Railroad, the Sioux, and the Panic of 1873* (Norman: University of Oklahoma Press, 2006), 287; Sobel, *Panic on Wall Street*, 164–66, 174–75.

8. Sir George Campbell, *White and Black: The Outcome of a Visit to the United States* (New York: R. Worthington, 1879), 179; Nevins, *Emergence of Modern America*, 312–13; Samuel P. Orth, *The Boss and the Machine* (New Haven: Yale University Press, 1920), 93–118.

9. Lynch, *Wild Seventies*, 97; Mark Twain and Charles Dudley Warner, *The Gilded Age* (Hartford, CT: American Publishing Co., 1874).

10. *Commercial and Financial Chronicle*, January 10, 1874, p. 28; *Commercial and Financial Chronicle*, April 11, 1873, p. 445 (quote); Lubetkin, *Jay Cooke's Gamble*, 275; Larson, *Jay Cooke*, 397; Nevins, *Emergence of Modern America*, 294–95; Fels, *American Business Cycles*, 99; Sobel, *Panic on Wall Street*, 171–73.

11. "Financial Affairs," *New York Times*, September 17, 1873, p. 2 (quote); "Financial Affairs," *New York Times*, September 12, 1873; "Financial Affairs," *New York Times*, September 13, 1873; "Railroad Bonds and United States Securities Strong," *New York Herald*, September 12, 1873; "Shall We Have Another Black Friday?" *Harper's Weekly*, September 6, 1873; "The Week in Trade and Finance," *The Nation*, September 11, 1873; Sobel, *Panic on Wall Street*, 175–77; Lubetkin, *Jay Cooke's Gamble*, 276, 279.

12. "Cooke's Crash," *New York Herald*, September 19, 1873 (quote); "Washington: The Suspension of Henry Cooke," *New York Herald*, September 19, 1873; "The Panic," *New York Times*, September 19, 1873; "The Northern Pacific Railroad," *New York Times*, September 20, 1873, p. 4; Lubetkin, *Jay Cooke's Gamble*, 279–85; Ellis Paxson Oberholtzer, *Jay Cooke: Financier of the Civil War*, 2 vols. (Philadelphia: George W. Jacobs & Co., 1907), 2:181n2, 352–57, 421–22; Sobel, *Panic on Wall Street*, 178, 185; Nevins, *Emergence of Modern America*, 295. Jay Cooke lost his extravagant home and moved in with his daughter, where he spent the remaining thirty-one years of his life. He either hid $2 million of his money or made a killing in an investment with Jay Gould, but by 1880 he was once more a rich man. Lubetkin, *Jay Cooke's Gamble*, 285, 291–92; Oberholtzer, *Jay Cooke* 2:523–26; Larson, *Jay Cooke*, 424–25.

13. *New York Tribune*, September 19, 1873.

14. *Philadelphia Press*, probably September 19, 1873.

15. *Philadelphia Press*, September 19, 1873.

16. *New York Tribune*, September 19, 1873.

17. Lubetkin, *Jay Cooke's Gamble*, 283; Oberholtzer, *Jay Cooke*, 2:422–25, 429, 432–34.

18. Oberholtzer, *Jay Cooke*, 2:432–33.

19. Horace White, "The Financial Crisis in America," from *Fortnightly Review* in *Milwaukee Daily Sentinel*, June 27, 1876, p. 3; "Washington: The Suspension of Henry Cooke," *New York Herald*, September 19, 1873; Harvey O'Connor, *Mellon's Millions: The Biography of a Fortune* (New York: Blue Ribbon Books, 1933), 30–31; Nevins, *Emergence of Modern America*, 295–96; Oberholtzer, *Jay Cooke*, 2:421–22, 428–30; Lubetkin, *Jay Cooke's Gamble*, 283; Fels, *American Business Cycles*, 101–2.

20. *The Nation*, September 25, 1873; Sobel, *Panic on Wall Street*, 178–86; 191; Nevins, *Emergence of Modern America*, 290–304; Oberholtzer, *Jay Cooke*, 2:432; Theodore Roosevelt Sr. to Anna Roosevelt Cowles, September 24, 1873, in David McCullough, *Mornings on Horseback* (New York: Simon & Schuster, 1981), 134.

21. David Nasaw, *Andrew Carnegie* (New York: Penguin Press, 2006), 151–53.

22. Nasaw, *Andrew Carnegie*, 151–55 (quote, 153); James A Ward, *J. Edgar Thomson, Master of the Pennsylvania* (Westport, CT: Greenwood Press, 1980), 207–8.

23. O'Connor, *Mellon's Millions*, 33–34 (quote, 32); Fels, *American Business Cycles*, 102; Sobel, *Panic on Wall Street*, 188–93; Moody, *Land and Labor*, 224–29.

24. Miriam Leslie, *California: A Pleasure Trip from Gotham to the Golden Gate* (New York: G.W. Carleton & Co., 1877), 127; "Jay Cooke's Crash," *San Francisco Daily Evening Bulletin*, October 3, 1873; *Commercial and Financial Chronicle*, January 10, 1874; *Commercial and Financial Chronicle*, January 24, 1874; *Commercial and Financial Chronicle*, January 15, 1876; *Commercial and Financial Chronicle*, July 1, 1876; *Commercial*

and Financial Chronicle, January 5, 1878; *Commercial and Financial Chronicle*, January 19, 1878; "Alleged Conspiracy: A Great Company Doing Business Without Capital," *North American* (Philadelphia), September 27, 1877; Nevins, *Emergence of Modern America*, 298n2, 303; Sobel, *Panic on Wall Street*, 185, 187, 191–94.

25. Nevins, *Emergence of Modern America*, 290. On the spread of the depression, see Walter Nugent, *Money and American Society, 1865–1880* (New York: Free Press, 1968), 176–84.

26. Campbell, *White and Black*, 104; "Who Is Responsible—Hard Times Ahead," *Georgia Weekly Telegraph and Georgia Journal & Messenger* (Macon), November 11, 1873; "What Can We Do?" *Idaho Signal* (Lewiston), April 11, 1874; O'Connor, *Mellon's Millions*, 32.

27. Vanderbilt quoted in Sobel, *Panic on Wall Street*, 180; "The Mystery of Hard Times," *Lowell Daily Citizen and News*, November 22, 1873; Nevins, *Emergence of Modern America*, 291; Charles Dickens, *Hard Times* (New York: Harper & Brothers, 1854).

28. *Commercial and Financial Chronicle*, November 15, 1873, p. 647 (quote); "The Panic," *New York Times*, September 20, 1873 (quote); *Commercial and Financial Chronicle*, January 10, 1874, p. 36.

29. "The Panic," *New York Times*, September 20, 1873. See also "The Panic," *San Francisco Daily Evening Bulletin*, September 20, 1873; "The Financial Crisis," *Independent Statesman* (Concord, NH), September 25, 1873, p. 412; Nevins, *Emergence of Modern America*, 29; Campbell, *White and Black*, 33.

30. Carnegie, *Autobiography*, 189–90; Sobel, *Panic on Wall Street*, 188–99; Nevins, *Emergence of Modern America*, 297; Oberholtzer, *Jay Cooke*, 2:431–32; Alexander Dana Noyes, *Forty Years of American Finance* (New York: G.P. Putnam's Sons, 1909), 19–20. On the confusion in Congress, see John Sherman, *Recollections of Forty Years in the House, Senate and Cabinet*, 2 vols. (Chicago: Werner Co., 1895), 1:490–506.

31. Carnegie, *Autobiography*, 190, 192; *New York Times*, December 11, 1874, p. 5; "The American Iron and Steel Association," *North American and United States Gazette* (Philadelphia), February 12, 1875; Nasaw, *Andrew Carnegie*, 161–63, 175.

32. "The Week," *The Nation*, July 1, 1875, p. 1; Stephen Thernstrom, *Progress and Poverty: Social Mobility in a Nineteenth-Century City* (New York: Atheneum, 1970), 20. A survey of workingmen by the Ohio Bureau of Labor Statistics in 1880 found that they had lost an average of eight weeks of work the previous year, even after the depression was over. Eric H. Monkkonen, *The Dangerous Class: Crime and Poverty in Columbus, Ohio, 1860–1885* (Cambridge, MA: Harvard University Press, 1975), 142; Ohio Bureau of Labor Statistics, *Third Annual Report, 1879* (Columbus: State of Ohio, 1880), 219.

33. Senate Committee on Finance [the Aldrich Committee], *Report on Wholesale Prices, Wages, and Transportation*, 52nd Cong., 2nd sess., 3, pt. 1 (Washington, DC: GPO, 1893); Nevins, *Emergence of Modern America*, 302; *Report on the Statistics of Wages in Manufacturing Industries*, vol. 20, Tenth Census of the United States (Washington, DC: GPO, 1886); Nasaw, *Andrew Carnegie*, 174; Thomas J. Misa, *A Nation of Steel: The Making of Modern America, 1865–1925* (Baltimore: Johns Hopkins University Press, 1995), 31; Fels, *American Business Cycles*, 90, 93, 97–98; Sobel, *Panic on Wall Street*, 195. H.R. 2934, known as the Fourth Coinage Act and the Mint Act, was an exceedingly complex piece of legislation that basically placed the United States on the gold standard. Nugent, *Money and American Society*, 140–71.

34. *Commercial and Financial Chronicle*, August 22, 1874; *The Economist*, December 26, 1874; *The Economist*, September 21, 1878; Nevins, *Emergence of Modern America*,

299–305; Dewey, *Financial History*, 371–73; Campbell, *White and Black*, 349; Nasaw, *Andrew Carnegie*, 173; Edith A. Abbott, *Wages of Unskilled Labor in the United States* (Chicago: University of Chicago Press, 1905), 363; C.D. Wright, *Comparative Wages, Prices, and Cost of Living* (Boston: Wright & Potter, 1889); *Report on the Defective, Dependent and Delinquent Classes of the Population of the United States*, vol. 21, Tenth Census of the United States (Washington, DC: GPO, 1888), ix–xxi; Moody, *Land and Labor*, 215–35.

35. Campbell, *White and Black*, 97–103, 237, 241–42, 309–10 (quotes, 97, 99); *Commercial and Financial Chronicle*, August 7, 1875; Nevins, *Emergence of Modern America*, 299.

36. *Colorado Springs Gazette*, May 12, 1877, p. 2; "The Times Growing Worse and Worse," *Georgia Weekly Telegraph and Georgia Journal & Messenger* (Macon), May 8, 1877. See also "Gaunt Famine," *St. Louis Globe-Democrat*, January 14, 1877, p. 2.

37. Campbell, *White and Black*, 238, 245, 257; Barry Werth, *Banquet at Delmonico's: Great Minds, the Gilded Age, and the Triumph of Evolution in America* (New York: Random House, 2009), 166; Carolyn Ashbaugh, *Lucy Parsons: American Revolutionary* (Chicago: Charles Kerr, 1976), 16; Denis Tilden Lynch, *The Wild Seventies* (New York: D. Appleton–Century Co., 1941), 266.

38. Jules Leclercq, "L'empereur de la ville impériale, c'est le dollar" and "le même culte au dieu Greenback," in *Un Été en Amérique de l'Atlantique aux Montagnes Rocheux* (Paris: Plon, 1877), 76. See also ibid., 27–28, 41–43, 72–81, 140; John E. Van Sant, ed., *Mori Arinori's Life and Resources in America* (Lanham, MD: Lexington Books, 2004), 68; H. Husey Vivian, *Notes of a Tour in America from August 7th to November 17th, 1877* (London: Edward Stanford, 1878), 247; Henry Sienkiewicz, *Portrait of America: Letters of Henry Sienkiewicz*, ed. and trans. Charles Morley (New York: Columbia University Press, 1959), 28–29.

39. Smith, "The Labour War in the United States," 532. This passage is a bit ambiguous, but its context of condemning the conduct of the railroads seems to support this reading.

40. Sienkiewicz, *Portrait of America*, 12–13. There were many such instances of people getting arrested in order to gain food and shelter in jail. See, for instance, "A Sample of Hard Times," *Daily Rocky Mountain News* (Denver), November 13, 1873; *Frank Leslie's Illustrated Newspaper* (New York), February 10, 1877.

41. William Peirce Randel, *Centennial: American Life in 1876* (Philadelphia: Chilton Books, 1969), 10; Thomas J. Schlereth, *Victorian America: Transformations in Everyday Life, 1876–1915* (New York: HarperCollins, 1991), 5. For a contrary view, which does not reference any specific exhibits or contemporary published statements, see Dee Brown, *The Year of the Century: 1876* (New York: Charles Scribner's Sons, 1966), 2: "In 1876, almost as if by common consent the people of the United States chose the centennial of the nation's birth as a year for taking stock of the past by means of celebrations both solemn and gay."

42. Randel, *Centennial*, 293; John D. McCabe, *The Illustrated History of the Centennial Exhibition* (Philadelphia: National Publishing Co., 1876); "Characteristics of the International Fair," *Atlantic Monthly* 38 (1876): 85–91, 233–40, 350–60, 492–502; Frank H. Norton, *Frank Leslie's Historical Register of the United States Centennial Exposition, 1876* (New York: Frank Leslie, 1877), which has 800 illustrations of the exposition. The Chicago World's Fair drew 27 million people and covered 685 acres; Lilia Moritz Schwarcz, *The Emperor's Beard: Dom Pedro II and the Tropical Monarchy of Brazil*, trans. John Gledson (New York: Hill & Wang, 2004), 287.

43. "Characteristics of the International Fair," *Atlantic Monthly* 38 (1876): 85–91 (quote, 91); *Harper's Weekly*, October 14, 1876; Randel, *Centennial*, 189, 294, 299, 327; McCabe, *Illustrated History of the Centennial Exhibition*.

44. Wagner called this piece "Fest Marsche." Randel, *Centennial*, 343; Mary Wilhelmine Williams, *Dom Pedro the Magnanimous: Second Emperor of Brazil* (Chapel Hill: University of North Carolina Press, 1937), 196; Schwarcz, *Emperor's Beard*, 275.

45. Brown, *Year of the Century*, 127.

46. Pedro on Corliss engines: Williams, *Dom Pedro the Magnanimous*, 197; Pedro's private opinion: Roderick J. Barman, *Citizen Emperor: Pedro II and the Making of Brazil, 1825–91* (Stanford: Stanford University Press, 1999), 279; *Baltimore Sun*, May 12, 1876; *Public Ledger*, May 11, 1876; *Baltimore Weekly American*, May 13, 1876; Brown, *Year of the Century*, 122–29.

47. Sidney Kirkpatrick, *The Revenge of Thomas Eakins* (Binghamton, NY: Vail-Ballou Press, 2006), 191–97; William Howe Downes, *The Life and Works of Winslow Homer* (Boston: Houghton Mifflin, 1911), 81–82.

48. Samuel T. Pickard, *Life and Letters of John Greenleaf Whittier*, 2 vols. (London: Samson Low, Marston & Co., 1895), 2:613; Howells, "A Sennight of the Centennial," *Atlantic Monthly* 38 (1876): 96, 107; Brown, *Year of the Century*, 43–45.

49. Randel, *Centennial*, 241, 244, 246; Brown, *Year of the Century*, 169.

50. Brown, *Year of the Century*, 2; Schlereth, *Victorian America*, 1. In contrast, the Paris Exhibition of 1878 drew 16 million people; Schwarcz, *Emperor's Beard*, 287. Randel, *Centennial*, 188, estimates one in fifteen Americans visited.

51. Emerson quoted in Randel, *Centennial*, 352; Herbert S. Gorman, *A Victorian American: Henry Wadsworth Longfellow* (New York: Doran, 1926), 334; Makato quoted in *Harper's Weekly*, July 15, 1876, p. 579; Brown, *Year of the Century*, 131n.

52. John Leng, *America in 1876: Pencillings During a Tour in the Centennial Year* (Dundee, Scotland: Dundee Advertiser, 1877), 28–30.

53. Schlereth, *Victorian America*, 5; Randel, *Centennial*, 180, 295; James Blaine Walker, *The Epic of American Industry* (New York: Harper & Brothers, 1949), 272–76; Brown, *Year of the Century*, 132–33; Randel, *Centennial*, 294; McCabe, *Illustrated History of the Centennial Exhibition*.

54. Williams, *Dom Pedro the Magnanimous*, 210–11; Catherine Mackenzie, *Alexander Graham Bell: The Man Who Contracted Space* (Boston: Houghton Mifflin, 1928), 122–24, 158; Barman, *Citizen Emperor*, 280, 479n20; Walker, *Epic of American Industry*, 261–69.

55. George Augustus Sala, *America Revisited: From the Bay of New York to the Gulf of Mexico, and From Lake Michigan to the Pacific*, 3d ed., 2 vols. (London: Vizetelly & Co., 1883), 1:126, 129; Schlereth, *Victorian America*, 2, 5; Randel, *Centennial*, 289; Jacques Offenbach, *Orpheus in America: Offenbach's Diary of His Journey to the New World*, trans. Lander MacClintock (Bloomington: Indiana University Press, 1957), 95; Vivian, *Notes of a Tour*, 248.

56. Campbell, *White and Black*, 222.

57. "Pharasaisme americain," Leclercq, *Un Ete en Amerique*, 72. See also Campbell, *White and Black*, 384.

58. Campbell, *White and Black*, 243.

59. Offenbach, *Orpheus in America*, 129.

60. Leng, *America in 1876*, 318.

61. Brown, *Year of the Century*, 141–43. Women were generally not allowed in most

theaters and bars, and often were consigned to separate rooms in restaurants, while large hotels had side entrances for women so that they would not have to mingle among men in the lobby. George Sala saw this conduct as "thoughtful courtesy" and a "well-deserved homage" to women, assuming that men like himself were so awful that women should not come near them except through marriage. Sala, *America Revisited*, 1:171. Sir George Campbell also noticed this separation of the genders, but was shocked that it did not extend to the sleeping cars on trains; Campbell, *White and Black*, 218.

62. R. David Arkush and Leo O. Lee, ed. and trans., *Land Without Ghosts: Chinese Impressions of America from the Mid-Nineteenth Century to the Present* (Berkeley: University of California Press, 1989), 42–44. See also Campbell, *White and Black*, 29.

63. Friedrich Ratzel, *Sketches of Urban and Cultural Life in North America*, trans. and ed. Stewart A. Stehlin (New Brunswick, NJ: Rutgers University Press, 1988), 188–89; M. Philips Price, *America After Sixty Years: The Travel Diaries of Two Generations of Englishmen* (London: Allen & Unwin, 1936), 54–55; Paul Toutain, *Un Français en Amérique: Yankees, Indiens, Mormons* (Paris: Plon, 1876), 64–68.

64. Elizabeth Cady Stanton et al., eds., *History of Woman Suffrage*, 6 vols. (Rochester, NY: Susan B. Anthony, 1881–1922), 3:18–20; Brown, *Year of the Century*, 143–45.

65. "Not Yet Named," *Inter Ocean* (Chicago), June 16, 1876; "The Political Pot," *St. Louis Globe-Democrat*, June 25, 1876, p. 3; "The Women's Memorial," *Daily Arkansas Gazette*, June 30, 1876.

66. "Characteristics of the International Fair," *Atlantic Monthly* 38 (1876): 357; Randel, *Centennial*, 301; McCabe, *Illustrated History of the Centennial Exhibition*, 671.

67. Stanton et al., *History of Woman Suffrage*, 3:29–34.

68. William Saunders, *Through the Light Continent; or, the United States in 1877–78* (London: Cassell, Petter, and Galpin, 1879), 393; Lady Duffus Hardy [Mary McDowell], *Through Cities and Prairie Lands: Sketches of an American Tour* (New York: Worthington, 1881), 168; Randel, *Centennial*, 59; Toutain, *Un Français en Amérique*.

69. James D. Richardson, comp., *A Compilation of the Messages and Papers of the Presidents, 1789–1902*, 10 vols. (New York: Bureau of National Literature and Art, 1903), 10:4364–65, 4367.

70. See, for example, "Louisiana . . . A Suppressed Volcano," *Chicago Tribune*, September 18, 1876, p. 2; "A Volcano in Pennsylvania," *Chicago Tribune*, January 8, 1877, p. 8; "a volcano which may yet bring ruin on their households," from "The 'Color Line' Policy," *New York Times*, January 2, 1877, p. 4; "a political volcano," from "A Republic in Chaos," *New York Times*, January 30, 1877, p. 4.

71. *Philadelphia Inquirer*, December 30, 1876; *Baltimore Sun*, December 30, 1876. Since December 31, 1876, fell on a Sunday, the final issue of the year for most papers was December 30; weekly papers tended to come out on Wednesday or Friday.

72. *New York Sun*, January 13, 1877.

73. "Poor Men's Day at the Exhibition," *Philadelphia Inquirer*, September 8, 1876, quoted in Kevin Kenny, *Making Sense of the Molly Maguires* (New York: Oxford University Press, 1998), 244; Samuel Gompers, *Seventy Years of Life and Labour: An Autobiography* (New York: E.P. Dutton, 1925), 138.

74. *Wheeling Daily Register*, December 30, 1876; *Macon Weekly Telegraph*, December 26, 1876; *Duluth Weekly Tribune*, December 29, 1876; *Salt Lake Weekly Tribune*, December 30, 1876; *Pomeroy's Democrat*, December 30, 1876. See also the *Mobile Register*, December 12, 1876; "The Tramp," *Daily Arkansas Gazette* (Little Rock), January 24, 1877. On the press's obsession with the illusory idea that Grant sought a third term, see

Mark Wahlgren Summers, *The Press Gang: Newspapers and Politics, 1865–1878* (Chapel Hill: University of North Carolina Press, 1994), 256–78.

75. Quoted in the *Wheeling Daily Register*, December 30, 1876.

76. *Pomeroy's Democrat*, December 30, 1876.

Chapter 2: Seeking White Unity

1. Samuel Gompers, *Seventy Years of Life and Labour: An Autobiography* (New York: E.P. Dutton, 1925), 138.

2. I would like to thank Nell Irvin Painter for bringing Henry Adams's testimony to my attention. His entire list is reprinted in Senate Report no. 693, 46th Cong., 2nd sess., *Report and Testimony of the Select Committee of the United States Senate to Investigate the Causes of the Removal of the Negroes from the Southern States to the Northern States*, 3 parts (Washington, DC: GPO, 1880), pt. 2:192–211; examples from 201, 204–5, 208.

3. *Report and Testimony of the Select Committee . . . to Investigate the Causes of the Removal of the Negroes*, pt. 2:127.

4. Ibid., 153–54, 113–14, 127–28.

5. Ibid., 176–92.

6. Ibid., 184–85.

7. Edmund S. Morgan, *American Slavery, American Freedom: The Ordeal of Colonial Virginia* (New York: Norton, 1975); C. Vann Woodward, *The Strange Career of Jim Crow* (New York: Oxford University Press, 1955); Dan T. Carter, *The Politics of Rage: George Wallace, the Origins of the New Conservatism, and the Transformation of American Politics* (New York: Simon & Schuster, 1995).

8. There are numerous histories of the 1876 election, but they focus overwhelmingly on the political maneuvering and very little on the violence of the campaign. Even recent histories give scant attention to the outrageous violations of democratic principles and of the law by Southern Democrats. In one of the classic accounts of the election, Allan Nevins portrayed the contest as a "bracing new wind blowing through the country," since the public turned against corruption. Angrily accusing the Republicans of attempting to "revive the hatreds of the Civil War," Nevins maintained that the election "brought out the essential stuff of the American people," by which he seems to mean something other than the policy of terrorism employed by the Democrats. While acknowledging "the atrocities committed on helpless blacks," Nevins concludes "the whole controversy was ended without the slightest disturbance," and suggests that it may have been wisest to have just counted the white vote. Allan Nevins, *The Emergence of Modern America, 1865–1878* (New York: Macmillan, 1927), 314–17.

9. "Scalawag" is an old Scottish word referring to a rootless scoundrel and was first applied to white Southerners who supported Reconstruction in 1867. "Carpetbagger" identified Northerners who came south after the war, the term being based on their cheap luggage, with the implication that they held no other property before arriving and were just passing through. Both terms carried a heavy opprobrium for Southern Democrats. Ted Tunnell, *War, Radicalism, and Race in Louisiana, 1862–1877* (Baton Rouge: Louisiana State University Press, 1984), 138–40; James Alex Baggett, *The Scalawags: Southern Dissenters in the Civil War and Reconstruction* (Baton Rouge: Louisiana State University Press, 2003), 1–2.

10. Edward J. Blum, *Reforging the White Republic: Race, Religion, and American Nationalism, 1865–1898* (Baton Rouge: Louisiana State University Press, 2005), 12–13; Sir

George Campbell, *White and Black: The Outcome of a Visit to the United States* (New York: R. Worthington, 1879), 364. In general, see Eric Foner, *Reconstruction: America's Unfinished Revolution, 1863–1877* (New York: Harper & Row, 1988).

11. Lou Falkner Williams, *The Great South Carolina Ku Klux Klan Trials, 1871–1872* (Athens: University of Georgia Press, 1996); Foner, *Reconstruction*, 425–59; William H. Rehnquist, *Centennial Crisis: The Disputed Election of 1876* (New York: Knopf, 2004), 18.

12. Stephen Budiansky, *The Bloody Shirt: Terror After Appomattox* (New York: Viking, 2008), 221–25; Green B. Raum, *The Existing Conflict Between Republican Government and Southern Oligarchy* (Washington, DC: Greene Printing, 1884), 231–87; Nicholas Lemann, *Redemption: The Last Battle of the Civil War* (New York: Farrar, Straus and Giroux, 2006), 170–80.

13. Foner, *Reconstruction*, 558–63; Mark Wahlgren Summers, *The Press Gang: Newspapers and Politics, 1865–1878* (Chapel Hill: University of North Carolina Press, 1994), 4–6, 47, 191–222; Campbell, *White and Black*, 332.

14. William Gillette, *Retreat from Reconstruction, 1869–1879* (Baton Rouge: Louisiana State University Press, 1979), 312–13.

15. Akerman to John Sherman, June 17, 1876, in Gillette, *Retreat from Reconstruction*, 313.

16. "Funding the National Debt," *Independent Statesman* (Concord, NH), November 2, 1876, p. 34; Gillette, *Retreat from Reconstruction*, 301–2.

17. *New York Times* quoted in Blum, *Reforging the White Republic*, 125–26; Fanueil Hall protest quoted in Jack Beatty, *Age of Betrayal: The Triumph of Money in America, 1865–1900* (New York: Knopf, 2007), 144; Morton Keller, *Affairs of State: Public Life in Late Nineteenth-Century America* (Cambridge, MA: Harvard University Press, 1977), 30, 44, 161; Foner, *Reconstruction*, 554.

18. Foner, *Reconstruction*, 569–70; *U.S. v. Reese* (1876) 92 US 214. The case challenged the right of a Kentucky Democratic election official to refuse to register black voters so long as it was not a federal election, thereby negating the Fifteenth Amendment.

19. Waite quoted in Samuel T. Spear, "The Elective Franchise," *Albany Law Journal* 16 (1877): 27; Gillette, *Retreat from Reconstruction*, 295–97; C. Peter Magrath, *Morrison R. Waite: The Triumph of Character* (New York: Macmillan, 1963), 122–34; Ward E.Y. Elliott, *The Rise of Guardian Democracy: The Supreme Court's Role in Voting Rights Disputes, 1845–1969* (Cambridge, MA: Harvard University Press, 1974), 64–71; Beatty, *Age of Betrayal*, 143; Everette Swinney, "Enforcing the Fifteenth Amendment," *Journal of Southern History* 28 (1962): 208.

20. Ari Hoogenboom, *The Presidency of Rutherford B. Hayes* (Lawrence: University Press of Kansas, 1988), 6–8; Mark Twain and Charles Dudley Warner, *The Gilded Age* (Hartford: American Publishing Co., 1874); John De Forest, *Honest John Vane* (New Haven: Richmond & Patten, 1875); De Forest, *Playing the Mischief* (New York: Harper & Brothers, 1875); Edmund Wilson, *Patriotic Gore: Studies in the Literature of the American Civil War* (New York: Oxford University Press, 1962), 709–14.

21. Carl Schurz to B.B. Cahoon, March 3, 1876, and "Address to the People," May 16, 1876, in *Speeches, Correspondence and Political Papers of Carl Schurz*, 6 vols., ed. Frederic Bancroft (New York: G.P. Putnam's Sons, 1913), 3:222, 248; "Mark Twain in Politics," *Boston Daily Advertiser*, October 3, 1876.

22. Hoogenboom, *Presidency of Hayes*, 260, 262.

23. John W. Blassingame and John R. McKivigan, eds., *The Frederick Douglass Papers: Series One: Speeches, Debates, and Interviews*, 5 vols. (New Haven: Yale University Press,

1979–1992), 4:441; "Hayes' Manifesto," *Daily Rocky Mountain* News (Denver), July 13, 1876; *Cincinnati Commercial*, July 10, 1876; *Cincinnati Commercial*, July 19, 1876; *Cincinnati Commercial*, September 2, 1876; "Political," *Milwaukee Daily Sentinel*, July 10, 1876; "Pith of the Press," *Milwaukee Daily Sentinel*, July 24, 1876, p. 4; "Sound Sense," *St. Louis Globe-Democrat*, July 10, 1876; "Notes and Opinions," *Galveston Daily News*, July 14, 1876; "Notes and Opinions," *Galveston Daily News*, July 18, 1876; "Gov. Hayes' Letter of Acceptance," *Southwestern Advocate* (New Orleans), July 20, 1876; "Political Notes," *Inter Ocean* (Chicago), July 22, 1876, p. 2; Republican National Convention, *Official Proceedings of the National Republican Conventions of 1868, 1872, 1876 and 1880* (Minneapolis: Charles W. Johnson, 1903), 234, 293, 334–35. Many delegates at the convention attempted to raise the issue of Democratic conduct; ibid., 236, 248, 252, 290–91, 382, 414–15

24. Blassingame and McKivigan, *Frederick Douglass Papers*, 4:442; *Cincinnati Commercial*, June 15, 1876; Gillette, *Retreat from Reconstruction*, 304.

25. Hoogenboom, *Presidency of Hayes*, 265; Alexander C. Flick, *Samuel Jones Tilden: A Study in Political Sagacity* (New York: Dodd, Mead & Co., 1939), 255–78, 280–86, 291, 303–4.

26. Most observers predicted a close election, leading the Republicans to push Colorado into statehood by August 1876, just in time to pick up its three electoral votes in the presidential election. William Peirce Randel, *Centennial: American Life in 1876* (Philadelphia: Chilton Books, 1969), 116; Roy Morris Jr., *Fraud of the Century: Rutherford B. Hayes, Samuel Tilden, and the Stolen Election of 1876* (New York: Simon & Schuster, 2003), 155–56; "Republican Victory in Colorado Confirmed," *St. Louis Globe-Democrat*, October 9, 1876; Flick, *Samuel Jones Tilden*, 297–304, 315–17 (quote, 299).

27. Keith Ian Polakoff, *The Politics of Inertia: The Election of 1876 and the End of Reconstruction* (Baton Rouge: Louisiana State University Press, 1973), 116–26; Summers, *Press Gang*, 301–2; Hoogenboom, *Presidency of Hayes*, 266.

28. Hoogenboom, *Presidency of Hayes*, 267.

29. Ibid., 267 ("danger"), 269 (Nordhoff); letter to Blaine quoted in Gillette, *Retreat from Reconstruction*, 316; Douglass to Chandler, in Philip S. Foner, ed., *Life and Writings of Frederick Douglass*, 5 vols. (New York: International Publishers, 1950–1955), 4:536n42. I have located more than 400 articles written during the election that reference this fear of a "Solid South." See especially Redfield's articles in the *Cincinnati Commercial*, August 3 and December 23, 1876; "The 'Solid South,'" *North American* (Philadelphia), August 22, 1876; "The Southern Question," *St. Louis Globe-Democrat*, September 12, 1876, p. 3; "The Solid South," *St. Louis Globe-Democrat*, October 2, 1876, p. 4; "The Solid South," *Galveston Daily News*, October 4, 1876; "What a Solid South Implies," *Bangor Daily Whig & Courier*, October 9, 1876; "The 'Solid South,'" *Inter Ocean* (Chicago), October 17, 1876; "Fears of a 'Solid South,'" *Georgia Weekly Telegraph and Georgia Journal & Messenger* (Macon), October 17, 1876; Gillette, *Retreat from Reconstruction*, 321.

30. Flick, *Samuel Jones Tilden*, 288–89, 301–2, 307–8. Traditional histories of the 1876 election portray reform as the only significant issue, avoiding the question of "home rule" versus "the Solid South," as well as economic issues. Flick, for instance, maintained that Americans cared most deeply about reform in 1876; ibid., 332–33.

31. Hoogenboom, *Presidency of Hayes*, 270.

32. Ari Hoogenboom, *Rutherford B. Hayes: Warrior and President* (Lawrence: University Press of Kansas, 1995), 259 (quote); Hoogenboom, *Presidency of Hayes*, 272; Polakoff,

Politics of Inertia, 197–98; Flick, *Samuel Jones Tilden,* 307–14; Polakoff, *Politics of Inertia,* 116–18; *Harper's Weekly,* July 15, 1876; *Harper's Weekly,* August 19, 1876; "Tilden a Secessionist," *Inter Ocean* (Chicago), July 25, 1876, p. 4. On the Mississippi election of 1875, see Vernon L. Wharton, *The Negro in Mississippi, 1865–1890* (Chapel Hill: University of North Carolina Press, 1947), 182–90; William C. Harris, *The Day of the Carpetbagger: Republican Reconstruction in Mississippi* (Baton Rouge: Louisiana State University Press, 1979), 670–96; Foner, *Reconstruction,* 558–63.

33. Quoted in "Political Miscellany," *Milwaukee Daily Sentinel,* October 10, 1876, p. 3; *Lowell Daily Citizen,* November 6, 1876; Gillette, *Retreat from Reconstruction,* 314.

34. Quoted in "A Terrible Indictment," *Bangor Daily Whig & Courier,* August 10, 1876, which identifies the source as the *Augusta Constitutionalist;* Richard Zuczek, *State of Rebellion: Reconstruction in South Carolina* (Columbia: University of South Carolina Press, 1996), 168.

35. *Opelousas Courier,* quoted in Otis A. Singletary, *Negro Militia and Reconstruction* (New York: McGraw-Hill, 1963), 135; Zuczek, *State of Rebellion,* 169–70; Francis Butler Simkins and Robert H. Woody, *South Carolina during Reconstruction* (Chapel Hill: University of North Carolina Press, 1932), 501.

36. Senate Report no. 527, 44th Cong., 1st sess., *Mississippi in 1875: Report of the Select Committee to Inquire into the Mississippi Election of 1875,* 2 vols. (Washington, DC: GPO, 1876), 1:xiv, xx–xxii; Singletary, *Negro Militia,* 131 (quote), 136; Gillette, *Retreat from Reconstruction,* 316; testimony of Jerry Thornton Moore, Edward Dunbar, L.L. Guffin, Alexander S. Richardson, Cornelius Arnold, and David Graham, Senate Miscellaneous Document no. 48, 44th Cong., 2nd sess., *South Carolina in 1876: Testimony as to the Denial of the Elective Franchise in South Carolina at the Elections of 1875 and 1876,* 3 vols. (Washington, DC: GPO, 1877), 1:11–15, 19, 22–26, 315–20, 450–52, 456–59, 464–67, 509–11. Wealthy whites often bought firearms for the gun clubs; for instance, the White League in New Orleans had two thousand members, two-thirds of whom were armed with pistols and Belgian muskets purchased in New York. They also had two cannon. Singletary, *Negro Militia,* 136.

37. Zuczek, *State of Rebellion,* 168, 170–73, 190; Francis Butler Simkins, *Pitchfork Ben Tillman: South Carolinian* (Baton Rouge: Louisiana State University Press, 1944), 59–60; Gillette, *Retreat from Reconstruction,* 311; *Augusta Constitutionalist,* September 19, 1876; *Atlanta Constitution,* October 18, 1876.

38. Singletary, *Negro Militia,* 114–128; J.A. Sharp, "The Downfall of the Radicals in Tennessee," *East Tennessee Historical Society's Publications,* no. 5 (1933): 108; Ella Lonn, *Reconstruction in Louisiana after 1868* (Gloucester, MA: P. Smith, 1967), 67; James W. Garner, *Reconstruction in Mississippi* (Baton Rouge: Louisiana State University Press, 1968), 297, 328, 384, 411; Joseph Hamilton, *Reconstruction in North Carolina* (Gloucester, MA: P. Smith, 1964), 531, 559; Ramsdell, *Reconstruction in Texas,* 313; Zuczek, *State of Rebellion,* 170–71; Nell Irvin Painter, *Exodusters: Black Migration to Kansas after Reconstruction* (New York: Norton, 1992), 23n13; John G. Fletcher, *Arkansas* (Chapel Hill: University of North Carolina Press, 1947), 218–19; William Watson Davis, *The Civil War and Reconstruction in Florida* (New York: Longmans, Green & Co., 1913), 566–70; Alfred B. Williams, *Hampton and his Red Shirts: South Carolina's Deliverance in 1876* (Freeport, NY: Books for Libraries Press, 1970), 224–27; Simkins, *Pitchfork Ben Tillman,* 60–61; testimony of Jesse Jones, *South Carolina in 1876,* 1:857–58; testimony of H.P. Hurst, *Mississippi in 1875,* 1:95–99; Benjamin S. Johnson, "The Brooks-Baxter War," *Publications of the Arkansas Historical Association* 2 (1908): 122–73.

39. Zuczek, *State of Rebellion*, 168, 171–72, 174 (quote); Simkins, *Pitchfork Ben Tillman*, 64–65; Painter, *Exodusters*, 101; Singletary, *Negro Militia*, 118, 122–27; Wharton, *Negro in Mississippi*, 188–90; Garner, *Reconstruction in Mississippi*, 374; testimony of Henry Mays, *South Carolina in 1876*, 1:31–34; Gillette, *Retreat from Reconstruction*, 295–97, 312; Hamilton, *Reconstruction in North Carolina*, 470.

40. Randel, *Centennial*, 254; Zuczek, *State of Rebellion*, 166–68, 172, 175; Gillette, *Retreat from Reconstruction*, 312; Hoogenboom, *Presidency of Hayes*, 20–21; Singletary, *Negro Militia*, 122–27; John S. Reynolds, *Reconstruction in South Carolina, 1865–1877* (Columbia, SC: State Co., 1905), 184–90, 201, 305, 311–13; Simkins and Woody, *South Carolina during Reconstruction*, 444; Powell Clayton, *The Aftermath of the Civil War in Arkansas* (New York: Neale, 1915), 99–102; Hamilton, *Reconstruction in North Carolina*, 468–72; Louis F. Post, "A Carpetbagger in South Carolina," *Journal of Negro History* 10 (1925): 61; John A. Leland, *A Voice from South Carolina* (Charleston, SC: Walker, Evans & Cogswell, 1879), 51–74, 134; testimony of Margaret Ann Caldwell, *Mississippi in 1875*, 1:435–40.

41. Where Dee Brown treats Butler as a hero, Singletary identifies him as the leader of a "deliberately incited race riot" intent "to strike terror." Singletary, *Negro Militia*, 139–40; Dee Brown, *The Year of the Century: 1876* (New York: Charles Scribner's Sons, 1966), 269–71, 274; Zuczek, *State of Rebellion*, 163–65; Simkins and Woody, *South Carolina during Reconstruction*, 487; Joel Williamson, *After Slavery: The Negro in South Carolina During Reconstruction* (Chapel Hill: University of North Carolina Press, 1965), 267–69; Raum, *Existing Conflict*, 322–25; Simkins, *Pitchfork Ben Tillman*, 61–63; Rehnquist, *Centennial Crisis*, 108.

42. Democrats blamed the victims. So convincing was Southern white propaganda that an historian writing nearly a century later would blame the town's black "thieves and criminals" for the confrontation. Brown, *Year of the Century*, 273–74; *Augusta Constitutionalist*, July 14, 1876; Foner, *Reconstruction*, 570–72 (quote, 572); Gillette, *Retreat from Reconstruction*, 308; Summers, *Press Gang*, 201–2.

43. "The Old Rebel Spirit," *New York Times*, July 14, 1876. See also "Southern Troubles," *St. Louis Globe-Democrat*, August 3, 1876, p. 4; *Boston Journal*, September 11, 1876; testimony of Edward Dunbar and D.L. Adams, *South Carolina in 1876*, 1:22–42; Hoogenboom, *Presidency of Hayes*, 66–73; Zuczek, *State of Rebellion*, 173; Gillette, *Retreat from Reconstruction*, 307–9, 316.

44. Grant to Chamberlain, in Walter Allen, *Governor Chamberlain's Administration in South Carolina* (New York: G.P. Putnam's Sons, 1888), 325–26; Randel, *Centennial*, 253; "Wade Hampton's Canvass," *New York Times*, October 13, 1876; "The Troops in South Carolina," *New York Times*, October 15, 1876; "The Rebels in Power" and "The Terror in the South," *New York Times*, October 16, 1876; Singletary, *Negro Militia*, 140–41; Benjamin R. Tillman, *The Struggles of '76: How South Carolina Was Delivered from Carpetbag and Negro Rule* (n.p., n.d.), 15; Reynolds, *Reconstruction in South Carolina*, 344–47; Anderson (SC) *Intelligencer*, July 13, 1876; *South Carolina in 1876*, 1:3–102; Singletary, *Negro Militia*, 143; Zuczek, *State of Rebellion*, 177–79; proclamation in *Appleton's Annual Cyclopædia and Register of Important Events of the Year 1876* (New York: D. Appleton & Co., 1877), 721; Garner, *Reconstruction in Mississippi*, 378; Simkins and Woody, *South Carolina during Reconstruction*, 509. Chamberlain wrote bitterly about these matters years later in "Reconstruction in South Carolina," *Atlantic Monthly* 87 (1904): 473–84.

45. Gillette, *Retreat from Reconstruction*, 317 (quote); Zuczek, *State of Rebellion*, 165, 179.

46. Many later historians, such as Dee Brown, continued to accept the Democrats' version of events; Brown, *Year of the Century*, 279–80. In contrast, see Mark M. Smith, "'All Is Quiet in Our Hellish County': Facts, Fiction, Politics, and Race—the Ellenton Riot of 1876," *South Carolina Historical Magazine* 95 (1994): 142–55; Zuczek, *State of Rebellion*, 176; Raum, *Existing Conflict*, 325–32; Simkins, *Pitchfork Ben Tillman*, 66; *South Carolina in 1876*, 1:103–43.

47. Robert M. Utley, *Lone Star Justice: The First Century of the Texas Rangers* (New York: Oxford University Press, 2002), 156–57. The vicious nature of the Texas Ku Klux Klan was legendary; in addition to the notorious mass murder at Waco in 1868, in which they killed thirteen freedmen, they routinely beat and raped women and girls, not hesitating to steal the change from the pockets of their victims. Carolyn Ashbaugh, *Lucy Parsons: American Revolutionary* (Chicago: Charles Kerr, 1976), 14–15.

48. Utley, *Lone Star Justice*, 157; James B. Gillett, *Six Years with the Texas Rangers, 1875 to 1881*, ed. Milo M. Quaife (New Haven: Yale University Press, 1925), 69–77; C.L. Sonnichsen, *Ten Texas Feuds* (Albuquerque: University of New Mexico Press, 1957), 87–107; Walter Prescott Webb, *The Texas Rangers: A Century of Frontier Defense* (Boston: Houghton Mifflin, 1935), 325–28.

49. *Charleston News and Courier*, May 8, 1876, quoted in Allen, *Governor Chamberlain's Administration*, 275. As Mark Summers wrote, the bias of the *Charleston News and Courier* was so intense that "its support for the Democratic ticket could not be separated from its reports." Summers, *Press Gang*, 219.

50. Budiansky, *Bloody Shirt*, 221 (emphasis in original).

51. Quoted in Zuczek, *State of Rebellion*, 167; Singletary, *Negro Militia*, 133, 139; Simkins and Woody, *South Carolina during Reconstruction*, 564–69. Francis Butler Simkins called the Shotgun Plan a "hard necessity"; Simkins, *Pitchfork Ben Tillman*, 56. The complete plan is in Sheppard, *Red Shirts Remembered*, 47–50.

52. Tillman, *Struggles of '76*, 17; Singletary, *Negro Militia*, 142. See also testimony of William A. Hayne, *South Carolina in 1876*, 2:169; John R. Lynch, *The Facts of Reconstruction* (New York: Neale, 1913) 137–46; Henry W. Warren, *Reminiscences of a Mississippi Carpet-Bagger* (Holden, MA: for the author, 1914), 68–71; Allen, *Governor Chamberlain's Administration*, 365–427; testimony of W.B. Cunningham, *Mississippi in 1875*, 2:836–37.

53. "Must be exterminated": *Vicksburg Herald*, quoted in "The Reign of Hate," *Inter Ocean* (Chicago), September 2, 1874; Wallace quoted in Zuczek, *State of Rebellion*, 172. For other acts of racial violence in the 1876 election, see "A Warning to Corrupt and Dishonest County Officers," *Hinds County Gazette* (Raymond, MS), September 9, 1874; Melinda M. Hennessey, "Racial Violence during Reconstruction: The 1876 Riots in Charleston and Cainhoy," *South Carolina Historical Magazine* 86 (1985): 100–12; Orville V. Burton, "Race and Reconstruction in Edgefield County, South Carolina," *Journal of Social History* 12 (1978): 31–56; Randel, *Centennial*, 254; Budiansky, *Bloody Shirt*, 224–48; Zuczek, *State of Rebellion*, 177–78.

54. Singletary, *Negro Militia*, 143–44; Zuczek, *State of Rebellion*, 197.

55. Edward McPherson, *A Hand-Book of Politics for 1876* (Washington, DC: Solomons & Chapman, 1876), 256. See also Gillette, *Retreat from Reconstruction*, 317–18; Zuczek, *State of Rebellion*, 178–79; "South Carolina," *San Francisco Daily Evening Bulletin*, October 18, 1876; "The Prostrate State," *Galveston Daily News*, October 18, 1876; "The New Rebellion," *Inter Ocean* (Chicago), October 19, 1876, p. 4; *Cincinnati Commercial*, October 23, 1876; "Grant's Southern Campaign," *Hinds County Gazette* (Raymond, MS), October 25, 1876.

56. Zuczek, *State of Rebellion*, 173–74; *Spartanburg Herald*, August 23, 1876; *Charleston News and Courier*, September 18, 1876; *Charleston News and Courier*, October 2, 1876; *Charleston News and Courier*, October 3, 1876; *Charleston News and Courier*, October 17, 1876; *Charleston News and Courier*, October 20, 1876.

57. Hoogenboom, *Rutherford B. Hayes*, 308, 315. As William Gillette wrote about the vote in Louisiana, "Intimidation, irregularities, and murders of Republicans there were so prevalent and so publicized that they popularized the word 'bulldoze,' and the validity of the outcome would of course be highly questionable." Gillette, *Retreat from Reconstruction*, 315.

58. *Cincinnati Commercial*, November 10, 1876 (story dated November 7); *Cincinnati Commercial*, September 15, 1876; *Cincinnati Commercial*, November 6, 1876; Gillette, *Retreat from Reconstruction*, 317–20. Michael Holt feels that the contested election made no difference as far as the end of Reconstruction is concerned—that the Republicans would have behaved the same regardless of the election results; Michael F. Holt, *By One Vote: The Disputed Election of 1876* (Lawrence: University Press of Kansas, 2008), 246–47.

59. *Cincinnati Commercial*, March 6, 1877; *Cincinnati Commercial*, March 26, 1877; *Springfield Republican*, February 16, 1877; Gillette, *Retreat from Reconstruction*, 320–32, 423n63; J.F. Cleveland, comp., *Tribune Almanac and Political Register for 1877* (New York: New York Tribune, 1877), 46–52; Brown, *Year of the Century*, 288. Many historians believe that Tilden won the election, holding that the Republicans alone stole the election through "the post-election abuses in Florida and Louisiana." Morris, *Fraud of the Century*, 249. This perspective requires full faith in the official tabulation of votes in the South, which in turn necessitates ignoring the efforts of Democrats to suppress the Republican vote. Officially, the results were astoundingly one-sided in several Southern states, the Democrats receiving 72 percent of the Georgia vote, 70 percent in Texas, and 68 percent in Mississippi. Holt, *By One Vote*, 167. Given that the last state had a black majority and Georgia was about 40 percent black, these results surely indicate some finagling with the results. The turnout for the Democrats was enormous, exceeding 100 percent in many Southern precincts. Most scholars present figures such as these without noting the degree to which they were the result of violence and fraud. While Holt admits that "some fraction of those recorded votes, and not just in the South, was undoubtedly fraudulent," he maintains that "Republicans' Reconstruction programs also best explain the breathtaking jump in white support for Democrats in the South." Holt, *By One Vote*, 244–45.

60. Hoogenboom, *Rutherford B. Hayes*, 272–73.

61. Ibid., 274; Polakoff, *Politics of Inertia*, 199–202; Jerome L. Sernstein, ed., "The Sickles Memorandum: Another Look at the Hayes-Tilden Election-Night Conspiracy," *Journal of Southern History* 32 (1966): 342–57.

62. *New York Tribune*, November 8, 1876; *New York Sun*, November 8, 1876; *New York Evening Post*, November 8, 1876; *New York Times*, November 8, 1876; *New York Herald*, November 8, 1876; Hoogenboom, *Rutherford B. Hayes*, 275; Polakoff, *Politics of Inertia*, 202–4; Sernstein, "Sickles Memorandum," 342–45. Reid later tried to take all the credit for motivating the Republicans to act on the morning of November 11; Flick, *Samuel Jones Tilden*, 324–26; Elmer Davis, *History of the New York Times, 1851–1921* (New York: New York Times, 1921), 131–36.

63. Hoogenboom, *Rutherford B. Hayes*, 276; Flick, *Samuel Jones Tilden*, 327.

64. Gillette, *Retreat from Reconstruction*, 314–15; *Cincinnati Commercial*, December 30, 1876, March 3, 1877.

65. Flick, *Samuel Jones Tilden*, 328, 336–44; Hoogenboom, *Rutherford B. Hayes*, 278; Rehnquist, *Centennial Crisis*, 103; Paul Leland Haworth, *The Hayes-Tilden Disputed Presidential Election of 1876* (Cleveland: Burrows Brothers, 1906), 111–12, 318; James Ford Rhodes, *History of the United States from the Compromise of 1850 to the Final Restoration of Home Rule at the South in 1877*, 7 vols. (New York: Macmillan, 1920), 7:231; Randel, *Centennial*, 231–32; Polakoff, *Politics of Inertia*, 210–14. The efforts of Tilden's nephew to buy off the Florida and Louisiana election boards became national scandals in 1878; Summers, *Press Gang*, 308; Flick, *Samuel Jones Tilden*, 429–42.

66. Rehnquist, *Centennial Crisis*, 107–8; Hoogenboom, *Rutherford B. Hayes*, 277–78; Polakoff, *Politics of Inertia*, 210–14. Georgia and Alabama had nearly equal proportions of black and white voters.

67. Zuczek, *State of Rebellion*, 194–97; Hoogenboom, *Rutherford B. Hayes*, 278; Polakoff, *Politics of Inertia*, 219–20; Brown, *Year of the Century*, 326–27. By acting quickly, the election board undermined the Democrats' plan of having the state supreme court issue an injunction. Furious, the court fined the board's members $1,500 and sentenced them all to jail. Rehnquist, *Centennial Crisis*, 108–9.

68. Gillette, *Retreat from Reconstruction*, 424n80; see Redfield's reporting in *Cincinnati Commercial*, November 25, November 27, December 2, December 4, December 30, 1876, February 18, 1877, and March 6, 1877. Haworth made much the same point about the Florida election: "While a *fair count* of the votes cast in the state of Florida might have resulted in a small majority for Tilden, a *free election* would with far greater certainty have resulted in a substantial majority for Hayes." Haworth, *Hayes-Tilden Disputed Presidential Election*, 76. After studying the Louisiana election returns closely, Haworth came to the conclusion that a fair election in that state would have produced a Republican majority of between five thousand and fifteen thousand votes; ibid., 116–21.

69. Hoogenboom, *Rutherford B. Hayes*, 277–79; Polakoff, *Politics of Inertia*, 214–19; Haworth, *Hayes-Tilden Disputed Presidential Election*, 64–80; Flick, *Samuel Jones Tilden*, 344–46; Jerrell H. Shofner, "Fraud and Intimidation: The Florida Election of 1876," *Florida Historical Quarterly* 42 (1964): 321–30; Rehnquist, *Centennial Crisis*, 105–6.

70. Hoogenboom, *Rutherford B. Hayes*, 279–80; Polakoff, *Politics of Inertia*, 220–41; Rehnquist, *Centennial Crisis*, 111; Flick, *Samuel Jones Tilden*, 348–49. One of Hayes's Oregon electors, John W. Watts, served as a postmaster. Since Article 2, Section 1 of the Constitution forbids a federal officeholder from serving as a presidential elector, Watts immediately resigned as postmaster upon his election—as was often done. Democratic Party chairman Abram Hewitt wired Oregon's Democratic governor suggesting that he disqualify Watts and replace him with a Democrat. Though no law supported this action, Oregon governor LaFayette Grover did as requested, throwing the election back to Tilden by one vote. Rehnquist, *Centennial Crisis*, 110–11; Hoogenboom, *Rutherford B. Hayes*, 279; Polakoff, *Politics of Inertia*, 225–27; Flick, *Samuel Jones Tilden*, 349; Allan Nevins, *Abram S. Hewitt* (New York: Harper & Brothers, 1935), 327.

71. Brown, *Year of the Century*, 325; Nevins, *Abram S. Hewitt*, 338–40; Flick, *Samuel Jones Tilden*, 369–73.

72. On the negotiations, which were sometimes conducted in the press, see *New York Herald*, December 3, 1876, in "Hayes' Bid for the Presidency," *Georgia Weekly Telegraph and Georgia Journal & Messenger* (Macon), December 12, 1876; *New York Tribune*, December 4, 1876; "A Carnival of Lies," *Bangor Daily Whig & Courier*, December 5, 1876; Summers, *Press Gang*, 303–4; Hoogenboom, *Rutherford B. Hayes*, 281–84, 288–89, 291, 296; Hoogenboom, *Presidency of Hayes*, 45–50, 60–61, 65; Polakoff, *Politics of Inertia*,

244–45, 290–92, 301–5; Gillette, *Retreat from Reconstruction*, 331; Holt, *By One Vote*, 238–42, 277–78n56; Charles Richard Williams, ed., *Diary and Letters of Rutherford B. Hayes*, 6 vols. (Columbus: Ohio State Archaeological and Historical Society, 1924), 3:417; Flick, *Samuel Jones Tilden*, 332.

73. Flick, *Samuel Jones Tilden*, 330; Hoogenboom, *Rutherford B. Hayes*, 280–84; Polakoff, *Politics of Inertia*, 259; Bancroft, *Speeches, Correspondence and Political Papers of Carl Schurz*, 3:387. Some historians argue that there was no deal involved in Hayes's attaining the presidency, particularly as Reconstruction "was already dead in eight of the eleven former Confederate states" at the time of the election; Holt, *By One Vote*, 277n56.

74. Tilden quoted in Rehnquist, *Centennial Crisis*, 115; Haworth, *Hayes-Tilden Disputed Presidential Election*, 168–203; Flick, *Samuel Jones Tilden*, 365–69, 375. The idea for the commission is generally credited to Republican representative George W. McCrary of Iowa. Flick, *Samuel Jones Tilden*, 365–67; Haworth, *Hayes-Tilden Disputed Presidential Election*, 190–98.

75. *Nashville Weekly American*, January 25, 1877, p. 2; "The Difficulty of a Settlement," *The Nation*, January 4, 1877, p. 4–5; *Washington National Republican*, January 24, 1877, p. 2; *Congressional Record* (1877): 5:799–801, 820–25; Michael Les Benedict, "Southern Democrats in the Crisis of 1876–1877: A Reconsideration of *Reunion and Reaction*," *Journal of Southern History* 46 (1980): 508–11; Rehnquist, *Centennial Crisis*, 115–16; Haworth, *Hayes-Tilden Disputed Presidential Election*, 204–12; Flick, *Samuel Jones Tilden*, 369–76, 382. The House vote was 191 to 86, with 160 Democrats in favor and 17 opposed, and 31 Republicans voting yes compared to 69 opposed. In the Senate, the vote was 47 to 17, with the Democrats voting 26 to 1 in favor, and the Republicans 21 to 16. Haworth, *Hayes-Tilden Disputed Presidential Election*, 210–19. The commission consisted of Senators Thurman (D-OH), Bayard (D-DE), Frelinghuysen (R-NJ), Morton (R-IN), and Edmunds (R-VT); Representatives Payne (D-OH), Hunton (D-VA), Abbott (D-MA), Garfield (R-OH), Hoar (R-MA); and Justices William Strong of Pennsylvania (R), Samuel F. Miller of Iowa (R), Nathan Clifford of Maine (D), Stephen J. Field of California (D), and David Davis of Illinois (Greenback). Thurman retired from the Senate and was replaced by Senator Kernan (D-NY).

76. Tilden quoted in Flick, *Samuel Jones Tilden*, 376; Brown, *Year of the Century*, 333; Nevins, *Abram S. Hewitt*, 361–63; Simpson, "Grant and the Electoral Crisis," 13–15; Hoogenboom, *Rutherford B. Hayes*, 285–86; John Sherman, *Recollections of Forty Years in the House, Senate and Cabinet*, 2 vols. (Chicago: Werner Co., 1895), 1:560–61. David Barry saw the Electoral Commission as a Republican trap into which the Democrats stepped, having been cleverly maneuvered into putting the bill forth. The only Democratic senator to vote against the bill, William Eaton of Connecticut, took the same position at the time. David Barry, *Forty Years in Washington* (1924; New York: Beekman Publishers, 1974), 11. Since the commission was to be evenly divided between Democrats and Republicans except for the independent justice David Davis, everyone assumed that the presidential election would be decided by this one man. Hoogenboom, *Rutherford B. Hayes*, 285; Polakoff, *Politics of Inertia*, 268–75; Barry, *Forty Years in Washington*, 13.

77. "Our Political Drama," *Galveston Daily News*, December 5, 1876; *New York Herald* December 18, 1876; "The Tilden Conspiracy," *Bangor Daily Whig & Courier*, December 19, 1876; Brown, *Year of the Century*, 328–30; Flick, *Samuel Jones Tilden*, 330.

78. *Sunday Capital*, February 18, 1877; "Piatt's Incendiary Talk," *Inter Ocean* (Chicago), February 20, 1877; "Urging Assassination," *Inter Ocean*, February 20, 1877, p. 4; "Inciting to Murder," *Inter Ocean*, February 21, 1877, p. 4; *Cincinnati Enquirer*,

February 22, 1877; *Cincinnati Enquirer*, February 23, 1877; *Cincinnati Enquirer*, February 25, 1877; *Cincinnati Enquirer*, February 28, 1877; *Cincinnati Enquirer*, March 9, 1877; "How the Props Fell Out," *St. Louis Globe-Democrat*, January 12, 1877, p. 3; "Political Mention," *Independent Statesman* (Concord, NH), January 25, 1877, p. 132; *North American* (Philadelphia), February 24, 1877; Summers, *Press Gang*, 299; Rehnquist, *Centennial Crisis*, 114. Nast mocked Piatt's call for blood in a cartoon in *Harper's Weekly*, while the *St. Louis Globe-Democrat* charged him with being "a fierce advocate of assassination." *Bangor Daily Whig & Courier*, February 10, 1877; "Evading the Issue," *St. Louis Globe-Democrat*, February 20, 1877.

79. *Atlanta Constitution*, December 24, 1876; "Ben Hill," *St. Louis Globe-Democrat*, December 29, 1876, p. 4; "Insidious and Devilish," *Georgia Weekly Telegraph and Georgia Journal & Messenger* (Macon), January 9, 1877; *Colorado Springs Gazette*, February 10, 1877, p. 2.

80. Barry, *Forty Years in Washington*, 7–8, 10. For additional fears of, and calls for, civil war, see *Richmond Daily Dispatch*, January 13, 1877, in "The Fighting Phalanx," *Georgia Weekly Telegraph and Georgia Journal & Messenger* (Macon), January 23, 1877; "L.Q.W.," *Louisville Courier-Journal*, April 10, 1877, p. 3; *Atlanta Constitution*, February 22, 1877; Flick, *Samuel Jones Tilden*, 330–32, 339–40, 351, 359, 390–92, 400–401; Nevins, *Abram S. Hewitt*, 330.

81. *New York Herald* quoted in Brown, *Year of the Century*, 321; Sherman quoted in Gillette, *Retreat from Reconstruction*, 331–32; Hoogenboom, *Presidency of Hayes*, 57, 70.

82. Gillette, *Retreat from Reconstruction*, 325–26, 331–32. Any newspaper from this period will give a sense of anxiety and attention to Grant's actions: for example, "General Grant and the Presidential Crisis," *San Francisco Daily Evening Bulletin*, December 1, 1876; "Will Grant Interfere?" *Georgia Weekly Telegraph and Georgia Journal & Messenger* (Macon), December 5, 1876; "Grant's Coup Detat" and "Grant's Latest Outrage," *Georgia Weekly Telegraph and Georgia Journal & Messenger*, December 12, 1876; "Hewitt's Interview with Grant," *Lowell Daily Citizen*, December 9, 1876; "Grant Speaks," *North American* (Philadelphia), December 11, 1876; "Grant to the Front," *Newark Advocate* (Newark, OH), December 15, 1876.

83. Sherman quoted in Nevins, *Abram S. Hewitt*, 380–81; Rehnquist, *Centennial Crisis*, 176.

84. See particularly Charles Fairman, *Five Justices and the Electoral Commission of 1877* (New York: Macmillan, 1988); U.S. Congress, *Electoral Count of 1877: Proceedings of the Electoral Commission and of the Two Houses of Congress in Joint Meeting* (Washington, DC: GPO, 1877).

85. Barry, *Forty Years in Washington*, 13–14; Hoogenboom, *Rutherford B. Hayes*, 293. Hoping, no doubt, to justify his own unorthodox actions in *Bush v. Gore*, Rehnquist concludes, "This outcome was a testament to the ability of the American system of government to improvise solutions to even the most difficult and important problems"; Rehnquist, *Centennial Crisis*, 219.

86. Barry, *Forty Years in Washington*, 8–9, 15.

87. Ibid., 9; Hoogenboom, *Rutherford B. Hayes*, 294; Polakoff, *Politics of Inertia*, 312; Simpson, "Grant and the Electoral Crisis," 18–19.

88. Hoogenboom, *Presidency of Hayes*, 70; Hoogenboom, *Rutherford B. Hayes*, 295.

89. James D. Richardson, ed., *Messages and Papers of the Presidents of the United States*, 20 vols. (New York: Bureau of National Literature, 1897–1918), 10:4394–99. Hayes paraphrased a line of Carl Schurz's in a letter to Hayes, January 25, 1877: "You will serve

that party best by serving the public interest best"; Bancroft, *Speeches, Correspondence and Political Papers of Carl Schurz*, 3:372.

90. Brown, *Year of the Century*, 342.

91. Barry, *Forty Years in Washington*, 25; Hoogenboom, *Rutherford B. Hayes*, 297, 324.

92. *Cincinnati Enquirer*, March 2, 1877, quoted in Flick, *Samuel Jones Tilden*, 396; Hoogenboom, *Rutherford B. Hayes*, 89. Justice Nathan Clifford showed his pique by never setting foot in the White House during Hayes's presidency, while Abram Hewitt refused to meet Hayes. Flick, *Samuel Jones Tilden*, 397; Nevins, *Abram S. Hewitt*, 389.

93. Summers, *Press Gang*, 315.

94. Chamberlain to F.J. Garrison, March 18, 1877, in Gillette, *Retreat from Reconstruction*, 340, 349.

95. *New York Herald*, March 8, 1877; *Indiana Progress* (Indiana, PA), March 15, 1877, p. 4; Gillette, *Retreat from Reconstruction*, 337–38. On Republican dissent over Hayes's cabinet, see Hoogenboom, *Rutherford B. Hayes*, 301–2.

96. Butler to L. Stiger, March 23, 1877, in Gillette, *Retreat from Reconstruction*, 349; Hoogenboom, *Rutherford B. Hayes*, 296–97. Richard W. Thompson of Indiana was named secretary of the navy, Representative George W. McCrary of Iowa secretary of war, and Judge Charles Devans of Massachusetts attorney general.

97. "The President's Tour," *Lowell Daily Citizen*, September 24, 1877; *Atlanta Constitution*, September 22, 1877, p. 2; "The Georgia Press," *Georgia Weekly Telegraph and Georgia Journal & Messenger* (Macon), October 2, 1877; Gillette, *Retreat from Reconstruction*, 348–49; Rayford W. Logan, *The Betrayal of the Negro: From Rutherford B. Hayes to Woodrow Wilson* (New York: Collier Books, 1965), 28; *New York Tribune*, September 23, 1877, p. 4.

98. "Speech of President Hayes at Atlanta," *Independent Statesman* (Concord, NH), September 27, 1877, p. 416. For a Southern view of this speech, see Sue Harper Mims in *Atlanta Constitution*, January 25, 1914. When Hayes spoke in Louisville, he received lusty cheers for his policy from the white section of the audience, while the black members of the audience were "less enthusiastic." *New York Tribune*, September 19, 1877; Logan, *Betrayal of the Negro*, 24. Hayes gave very different kinds of speeches in the North; see *Cincinnati Commercial*, September 8, 1877; *Washington National Republican*, September 15, 1877. Many papers responded angrily to Hayes stating that there was no difference between Union and Confederate soldiers. "The Peace of Surrender," *Bangor Daily Whig & Courier*, September 29, 1877; "President Hayes' Policy, William Lloyd Garrison's Views," *Bangor Daily Whig & Courier*, November 2, 1877; "God Forbid," *Colorado Springs Gazette*, October 20, 1877; *Colorado Springs Gazette*, November 11, 1877, p. 2.

99. Hayes to William Bickham, May 3, 1877, in Williams, *Diary and Letters of Rutherford B. Hayes*, 3:432; ibid., 3:450; Gillette, *Retreat from Reconstruction*, 351. Logan writes that the Southern white leadership took advantage of Hayes's weakness, his "horror of bloodshed." The old Civil War general did not want a repetition of the battles he had survived; Logan, *Betrayal of the Negro*, 29.

100. "Governor Chamberlain's Inaugural," *Bangor Daily Whig & Courier*, December 11, 1876; *Cincinnati Commercial*, February 18, 1877; *Columbia Union-Herald*, January 17, 1877; *Louisville Courier-Journal*, March 2, 1877; *Memphis Appeal*, March 4, 1877; "Boston Calipers," *Bangor Daily Whig & Courier*, March 15, 1877; "Blaine," *Inter Ocean* (Chicago), March 8, 1877, p. 4; Gillette, *Retreat from Reconstruction*, 336–37.

101. "Political," *Inter Ocean* (Chicago), September 11, 1877; "The President Inter-

viewed," *Boston Daily Advertiser,* September 11, 1877; "President Hayes," *North American* (Philadelphia), September 11, 1877; "Hayes' Policy," *Milwaukee Daily Sentinel,* September 11, 1877, p. 4; "Hayes' Solution of the Southern Problem," *St. Louis Globe-Democrat,* September 11, 1877, p. 5; "How the President Came to Adopt His Southern Policy," *Independent Statesman* (Concord, NH), September 13, 1877, p. 396.

102. "Hayes Tells How He Came to Weaken So Terribly," *Daily Rocky Mountain News* (Denver), September 11, 1877; "A New Coalition Invited: The Hayes Republicans Offering to Form a Compact with the Master Class of the South," *Newark Advocate* (Newark, OH), February 23, 1877. The *New York Herald* observed that Hayes was more useful to the white Democrats than Tilden would ever have been as president; *New York Herald,* September 24, 1877, p. 4; Logan, *Betrayal of the Negro,* 28. See also "The New South," *St. Louis Globe-Democrat,* March 26, 1877, p. 4; "Seated," *Inter Ocean* (Chicago), December 1, 1877.

103. Methodists quoted in *Galveston Daily News,* April 12, 1877. See also "Washington," *Inter Ocean* (Chicago), April 5, 1877; "The Southern Policy," *Raleigh Register,* September 20, 1877; Wade quoted in "Southern Policy," *Inter Ocean,* April 23, 1877. Northern Democrats and many Northern newspapers approved of Hayes's policies ending Reconstruction; "Effects of the President's Southern Pacification," *Frank Leslie's Illustrated Newspaper* (New York), July 7, 1877, p. 298; Logan, *Betrayal of the Negro,* 20–21.

104. "Uneventful," *Milwaukee Daily Sentinel,* March 10, 1877; "Washington," *Galveston Daily News,* March 11, 1877; *Charleston News and Courier,* March 12, 1877; "By Telegraph," *Georgia Weekly Telegraph and Georgia Journal & Messenger* (Macon), March 13, 1877; Gillette, *Retreat from Reconstruction,* 339; *New York Herald,* March 7, 1877; *New York Times,* March 11, 1877; *New York Times,* March 15, 1877; *New York Times,* March 26, 1877; *New York World,* March 12, 1877; "Hampton and Nicholls," *Daily Arkansas Gazette* (Little Rock), March 3, 1877; "Packard or No Packard," *Georgia Weekly Telegraph and Georgia Journal & Messenger* (Macon), March 6, 1877; "The New Heads," *Milwaukee Daily Sentinel,* March 13, 1877; "The Louisiana Bother," *San Francisco Daily Evening Bulletin,* March 27, 1877.

105. *Spartanburg Herald,* January 3, 1877; Zuczek, *State of Rebellion,* 198; Simkins and Woody, *South Carolina during Reconstruction,* 535; *Charleston News and Courier,* December 16, 18, 1876; "South Carolina," *Milwaukee Daily Sentinel,* December 27, 1876; "South Carolina," *Milwaukee Daily Sentinel,* January 9, 1877; "Hampton Taxes," *Georgia Weekly Telegraph and Georgia Journal & Messenger* (Macon), January 30, 1877; "Southern News," *Galveston Daily News,* February 10, 1877.

106. *Spartanburg Herald,* January 17, 1877; Zuczek, *State of Rebellion,* 198.

107. *Charleston News and Courier,* April 4, 1877; Zuczek, *State of Rebellion,* 200; Simkins and Woody, *South Carolina during Reconstruction,* 540–41; Hoogenboom, *Rutherford B. Hayes,* 309–10.

108. Williams, *Diary and Letters of Rutherford B. Hayes,* 3:428, 449; *Washington National Republican,* March 16, 1877; Hoogenboom, *Presidency of Hayes,* 64; Gillette, *Retreat from Reconstruction,* 339; "South Carolina," *North American* (Philadelphia), April 4, 1877; "Words of Warning," *Daily Rocky Mountain News* (Denver), April 4, 1777.

109. "National Affairs," *Inter Ocean* (Chicago), April 4, 1877; Chamberlain to Hayes, April 1877, and Hampton to Hayes, March 29 and March 31, 1877, in Gillette, *Retreat from Reconstruction,* 344, 429n27; "Washington," *Daily Arkansas Gazette* (Little Rock), April 10, 1877; "South Carolina," *Daily Arkansas Gazette,* April 25, 1877; "Free Carolina,"

Daily Arkansas Gazette, April 11, 1877; "South Carolina," *Boston Daily Advertiser*, April 11, 1877; "The South Carolina Legislature," *Boston Daily Advertiser*, April 26, 1877; "South Carolina Free!" *Galveston Daily News*, April 11, 1877; "Left in the Lurch," *St. Louis Globe-Democrat*, April 11, 1877, p. 3; "The New South Carolina," *Hinds County Gazette* (Raymond, MS), May 9, 1877; "South Carolina," *Inter Ocean* (Chicago), May 15, 1877, p. 2; *North American* (Philadelphia), May 19, 1877; "The Week," *The Nation*, July 5, 1877, pp. 1–2.

110. "South Carolina," *Southwestern Christian Advocate*, April 19, 1877; Akerman to Chamberlain, April 16, 1877, in Hoogenboom, *Presidency of Hayes*, 68; Zuczek, *State of Rebellion*, 201.

111. Hoogenboom, *Presidency of Hayes*, 65; Hoogenboom, *Rutherford B. Hayes*, 310–12, 314.

112. "Governor Packard's Proclamation," *Bangor Daily Whig & Courier*, April 26, 1877; "Nicholls Is Happy," *Milwaukee Daily Sentinel*, April 25, 1877, p. 4; "Louisiana," *Wisconsin State Register* (Portage), April 28, 1877; "National Notes," *St. Louis Globe-Democrat*, April 21, 1877, p. 4; "Washington," *Inter Ocean* (Chicago), April 24, 1877, p. 5; Gillette, *Retreat from Reconstruction*, 344–45; Hoogenboom, *Rutherford B. Hayes*, 314.

113. Zuczek, *State of Rebellion*, 188; "The Warning," *St. Louis Globe-Democrat*, March 31, 1877, p. 4. The *Globe-Democrat* was a Republican paper despite its name.

114. Richard Hofstadter, *Social Darwinism in American Thought* (New York: George Braziller, 1965), 85–104.

115. Rhodes, *History of the United States*, 6:36–39; "Wade Hampton," *Boston Daily Advertiser*, March 29, 1877.

116. Gillette, *Retreat from Reconstruction*, 302, 345–46; Painter, *Exodusters*, 249.

117. William S. McFeely, *Frederick Douglass* (New York: Norton, 1991), 289, 291; Gillette, *Retreat from Reconstruction*, 338; Foner, *Life and Writings of Frederick Douglass*, 4:101; "Frederick Douglass, United States Marshall for the District of Columbia," *Frank Leslie's Illustrated Newspaper* (New York), April 7, 1877, p. 85; *Inter Ocean* (Chicago), May 5, 1877, p. 4. Oddly, the standard biographies of Hayes fail to mention this aspect of the Douglass appointment.

118. Blassingame and McKivigan, *Frederick Douglass Papers*, 4:454–55, 460, 467. There is some disagreement on the date of the speech. McFeely places it in March 1877 (*Frederick Douglass*, 292), while Blassingame and McKivigan put it in May (*Frederick Douglass Papers*, 4:443).

119. Blassingame and McKivigan, *Frederick Douglass Papers*, 4:443, 618; *Washington Evening Star*, May 11, 1877; *Washington Evening Star*, May 14, 1877; *Washington National Republican*, May 11, 1877; *Washington National Republican*, May 12, 1877; *New York Times*, May 13, 1877; *New York Times*, May 18, 1877; *New York Times*, May 19, 1877; *Christian Recorder*, May 17, 1877; *New York Times*, May 24, 1877; "Blow for Blow," *North American* (Philadelphia), May 14, 1877; "The Capital," *Milwaukee Daily Sentinel*, May 14, 1877, p. 4; "Distinction on Account of Color," *Georgia Weekly Telegraph and Georgia Journal & Messenger* (Macon), May 22, 1877.

120. Douglass quoted in "The Capital," *Milwaukee Daily Sentinel*, May 14, 1877, p. 4; "Quiet in Washington," *New York Times*, June 1, 1877, p. 4. See also *Washington National Republican*, May 13, 1877; *New York Times*, May 13, 1877; *New York Times*, May 18, 1877; *New York Times*, May 19, 1877; *New York Times*, May 31, 1877; *New York Times*, June 1, 1877; *Christian Recorder*, May 17, 1877; *Christian Recorder*, May 24, 1877; Blassingame and McKivigan, *Frederick Douglass Papers*, 4:475, 617–20.

121. "Quiet in Washington," *New York Times*, June 1, 1877, p. 4. Douglass dealt with this controversy in *Life and Times*, 463–70.

122. "Packard's Downfall," *Inter Ocean* (Chicago), April 23, 1877. Some of the best articles on the consequences of Hayes's Southern policies were written by the journalist Grace Greenwood of the *New York Times*; see April 7, April 21, May 5, May 15, May 26, June 2, and June 23, 1877. Her articles circulated widely in other newspapers; for example, "Progress of the Surrender," *Bangor Daily Whig & Courier*, April 24, 1877; "Notes on the New Policy," *Bangor Daily Whig & Courier*, May 8, 1877; "The Forty-Fifth Congress," *Daily Rocky Mountain News* (Denver), May 12, 1877; "Grace Greenwood on the Chisholm Tragedy," *Daily Rocky Mountain News*, May 26, 1877; "Patriotic Words by Grace Greenwood," *Independent Statesman* (Concord, NH), June 7, 1877, p. 282; "The Kemper County, Mississippi, Butchery," *Independent Statesman*, June 28, 1877, p. 308; "Grace Greenwood on Morton," *Daily Arkansas Gazette* (Little Rock), June 10, 1877. There was a great deal of interest in the success of Greenwood and her fellow women journalists Jane Swisshelm and Mary Clemmer Ames; for example, "The Three Graces of Journalism," *Daily Rocky Mountain News*, April 29, 1877.

123. *Philadelphia Weekly Times*, March 24, 1877, Gillette, *Retreat from Reconstruction*, 379. George Alfred Townsend wrote under the pseudonym "Gath." Summers, *Press Gang*, 82–85. For a contrary judgment, see Holt, *By One Vote*, 248, who argues that there was no significant "voter realignment" as a consequence of the election of 1876; rather, the Democrats triumphed by getting more white voters to the poll—and African Americans would have been disenfranchised anyway.

124. Testimony of William Murrell, *Report and Testimony of the Select Committee . . . to Investigate the Causes of the Removal of the Negroes*, pt. 2:521; Painter, *Exodusters*, 166–67.

125. Senate Report no. 855, 45th Cong., 3rd sess., *Report of the United States Senate Committee to Inquire into Alleged Frauds and Violence in the Elections of 1878* (Washington, DC: GPO, 1879), 1:xxviii; Painter, *Exodusters*, 30, 168–69, 99–100; Beatty, *Age of Betrayal*, 213; Gilles Vandal, "The Policy of Violence in Caddo Parish, 1865–1884," *Louisiana History* 32 (1991): 159–82.

126. *Brenham Weekly Banner*, December 20, 1878, quoted in Painter, *Exodusters*, 36–37.

127. Painter, *Exodusters*, 36–39 (quote, 39); *Report of the United States Senate Committee to Inquire into Alleged Frauds and Violence in the Elections of 1878*, 1:140–42.

128. *New Orleans Times*, April 29, 1879; Painter, *Exodusters*, 170, 172–73, 240–41. This tendency to blame black victims started with the 1876 election; for example, "A Merciless Massacre," *Atlanta Constitution*, October 18, 1876. As the *St. Louis Times* said, "In every instance the negroes have been the aggressors; in every instance the white men have acted on the defensive"; quoted in "About Republican Misrule," *Milwaukee Daily Sentinel*, October 2, 1876, p. 4. White Southern historians also tended to blame the blacks for violence; for example, John S. Reynolds, *Reconstruction in South Carolina, 1865–1877* (Columbia, SC: State Co., 1905), 188–90, 344–46, 374–78.

129. Painter, *Exodusters*, 163. Speaking of the 1877 elections, Sir George Campbell wrote, "It is notorious that in the late elections the free exercise of that vote has been abridged and destroyed by violence and fraud." Campbell, *White and Black*, x–xi; see also 225–27, 316–18, 321–22, 330–33, 341–42.

130. Painter, *Exodusters*, 96–99, 160–74 (quote, 164).

131. Leslie H. Fishel Jr., "The African-American Experience," in *The Gilded Age: Essays on the Origins of Modern America*, ed. Charles W. Calhoun (Wilmington, DE: Scholarly

Resources, 2000), 139; quoting Edgar T. Thompson, *Plantation Societies, Race Relations, and the South: The Regimentation of Populations* (Durham, NC: Duke University Press, 1975), 217; Randel, *Centennial*, 257; C. Vann Woodward, *Reunion and Reaction: The Compromise of 1877 and the End of Reconstruction* (Boston: Little, Brown, 1951), 53–54; Paul W. Gates, "Federal Land Policy in the South, 1866–88," *Journal of Southern History* 6 (1940): 303–30.

132. Painter, *Exodusters*, 101.

133. Ibid., 2.

134. Testimony of William Murrell, *Report and Testimony of the Select Committee . . . to Investigate the Causes of the Removal of the Negroes*, pt. 2:517.

135. Painter, *Exodusters*, 39, 134.

136. Ibid., 39, 88–93, 137–45 (quote, 138); Campbell, *White and Black*, 304, 321, 330, 332; George B. Tindall, "The Liberian Exodus of 1878," *South Carolina Historical Magazine* 53 (July 1952): 133–45 (quote, 139); De Santis, "The Republican Party and the Southern Negro," 77.

137. *Report and Testimony of the Select Committee . . . to Investigate the Causes of the Removal of the Negroes*, 2:187; Painter, *Exodusters*, 83–88.

138. *Report and Testimony of the Select Committee . . . to Investigate the Causes of the Removal of the Negroes*, 2:108.

139. Testimony of William Murrell, *Report and Testimony of the Select Committee . . . to Investigate the Causes of the Removal of the Negroes*, 2:529. Murrell had the vain hope that leaving would serve some purpose in Louisiana, for he added, "As I said to one white man, . . . 'It is of no use talking; the best thing the negro can do now is to get out of the State and teach these white people a lesson'" (ibid.). See also Painter, *Exodusters*, 23–24, 92–93.

140. Petition written in Shreveport, September 15, 1877, in *Report and Testimony of the Select Committee . . . to Investigate the Causes of the Removal of the Negroes*, 2:156.

141. Painter, *Exodusters*, 115–16.

142. Ibid., 154–56, 159 (quote), 163n6.

143. Edwards, *New Spirits*, 31; Fishel, "African-American Experience," 139; Painter, *Exodusters*, 147.

144. "Relief for the Refugees," *St. Louis Globe-Democrat*, March 18, 1879, p. 3. See also "Our Colored Visitors," *St. Louis Globe-Democrat*, March 21, 1879, p. 5; "Africa's Hegira," *St. Louis Globe-Democrat*, April 17, 1879, p. 6; New Hampshire Methodists," *Independent Statesman* (Concord, NH), April 17, 1879, p. 226; "By Telegraph," *Georgia Weekly Telegraph and Georgia Journal & Messenger* (Macon), April 22, 1879; "The Exodus," *Southwestern Christian Advocate* (New Orleans), May 29, 1879.

145. Campbell, *White and Black*, 283–84, 187–88, 302, 305–6, 319, 344–45, 357; Painter, *Exodusters*, 44–53.

146. Blassingame and McKivigan, *Frederick Douglass Papers*, 4:468; Edwards, *New Spirits*, 117; Fishel, "African-American Experience," 144; Blum, *Reforging the White Republic*, 83–84, 107; Elizabeth Hyde Botume, *First Days Amongst the Contrabands* (Boston: Lee & Shepard, 1893) 286; Rayford W. Logan, *The Negro in American Life and Thought: The Nadir, 1877–1901* (New York: Dial Press, 1954), 328; Antonio Vinao Frago, "The History of Literacy in Spain: Evolution, Traits, and Questions," *History of Education Quarterly* 30 (1990): 586; Harvey J. Gruff, *The Legacies of Literacy: Continuities and Contradictions in Western Culture and Society* (Bloomington: Indiana University Press, 1987): 299, 361–66.

147. "Women who dared": W.E.B. Du Bois, *Dusk of Dawn: An Essay toward an Au-*

tobiography of a Race Concept (New York, Schocken Books, 1968), 24; "thread of brave": W.E.B. Du Bois, *Black Reconstruction in America: An Essay Toward a History of the Part Which Black Folk Played in the Attempt to Reconstruct Democracy in America, 1860–1880* (New York: Harcourt, Brace and Co., 1935), 708; Booker T. Washington, *Up from Slavery: An Autobiography* (Garden City, NY: Doubleday, Page & Co., 1919), 62.

148. Blum, *Reforging the White Republic*, 84 (quote); Botume, *First Days Amongst the Contrabands*, 286; Hoogenboom, *Rutherford B. Hayes*, 317; Williams, *Diary and Letters of Rutherford B. Hayes*, 2:245–53, 351; Louis D. Rubin, ed., *Teach the Freeman: The Correspondence of Rutherford B. Hayes and the Slater Fund for Negro Education, 1881–1887*, 2 vols. (Baton Rouge: Louisiana State University Press, 1959).

149. Hoogenboom, *Rutherford B. Hayes*, 317; "The Political South Hereafter," *The Nation*, April 5, 1877, p. 202; Blum, *Reforging the White Republic*, 150; Stanley P. Hirshson, *Farewell to the Bloody Shirt: Northern Republicans and the Southern Negro, 1877–1893* (Bloomington: Indiana University Press, 1962), 21–44; Foner, *Reconstruction*, 582.

150. Beatty, *Age of Betrayal*, 216; Peter H. Argersinger, "New Perspectives on Election Fraud in the Gilded Age," *Political Science Quarterly* 100 (1985): 673–82; Henry George, "Money in Elections," *North American Review* 86 (1883): 210–12; Richard F. Bensel, *The American Ballot Box in the Mid-Nineteenth Century* (New York: Cambridge University Press, 2004), 194–95, 290.

151. "Outcast states" and "bitterness": William C. Beecher and Samuel Scoville, *A Biography of Rev. Henry Ward Beecher* (New York: Charles L. Webster, 1888), 460; "You must not be disappointed" and "patience": Henry Ward Beecher, "Reconstruction," *New York Independent*, July 6, 1865, p. 8; Blum, *Reforging the White Republic*, 88.

152. Blum, *Reforging the White Republic*, 89–97 (quote, 90).

153. Harriet Beecher Stowe, *Palmetto Leaves* (Gainesville: University Press of Florida, 1999); Stowe, "Our Florida Plantation," *Atlantic Monthly* 43 (1879): 648; Blum, *Reforging the White Republic*, 100–103. Ann Rowe sees continuity in Stowe's writings based around a romantic vision, but that seems rather hard to accept in light of her attitudes toward the two races and political involvement. Ann Rowe, *Enchanted Country: Northern Writers in the South, 1865–1910* (Baton Rouge: Louisiana State University Press, 1978), 1–19.

154. Harriet Beecher Stowe, "Life in Florida," *New York Tribune*, February 17, 1877, p. 3; Blum, *Reforging the White Republic*, 101. Stowe claimed credit for persuading fourteen thousand Northerners to follow her example, a view shared by several scholars. *Palmetto Leaves*, xv; John T. Foster Jr. and Sarah Whitmer Foster, *Beechers, Stowes, and Yankee Strangers: The Transformation of Florida* (Gainesville: University Press of Florida, 1999), xvii.

155. *Atlanta Constitution* quoted in Hunter D. Farish, *The Circuit Rider Dismounts: A Social History of Southern Methodism, 1865–1900* (Richmond, VA: Dietz Press, 1938), 90–91; Thomas Cary Johnson, *The Life and Letters of Robert Lewis Dabney* (Richmond, VA: Presbyterian Committee of Publication, 1903), 378; Blum, *Reforging the White Republic*, 106; Sean Michael Lewis, "'Old Times Are Not Forgotten': Robert Lewis Dabney's Public Theology for a Reconstructed South," *Journal of Presbyterian History* 81 (2003): 163–77.

156. Scholars often miss the racial message of Moody's revivals, which gave a Christian veneer to the reactionary effort to reclassify blacks as inferior while encouraging the unification of America's whites. Moody's explicit rejection of political activism and the

integrative goals of Reconstruction carried enormous weight. Edward Blum observed that in "a political and social atmosphere depressed by financial hard times, class conflict, and seemingly interminable sectional bickering, Moody discouraged Protestants from taking an active interest in social reform and instead focused on the conciliatory message of the Christian gospel." Blum, *Reforging the White Republic*, 13; William G. McLoughlin, *Modern Revivalism: Charles Grandison Finney to Billy Graham* (New York: Ronald Press, 1959), 10, 167–70, 229, 272; Martin E. Marty, *Righteous Empire: The Protestant Experience in America* (New York: Dial Press, 1970), 162–63, 180, 256; Sidney Ahlstrom, *A Religious History of the American People* (New Haven: Yale University Press, 1972), 738–46.

157. "Our Augusta Letter," *Atlanta Constitution*, May 4, 1876; "A Respector of Persons," *Daily Rocky Mountain News* (Denver), May 16, 1876; "A Revival Incident," *New York Times*, May 10, 1876, p. 2; *Bangor Daily Whig & Courier*, May 13, 1876; Blum, *Reforging the White Republic*, 141.

158. Albert Taylor Bledsoe, "Moody and Sankey," *Southern Review* (Baltimore) 19 (1876): 186; Blum, *Reforging the White Republic*, 136, 141.

159. A.M.E. conference quotes in "Hasty Action," *Inter Ocean* (Chicago), June 21, 1887, p. 7; "Mr. Douglass' Great Speech," *New York Freeman*, May 2, 1885; "The Action Not Hasty," *Inter Ocean*, June 25, 1887, p. 16; Blum, *Reforging the White Republic*, 142.

160. Blum, *Reforging the White Republic*, 16–18, 124 (quote), 132–35.

161. Du Bois *Black Reconstruction*, 634, 707; Zuczek, *State of Rebellion*, 6; Michael Perman, "Counter-Reconstruction: The Role of Violence in Southern Redemption," in *The Facts of Reconstruction: Essays in Honor of John Hope Franklin*, ed. Eric Anderson and Alfred A. Moss (Baton Rouge: Louisiana State University Press, 1991), 121–40.

Chapter 3: Bringing Order to the West

1. Alexander Saxton, *The Indispensable Enemy: Labor and the Anti-Chinese Movement in California* (Berkeley: University of California Press, 1971), 118.

2. *Colorado Springs Gazette*, April 7, 1877, p. 2; *Colorado Springs Gazette*, August 4, 1877, p. 2.

3. See, for example, multiple articles in the *Colorado Springs Gazette*, February 10, February 17, February 24, and March 31, 1877. On the settlement of Colorado Springs, see *Colorado Springs Gazette*, August 4, 1877, p. 2.

4. Miriam Leslie, *California: A Pleasure Trip from Gotham to the Golden Gate* (New York: G.W. Carleton & Co., 1877), 56; *Colorado Springs Gazette*, March 17, 1877, p. 2. "Those of us who are opposed on principle to the sale of liquor, class such sale with the crimes of arson, theft, and murder, and we have a right to do so; for he who furnished the demon which men put in their mouths to steal away their brains and burn up their manhood, is an accomplice in whatever villainies may flow from indulgence in intoxicating drinks." *Colorado Springs Gazette*, February 24, 1877, p. 2; Clare V. McKanna, *Homicide, Race, and Justice in the American West, 1880–1920* (Tucson: University of Arizona Press, 1997); Clare V. McKanna, *Race and Homicide in Nineteenth-Century California* (Reno: University of Nevada Press, 2002); Richard W. Slatta, "Comparative Frontier Social Life: Western Saloons and Argentine Pulperias," *Great Plains Quarterly* 7 (1987): 155–65.

5. *Colorado Springs Gazette*, February 24, 1877, p. 2.

6. *Colorado Springs Gazette*, February 17, 1877, p. 3; *Colorado Springs Gazette*, March 10, 1877, p. 2; *Colorado Springs Gazette*, April 7, 1877, p. 2.

7. For example, *Colorado Springs Gazette*, February 10, 1877, pp. 2–3; *Colorado Springs Gazette*, March 17, 1877, p. 3; *Colorado Springs Gazette*, April 21, 1877; *Colorado Springs Gazette*, May 12, 1877, p. 2, *Colorado Springs Gazette*, June 9, 1877, p. 2, *Colorado Springs Gazette*, July 28, 1877, pp. 1–2, *Colorado Springs Gazette*, August 4, 1877, pp. 2–3; *Colorado Springs Gazette*, December 1, 1877; *Colorado Springs Gazette*, December 29, 1877.

8. *Colorado Springs Gazette*, August 4, 1877, p. 2; *Colorado Springs Gazette*, August 18, 1877, p. 2; *Colorado Springs Gazette*, August 25, 1877, p. 2; *Colorado Springs Gazette*, December 1, 1877, p. 2.

9. *Colorado Springs Gazette*, July 28, 1877, p. 4; *Colorado Springs Gazette*, November 17, 1877, p. 4 (quote); *Colorado Springs Gazette*, December 22, 1877, p. 2.

10. W. Eugene Hollon, *Frontier Violence: Another Look* (New York: Oxford University Press, 1974); Patricia Nelson Limerick, *The Legacy of Conquest: The Unbroken Past of the American West* (New York: Norton, 1987); Richard Slotkin, *The Fatal Environment: The Myth of the Frontier in the Age of Industrialization, 1800–1890* (Norman: University of Oklahoma Press, 1985); Frank R. Prassel, *The Great American Outlaw: A Legacy of Fact and Fiction* (Norman: University of Oklahoma Press, 1993); Robert R. Dykstra, *The Cattle Towns* (New York: Knopf, 1968); Richard White, *"It's Your Misfortune and None of My Own": A History of the American West* (Norman: University of Oklahoma Press, 1991); Rebecca Edwards, *New Spirits: Americans in the Gilded Age, 1865–1905* (New York: Oxford University Press, 2006), 209–10.

11. Wallace Stegner, *Beyond the Hundredth Meridian: John Wesley Powell and the Second Opening of the West* (New York: Penguin, 1992).

12. Ari Hoogenboom, *The Presidency of Rutherford B. Hayes* (Lawrence: University Press of Kansas, 1988), 153, 173; Edwards, *New Spirits*, 260. Congress actually voted for an army of thirty thousand but refused to allocate the additional funds to pay for those troops. Russell Weigley, *History of the United States Army* (New York: Macmillan, 1967), 275–81.

13. Ray Raphael and Freeman House, *Two Peoples, One Place* (Eureka, CA: Humboldt County Historical Society, 2007), 286–88; Byron Nelson Jr., *Our Home Forever: A Hupa Tribal History* (Hoopa, CA: Hupa Tribe, 1978). The Hupa are also known as the Hoopa; Sarah Steinberg et al., *In Hoopa Territory* (Hoopa, CA: Hoopa Valley Tribe, 2000).

14. "Our Indian Wards," *The Nation*, July 13, 1876, pp. 21–22; Othniel C. Marsh, *A Statement of Affairs at the Red Cloud Agency, Made to the President of the United States* (n.p., 1875); *Report of the Special Commission Appointed to Investigate the Affairs of the Red Cloud Agency* (Washington, DC: GPO, 1875); "Swindling the Indians," *Boston Daily Advertiser*, May 29, 1875; *Daily Rocky Mountain News* (Denver), June 2, 1875; "Indian Affairs," *San Francisco Daily Evening Bulletin*, July 14, 1875; "The Red Cloud Investigation," *The Congregationalist* (Boston), October 28, 1875, p. 4.

15. Sherman quoted in Stephen E. Ambrose, *Crazy Horse and Custer: The Parallel Lives of Two American Warriors* (New York: Doubleday, 1975), 292; *Colorado Springs Gazette*, February 10, 1877; Edmund J. Danziger Jr., "Native American Resistance and Accommodation during the Late Nineteenth Century," in *The Gilded Age: Essays on the Origins of Modern America*, ed. Charles W. Calhoun (Wilmington, DE: Scholarly Resources, 2000), 164; Edwards, *New Spirits*, 37.

16. Paul I. Wellman, *Death on the Prairie: The Thirty Years' Struggle for the Western Plains* (Lincoln: University of Nebraska Press, 1987), 130–31, 135–36; Walter Nugent, *Into the West: The Story of Its People* (New York: Knopf, 1999), 71; Ambrose, *Crazy Horse and Custer*, 374–81, 390–97; Edwards, *New Spirits*, 81; Joseph M. Marshall III, *The Day*

the World Ended at Little Bighorn: A Lakota History (New York: Viking, 2007), 31. Historians often shared the view that "something also had to be done about the Indians"; see Dee Brown, *The Year of the Century: 1876* (New York: Charles Scribner's Sons, 1966), 17. Robert Utley blamed the Sioux for the war, as they continued to launch raids, "disrupted the management of the reservation Indians," and "interfered with the sale of the Black Hills"; see Robert M. Utley, *Frontier Regulars: The United States Army and the Indian, 1866–1891* (New York: Macmillan, 1973), 246. The *Chicago Times* reporter also lay the war at the feet of the Sioux, whose "ungovernable pride" led them to unfairly exclude white men from the northern Plains; see John F. Finerty, *War-Path and Bivouac, or: The Conquest of the Sioux* (Chicago: Donohue & Henneberry, 1890), 37–38.

17. Perry Belmont, *An American Democrat: The Recollections of Perry Belmont* (New York: Columbia University Press, 1940), 158; Ambrose, *Crazy Horse and Custer*, 375, 396–97.

18. Wellman, *Death on the Prairie*, 129; Ambrose, *Crazy Horse and Custer*, 247 (Sherman quote), 281–82, 305; Utley, *Frontier Regulars*, 111.

19. On Sitting Bull, see Stanley Vestal, *Sitting Bull: Champion of the Sioux* (Boston: Houghton Mifflin, 1932); Robert M. Utley, *The Lance and the Shield: The Life and Times of Sitting Bull* (New York: Henry Holt, 1993).

20. On Crazy Horse, see Ambrose, *Crazy Horse and Custer*; Kingsley M. Bray, *Crazy Horse: A Lakota Life* (Norman: University of Oklahoma, 2006). On the Little Bighorn, see Ambrose, *Crazy Horse and Custer*, 435–47; Wellman, *Death on the Prairie*, 147–61. There is some debate about whether the Battle of the Rosebud should be credited as a victory for the Sioux, but given that the battle stopped General Crook's advance, breaking up the planned conjunction with Custer's forces, it seems fair to consider it a strategic as well as tactical victory for the Sioux. Ambrose, *Crazy Horse and Custer*, 420–24; Marshall, *Day the World Ended at Little Bighorn*, 85–86, 130–31; Wellman, *Death on the Prairie*, 139–46. For the contemporary debate, see "Horrible Catastrophe in the Lower Platte Valley," *Daily Rocky Mountain News* (Denver), July 25, 1876; "Belligerent Bohemians," *Daily Rocky Mountain News*, August 8, 1876; "Gen. Crook and the Rosebud Fight," *Arizona Weekly Miner* (Prescott), July 28, 1876; "Crook Corraled," *St. Louis Globe-Democrat*, July 29, 1876; "Treating with Crazy Horse," *St. Louis Globe-Democrat*, July 31, 1876, p. 4; "The Indian War," *Inter Ocean* (Chicago), August 2, 1876, p. 5; *Inter Ocean*, August 3, 1876, p. 2; "Marching upon the Sioux," *Inter Ocean*, August 5, 1876, p. 3; "What the Sioux Say," *Wisconsin State Register* (Portage), August 5, 1876; Finerty, *War-Path and Bivouac*, 111–19; John G. Bourke, *On the Border with Crook* (New York: Charles Scribner's Sons, 1896), 309–16.

21. Kingsley M. Bray, "Crazy Horse and the End of the Great Sioux War," in *American Nations: Encounters in Indian Country, 1850 to the Present*, ed. Frederick E. Hoxie et al. (New York: Routledge, 2001), 21n17.

22. Jack Crawford, *The Poet Scout* (San Francisco: H. Keller & Co., 1879), 79. The painting is often credited to Otto Becker, as in William Peirce Randel, *Centennial: American Life in 1876* (Philadelphia: Chilton Books, 1969), 134, but Becker was the lithographer. Robert Taft, *Artists and Illustrators of the Old West, 1850–1900* (New York: Charles Scribner's Sons, 1953), 129–48; Michael A. Elliot, *Custerology: The Enduring Legacy of the Indian Wars and George Armstrong Custer* (Chicago: University of Chicago Press, 2007), 34–35.

23. *New York Herald*, July 7, 1876; Oliver Knight, *Following the Indian Wars: The Story of the Newspaper Correspondents among the Indian Campaigners* (Norman: University of Oklahoma Press, 1960), 219.

24. Sturgis quoted in "The Sioux Slaughter," *St. Louis Globe-Democrat*, July 19, 1876, p. 4; Knight, *Following the Indian Wars*, 221; Charles S. Diehl, *The Staff Correspondent* (San Antonio: Clegg Co., 1931), 107; Lewis Henry Morgan, "The Hue and Cry Against the Indians," *The Nation*, July 20, 1876, pp. 40–41; Lewis Henry Morgan, "The Factory System for Indian Reservations," *The Nation*, July 27, 1876, pp. 58–59.

25. Emily FitzGerald to Aunt Annie, September 30, 1876, in Emily McCorkle FitzGerald, *An Army Doctor's Wife on the Frontier: Letters from Alaska and the Far West, 1874–1878*, ed. Abe Laufe (Pittsburgh: University of Pittsburgh Press, 1962), 207. See also Sherry Lynn Smith, *The View from Officers' Row: Army Perceptions of Western Indians* (Tucson: University of Arizona Press, 1991), 144–47.

26. *Chicago Times*, July 5, 1876; Knight, *Following the Indian Wars*, 246. Finerty compared Little Bighorn to Thermopylae and Custer to Leonidas; see Finerty, *War-Path and Bivouac*, v. For more of his negative opinions on the Sioux, see ibid., 106–8.

27. Finerty, *War-Path and Bivouac*, 228; *Chicago Times*, September 5, 1876; *New York Herald*, September 12, 1876; Knight, *Following the Indian Wars*, 257, 262. See also *Alta California*, September 26, 1876; *San Francisco Evening Bulletin*, September 4, 1876; *San Francisco Evening Bulletin*, September 5, 1876; *New York Herald*, August 24, 1876; *New York Herald*, September 17, 1876; *New York Herald*, September 21, 1876; *Chicago Tribune*, September 5, 1876; Finerty, *War-Path and Bivouac*, 226–32.

28. Charles A. King, *Campaigning with Crook and Stories of Army Life* (New York: Harper & Brothers, 1890), 167. Crook's view that the Indians were basically welfare cheats is "a shocking travesty of the facts," as Stephen Ambrose put it, given that the "Sioux had just signed over lands worth their keep for one hundred years or more, and got nothing in return"; Ambrose, *Crazy Horse and Custer*, 455.

29. *Chicago Times*, July 12, 1876; *Chicago Times*, September 16, 1876; Knight, *Following the Indian Wars*, 233–34, 286–87.

30. Knight, *Following the Indian Wars*, 220, 272.

31. Ibid., 223–24, 241–42, 249.

32. *New York Herald*, July 16, 1876; Knight, *Following the Indian Wars*, 241.

33. Knight, *Following the Indian Wars*, 232–33, 244, 251–53; Ambrose, *Crazy Horse and Custer*, 453–56; *New York Tribune*, July 27, 1876; *New York Herald*, August 18, 1876; *Alta California*, August 1, 1876; "Battle Echoes from Montana," *San Francisco Daily Evening Bulletin*, August 30, 1877; "Another Sensation," *Inter Ocean* (Chicago), January 24, 1878, p. 4; "Sitting Bull on the Warpath," *Daily Rocky Mountain News* (Denver), January 29, 1878; "An Indian Congress," *Bangor Daily Whig & Courier*, June 11, 1878; *Weekly Register-Call* (Central City, CO), June 22, 1878; Bourke, *On the Border with Crook*, 316–19, 338–39, 393–94.

34. Bourke, *On the Border with Crook*, 415; Wellman, *Death on the Prairie*, 132–35.

35. *Colorado Springs Gazette*, March 17, 1877, p. 3. See also Jerome A. Greene, *Nez Perce Summer 1877: The U.S. Army and the Nee-Me-Poo Crisis* (Helena: Montana Historical Society Press, 2000), 95–96; Ambrose, *Crazy Horse and Custer*, 145–64.

36. Knight, *Following the Indian Wars*, 289; Wellman, *Death on the Prairie*, 162, 172. There is of course some disagreement on the number of warriors. Marshall, *Day the World Ended at Little Bighorn*, 136–37; Ambrose, *Crazy Horse and Custer*, 456–58, 462.

37. Wellman, *Death on the Prairie*, 162n1 (quote), 166–67; Stanley Vestal, *Sitting Bull: Champion of the Sioux* (Norman: University of Oklahoma Press, 1989), 203–5; Nelson A. Miles, *Serving the Republic: Memoirs of the Civil and Military Life of Nelson A. Miles* (New York: Harper & Brothers, 1911), 157–60.

38. Iron Horse quoted in Bray, "Crazy Horse and the End of the Great Sioux War," 35n81; Ambrose, *Crazy Horse and Custer*, 458–59.

39. Bray, "Crazy Horse and the End of the Great Sioux War," 32n68, 36n86.

40. Ambrose, *Crazy Horse and Custer*, 459–63 (quote, 462); Marshall, *Day the World Ended at Little Bighorn*, 136–38; Bray, "Crazy Horse and the End of the Great Sioux War," 38–39; Wellman, *Death on the Prairie*, 174–75; Belmont, *American Democrat*, 157–81.

41. Marshall, *Day the World Ended at Little Bighorn*, 139, 141–42; Wellman, *Death on the Prairie*, 176–79; Ambrose, *Crazy Horse and Custer*, 463–68.

42. Ambrose, *Crazy Horse and Custer*, 469–72. For several eyewitness accounts, see Robert A. Clark, ed., *The Killing of Chief Crazy Horse* (Lincoln: University of Nebraska Press, 1988).

43. Touch-the-Clouds quoted in Ambrose, *Crazy Horse and Custer*, 473; Crazy Horse quoted in Homer W. Wheeler, *Buffalo Days: Forty Years in the Old West* (Brooklyn: A.L. Burt, 1925), 200; Marshall, *Day the World Ended at Little Bighorn*, 138, 152; Wellman, *Death on the Prairie*, 176–78.

44. Marshall, *Day the World Ended at Little Bighorn*, 142–43; Ambrose, *Crazy Horse and Custer*, 454; Greene, *Nez Perce Summer*, 246.

45. Greene, *Nez Perce Summer*, 236; *Fort Benton Record*, October 5, 1877.

46. Molchert quoted in Greene, *Nez Perce Summer*, 237; L.V. McWhorter, *Yellow Wolf: His Own Story* (Caldwell, ID: Caxton Press, 2000), 199; *New York Herald*, September 29, 1877; *Fort Benton Record*, October 5, 1877; L.V. McWhorter, *Hear Me, My Chiefs: Nez Perce Legend and History* (Caldwell, ID: Caxton Press, 1984), 469–72; Alvin M. Josephy Jr., *The Nez Perce Indians and the Opening of the Northwest* (Boston: Houghton Mifflin, 1997), 611–15. The Nez Perce called themselves the Nee-Me-Poo.

47. See, for instance, "The Indians," *The Congregationalist* (Boston), October 10, 1877; "The Last Indian War," *Frank Leslie's Illustrated Newspaper* (New York), October 27, 1877; "Chief Joseph," *Colorado Springs Gazette*, December 22, 1877; "The Indian Question," *Milwaukee Daily Sentinel*, October 4, 1878; Greene, *Nez Perce Summer*, 350–51.

48. *Colorado Springs Gazette*, June 9, 1877, p. 2. See also "Responsibility for the Idaho War," *The Nation*, August 2, 1877, p. 69; "A Lesson from the Nez Perces," *New York Times*, October 15, 1877, p. 4; Hoogenboom, *Presidency of Hayes*, 158; Josephy, *Nez Perce Indians*, xix–xx, 5–15, 543, 557.

49. Hoogenboom, *Presidency of Hayes*, 154–55; Josephy, *Nez Perce Indians*, 445–58, 512–13; Greene, *Nez Perce Summer*, 13–14, 25; Charles C. Royce, "Indian Land Cessions in the United States," *Eighteenth Annual Report of the Bureau of American Ethnology, 1896–97* (Washington, DC: GPO, 1899), pt. 2:864–65.

50. Greene, *Nez Perce Summer*, 14–15; *Army and Navy Journal*, July 7, 1877; *Army and Navy Journal*, September 8, 1877; *Eighth Annual Report of the Board of Indian Commissioners for the Year 1876* (Washington, DC: GPO, 1877), 60.

51. Italics in original; McDowell's words appear as well in the instructions of the Department of the Interior to J.B. Monteith, the Indian agent in Lewiston. *Report of the Secretary of War on the Operations of the Department for the Fiscal Year Ending June 30, 1877*, 2 vols. (Washington, DC: GPO, 1877), 1:7–9, 585–86; *The Teller* (Lewiston, ID), February 17, 1877.

52. Wilkinson quoted in Greene, *Nez Perce Summer*, 382–83n45; *Army and Navy Journal*, August 18, 1877; General O.O. Howard Report, *Report of the Secretary of War . . . 1877*, 1:588–97, 594 (Howard quote); O.O. Howard, *My Life and Experiences*

among Our Hostile Indians (Hartford, CT: A.D. Worthington & Co., 1907), 249–56; Joseph, "An Indian's Views of Indian Affairs," *North American Review* 128 (1879): 421–22; Josephy, *Nez Perce Indians*, 491–92; Frederick Bancroft, *Speeches, Correspondence and Political Papers of Carl Schurz*, 6 vols. (New York: Putnam's Sons, 1913), 4:55.

53. George Crook, *General George Crook: His Autobiography*, ed. Martin F. Schmitt (Norman: University of Oklahoma, 1986), 169; Greene, *Nez Perce Summer*, 23.

54. Joseph, "Indian's Views of Indian Affairs," 422; Howard Report, *Report of the Secretary of War . . . 1877*, 1:594–95; Howard, *My Life and Experiences*, 256–57; Hoogenboom, *Presidency of Hayes*, 155–56; Greene, *Nez Perce Summer*, 26 (McCarthy quote), 28–29.

55. John D. McDermott, *Forlorn Hope: The Nez Perce Victory at White Bird Canyon* (1878; Caldwell, ID: Caxton Press, 2003), 3–43; Hoogenboom, *Presidency of Hayes*, 156, 158; Greene, *Nez Perce Summer*, 30–32. The three murderers and rapists were Shore Crossing, Red Moccasin Top, and Swan Necklace.

56. Greene, *Nez Perce Summer*, 33.

57. Settles to Captain Perry, *Report of the Secretary of War . . . 1877*, 1:601; O.O. Howard, *Nez Perce Joseph* (Boston: Lee and Shepard, 1881), 98; *Army and Navy Journal*, August 18, 1877; McDermott, *Forlorn Hope*, 49–68.

58. McDermott, *Forlorn Hope*, 57–68; "The Indians," *Daily Rocky Mountain News* (Denver), August 22, 1877; Hoogenboom, *Presidency of Hayes*, 156–57; Greene, *Nez Perce Summer*, 34–42 (quote, 39); McWhorter, *Hear Me*, 53–54, 239–52; William R. Parnell, "The Nez Perce War, 1877: Battle of White Bird Canyon," *Eyewitnesses to the Indian Wars, 1865–1890: The Wars for the Pacific Northwest*, 2 vols., ed. Peter Cozzens (Mechanicsburg, PA: Stackpole Books, 2002), 2:344–55; Howard, *My Life and Experiences*, 283–86. The Battle of White Bird Creek is also known as the Battle of White Bird Canyon.

59. Howard, *Nez Perce Joseph*, 117; *Report of the Secretary of War . . . 1877*, 1:358–59; Greene, *Nez Perce Summer*, 42–43 (McCarthy quote), 46–48, 389n43.

60. *New York Herald*, September 10, 1877; Greene, *Nez Perce Summer*, 387n31.

61. "The Week," *The Nation*, July 5, 1877, p. 1; "Responsibility for the Idaho War," *The Nation*, August 2, 1877, 69–70; McWhorter, *Hear Me*, 239–41; Greene, *Nez Perce Summer*, 36, 41, 388n37; Walter F. Beyer and Oscar Frederick Keydel, *Deeds of Valor: From Records in the Archives of the United States Government*, 2 vols. (Detroit: Perrien-Keydel Co., 1907), 2:239–44. There was a general sense that Joseph was a superior military commander to General Howard; see "The War in the West: Howard Outgeneraled by Joseph," *Galveston Daily News*, July 20, 1877.

62. *Colorado Springs Gazette*, September 1, 1877, p. 2; Greene, *Nez Perce Summer*, 44, 50 (McCarthy quote).

63. McWhorter, *Hear Me*, 261–73; *Army and Navy Journal*, July 14, 1877; Greene, *Nez Perce Summer*, 51–58 (quote, 58); McWhorter, *Hear Me*, 267–71; Josephy, *Nez Perce*, 535–37; *Boise Tri-Weekly Statesman*, July 14, 1877. Bird Alighting was also known as Peopeo Tholekt.

64. McWhorter, *Hear Me*, 279; *Boise Tri-Weekly Statesman*, July 21, 1877; Greene, *Nez Perce Summer*, 73–75, 399n6–7.

65. McCarthy quoted in Greene, *Nez Perce Summer*, 81–82, 91. See also *Army and Navy Journal*, July 14, 1877; *Army and Navy Journal*, August 18, 1877; McWhorter, *Hear Me*, 298–303, 318–20; *Boise Tri-Weekly Statesman*, July 14, 1877; "The Walla Walla Region," *Galveston Daily News*, July 14, 1877; Greene, *Nez Perce Summer*, 67–68, 77–82, 88–91.

66. McWhorter, *Yellow Wolf,* 88–91 (quote, 88); McWhorter, *Hear Me,* 305, 309–13.

67. C.E.S. Wood, "Chief Joseph, the Nez Perce," *The Century Illustrated Monthly Magazine* 28 (1884): 137; McWhorter, *Hear Me,* 314–15 (Bird Alighting quote), 323; Greene, *Nez Perce Summer,* 86–97, 105 McWhorter, *Yellow Wolf,* 98–100; Joseph, "An Indian's Views," 426.

68. Greene, *Nez Perce Summer,* 100, 106–7 (quote, 107); McWhorter, *Hear Me,* 332–40; McWhorter, *Yellow Wolf,* 104–5, 310–12; Duncan MacDonald, "The Nez Perces: The History of Their Troubles and the Campaign of 1877," Linwood Laughy, comp., *In Pursuit of the Nez Perces: The Nez Perce War of 1877* (Wrangell, AK: Mountain Meadow Press, 1993), 247; Josephy, *Nez Perce Indians,* 555–57. The Lolo Trail ran from Montana's Bitterroot Valley into central Idaho.

69. Greene, *Nez Perce Summer,* 108.

70. Ibid., 110–11; McWhorter, *Hear Me,* 351n21, 352; Josephy, *Nez Perce Indians,* 567–72.

71. *Boise Tri-Weekly Statesman,* August 21, 1877; *Helena Daily Herald* July 30, 1877; *Portland Daily Standard,* September 6, 1877; Greene, *Nez Perce Summer,* 112–13, 121–22, 124–27; MacDonald, "Nez Perces," 251; Report of Colonel Gibbon, September 2, 1877, *Report of the Secretary of War . . . 1877,* 1:68–69.

72. Charles A. Woodruff, "Battle of the Big Hole," *Contributions to the Historical Society of Montana* 7 (1910): 109; Greene, *Nez Perce Summer,* 126–33; McWhorter, *Yellow Wolf,* 115.

73. Woodruff, "Battle of the Big Hole," 109; "Battle Briefs," *Helena Daily Herald,* August 23, 1877.

74. Greene, *Nez Perce Summer,* 132–33.

75. Ibid., 131–34; McWhorter, *Yellow Wolf,* 118; McWhorter, *Hear Me,* 376; Beyer and Keydel, *Deeds of Valor,* 2:244–48.

76. Report of Colonel Gibbon, September 2, 1877, *Report of the Secretary of War . . . 1877,* 1:70–71; MacDonald, "Nez Perces," 260–61; Greene, *Nez Perce Summer,* 135–38.

77. *Report of the Secretary of War . . . 1877,* 1:56 (quote), 71, 521–22, 553, 562; Gibbon, "Pursuit of Joseph," 341–43; *Army and Navy Journal,* August 18, 1877; *Army and Navy Journal,* August 25, 1877; *Army and Navy Journal,* September 22, 1877; McWhorter, *Hear Me,* 384–88; Greene, *Nez Perce Summer,* 138–40, 144–45; McWhorter, *Yellow Wolf,* 134–46; Josephy, *Nez Perce Indians,* 579–90; August 18, 1877; Beyer and Keydel, *Deeds of Valor,* 2:244–48.

78. Report of Colonel Gibbon, September 2, 1877, *Report of the Secretary of War . . . 1877,* 1:9; John Gibbon, "The Pursuit of Joseph," *American Catholic Quarterly Review* 4 (1879): 327–29; "Tecumseh's Tour," *St. Louis Globe-Democrat,* October 21, 1877, p. 11; Greene, *Nez Perce Summer,* 120–24; Rex C. Myers, "The Settlers and the Nez Perce," *Montana: The Magazine of Western History* 27 (1977): 20–29.

79. *Bozeman Times,* September 13, 1877; *Deer Lodge New North-West,* September 14, 1877; "Howard and the Volunteers," *Butte Miner,* September 25, 1877, p. 2; *Boise Tri-Weekly Statesman,* September 18, 1877; *New York Herald,* September 10, 1877; *Cheyenne Daily Leader,* August 31, 1877; *Cheyenne Daily Leader,* November 2, 1877; *Helena Daily Independent,* June 13, 1896; McWhorter, *Yellow Wolf,* 187–88, 194; Greene, *Nez Perce Summer,* 139, 151–216, 232; *Report of the Secretary of War . . . 1877,* 1:13, 609–10; O.O. Howard, *Nez Perce Joseph: An Account of his Ancestors, His Lands, His Confederates, His Enemies, His Murders, His War, His Pursuit and Capture* (Boston: Lee and Shepard, 1881), 225–29.

80. Greene, *Nez Perce Summer*, 206–9, 216–33, 242–43 (quote, 229); *Report of the Secretary of War . . . 1877*, 1:508, 525–27, 627; *Bozeman Times*, September 13, 1877; *New York Herald*, September 29, 1877; Nelson A. Miles, *Personal Recollections and Observations of General Nelson A. Miles* (Chicago: Werner Co., 1896), 260; McWhorter, *Yellow Wolf*, 202–3; McWhorter, *Hear Me*, 473–74.

81. Miles, *Personal Recollections*, 265–67; Henry Romeyn, "The Capture of Chief Joseph and the Nez Perce Indians," *Contributions to the Historical Society of Montana* (Helena: State Publishing Co., 1896), 2:285–87; Sturgis to Miles, September 13, 1877, *Report of the Secretary of War . . . 1877*, 1:74; Greene, *Nez Perce Summer*, 245–66; Jerome A. Greene, *Yellowstone Command: Colonel Nelson A. Miles and the Great Sioux War, 1876–1877* (Norman: University of Oklahoma Press , 2006), 205–13. On this approach to combat, see Robert Wooster, *The Military and United States Indian Policy, 1865–1903* (New Haven: Yale University Press, 1988), 127, 135–43; Greene, *Yellowstone Command*, 10–12. On the Washita, see Ambrose, *Crazy Horse and Custer*, 313–24.

82. McWhorter, *Yellow Wolf*, 205–6; Joseph, "Indian's Views," 428; McWhorter, *Hear Me*, 478–81; MacDonald, "The Nez Perces," 269.

83. McWhorter, *Yellow Wolf*, 207; Greene, *Nez Perce Summer*, 271–88 (quotes, 274, 282); *Portland Daily Standard*, November 4, 1877; *New York Herald*, October 11, 1877; *Army and Navy Journal*, December 8, 1877; *Army and Navy Journal*, April 27, 1878; McWhorter, *Hear Me*, 479–80; Miles, *Personal Recollections*, 268; *Harper's Weekly*, November 17, 1877.

84. Miles, "Report," *Report of the Secretary of War . . . 1877*, 1:528; McWhorter, *Hear Me*, 485; *Army and Navy Journal*, October 13, 1877; Greene, *Nez Perce Summer*, 280–88, 293–94, 299, 306 (quote, 281); Romeyn, "Capture of Chief Joseph," 287–89; *Army and Navy Journal*, March 9, 1878; Utley, *Lance and the Shield*, 193, 371–72n14.

85. Greene, *Nez Perce Summer*, 288–89; *New York Herald*, October 11, 1877; *Portland Daily Standard*, November 4, 1877.

86. McWhorter, *Yellow Wolf*, 211 (quote), 215–16, 218; Greene, *Nez Perce Summer*, 285–308, 300–301, 477n28; War Department, *Rules of Land Warfare* (Washington, DC: GPO, 1914), 88–96; Thomas Wilhelm, *A Military Dictionary and Gazetteer: Comprising Ancient and Modern Military Technical Terms, Historical Accounts of All North American Indians, as Well as Ancient Warlike Tribes* (Philadelphia: L.R. Hamersly & Co., 1881), 163, 602; report of Colonel Miles, *Report of the Secretary of War . . . 1877*, 1:528; Miles, *Personal Recollections*, 274; McWhorter, *Hear Me*, 488; William F. Zimmer, *Frontier Soldier: An Enlisted Man's Journal of the Sioux and Nez Perce Campaigns, 1877* (Helena: Montana Historical Society, 1998), 123; Joseph, "Indian's Views," 428–29; *New York Herald*, October 30, 1877.

87. Miles quoted in "The Bloody Nez Perces," *Milwaukee Daily Sentinel*, October 8, 1877, p. 4; Joseph, "Indian's Views," 429; Greene, *Nez Perce Summer*, 304–6; Greene, *Yellowstone Command*, 166–76; *Army and Navy Journal*, December 8, 1877; *Fort Benton Record*, October 12, 1877; Romeyn, "The Capture of Chief Joseph," 289–91; McWhorter, *Yellow Wolf*, 220; McWhorter, *Hear Me*, 495.

88. General O.O. Howard, Supplementary Report, *Report of the Secretary of War . . . 1877*, 1:630. The *Bismarck Tri-Weekly Tribune*, October 26, 1877, had the earliest published version of Joseph's surrender speech, which is similar to this one. Greene, *Nez Perce Summer*, 306–12; *Harper's Weekly*, November 17, 1877; Miles, *Serving the Republic*, 178–79; McWhorter, *Yellow Wolf*, 222–24; McWhorter, *Hear Me*, 493–94.

89. Howard, *My Life and Experiences*, 299; *Inter Ocean* (Chicago), October 26, 1877, p. 4; Greene, *Nez Perce Summer*, 310–12, 334; Joseph, "Indian's Views," 429; Howard, Supplementary Report, *Report of the Secretary of War . . . 1877*, 1:630–31; McWhorter, *Yellow Wolf,* 224–26; McWhorter, *Hear Me*, 496–98; Miles, *Personal Recollections*, 275; *Harper's Weekly*, November 17, 1877. Miles reported a total of 448 prisoners; see Greene, *Nez Perce Summer*, 313.

90. Greene, *Nez Perce Summer*, 312; Miles to Terry, October 5, 1877, *Report of the Secretary of War . . . 1877*, 1:515.

91. Walsh quoted in Greene, *Nez Perce Summer*, 341; Nez Perce woman quoted in McWhorter, *Hear Me*, 509; McWhorter, *Yellow Wolf,* 225–26; Zimmer, *Frontier Soldier*, 128–30; Howard, Supplementary Report, *Report of the Secretary of War . . . 1877*, 1:631.

92. Report of Colonel Miles, October 6, 1877, and Howard, Supplementary Report, *Report of the Secretary of War . . . 1877*, 1:74–75, 632–33; McWhorter, *Hear Me*, 486, 501; *Fort Benton Record*, October 5, 1877; *Fort Benton Record*, October 12, 1877; *Army and Navy Journal*, November 24, 1877; *Leavenworth Daily Times*, November 29, 1877; *New York Herald*, October 23, 1877; Greene, *Nez Perce Summer*, 290–91, 315, 317–19, 325, 332, 350, 368–71, 375–76, 495n28; Hoogenboom, *Presidency of Hayes*, 158–59.

93. Miles to Terry, October 17, 1877, in Greene, *Nez Perce Summer*, 350.

94. Greene, *Nez Perce Summer*, 334; "The Captured Nez Perces," *Inter Ocean* (Chicago), October 19, 1877; *Chicago Tribune*, October 25, 1877; Joseph, "Indian's Views," 430–31.

95. Robert H. Steinbach, *A Long March: The Lives of Frank and Alice Baldwin* (Austin: University of Texas Press, 1989), 132; Joseph quoted in "Breaking Promises with the Indians," *Inter Ocean* (Chicago), November 23, 1877; Miles, *Personal Recollections*, 279–80; *Bismarck Tri-Weekly Tribune*, November 21, 1877; *Bismarck Tri-Weekly Tribune*, November 23, 1877; Greene, *Nez Perce Summer*, 335–36; *Army and Navy Journal*, December 1, 1877.

96. Greene, *Nez Perce Summer*, xi (quote), 337; Hoogenboom, *Presidency of Hayes*, 160. The Nez Perce split into two groups—150 of them, including Joseph, settling on the Colville reservation in Washington, the remaining 118 moving to the Lapwai reservation. Joseph, "An Indian's Views," 431–33; J. Stanley Clark, "The Nez Perces in Exile," *Pacific Northwest Quarterly* 26 (1945): 213–32; Josephy, *Nez Perce Indians*, 637–42.

97. *Report of the Secretary of War . . . 1877*, 1:xv.

98. Utley, *Lance and the Shield*, 260–67, 291–307; Candy Moulton, *Chief Joseph: Guardian of the People* (New York: Forge Books, 2005), 216–22.

99. Robert W. Larson, *New Mexico's Quest for Statehood, 1846–1912* (Albuquerque: University of New Mexico Press, 1968), 13, 28–29, 54, 117; Article IX of the Treaty of Guadalupe Hidalgo, U.S. Congress, Senate Doc. no. 357, 61st Cong., 2nd sess., *Treaties, Conventions, International Acts, Protocols and Agreements Between the United States of America and Other Powers, 1776–1909*, 2 vols. (Washington, DC: GPO, 1910), 1:1112. New Mexico had a larger population than Colorado and Nevada. Department of the Interior, *Statistics of the Population of the United States at the Tenth Census* (Washington, DC: GPO, 1882), 3. The census almost certainly undercounted the number of Indians in New Mexico at just 9,772. There was continual debate over the accuracy and methods of counting the population in New Mexico; see Larson, *New Mexico's Quest for Statehood*, 108, 116–19, 124, 212–16.

100. "The State of Colorado," *New York Times*, March 5, 1875, p. 4; *Cincinnati Com-*

mercial, March 3, 1875; Larson, *New Mexico's Quest for Statehood,* 121–28. See also *Daily Arkansas Gazette* (Little Rock), February 5, 1875; *Chicago Tribune,* February 26, 1875; *Milwaukee Daily Sentinel,* March 5, 1875, p. 4.

101. For an overview of New Mexico's development, see Warren A. Beck, *New Mexico: A History of Four Centuries* (Norman: University of Oklahoma Press, 1962); Marc Simmons, *New Mexico: A Bicentennial History* (New York: Norton, 1977); Thomas E. Chavez, *New Mexico Past and Future* (Albuquerque: University of New Mexico Press, 2006).

102. Robert J. Rosenbaum, *Mexicano Resistance in the Southwest: "The Sacred Right of Self-Preservation"* (Austin: University of Texas Press, 1981), 90. Chisum's nickname came from the odd shape in which the ears of his cattle were cut, serving as an identifying mark to forestall rustling. Rustlers responded by simply cutting off the ears of Chisum's cattle.

103. Rosenbaum, *Mexicano Resistance in the Southwest,* 93, 95; Phillip J. Rasch, "The Horrell War," *New Mexico Historical Review* 30 (1956): 223–31.

104. Rasch, "Horrell War," 229; Frederick Nolan, *The Lincoln County War: A Documentary History* (Norman: University of Oklahoma Press, 1992), 48–54, 306–10, 469, 531n53, 532n61; Rosenbaum, *Mexicano Resistance in the Southwest,* 93–94; William A. Keleher, *Violence in Lincoln County, 1869–1881* (Albuquerque: University of New Mexico Press, 1957), 13–15.

105. Rosenbaum, *Mexicano Resistance in the Southwest,* 92–95 (quote, 95); Keleher, *Violence in Lincoln County,* 38–40; "Pat Garrett's Version of the Lincoln County War, 1877," in *Documenting American Violence: A Sourcebook,* ed. Michael Bellesiles and Christopher Waldrep (New York: Oxford University Press, 2006), 227.

106. Larson, *New Mexico's Quest for Statehood,* 143–45, 170–71, 300 (quote); Rosenbaum, *Mexicano Resistance in the Southwest,* 202–3n47; Phillip J. Rasch, "The People of the Territory of New Mexico versus the Santa Fe Ring," *New Mexico Historical Review* 47 (1972): 185–201; "Pat Garrett's Version," 227; Nolan, *Lincoln County War,* 47, 178, 181, 230–31, 236–39.

107. "Pat Garrett's Version," 227; Nolan, *Lincoln County War,* 120–21; *Mesilla Valley Independent* (Mesilla, NM), June 23, 1877.

108. Nolan, *Lincoln County War,* 121, 505, 536n16; *Weekly New Mexican* (Santa Fe), January 30, 1877.

109. "Pat Garrett's Version," 227; Nolan, *Lincoln County War,* 540–41n9; *Weekly New Mexican* (Santa Fe), January 6, 1877.

110. "Pat Garrett's Version," 228; Nolan, *Lincoln County War,* 148–49; *Arizona Weekly Star* (Tucson), August 23, 1877; *Arizona Weekly Star,* August 25, 1877. Bonney was born Henry McCarty in New York City in 1859.

111. Nolan, *Lincoln County War,* 64, 154–55, 175–76, 507–8, 542n32, 544n19 (quotes, 64, 175); *Mesilla Valley Independent* (Mesilla, NM), August 8, 1877; *Mesilla Valley Independent,* September 8, 1877; *Mesilla Valley Independent,* November 3, 1877; *Mesilla Valley Independent,* November 10, 1877.

112. "Pat Garrett's Version," 229. The story of the Lincoln County War is further confused by the misidentification of several key figures. For instance, many accounts of Tunstall's murder state that William Brady led the posse; e.g., see Larson, *New Mexico's Quest for Statehood,* 138–39. But Frederick Nolan's meticulous documentary reconstruction of these events shows that Brady was not present at the murder; see *Lincoln County War,* 196–99. Pat Garrett also states that Morton led the posse; see "Pat Garrett's Version," 229.

113. "Pat Garrett's Version," 229; Nolan, *Lincoln County War,* 219–20, 228.

114. Nolan, *Lincoln County War*, 220–23, 233–49, 257–58, 320–331; "Pat Garrett's Version," 229–30.

115. Larson, *New Mexico's Quest for Statehood*, 123, 299–300; "Colorado," *New York Times*, March 5, 1875, p. 4; Nolan, *Lincoln County War*, 347–48, 402–26; Bellesiles and Waldrep, *Documenting American Violence*, 225–26, 230; Rosenbaum, *Mexicano Resistance in the Southwest*, 94–98 (see also 99–110 for similar violence in another part of New Mexico). Catron would live long enough to be one of the first U.S. senators from New Mexico in 1912.

116. Nolan, *Lincoln County War*, 72, 534n20.

117. Rosenbaum, *Mexicano Resistance in the Southwest*, 37–52, 68–90.

118. James B. Gillett, *Six Years with the Texas Rangers, 1875 to 1881*, ed. Milo M. Quaife (New Haven: Yale University Press, 1925), 130; Walter Prescott Webb, *The Texas Rangers: A Century of Frontier Defense* (Boston: Houghton Mifflin, 1935), 307. The bias of Webb is further demonstrated when he falsely states, "The people, resenting the presence of federal troops and hating the 'buffalo soldiers' in the army posts, were ready to call their Rangers and willing to pay them." Webb also denies the legitimacy of Republican governor Davis since he was elected only by "enfranchising their former slaves." See ibid., 220.

119. Robert M. Utley, *Lone Star Justice: The First Century of the Texas Rangers* (New York: Oxford University Press, 2002), 143–44 (quote), 169–70; Webb, *Texas Rangers*, 292–93.

120. Gillett, *Six Years with the Texas Rangers*, 130–32, 239; Webb, *Texas Rangers*, 292.

121. Webb, *Texas Rangers*, 293–94.

122. James D. Richardson, comp., *A Compilation of the Messages and Papers of the Presidents, 1789–1897*, 10 vols. (New York: Bureau of National Literature and Art, 1897), 10:4358; Rebecca Edwards, *New Spirits: Americans in the Gilded Age, 1865–1905* (New York: Oxford University Press, 2006), 46; William Peirce Randel, *Centennial: American Life in 1876* (Philadelphia: Chilton Books, 1969), 271.

123. "Ord's Orders," *St. Louis Globe-Democrat*, June 2, 1877; Utley, *Lone Star Justice*, 164, 168, 192–93; Webb, *Texas Rangers*, 259; "The Raids Across the Rio Grande," *New York Times*, June 25, 1877, p. 5; "Editorial Brevities," *Galveston Daily News*, July 31, 1877; "The Frontier Imbroglio," *Milwaukee Daily Sentinel*, December 18, 1877; Ari Hoogenboom, *The Presidency of Rutherford B. Hayes* (Lawrence: University Press of Kansas, 1988), 174–76.

124. "What May Lead to War," *Galveston Daily News*, August 14, 1877; Utley, *Lone Star Justice*, 161. See also ibid., 163–64; "How Is This, Diaz?" *St. Louis Globe-Democrat*, August 14, 1877; p. 4; "Washington: The Mexican Revolutionists," *North American* (Philadelphia), August 15, 1877; "Outrage by the Mexicans at Rio Grande City," *San Francisco Daily Evening Bulletin*, August 14, 1877; "Lively Times in Mexico," *Galveston Daily News*, August 16, 1877; "The Mexican Question," *Galveston Daily News*, August 17, 1877; "The Rio Grande Frontier," *Galveston Daily News*, August 21, 1877; *Colorado Springs Gazette*, August 18, 1877, p. 2; "Mexican Border," *Georgia Weekly Telegraph and Georgia Journal & Messenger* (Macon), August 21, 1877.

125. *Colorado Springs Gazette*, December 1, 1877, p. 2. See also *Colorado Springs Gazette*, August 25, 1877, p. 2; "The Mexican Border," *New York Times*, November 13, 1877, p. 5; "Hankering for Mexican Territory," *Milwaukee Daily Sentinel*, October 5, 1877, p. 5; "The Mexican Question," *Galveston Daily News*, October 12, 1877; "Notes and Opinions," *Galveston Daily News*, December 25, 1877.

126. "The Lerdo Revolution," *Galveston Daily News*, July 8, 1877; "Texas News by Telegraph," *Galveston Daily News*, July 20, 1877; "The Mexican Problem," *Galveston Daily News*, July 28, 1877; "Border and Frontier," *Galveston Daily News*, August 3, 1877; Utley, *Lone Star Justice*, 168, 192–93; Hoogenboom, *Presidency of Hayes*, 174–76; Gillett, *Six Years with the Texas Rangers*, 104.

127. These population figures remain in dispute; see Utley, *Lone Star Justice*, 188–89; Webb, *Texas Rangers*, 345. There is also some disagreement on the distance and travel time: Webb puts it at 600 miles requiring "thirty or more days" to reach El Paso; see Webb, *Texas Rangers*, 345. Utley states it is 500 miles; Utley, *Lone Star Justice*, 188. Gillett held El Paso was 750 miles from Austin yet took only a week to get there; Gillett, *Six Years with the Texas Rangers*, 197. Mapquest places the distance at 580 miles.

128. Webb, *Texas Rangers*, 346; C.L. Sonnichsen, *Ten Texas Feuds* (Albuquerque: University of New Mexico Press, 2000), 112–13; Gillett, *Six Years with the Texas Rangers*, 194; Utley, *Lone Star Justice*, 191. Webb disagrees, insisting that the salt lakes had been discovered only in 1862, apparently assuming the building of the road indicated the acknowledgment of the lake's existence; Webb, *Texas Rangers*, 347.

129. Gillett, *Six Years with the Texas Rangers*, 195; Utley, *Lone Star Justice*, 190–91, 196; Webb, *Texas Rangers*, 351, 356; Sonnichsen, *Ten Texas Feuds*, 113–14, 119–23, 127–28; testimony of G.N. Garcia, U.S. Congress, House Exec. Doc. no. 93, 45th Cong., 2nd sess., *El Paso Troubles in Texas* (Washington, DC: GPO, 1878), 106–7. Webb credits Cardis with controlling the Hispanic vote in the region, labeling him "a Machiavelli," praising Howard as "a man of undoubted courage . . . and an excellent pistol shot"; Webb, *Texas Rangers*, 348–49.

130. Webb, *Texas Rangers*, 345.

131. A few days before the onset of violence around El Paso, the *Galveston Daily News* reported that the county's grand jury heard just a single indictment, which they took as evidence "that the population of El Paso county is composed of good, peaceable and law-abiding citizens"; "State News," *Galveston Daily News*, September 28, 1877.

132. *El Paso Troubles*, 3–4, 50–54, 68–78, 100, 106; Gillett, *Six Years with the Texas Rangers*, 195–96; Utley, *Lone Star Justice*, 191, 196; Sonnichsen, *Ten Texas Feuds*, 111–12, 122–23, 127–30. Webb, *Texas Rangers*, 351, 356; "State Press," *Galveston Daily News*, September 20, 1877.

133. "Howard's Statement," *Mesilla Independent*, October 6, 1877; Sonnichsen, *Ten Texas Feuds*, 130.

134. Testimony of Father "Peter" Bourgade, *El Paso Troubles*, 100; see also 26–27, 98–101. Traditional narratives of the Salt War grant "sinister power" to Father Antonio Borajo, a sort of Mexican Rasputin; see Utley, *Lone Star Justice*, 190. Webb called him "an evil spirit" who manipulated the "ignorant rabble" of Mexicans into acts of violence; Webb, *Texas Rangers*, 348, 350. But the evidence for his machinations is largely nonexistent, based on the statements of white Democrats, and clearly intended to imply that the Hispanics were unjustified in their uprising. See, for instance, the letter of A.J. Fountain to Major John Jones, March 4, 1878, *El Paso Troubles*, 127–29, which states that Borajo conspired to bring the salt lakes under his control for monetary purposes. See also ibid., 24–25.

135. "Mexican Invasion of Texas," *North American* (Philadelphia), October 8, 1877; "Mexico," *North American*, October 9, 1877; "Death to Gringos!" *Daily Arkansas Gazette* (Little Rock), October 7, 1877; "Death to Gringos," *St. Louis Globe-Democrat*, October 7, 1877; "Texas News by Telegraph," *Galveston Daily News*, October 3, 1877; "Texas News by Telegraph," *Galveston Daily News*, October 6, 1877; "The El Paso Trouble,"

Galveston Daily News, October 7, 1877; "Texas," *Daily Rocky Mountain News* (Denver), October 7, 1877; "Foreign News," *Boston Daily Advertiser*, October 8, 1877; *Milwaukee Daily Sentinel*, October 8, 1877; "Trouble on the Mexican Border," *Lowell Daily Citizen*, October 8, 1877. Most newspaper accounts of the crisis were based on the reporting of the *Galveston Daily News*. Sonnichsen, *Ten Texas Feuds, 130–31*; "Howard's Statement," *Mesilla Independent*, October 6, 1877; Utley, *Lone Star Justice*, 191–92; Webb, Texas Rangers, 351–52; testimony of Jesus Cobas, Vidal Garcia, *Father Bourgade, and G.N.* Garcia, *El Paso Troubles*, 71–74, 98–108; Kerber to Steele, October 5, 1877, *El Paso Troubles*, 151–52. Sheriff Kerber published his version of these events, which had Cardis targeting Howard for assassination; see "Cardis Against Howard," *Galveston Daily News*, October 24, 1877.

136. Blacker to Hubbard, October 9, 1877, and Kerber to Hubbard, October 10, 1877, *El Paso Troubles*, 141–42.

137. Webb, *Texas Rangers*, 352; Sonnichsen, *Ten Texas Feuds*, 132.

138. The *Daily News* had the integrity to print this article; "An End of Extradition," *Galveston Daily News*, October 9, 1877; "Shall We Invade?" *Galveston Daily News*, October 13, 1877.

139. Sheridan quoted in "Washington," *North American* (Philadelphia), October 17, 1877; Utley, *Lone Star Justice*, 193, 333n11. Sheridan's comments persuaded many commentators that the war scare was overblown. *North American*, October 8, 1877; "The Affair at El Paso," *North American*, October 10, 1877; *The Congregationalist* (Boston), October 10, 1877, p. 8; "The Mexican Imbroglio," *Galveston Daily News*, October 14, 1877; "Troubles Between Mexicans and Americans," *Milwaukee Daily Sentinel*, October 18, 1877, p. 2.

140. Utley, *Lone Star Justice*, 193; *El Paso Troubles*, 102, 151–54; "The El Paso Trouble," *Galveston Daily News*, October 11, 1877.

141. "El Paso Troubles," *Mesilla Independent*, October 6, 1877; testimony of Wesley Owens, *El Paso Troubles*, 59; Sonnichsen, *Ten Texas Feuds*, 132.

142. Testimony of Lt. Leonard Hay, *El Paso Troubles*, 62.

143. Testimony of Jesus Gonzales, A. Krakauer, Leopold Sender, and Wesley Owens, *El Paso Troubles*, 59–64 (quote, 59); Gillett, *Six Years with the Texas Rangers*, 196; Utley, *Lone Star Justice*, 193–94; *Mesilla Independent*, October 18, 1877; Webb, *Texas Rangers*, 353. Curiously, in reporting on Cardis's murder, the *Galveston Daily News* did not identify him as a member of the state legislature, but as "the leader of the mob" in El Paso; "The El Paso Imbroglio," *Galveston Daily News*, October 13, 1877. See also "Mexican Mobs: A Reign of Terror at El Paso," *St. Louis Globe-Democrat*, October 15, 1877.

144. *El Paso Troubles*, 64.

145. Kerber to Steele, November 14, 1877, *El Paso Troubles*, 156.

146. Gillett, *Six Years with the Texas Rangers*, 197–98; Utley, *Lone Star Justice*, 194–95; Webb, *Texas Rangers*, 354–56, 355–56. Major Jones did accept a bond from Howard for his good behavior. Sonnichsen, *Ten Texas Feuds*, 139; testimony of Joseph Magoffin, *El Paso Troubles*, 80.

147. Kerber quoted in Webb, *Texas Rangers*, 355; Gillett, *Six Years with the Texas Rangers*, 197–98; Utley, *Lone Star Justice*, 194; Sonnichsen, *Ten Texas Feuds*, 137–38.

148. Sonnichsen, *Ten Texas Feuds*, 141–42; Testimony of Jesus Cobas, *El Paso Troubles*, 71–72; Gillett, *Six Years with the Texas Rangers*, 198.

149. Sonnichsen, *Ten Texas Feuds*, 137, 141–42 (Bourgarde quote); Jones to Steele, *El Paso Troubles*, 99, 154–55; Utley, *Lone Star Justice*, 196.

150. *El Paso Troubles*, 55–59, 78–79, 100–109, 157–58; Utley, *Lone Star Justice*, 196–97; "The El Paso Trouble—A Salt Riot," *Galveston Daily News*, October 13, 1877; "State Press," *Galveston Daily News*, October 13, 1877; Sonnichsen, *Ten Texas Feuds*, 142; Webb, *Texas Rangers*, 358; *Mesilla Independent*, January 5, 1878.

151. "War in El Paso Again!" *Galveston Daily News*, December 15, 1877; Governor Hubbard's telegrams, *El Paso Troubles*, 144–48; Sonnichsen, *Ten Texas Feuds*, 144; Utley, *Lone Star Justice*, 201. The *Daily News* argued that there was no contradiction between wanting a weak central government and calling for its aid to deal with "foreign aggression"; see "Texas, Federal Protection and a 'Strong Government,'" *Galveston Daily News*, October 25, 1877.

152. Unsigned letter from Juan Nepa Garcia to *Mesilla Independent*, January 7, 1878, *El Paso Trouble*, 97–98; Gillett, *Six Years with the Texas Rangers*, 198; Utley, *Lone Star Justice*, 197; Sonnichsen, *Ten Texas Feuds*, 145.

153. *El Paso Troubles*, 37, 57, 81, 96–101; *Mesilla Independent*, December 22, 1877; *Mesilla Independent*, January 5, 1878; *Mesilla Independent*, January 17, 1878; Sonnichsen, *Ten Texas Feuds*, 146 *Mesilla Independent*, 48; Utley, *Lone Star Justice*, 198.

154. Testimony of J.B. Tays, *El Paso Troubles*, 81. See also *El Paso Troubles*, 55–58, 72–74, 82, 98–102; *Mesilla Independent*, January 5, 1878; Utley, *Lone Star Justice*, 198–99; Sonnichsen, *Ten Texas Feuds*, 148–49.

155. Testimony of Mary A. Cooper, *El Paso Troubles*, 74. See also *El Paso Troubles*, 30, 57, 66, 74, 78–79, 96–98, 158; Webb, *Texas Rangers*, 361–62; Sonnichsen, *Ten Texas Feuds*, 149–52; *Mesilla Independent*, January 5, 1878; *Mesilla Independent*, January 12, 1878; Gillett, *Six Years with the Texas Rangers*, 199–200; Utley, *Lone Star Justice*, 199–200, 205.

156. Tays quoted in Utley, *Lone Star Justice*, 201; Webb, *Texas Rangers*, 362; Sonnichsen, *Ten Texas Feuds*, 152–53; *Mesilla Independent*, January 5, 1878; *El Paso Troubles*, 82, 113, 158.

157. Sonnichsen, *Ten Texas Feuds*, 153; Utley, *Lone Star Justice*, 201, 334n31.

158. Colonel Edward Hatch to Colonel Jonathan King, February 8, 1878, "Orders of December 24, 1877," *El Paso Troubles*, 87–88. See also *El Paso Troubles*, 28, 78–79, 83–95, 102–3, 112–17, 145–50; Utley, *Lone Star Justice*, 201–3; Sonnichsen, *Ten Texas Feuds*, 152–54; Gillett, *Six Years with the Texas Rangers*, 200–201; Mesilla *Independent*, January 5, 1878; Webb, *Texas Rangers*, 362–63.

159. Col. Edward Hatch, commander of U.S. forces in New Mexico, and Lt. Col. William H. Lewis compiled a report in *Annual Report of the Secretary of War for the Year 1878* (Washington, DC: GPO, 1878), 50–57. See also *El Paso Troubles*, 1–33; Webb, *Texas Rangers*, 366–67; Gillett, *Six Years with the Texas Rangers*, 214; Utley, *Lone Star Justice*, 203–5. Most of the sources on the Salt War are by Anglos, but there are some documents from Hispanics and Mexicans in *El Paso Troubles*.

160. Edwards, *New Spirits*, 46; Utley, *Lone Star Justice*, 168, 192–93; Hoogenboom, *Presidency of Hayes*, 174–76. There had been numerous suggestions that the best solution to the border problems was to expand the railroad network, which would bring progress and prosperity to the region; see "Railroads and the Mexican Problem," *Galveston Daily News*, October 12, 1877.

161. Richard Buitron Jr., *The Quest for Tejano Identity in San Antonio, Texas, 1913–2000* (New York: Routledge, 2004); Julio Noboa, *Leaving Latinos Out of History: Teaching U.S. History in Texas* (New York: Routledge, 2005).

162. Ken Gonzales-Day, *Lynching in the West, 1850–1935* (Durham, NC: Duke University Press, 2006), 235.

163. Ibid., 93–94. The postcard can be seen in plate 4.

164. Ibid., 93–95, 99 (quote). The *Colorado Springs Gazette* justified the lynching of a murderer—who had been identified by a surviving victim—as "quiet and orderly but determined"; see "Lynching at La Veta," *Colorado Springs Gazette* July 28, 1877, p. 4.

165. Gonzales-Day, *Lynching in the West*, 99–100; "A Desperado Lynched," *Inter Ocean* (Chicago) July 14, 1877, p. 2. There were three known lynchings in 1879 and none in 1880; see Gonzales-Day, *Lynching in the West*, 235.

166. Josiah Royce, *California, from the Conquest in 1846 to the Second Vigilance Committee in San Francisco: A Study of American Character* (Boston: Houghton Mifflin, 1886), 263–64.

167. "The Chinese," *San Francisco Daily Evening Bulletin*, March 1, 1877; "The Workingmen," *San Francisco Daily Evening Bulletin*, December 29, 1877; "The Mongolian Workingmen," *San Francisco Daily Evening Bulletin*, January 15, 1878; "Romish Plans," *The Congregationalist* (Boston), August 7, 1878; p. 5; Saxton, *Indispensible Enemy*, 3, 53–66; Lucy M. Cohen, *Chinese in Post-Civil War South: A People Without History* (Baton Rouge: Louisiana State University Press, 1984); Ronald T. Takaki, *Strangers from a Different Shore: A History of Asian Americans* (Boston: Little, Brown, 1989); Sucheng Chan, *The Bittersweet Soil: The Chinese in California Agriculture, 1860–1910* (Berkeley: University of California Press, 1989).

168. Mary Roberts Coolidge, *Chinese Immigration* (New York: Henry Holt & Co., 1909), 498–504; George Anthony Peffer, *If They Don't Bring Their Women Here: Chinese Female Immigration before Exclusion* (Urbana: University of Illinois, 1999), 43–56; Najia Aarim-Heriot, *Chinese Immigrants, African Americans, and Racial Anxiety in the United States, 1848–82* (Urbana: University of Illinois Press, 2003), 178–79; Saxton, *Indispensible Enemy*, 3–8.

169. Sidney I. Pomerantz, "Election of 1876," in *History of American Presidential Elections, 1789–1968*, ed. Arthur M. Schlesinger (New York: Chelsea House, 1971), 2:1439, 1442; Aarim-Heriot, *Chinese Immigrants*, 180–86; U.S. Senate Report no. 689, 44th Cong., 2nd sess., *Report of the Joint Special Committee to Investigate Chinese Immigration, Feb. 27, 1877* (Washington, DC: GPO, 1877), 275–88, 942, 951–68, 1133–34, 1241–48; Roger Daniels, *Asian America: Chinese and Japanese in the United States since 1850* (Seattle: University of Washington Press, 1990), 45–54.

170. *Report of the Joint Special Committee to Investigate Chinese Immigration*, 1051; Aarim-Heriot, *Chinese Immigrants*, 185.

171. *Report of the Joint Special Committee to Investigate Chinese Immigration*, v; Aarim-Heriot, *Chinese Immigrants*, 183. In August 1877, the California legislature conducted its own investigation, hearing John Boalt, for whom the University of California at Berkeley Law School is named, inform the committee that contact with the "Mongolians" aroused "an unconquerable repulsion" among whites and was reason enough to not only end all Chinese immigration, but also expel those Chinese already living in the United States. State of California, Senate, *Chinese Immigration: Its Social, Moral, and Political Effect* (Sacramento: State Office, 1878), 258–84. The state delivered ten thousand copies to members of Congress and the newspapers. Aarim-Heriot, *Chinese Immigrants*, 187–89.

172. Winfield J. Davis, *History of Political Conventions in California, 1849–1892* (Sacramento: State of California, 1893), 365–93; Ira B. Cross, *A History of the Labor Movement in California* (Berkeley: University of California Press, 1935), 88–129; Saxton, *Indispensible Enemy*, 113–32; Aarim-Heriot, *Chinese Immigrants*, 190; Kenneth C.

Wenzer, ed., *Henry George: Collected Journalistic Writings*, 4 vols. (Armonk, NY: M.E. Sharpe, 2003), 1:161–68, 175, 179–81.

173. Wenzer, *Henry George*, 1:169–70, 173.

174. "A Chinese Massacre Exciting California," *Daily Rocky Mountain News* (Denver), March 17, 1877; *Butte Record*, March 18, 1877; "Woe and Wickedness," *Milwaukee Daily Sentinel*, April 6, 1877, p. 4; "Outrage on Chinamen," *New York Times*, March 16, 1877; "The Massacre of Chinamen," *New York Times*, March 17, 1877; "The California Massacre," editorial, *New York Times*, March 18, 1877, p. 4; *New York Times*, March 19, 1877; "The Chinese Question," *New York Times*, March 21, 1877, p. 2; "Gleanings from the Mail," *New York Times*, March 24, 1877, p. 2; Jean Pfaelzer, *Driven Out: The Forgotten War Against Chinese Americans* (New York: Random House, 2007), 64–74; Saxton, *Indispensible Enemy*, 8–9.

175. There are numerous stories on these riots in the *San Francisco Daily Evening Bulletin*, July 24–28, 1877; Saxton, *Indispensible Enemy*, 114–16. Several prominent West Coast ministers defended Kearney; see, e.g., "The San Francisco Pulpit," *San Francisco Daily Evening Bulletin*, November 19, 1877.

176. "Irishmen vs. Chinamen," *Colorado Springs Gazette*, November 24, 1877; *Colorado Springs Gazette*, August 4, 1877, p. 2; "Communism in California," *New York Times*, November 4, 1877; William Deverell, *Railroad Crossing: Californians and the Railroad, 1850–1910* (Berkeley: University of California Press, 1994), 34.

177. Henry George, "The Kearney Agitation in California," *Popular Science Monthly* 17 (1880): 448, 451; "Trial of the Agitators," *San Francisco Daily Evening Bulletin*, January 18, 1878; Davis, *History of Political Conventions in California*, 367.

178. Kearney quoted in Deverell, *Railroad Crossing*, 44; Neil L. Shumsky, "Dissatisfaction, Mobility, and Expectation: San Francisco Workingmen in the 1870s," *Pacific Historian* 30 (1986): 21–28.

179. "Order or Disorder?" *San Francisco Daily Evening Bulletin*, November 1, 1877; "Arrest of a Communist," *St. Louis Globe-Democrat*, November 4, 1877, p. 3; "California: Communism in San Francisco," *North American* (Philadelphia), November 5, 1877; "The Incendiary Agitators," *San Francisco Daily Evening Bulletin*, November 5, 1877; "The Interior Press on the San Francisco Incendiaries," *San Francisco Daily Evening Bulletin*, November 6, 1877; "Putting the Case Upside Down," *San Francisco Daily Evening Bulletin*, November 9, 1877; Saxton, *Indispensible Enemy*, 116, 119–20.

180. "The Incendiary Agitators"; "Denis Kearney: An Interview with Him in the County Jail," *San Francisco Daily Evening Bulletin*, November 6, 1877; "The Incendiary Business," *San Francisco Daily Evening Bulletin*, November 8, 1877; "Kearney in the Criminal Court," *San Francisco Daily Evening Bulletin*, November 13, 1877; "Kearney and Confederates," *San Francisco Daily Evening Bulletin*, November 14, 1877; "Careless Law Making," *San Francisco Daily Evening Bulletin*, November 15, 1877; "Open Air Meeting," *San Francisco Daily Evening Bulletin*, November 16, 1877; Saxton, *Indispensible Enemy*, 119–21.

181. Kearney was mentioned in the *San Francisco Daily Evening Bulletin* nearly every day through the last three months of 1877, often several times. See, for instance, "Order or Disorder?" November 1, 1877; "The Incendiary Agitators"; "Kearney Shows His Teeth," November 6, 1877; "Kearney's Sedition," November 9, 1877; "The Labor Agitation," November 14, 1877; "Workingmen's Parties," November 24, 1877; "Kearney Meetings: Communistic Ideas Expressed," November 26, 1877.

182. It is difficult to determine the party loyalty of many of the convention delegates, which leads to some contrary figures. See Deverell, *Railroad Crossing*, 47 (quote); Carl B. Swisher, *Motivation and Political Technique in the California Constitutional Convention, 1878–1879* (Claremont, CA: Pomona College, 1930), 24; Saxton, *Indispensible Enemy*, 123–27.

183. The first quote is by William White of Santa Cruz, the Workingmen's Party candidate for governor in 1880; the second is by Charles Kleine of San Francisco. E.B. Willis and P.K. Stockton, comp., *Debates and Proceedings of the Constitutional Convention of the State of California*, 3 vols. (Sacramento: State Office, 1881), 1:569, 600.

184. Deverell, *Railroad Crossing*, 49; Davis, *History of Political Conventions in California*, 374–93; Aarim-Heriot, *Chinese Immigrants*, 191–92; *Debates and Proceedings of the 1878 Constitutional Convention of the State of California*; Saxton, *Indispensible Enemy*, 127–32.

185. Henry George, "The Kearney Agitation in California," *Popular Science Monthly* 17 (1880): 448; Davis, *History of Political Conventions in California*, 393–421; Raphael and House, *Two Peoples*, 263; Daniel Cornfield, *Workers and Dissent in the Redwood Empire* (Philadelphia: Temple University Press, 1987); Saxton, *Indispensible Enemy*, 129–30; Swisher, *Motivation and Political Technique*, 101–10.

186. Richardson, *Compilation of the Messages and Papers of the Presidents*, 9:4466–72; Hoogenboom, *Presidency of Hayes*, 177–81; Saxton, *Indispensible Enemy*, 133, 137.

187. Lucile Eaves, *A History of California Labor Legislation* (Berkeley: University of California Press, 1910), 158–59; Saxton, *Indispensible Enemy*, 138–39; Swisher, *Motivation and Political Technique*, 112–14; Aarim-Heriot, *Chinese Immigrants*, 192; Eaves, *History of California Labor Legislation*, 159–60.

188. R. David Arkush and Leo O. Lee, ed. and trans., *Land Without Ghosts: Chinese Impressions of America from the Mid-Nineteenth Century to the Present* (Berkeley: University of California Press, 1989), 57; Henry Sienkiewicz, *Portrait of America: Letters of Henry Sienkiewicz*, ed. and trans. Charles Morley (New York: Columbia University Press, 1959), 264n6; Aarim-Heriot, *Chinese Immigrants*, 5; Charles J. McCalin, *In Search of Equality: The Chinese Struggle against Discrimination in Nineteenth-Century America* (Berkeley: University of California Press, 1996), 147–220. On expulsion of the Chinese from Western communities, see the outstanding work of Jean Pfaelzer, *Driven Out*.

Chapter 4: The Terror of Poverty

1. Terence Powderly, *The Path I Trod: The Autobiography of Terence V. Powderly* (Brooklyn: AMS Press, 1968), 27.

2. "Some Pictures of Poverty," *Cincinnati Commercial*, January 7, 1877, reprinted in *Lafcadio Hearn's America: Ethnographic Sketches and Editorials*, ed. Simon J. Bronner (Lexington: University Press of Kentucky, 2002), 78–86 (quotes, 83–84).

3. See for instance, "Sicilians in New Orleans," *Cincinnati Commercial*, December 27, 1877, in *Lafcadio Hearn's America*, 63–65.

4. Elizabeth Bisland, ed., *Life and Letters of Lafcadio Hearn* (Boston: Houghton Mifflin Co., 1923), 155; Adam Rothman, "Lafcadio Hearn in New Orleans and the Caribbean," *Atlantic Studies* 5 (2008): 265–83. Helen Campbell and Jacob Riis wrote their exposés of poverty in the 1880s, publishing them as books in 1887 and 1890, respectively: Helen Campbell, *Prisoners of Poverty: Women Wage-Workers, Their Trades and Their Lives* (Boston: Little, Brown, 1887); Jacob Riis, *How the Other Half Live: Studies Among the Tenements of New York* (New York: Charles Scribner's Sons, 1890).

5. Bisland, *Life and Letters of Lafcadio Hearn*, 59.

6. Oliver P. Morton, "American Constitution," *North American Review* 124 (1877): 345; "Macaulay on Democracy," *Milwaukee Daily Sentinel*, January 29, 1877, p. 4; "Concerning Tenements," *Boston Daily Advertiser*, June 6, 1877; "Middlemen and Laborers," *Inter Ocean* (Chicago), July 26, 1877, p. 6; Henry Carey Baird, "Money and Its Substitutes: Commerce and Its Instruments of Adjustment," *Atlantic Monthly* 37 (1876): 355; William A. Zulker, *John Wanamaker, King of Merchants* (Wayne, PA: Eaglecrest Press, 1993), 17–38; "New Books," *St. Louis Globe-Democrat*, November 26, 1877, p. 3; "Literary Notices," *North American* (Philadelphia), March 16, 1877.

7. "The French Bourgeoisie," *Daily Arkansas Gazette* (Little Rock), April 4, 1877; "Gov. Rice's Address," *Boston Daily Advertiser*, January 5, 1877; Baird, "Money and Its Substitutes," 355; Bond quoted in "The Labor Question," *St. Louis Globe-Democrat*, August 27, 1877, p. 3; "Gotham's Gloomy Outlook," *Georgia Weekly Telegraph and Georgia Journal & Messenger* (Macon), May 8, 1877.

8. "Beggared": "California's Dark Days," *Lowell Daily Citizen*, May 25, 1877; "Financial Freaks," *St. Louis Globe-Democrat*, July 15, 1877, p. 3; visit to secondhand dealers in "The Pressure on the Middle Class," from the *New York Graphic*, *Boston Daily Advertiser*, August 9, 1877; "The General Court," *Boston Daily Advertiser*, March 13, 1877; "The Ideal House," *San Francisco Daily Evening Bulletin*, February 17, 1877; "Real Estate," *Inter Ocean* (Chicago), February 17, 1877, p. 7; "Business in Philadelphia," *North American* (Philadelphia), April 5, 1877; "Real Estate: The Market Still Apathetic," *Inter Ocean* (Chicago) April 28, 1877, p. 6.

9. "Home Politics," *Boston Daily Advertiser*, October 29, 1877; "Wendell Phillips on the Labor Question," *Chicago Daily Tribune*, September 19, 1877.

10. "Help, or We Perish!" *Inter Ocean* (Chicago), January 13, 1877, p. 6.

11. Quotes from the following sources, in order: "Tramps Raiding in Pennsylvania," *Galveston Daily News*, September 11, 1877; "The Tramp," *Daily Arkansas Gazette* (Little Rock), January 24, 1877; "Tramps," *Bangor Daily Whig & Courier*, April 21, 1877.

12. Quotes from the following sources, in order: "A War with the Tramps," *Georgia Weekly Telegraph and Georgia Journal & Messenger* (Macon), September 18, 1877; "March of the Tramps"; "Encouraging Tramps," *St. Louis Globe-Democrat*, March 12, 1877, p. 4; "The Tramp Question and Wholesale Pauperism," *Galveston Daily News*, December 30, 1877.

13. Even fifty years later, the excellent historian Allan Nevins took what he read in the newspapers of the late 1870s as fact and reported on the "tramp evil" sweeping the country, with its hordes of criminals raping, pillaging, and murdering across the country. Allan Nevins, *The Emergence of Modern America, 1865–1878* (New York: Macmillan, 1927), 301–2.

14. Board of Charities quoted in "The Tramp Nuisance," *Frank Leslie's Illustrated Newspaper* (New York), July 21, 1877, p. 341; "people will be overrun": "The Tramps," *Bangor Daily Whig & Courier*, April 21, 1877.

15. Eric H. Monkkonen, ed., *Walking to Work: Tramps in America, 1790–1935* (Lincoln: University of Nebraska Press, 1984), 5.

16. Monkkonen, *Walking to Work*, 9; Walter Van Bru, ed., *Duluth and St. Louis County Minnesota: Their Story and People*, 3 vols. (Chicago: American Historical Society, 1921), 1:243–44; Michael Davis, "Forced to Tramp: The Perspective of the Labor Press, 1870–1900,"in Monkkonen, *Walking to Work*, 156–57; *National Labor Tribune* (Pittsburgh), December 1, 1877 (quote). Allan Pinkerton also used this wording in his *Strikers, Communists, Tramps and Detectives* (New York: G.W. Carleton & Co., 1878), 134.

17. The first such use of "tramps" as a pejorative noun that I can locate is in the *Eighth Annual Report of the Board of State Charities of Massachusetts* (Boston: Wright & Potter, 1872), lxxviii, which speaks of the need to "accurately discriminate between the worthy traveler and the professional tramp." The first use in a newspaper appears to be "Tramps in Maine," *Yankton* (SD) *Press and Union and Dakotaian*, December 4, 1873. Though he offers no supportive citation, Jack Beatty places the first use of "tramp" in the *New York Times* sometime in 1874; see Jack Beatty, *Age of Betrayal: The Triumph of Money in America, 1865–1900* (New York: Knopf, 2007), 293. Paul T. Ringenbach locates that first usage of "tramp" in the *New York Times*, February 6, 1875, as does Tim Cresswell. See Paul T. Ringenbach, *Tramps and Reformers, 1873–1916: The Discovery of Unemployment in New York* (Westport, CT: Greenwood Press, 1973), 4; Tim Cresswell, *The Tramp in America* (London: Reaktion Books, 2001), 48.

18. *The Congregationalist* (Boston), November 26, 1874, p. 8; *Lowell Daily Citizen and News*, August 4, 1875; "The Tramp," *Daily Arkansas Gazette* (Little Rock), January 24, 1877; "the tramp nuisance": *Boston Daily Advertiser*, November 23, 1877; "The Tramp Evil," *The Nation*, January 24, 1878, p. 50. This analysis is based on a study of just over two thousand articles in thirty-two newspapers and magazines, 1875–1878.

19. Priscilla Ferguson Clement, "The Transformation of the Wandering Poor in Nineteenth-Century Philadelphia," in Monkkonen, *Walking to Work*, 59–61; Monkkonen, "Introduction," *Walking to Work*, 8.

20. Clement, "Transformation of the Wandering Poor," 56–84; Josiah Flynt Willard, *Tramping with Tramps* (New York: Century Co., 1899), 99; *Philadelphia Telegraph*, June 19, 1876; Monkkonen, *Walking to Work*, 9–10.

21. "The Tramp," *Daily Arkansas Gazette* (Little Rock), January 24, 1877; Karl Marx, *The Civil War in France: The Paris Commune* (New York: International Publishers, 1984); Martin Phillip Johnson, *The Paradise of Association: Political Culture and Popular Organizations in the Paris Commune of 1871* (Ann Arbor: University of Michigan Press, 1996); Beatty, *Age of Betrayal*, 153; Howard Jay Graham, *Everyman's Constitution: Historical Essays on the Fourteenth Amendment, the "Conspiracy Theory," and American Constitutionalism* (Madison: State Historical Society of Wisconsin, 1968), 124–25; George L. Cherry, "American Metropolitan Press Reaction to the Paris Commune of 1871," *Mid-America* 32 (1950): 3–12.

22. First three quotes from "The Tramp," *Daily Arkansas Gazette* (Little Rock), March 18, 1877; remaining three quotes from "Vagrants and Tramps," *Daily Arkansas Gazette* (Little Rock), February 4, 1877.

23. "Disgusted Tramps," *St. Louis Globe-Democrat*, January 1, 1877, p. 2; *San Francisco Daily Evening Bulletin*, January 11, 1877; *San Francisco Daily Evening Bulletin*, June 15, 1877, citing the *Buffalo Express*.

24. "Tramps," *Daily Arkansas Gazette* (Little Rock), July 14, 1877; "Tramp Nuisance." See also *San Francisco Daily Evening Bulletin*, August 1, 1877; *Galveston Daily News*, August 25, September 11, 1877.

25. "Tramp Nuisance"; "Depredations of Tramps," *Boston Daily Advertiser*, September 22, 1877; "Virginia Outrages by a Gang of Tramps," *North American* (Philadelphia), September 22, 1877.

26. "Fond du Lac Tramps," *Milwaukee Daily Sentinel*, July 30, 1877, p. 5; "Tramp Nuisance."

27. *Lowell Daily Citizen*, September 7, 1877; Davis, "Forced to Tramp," 141–70;

Henry James to William James, January 12, 1877, in *Henry James Letters*, 4 vols., ed. Leon Edel (Cambridge, MA: Harvard University Press, 1974–84), 91.

28. *San Francisco Daily Evening Bulletin*, from the *Albany Argus*, February 17, 1877; "Depravity Grouped," *Inter Ocean* (Chicago), April 23, 1877; "Robbed by a Tramp," *St. Louis Globe-Democrat*, November 24, 1877; "A War on the Nomads," *North American* (Philadelphia) November 20, 1877.

29. "Crime and Criminals," *Inter Ocean* (Chicago), February 14, 1877, p. 5; "Robbery in Foxborough: Arrest of the Thieves," *Boston Daily Advertiser*, March 13, 1877; *St. Louis Globe-Democrat*, April 28, 1877, p. 8.

30. "A Freight Train Boarded by Half a Hundred Tramps," *St. Louis Globe-Democrat*, August 3, 1877, p. 3; "Tramps Robbing Mongolian Graves," *San Francisco Daily Evening Bulletin*, December 27, 1877; "Tramps," *Daily Arkansas Gazette* (Little Rock), July 14, 1877.

31. "Ragamuffins": *North American* (Philadelphia) July 26, 1877; Macon City taken over by tramps: *St. Louis Globe-Democrat*, August 3, 1877, p. 3; *Inter Ocean* (Chicago) July 28, 1877, p. 11; "Depredations of Tramps," *Boston Daily Advertiser*, September 22, 1877; "Curiosities of Crime," *Inter Ocean* (Chicago), February 8, 1877, p. 5; *Inter Ocean*, July 28, 1877, p. 11.

32. "Villainous tramp": "The General Criminal Calendar," *Inter Ocean* (Chicago), July 14, 1877, p. 2; "an Inoffensive Young Man": "Lawlessness," *Inter Ocean*, August 22, 1877 "Murder and Suicide," *Boston Daily Advertiser*, May 14, 1877.

33. "Tramps," *Daily Arkansas Gazette* (Little Rock), July 14, 1877; "Tramps Raiding in Pennsylvania"; *Georgia Weekly Telegraph and Georgia Journal & Messenger* (Macon), November 6, 1877; "Virginia: Tramps behind the Bars," *North American* (Philadelphia), September 24, 1877.

34. "Depredations of Tramps," *Boston Daily Advertiser*, September 22, 1877; "Virginia: Outrages by a Gang of Tramps," *North American* (Philadelphia), September 22, 1877; "Virginia: Tramps behind the Bars"; *San Francisco Daily Evening Bulletin*, October 5, 1877; "Depredations of Tramps," *Boston Daily Advertiser*, September 22, 1877. For similarly undramatic stories, see "How a Thieving Gang of Tramps Were [sic] Foiled by a Telegrapher," *St. Louis Globe-Democrat*, August 31, 1877, p. 3; "A Thieving Tramp," *Inter Ocean* (Chicago), September 18, 1877, p. 5; "A Party of Tramps Routed by Chinamen," *San Francisco Daily Evening Bulletin*, October 5, 1877.

35. "Ingratitude of a Tramp," *Inter Ocean* (Chicago), August 27, 1877, p. 5; "Eloped with a Tramp," *St. Louis Globe-Democrat*, August 27, 1877.

36. *Hartford Times* quoted in the *Bangor Daily Whig & Courier*, April 21, 1877. See also "Organized Tramps," *Wisconsin State Register* (Portage), September 8, 1877; "Tramps Raiding in Pennsylvania."

37. "Tramp Nuisance."

38. "Swarm": "Virginia," *North American* (Philadelphia), September 24, 1877; remaining quotes from *Galveston Daily News*, August 25, 1877. See also "Organized Tramps"; "The Third Day of the American Association at Saratoga," *Boston Daily Advertiser*, September 7, 1877.

39. "Tramps," *Galveston Daily News*, September 25, 1877; David R. Johnson, *American Law Enforcement: A History* (St. Louis: Forum Press, 1981), 41–43; Kenneth L. Kusmer, *Down and Out, On the Road: The Homeless in American History* (New York: Oxford University Press, 2002), 43.

40. "The Tramp," *Daily Arkansas Gazette* (Little Rock), March 18, 1877; "Utilising the Tramps," from *New York World, Daily Arkansas Gazette* (Little Rock) September 9, 1877.

41. *Hartford Times* quoted in the *Bangor Daily Whig & Courier*, April 21, 1877; *Galveston Daily News*, January 14, 1877 (this paper favored the same policy for Galveston).

42. "The Tramp Question," *Inter Ocean* (Chicago), February 1, 1877, p. 3; "To Suppress Tramps," *Wisconsin State Register* (Portage), May 5, 1877; McCook, "Tramp Census and its Revelations," *Forum* 15 (August 1893): 156, 765; Cresswell, *Tramp in America*, 52; Harry A. Millis, "The Law Affecting Immigrants and Tramps," *Charities Review* 7 (September 1897): 587–94.

43. "Utilising the Tramps"; "The Tramp Question," *Inter Ocean* (Chicago), February 1, 1877, p. 3; "The Tramp Question and Wholesale Pauperism," *Galveston Daily News*, December 30, 1877.

44. The South being "overrun" and "whipping post" in *New York Tribune* quoted in *North American* (Philadelphia), July 26, 1877; *St. Louis Globe-Democrat*, September 11, 1877, p. 4; Beatty, *Age of Betrayal*, 294; Kusmer, *Down and Out*, 99; Amy Dru Stanley, "Beggars Can't Be Choosers: Compulsion and Contract in Post-Bellum America," *Journal of American History* 78 (1992): 1265–93.

45. For these laws, see Orlando F. Lewis, *Vagrancy in the United States* (New York: for the author, 1907); Michigan State Library, *Laws of the Various States Relating to Vagrancy* (n.p.: Michigan State Library, 1910); Jeffrey S. Adler, "A Historical Analysis of the Law of Vagrancy," *Criminology* 27 (1989), 209–29; Elbert Hubbard, "The Rights of Tramps," *Arena* 9 (April 1894): 593–600.

46. Beatty, *Age of Betrayal*, 295; William Cohen, "Negro Involuntary Servitude in the South, 1865–1940: A Preliminary Analysis," *Journal of Southern History* 42 (1976): 31–60; "The Tramp Question and Wholesale Pauperism," *Galveston Daily News*, December 30, 1877; *Boston Daily Advertiser*, November 23, 1877; Douglas A. Blackmon, *Slavery by Another Name: The Re-Enslavement of Black Americans from the Civil War to World War II* (New York: Doubleday, 2008), 39–83.

47. *Third Annual Report of the Bureau of Labor Statistics of the State of Connecticut* (Hartford: The Bureau, 1887), 140–42; "Virginia: Tramps behind the Bars"; Davis, "Forced to Tramp," 162.

48. Lucilius Emery, "The Constitutional Right to Bear Arms," *Harvard Law Review* 28 (1915): 476; Davis, "Forced to Tramp," 162; Samuel Leavitt, "Tramps and the Law," *Forum* 2 (1886): 190–200.

49. *National Labor Tribune*, November 10, 1877.

50. *State v. Hogan*, 63 Ohio (1900) 215; *National Labor Tribune*, December 1, 1877; *National Labor Tribune*, January 12, 1878; Davis, "Forced to Tramp," 162–63.

51. Davis, "Forced to Tramp," 144.

52. The *North American* (Philadelphia), July 10, 1877, published two articles on this meeting, "The Tramp" and "The Tramp Nuisance."

53. "Tramps," *Daily Arkansas Gazette* (Little Rock), July 14, 1877; "The Tramp Nuisance," *North American* (Philadelphia), July 10, 1877; Beatty, *Age of Betrayal*, 293; Robert V. Bruce, *1877: Year of Violence* (Indianapolis: Bobbs-Merrill, 1959), 68–69.

54. "The Tramp Nuisance," *North American* (Philadelphia), July 10, 1877; "The Tramp," *North American*, July 10, 1877.

55. "Move On: The War on the Pestiferous Tramp—He Must Be Suppressed," *North American* (Philadelphia), July 14, 1877; "The Tramp: What Will Be Done with Him," *North American*, July 23, 1877; *San Francisco Daily Evening Bulletin*, August 1, 1877.

56. "Tramps," *Daily Arkansas Gazette* (Little Rock), July 14, 1877; "March of the Tramps"; "Tramps Raiding in Pennsylvania."

57. "No fear": "March of the Tramps"; "vigilance committees": "Tramps," *Galveston Daily News*, September 25, 1877 (this article attributes a similar opinion to the *Pittsburgh Post*). See also "A War on the Nomads," *North American* (Philadelphia), November 20, 1877.

58. "A War with the Tramps"; *Georgia Weekly Telegraph and Georgia Journal & Messenger*, October 30, 1877; "A War on the Nomads," *North American* (Philadelphia), November 20, 1877.

59. First four quotes from *Boston Daily Advertiser*, November 23, 1877; remaining two quotes in "Utilising the Tramps."

60. "The Tramp," *Daily Arkansas Gazette* (Little Rock), March 18, 1877. See also Rev. W.H. Throop, "Pious Pabulum," *Milwaukee Daily Sentinel*, November 26, 1877, p. 3; *Christian Union*, November 7, 1877, p. 392; "Shelter for the Idle," *New York Times*, February 12, 1877, p. 2.

61. *Boston Daily Advertiser*, November 23, 1877. On the anti-charity campaign, see Leah H. Feder, *Unemployment Relief in Periods of Depression: A Study of Measures Adopted in Certain American Cities, 1857 through 1922* (New York: Russell Sage, 1936), 41–44, 47.

62. Quoted in "Utilising the Tramps."

63. *Lowell Daily Citizen*, January 18, 1877. The more common form is that a granite contractor offers six tramps at a police station work, and they all make excuses for not taking the job; "The Non-Laboring Class," *Frank Leslie's Illustrated Newspaper* (New York), December 15, 1877; p. 239.

64. "Encouraging Tramps"; "The Tramp's Paradise," *Boston Daily Advertiser*, November 15, 1877.

65. "Paupers and Tramps," *St. Louis Globe-Democrat*, November 18, 1877, p. 7; "Tramp's Paradise"; "Utilising the Tramps"; Feder, *Unemployment Relief in Periods of Depression*, 50.

66. Murray: *Milwaukee Daily Sentinel*, March 31, 1877; "sack and burn": "Synopsis of a Practical Sermon," *Wisconsin State Register* (Portage), July 27, 1878; Hill: "Tramps," *North American* (Philadelphia), July 30, 1877.

67. Quoted in "The Tramp," *Daily Arkansas Gazette* (Little Rock), January 24, 1877.

68. Indianapolis: Feder, *Unemployment Relief in Periods of Depression*, 47, 49, 52–53, 57; Davis, "Forced to Tramp," 147; "tramping for several months": "Tramps Fire a Barn in Order to Get into Prison," *North American* (Philadelphia), August 30, 1877; "A Hero and a Martyr," *New York Times*, March 20, 1877, p. 4.

69. Daniel S. Gregory, *Christian Ethics: or, The True Moral Manhood and Life of Duty* (1875; Philadelphia: Eldridge & Brother, 1883), 224; Henry Ward Beecher, *Plymouth Pulpit: Sermons Preached in Plymouth Church, Brooklyn*, 4 vols. (Boston: Pilgrim Press, 1875), 4:463. On this point, see Henry F. May, *Protestant Churches and Industrial America* (New York: Harper & Row, 1967), 65–70; Richard T. Hughes, *Myths America Lives By* (Urbana: University of Illinois Press, 2004), 126–30.

70. "On the Tramp," *Milwaukee Daily Sentinel*, March 30, 1877, p. 4, is the first use of "social Darwinism" I can locate. See also *Milwaukee Daily Sentinel*, June 18, 1877, p. 7. Generally "social Darwinism" is said to have first appeared in an 1879 article by Oscar Schmidt in *Popular Science*, which is clearly not the case. In her brilliant book *The Age of American Unreason* (New York: Pantheon Books, 2008), 61, Susan Jacoby states, "I use the phrase 'social Darwinism' even though no one employed it in nineteenth-century

America or England." On Spencer's influence, see Richard Hofstadter, *Social Darwinism in American Thought* (New York: George Braziller, 1965); Barry Werth, *Banquet at Delmonico's: Great Minds, the Gilded Age, and the Triumph of Evolution in America* (New York: Random House, 2009); Louis Menand, *The Metaphysical Club: A Story of Ideas in America* (New York: Farrar, Straus and Giroux, 2001), 141–43, 177–200, 210–11.

71. "Universal Suffrage," *The Nation*, December 27, 1877, p. 391.

72. Henry Adams, *The Education of Henry Adams* (New York: Vintage, 1954), 211–12.

73. "Truth and Life," *The Congregationalist* (Boston), January 17, 1877, p. 2; "Philosophy and Science in American Colleges," *The Congregationalist* (Boston), April 4, 1877, p. 2; "Religious," *Milwaukee Daily Sentinel*, April 9, 1877, p. 7; *Milwaukee Daily Sentinel*, July 19, 1877, p. 7; "Boston Monday Lectures," *Boston Daily Advertiser*, October 31, 1877; "Church and Pulpit," *Inter Ocean* (Chicago), June 16, 1877, p. 9.

74. "Educational," *Milwaukee Daily Sentinel*, March 23, 1877, p. 7. See also, "In Memoriam," *Inter Ocean* (Chicago), April 20, 1877, p. 5; "Our Curiosity Shop," *Inter Ocean*, May 26, 1877, p. 12.

75. William A. Halliday, "Theories of Labor Reform and Social Improvement," *Presbyterian Quarterly and Princeton Review* 5 (1876): 425. In the same journal J. Elliot Condit noted that while the Presbyterian church conducted eleven missions among the Indians, it spent one-fifth what it did in 1857. "Our Indians and the Duty of the Presbyterian Church to Them," *Presbyterian Quarterly and Princeton Review* 5 (1876): 76–92.

76. "Literary," *Boston Daily Advertiser*, March 1, 1877; *Milwaukee Daily Sentinel*, March 8, 1877, p. 3; "Spencer's Sociology," *Boston Daily Advertiser*, May 21, 1877; "At Home and Abroad," *Frank Leslie's Illustrated Newspaper* (New York), September 8, 1877, p. 7; *St. Louis Globe-Democrat*, October 7, 1877, p. 4; "Mining," *Daily Rocky Mountain News* (Denver), March 1, 1877; "A Stroke of Love Lightning," *San Francisco Daily Evening Bulletin*, August 17, 1877.

77. Jacoby, *Age of American Unreason*, 68–73; Hofstadter, *Social Darwinism in American Thought*, 29–31, 51–70 (quote, 54); Werth, *Banquet at Delmonico's*, 126–27.

78. *Henry James Letters*, 2:98, 102.

79. Jacoby, *Age of American Unreason*, 61–81; Dee Brown, *The Year of the Century: 1876* (New York: Charles Scribner's Sons, 1966), 306; Steven Mintz and Susan Kellogg, *Domestic Revolutions: A Social History of American Family Life* (New York: Free Press, 1988), 104–5; Thomas J. Schlereth, *Victorian America: Transformations in Everyday Life, 1876–1915* (New York: HarperCollins, 1991), 288. On Sumner's influence, see the extended discussions in Hofstadter, *Social Darwinism in American Thought*, and Werth, *Banquet at Delmonico's*.

80. Darwin's 1871 edition of *The Descent of Man* seems to have anticipated and dismissed the direction in which Spencer was taking his work with a discussion of the "instinct of sympathy"; see Charles Darwin, *The Descent of Man and Selection in Relation to Sex* (New York: D. Appleton, 1909), 100–136, 624–26.

81. Herbert Spencer, *Social Statics: Or, the Conditions Essential to Human Happiness Specified, and the First of Them Developed* (New York: Appleton, 1865), 414–15; Henry Demarest Lloyd, "The New Conscience," *North American Review* 147 (1888): 336.

82. "Bloomington Brevities," *Inter Ocean* (Chicago), January 3, 1877, p. 6; "The President's Order," *Inter Ocean*, June 26, 1877, p. 4; *Milwaukee Daily Sentinel*, December 19, 1877, p. 7; *Inter Ocean*, December 31, 1877, p. 2; *Inter Ocean*, January 1, 1878, p. 4.

83. "Wanderlust": Monkkonen, *Walking to Work*, 6; "The Tramp: The Disease of Mendicancy a Result of the War," reprinted from *Scribner's Monthly* in the *Daily*

Arkansas Gazette (Little Rock), January 26, 1877; reprinted as "The Tramp" without attribution in the *Hinds County Gazette* (Raymond, MS), February 28, 1877. See also Joaquin Miller's poem "The Tramp of Shiloh," *Frank Leslie's Illustrated Newspaper* (New York), January 3, 1880, p. 324.

84. First two quotes from "The Tramp Question and Wholesale Pauperism," *Galveston Daily News*, December 30, 1877; "The Tramp," *Daily Arkansas Gazette* (Little Rock), March 18, 1877.

85. *National Labor Tribune*, January 13, 1875; *National Labor Tribune*, December 23, 1876, Davis, "Forced to Tramp,"147–48.

86. "South St. Louis Tramps," *St. Louis Globe-Democrat*, February 5, 1877, p. 8; Clement, "Transformation of the Wandering Poor," 65, 77; Eric H. Monkkonen, *The Dangerous Class: Crime and Poverty in Columbus, Ohio, 1860–1885* (Cambridge, MA: Harvard University Press, 1975), 112–16, 132, 143–44, 147, 160.

87. "The Third Day of the American Association at Saratoga," *Boston Daily Advertiser*, September 7, 1877. See also "Tramps," *Lowell Daily Citizen*, September 7, 1877. Wayland's name is often spelled Weyland; see, e.g., Cresswell, *Tramp in America*, 94.

88. "Treatment of Tramps," *Daily Arkansas Gazette* (Little Rock), September 13, 1877; *Lowell Daily Citizen*, September 7, 1877. See also "Tramps," *Galveston Daily News*, September 25, 1877.

89. "The Molly Maguires," *San Francisco Daily Evening Bulletin*, May 1, 1877; Kevin Kenny, *Making Sense of the Molly Maguires* (New York: Oxford University Press, 1998), 10–12.

90. Kenny, *Making Sense of the Molly Maguires*, 103, 111–12, 117–20, 126–28, 202–3 (quote, 112); Anthony F.C. Wallace, *St. Clair: A Nineteenth-Century Coal Town's Experience with a Disaster-Prone Industry* (Ithaca, NY: Cornell University Press, 1988), 249–313; Alexander Trachtenberg, *The History of Legislation for the Protection of Coal Miners in Pennsylvania, 1824–1915* (New York: International Publishers, 1942), 38–39, 53–60.

91. Francis P. Dewees, *The Molly Maguires: The Origin, Growth, and Character of the Organization* (Philadelphia: J.B. Lippincott & Co., 1877), 44; Allan Pinkerton, *The Molly Maguires and the Detectives* (1877; New York: G.W. Dillingham, 1905).

92. Pinkerton, *Molly Maguires and the Detectives*, 13–17, 148, 152, 235, 243, 258, 334, 455.

93. Kenny, *Making Sense of the Molly Maguires*, 156, 167, 170–73.

94. Ibid., 129, 131–32, 143, 148.

95. *New York Labor Standard*, March 17, 1877; Kenny, *Making Sense of the Molly Maguires*, 181–82; Wallace, *St. Clair*, 403–31.

96. Kenny, *Making Sense of the Molly Maguires*, 8–10, 13, 62; Wallace, *St. Clair*, 133–41, 372–75; Pinkerton, *Molly Maguires and the Detectives*, 355–56.

97. Pinkerton, *Molly Maguires and the Detectives*, 457–58.

98. Kenny, *Making Sense of the Molly Maguires*, 210–11.

99. James D. Horan and Howard Swiggett, *The Pinkerton Story* (New York: Putnam, 1951), 139–54; Kenny, *Making Sense of the Molly Maguires*, 5, 10, 110–17.

100. Kenny, *Making Sense of the Molly Maguires*, 213.

101. Harold D. Aurand, "The Anthracite Mine Workers, 1869–1897," PhD diss., Pennsylvania State University, 1969, 57; quoted in Kenny, *Making Sense of the Molly Maguires*, 213.

102. Pinkerton, *Molly Maguires and the Detectives*, 506, 508, 553; Kenny, *Making Sense of the Molly Maguires*, 235. Pinkerton published one of Gowen's closing statements; see Pinkerton, *Molly Maguires and the Detectives*, 510–41.

103. Aurand, "Anthracite Mine Workers," 57; quoted in Kenny, *Making Sense of the Molly Maguires*, 213; see also ibid., 95, 215.

104. "The Mollie Maguires," *New York Times*, May 14, 1876, p. 6; Kenny, *Making Sense of the Molly Maguires*, 213–15.

105. Kenny, *Making Sense of the Molly Maguires*, 229–33.

106. Ibid., 213–14, 231, 270.

107. Ibid., 8, 85. Some records indicate a total of fifty arrests; see ibid., 186. The earliest reference to the Molly Maguires I can locate in a U.S. newspaper is in reference to events in Ireland: "News from England," *Boston Daily Atlas*, January 25, 1845. In 1857, a Mississippi newspaper refers to a new Democratic political club in Philadelphia called the Molly Maguires; "The 'Molly Maguires,'" *Hinds County Gazette* (Raymond, MS), November 4, 1857; see also the *Ripley* (OH) *Bee*, November 7, 1857; "A New Secret Order," *San Francisco Daily Evening Bulletin*, December 9, 1857. The first reference to a workers organization called the Molly Maguires is in the *New York Times*, March 22, 1867; see also *Bangor Daily Whig & Courier*, March 23, 1867.

108. Kenny, *Making Sense of the Molly Maguires*, 85.

109. Pinkerton, *Molly Maguires and the Detectives*, 510; "Jack Kehoe's Doom," *Galveston Daily News*, February 1, 1877; Kenny, *Making Sense of the Molly Maguires*, 85, 226–28.

110. Kenny, *Making Sense of the Molly Maguires*, 272–74; "A Jack in a Box," *St. Louis Globe-Democrat*, December 18, 1878, p. 5; "Eternity Entered," *St. Louis Globe-Democrat*, December 19, 1878, p. 5; "Kehoe's Last Day," *New York Times*, December 18, 1878; "The Dance of Death," *Milwaukee Daily Sentinel*, December 19, 1878, p. 4.

111. Kenny, *Making Sense of the Molly Maguires*, 238; John T. Morse Jr., "The 'Molly Maguire' Trials," *American Law Review* 11 (1877): 233–60.

112. Kenny, *Making Sense of the Molly Maguires*, 241–42; "What's This For?" *Inter Ocean* (Chicago), February 12, 1877, p. 5; *Catholic Standard* (Philadelphia), February 17, 1877; "State Items," *North American* (Philadelphia), March 16, 1877.

113. The governor seeks "to dispatch as many murderers on the same day as the circumstances would admit"; see "The Doomed Molly Maguires," *Frank Leslie's Illustrated Newspaper* (New York), June 16, 1877, p. 253. See also *Frank Leslie's Illustrated Newspaper*, June 16, 1877; *Frank Leslie's Illustrated Newspaper*, June 30, 1877; *Frank Leslie's Illustrated Newspaper*, July 7, 1877; "Ten Drops," *St. Louis Globe-Democrat*, June 21, 1877; "The End of the 'Mollie Maguires,'" *Boston Daily Advertiser*, June 21, 1877; numerous articles in the *New York Times*, June 19–22, 1877; "Stern Justice," *Inter Ocean* (Chicago), June 22, 1877; Kenny, *Making Sense of the Molly Maguires*, 246–51, 254.

114. "The Mollie Maguires," *Boston Daily Advertiser*, June 18, 1877; "Artistic Neckties," *Daily Arkansas Gazette* (Little Rock), June 19, 1877; "Gone to Glory," *Daily Arkansas Gazette*, June 22, 1877; "Retribution," *Milwaukee Daily Sentinel*, June 22, 1877; "The Molly Maguires Will Swing on the Day Appointed for Their Execution," *St. Louis Globe-Democrat*, June 19, 1877; Kenny, *Making Sense of the Molly Maguires*, 245–46, 249, 253; "We Are Eleven," *St. Louis Globe-Democrat*, June 22, 1877; "Death on the Gallows," *New York Times*, June 22, 1877.

115. *New York Herald*, June 22, 1877; Kenny, *Making Sense of the Molly Maguires*, 240–42, 254–55, 268–69; "Death on the Gallows," *New York Times*, June 22, 1877.

116. "Molly Maguires Will Swing on the Day Appointed for Their Execution"; "Artistic Neckties," *Daily Arkansas Gazette* (Little Rock), June 19, 1877; *New York Sun*, June 22, 1877, quoted in Kenny, *Making Sense of the Molly Maguires*, 256.

117. *Philadelphia Public Ledger*, June 21, 1877; *Philadelphia Inquirer*, June 22, 1877; *North American* (Philadelphia), May 24, 1877; *Chicago Tribune*, June 22, 1877; Kenny, *Making Sense of the Molly Maguires*, 258.

118. "More Molly Maguires," *Newark Advocate* (Newark, OH), February 23, 1877; "The Molly Maguires," *San Francisco Daily Evening Bulletin*, May 1, 1877.

119. "Molly Maguires at Home," from *Baltimore Gazette*, in *St. Louis Globe-Democrat*, February 24, 1877, p. 2; "Molly Maguireism," *Daily Rocky Mountain News* (Denver), March 31, 1877. See also "Molly Maguires," *Daily Rocky Mountain News*, April 27, 1877.

120. *Miner's Journal*, June 14, 1878, quoted in Kenny, *Making Sense of the Molly Maguires*, 272. Donnelly's execution evoked a single sentence in the *North American* (Philadelphia), June 12, 1878.

121. Kenny, *Making Sense of the Molly Maguires*, 272.

122. "The Vilest of the Vile," *New York Times*, January 7, 1877; *Irish World*, June 3, 1876; *Boston Pilot*, June 28, 1877; *Boston Pilot*, June 30, 1877; Samuel Gompers, *Seventy Years of Life and Labour: An Autobiography* (New York: E.P. Dutton, 1925), 139; "Molly Maguires," *Milwaukee Daily Sentinel*, March 14, 1877; multiple stories in the *New York Herald*, June and July 1877; *New York Tribune*, June 26, 1877. These conflicted sentiments were shared in the novel by Rollin Edwards, *Twice Defeated: Or, the Story of a Dark Society in Two Countries* (Philadelphia: J.B. Lippincott & Co., 1877).

123. "The Tramp on the War Path," *Galveston Daily News*, September 11, 1877; Carolyn Ashbaugh, *Lucy Parsons: American Revolutionary* (Chicago: Charles Kerr, 1976), 55.

Chapter 5: The Great Insurrection

1. Twain to Mrs. Fairbanks, August 6, 1877, in *Mark Twain to Mrs. Fairbanks*, ed. Dixon Wecter (San Marino, CA: Huntington Library, 1949), 208.

2. *Washington National Republican*, August 4, 1877; Philip S. Foner, *The Great Labor Uprising of 1877* (New York: Monad Press, 1977), 211; "The No Property Flag Raised," *Georgia Weekly Telegraph and Georgia Journal & Messenger* (Macon), August 14, 1877; "Our Labor Troubles," *Cedar Rapids Times*, August 9, 1877, p. 2; "The Workingmen's Party," *Chicago Daily Tribune*, August 27, 1877, p. 4; "Communism in America," *Georgia Weekly Telegraph and Georgia Journal & Messenger*, April 30, 1878; "Communism in America," *San Francisco Daily Evening Bulletin*, May 17, 1878.

3. W.W. Grosvenor, "The Communist and the Railway," *International Review* 4 (1877): 585–86. Grosvenor was widely quoted; see, for instance, "Magazines and Books," *Boston Daily Advertiser*, August 25, 1877; "Literary Review," *The Congregationalist* (Boston), August 29, 1877, p. 6; *Inter Ocean* (Chicago), September 3, 1877, p. 4. On the Grangers as communists, see *Inter Ocean*, September 3, 1877, p. 4; *Daily Rocky Mountain News* (Denver), August 14, 1877.

4. *Louisville Courier-Journal*, July 30, 1877; "Table Talk," *North American* (Philadelphia), September 15, 1877; "St. Louis Communism," *Chicago Tribune*, July 29, 1877, p. 4. The *Tribune* added, "The Communist anywhere is a lazy, dissolute, sneaking, dangerous vagabond, and the St. Louis Communist seems to be the worst of the whole worthless class."

5. *Pittsburgh Leader*, July 20, 1877, reprinted in "The Commune in the United States," *New York Tribune*, July 25, 1877; Secretary of the Navy Richard W. Thompson to Tom Scott, August 5, 1877, in Foner, *Great Labor Uprising*, 101; Gerald Grob, "The Railroad Strike of 1877," *Midwest Journal* 6 (1954–55): 16–34; "The American Commune," *Washington National Republican*, July 21; "The American Commune," *Galveston Daily News*, August 14, 1877; *Inter Ocean* (Chicago), July 25, 1877; *St. Louis Globe-Democrat*, July 28, 1877.

6. "St. Louis . . . The Commune," *Chicago Daily Tribune*, July 27, 1877, p. 5; "The American Commune," *Galveston Daily News*, August 2, 1877; "A Colored Woman Joins the Commune and Defies Her Husband's Authority," *St. Louis Globe-Democrat*, August 5, 1877, p. 2.

7. On the place of the strikes of 1877 in labor history, see Jeremy Brecher, *Strike!*, rev. ed. (Cambridge, MA: South End Press, 1997), 13–37; Philip S. Foner, *History of the Labor Movement in the United States*, 2 vols. (New York: International Publishers, 1998), 1:464–74; Joseph G. Rayback, *A History of American Labor* (New York: Free Press, 1966), 129–44.

8. Troops were used during the Civil War against employees of the Reading Railroad and in the coal mines of Pennsylvania, and in smaller strikes in St. Louis, Louisville, and Cold Springs, New York; Richard B. Morris, "Andrew Jackson, Strikebreaker," *American Historical Review* 55 (1949): 54–68; Foner, *History of the Labor Movement*, 1:327–29.

9. "The Value of Railroad Transportation," *Chicago Tribune*, July 23, 1877, p. 4; John L. Ringwalt, *Development of Transportation Systems in the United States* (Philadelphia: Railway World, 1888), 211–22, 258–61; Thomas C. Cochran, *Railroad Leaders, 1845–1890: The Business Mind in Action* (Cambridge, MA: Harvard University Press, 1953), 94–108, 126–40; John F. Stover, *American Railroads* (Chicago: University of Chicago Press, 1997), 61–132; John F. Stover, *The Routledge Historical Atlas of the American Railroads* (New York: Routledge, 1999), 32–43.

10. *Poor's Manual of Railroads for 1877* (New York: Henry V. Poor, 1877); "Railroad Earnings," *Commercial and Financial Chronicle* (New York), July 14, 1877, pp. 30–31, "Shall the Railroad Interest Support Labor," *Commercial and Financial Chronicle*, August 11, 1877, pp. 125–27; "What Shall Limit Railroad Dividends," August 18, 1877, pp. 148–49; *Railroad Gazette* 9 (August 10, 1877): 365; "Railroad Wages," *The Nation*, August 16, 1877, pp. 99–100.

11. "Interview with J.M. McCullough," *Chicago Times*, December 28, 1873; Foner, *Great Labor Uprising*, 21; "Probable Strike of the Railroad Engineers," *New York Times*, November 19, 1873, p. 2.

12. Foner, *Great Labor Uprising*, 18 (quote); John F. Stover, *History of the Baltimore and Ohio Railroad* (West Lafayette, IN: Purdue University Press, 1987), 62, 135–36; "Railroad Wages," p. 99; Edith Abbott, "The Wages of Unskilled Labor in the United States," *Journal of Political Economy* 13 (1905): 363.

13. "We have sympathized": "The Employes' Complaint," from *Pittsburgh Commercial*, in *Daily Rocky Mountain News* (Denver), July 27, 1877; "simply that the men": Thomas A. Scott, "The Recent Strikes," *North American Review* 125 (1877): 353–54; "The Rights of Labor," *Inter Ocean* (Chicago), August 2, 1877, p. 4; Pennsylvania General Assembly, *Report of the Committee Appointed to Investigate the Railroad Riots in July, 1877* (Harrisburg: State of Pennsylvania, 1878), 903–5.

14. *Report of the Committee Appointed to Investigate the Railroad Riots*, 671. The significance of Ammon's organizing is clearly reflected in the official investigation; see *Report*

of the Committee Appointed to Investigate the Railroad Riots, 3, 21–22, 460, 464–65, 507–9, 661–90, 791–97, 826–29, 949–54.

15. Ibid., 671–75, 684 (quote); *Baltimore Sun*, July 15, 1877; *Baltimore Sun*, July 16, 1877; Foner, *Great Labor Uprising*, 34; "The Railroads," *Inter Ocean* (Chicago), July 13, 1877, p. 8.

16. "Railroad Strikers," *North American* (Philadelphia), July 17, 1877; "Railroad Employes on a Strike," *New York Times*, July 17, 1877.

17. "Railway News," *St. Louis Globe-Democrat*, July 17, 1877, p. 3; *Chicago Daily Tribune*, July 18, 1877, p. 4; "Firemen's Fight," *Inter Ocean* (Chicago), July 18, 1877.

18. *Martinsburg Statesman*, July 17, 1877; Foner, *Great Labor Uprising*, 35; "Cause of the Strike, and a Remedy," *Chicago Tribune*, July 23, 1877, p. 4; *Biennial Message of Governor Henry M. Mathews to the Legislature of West Virginia* (Wheeling: State of West Virginia, 1879), 1–2; "Serious Railroad Strike," *New York Times*, July 18, 1877, p. 5; "The Railroad Men's War," *New York Times*, July 19, 1877; "The Baltimore and Ohio Strike," *New York Times*, July 18, 1877, p. 4; *Wheeling Intelligencer*, July 17, 1877; *Wheeling Intelligencer*, July 18, 1877; "Riotous Strikers," *Chicago Daily Tribune*, July 18, 1877, p. 5; "A Real Railroad War," *Galveston Daily News*, July 18, 1877; "A Desperate Band," *St. Louis Globe-Democrat*, July 19, 1877.

19. *Martinsburg Statesman*, July 24, 1877; *Martinsburg Statesman*, July 31, 1877, Foner, *Great Labor Uprising*, 36; "The Stokers' Strike," *Inter Ocean* (Chicago), July 19, 1877; "Railroad Rioters," *Milwaukee Daily Sentinel*, July 19, 1877, p. 4; *Biennial Message of Governor Henry M. Mathews*, 3.

20. "The Railroad Outbreaks," *Commercial and Financial Chronicle* (New York), July 28, 1877, p. 73 (quote); *Biennial Message of Governor Henry M. Mathews*, 4; "'Stop Her!'" *Inter Ocean* (Chicago), July 20, 1877; "A Railroad War," *Milwaukee Daily Sentinel*, July 20, 1877.

21. *Scranton Republican*, July 29, 1877, from the *Baltimore Gazette*; *Baltimore Sun*, July 19, 1877 (quote); Foner, *Great Labor Uprising*, 37–38; "Furious Firemen," *Milwaukee Daily Sentinel*, July 18, 1877, p. 4; "Desperate Men on Strike," *New York Times*, July 20, 1877; "West Virginia," *Chicago Daily Tribune*, July 21, 1877; *Biennial Message of Governor Henry M. Mathews*, 4; "A Real Railroad War Strike at Martinsburg," *Galveston Daily News*, July 18, 1877; "Long and Strong," *St. Louis Globe-Democrat*, July 20, 1877; "By Telegraph," *Georgia Weekly Telegraph and Georgia Journal & Messenger* (Macon), July 24, 1877.

22. "The Railway Riot," *Boston Daily Advertiser*, July 19, 1877 (quote); "'Stop Her!'"

23. Hayes's proclamation was published in most newspapers; see, for instance, "Strike on the B. & O. Road," *Galveston Daily News*, July 19, 1877. Ari Hoogenboom, *Rutherford B. Hayes: Warrior and President* (Lawrence: University Press of Kansas, 1995), 295–302; "The States and Their Domestic Police," *Galveston Daily News*, July 20, 1877; "Insurrection," *Galveston Daily News*, July 21, 1877; "In Washington," *Chicago Daily Tribune*, July 22, 1877, p. 2; "The Strikers' Insurrection," *Bangor Daily Whig & Courier*, July 23, 1877; "The Railway Disorders," *Hartford Daily Courant*, July 23, 1877, p. 2; "The New Rebellion," *Boston Daily Advertiser*, July 24, 1877; "Is This a Rebellion?" *Chicago Daily Tribune*, July 27, 1877, p. 8.

24. "Heroines"?: *New York Sun*, July 20, 1877; King quoted in *Baltimore Sun*, July 20, 1877; Foner, *Great Labor Uprising*, 43–44; "'Stop Her!'" On July 21, King had to admit that the strike was far from broken; see "The Great Riots," *Bangor Daily Whig & Courier*, July 23, 1877.

25. *Wheeling Register*, July 21, 1877; *New York Herald*, July 20, 1877; *Reading Daily Eagle*, July 21, 1877 (quotes); Foner, *Great Labor Uprising*, 4, 44–45.

26. "The Afflicted Railroads," *Hartford Daily Courant*, July 21, 1877, p. 3; "Bloodshed," *Chicago Daily Tribune*, July 21, 1877; "Maryland," *Chicago Daily Tribune*, July 22, 1877, p. 2; "Like Wild-Fire: Strikes Spreading with Frightful Rapidity," *St. Louis Globe-Democrat*, July 21, 1877; *Wheeling Intelligencer*, July 21, 1877 (quote); Foner, *Great Labor Uprising*, 37.

27. "Working people everywhere": *Philadelphia Inquirer*, July 23, 1877; "a respectable body": *Wheeling Intelligencer*, July 20, 1877; Foner, *Great Labor Uprising*, 37, 45–46; "there is no disguising": "Glutted with Gore!" *St. Louis Globe-Democrat*, July 22, 1877; "Precautions of the Government," *New York Times*, July 22, 1877, p. 7.

28. "Shot Down," *Inter Ocean* (Chicago), July 21, 1877; "Insurrection," *North American* (Philadelphia), July 21, 1877.

29. *Baltimore Sun*, July 21, 1877; *Baltimore Sun*, July 22, 1877; Foner, *Great Labor Uprising*, 46–48; "The Great Riots"; "The Nation's Woe," *St. Louis Globe-Democrat*, July 23, 1877.

30. "Glutted with Gore!"; "The Nation's Woe"; "Bread or Blood!" *Daily Arkansas Gazette* (Little Rock), July 22, 1877.

31. "The Great Railroad Strike Still Growing," *Daily Rocky Mountain News* (Denver), July 22, 1877; "The Nation's Woe"; "Go Slow!" *Inter Ocean* (Chicago), July 24, 1877; "Crush It Out," *Inter Ocean*, July 27, 1877.

32. Joseph A. Dacus, *Annals of the Great Strikes in the United States* (Chicago: L.T. Palmer, 1877), iii; *Daily Rocky Mountain News* (Denver), July 19, 1877; "King Mob, the Strike Degenerating into Lawlessness," *San Francisco Daily Evening Bulletin*, July 23, 1877; "The Strike Spreading," *Lowell Daily Citizen*, July 23, 1877; "The Great Strike: It Is Still Spreading with Frightful Rapidity," *Daily Arkansas Gazette* (Little Rock), July 24, 1877; "The Great Strike: It is Still Spreading in All Directions," *San Francisco Daily Evening Bulletin*, July 24, 1877; "The New Rebellion"; "Riotous Outbreaks Still Increasing," *Lowell Daily Citizen*, July 24, 1877; "The Contagion Still Spreading," *San Francisco Daily Evening Bulletin*, July 25, 1877; "Bloodshed," *Milwaukee Daily Sentinel*, July 26, 1877; "Fire and Blood, Pillage, Confusion, Anarchy," *North American* (Philadelphia), July 23, 1877; "Chaos Reigns Supreme," *St. Louis Globe-Democrat*, July 20, 1877; "The Strike in the East," *Colorado Springs Gazette*, July 28, 1877; "The Railroad Commune," *Galveston Daily News*, July 24, 1877. The subheads to this last article give a sense of the panic: The Great Conspiracy, Reign of Terror, Triumph of the Torch, Disastrous Defeat of the State Militia, Millions of Magnificent Railroad Property Give to the Flames, Uncle Sam the Country's Only Hope of Deliverance!

33. *Report of the Committee Appointed to Investigate the Railroad Riots*, 273–74; see also 817–23.

34. William B. Sipes, *The Pennsylvania Railroad: Its Origin, Construction, Condition, and Connections* (Philadelphia: Passenger Department, 1875), 255; Foner, *Great Labor Uprising*, 55–56. Starting with *Farwell v. Boston & Worcester Railroad*, 45 Mass. 49 (1842), in which Justice Lemuel Shaw reasoned that workers had to be aware of the dangers and "bargained" away safety for income: "In legal presumption, the compensation is adjusted accordingly." See also *Lossee v. Buchanan et al.*, 51 N.Y. 476 (1873), 484. In general, on this point, see Morton J. Horwitz, *The Transformation of American Law, 1780–1860* (Cambridge, MA: Harvard University Press, 1981).

35. David Nasaw, *Andrew Carnegie* (New York: Penguin, 2006), 178, 180.

36. *Report of the Committee Appointed to Investigate the Railroad Riots*, 60.

37. Ibid., 75–76, 140 (quote), 143–46, 389–91, 442–46; "The Labor Outbreak: The City of Pittsburgh vs. The Pennsylvania Railroad," *Inter Ocean* (Chicago), September 11, 1877, p. 5.

38. "Reckless to the verge of criminality": "Causes of the Strike," *Milwaukee Daily Sentinel*, July 25, 1877, p. 4; *Report of the Committee Appointed to Investigate the Railroad Riots*, 59–60, 75–80, 139–46, 176–79, 184 (Fife quote), 373–81, 387–89, 818 (*Pittsburgh Critic* quote).

39. *Report of the Committee Appointed to Investigate the Railroad Riots*, 18 (quote); "Military Blunder—Uncalled for Bloodshed," *Pittsburgh Critic*, July 22, 1877.

40. *Report of the Committee Appointed to Investigate the Railroad Riots*, 7–11, 19–20, 52–54, 176–79, 610, 698–99, 822–23, 907–10.

41. "Incidental," *Chicago Daily Tribune*, July 22, 1877, p. 2 (quote); "A Terrible Day in Pittsburgh," *New York Times*, July 22, 1877; *Army Journal*, August 4, 1877; *Report of the Committee Appointed to Investigate the Railroad Riots*, 10–11, 377, 477, 480–81, 620, 631, 786–88.

42. Grand jury report in "The Pittsburgh Riots," *Inter Ocean* (Chicago), November 20, 1877, p. 4; "Relic of the Riots," *Chicago Daily Tribune*, September 28, 1877; *Report of the Committee Appointed to Investigate the Railroad Riots*, 785–816; multiple articles, *New York Times* and *Chicago Daily Tribune*, July 22–24, 1877; *Army Journal*, August 4, 1877; Dacus, *Annals of the Great Strikes*, 112–28; Foner, *Great Labor Uprising*, 59–63.

43. "Labor Outbreak"; "Increase the National Army," *Chicago Daily Tribune*, July 26, 1877, p. 4; "Gen. Pearson's Arraignment," *Chicago Daily Tribune*, October 1, 1877, p. 4: "First Blood," *Pittsburgh Sunday Globe*, July 22, 1877; *Report of the Committee Appointed to Investigate the Railroad Riots*, 806–7 (quotes).

44. Multiple articles, *New York Times* and *Chicago Daily Tribune*, July 22–24, 1877; *Report of the Committee Appointed to Investigate the Railroad Riots*, 13–19, 54–56, 88–93, 192–95, 242–45, 253–56, 326–29, 881–903; James A. Henderson, "The Railroad Riots in Pittsburgh: Saturday and Sunday, July 21st and 22nd, 1877," *Western Pennsylvania Historical Magazine* 40 (1928): 194–97.

45. "The Great Strikes," *Bangor Daily Whig & Courier*, July 24, 1877; *Daily Rocky Mountain News* (Denver), August 3, 1877; "By-the-By, Where Is Major Buffington?" *North American* (Philadelphia), August 20, 1877; "The Labor Riots," *North American*, March 23, 1878; *Report of the Committee Appointed to Investigate the Railroad Riots*, 14, 254–55, 264–70, 450–60, 522, 914–15, 960–62, 978–82; Dacus, *Annals of the Great Strikes*, 129–42.

46. "The Railway Troubles," *Galveston Daily News*, July 28, 1877; "Echoes of the Strikes," *Galveston Daily News*, July 31, 1877; multiple articles, *New York Times* and *Chicago Daily Tribune*, July 26–27, 1877; Michael Bellesiles and Christopher Waldrep, eds., *Documenting American Violence: A Sourcebook* (New York: Oxford University Press, 2006), 160–64.

47. Quotes from the following sources, in order: "King Mob"; "The Strikers' Insurrection"; "The Contagion of Violence," *Boston Daily Advertiser*, July 25, 1877; "Local Aspect of the Strike," *New York Times*, July 23, 1877, p. 2. On the collapse of civilization, see "The Lessons of the Week," *New York Times*, July 29, 1877, p. 6; Dacus, *Annals of the Great Strikes*, 328; "The Great Strike," *Inter-Ocean* (Chicago), July 23, 1877, p. 4.

48. "The New Rebellion"; "Carnival of Blood," *North American* (Philadelphia), July 24, 1877; *Pittsburgh Post*, July 24–26, 1877; *Report of the Committee Appointed to Investigate the Railroad Riots*, 493–95, 514–16.

49. Foner, *Great Labor Uprising*, 69–70; Philip English Mackey, "Law and Order, 1877: Philadelphia's Response to the Railroad Riots," *Pennsylvania Magazine of History and Biography* 96 (1972): 183–202; George B. Stitchter, "The Schuylkill County Soldiery in the Industrial Disturbances in 1877, or the Railroad Riot War," *Publications of the Historical Society of Schuylkill County* 1 (1907): 193–215.

50. Hartranft quoted in Gerald G. Eggert, *Railroad Labor Disputes: The Beginnings of Federal Strike Policy* (Ann Arbor: University of Michigan Press, 1967), 32; Dacus, *Annals of the Great Strikes*, 172–73. Hoogenboom writes that Hayes did not supply troops "to break the strike" but to keep the peace, a distinction lost on the striking workers; see Hoogenboom, *Rutherford B. Hayes*, 330.

51. All quotes from *Reading Daily Eagle*, July 23–24, and July 27–29, 1877; Foner, *Great Labor Uprising*, 72–73; "By Telegraph," *Bangor Daily Whig & Courier*, August 9, 1877; "Dwindling Away," *North American* (Philadelphia), July 28, 1877; "The Situation," *North American*, August 8, 1877.

52. *Terre Haute Express*, July 25–26, 1877; Foner, *Great Labor Uprising*, 96–97; "Railroad Employes," *St. Louis Globe-Democrat*, July 1, 1877, p. 3; "Glutted with Gore!" and "Situation in St. Louis," *St. Louis Globe-Democrat*, July 22, 1877; "The Nation's Woe"; "Rough Raillery," *St. Louis Globe-Democrat*, July 24, 1877; "Go Slow!"; "Railraiders," *Milwaukee Daily Sentinel*, July 24, 1877.

53. *Terre Haute Express*, July 25–27, 1877; Foner, *Great Labor Uprising*, 96–97; Dacus, *Annals of the Great Strikes*, 292–94.

54. "An Afflicted City," *Inter Ocean* (Chicago), January 10, 1877, p. 4; quotes from *Indianapolis Sentinel*, July 24–25, 1877; Foner, *Great Labor Uprising*, 98–99, 194; "Go Slow!"; "Rail Rulers," *Milwaukee Daily Sentinel*, July 25, 1877; "Line Entering Indianapolis," *New York Times*, July 25, 1877, p. 5; Dacus, *Annals of the Great Strikes*, 293–95, 305–6; Matilda Gresham, *The Life of Walter Quintin Gresham, 1832–1895*, 2 vols. (Chicago: Rand McNally & Co., 1919), 1:382–90; Hoogenboom, *Rutherford B. Hayes*, 333; Robert V. Bruce, *1877: Year of Violence* (Indianapolis: Bobbs-Merrill, 1959), 288–89.

55. Multiple articles, *Indianapolis Sentinel*, July 26–29, 1877; "No Temporizing," *Inter Ocean* (Chicago), July 28, 1877, p. 5; "Crush It Out"; "More Bloodshed," *Inter Ocean*, August 2, 1877, p. 5; "The Situation in Indianapolis," *New York Times*, July 27, 1877, p. 5; *Terre Haute Express*, July 30–31, 1877; Gresham, *Life of Walter Quintin Gresham*, 1:390–408.

56. Multiple articles, *Louisville Courier-Journal*, July 23–27, 1877; "Cease Firing," *Inter Ocean* (Chicago), July 25, 1877; "Nearly Over," *Inter Ocean*, July 28, 1877; "The Climax," *St. Louis Globe-Democrat*, July 27, 1877; "Riotous Crowds in Louisville," *New York Times*, July 25, 1877, p. 5; "The Situation in Louisville," *New York Times*, July 26, 1877, p. 5; Foner, *Great Labor Uprising*, 124–25; Bill L. Weaver, "Louisville's Labor Disturbance, July 1877," *Filson Club Historical Quarterly* 48 (1974): 177–86; Lewis J. Paper, *Brandeis* (Englewood Cliffs, NJ: Prentice-Hall, 1983), 16.

57. "Railway News," *St. Louis Globe-Democrat*, June 6, 1877, p. 3; "By Telegraph," *Georgia Weekly Telegraph and Georgia Journal & Messenger* (Macon), July 3, 1877; "Affairs Along the Erie Road," *New York Times*, July 22, 1877, p. 7; "Military Sent from New York," *New York Times*, July 23, 1877, p. 2; "The Trouble on the Erie Road," *New York Times*,

p. 2; "Hornellsville," *Chicago Daily Tribune*, July 24, 1877; "The New Rebellion"; "Cease Firing"; Foner, *Great Labor Uprising*, 79–83; Dacus, *Annals of the Great Strikes*, 196–99.

58. "In a Ferment," *Inter Ocean* (Chicago), July 26, 1877; "A Leaden Rebuke," *Inter Ocean*, July 27, 1877; "Mob Law," *North American* (Philadelphia), July 26, 1877; *Frank Leslie's Illustrated Newspaper* (New York), August 4, 1877, p. 4; Foner, *Great Labor Uprising*, 83–84; Dacus, *Annals of the Great Strikes*, 199–204.

59. Multiple articles and editorials, *New York Times*, July 23–25, 1877.

60. "The Striker Donahue in Court," *New York Times*, July 29, 1877, p. 2; "Desperate Working Men," *New York Times*, August 10, 1877, p. 3; "Donahue the Striker," *New York Times*, August 23, 1877, p. 3; "Penitent Peorians," *Chicago Daily Tribune*, July 31, 1877, p. 2; "The Law in the Case," *Chicago Daily Tribune*, August 1, 1877; "The End of the Strike," *Hartford Daily Courant*, July 31, 1877, p. 3.

61. "Law Reports," *New York Times*, August 3, 1877, p. 3; "A Striker's Story," from the *New York Tribune*, in *North American* (Philadelphia), August 2, 1877; "The Brotherhood," *Inter Ocean* (Chicago), August 3, 1877, p. 2; "A Striker Speaks," *St. Louis Globe-Democrat*, August 16, 1877; Foner, *Great Labor Uprising*, 85–89.

62. *Brooklyn Daily Eagle*, July 23, 1877; Foner, *Great Labor Uprising*, 104, 192; "The Week," *The Nation*, July 26, 1877, p. 49; *Railroad Gazette* 9 (July 27, 1877), 50.

63. These appellations appear in several different articles in the *New York Times* in one issue, July 26, 1877. The list was compiled by Samuel Yellen in *American Labor Struggles* (New York: Harcourt, Brace, 1936), 21–22.

64. "Scant pay" and next two quotes from "The Railroad Outbreaks"; "the interests of the monopolies": "The Mob," *Inter Ocean* (Chicago), July 23, 1877; McBride quoted in "On the Ragged Edge," *St. Louis Globe-Democrat*, July 25, 1877, p. 4; "The Strike at Home," *St. Louis Globe-Democrat*, July 24, 1877, p. 4; "On a Volcano," *St. Louis Globe-Democrat*, July 26, 1877, p. 4.

65. "Military Blunder—Uncalled for Bloodshed"; *Report of the Committee Appointed to Investigate the Railroad Riots*, 819.

66. *Missouri Republican* (St. Louis), July 19, 1877; Foner, *Great Labor Uprising*, 104; "Public Sentiment," *Chicago Daily Tribune*, July 29, 1877, p. 2; "Chicago," *Inter Ocean* (Chicago), July 24, 1877, p. 5. See in general the tone of coverage in these two newspapers, plus the *Chicago Times* and *Chicago Daily News* for July 20 and 21, 1877.

67. Multiple articles in the *Inter Ocean* (Chicago), *Chicago Daily Tribune*, *Chicago Daily News*, and *Chicago Times*, July 23, 1877; Dacus, *Annals of the Great Strikes*, 312–15; Foner, *Great Labor Uprising*, 141–42; Fogelson, *America's Armories*, 28.

68. "Public Sentiment" and "The Mass Meeting," *Chicago Daily Tribune*, July 24, 1877, pp. 3, 5; "Chicago." "Grand Army of Starvation" appears to have originated with Albert Parsons; see "Rioting Roughs," *Inter Ocean* (Chicago), July 25, 1877.

69. "The Mass Meeting." The *Inter Ocean* thought it went over that line into "incendiary"; see "Chicago."

70. "Rioting Roughs"; "The Mass Meeting." There is some disagreement whether Parsons said "exploiting us" in the penultimate quotation.

71. "Rioting Roughs"; "It Is Here," *Chicago Daily Tribune*, July 25, 1877, p. 3; Foner, *Great Labor Uprising*, 144–46.

72. "At the Bridge," *Chicago Daily Tribune*, July 27, 1877, p. 2. See also "It Is Here"; "Ninth and Tenth Wards," *Chicago Daily Tribune*, July 25, 1877, p. 5; "The Strikers and the Mob," *Chicago Daily Tribune*, July 26, p. 4; "Halsted Street" and "Plain Words with

Strikers," *Chicago Daily Tribune*, July 27, 1877, pp. 2, 8; "The Mob's Madness," *Inter Ocean* (Chicago), July 26, 1877; "A Leaden Rebuke."

73. "Better class": "In a Ferment"; "the neighborhood": "The Cavalry Fight," *Chicago Daily Tribune*, July 27, 1877, p. 2; multiple articles, *Chicago Daily Tribune*, July 25, 1877, pp. 3, 7; "Red War," *Chicago Daily Tribune*, July 26, 1877; "Rioting Roughs"; "The Mob's Madness."

74. Common Council quoted in "The Mob's Madness"; Tabernacle meeting quoted in "Meetings," *Chicago Daily Tribune*, July 26, 1877, p. 3; "Volunteers for Our Defense," *Inter Ocean* (Chicago), July 26, 1877, p. 6; Dacus, *Annals of the Great Strikes*, 315–31.

75. "A Leaden Rebuke"; "The Mob's Madness"; "In a Ferment"; "No Temporizing"; "The First Regime," *Chicago Daily Tribune*, July 26, 1877, p. 3; "The Regulars," *Chicago Daily Tribune*, July 27, 1877, p. 4.

76. "Pitched Battles," "Arrests," and "Turner Hall," *Chicago Daily Tribune*, July 27, 1877; "A Leaden Rebuke"; "Crush It Out"; Dacus, *Annals of the Great Strikes*, 331–36. When the Cigarmakers Union attempted to hold a meeting in Turner Hall that evening, the police stated they would arrest all of them if they did not leave. "The Cigar-Makers," *Inter Ocean* (Chicago), July 27, 1877, p. 7.

77. Multiple articles, *Inter Ocean* (Chicago), July 27–28, 1877; *Chicago Daily News*, July 27–29, 1877; *Chicago Times*, July 27 and 28, 1877; Dacus, *Annals of the Great Strikes*, 336–40; Bruce, *1877*, 250.

78. "Cavalry Fight"; "Struck Out," *Chicago Daily Tribune*, July 28, 1877; "The Labor Outbreak," *Inter Ocean* (Chicago), September 11, 1877, p. 5; "Communism," *Inter Ocean*, August 8, 1877; "The Labor Outbreak," *Inter Ocean*, August 15, 1877, p. 3. Because of such misleading reporting, workers found it necessary to make clear that they were not communists; see "Labor's Complaint," *Inter Ocean*, August 24, 1877, p. 8; *Chicago Daily News*, July 27, 1877; Foner, *Great Labor Uprising*, 156.

79. William Roscoe Thayer, *The Life and Letters of John Hay*, 2 vols. (Boston: Houghton Mifflin, 1915), 2:3. The CCC & I translates to the Cleveland, Columbus, Cincinnati & Indianapolis Railroad. "The Mob"; "Go Slow!"; "Cease Firing"; "Peace Prospects," *St. Louis Globe-Democrat*, July 26, 1877; "Near the End," *Milwaukee Daily Sentinel*, July 30, 1877; Victor R. Greene, *The Slavic Community on Strike: Immigrant Labor in Pennsylvania Anthracite* (Notre Dame, IN: University of Notre Dame Press, 1968), 71–82; Nasaw, *Andrew Carnegie*, 182–83.

80. Multiple articles, *Pittsburgh Post*, July 28–30, 1877; "Action of the Government," *New York Times*, July 25, 1877, p. 2; "Gov. Hartranft's Order," *New York Times*, July 27, 1877, p. 2; "Trains Moving from Pittsburgh," *New York Times*, July 30, 1877; "The Campaign in the Coal Region," *New York Times*, August 3, 1877; "Railway Troubles"; "The Strikers," *Milwaukee Daily Sentinel*, August 6, 1877, p. 5; "After the Strike," *Frank Leslie's Illustrated Newspaper* (New York), August 18, 1877, p. 409; "A Thrilling Ride," *Lowell Daily Citizen*, September 4, 1877; Foner, *Great Labor Uprising*, 74–77, 156; Hoogenboom, *Rutherford B. Hayes*, 332–35.

81. "Missouri Strike," *North American* (Philadelphia), July 25, 1877; "In a Ferment"; "No Temporizing"; "After the Storm," *St. Louis Globe-Democrat*, July 31, 1877.

82. Worker quoted in "The Misery of the Mines," *New York Times*, August 5, 1877; multiple articles, *Scranton Republican*, July 26–30, 1877; "Scranton: Intense Excitement," *San Francisco Daily Evening Bulletin*, July 25, 1877; "Bloody Work at Scranton," *San Francisco Daily Evening Bulletin*, August 2, 1877; "A Fresh Outbreak: Bloody Riot at Scranton," *North American* (Philadelphia), August 2, 1877; "The Scranton Riot," *North*

American, August 3, 1877; "The Pennsylvania Miners," *Boston Daily Advertiser*, August 7, 1877; "The Collapsed Strikes," *Boston Daily Advertiser*, August 8, 1877.

83. Samuel C. Logan, *A City's Danger and Defense: Or, Issues and Results of the Strikes of 1877* (Scranton, PA: Rodgers Printing, 1887), 79.

84. Ibid., 35–38, 104–31 (quote, 111–12); *Report of the Committee Appointed to Investigate the Railroad Riots*, 155–60, 708–11, 734–35, 755–59; multiple articles, *Scranton Republican*, October 1–5, 1877.

85. "The Nation's Woe." St. Louis was not the first general strike; the Philadelphia strike for the ten-hour day in 1835 deserves that honor.

86. Multiple articles, *St. Louis Globe-Democrat*, July 23, 1877; "The Situation at St. Louis," *New York Times*, July 25, 1877, p. 5; "At St. Louis," *Hartford Daily Courant*, July 25, 1877, p. 3.

87. Wilson quoted in Bruce, *1877*, 258; "On the Ragged Edge."

88. "Riot's Ruin," *Milwaukee Daily Sentinel*, July 23, 1877. Peter A. Lofgreen's real name was Laurence A. Gronlund.

89. *Missouri Republican* (St. Louis), July 24, 1877; "The Strike at Home"; Foner, *Great Labor Uprising*, 166–68.

90. Multiple articles, *St. Louis Globe-Democrat*, July 23–26, 1877, especially "On the Ragged Edge"; "Mad Strikers," *Missouri Republican* (St. Louis), July 26, 1877; Foner, *Great Labor Uprising*, 163–64, 170–76.

91. David T. Burbank, *Reign of the Rabble: The St. Louis General Strike of 1877* (New York: Augustus M. Kelley, 1966), frontispiece; "On a Volcano"; "Progress of the Strike," *St. Louis Globe-Democrat*, July 24, 1877, p. 4.

92. "On a Volcano" multiple articles, *Missouri Republican* (St. Louis), July 27–29, 1877; Foner, *Great Labor Uprising*, 179–82. For a similar call for the nationalization of the railroads, see "The Workingmen's Convention in Ohio," *Lowell Daily Citizen*, August 15, 1877.

93. "Albert the Agitator," *St. Louis Times*, August 4, 1877; Foner, *Great Labor Uprising*, 182, 208.

94. George Crump, British consul, to the Earl of Derby, July 27, 1877, in *Reports Respecting the Late Industrial Conflicts in the United States* (London: Harrison and Sons, 1877), 3; "The Strike at Home"; "On a Volcano"; "Rail Rulers."

95. Quotes, in order, from "On the Ragged Edge"; "On a Volcano"; "Reign of the Mob," *St. Louis Globe-Democrat*, July 27, 1877, p. 4.

96. "Rough Raillery," *St. Louis Globe-Democrat*, July 24, 1877; "On a Volcano"; "Reign of the Mob"; "Extra," *Inter Ocean* (Chicago), July 24, 1877, p. 8; Foner, *Great Labor Uprising*, 165–70; Burbank, *Reign of the Rabble*, 21–22.

97. Foner, *Great Labor Uprising*, 175, 184; "Crush It Out"; "No Temporizing"; "Peace Prospects"; "Reign of the Mob"; "In Full Retreat," *St. Louis Globe-Democrat*, July 29, 1877, p. 4.

98. *Missouri Republican* (St. Louis), July 28, 1877; Foner, *Great Labor Uprising*, 185–86. A more heroic portrait appears in "The Bubble Bursted," *St. Louis Globe-Democrat*, July 28, 1877, p. 4.

99. *Reports Respecting the Late Industrial Conflicts*, 47; multiple articles, *Missouri Republican* (St. Louis) and *St. Louis Globe-Democrat*, July 29–31, 1877; Foner, *Great Labor Uprising*, 209.

100. "The Bubble Bursted"; "A Splendid Pageant," *St. Louis Globe-Democrat*, August 1, 1877, p. 4; "The St. Louis Roads Open," *New York Times,* July 29, 1877, p. 2;

"The Right of Self Preservation," *St. Louis Journal*, in *Daily Rocky Mountain News* (Denver), July 26, 1877; "Crush It Out"; *Missouri Republican* (St. Louis), July 28, 1877; "The Drama of the Strike," *North American* (Philadelphia), August 1, 1877; Burbank, *Reign of the Rabble*, 177–78.

101. "Sherman's Say," *St. Louis Globe-Democrat*, August 18, 1877, p. 4. Some workers also compared the Great Strike with the French Revolution; see "On the Ragged Edge."

102. *New York Herald*, July 27, 1877; *Labor Standard* (New York), August 4, 1877, Foner, *Great Labor Uprising*, 122. Similar sentiments were expressed at a meeting of workers in Cincinnati; see "Political Notes," *Inter Ocean* (Chicago), August 13, 1877, p. 5.

103. Edward Winslow Martin, *The History of the Great Riots* (Philadelphia: National Publishing Co., 1877), 117–18, 177; Foner, *Great Labor Uprising of 1877*, 204; *Labor Standard* (New York), August 4, 1877; *Labor Standard*, August 11, 1877. The following numbers represent the minimum known killed in the Great Strike: Martinsburg, one; Baltimore, twelve; Pittsburgh, forty-two to fifty-three; Reading, twelve; Scranton, six; Chicago, thirty to fifty; Buffalo, eight; Philadelphia, one; and San Francisco, five. Beyond these estimates there is a great deal of disagreement in both contemporary and scholarly works.

104. Robert M. Fogelson, *America's Armories: Architecture, Society, and Public Order* (Cambridge, MA: Harvard University Press, 1989), 21; William H. Riker, *Soldiers of the States: The Role of the National Guard in American Democracy* (Washington, DC: Public Affairs Press, 1957), 47–51; Robert Reinders, "Militia and Public Order in Nineteenth-Century America," *Journal of American Studies* 11 (1977): 81–101; "Law and Order," *Inter Ocean* (Chicago), July 30, 1877; "Wheels of Commerce," *Inter Ocean*, July 31, 1877, p. 5; "The Expiring Strike," *Boston Daily Advertiser*, July 30, 1877; "The Strikes," *Boston Daily Advertiser*, July 31, 1877; "Almost Over," *North American* (Philadelphia), July 30, 1877; "After the Storm"; Jerry M. Cooper, "The Army as Strikebreaker—the Railroad Strike of 1877 and 1894," *Labor History* 18 (1977): 179–96.

105. *Reading Daily Eagle*, July 32, 1877; Ronald L. Filippeli, "The Railroad Strike of 1877 in Reading," *Historical Society of Berks County* 37 (1972): 51. Foner, *Great Labor Uprising*, 71, has a different version of this quote.

106. Thayer, *Life and Letters of John Hay*, 2:2.

107. *Independent*, August 2, 1877, quoted in Foner, *Great Labor Uprising*, 205. The national press tended not to cover this story of workers being fired and blackballed, though the two leading labor newspapers did; see multiple articles, *National Labor Tribune* (Pittsburgh), August 4, 11, 18, and 25, 1877; *Labor Standard* (New York), August 4, 11, and 18, 1877; Foner, *Great Labor Uprising*, 189, 204.

108. *Martinsburg Statesman* quoted in Foner, *Great Labor Uprising*, 54; Samuel Gompers, *Seventy Years of Life and Labour: An Autobiography* (New York: E.P. Dutton, 1925), 150–51; Scott, "Recent Strikes," 357.

109. "Is This a Rebellion?"; Wecter, *Mark Twain to Mrs. Fairbanks*, 208.

110. Debby Applegate, *The Most Famous Man in America: The Biography of Henry Ward Beecher* (New York: Doubleday, 2006); Rebecca Edwards, *New Spirits: Americans in the Gilded Age, 1865–1905* (New York: Oxford University Press, 2006), 312–14. The full sermon is in *Christian Union*, August 1, 1877, pp. 92–94, and August 8, 1877, pp. 112–14.

111. For example, "What Beecher Says," *Daily Rocky Mountain News* (Denver), July 29, 1877; "A Card from Henry Ward Beecher," *Daily Arkansas Gazette* (Little Rock), July 31, 1877; "Communism Considered," *Milwaukee Daily Sentinel*, August 4, 1877;

"Henry Ward Beecher," *Wisconsin State Register* (Portage), August 11, 1877; "Beecher's Preaching Nowadays," *San Francisco Daily Evening Bulletin*, August 17, 1877.

112. "Joseph Cook's Lectures," *The Congregationalist* (Boston), October 17, 1877, p. 3; Sven Beckert, *The Monied Metropolis: New York City and the Consolidation of the American Bourgeoisie, 1850–1896* (New York: Cambridge University Press, 2003), 233.

113. "The Railroad Outbreaks." To many newspapers, Swinton was just another communist addressing his fellow radicals. "Communists' Meeting," *Milwaukee Daily Sentinel*, July 26, 1877; "The New York Communists," *St. Louis Globe-Democrat*, July 26, 1877. Of course, the *New York Sun*, July 26, 1877, took a contrary view, holding the audience to be composed of workers.

114. "Henry Ward Beecher and the Laboring Men," *Raleigh Register*, July 31, 1877; *New York World* quoted in *Raleigh Register*, July 31, 1877; *Indianapolis Sentinel* quoted in *Galveston Daily News*, August 4, 1877; *Independent Statesman* (Concord, NH), December 13, 1877.

115. "Communism Denounced," *New York Times*, July 30, 1877, p. 8; Gompers, *Seventy Years of Life and Labour*, 141–42.

116. John S. Duss, *The Harmonists: A Personal History* (Harrisburg: Pennsylvania Book Service, 1943), 185; "Political Plunder," *New York Tribune*, in *Milwaukee Daily Sentinel*, August 16, 1877, p. 4. See also "Riot's Ruin"; "The Great Strike," *San Francisco Daily Evening Bulletin*, July 25, 1877; "Rioting Roughs"; "A Splendid Pageant"; "Exactly So," *Georgia Weekly Telegraph and Georgia Journal & Messenger* (Macon), August 7, 1877.

117. *Labor Standard*, August 4, 1877; Eric Arnesen, "American Workers and the Labor Movement in the Late Nineteenth Century," in *The Gilded Age: Essays on the Origins of Modern America*, 2nd ed., ed. Charles W. Calhoun (Lanham, MD: Rowman & Littlefield, 2007), 55; *New York Sun*, July 26, 1877, quoted in Foner, *Great Labor Uprising*, 9.

118. "At the Bridge" (quotes); "Cavalry Fight"; *Report of the Committee Appointed to Investigate the Railroad Riots*, 15, 36–37, 68–69, 93, 158, 178, 244–45, 252–56, 375–77, 382, 387, 479, 939, 976–79; Henderson, "Railroad Riots in Pittsburgh," 195–96.

119. *Baltimore Sun*, July 22, 1877; Foner, *History of the Labor Movement in the United States*, 1:465.

120. "A Leaden Rebuke," reprinted over the next few days in the *New York Sun*, *New York Times*, *Baltimore Sun*, and *Bangor Daily Whig & Courier*.

121. Quotes, in order, from Hoogenboom, *Rutherford B. Hayes*, 331; Charles Richard Williams, ed., *Diary and Letters of Rutherford B. Hayes*, 6 vols. (Columbus: Ohio State Archaeological and Historical Society, 1924), 3:93; *Martinsburg Statesman*, July 31, 1877; Foner, *Great Labor Uprising*, 192. The *Martinsburg Statesman* was one of the few papers to understand the workers' position, for which it received the thanks of numerous workers; see *Martinsburg Statesman*, August 7, 21, and 28, 1877.

122. Multiple articles, *North American* (Philadelphia), July 24–27, 1877, especially "A Story of Riot," *North American*, July 25, 1877; "McBridge the Rioter," *North American*, August 11, 1877; *Labor Standard* (New York), August 4, 1877; *Labor Standard*, August 11, 1877; "The Strike in Philadelphia," *New York Times*, July 23, 1877, p. 2; "The Excitement in Philadelphia," *New York Times*, July 24, 1877; "The Philadelphia Strikers," *New York Times*, July 25, 1877, p. 2; "Affairs in Philadelphia," *New York Times*, July 29, 1877, p. 2; "Incidents of Recent Riots," *New York Times*, August 5, 1877, p. 2.

123. Philip English Mackey, "Law and Order, 1877: Philadelphia's Response to the Railroad Riots," *Pennsylvania Magazine of History and Biography* 46 (1972): 198–200.

124. Scott to Hayes, July 31, 1877, in Jack Beatty, *Age of Betrayal: The Triumph of Money in America, 1865–1900* (New York: Knopf, 2007), 296; Gerald G. Eggert, *Railroad Labor Disputes: The Beginnings of Federal Strike Policy* (Ann Arbor: University of Michigan Press, 1969), 31–32, 39–42, 55–56.

125. Lucy Stone, "The Strikers and the Mob," *Woman's Journal*, July 28, 1877, p. 236; Leslie Wheeler, ed., *Loving Warriors: Selected Letters of Lucy Stone and Henry B. Blackwell, 1853 to 1893* (New York: Dial Press, 1981), 397; "The Issue and the Remedy," *Independent* (New York), August 2, 1877, p. 16. The Reverend Joseph Cook stated, "A republic must treat them [strikers] with that kind of mercy which Napoleon showed toward the original Communists of Paris, when he closed the French Revolution by a whiff of grapeshot." See "Joseph Cook's Lectures." See also "The Great Riots"; "The Climax"; "The Mob's Madness"; "A Leaden Rebuke"; "Chicago and Its Rioters," *Inter Ocean*, July 31, 1877, p. 4.

126. James F. Richardson, *The New York Police: Colonial Times to 1901* (New York: Oxford University Press, 1970), 198–99; "The Week," *The Nation*, July 26, 1877, p. 49; "Mob Law"; David Austen, *Manual for Street Fighting* (New York: New York National Guard, 1877); *Harper's Weekly* 21 (1877): 617.

127. "Irish workingmen": "Volunteer Militia and Riots," *New York Times*, July 26, 1877, p. 4; "unfit to bear arms": "The Rioters and the Regular Army," *The Nation*, August 9, 1877, 85–86; *Report of the Committee Appointed to Investigate the Railroad Riots*, 8–10, 18, 27–28 ("intention, in case of further trouble"), 34–35, 117, 266, 385; *Annual Report of the Adjutant General of Pennsylvania* (Harrisburg, PA: State of Pennsylvania, 1878), 89 ("disgraceful" and "humiliating"); Fogelson, *America's Armories*, 38.

128. A spectator, *The Commune in 1880, Downfall of the Republic* (New York: n.p., 1877), 10; "Debate on the Army Bill," *Galveston Daily News*, November 16, 1877; "The Army in Congress," *Boston Daily Advertiser*, November 12, 1877; Matthew Josephson, *The Politicos, 1865–1896* (New York: Harcourt, Brace & World, 1938), 254–58; Scott, "Recent Strikes," 360–61.

129. "Getting Grant into the Field Again," from the *Baltimore Sun* and *Raleigh Register*, July 17, 1877; "Notes on Public Affairs," *The Congregationalist* (Boston), July 18, 1877, p. 8; "Blaine on a Third Term for Grant," from the *Boston Herald* and *Galveston Daily News*, August 25, 1877; "Washington Letter," *St. Louis Globe-Democrat*, October 22, 1877, p. 4; Gresham, *Life of Walter Quintin Gresham*, 1:408.

130. Melvyn Dubofsky, *The State and Labor in Modern America* (Chapel Hill: University of North Carolina Press, 1994), 12; "Missouri Democracy," *St. Louis Globe-Democrat*, December 5, 1877, p. 3.

131. "What they demand": *National Labor Tribune*, September 22, 1877; Bond quoted in "The Labor Question," *St. Louis Globe-Democrat*, August 27, 1877, p. 3; "The Railroad Outbreaks." See also the *Philadelphia Commonwealth* quoted in *Martinsburg Statesman*, August 28, 1877; *Cincinnati Enquirer*, August 28, 1877; *Pittsburgh Press*, July 30, 1877; *New York Tribune*, September 22, 1877.

132. "After the Battle," *Railroad Gazette*, August 12, 1877; *New York Sun*, August 12, 1877.

133. Quotes from "The Army in Congress"; "Pictures That Speak," *Bangor Daily Whig & Courier*, November 24, 1877.

134. "Trade Union Fallacies," *Galveston Daily News*, July 22, 1877, from the *Philadelphia Ledger* and *Inter Ocean* (Chicago), July 31, 1877, p. 4; "The Dangerous Classes," *Chicago Daily Tribune*, July 29, 1877, p. 4.

135. W.M. Grosvenor in the *International Review*, quoted in "Literary Review," *The Congregationalist* (Boston), August 29, 1877, p. 6. See, for instance, "The Practical and the Abstract in Politics," *Galveston Daily News*, April 8, 1877; "Liberty of Labor," *Galveston Daily News*, July 17, 1877; "Notes and Opinions," *Galveston Daily News*, August 25, 1877; *St. Louis Globe-Democrat*, July 30, 1877, p. 4; "Surplus Population," *North American* (Philadelphia), August 1, 1877; "Communism," *Inter Ocean* (Chicago), August 8, 1877; "Communism," *The Congregationalist* (Boston), August 29, 1877, p. 4.

136. "No Property Flag Raised"; "Female Communists," *Georgia Weekly Telegraph and Georgia Journal & Messenger*, October 15, 1877; "The Anti-Hayes Party in Ohio," *North American* (Philadelphia), August 17, 1877; "Views of New Hampshire Politicians and the People," *Independent Statesman* (Concord, NH), August 30, 1877; *Milwaukee Daily Sentinel*, October 11, 1877, p. 4; "It's Booming," *Inter Ocean* (Chicago), March 28, 1877, p. 2.

137. "Limits to Local Authority," *Galveston Daily News*, July 18, 1877; "Boston Monday Lectures," *Boston Daily Advertiser*, October 10, 1877; "Mock Mothers," *St. Louis Globe-Democrat*, November 18, 1877, p. 12; "Money," *St. Louis Globe-Democrat*, November 26, 1877, p. 3; "Pious Pabulum," *Milwaukee Daily Sentinel*, November 26, 1877, p. 3; "Voices of the Pulpit," *Inter Ocean* (Chicago), March 19, 1877, p. 2.

138. "Hawkeye Happenings," *St. Louis Globe-Democrat*, August 11, 1877, p. 7; "Arrest of a Communist," *St. Louis Globe-Democrat*, November 4, 1877, p. 3; "The Example of France," *St. Louis Globe-Democrat*, November 19, 1877, p. 4; "Wisconsin News," *Milwaukee Daily Sentinel*, November 5, 1877, p. 7; "Political Paragraphs," *Milwaukee Daily Sentinel*, November 29, 1877, p. 4; *North American* (Philadelphia), November 1, 1877; "The Other Scheme That Is to Be Urged," *North American*, December 26, 1877; "Editorial Correspondence," *Georgia Weekly Telegraph and Georgia Journal & Messenger* (Macon), December 11, 1877; "City Brevities," *Inter Ocean* (Chicago), December 4, 1877, p. 8; "gray-bearded communist": "A State Stolen," *Inter Ocean*, December 14, 1877; "Communist of the Plains": *Daily Arkansas Gazette* (Little Rock), August 10, 1877.

139. *Bangor Daily Whig & Courier*, August 1, 1877, attributed to *Lowell Courier*, repeated in *Independent Statesman* (Concord, NH), August 2, 1877, p. 352.

140. "Communism," *Inter Ocean* (Chicago), August 8, 1877. See also a poem written on this theme: "The Communist Citizen," *Georgia Weekly Telegraph and Georgia Journal & Messenger* (Macon), October 2, 1877; "The Communist Citizen," *Daily Arkansas Gazette* (Little Rock), August 12, 1877.

141. *Pittsburgh Post* quoted in Philip M. Katz, *From Appomattox to Montmartre: Americans and the Paris Commune* (Cambridge, MA: Harvard University Press, 1998); Robert P. Porter, "The Truth About the Strike," *The Galaxy* 24 (1877): 727; Bond quoted in "The Labor Question," *St. Louis Globe-Democrat*, August 27, 1877, p. 3; "Political Plunder."

142. *Inter Ocean* (Chicago), July 30, 1877, p. 4; "The Communist Proposition," *Weekly Arizona Miner* (Prescott), August 31, 1877; "A Surviving Danger," *Galveston Daily News*, August 9, 1877.

143. "Indiana," *Chicago Daily Tribune*, August 2, 1877, p. 2; "Judge Drummond and the Riot," *Milwaukee Daily Sentinel*, August 2, 1877, p. 4; "The Labor Troubles," *Boston Daily Advertiser*, August 4, 1877; Gresham, *Life of Walter Quintin Gresham*, 2:230–31; Elwin W. Sigmund, "Railroad Strikers in Court: Unreported Contempt Cases in Illinois in 1877," *Illinois State Historical Journal* 49 (1956): 190–209; "The Strikes in Pennsylvania,"

New York Times, August 1, 1877; "The Campaign in the Oil Regions," *New York Times*, August 2, 1877; "The Great Labor Strike," *New York Times*, August 6, 1877; "Notes of the Strike," *North American* (Philadelphia), August 3, 1877; multiple articles, *St. Louis Globe-Democrat*, August 1–3, 1877; Burbank, *Rabble*, 176–77.

144. Filippeli, "Railroad Strike of 1877 in Reading," 69–71.

145. *Pittsburgh Telegraph*, August 12, 1877 (quote); Foner, *Great Labor Uprising*, 229; "Latest Dispatches," *San Francisco Daily Evening Bulletin*, August 10, 1877; "Associated Working Men," *New York Times*, August 13, 1877, p. 3; "The Trades," *Chicago Daily Tribune*, December 2, 1877, p. 3. On the existence of the blacklist, see Herbert G. Gutman, "Trouble on the Railroads in 1873–1874: Prelude to the 1877 Crisis?" *Labor History* 2 (1961): 215–35.

146. Foner, *History of the Labor Movement*, 1:438, 504–8; Terence V. Powderly, *Thirty Years of Labor, 1859 to 1889* (Columbus, OH: Excelsior Publishing House, 1889), 213–22; Leon Fink, *Workingmen's Democracy: The Knights of Labor and American Politics* (Champaign, IL: University of Illinois Press, 1985).

147. "Springfield rifles": *National Labor Tribune*, September 22, 1877, Foner, *The Great Labor Uprising*, 227; "Political Matters," *Inter Ocean* (Chicago), September 12, 1877, p. 8; Marx to Engels, July 24, 1877, Barry Werth, *Banquet at Delmonico's: Great Minds, the Gilded Age, and the Triumph of Evolution in America* (New York: Random House, 2009), 167.

148. Morris Hillquit, *History of Socialism in the United States* (New York: Funk & Wagnalls, 1910), 203–5. Powderly is modest about his accomplishment and does not discuss his remarkable election in his autobiography, just alluding to the electoral victories of workers; Powderly, *Thirty Years of Labor*, 272–73.

149. Multiple articles, *Louisville Courier-Journal*, August 2–7, 1877; Foner, *Great Labor Uprising*, 220–21; "Political Points," *St. Louis Globe-Democrat*, August 7, 1877; "The Louisville Election," *St. Louis Globe-Democrat*, August 8, 1877, p. 4; *North American* (Philadelphia), August 9, 1877.

150. Foner, *Great Labor Uprising*, 221–22; *Louisville Courier-Journal*, August 6–10, 1877.

151. To take just St. Louis as an example, see the following articles in the *St. Louis Globe-Democrat*: "The Late City Election," August 14, 1877, p. 4; "Associated Workingmen," August 16, 1877, p. 2; "Baits for Workingmen," August 19, 1877, p. 4; "Labor's Logic," August 20, 1877, p. 8; "The Labor Platforms," August 23, 1877, p. 4; "The Labor Question," August 25, 1877, p. 3; "The Workingmen's Party," August 25, 1877, p. 8; "The Labor Question," August 27, 1877, p. 3; "The Workingmen Convention," August 27, 1877, p. 5.

152. Multiple articles, *Labor Standard* (New York), August 7, 12, and 19, 1877; Hillquit, *History of Socialism*, 204–6, 242–46; *Emancipator* (Cincinnati), August 18, 1877, quoted in Foner, *Great Labor Uprising*, 223.

153. *Cincinnati Commercial*, July 24, 1877; Philip S. Foner, *American Socialism and Black Americans: From the Age of Jackson to World War II* (Westport, CT: Greenwood Press, 1977), 46–51; "Political Points," *St. Louis Globe-Democrat*, August 12, 1877, p. 7; "The Labor Question," *Milwaukee Daily Sentinel*, August 13, 1877, p. 3; *Inter Ocean* (Chicago), August 14, 1877, p. 4; "Socialism: The Remedy for the Evils of Society," *Cincinnati Commercial*, July 23, 1877; Philip S. Foner, ed., *The Voice of Black America: Major Speeches of Blacks in the United States, 1797–1973* (New York: Simon & Schuster, 1975), 1:481–87; Herbert G. Gutman, "Peter H. Clark: Pioneer Negro Socialist, 1877," *Journal of Negro*

Education 34 (1965): 413–18; "Political Points," *St. Louis Globe-Democrat*, August 12, 1877, p. 7; "Political Points," *Inter Ocean* (Chicago), August 13, 1877, p. 5; *Emancipator* (Cincinnati), August 4, 11, and 18, 1877, quoted in Foner, *Great Labor Uprising*, 224.

154. "A Plea for the Strikers," *Cincinnati Commercial*, July 26, 1877.

155. Multiple articles, *New York Times*, November 8–15, 1877; Hillquit, *History of Socialism in the United States*, 237–41; Foner, *Great Labor Uprising*, 224–26; Burbank, *Rabble*, 189.

156. For some reason this quotation is often used but rarely cited or recorded correctly: Jane Addams, "Trade Unions and Public Duty," *American Journal of Sociology* 4 (1899): 458.

157. Roscoe Pound, "Liberty of Contract," *Yale Law Journal* 18 (1909): 454–87; William Forbath, "The Shaping of the American Labor Movement," *Harvard Law Review* 102 (1989): 1134–45; Morton J. Horwitz, *The Transformation of American Law, 1870–1960: The Crisis of Legal Orthodoxy* (New York: Oxford University Press, 1992), 9–32; Beatty, *Age of Betrayal*, 160–61.

158. Gompers, *Seventy Years of Life and Labour*, 139; Edwards, *New Spirits*, 318; Powderly, *Thirty Years of Labor*, 186–202.

159. Gompers, *Seventy Years of Life and Labour*, 139, 140, 148–54.

160. Ibid., 135, 142–54 (quote, 140); Foner, *Great Labor Uprising*, 228.

161. *Washington Capital*, reprinted in *Martinsburg Statesman*, September 4, 1877; Foner, *Great Labor Uprising*, 230; "Reign of the Mob"; "No Temporizing"; "The Seeds of Sedition," *Idaho Avalanche* (Silver City, ID), August 4, 1877; "Home Again," *North American* (Philadelphia), August 6, 1877; "The Demagogue's Opportunity," *Milwaukee Daily Sentinel*, August 13, 1877, p. 4; "A Lesson from the Riots," *Frank Leslie's Illustrated Newspaper* (New York), August 18, 1877, p. 398.

162. *Commercial and Financial Chronicle*, quoted in Foner, *History of the Labor Movement*, 1:464.

163. F.R. Plunkett to the Earl of Derby, July 31, 1877, in *Reports Respecting the Late Industrial Conflicts*, 6.

164. Williams, *Diary and Letters of Rutherford B. Hayes*, 5:440.

Chapter 6: Homicidal Nation

1. "Demonology," *St. Louis Globe-Democrat*, March 18, 1877, p. 9, from the *North American Review*.

2. On Clay's political move to the Democratic Party by way of the Liberal Party, see David L. Smiley, *Lion of White Hall: The Life of Cassius M. Clay* (Madison: University of Wisconsin Press, 1962), 223–29.

3. Cassius M. Clay, *The Life of Cassius Marcellus Clay: Memoirs, Writings, and Speeches* (New York: Negro Universities Press, 1969), 557, 565. His memoirs mix the two versions, charging that the Whites had been stealing from him for years while trying to poison his son at the behest of his political enemies. See ibid., 557–63.

4. Ibid., 563 (quote); Smiley, *Lion of White Hall*, 234–35. Clay states that after reading this letter the whole plot of theft and the poisoning of his son came to him "like a flash of lightning." Clay, *Life of Cassius Marcellus Clay*, 564.

5. In his memoir, Clay did not actually say what happened during the shooting; instead he reprinted the account written from the *Cincinnati Commercial*, even though this article holds that theft and not poisoning was the cause of the confrontation. This ver-

sion states that Clay was questioning White when "Perry jumped to his feet and attempted to draw his weapons," whereupon Clay shot White in the neck and heart. The article does not note what Perry was doing lying on the ground or what weapons White attempted to draw. Clay, *Life of Cassius Marcellus Clay*, 568–69.

6. "High-Toned Homicide," *Milwaukee Daily Sentinel*, October 10, 1877, p. 3. See also "Wickedness," *Milwaukee Daily Sentinel*, October 2, 1877; "The Shooting of a Negro by the Hon. Cassius M. Clay," *Boston Daily Advertiser*, October 2, 1877; "A Sad Affair," *Galveston Daily News*, October 2, 1877; "Gen. Clay's Deadly Fight," *St. Louis Globe-Democrat*, October 17, 1877, p. 2; "Cassius M. Clay: The True Story of His Killing the Negro Perry White," *San Francisco Daily Evening Bulletin*, October 27, 1877; "The Clay-Wickliffe Duel," *Raleigh Register*, November 1, 1877.

7. *Boston Globe* quoted in "The Homicide by Cassius M. Clay," *Bangor Daily Whig & Courier*, November 21, 1877; "Cassius M. Clay's Crime," *Inter Ocean* (Chicago), November 14, 1877, p. 2; "gloomy": "People and Things," *Daily Rocky Mountain News* (Denver), November 1, 1877; "Political and Personal," *Bangor Daily Whig & Courier*, October 10, 1877; "Cassius M. Clay's Pistol," *Bangor Daily Whig & Courier*, October 4, 1877; "Discouraged with the Negro," *Inter Ocean*, November 6, 1877, p. 4; "Gen. Cassius M. Clay," *St. Louis Globe-Democrat*, October 8, 1877, p. 2; "Notes and Opinions," *Galveston Daily News*, October 30, 1877; Clay, *Life of Cassius Marcellus Clay*, 569. There was some disagreement as to the presence of witnesses other than Clay's son; ibid., 567.

8. "Trial of J. Wesley Hardin," *Galveston Daily News*, October 7, 1877 ; "A Bad 'Un," *St. Louis Globe-Democrat*, October 15, 1877; Robert M. Utley, *Lone Star Justice: The First Century of the Texas Rangers* (New York: Oxford University Press, 2002), 172; Leon Metz, *John Wesley Hardin: Dark Angel of Texas* (El Paso: Mangan, 1996); Walter Prescott Webb, *The Texas Rangers: A Century of Frontier Defense* (Boston: Houghton Mifflin, 1935), 298.

9. Shortly thereafter Hardin organized a mass jailbreak in Brownwood, Texas. "Brown County," *Galveston Daily News*, May 19, 1877; "State News," *Galveston Daily News*, May 22, 1877.

10. "John Wesley Hardin," *Galveston Daily News*, August 28, 1877; Webb, *Texas Rangers*, 298–99; Utley, *Lone Star Justice*, 173–74; Metz, *John Wesley Hardin*, 158–72; Chuck Parsons, *The Capture of John Wesley Hardin* (College Station, TX: Creative, 1978). For an unlikely version of these events in which Armstrong single-handedly overcomes all four men, see Webb, *Texas Rangers*, 299.

11. "John Wesley Hardin at Comanche," *Galveston Daily News*, October 3, 1877; "Trial of J. Wesley Hardin"; "Houston Local Items," *Galveston Daily News*, October 13, 1877; "State News," *Galveston Daily News*, October 18, 1877; "State Press," *Galveston Daily News*, October 19, 1877; Webb, *Texas Rangers*, 302–3; James B. Gillett, *Six Years with the Texas Rangers, 1875 to 1881*, ed. Milo M. Quaife (New Haven: Yale University Press, 1925), 124–25.

12. "State Press," *Galveston Daily News*, November 13, 1877.

13. "Trial of J. Wesley Hardin"; Metz, *John Wesley Hardin*, 185–65.

14. Quotes from *Daily Arkansas Gazette* (Little Rock), August 17, 1877; "Jay Gould at Home," *Galveston Daily News*, August 31, 1877. See also Denis Tilden Lynch, *The Wild Seventies* (New York: D. Appleton-Century Co., 1941), 491; "Jay Gould," *North American* (Philadelphia), August 14, 1877.

15. "Jay Gould's Railroad Operations," *San Francisco Daily Evening Bulletin*, March 6, 1877; "The Railroads: Jay Gould's Capture of Two of the Iowa Pool Lines," *St. Louis*

Globe-Democrat, March 7, 1877, p. 3; "Jay Gould's Game," *St. Louis Globe-Democrat*, October 22, 1877; "Jay Gould's Railroad Scheme," *Weekly Arizona Miner* (Prescott), March 23, 1877; *Galveston Daily News*, April 28, 1877; *Daily Rocky Mountain News* (Denver), July 28, 1877; "Jay Gould's Last," *Daily Rocky Mountain News*, October 26, 1877; *Daily Arkansas Gazette* (Little Rock), August 17, 1877.

16. Lynch, *Wild Seventies*, 495–97. Most newspapers covered the attack, but the most coherent account is "Gould's Ghost," *Inter Ocean* (Chicago), August 4, 1877, p. 5.

17. "Mauling a Millionaire: The Assault upon Jay Gould in New York," *St. Louis Globe-Democrat*, August 4, 1877, p. 4; "A Racy Scandal," *St. Louis Globe-Democrat*, August 3, 1877.

18. "Mauling a Millionaire" (quote); "A Racy Scandal"; "Jay Gould Assaulted and Slightly Injured by a Rival Speculator," *Boston Daily Advertiser*, August 3, 1877; "The Jay Gould Assault," *San Francisco Daily Evening Bulletin*, August 3, 1877; "Assault on Jay Gould," *North American* (Philadelphia), August 3, 1877; *North American*, August 9, 1877; "New York," *Daily Arkansas Gazette* (Little Rock), August 3, 1877.

19. First three quotes from "Mauling a Millionaire"; "the worst man": "Keene and Selover," *San Francisco Daily Evening Bulletin*, August 13, 1877; "Jay Gould," *San Francisco Daily Evening Bulletin*, August 27, 1877.

20. "Jay Gould," *Independent Statesman* (Concord, NH), August 9, 1877; "The Jay Gould Assault"; "Keene and Selover."

21. "Jay Gould," *Independent Statesman* (Concord, NH), August 9, 1877.

22. The *Inter Ocean* tried the heading "Era of Accident" starting on January 4, 1877, and by January 13 carried a subhead reading, "The 'Head-writer' Is Anxious to Do Away with This Caption, but Cannot at Present," including "Casualty Calendar" as a subhead. "Era of Accident," *Inter Ocean* (Chicago), January 13, 1877, p. 5. "Criminal Calendar" appeared on February 1, 1877, p. 5; "Casualty Calendar" appeared as a heading on July 13, 1877, p. 5. The *St. Louis Globe-Democrat* used "Rogues and Roughs," "Rogues and Assassins," and "The Rogues' Register."

23. H.V. Redfield, *Homicide, North and South* (Columbus: Ohio State University Press, 2000), 100.

24. See, for instance, *Inter Ocean* (Chicago), August 30, 1877, p. 4, quoting the *Houston Age*; "Iowa Inklings," *St. Louis Globe-Democrat*, November 23, 1877, p. 3; "Words of Warning," *Daily Rocky Mountain News* (Denver), April 4, 1877; "Lawlessness in Lee County," *Galveston Daily News*, July 10, 1877; *St. Louis Globe-Democrat*, July 18, 1877, p. 4; "State News in Brief," *San Francisco Daily Evening Bulletin*, March 15, 1877; "Crime and Poverty," *Milwaukee Daily Sentinel*, April 25, 1877, p. 2.

25. Robert V. Bruce, *1877: Year of Violence* (Indianapolis: Bobbs-Merrill, 1959), 10.

26. "The Poplar-Street Homicide of Last October," *St. Louis Globe-Democrat*, October 10, 1877, p. 7; "Criminal Calendar," *St. Louis Globe-Democrat*, August 31, 1877, p. 3; "Homicide at Bryan," *Galveston Daily News*, March 3, 1877; "A Remorseless Decapitator," from the *New Orleans Democrat*, *North American* (Philadelphia), August 31, 1877; "Murdered for Money," *St. Louis Globe-Democrat*, March 15, 1877, p. 3.

27. "Homicide Cases to Be Tried," *North American* (Philadelphia), April 4, 1877; "Homicide," *North American*, August 21, 1877 (quote).

28. "San Buenaventura Matters," *San Francisco Daily Evening Bulletin*, June 13, 1877; "Judge Lynch," *Colorado Springs Gazette*, December 22, 1877, p. 2; "Another Homicide," *Raleigh Register*, September 13, 1877. Murder filled the newspapers; this study is based on more than one thousand articles in 1877 addressing homicides from the follow-

ing papers: *Bangor Daily Whig & Courier, Boston Daily Advertiser, Boston Pilot, Cedar Rapids Times, Chicago Tribune, Cincinnati Commercial, Colorado Springs Gazette, Commercial and Financial Chronicle and Hunt's Merchant's Magazine* (New York), *The Congregationalist* (Boston), *Daily Arkansas Gazette* (Little Rock), *Daily Rocky Mountain News* (Denver), *Frank Leslie's Illustrated Newspaper* (New York), *National Labor Tribune* (Pittsburgh), *Galveston Daily News, Georgia Weekly Telegraph and Georgia Journal & Messenger* (Macon), *Hartford Daily Courant, Hinds County Gazette* (Raymond, MS), *Inter Ocean* (Chicago), *Irish World* (New York), *Lowell Daily Citizen and News, Mesilla Valley Independent* (Mesilla, NM), *Milwaukee Daily Sentinel, New York Times, Newark Advocate* (Newark, OH), *North American* (Philadelphia), *Raleigh Register, St. Louis Globe-Democrat, San Francisco Daily Evening Bulletin, The Teller* (Lewiston, ID), *Wisconsin State Register* (Portage, WI), and *Yankton Press and Union and Dakotaian.*

29. *Galveston Daily News* quoted in Redfield, *Homicide,* 81–82; "Homicide by an Infant: A Boy Four Years Old Shoots His Six-Years-Old Playfellow through the Head," *St. Louis Globe-Democrat,* April 25, 1877, p. 2.

30. *Milwaukee Daily Sentinel,* December 28, 1877, p. 4.

31. "A Rope for Roper," *St. Louis Globe-Democrat,* November 28, 1877, p. 5; "The Criminal Record," *Milwaukee Daily Sentinel,* November 28, 1877, p. 5; "By Telegraph," *Georgia Weekly Telegraph* (Macon), December 4, 1877.

32. "Lynching at La Veta," *Colorado Springs Gazette,* July 28, 1877, p. 4; "Judge Lynch," *Colorado Springs Gazette,* December 22, 1877, p. 2. On American popular attitudes toward lynching, see Christopher Waldrep, *The Many Faces of Judge Lynch: Extralegal Violence and Punishment in America* (New York: Palgrave Macmillan, 2002); Jacqueline Goldsby, *A Spectacular Secret: Lynching in American Life and Literature* (Chicago: University of Chicago Press, 2006).

33. Michael J. Pfeifer, *Rough Justice: Lynching and American Society, 1874–1947* (Urbana: University of Illinois Press, 2004), 1–12 (quote, 3).

34. Pfeifer, *Rough Justice,* 14; Christopher Waldrep, *Roots of Disorder: Race and Criminal Justice in the American South, 1817–80* (Urbana: University of Illinois Press, 1998), 172–74; Waldrep, *Many Faces of Judge Lynch*; Christopher Waldrep, *Lynching in America: A History in Documents* (New York: New York University Press, 2006); Ken Gonzales-Day, *Lynching in the West, 1850–1935* (Durham, NC: Duke University Press, 2006).

35. *San Francisco Daily Alta California,* May 4, 1877; Pfeifer, *Rough Justice,* 4, 14–15, 66 (quote); "Lawlessness in Lee County," *Galveston Daily News,* July 10, 1877; Frederick Allen, *A Decent, Orderly Lynching: The Montana Vigilantes* (Norman: University of Oklahoma Press, 2004).

36. "A Virginia City Homicide," *San Francisco Daily Evening Bulletin,* October 9, 1877; "The Davis-Ash Homicide," *San Francisco Daily Evening Bulletin,* October 10, 1877; "A Texas Sheriff Eludes a Mob," *St. Louis Globe-Democrat,* March 20, 1877, p. 2; "Judge Pleasants and Three Other Citizens Threatened with Assassination," *Galveston Daily News,* January 26, 1877; "Bill Longley Interviewed," *Galveston Daily News,* September 16, 1877; Webb, *Texas Rangers,* 289–94; Utley, *Lone Star Justice,* 153–54, 176.

37. "State Press," *Galveston Daily News,* February 6, 1877; Gillett, *Six Years with the Texas Rangers,* 137, 162–63.

38. "Letter from New York," *The Congregationalist* (Boston), February 21, 1877; Robert Fletcher, "The New School of Criminal Anthropology," *American Anthropologist* 4 (July 1891): 231.

39. "Break in the Carson Prison," *San Francisco Daily Evening Bulletin,* October 30,

1877; "Escape of the Connecticut Borgia," *Inter Ocean* (Chicago), June 9, 1877, p. 14; "Mrs. Lydia Sherman at Large," *St. Louis Globe-Democrat*, June 4, 1877, p. 2; "A Murderess of Eight Persons," *Newark Advocate* (Newark, OH), June 8, 1877. There was some disagreement in the press about how many people she murdered; see "This Morning's News," *North American* (Philadelphia), May 31, 1877; "New England," *Boston Daily Advertiser*, May 31, 1877. Sherman was free for a week, making it as far as Providence before being captured; see "Bulletin of the News," *Boston Daily Advertiser*, June 6, 1877; "Recapture of Lydia Sherman," *St. Louis Globe-Democrat*, June 9, 1877, p. 2. Sherman died in prison the following year; see "Death of Lydia Sherman, the Poisoner," *San Francisco Daily Evening Bulletin*, May 29, 1878.

40. "An Escape from Prison," *Boston Daily Advertiser*, July 25, 1877; Webb, *Texas Rangers*, 293, 333; "State News," *Galveston Daily News*, March 17, 1877; "State News," *Galveston Daily News*, August 1, 1877; "A Texas Sheriff Eludes a Mob," *St. Louis Globe-Democrat*, March 20, 1877, p. 2; "City and Vicinity," *Daily Rocky Mountain News* (Denver), December 23, 1877; "The Police Force," *San Francisco Daily Evening Bulletin*, August 27, 1877; "The Crooks' Corner," *St. Louis Globe-Democrat*, August 26, 1877, p. 4; "Three Bad Kentuckians Escape," *St. Louis Globe-Democrat*, December 30, 1877, p. 7; "The Chisholm Murderers Baffled," *Inter Ocean* (Chicago), December 14, 1877, p. 4; "The Farmington Jail Delivery," *St. Louis Globe-Democrat*, April 6, 1877; "A Jail Escape in Dodge County," *Milwaukee Daily Sentinel*, April 21, 1877, p. 2; "This Morning's News," *North American* (Philadelphia), May 10, 1877; "Criminal Calendar," *Inter Ocean*, August 20, 1877, p. 5; "The Court Record," *Inter Ocean*, January 24, 1877, p. 3; "Escape from Jail," *Lowell Daily Citizen*, March 27, 1877; "Escape from Jail, at Manchester," *Boston Daily Advertiser*, April 16, 1877; "Sundries," *Newark Advocate* (Newark, OH), February 23, 1877.

41. "Crime and Poverty," *Milwaukee Daily Sentinel*, April 25, 1877, p. 2.

42. Roger Lane, *Violent Death in the City: Suicide, Accident, and Murder in Nineteenth-Century Philadelphia* (Columbus: Ohio State University Press, 1999), 59–62, 84–90, 98–100, 131 (quote).

43. Eric H. Monkkonen, *Police in Urban America, 1860–1920* (Cambridge: Cambridge University Press, 1981), 21; Eric H. Monkkonen, *The Dangerous Class: Crime and Poverty in Columbus, Ohio, 1860–1885* (Cambridge, MA: Harvard University Press, 1975), 72; Marx from Paul Hirst, "Marx and Engels on Law, Crime and Morality," in Ian Taylor et al., *The New Criminology: For a Social Theory of Deviance* (London: Routledge and Kegan Paul, 1973), 215–16; Christopher G. Tiedeman, "Police Control of Dangerous Classes, Other than by Criminal Prosecutions," *American Law Review* 19 (1885): 547–70.

44. "Louisiana," *Boston Daily Advertiser*, January 20, 1877; "Silence," *St. Louis Globe-Democrat*, March 4, 1877, p. 10; "A Black Thursday," *North American* (Philadelphia), June 23, 1877; *North American*, July 25, 1877; "Changing Aspect of the Great Strike," *San Francisco Daily Evening Bulletin*, July 24, 1877. The phrase "criminal class" dates back to at least 1830 and was often used in the context of drunkenness. The earliest use I can find is in "Temperance Department," *Observer and Telegraph* (Hudson, OH), April 23, 1830.

45. Thomas Byrnes, *1886 Professional Criminals of America* (New York: Chelsea House, 1969); Monkkonen, *Police in Urban America*, 25, 31, 42. See, for instance, "An American Detective," *Bangor Daily Whig & Courier*, January 21, 1886; "The Bribers' Nemesis," *Milwaukee Daily Journal*, April 9, 1886; "Inspector Byrnes," *Atchison Daily Globe*, January 13, 1887.

46. Byrnes, *1886 Professional Criminals*, 55.

47. "The Public Library," *Boston Daily Advertiser*, February 14, 1877 (quotes); "The Criminal Class," *San Francisco Daily Evening Bulletin*, August 9, 1877. Eric Monkkonen found that in East Coast cities 65 percent of the "criminal class" was native-born, 9 percent Irish, 6 percent German, and just 4 percent black; see Monkkonen, *Dangerous Class*, 154.

48. "The Criminal Class," *San Francisco Daily Evening Bulletin*, August 9 and September 25, 1877.

49. "Attempt to Obtain a Pardon for the Murderer Pryce," *Daily Rocky Mountain News* (Denver) December 27, 1877; "The Police Department," *San Francisco Daily Evening Bulletin*, May 19, 1877; "Power of the Criminal Classes," *Lowell Daily Citizen*, January 5, 1877.

50. "The Police Department"; "The Dangerous Elements," *San Francisco Daily Evening Bulletin*, July 26, 1877 (quote); "The Criminal Class," *San Francisco Daily Evening Bulletin*, August 9, 1877; "Louisiana."

51. "American Tramps—An English View," *San Francisco Daily Evening Bulletin*, November 13, 1877; *Bangor Daily Whig & Courier*, December 12, 1877; "Power of the Criminal Classes"; *Lowell Daily Citizen*, September 1, 1877.

52. Herbert Asbury, *The Gangs of New York* (New York: Capricorn Books, 1970), 233, 238–43.

53. George Augustus Sala, *America Revisited: From the Bay of New York to the Gulf of Mexico, and From Lake Michigan to the Pacific*, 3d. ed., 2 vols. (London: Vizetelly & Co., 1883), 1:74; "Treatment of Habitual Criminals," *The Nation*, July 12, 1877, p. 24; Asbury, *Gangs of New York*, 174.

54. Asbury, *Gangs of New York*, 191; Byrnes, *1886 Professional Criminals*, 183–84.

55. George W. Walling, *Recollections of a New York Chief of Police* (New York: Caxton Book Concern, 1887), 534–37.

56. David J. Cook, *Hands Up! or Thirty-Five Years of Detective Work in the Mountains and on the Plains* (1882; Denver: W.F. Robinson Printing, 1897), 10.

57. "Justifiable Homicide," *San Francisco Daily Evening Bulletin*, January 3, 1877; "Sunday's Homicide," *St. Louis Globe-Democrat*, June 5, 1877, p. 8; "Trial of the J.F. Morris Homicide Matter," *Galveston Daily News*, June 22, 1877. See also "The Criminal Record: Probable Homicide by a Police Officer in Charlestown," *Boston Daily Advertiser*, February 28, 1877; "Criminal News: The Charlestown Homicide," *Boston Daily Advertiser*, March 1, 1877; "The Charlestown Homicide Officer Freeman's Course Fully Vindicated by the Coroner's Jury," *Boston Daily Advertiser*, March 2, 1877.

58. Sala, *America Revisited*, 1:65, 188.

59. "Major John B. Jones," *Galveston Daily News*, May 25, 1878; Utley, *Lone Star Justice*, 152–54; Webb, *Texas Rangers*, 288–89, 297. Section 23 of the Constitution of the State of Texas, *The Revised Statutes of Texas: Adopted by the Regular Session of the Sixteenth Legislature, A.D. 1879* (Galveston: A.H. Belo & Co., 1879), 10; Gillett, *Six Years with the Texas Rangers*, 177–78; Utley, *Lone Star Justice*, 155. The wording of the Texas constitution on this point is identical with that of the Tennessee constitution; see "The Right to Keep and Bear Arms for Private and Public Defense," *Central Law Journal* 1 (1874): 273. A later Texas act allowed city councils "full power and authority by ordinance to regulate, control and prohibit the carrying of firearms and other weapons within the city limits." *General Laws of the State of Texas Passed at the Regular Session of the Twenty-second Legislature* (Austin: Henry Hutchings, 1891), 43.

60. Napoleon A. Jennings, *A Texas Ranger* (Norman: University of Oklahoma Press, 1997), 108–15; George Durham, *Taming the Nueces Strip: The Story of McNelly's Rangers* (Austin: University of Texas Press, 1962), 129–37; Utley, *Lone Star Justice*, 176–78; Webb, *Texas Rangers*, 333; Gillett, *Six Years with the Texas Rangers*, 104–6, 115–16; Ovie C. Fisher and Jeff Dykes, *King Fisher: His Life and Times* (Norman: University of Oklahoma Press, 1967), 95–116.

61. Jennings, *Texas Ranger*, 109 (quote); C.L. Sonnichsen, *I'll Die Before I'll Run: The Story of the Great Feuds of Texas* (Lincoln: University of Nebraska Press, 1988), 90–115; Utley, *Lone Star Justice*, 175.

62. Utley, *Lone Star Justice*, 181; Sonnichsen, *I'll Die Before I'll Run*, 125–49; Gillett, *Six Years with the Texas Rangers*, 101–17; Webb, *Texas Rangers*, 334–35.

63. Utley, *Lone Star Justice*, 181–82; Bill O'Neal, *The Bloody Legacy of Pink Higgins: A Half Century of Violence in Texas* (Austin: Eakin, 1999), 44–48. The Horrell letter promised "to abstain from insulting or injuring you and your friends, to bury the bitter past forever, and join with you as good citizens in undoing the evil which has resulted from our quarrel," while the Higgins letter stated, "It would be difficult for us to express in words the mental disturbance to ourselves which the sad quarrel with its fatal consequences . . . occasioned" and promised to become "good law-abiding citizens and preservers of peace and order." Webb, *Texas Rangers*, 337–38.

64. Utley, *Lone Star Justice*, 166 (quote), 182–83; Webb, *Texas Rangers*, 335–38.

65. Gillett, *Six Years with the Texas Rangers*, 156–58 (quote, 157); Webb, *Texas Rangers*, 371–73; "A Desperado's Death," *Milwaukee Daily Sentinel*, July 26, 1878, p. 7.

66. Gillett, *Six Years with the Texas Rangers*, 158–68; Webb, *Texas Rangers*, 373–74; "Through 'Em a Third Time," *Galveston Daily News*, April 6, 1878; "Texas News," *Galveston Daily News*, April 18, 1878; "The Train Robbers," *Galveston Daily News*, April 19, 1878; "Texas News," *Galveston Daily News*, April 20, 1878.

67. Webb, *Texas Rangers*, 375–79 (quote, 376); "Denton as Good as Dallas," *Galveston Daily News*, April 27, 1878; "Rumors of a Skirmish with the Bass Gang," *Galveston Daily News*, April 30, 1878; "Texas News," *Galveston Daily News*, May 1, 1878; "Sherman," *Galveston Daily News*, May 4, 1878; "Dallas Letter," *Galveston Daily News*, May 7, 1878; "Sam Bass Heard From," *Galveston Daily News*, May 29, 1878; "Bass Not in Such a Bad Box," *Galveston Daily News*, June 5, 1878; "Sam Bass and His Band," *Galveston Daily News*, June 7, 1878.

68. "Battle with Sam Bass the Bold Brigand," *Galveston Daily News*, July 20, 1878; "Bass at Length Bagged," *Galveston Daily News*, July 21, 1878; "Sam Bass and His Band," *Galveston Daily News*, July 24, 1878; "The Fight with Bass," *Galveston Daily News*, July 25, 1878; Utley, *Lone Star Justice*, 183–87; Gillett, *Six Years with the Texas Rangers*, 168–84; Webb, *Texas Rangers*, 379–89.

69. David R. Johnson, *American Law Enforcement: A History* (St. Louis: Forum Press, 1981), 55, 62–63. Monkkonen works on the assumption that the amount of crime is constant; see Monkkonen, *Police in Urban America*, 22. This formulation is useful in that variations from that constant must be demonstrated and explained, though a great deal depends on definitions. If political murders, such as occurred in the South in 1877, are not labeled "homicides," then the totals may remain constant, while their inclusion indicates a dramatic rise in the murder rate.

70. Monkkonen, *Dangerous Class*, 151; "Robbers," *Colorado Springs Gazette*, November 17, 1877, p. 4; Robert R. Dykstra, *The Cattle Towns* (Lincoln: University of Nebraska Press, 1968), 143–48.

71. "The Dangerous Elements," *San Francisco Daily Evening Bulletin*, July 26, 1877; "Treatment of Habitual Criminals," *The Nation*, July 12, 1877, pp. 23–24; Byrnes, *1886 Professional Criminals*, xxii–xxiv; Marilynn S. Johnson, *Street Justice: A History of Police Violence in New York City* (Boston: Beacon Press, 2003), 12–56; Johnson, *Street Justice*, 40.

72. Asbury, *Gangs of New York*, 235–37 (quote, 237); Johnson, *Street Justice*, 42–43; James F. Richardson, *The New York Police: Colonial Times to 1901* (New York: Oxford University Press, 1970), 167, 181, 204–5.

73. *National Police Gazette*, November 1, 1879; Johnson, *Street Justice*, 45; Asbury, *Gangs of New York*, 235–37; Richardson, *New York Police*, 204–7.

74. Johnson, *Street Justice*, 22, 27. Johnson found that the victims of police brutality in New York City in this period were 32 percent Irish, 15 percent Germans, and 7 percent Jews, while Anglo-Americans and British immigrants accounted for 36 percent of the total, well below their percentage of the population; see ibid., 27.

75. Compared with 22 percent clerical and 8 percent professional; see Johnson, *Street Justice*, 31.

76. Johnson, *Street Justice*, 37, 40; Richardson, *New York Police*, 166–67, 190, 195–98.

77. *New York World* quoted in Johnson, *Street Justice*, 38.

78. "Miscellaneous City News," *New York Times*, October 15, 1877, p. 8; "City Hall Notes," *New York Times*, October 16, 1877, p. 8; "Political Assessments," *New York Times*, October 17, 1877, p. 5; Richardson, *New York Police*, 176–77.

79. "State News," *Galveston Daily News*, January 16 and August 23, 1877; Webb, *Texas Rangers*, 296–97.

80. Ord quoted in Utley, *Lone Star Justice*, 163; "this treatment": Webb, *Texas Rangers*, 243. For additional material on torture and terror tactics, see the accounts by two former Rangers in Durham, *Taming the Nueces Strip*, 103–28; Jennings, *Texas Ranger*, 71–79.

81. Richardson, *New York Police*, 168–73.

82. William Stanton, *The Leopard's Spots: Scientific Attitudes Toward Race in America, 1815–1859* (Chicago: University of Chicago Press, 1960); Stephen Jay Gould, *The Mismeasure of Man* (New York: Norton, 1981); G.J. Barker-Benfield, *The Horrors of the Half-Known Life: Male Attitudes Toward Women and Sexuality in Nineteenth-Century America* (New York: Routledge, 1999).

83. Gould, *Mismeasure of Man*, 154; Cesare Lombroso, *Criminal Man*, trans. Mary Gibson and Nicole Hahn Rafter (Durham, NC: Duke University Press, 2006).

84. "A distinctive type": "Encouraging Tramps," *St. Louis Globe-Democrat*, March 12, 1877, p. 4; "Demonology"; "Dr. Joseph Simms, Physiognomist," *Frank Leslie's Illustrated Newspaper* (New York), September 14, 1878, p. 29; "Dr. Schliemann's Appearance on the Platform," *Daily Arkansas Gazette* (Little Rock), April 14, 1877; "American and English Physique," *Chicago Daily Tribune*, April 29, 1877, p. 9; "A Felon's Fate," from the *Columbus* (GA) *Times*, *St. Louis Globe-Democrat*, November 8, 1877, p. 2; "The Moral Effects of Hard Times," *New York Times*, July 27, 1877, p. 4.

85. Fletcher, "New School of Criminal Anthropology," 206.

86. And was the basis for many who rejected Lombroso as inaccurate; e.g., "Vienna's Rogues' Gallery," from the *New York Sun*, *St. Louis Globe-Democrat*, May 6, 1877, p. 9.

87. "Barbara Schneller," *St. Louis Globe-Democrat*, October 29, 1878, p. 8; "Police Proceedings," *Daily Arkansas Gazette* (Little Rock), May 2, 1878; "Evil Lines in the Face," *Daily Arkansas Gazette*, December 30, 1887; "Dunham to Die," *Daily Rocky Mountain News* (Denver), September 27, 1878.

88. "Rogues' Gallery," *Inter Ocean* (Chicago), December 18, 1877, p. 8.

89. Fletcher, "New School of Criminal Anthropology," 207. Every edition of the book published by G.P. Putnam's Sons that I have examined uses the same pagination as the original 1877 edition. The only differences are the introductions and the correction of a few typos and spelling errors. For the following quotations I have used the 1910 edition, which appears to be the most correct version of the text. Richard L. Dugdale, *The Jukes: A Study in Crime, Pauperism, Disease, and Heredity*, 4th ed. (1887; New York: G.P. Putnam's Sons, 1910), 15.

90. Dugdale, *Jukes*, 8; Fletcher, "The New School of Criminal Anthropology," 207. Allan Nevins praised Dugdale as the founder of "the new scientific sociology"; Allan Nevins, *The Emergence of Modern America, 1865–1878* (New York: Macmillan, 1927), 327.

91. Dugdale, *Jukes*, 47–48.

92. Ibid., 63, 67–70.

93. Ibid., 10, 49, 65 (quote). The word "genetics" first appeared in American discourse in 1875 within debates over Darwinian theory: "Scientific Objections to Mr. Darwin's Theory of Development," *Inter Ocean* (Chicago), August 23, 1875, p. 2; "Matter and Life," *St. Louis Globe-Democrat*, November 28, 1875, p. 12.

94. Dugdale, *Jukes*, 12.

95. Ibid., 59–60.

96. Ibid., 37 (quote), 49.

97. Ibid., 60–62.

98. Ibid., 117–19 (quote, 118).

99. Ibid., 71–73 (quote, 72).

100. Ibid., 73, 80–91 (quote, 86–87). On page 100 he gives the figure as 75.6 percent.

101. Ibid., 106–9.

102. Ibid., 62.

103. Ibid., 112–15.

104. Richard L. Dugdale, *"The Jukes": A Study in Crime, Pauperism, Disease and Heredity*, 5th ed. (New York: G.P. Putnam's Sons, 1891), vi–vii.

105. Fletcher, "New School of Criminal Anthropology," 208, 210.

106. Ibid., 210–12; Stuart Banner, *The Death Penalty: An American History* (Cambridge, MA: Harvard University Press, 2003); Carl N. Degler, *In Search of Human Nature: The Decline and Revival of Darwinism in American Social Thought* (New York: Oxford University Press, 1991), 37; Mark H. Haller, *Eugenics: Hereditarian Attitudes in American Thought* (New Brunswick, NJ: Rutgers University Press, 1963), 22–23; Tim Cresswell, *The Tramp in America* (London: Reaktion Books, 2001), 114.

107. Dugdale, *Jukes*, 96, 105.

108. *Ninth Census: The Statistics of the Population of the United States* (Washington, DC: GPO, 1872), 1:567.

109. Redfield, *Homicide*, 9–10, 100.

110. Ibid., 14, 26–28, 31, 73–74, 86–87, 147.

111. Ibid., 63–64, 72.

112. Ibid., 69, 83–84.

113. Ibid., 75–76.

114. Ibid., 39, 101, 117.

115. Ibid., 18, 121.

116. Redfield appears to have been influenced in this view by Kentucky's Episcopal Bishop Smith, who in 1835 had reached roughly the same conclusion. Redfield interviewed Smith in 1879: "The Stain on Kentucky," *New York World*, June 16, 1879.

117. Redfield, *Homicide*, 77.

118. Ibid., 32–35 (quote, 34).

119. Ibid., 46, 81–82; quoting *Galveston Daily News*, February 11, 1870.

120. Ibid., 91, 159; *Vicksburg Herald*, February 28, 1880.

121. Ibid., 81–82 (quoting *Galveston Daily News*, February 11, 1870), 155.

122. Ibid., 74–75, 101 (quote), 106.

123. Ibid., 74–75 (quote), 95.

124. Ibid., 127–28.

125. Charles Dickens, *American Notes for General Circulation* (New York: D. Appleton and Co., 1868), 100; Redfield, *Homicide*, 115.

126. Redfield, *Homicide*, 81; James B. Cranfill, *Dr. J.B. Cranfill's Chronicle: A Story of Life in Texas* (New York: Fleming R. Revell Co., 1916), 315.

127. Redfield, *Homicide*, 160–61.

128. Ibid., 75–76 (quote), 116–17, 152–55. For contemporary support for Redfield's position on the death penalty, see, for instance, *St. Louis Globe-Democrat*, April 22, 1877, p. 4; "The Death Penalty," *St. Louis Globe-Democrat*, July 16, 1877; "Iowa Inklings," *St. Louis Globe-Democrat*, November 23, 1877, p. 3; "People and Things," *Daily Rocky Mountain News* (Denver), October 20, 1877; *San Francisco Daily Evening Bulletin*, November 7, 1877. On laws outlawing the carrying of concealed firearms, see "Carrying Concealed Weapons," *San Francisco Daily Evening Bulletin*, January 19, 1877; *St. Louis Globe-Democrat*, January 23, 1877, p. 3; "Rights of the Races," *St. Louis Globe-Democrat*, May 16, 1877, p. 8; "Catching a Tartar," *Independent Statesman* (Concord, NH), March 29, 1877, p. 207; "Houston," *Galveston Daily News*, May 16, 1877; "Number of Arrests," *Galveston Daily News*, July 8, 1877; *Inter Ocean* (Chicago), July 8, 1878, p. 4; "The Bloomington Tragedy," *Inter Ocean*, December 31, 1877, p. 5.

129. Redfield, *Homicide*, 117.

130. Miller quoted in Jack Beatty, *Age of Betrayal: The Triumph of Money in America, 1865–1900* (New York: Knopf, 2007), 133; U.S. attorney quoted in Robert J. Kaczorowski, *The Politics of Judicial Interpretation: The Federal Courts, Department of Justice, and Civil Rights, 1866–1876* (New York: Fordham University Press, 2005), 156; "fiendish hatred": *Milwaukee Daily Sentinel*, December 3, 1877, quoting Henry Watterson of the *Louisville Courier-Journal*.

131. "An Altercation Resulting in a Homicide," *Galveston Daily News*, January 25, 1877; "Homicide in Macon County," *Georgia Weekly Telegraph and Georgia Journal & Messenger* (Macon), November 6, 1877.

132. Newspapers throughout the country treated lynchings as prominent news stories. For instance, some random examples from the first half of April 1877: "Lynch Law in Kentucky," *St. Louis Globe-Democrat*, April 2, 1877, p. 3; "Three Cruel Murders," *St. Louis Globe-Democrat*, April 2, 1877, p. 4; "Lynched," *St. Louis Globe-Democrat*, April 3, 1877, p. 5; "Crime in Iowa," *St. Louis Globe-Democrat*, April 6, 1877; "Belial's Bull-Dozers," *St. Louis Globe-Democrat*, April 11, 1877; "This Morning's News," *North American* (Philadelphia), April 3, 1877; "Lynched," *Daily Arkansas Gazette* (Little Rock), April 3, 1877; "By Telegraph," *Daily Rocky Mountain News* (Denver), April 3, 1877; "Crime and Criminals," *Inter Ocean* (Chicago), April 7, 1877, p. 2; "Colored People and the President," *New York Times*, April 4, 1877; "Crimes and Casualties," *Hartford Daily Courant*, April 12, 1877, p. 3; "The Benders," *Chicago Daily Tribune*, April 8 and 9, 1877; "Edward Lee," *Chicago Daily Tribune*, April 11, 1877, p. 5.

133. Utley, *Lone Star Justice*, 171–72, 179–80; Webb, *Texas Rangers*, 328–32 (quote, 331); Gillett, *Six Years with the Texas Rangers*, 101–2.

134. See, for instance, Douglas Eckberg, "Stalking the Elusive Homicide: A Capture-Recapture Approach to the Estimation of Post-Reconstruction South Carolina Killings," *Social Science History* 25 (2001): 67–91; Roger Lane, "Crime and Criminal Statistics in Nineteenth-Century Massachusetts," *Journal of Social History* 2 (1968): 156–63.

135. While there were some isolated references to Redfield's work in the 1950s and 1960s, Sheldon Hackney deserves credit for bringing Redfield to the attention of scholars in several fields with his article "Southern Violence," *American Historical Review* 74 (1969): 906–25; Redfield, *Homicide*, vii–viii, xxiii–xxviii, xxxiii–xxxiv; Raymond Gastil, "Homicide and the Regional Culture of Violence," *American Sociological Review* 36 (1971): 412–27; Edward L. Ayers, *Vengeance and Justice: Crime and Punishment in the Nineteenth-Century South* (New York: Oxford University Press, 1984); Gilles Vandal, "'Bloody Caddo': White Violence against Blacks in a Louisiana Parish, 1865–1876," *Journal of Social History* 25 (1991): 373–88; Gilles Vandal, "Black Violence in Post–Civil War Louisiana," *Journal of Interdisciplinary History* 25 (1994): 45–64; Roger Lane, *Murder in America: A History* (Columbus: Ohio State University Press, 1997).

136. Redfield, *Homicide*, 170, 176. The *Hinds County Gazette* argued the complete opposite, insisting that more murders were committed in New York City in one day than "in the whole state of Mississippi in a week"—since Northern murders are so common they are "barely noticed," while Southern crimes "are magnified by the Northern press much to our injury." "Persecution of the South," *Hinds County Gazette* (Raymond, MS), January 10, 1877.

137. Redfield, *Homicide*, 176, 177. Redfield does not give the name of the murderer, and the only article I can locate on the case refers to her only as "the wife of James Adams"; see *Boston Investigator*, November 26, 1879, p. 5. See also "Freeman's Fanaticism," *Inter Ocean* (Chicago), May 5, 1879; "Delusional Insanity," *Inter Ocean*, February 2, 1880, p. 4; "The Pocasset Tragedy," *Boston Daily Advertiser*, May 7, 1879; "Edith Freeman's Murder," *Louisville Courier-Journal*, May 19, 1879.

138. "Party Plots," *St. Louis Globe-Democrat*, March 14, 1877, p. 5; "Robbers."

139. "Demonology."

140. Ibid.

Chapter 7: Breaking the Spell

1. George Augustus Sala, *America Revisited: From the Bay of New York to the Gulf of Mexico, and from Lake Michigan to the Pacific*, 3d. ed., 2 vols. (London: Vizetelly & Co., 1883), 2:45–46.

2. "Our Chronological Review," *Inter Ocean* (Chicago), December 27, 1877; "The New Year," *Inter Ocean*, January 1, 1878, p. 4; "A Happy New Year," *Milwaukee Daily Sentinel*, January 1, 1878, p. 4; "1877," *Boston Daily Advertiser*, December 29, 1877; "The New Year," *Independent Statesman* (Concord, NH), January 3, 1878, p. 108; "The New Year," *Boston Daily Advertiser* (Boston), January 1, 1878; "End of the Year," *San Francisco Daily Evening Bulletin*, December 31, 1877.

3. "A Terrible Record," *Georgia Weekly Telegraph and Georgia Journal & Messenger* (Macon), January 8, 1878; "Washington Notes," *Daily Rocky Mountain News* (Denver), January 10, 1878; William Godwin Moody, *Land and Labor in the United States* (New York: Charles Scribner's Sons, 1883), 189–92.

4. "Who's Next," *Inter Ocean* (Chicago), December 12, 1877; "The Street and the Market," *North American* (Philadelphia), December 24 and 31, 1877; "1877–1878," *North American*, January 1, 1878; "A Year's Business," *North American*, January 1, 1878.

5. "The New Year," *Independent Statesman* (Concord, NH), January 3, 1878, p. 108; "A Year's Business," *North American* (Philadelphia), January 1, 1878. See also Rendig Fels, "The Long-Wave Depression, 1873–79," *Review of Economic and Statistics* 31 (1949): 69–73.

6. "1877–1878," *North American* (Philadelphia), January 1, 1878; Horace White, "The Tariff Question," *Journal of Social Science* 9 (1878): 117–31; Moody, *Land and Labor in the United States*, 189–92, 201–12.

7. "1877," *Boston Daily Advertiser*, December 29, 1877.

8. "A Review of the Trade of the Country the Past Year," *Inter Ocean* (Chicago), January 5, 1878, p. 5; "The New Year," *Independent Statesman* (Concord, NH), January 3, 1878, p. 108; "1877," *Boston Daily Advertiser*, December 29, 1877; "A Review of the Trade of the Country the past Year," *Inter Ocean* (Chicago), January 5, 1878, p. 5; "The New Year," Boston *Daily Advertiser*, January 1, 1878.

9. "1877–1878," *North American* (Philadelphia), January 1, 1878.

10. "1877," *Boston Daily Advertiser*, December 29, 1877.

11. Theodore Parker, *Sermons of Religion* (Boston: American Unitarian Association, 1908), 64.

12. Carol Mattingly, *Well-Tempered Women: Nineteenth-Century Temperance Rhetoric* (Carbondale: Southern Illinois University Press, 1998), 58 (quote); Ruth Bordin, *Frances Willard: A Biography* (Chapel Hill: University of North Carolina Press, 1986), 34–37, 54–64.

13. Rebecca Edwards, *New Spirits: Americans in the Gilded Age, 1865–1905* (New York: Oxford University Press, 2006), 118, 121; Mattingly, *Well-Tempered Women*, 58–59.

14. *Bradwell v. Illinois*, in John W. Wallace, ed., *Cases Argued and Adjudged in the Supreme Court of the United States* (often known as *United States Reports*) 16 (Washington, DC: W.H. & O.H. Morrison, 1873), 141–42. On American legal attitudes toward women, see Linda K. Kerber, *No Constitutional Right to Be Ladies: Women and the Obligations of Citizenship* (New York: Hill & Wang, 1999).

15. Bordin, *Frances Willard*, 64, 72.

16. "Barnum on Temperance," *Daily Rocky Mountain News* (Denver), September 18, 1877; *Colorado Springs Gazette*, March 17, 1877, p. 2; "State Temperance Convention," *Bangor Daily Whig & Courier*, January 27, 1877; *The Congregationalist* (Boston), January 2, 1878, p. 7; Robert C. Pitman, *Alcohol and the State* (New York: National Temperance Society, 1877); James J. Collins Jr., ed., *Drinking and Crime: Perspectives on the Relationships between Alcohol Consumption and Criminal Behavior* (New York: Guilford Press, 1981); Robert Nash Parker and Linda-Anne Rebhun, *Alcohol and Homicide: A Deadly Combination of Two American Traditions* (Albany: State University of New York Press, 1995).

17. "Incapable of controlling": "Edgar M. Moore," *St. Louis Globe-Democrat*, January 28, 1877; Washingtonian Home report quoted in "Reclaiming Drunkards," *Independent Statesman* (Concord, NH), May 24, 1877, p. 271. See also "State Press," *Galveston Daily News*, January 31, 1877; "Whisky and Lawlessness," *Galveston Daily News*, February 13, 1877; "Somebody's Wife Speaks," *Galveston Daily News*, February 3, 1878; "Gathering Them In," *Daily Rocky Mountain News* (Denver), August 28, 1877; "Temperance Con-

vention," *Lowell Daily Citizen*, October 11, 1877; "Boys and Girls Drunk in the Streets of Chicago," *Inter Ocean* (Chicago), October 16, 1877, p. 8; "On with the Good Work," *Inter Ocean*, November 28, 1877, p. 2; "The New Gospel," *St. Louis Globe-Democrat*, February 18, 1878, p. 5; "Ingersoll on Intemperance," *St. Louis Globe-Democrat*, October 29, 1877, p. 2; "M.E. District Conference," *Milwaukee Daily Sentinel*, November 28, 1877, p. 8; "Ingersoll on Alcohol," *Wisconsin State Register* (Portage), December 29, 1877.

18. "Close the Saloons!" *Inter Ocean* (Chicago), July 27, 1877; "Inebriate Asylums," *St. Louis Globe-Democrat*, April 23, 1877, p. 3. See also "King Alcohol Defended," *St. Louis Globe-Democrat*, March 16, 1877, p. 2; "The Brewers," *Milwaukee Daily Sentinel*, June 7, 1877, p. 2; "Rough Raillery," *St. Louis Globe-Democrat*, July 24, 1877; "The Strike at Home," *St. Louis Globe-Democrat*, July 24, 1877, p. 4; "Rioting Roughs," *Inter Ocean*, July 25, 1877; "The Great Strike," *San Francisco Daily Evening Bulletin*, July 27, 1877.

19. "Inebriate Asylums," *St. Louis Globe-Democrat*, April 23, 1877, p. 3. One sign of this gender shift in temperance is the decline of the Sons of Temperance, the male abstinence society, which had a quarter million members at the start of the Civil War and just over fifty thousand by 1877; D. Leigh Colvin, *Prohibition in the United States: A History of the Prohibition Party and of the Prohibition Movement* (New York: George H. Doran Co., 1926), 119.

20. "Drinking and Gambling in Nevada," *San Francisco Daily Evening Bulletin*, February 27, 1875; "Extent of the Liquor Business," *North American* (Philadelphia), December 20, 1877; "The Flowing Bowl," *Inter Ocean* (Chicago) December 20, 1877, p. 5; Mattingly, *Well-Tempered Women*, 123–24, 132–36, 149–51. On alcohol as a cause of domestic violence, see Claire Jo Hamilton and James J. Collins Jr., "The Role of Alcohol in Wife Beating and Child Abuse: A Review of the Literature," in *Drinking and Crime*, ed. James J. Collins (New York: Guilford Press, 1981), 253–87; Holly Berkley Fletcher, *Gender and the American Temperance Movement of the Nineteenth Century* (New York: Routledge, 2008), 15, 19–20, 24, 39–42.

21. "Woman's Kingdom," *Inter Ocean* (Chicago), July 7, 1877, p. 11. See also "Church and Pulpit," *Inter Ocean*, February 24, 1877, p. 6; "Number One Hundred," *Milwaukee Daily Sentinel*, January 26, 1877; "Letter from Worcester," *The Congregationalist* (Boston), January 31, 1877, p. 5; "A Gospel for the Lost," *The Congregationalist*, August 1, 1877, p. 2; *Colorado Springs Gazette*, February 10, 1877, p. 3. On the home as a safe retreat from a hostile world, see Mary P. Ryan, *Cradle of the Middle Class: The Family in Oneida County, New York, 1790–1865* (New York: Cambridge University Press, 1983).

22. Mother Stewart, *Memories of the Crusade: A Thrilling Account of the Great Uprising of the Women of Ohio in 1873, Against the Liquor Crime* (Chicago: H.H. Smith & Co., 1890); Jack S. Blocker Jr., *"Give to the Winds Thy Fears": The Women's Temperance Crusade, 1873–74* (Westport, CT: Greenwood, 1985).

23. Mattingly, *Well-Tempered Women*, 43; Jane Stebbins, *Fifty Years of the Temperance Cause* (Hartford: J.P. Fitch, 1876), 341–500; Herbert Asbury, *The Great Illusion: An Informal History of Prohibition* (Garden City, NY: Doubleday & Co., 1950), 68–87; Ruth Bordin, *Women and Temperance: The Quest for Power and Liberty, 1873–1900* (Philadelphia: Temple University Press, 1981), 15–33; Blocker, *"Give to the Winds Thy Fears"*, 76–77.

24. This loss of production cost the U.S. government an estimated $1 million in lost revenue. Asbury, *Great Illusion*, 85; Blocker, *"Give to the Winds Thy Fears"*, 24, 147–53, 236n40; Mattingly, *Well-Tempered Women*, 41–42.

25. Colvin, *Prohibition in the United States*, 116–18; Bordin, *Frances Willard*, 78–79.

26. Willard quoted in Asbury, *Great Illusion*, 86; Jean H. Baker, *Sisters: The Lives of American Suffragists* (New York: Hill & Wang, 2005), 159.

27. Frances Willard, *Glimpses of Fifty Years: The Autobiography of an American Woman* (Chicago: Woman's Christian Temperance Pub., 1889), 338; Bordin, *Frances Willard*, 70–73.

28. Anna Gordon, *The Life of Frances E. Willard* (Evanston, IL: National Woman's Christian Temperance Pub., 1914), 100–101.

29. Willard, *Glimpses of Fifty Years*, 342; Bordin, *Frances Willard*, 68–69, 74.

30. Bordin, *Frances Willard*, 75; Willard, *Glimpses of Fifty Years*, 345.

31. Bordin, *Frances Willard*, 76–82 (quote, 82); Willard, *Glimpses of Fifty Years*, 188; Baker, *Sisters*, 160; Carolyn De Swarte Gifford, ed., *Writing Out My Heart: Selections from the Journal of Frances E. Willard, 1855–96* (Urbana: University of Illinois Press, 1995), 5–7, 222–24, 229–31.

32. Bordin, *Frances Willard*, 83–86.

33. Vincent quoted in ibid., 254n14; Baker, *Sisters*, 163.

34. "The World of Religion," *Inter Ocean* (Chicago), January 20, 1877, p. 6; "The Tabernacle," *Boston Daily Advertiser*, January 26, 1877; Bordin, *Frances Willard*, 86. An indication of the sensation created by Moody is that his Boston revival was front-page news in Colorado; *Colorado Springs Gazette*, February 10, 1877.

35. "The World of Religion," *Inter Ocean* (Chicago), January 20, 1877, p. 6; "Christian Labor," *Inter Ocean*, January 27, 1877, p. 6; "Miss Willard's Work in Boston," *Inter Ocean*, April 28, 1877, p. 7; "Tabernacle Notes," *The Congregationalist* (Boston), February 21, 1877; "The Christian Convention," *The Congregationalist*, March 21, 1877; "Religious Intelligence," *The Congregationalist*, May 16, 1877; "Literary Review," *The Congregationalist*, May 16, 1877, p. 6; "Moody and Sankey," *Boston Daily Advertiser*, March 8, 1877; *Boston Daily Advertiser*, March 9, 1877; Bordin, *Frances Willard*, 87; Willard, *Glimpses of Fifty Years*, 354–57.

36. Dio (Dioclesian) Lewis, *Prohibition a Failure: Or, the True Solution of the Temperance Question* (Boston: James R. Osgood and Co., 1875), 109–52; Asbury, *Great Illusion*, 68; Bordin, *Frances Willard*, 68; Baker, *Sisters*, 164.

37. "Mr. Moody and the Woman's Christian Temperance Union," *Boston Daily Advertiser*, July 12, 1877; "Woman's Kingdom," *Inter Ocean* (Chicago), July 21, 1877, p. 9; Willard, *Glimpses of Fifty Years*, 359–60; Willard on "brethren": "Mrs. Frances E. Willard," *Review of Reviews* 6 (1892): 345.

38. Bordin, *Frances Willard*, 89–90.

39. "Total Abstinence," *Inter Ocean* (Chicago), October 26, 1877, p. 3; Willard, *Glimpses of Fifty Years*, 370, 458.

40. "Let your women keep silence in the churches: for it is not permitted unto them to speak; but they are commanded to be under obedience as also saith the law. And if they will learn anything, let them ask their husbands at home: for it is a shame for women to speak in the church." 1 Corinthians 14:34–35; "But I suffer not a woman to teach, nor to usurp authority over the man, but to be in silence," 1 Timothy 2:12. See, for example, *Daily Rocky Mountain News* (Denver), February 9, 1877; "The Woman's Column," *Daily Rocky Mountain News*, May 13, 1877; *The Congregationalist* (Boston), March 14, 1877, p. 4; "Shall Womanhood Be Abolished?" *The Congregationalist*, August 22, 1877, p. 2; "Woman's Work," *The Congregationalist*, November 7, 1877, p. 2.

41. "Women in the Pulpit," *St. Louis Globe-Democrat*, January 7, 1877, p. 5. For a

parody of this action by the Presbyterian Church, see "Let Women Keep Silence," *Daily Rocky Mountain News* (Denver), October 10, 1877. The Presbyterian Church would not ordain a woman until Margaret Towner in 1956.

42. Galatians 3:28; Berry quoted in "Women Preachers," *Lowell Daily Citizen*, January 12, 1877; WCTU response: "The Woman's Column," *Daily Rocky Mountain News* (Denver), May 13, 1877; "A Woman's Sermon," *Milwaukee Daily Sentinel*, October 18, 1877, p. 8; Mattingly, *Well-Tempered Women*, 49.

43. Julia R. Parish, ed., *The Poems and Written Addresses of Mary T. Lathrap* (n.p.: WCTU of Michigan, 1895), 399; Mattingly, *Well-Tempered Women*, 48; "The Congregational Council," *St. Louis Globe-Democrat*, October 22, 1877, p. 5. The Congregational Church ordained Antoinette Brown Blackwell as its first woman minister in 1853, though its journal, *The Congregationalist*, remained hostile to women ministers through most of the rest of the nineteenth century.

44. "Silly" and "extravagant": "Domestic Ruin," *Galveston Daily News*, July 26, 1877; "foolish and selfish": "Mock Mothers," *St. Louis Globe-Democrat*, November 18, 1877, p. 12; "busy-bodies": "Woman Suffrage and Colorado," *The Congregationalist* (Boston), December 26, 1877, p. 7; "filth": "Wisconsin News," *Milwaukee Daily Sentinel*, December 24, 1877, p. 2.

45. "Silly sentimental": "Preacher Moody's Children," *St. Louis Globe-Democrat*, January 8, 1877, p. 4; Moody quoted in "A Sermon by Mr. Moody," *Bangor Daily Whig & Courier*, May 2, 1877; "most dangerous": "The Untruthful Woman," *San Francisco Daily Evening Bulletin*, January 13, 1877; "New York Shysters," *St. Louis Globe-Democrat*, October 2, 1877, p. 2; "Philanthropic Works," *Inter Ocean* (Chicago), February 17, 1877, p. 6; Holmes quoted in *Inter Ocean*, September 10, 1877, p. 4.

46. Mattingly, *Well-Tempered Women*, 43; Parish, *Poems and Written Addresses of Mary T. Lathrap*, 355.

47. Mattingly, *Well-Tempered Women*, 40–42, 61 ("step to the front"); "women, sisters" and "women out of silence": Frances E. Willard, *Woman and Temperance: Or, the Work and Workers of the Woman's Christian Temperance Union* (Hartford: James Betts & Co., 1883), 624; "Total Abstinence"; "Woman's Temperance Work," *Inter Ocean*, October 27, 1877, p. 6; Stewart, *Memories of the Crusade*, 422.

48. Mattingly, *Well-Tempered Women*, 45, 56.

49. Willard, *Woman and Temperance*, 382; Frances E. Willard, "The Ideal of Womanhood," *Friends' Intelligencer and Journal* 47 (1890): 240.

50. Willard, *Glimpses of Fifty Years*, 446. Similar language was used by other temperance crusaders; see, e.g., "Bangor Woman's Crusade," *Bangor Daily Whig & Courier*, March 27, 1875; "A Victim of Starvation," *New York Times*, February 26, 1877, p. 8; "The Woman Suffrage Convention," *Hartford Daily Courant*, October 18, 1877, p. 2.

51. Clifford quoted in "Temperance Work," *Inter Ocean* (Chicago), September 15, 1877, p. 7; Baker, *Sisters*, 157–58.

52. George F. Hoar, *Autobiography of Seventy Years*, 2 vols. (New York: Charles Scribner's Sons, 1905), 2:15. However, Lucy Hayes found the WCTU too militant and her husband preferred that she avoid Willard. Betty Boyd Caroli, *First Ladies* (New York: Oxford University Press, 2003), 84, 92–93.

53. "State Temperance Convention," *Bangor Daily Whig & Courier*, January 27, 1877; "State Legislation," *Inter Ocean* (Chicago), February 15, 1877, p. 6; "Points from Pontiac," *Inter Ocean*, March 22, 1877, p. 5; "Rockford Items," *Inter Ocean*, October 20, 1877, p. 7; "Wendell Phillips," *Inter Ocean*, February 2, 1877; "The General Court,"

Boston Daily Advertiser, March 2, 1877; "Local Miscellany," *Milwaukee Daily Sentinel*, April 19, 1877, p. 8.

54. "Total Abstinence" (quote); Colvin, *Prohibition in the United States*, 101–6.

55. Colvin, *Prohibition in the United States*, 103. The Prohibition Party candidate for president, General Green Clay Smith, received just 9,737 votes in the 1876 election; see ibid., 114.

56. "Puritanical tyranny" in ibid., 104; Beer Congress: "The Brewers," *Milwaukee Daily Sentinel*, June 8, 1877, p. 2.

57. *Colorado Springs Gazette*, February 17, 1877, p. 2; *Colorado Springs Gazette*, February 24, 1877, p. 2; "Prohibition," *Bangor Daily Whig & Courier*, March 6, 1876; "Prohibition in Maine," *Lowell Daily Citizen*, April 13, 1877; "Prohibition in Maine," *Milwaukee Daily Sentinel*, August 31, 1877, p. 4.

58. Willard, *Glimpses of Fifty Years*, 351; Bordin, *Frances Willard*, 97.

59. Anna Dickinson, Lucy Stone, and Susan B. Anthony also influenced Willard's thinking on suffrage; Bordin, *Frances Willard*, 98, 101; Willard, *Glimpses of Fifty Years*, 380, 577–72, 590.

60. Willard, *Glimpses of Fifty Years*, 352 (quote); Willard, *Woman and Temperance*, 451–52; Bordin, *Frances Willard*, 98, 102–4.

61. "Total Abstinence."

62. Bordin, *Frances Willard*, 98. Elizabeth Cady Stanton made a similar argument in 1877; "Woman's Kingdom," *Inter Ocean* (Chicago), July 7, 1877, p. 11.

63. "Woman's Kingdom," *Inter Ocean* (Chicago), August 25, 1877, p. 9; Baker, *Sisters*, 164 (quote); "Total Abstinence"; Willard, *Glimpses of Fifty Years*, 48–49, 330–74, 393, 488–89; Bordin, *Frances Willard*, 103; Mattingly, *Well-Tempered Women*, 45.

64. Bordin, *Frances Willard*, 97–105 (quote, 100); Willard, *Glimpses of Fifty Years*, 351–52, 400–401, 437–53.

65. Ann D. Gordon, ed., *The Selected Papers of Susan B. Anthony and Elizabeth Cady Stanton*, 5 vols. (New Brunswick, NJ: Rutgers University Press, 1997–2009), 3:261 (quote); Bordin, *Frances Willard*, 99; Baker, *Sisters*, 164–65. On the significance of Willard's conversion to suffrage, see Stacy A. Cordery, "Women in Industrializing America," in *The Gilded Age: Essays on the Origins of Modern America*, ed. Charles W. Calhoun (Wilmington, DE: Scholarly Resources, 2000), 111–35.

66. "Total Abstinence"; "Woman's Temperance Work"; Willard, *Glimpses of Fifty Years*, 368–69; Willard, *Woman and Temperance*, 31–33, 355, 362–70; Bordin, *Frances Willard*, 104–8; Baker, *Sisters*, 165–66; Elizabeth Cady Stanton et al., eds., *History of Woman Suffrage*, 6 vols. (Rochester, NY: Susan B. Anthony, 1881–1922), 4:124–27, 140–42.

67. *Galveston Daily News*, January 7, 1877; "State Temperance Convention," *Bangor Daily Whig & Courier*, January 27, 1877; *Colorado Springs Gazette*, March 31, 1877, p. 4; "Inauguration of Governor Van Zandt of Rhode Island," *Boston Daily Advertiser*, May 30, 1877; Colvin, *Prohibition in the United States*, 115; Baker, *Sisters*, 163; Asbury, *Great Illusion*, 87.

68. Phillips quoted in Alexander Keyssar, *The Right to Vote: The Contested History of Democracy in the United States* (New York: Basic Books, 2000), 177; Ellen Carol DuBois, *Feminism and Suffrage: The Emergence of an Independent Women's Movement in America, 1848–1869* (Ithaca, NY: Cornell University Press, 1999), 59–61; Baker, *Sisters*, 125; Stanton et al., *History of Woman Suffrage*, 2:94–95, 104–5, 109–10, 349–55, 382–83.

69. Section 1. All persons born or naturalized in the United States, and subject to the jurisdiction thereof, are citizens of the United States and of the State wherein they reside.

No State shall make or enforce any law which shall abridge the privileges or immunities of citizens of the United States; nor shall any State deprive any person of life, liberty, or property, without due process of law; nor deny to any person within its jurisdiction the equal protection of the laws.

70. Section 2. Representatives shall be apportioned among the several States according to their respective numbers, counting the whole number of persons in each State, excluding Indians not taxed. But when the right to vote at any election for the choice of electors for President and Vice President of the United States, Representatives in Congress, the Executive and Judicial officers of a State, or the members of the Legislature thereof, is denied to any of the male inhabitants of such State, being twenty-one years of age, and citizens of the United States, or in any way abridged, except for participation in rebellion, or other crime, the basis of representation therein shall be reduced in the proportion which the number of such male citizens shall bear to the whole number of male citizens twenty-one years of age in such State.

71. Gordon, *Selected Papers of Susan B. Anthony and Elizabeth Cady Stanton*, 1:569; Keyssar, *Right to Vote*, 177, 179.

72. *Minor v. Happersett*, 88 U.S. 162 (1874).

73. Baker, *Sisters*, 84, 125.

74. "Ballot Seekers," *Milwaukee Daily Sentinel*, January 11, 1877, p. 2; "National News," *Milwaukee Daily Sentinel*, January 31, 1877; "The Sixteenth Amendment," *Milwaukee Daily Sentinel*, April 2, 1877; "Forty-Fourth Congress," *Boston Daily Advertiser*, January 31, 1877; "Senator Christiancy," *North American* (Philadelphia), January 31, 1877; "Woman and Temperance," *Inter Ocean* (Chicago), March 26, 1877, p. 4; "What Now?" *Inter Ocean*, December 13, 1877; Baker, *Sisters*, 41–46, 50–51.

75. "Toledo Woman Indignant," *Colorado Springs Gazette*, August 4, 1877.

76. Keyssar, *Right to Vote*, 182, 187; Kerber, *No Constitutional Right to be Ladies*, 81–112.

77. "The Bliss Theory of Government," *Daily Rocky Mountain News* (Denver), October 2, 1877; "Rev. Dr. Bliss, the Woman Hater," *Daily Rocky Mountain News*, November 16, 1877; Beverly Beeton, *Women Vote in the West: The Woman Suffrage Movement, 1869–1896* (New York: Garland, 1986), 106–7, 110.

78. "A Word from Lucy Stone," *Daily Rocky Mountain News* (Denver), October 9, 1877; *Daily Rocky Mountain News*, October 3, 1877; "Defeat of Woman Suffrage," *Daily Rocky Mountain News*, October 14, 1877; *Daily Rocky Mountain News*, October 18, 1877.

79. *Colorado Springs Gazette*, October 6, 1877, p. 2; "The Official Canvas," *Colorado Springs Gazette*, November 17, 1877, p. 4; "The Lost Cause," *Daily Rocky Mountain News* (Denver), October 4, 1877; "Defeat of Woman Suffrage," *Daily Rocky Mountain News*, October 14, 1877; Beeton, *Women Vote in the West*, 110; Billie Barnes Jensen, "Colorado Suffrage Campaigns of the 1870s," *Journal of the West* 12 (1973): 254–71.

80. *Debates and Proceedings of the Constitutional Convention of the State of California, Convened at the City of Sacramento, Saturday, September 28, 1878*, 3 vols. (Sacramento: J.D. Young, 1881), 2:832–34, 1003–19, 1365; Keyssar, *Right to Vote*, 186–87, 195, 390; Beeton, *Women Vote in the West*, 111–14. Idaho, also with substantial Populist support, passed suffrage in 1896; see ibid., 116–35.

81. "Woman Suffrage and Colorado," *The Congregationalist* (Boston), December 26, 1877, p. 7.

82. Watson quoted in "The Ground of the Right of Suffrage," *Colorado Springs Gazette*, August 25, 1877; Baker, *Sisters*, 177.

83. Marion Tinling, ed., *With Women's Eyes: Visitors to the New World, 1775–1918* (Hamden, CT: Archon Books, 1993), 121–23.

84. "Woman's Kingdom," *Inter Ocean* (Chicago), June 2, 1877, p. 6. They met again in January 1878 at what was called the "Sixteenth Amendment Convention"; see "The Silver Bill," *Inter Ocean*, November 21, 1877; "Woman's Kingdom," *Inter Ocean*, December 15, 1877, p. 9.

85. Keyssar, *Right to Vote*, 185; Bordin, *Frances Willard*, 90–93.

86. Louis R. Harlan et al., eds., *The Booker T. Washington Papers*, 14 vols. (Urbana: University of Illinois Press, 1972–1989), 2:69–70; Booker T. Washington, *Up from Slavery* (New York: Oxford University Press, 1995), 54.

87. Harlan et al., *Booker T. Washington Papers*, 2:67–69, 73 (quote); Washington, *Up from Slavery*, 54.

88. Harlan et al., *Booker T. Washington Papers*, 2:73–74.

89. Incredibly, Washington, writing in 1901, adds that "There are few places in the South now where public sentiment would permit such organizations to exist." Washington, *Up from Slavery*, 45–46.

90. Ibid., 47–49.

91. Quotes from ibid., 49–50; Harlan et al., *Booker T. Washington Papers*, 2:324–25.

92. Washington, *Up from Slavery*, 48, 51–52.

93. Ibid., 52–54 (quote, 54), 57–63.

94. First two quotes from "The Atlanta Exposition," *Daily Picayune* (New Orleans), September 19, 1895; "at the bottom": National Negro Business League, *Annual Report* (Nashville, TN: n.p., 1915), 74.

95. "The President's Policy," *Boston Daily Advertiser*, October 5, 1877 (quote); "So Fair, So Foolish," *North American* (Philadelphia), December 4, 1878; "A Voice from the Wilderness," *North American*, January 20, 1879; "The Refugees in Kansas," *Boston Daily Advertiser*, May 21, 1879.

96. "The President's Policy" (quotes); "The Prospect of New Industries at the South," *Boston Daily Advertiser*, June 22, 1878.

97. Quotes from "The Southern Situation," *The Congregationalist* (Boston), October 17, 1877, p. 2, quoting *American Missionary*; Charles Carleton Coffin, "The New South," *The Congregationalist* (Boston), May 8, 1878; "The New South," *San Francisco Daily Evening Bulletin*, June 29, 1878; "The Nation's Duty," *Weekly Register-Call* (Central City, CO), November 29, 1878.

98. "Reign of Terror in Mississippi," *Independent Statesman* (Concord, NH), June 14, 1877; "The Reign of Terror in South Carolina," *Independent Statesman*, October 31, 1878; "Tennessee: A Reign of Terror near Raleigh," *North American* (Philadelphia), November 13, 1877; "Reign of Terror in Raleigh County," *San Francisco Daily Evening Bulletin*, November 13, 1877; "Reigns of Terror," *St. Louis Globe-Democrat*, November 14, 1877, p. 4.

99. *Daily Rocky Mountain News* (Denver), March 19, 1878; "So Fair, So Foolish," *North American* (Philadelphia), December 4, 1878.

100. "The South in Congress," *Bangor Daily Whig & Courier*, November 12, 1878; "The Southern Republicans," *Bangor Daily Whig & Courier*, November 22, 1878; "Southern Outrages," *Boston Daily Advertiser*, November 13, 1878; "The Southern Frauds," *Boston Daily Advertiser*, November 13, 1878; John W. Blassingame and John R. McKivigan, eds., *The Frederick Douglass Papers: Series One: Speeches, Debates, and Interviews*, 5 vols. (New Haven: Yale University Press, 1979–1992), 4:493; Senate Report no. 855, 45th

Cong., 3rd sess., *Report of the United States Senate Committee to Inquire into Alleged Frauds and Violence in the Elections of 1878* (Washington, DC: GPO, 1879).

101. Charles W. Calhoun, "The Political Culture: Public Life and the Conduct of Politics," in Calhoun, *Gilded Age*, 188–89 (quote); U.S. Department of Commerce, *Statistical History of the United States: From Colonial Times to the Present* (Washington, DC: U.S. Department of Commerce, Bureau of the Census, 1976), 28, 30, 1073, 1079. Richard Hofstadter fostered this historical perspective of a conservative electorate in Richard Hofstadter, *The Age of Reform: From Bryan to F.D.R.* (New York: Knopf, 1959).

102. "The Old and the New South," *Independent Statesman* (Concord, NH), May 16, 1878, p. 258; "A New Party South," *North American* (Philadelphia), July 18, 1878.

103. Rod Andrew Jr., *Wade Hampton: Confederate Warrior to Southern Redeemer* (Chapel Hill: University of North Carolina Press, 2008), 440–41; Denis Tilden Lynch, *The Wild Seventies* (New York: D. Appleton-Century Co., 1941), 511; "South Carolina," *Boston Daily Advertiser*, November 14, 1878; "Will He Answer?" *Inter Ocean* (Chicago), November 20, 1878, p. 4; "Wanted, an Honest Democrat," *Inter Ocean*, Saturday, November 30, 1878, p. 4; "The South Carolina Frauds," *Bangor Daily Whig & Courier*, November 27, 1878.

104. Hampton quoted in "National Tourists," *Daily Arkansas Gazette* (Little Rock), September 16, 1877, and "Hampton and Nicholls," *Inter Ocean* (Chicago), September 17, 1877. See also "Its Effects in South Carolina," *New York Times*, May 8, 1877, p. 3; "Wade Hampton's Domain," *New York Times*, May 12, 1877, p. 4; "Fruits of the Policy," *New York Times*, October 12, 1877; "The South Carolina Militia," *New York Times*, October 20, 1877; *Harper's Weekly*, July 7, 1877, p. 518; Rayford W. Logan, *The Betrayal of the Negro: From Rutherford B. Hayes to Woodrow Wilson* (New York: Collier Books, 1965), 21; Andrew, *Wade Hampton*, 430–54.

105. Dee Brown, *The Year of the Century: 1876* (New York: Charles Scribner's Sons, 1966), 1, 4. In Brown's view, Reconstruction was the product of radical manipulation, with Blaine particularly to blame as he "kept the fires of sectional animosity burning for years, adroitly using the controlled conflagration as an excuse for continuing Reconstruction and radical Republican rule in the South." Ibid., 18.

106. William Peirce Randel, *Centennial: American Life in 1876* (Philadelphia: Chilton Books, 1969), 240; text of Hamburg Monument: Daniel S. Henderson, *The White Man's Revolution in South Carolina: Address of Hon. D.S. Henderson* (North Augusta, SC: n.p., 1916), 1.

107. One of most outrageous examples of the Reconstruction myth was written by the Mississippi state archivist Dunbar Rowland, *A Mississippi View of Race Relations in the South* (Jackson, MS: Mississippi Department of Archives and History, 1902). For an excellent analysis of the mythology, see Stephen Budiansky, *The Bloody Shirt: Terror After Appomattox* (New York: Viking, 2008), 268–78.

108. Charles Richard Williams, ed., *Diary and Letters of Rutherford B. Hayes*, 6 vols. (Columbus: Ohio State Archaeological and Historical Society, 1924), 2:68.

109. Budiansky, *Bloody Shirt*, 274–75. Interestingly, Andrews, who promoted the myth in his book, did not look at the records himself, but took the word of the sitting Democratic treasurer of Mississippi that the debt in 1876 was $1.4 million. He did, however, apologize for having "enormously exaggerated" the debt in an earlier magazine article; Benjamin Andrews, *A History of the Last Quarter-Century in the United States, 1870–1895*, 2 vols. (New York: Charles Scribner's Sons, 1896), 1:126.

110. Budiansky, *Bloody Shirt*, 277 (quote); John R. Lynch, *The Facts of Reconstruction* (New York: Neale Publishing Co., 1913), 88–89, 165–68.

111. Blassingame and McKivigan, *Frederick Douglass Papers*, 4:484–85, 488–89.

112. Philip S. Foner and Robert James Branham, eds., *Lift Every Voice: African American Oratory, 1787–1900* (Tuscaloosa: University of Alabama Press, 1998), 698. See also D.P. Brown's 1899 speech, ibid., 893–94.

113. Faith Berry, ed., *From Bondage to Liberation: Writings by and about Afro-Americans from 1700 to 1918* (New York: Continuum International Publishing, 2006), 447. Elsewhere Wells said, "The general government is willingly powerless to send troops to protect the lives of its black citizens, but the state governments are free to use state troops to shoot them down like cattle, when in desperation the black men attempt to defend themselves, and then tell the world that it was necessary to put down a 'race war.'" Richard T. Hughes, *Myths America Lives By* (Urbana: University of Illinois Press, 2004), 147.

114. Anna J. Cooper, *A Voice from the South* (Xenia, OH: Aldine Printing, 1892), 12.

115. Cooper added, "This I maintain in full knowledge of what at any time may be wrought by a sudden paroxysm of rage caused by the meaningless war whoop of some obscure politicians such as the rally word of 'Negro domination' which at times deafens and bemuddles all ears." Anna Julia Cooper, "Ethics of the Negro Question," in *The Voice of Anna Julia Cooper*, ed. Charles C. Lemert and Esme Bhan (Lanham, MD: Rowman & Littlefield, 1998), 214.

116. Historians are fortunate to have valuable insight into Hayes's thinking because of the diaries he kept while president. Williams, *Diary and Letters of Rutherford B. Hayes*.

117. Former vice president Schuyler Colfax blamed the "overbuilding of railroads and the enormous amount of money thus withdrawn from other uses." See "Hard Times: Their Cause and Cure," *Inter Ocean* (Chicago), September 6, 1877, p. 3. See also "Is the Tariff Responsible for Hard Times?" *Inter Ocean*, May 8, 1877; "The Money Problem," *Hinds County Gazette* (Raymond, MS), May 16, 1877; "Hard Times and Their Cause," *Newark Advocate* (Newark, OH), May 18, 1877; "The Hard Times," *Milwaukee Daily Sentinel*, May 24, 1877, p. 3; "Belford on Railroads," *Daily Rocky Mountain News* (Denver), August 28, 1877; "The Silver Question," *Wisconsin State Register* (Portage), September 15, 1877; Elizur Wright, "The Relations of Debt and Money," *North American Review* 124 (1877): 417–35; David A. Wells, "How Shall the Nation Regain Prosperity?" *North American Review* 125 (1877): 110–33; Charles Wyllys Elliott, "Hard Times," *The Galaxy* 23 (1877): 474–88.

118. For instance, "To the labor monopolies the hard times are mainly due," according to "Trades Unions," *Manufacturer and Builder* 9 (1877): 214; "The Silver Question," *Boston Daily Advertiser*, March 20, 1877; "The Good Time Coming," *San Francisco Daily Evening Bulletin*, April 20, 1877.

119. "The Silver Question," *Boston Daily Advertiser*, January 13, 1877; "Business," *Daily Rocky Mountain News* (Denver), January 16, 1877; "The Good Time Coming"; "The Silver Question," *San Francisco Daily Evening Bulletin*, October 18, 1877; "Thurman's Theories," *St. Louis Globe-Democrat*, September 24, 1877.

120. For example, "Resumption," *Daily Rocky Mountain News* (Denver), February 13, 1877; "The New Party Movement," *Hinds County Gazette* (Raymond, MS), May 2, 1877; "Our Flag Is There," *Inter Ocean* (Chicago), June 28, 1877; "Secretary Sherman's Speech," *Inter Ocean*, August 20, 1877, p. 4; "A Sound National Currency," *North American* (Philadelphia), July 3, 1877; "A Sound National Currency," *North American*, Au-

gust 20, 1878; "Silver Again Rising," *San Francisco Daily Evening Bulletin*, July 14, 1877; "The Money Power," *St. Louis Globe-Democrat*, August 24, 1877, p. 4.

121. "Gold and Silver Report of the Silver Commission to Congress," *Boston Daily Advertiser*, March 3, 1877; "The Silver Question," *Boston Daily Advertiser*, September 5, 1877; "Remonetization of Silver," *Georgia Weekly Telegraph and Georgia Journal & Messenger* (Macon), July 17, 1877; "A Voice from the past," *St. Louis Globe-Democrat*, April 26, 1877, p. 4; "The Ohio Campaign," *Inter Ocean* (Chicago), August 24, 1877, p. 2; "Silver," *Inter Ocean*, August 25, 1877, p. 4; Allen Weinstein, *Prelude to Populism: Origins of the Silver Issue, 1867–1878* (New Haven: Yale University Press, 1970). The leading economic treatises of the period included William Graham Sumner, *A History of American Currency* (New York: H. Holt and Co., 1874); William Graham Sumner, *Lectures on the History of Protection* (New York: G.P. Putnam's Sons, 1877); Julian M. Sturtevant, *Economics, or, the Science of Wealth* (New York: G.P. Putnam's Sons, 1877).

122. Diary entry for November 5, 1877, in Williams, *Diary and Letters of Rutherford B. Hayes*, 3:451.

123. Diary entries for February 3 and 6, 1878, in Williams, *Diary and Letters of Rutherford B. Hayes*, 3:459.

124. Diary entries for February 26 and March 1, 1878, in Williams, *Diary and Letters of Rutherford B. Hayes*, 3:461–62. On the Bland-Allison Act, see Ari Hoogenboom, *Rutherford B. Hayes: Warrior and President* (Lawrence: University Press of Kansas, 1995), 356–63.

125. Matthew Josephson, *The Politicos, 1865–1896* (New York: Harcourt, Brace & World, 1938); Stephen D. Kantrowitz, *Ben Tillman and the Reconstruction of White Supremacy* (Chapel Hill: University of North Carolina Press, 2000); Andrew, *Wade Hampton*, 430–43, 456–78, 482–87; diary entry for October 24, 1877, in Williams, *Diary and Letters of Rutherford B. Hayes*, 3:449.

126. Miller added, "I am losing interest in these matters. I will do my duty but will *fight* no more." See Michael A. Ross, *Justice of Shattered Dreams: Samuel Freeman Miller and the Supreme Court during the Civil War Era* (Baton Rouge: Louisiana State University Press, 2003), 175, 224; Ballard C. Campbell, "Public Policy and State Government," in Calhoun, *Gilded Age*, 309–29.

127. Hoogenboom, *Rutherford B. Hayes*, 494.

128. Robert H. Wiebe declares the Great Strike of 1877 "no more than a bad memory, an incident rather than an index to fear and failure," in *The Search for Order, 1877–1920* (New York: Hill & Wang, 1967), 10. Most workers would have respectfully dissented from this perspective.

129. "A Tough Customer," *St. Louis Globe-Democrat*, October 1, 1877, p. 4.

130. For example, "A Molly Maguire Gang: Another of the Murderous Mining Bands Unearthed," *Hartford Daily Courant*, February 26, 1878, p. 3; "Molly Maguires Colonizing," *San Francisco Daily Evening Bulletin*, Thursday, April 11, 1878; "The New Mollies," *Milwaukee Daily Sentinel*, April 12, 1878, p. 3; "Brigands in the Coal Fields," *Milwaukee Daily Sentinel*, November 25, 1878, p. 7. A much reproduced *Harper's Weekly* illustration of February 1, 1879, portrays communism as death.

131. Worth Robert Miller, "Farmers and Third-Party Politics," in Calhoun, *Gilded Age*, 235–60, 245; Lawrence Goodwyn, *The Populist Moment: A Short History of the Agrarian Revolt in America* (New York: Oxford University Press, 1978), 26–33; Robert C. McMath, *American Populism: A Social History, 1877–1898* (New York: Hill & Wang,

1992), 72–91; Edwards, *New Spirits*, 233–35; Allen S. Will, *Life of James Cardinal Gibbons* (Baltimore: John Murphy Co., 1911), 146–65.

132. Henry George, *Progress and Poverty: An Inquiry into the Cause of Industrial Depressions and of Increase of Want with Increase of Wealth* (1879; Garden City, NY: Doubleday, Page & Co., 1920); Hoogenboom, *Rutherford B. Hayes*, 493–95; Tom L. Johnson, *My Story* (Kent, OH: Kent State University Press, 1993), 48–58; Frederic C. Howe, *The Confessions of a Reformer* (New York: Charles Scribner's Sons, 1925), 95–98, 184–89.

133. Knights of Labor constitution: Nicholas N. Kittrie and Eldon D. Wedlock Jr., eds., *The Tree of Liberty: A Documentary History of Rebellion and Political Crime in America* (Baltimore: Johns Hopkins University Press, 1986), 240; statement on Tramps: Michael Davis, "Forced to Tramp: The Perspective of the Labor Press, 1870–1900," in *Walking to Work: Tramps in America, 1790–1935*, ed. Eric H. Monkkonen (Lincoln: University of Nebraska Press, 1984), 164; "The Knights of Liberty," *Galveston Daily News*, January 6, 1878.

134. Terence V. Powderly, *Thirty Years of Labor, 1859 to 1889* (Columbus, OH: Excelsior Publishing House, 1889); Leon Fink, *Workingmen's Democracy: The Knights of Labor and American Politics* (Champaign, IL: University of Illinois Press, 1985).

135. "Molly Maguires Colonizing," *San Francisco Daily Evening Bulletin*, April 11, 1878; "The New Mollies," *Milwaukee Daily Sentinel*, April 12, 1878, p. 3; "Communist Agitation," *Milwaukee Daily Sentinel*, May 2, 1878; "The Dreaded Commune," *Galveston Daily News*, April 28, 1878.

136. "Communist Agitation," *Milwaukee Daily Sentinel*, May 2, 1878; "Half a Million of Men," *Milwaukee Daily Sentinel*, May 8, 1878, p. 5; "Alive with Communists," *Milwaukee Daily Sentinel*, May 29, 1878, p. 7; *Lowell Daily Citizen*, May 14, 1878. A few public figures treated the Knights fairly in taking them at their word, even while disagreeing with their platform; e.g., the Rev. Joseph Cook, "Boston Monday Lectures," *Boston Daily Advertiser*, November 13, 1878.

137. The Knights of Labor resolution recognizing tramps as victims, "The Central Labor Union," *New York Times*, December 20, 1886, p. 8; the condemnation of this resolution, "Tramps and 'Labor,'" *New York Times*, December 23, 1886, p. 4.

138. Quotes, in order, from "The California Memorial," *Inter Ocean* (Chicago), January 3, 1878, p. 4; "On a Volcano," *St. Louis Globe-Democrat*, July 26, 1877, p. 4; "The Situation," *The Congregationalist* (Boston), August 22, 1877; "The Issues," *Inter Ocean*, August 17, 1877, p. 5.

139. "The beginning of a series": *New York Times*, July 26, 1877; "Communism": "The Moral from the Late Political Battle," *Boston Daily Advertiser*, November 11, 1878; Robert M. Fogelson, *America's Armories: Architecture, Society, and Public Order* (Cambridge, MA: Harvard University Press, 1989), 21.

140. Smith quoted in "Republicanism," *Milwaukee Daily Sentinel*, October 3, 1877; "The Issues," *Inter Ocean* (Chicago), August 17, 1877, p. 5; "The Money Power," *St. Louis Globe-Democrat*, August 24, 1877, p. 4; "A New Labor War," *Frank Leslie's Illustrated Newspaper* (New York), January 26, 1878, p. 350; "Good Advice," *Daily Arkansas Gazette* (Little Rock), May 12, 1878.

141. *St. Louis Globe-Democrat*, February 9, 1878, p. 4 (quote); "Strikes and Violence," *Inter Ocean* (Chicago), February 14, 1878; Campbell, "Public Policy and State Government," 323; Allan R. Millett and Peter Maslowski, *For the Common Defense: The Military History of the United States of America* (New York: Free Press, 1984), 249; Fogelson, *America's Armories*, 13–47.

142. Gould quoted in "Personals," *Hartford Daily Courant*, July 24, 1877, p. 2; *Georgia Weekly Telegraph and Georgia Journal & Messenger* (Macon), August 7, 1877. For Albert Parsons's response to Gould's comments, see "Rioting Roughs," *Inter Ocean* (Chicago), July 25, 1877.

143. "The Talk of the Desperate," *Pittsburgh Leader*, July 20, 1877, in *Report of the Committee Appointed to Investigate the Railroad Riots*, 798; Fogelson, *America's Armories*, 48–82.

144. "Remarks of Mr. Curtis," *New York Times*, November 18, 1879, p. 8; Fogelson, *America's Armories*, 2–3, 27.

145. Edwards, *New Spirits*, 27.

146. Kenton J. Clymer, *John Hay: The Gentleman as Diplomat* (Ann Arbor: The University of Michigan Press, 1975), 31, 37–38, 42, 47, 52.

147. John Hay, *The Bread-Winners* (New York: Harper & Brothers, 1899); Clymer, *John Hay*, 37 (quote). See also Frederic C. Jahar, "Industrialism and the American Aristocrat: A Study of John Hay and his Novel, *The Bread-winners*," *Journal of the Illinois State Historical Society* 65 (1972): 69–93. Other novels inspired by the strike include Lee Harris, *The Man Who Tramps* (Indianapolis: Douglass & Carlon, 1878); Frederick Whittaker, *Nemo, King of the Tramps: . . . A Story of the Great Railroad Riots* (n.p.: Beadle's Dime Library, 1881); T.S. Denison, *An Iron Crown* (Philadelphia: Potter & Co., 1885); Henry F. Keenan, *The Money-Makers: A Social Parable* (New York: Appleton & Co., 1885); Martin A. Foran, *The Other Side* (Cleveland: Ingham, Clarke & Co., 1886); George T. Dowling, *The Wreckers* (Philadelphia: J.P. Lippincott Co., 1886); Paul Leicester Ford, *The Honorable Peter Stirling* (New York: Henry Holt & Co., 1894); Captain Charles King, *A Tame Surrender: A Story of the Chicago Strike* (Philadelphia: J.P. Lippincott Co., 1896).

148. Diary entries for January 22, January 24, March 17–20, March 26, and April 6, 1886, in Williams, *Diary and Letters of Rutherford B. Hayes*, 4:261–62, 277–80.

149. Diary entries for May 2, 1886; December 4, 1887; December 10, 1887; and September 5–7, 1888, in Williams, *Diary and Letters of Rutherford B. Hayes*, 4: 282, 354–56, 405–6. See also ibid., 272–73, 278; Louis D. Rubin Jr., ed., *Teach the Freeman: The Correspondence of Rutherford B. Hayes and the Slater Fund for Negro Education, 1881–1887*, 2 vols. (Baton Rouge: Louisiana State University Press, 1959), 1:33n, 177, 179–81.

150. Hayes to Lucy Hayes, July 14–15, 1888, and diary entries for June 10, July 4, July 5, July 12, July 15, July 17, and July 22, 1888, in Williams, *Diary and Letters of Rutherford B. Hayes*, 4:391, 397–400. See also Hoogenboom, *Rutherford B. Hayes*, 493–507.

151. Diary entries for March 17–20 and March 26, 1886; June 10, July 4, July 5, July 12, July 15, July 17, and July 22, 1888; and Hayes to Lucy Hayes, July 14–15, 1888, in Williams, *Diary and Letters of Rutherford B. Hayes*, 4:277–78, 391, 397–400.

152. Hayes to William E. Dodge, February 1, 1887, and diary entries for November 6, December 4, and December 10, 1887, and March 11, 1888, in Williams, *Diary and Letters of Rutherford B. Hayes*, 4:309, 348, 354–56, 374.

153. Hoogenboom, *Rutherford B. Hayes*, 495; Hayes to William E. Dodge, February 1, 1887, and diary entries for November 6, December 4, and December 10, 1887; and March 11, 1888, in Williams, *Diary and Letters of Rutherford B. Hayes*, 4:309, 348, 354–56, 374 (quote).

154. Howard Zinn, *A People's History of the United States* (New York: Harper, 1980), 263–65.

155. Jacob A. Riis, *The Making of an American* (New York: Macmillan, 1902), 35, 38–39, 244.

156. Ibid., 39–49.

157. Ibid., 51–77 (quote, 66).

158. Ibid., 69, 75.

159. Ibid., 72–74.

160. For example, Paul T. Ringenbach, *Tramps and Reformers, 1873–1916: The Discovery of Unemployment in New York* (Westport, CT: Greenwood Press, 1973), 24.

161. "A Danger for Tramps," *New York Tribune*, March 19, 1882, p. 6; Kenneth L. Kusmer, *Down and Out, On the Road: The Homeless in American History* (New York: Oxford University Press, 2002), 44; Horatio Alger, *Tony the Tramp* (New York: A.L. Burt Co., 1890); "scum" and "able-bodied loafers": "Synopsis of a Practical Sermon," *Wisconsin State Register* (Portage), July 27, 1878.

162. "Nearly all cases of violence": "Tramps—How They Talk and How They Lodge," *Lowell Daily Citizen*, December 23, 1878; "furnishing support": "Synopsis of a Practical Sermon," *Wisconsin State Register* (Portage), July 27, 1878. See also "Fresh Local Breezes," *Milwaukee Daily Sentinel*, July 16, 1878, p. 8; Monkkonen, *Walking to Work*, 15n7. For a defense of tramps, see George F. Train, "Train on Tramps," *Milwaukee Daily Sentinel*, August 9, 1878, p. 7.

163. "Editorial," *New York Tribune*, November 28, 1877, p. 4; Allan Pinkerton, *Strikers, Communists, Tramps and Detectives* (New York: G.W. Carleton & Co., 1878); "Once More the Tramp," *Scribner's Monthly* 15 (1878): 883; W.H. Brewer, "What Shall We Do with Our Tramps," *New Englander* 37 (1878): 532; "From Another Point of View," *Rural New Yorker* 37 (July 13, 1878): 444; "Vilest of the Vile," *New York Times*, January 7, 1877, p. 5; "Apprehensions of a Strike," *New York Times*, June 18, 1878; "Communistic Tramps' Threats," *New York Times*, July 8, 1878; Kusmer, *Down and Out, On the Road*, 47–49.

164. Lee O. Harrris, *The Man Who Tramps: A Story of Today* (Indianapolis: Douglass & Carlon, 1878), 19, 43; Frank Bellew, *The Tramp: His Tricks, Tallies and Tell-Tales* (New York: Dick & Fitzgerald), quoted in Kusmer, *Down and Out, On the Road*, 49.

165. Eric H. Monkkonen, *Police in Urban America, 1860–1920* (Cambridge: Cambridge University Press, 1981), 4.

166. Francis Wayland and F.B. Sanborn, "Report on Tramp Laws and Indeterminate Sentences," *Seventh Annual Conference of Charities and Corrections* (Boston: A. Williams, 1880), 277–81; Monkkonen, *Walking to Work*, 10–11, 187; Kusmer, *Down and Out, On the Road*, 52, 100–101.

167. Kusmer, *Down and Out, On the Road*, 53–55.

168. Riis, *Making of an American*, 68 (quote), 122–25.

169. Ibid., 187, 189–90.

170. Ibid., 188–89, 197, 199.

171. Ibid., 236 (quote), 239–40, 245; Edwards, *New Spirits*, 166.

172. Archie Robertson, *That Old-Time Religion* (Boston: Houghton Mifflin, 1950); Aaron I. Abell, *The Urban Impact on American Protestantism, 1865–1900* (Cambridge, MA: Harvard University Press, 1943); Randel, *Centennial*, 436–40; Henry F. May, *Protestant Churches and Industrial America* (New York: Harper & Brothers, 1949), 30–59.

173. "Kearney in Brooklyn," *New York Times*, September 8, 1878; "Mrs. Tilton Pleads Guilty," *New York Times*, April 16, 1878; Barry Werth, *Banquet at Delmonico's: Great*

Minds, the Gilded Age, and the Triumph of Evolution in America (New York: Random House, 2009), 177–81.

174. May, *Protestant Churches and Industrial America*, 112.

175. *Watchman*, August 9, 1877, p. 252, quoted in May, *Protestant Churches and Industrial America*, 94; Emma Brace, *The Life of Charles Loring Brace: Chiefly Told in His Own Letters* (New York: Charles Scribner's Sons, 1894), 355; "Tupper," *Boston Daily Advertiser*, February 16, 1877; *Georgia Weekly Telegraph and Georgia Journal & Messenger* (Macon, GA), November 13, 1877.

176. *Inter Ocean* (Chicago), November 30, 1877, p. 4 (quote); *Inter Ocean*, December 12, 1877, p. 4, December 14, 1877, p. 4; Asbury, *Gangs of New York*, 174.

177. *Christian Advocate*, May 2, 1878, p. 280; *Christian Advocate*, June 13, 1878, p. 376; *Christian Advocate*, January 22, 1879, p. 74; *Christian Advocate*, December 16, 1880, p. 80; May, *Protestant Churches and Industrial America*, 95–96.

178. Riis, *Making of an American*, 246 (quote); Edward H. McKinley, *Marching to Glory: The History of the Salvation Army in the United States, 1880–1992* (Grand Rapids, MI: Wm. B. Eerdmans Publishing Co., 1995), 1–37; Jacob A. Riis, *How the Other Half Lives: Studies Among the Tenements of New York* (New York: Charles Scribner's Sons, 1890).

179. Riis, *Making of an American*, 244, 252–53, 256.

180. Theodore Roosevelt, *Theodore Roosevelt: An Autobiography* (New York: Macmillan, 1914), 64 (quote); Monkkonen, *Police in Urban America*, 107; Rosalie Butler, "Separating of Charities and Correction," *Charities Review* (1892): 164–70.

181. Roosevelt, *Theodore Roosevelt*, 64; Riis, *Making of an American*, 234, 250, 257–59. As Riis admits, many homeless suffered from the closing of the police lodgings, being "literally left out in the cold, cursing reform and its fruits." He dismissed those who felt such a measure was too harsh on the poor as a "few tender-hearted and soft-headed citizens." Jacob A. Riis, *The Battle with the Slum* (New York: Macmillan, 1902), 170; Riis, *Making of an American*, 260–61.

182. David McCullough, *Mornings on Horseback* (New York: Simon & Schuster, 1981), 140, 199 (quote).

183. Ibid., 191; Henry James, *Charles W. Eliot: President of Harvard University, 1869–1909*, 2 vols. (Cambridge, MA: Houghton Mifflin, 1930); Hugh Hawkins, *Between Harvard and America: The Educational Leadership of Charles W. Eliot* (New York: Oxford University Press, 1972).

184. John Woodbury quoted in McCullough, *Mornings on Horseback*, 160, 209–21 (quote, 208).

185. Donald Wilhelm, *Theodore Roosevelt as an Undergraduate* (Boston: John W. Luce, 1910), 35.

186. Theodore Roosevelt to Martha Bulloch Roosevelt, January 11, 1880, in McCullough, *Mornings on Horseback*, 212; Fogelson, *America's Armories*, 27–28; T.J. Jackson Lears, *No Place of Grace: Antimodernism and the Transformation of American Culture, 1880–1920* (Chicago: University of Chicago Press, 1981), 31.

187. McCullough, *Mornings on Horseback*, 206–7, 213–14.

188. Ibid., 21, 149, 182, 197–98, 213–15.

189. *New York Tribune*, August 28, 1877, quoted in McCullough, *Mornings on Horseback*, 149–50.

190. McCullough, *Mornings on Horseback*, 137–38 (quote, 137), 170.

191. "The Museum of Natural History," *New York Times*, May 16, 1877, p. 8.

192. Eleanor Butler Roosevelt, *Day Before Yesterday: The Reminiscences of Mrs. Theodore Roosevelt, Jr.* (Garden City, NY: Doubleday & Co., 1959), 37–38; McCullough, *Mornings on Horseback*, 205; James Blaine Walker, *The Epic of American Industry* (New York: Harper & Brothers, 1949), 265–68; Charlotte Gray, *Reluctant Genius: Alexander Graham Bell and the Passion for Invention* (New York: Arcade Publishing, 2006), 160–61; "A Telephonic Conversation," *Atlantic Monthly* 45 (1880): 841–843; Ithiel de Sola Pool, ed., *The Social Impact of the Telephone* (Cambridge, MA: MIT Press, 1981).

193. "Political Reformers: The Fifth Avenue Conference," *New York Times*, May 17, 1876; "The Schurz-Fest," *Bangor Daily Whig & Courier*, May 17, 1876; "The Fifth Avenue Conference," *North American* (Philadelphia), May 18, 1876; McCullough, *Mornings on Horseback*, 152, 155–58. For a nasty denunciation of the "Fifth Avenue Conference," see "The Ladies' Way," *St. Louis Globe-Democrat*, May 18, 1876, p. 4.

194. Thomas C. Reeves, *Gentleman Boss: The Life of Chester Alan Arthur* (New York: Knopf, 1975), 62–68, 82–83; Josephson, *Politicos*, 90–100, 154–77, 242–51, 305–13; McCullough, *Mornings on Horseback*, 170–80.

195. Josephson, *Politicos*, 247–49 (quotes); "Washington: The President's Nomination," *New York Times*, December 5, 1877; "The New York Nominations," *New York Times*, December 12, 1877; "The Senate and the President," *New York Times*, December 14, 1877; McCullough, *Mornings on Horseback*, 178–79; Josephson, *Politicos*, 248–49.

196. Theodore Roosevelt to Theodore Roosevelt Jr., December 16, 1877, in McCullough, *Mornings on Horseback*, 179–80.

197. McCullough, *Mornings on Horseback*, 177.

198. Ibid., 180–83, 188–90 (quote, 188). Historians speculate on the connection between the death of the senior Theodore Roosevelt and his son's later commitment to reform politics; see McCullough, *Mornings on Horseback*, 190; Josephson, *Politicos*, 249.

199. McCullough, *Mornings on Horseback*, 191 (diary quoted), 208; William Roscoe Thayer, *Theodore Roosevelt: An Intimate Biography* (Boston: Houghton Mifflin, 1919), 21.

200. Charles Francis Adams Jr., "An Erie Raid," in Charles Francis Adams Jr. and Henry Adams, *Chapters of Erie, and Other Essays* (New York: Henry Holt & Co., 1886), 135–36; Leonard D. White, *The Republican Era, 1869–1901: A Study in Administrative History* (New York: Macmillan, 1958), 366.

201. Henry Adams, *The Education of Henry Adams: An Autobiography* (Boston: Houghton Mifflin, 1918), 53; James Rodger Fleming, "Science and Technology in the Second Half of the Nineteenth Century," in Calhoun, *Gilded Age*, 19–21; Brown, *Year of the Century*, 51, 53 (Howells quoted).

202. McCullough, *Mornings on Horseback*, 120, 148, 317, 367. Roosevelt went on an earlier hunting trip with his brother Elliot in 1880 to Iowa and Minnesota; ibid., 228–29.

203. Joy S. Kasson, *Buffalo Bill's Wild West: Celebrity, Memory, and Popular History* (New York: Hill & Wang, 2001).

204. Susan Jacoby, *The Age of American Unreason* (New York: Pantheon Books, 2008), 68; John H. Ostrom and John S. McIntosh, *Marsh's Dinosaurs: The Collections from Como Bluff* (New Haven: Yale University Press, 1966); Edwards, *New Spirits*, 151–52.

205. O.C. Marsh, "Introduction and Succession of Vertebrate Life in America," *Popular Science Monthly* 12 (1877–1878): 513.

206. "New-York's New Museum," *New York Times*, December 23, 1877; William James, "Remarks on Spencer's Definition of Mind as Correspondence," *Journal of Specu-*

lative Philosophy 12 (1878): 1–18; Charles S. Peirce, "How to Make Our Ideas Clear," *Popular Science Monthly* 12 (1877–1878): 286–302.; Louis Menand, *The Metaphysical Club: A Story of Ideas in America* (New York: Farrar, Straus and Giroux, 2001), 219–20, 270; Wiebe, *Search for Order*; Fleming, "Science and Technology," 19–37; Michael Les Benedict, "Law and the Constitution in the Gilded Age," in Calhoun, *Gilded Age*, 289–308.

207. William James, "Great Men, Great Thoughts, and the Environment," *Atlantic Monthly* 46 (1880): 458; W.G. Sumner, "Suggestions on Social Subjects," *Popular Science Monthly* 24 (1883–1884): 168; Werth, *Banquet at Delmonico's*, 185.

208. Theodore Roosevelt, *The Strenuous Life: Essays and Addresses* (New York: Century Co., 1900), 18.

209. Though "overcivilized" seems to be a phrase that does not appear in the United States until the late 1890s; see, e.g., "Concessions to Expediency," *Daily Picayune* (New Orleans), August 18, 1889, p. 4; "Beatrice," *Wisconsin State Register* (Portage), February 22, 1890. "Neurasthenia" was coined by George Miller Beard in 1869; see "Neurasthenia, or Nervous Exhaustion," *Boston Medical and Surgical Journal* 80 (1869): 217–221; "Social Science," *Boston Daily Advertiser*, May 13, 1875; "More Doctors," *Inter Ocean* (Chicago), March 6, 1878, p. 3.

210. "Emigration or Desiccation [*sic*]," *Boston Daily Advertiser*, November 23, 1882, p. 4; "News Observations," *Raleigh News and Observer*, December 29, 1882; E. Anthony Rotundo, *American Manhood: Transformations in Masculinity from the Revolution to the Modern Era* (New York: Basic Books, 1993).

211. Henry James, *The Bostonians* (London: Penguin, 2000), 260; Edwards, *New Spirits*, 120.

212. "Muscular Christianity" is generally associated with Charles Kingsley, though he initially rejected the phrase when it was applied to his work in the late 1850s. The earliest American usage I can locate is an article on the Thomas Sayers v. John Heenan fight in 1860; see "The Fight for the Championship," *New York Herald*, Tuesday, May 1, 1860, p. 4.

213. T. DeWitt Talmage, *Sports That Kill* (New York: Harper & Bros., 1875). Talmage also attacked the theater as unhealthy, which led to a number of critical reviews; e.g. "Sports That Kill," *San Francisco Daily Evening Bulletin*, March 13 and March 20, 1875. See also J.J. Fleharty, *Social Impurity: The Sin of the World in All Ages, the Causes and the Remedy* (Cincinnati: the author, 1875).

214. "Peripatetic Learning," *North American* (Philadelphia), February 1, 1877; "new style": "Musical Church Notices," *Inter Ocean* (Chicago), March 17, 1877, p. 4; Ninde quoted in "Spiritual Teachings," *Inter Ocean*, June 18, 1877, p. 2.

215. "Muscular Christianity," *Milwaukee Daily Sentinel*, October 29, 1877, p. 3; Guy Lewis, "The Muscular Christianity Movement," *Journal of Health, Physical Education and Recreation* 5 (1966): 27–42; Clifford Putney, *Muscular Christianity: Manhood and Sports in Protestant America, 1880–1920* (Cambridge, MA: Harvard University Press, 2001); Elliot J. Gorn, *The Manly Art: Bare-Knuckle Prize Fighting in America* (Ithaca, NY: Cornell University Press, 1986), 180–81; Benjamin Rader, *American Sports: From Folk Games to the Age of Spectators* (Englewood Cliffs, NJ: Prentice-Hall, 1983), 146–69; Roderick Nash, "The American Cult of the Primitive," *American Quarterly* 18 (1966): 517–37. Dudley A. Sargent, who came to Harvard in 1879, led the way in developing college football; see Gorn, *Manly Art*, 188.

216. Theodore Roosevelt, "Professionalism in Sports," *North American Review* 15 (1890): 187, 191.

217. Roosevelt, *Strenuous Life*, 5; Fogelson, *America's Armories*, 27.

218. O'Neill quoted in Edwards, *New Spirits*, 245–46; Robert M. Utley, *The Last Days of the Sioux Nation* (New Haven: Yale University Press, 1966); Brian McAllister Linn, *The Philippine War, 1899–1902* (Lawrence: University Press of Kansas, 2002).

219. R. David Arkush and Leo O. Lee, ed. and trans., *Land Without Ghosts: Chinese Impressions of America from the Mid-Nineteenth Century to the Present* (Berkeley: University of California Press, 1989), 61, 64–65.

220. Sala, *America Revisited*, 2:210–12; Henry Sienkiewicz, *Portrait of America: Letters of Henry Sienkiewicz*, ed. and trans. Charles Morley (New York: Columbia University Press, 1959), 255; Edwards, *New Spirits*, 211.

221. Arkush and Lee, *Land Without Ghosts*, 1–12; Roger Daniels, *Coming to America: A History of Immigration and Ethnicity in American Life* (New York: HarperPerennial, 2002); Ronald Takai, *Strangers from a Different Shore: A History of Asian Americans* (New York: Back Bay Books, 1998); Aristide R. Zolberg, *A Nation by Design: Immigration Policy in the Fashioning of America* (Cambridge, MA: Harvard University Press, 2008).

222. Josiah Strong, *Our Country: Its Possible Future and Its Present Crisis* (New York: Baker & Taylor Co., 1885), 183; William Graham Sumner, *The Forgotten Man, and Other Essays* (New Haven: Yale University Press, 1969), 88–90; Francis Parkman, "The Failure of Universal Suffrage," *North American Review* 127 (1878): 4.

223. Donald L. Kinzer, *An Episode in Anti-Catholicism: The American Protective Association* (Seattle: University of Washington Press, 1964); James T. Fisher, *Communion of Immigrants: A History of Catholics in America* (New York: Oxford University Press, 2000).

224. Edwards, *New Spirits*, 243; J. Morgan Kousser, *The Shaping of Southern Politics: Suffrage Restriction and the Establishment of the One-Party South, 1880–1910* (New Haven: Yale University Press, 1976), 223–25; Francisco A. Rosales, *Chicano!: The History of the Mexican American Civil Rights Movement* (Houston: Arte Publico Press, 1997); Matt S. Meier and Feliciano Ribera, *Mexican Americans/American Mexicans: From Conquistadors to Chicanos* (New York: Hill & Wang, 1994).

225. Walt Whitman, *Democratic Vistas: And Other Papers* (London: Walter Scott, 1888), 12, 29.

226. James Ford Rhodes, *History of the United States from the Compromise of 1850 to McKinley, 1877–1896* (New York: Macmillan, 1919), 46; *The Nation*, August 2, 1877, p. 68; Thomas A. Scott, "The Recent Strikes," *North American Review* 125 (1877): 357.

227. "Princess Winnemucca Dead," *New York Times*, October 27, 1891.

228. Whitman, *Democratic Vistas*, 35–36, 40; Walt Whitman, "Facing West from California's Shores," in *Leaves of Grass* (New York: Modern Library, 1921), 96.

Index